PRAISE FOR *WALTHER'S HYMNAL*:

"*Remember your leaders, those who spoke to you the word of God. Consider the outcome of their way of life, and imitate their faith.*" The literary productivity of C. F. W. Walther is absolutely astounding. Of all the Missouri Synod presidents, I suspect only Franz Pieper (1899–1911) came anywhere close to Walther. Excluding Pieper, our venerable first president's output exceeds all the rest combined. That Walther turned his precious time and laser-like attention to the production of a hymnal at the very outset of the Missouri Synod's life, demonstrates that orthodox Lutheranism has orthodox worship in its very DNA. Thanks to Matthew Carver, we now have Walther's hymnal, which guided the life of the Synod through its German-speaking period—six decades blessed with exponential growth. And much more than that, the core German hymnody that Walther thought a Lutheran hymnal ought to contain has been preserved largely intact to this very day in *Lutheran Service Book*. That the Synod should have maintained Walther's deep convictions regarding freedom in matters of worship, while so broadly adopting similar practice through hymnals, is testimony to his Lutheran genius.

—Rev. Dr. Matthew C. Harrison
President, The Lutheran Church—Missouri Synod

Walther's hymnal, originally published in 1847, shaped the theology, graced the liturgy, and fostered the spirituality of The Lutheran Church—Missouri Synod almost from its beginnings, but did so in the German language. Until now English-speaking Missouri Lutherans have been unable to appreciate the significance of this collection of hymns, which, when it first appeared, was a pioneering anthology that sought to undo layers of editorial rewriting and truncation and give the texts in the language and length their authors gave to them. Matthew Carver has opened the closed door and provided English translations for all the hymns in Walther's hymnal, and many are translated for the first time.

—Dr. Robin A. Leaver
Yale Institute of Sacred Music

The text of Walther's hymnal (*Kirchengesangbuch*), first published in 1847 and appearing here in English translation, opens a window into the theology and piety of a group of nineteenth-century German Lutheran immigrants to America determined to establish and maintain a confessional orthodox Lutheranism in a new land. Drawing from a variety of English translations, many by the editor, *Walther's Hymnal* will soon find a place in the libraries of all interested in the development of Lutheran hymnody in America.

—Dr. Carl Schalk
Distinguished Professor of Church Music Emeritus
Concordia University Chicago

Matthew Carver has performed an extraordinary service to the English-speaking spiritual descendents of C. F. W. Walther, the first LCMS president. Through the compilation of existing translations and his original translations of the remaining hymns, Carver has made it possible for us to experience one of the most significant resources that shaped the piety of those first generations of Saxon Lutherans. *Walther's Hymnal* will serve not only as a rich devotional resource for our time but also as an impetus for future hymn writers as they add to our rich heritage.

—Rev. Dr. Paul J. Grime
Dean of the Chapel, Associate Professor
Concordia Theological Seminary, Fort Wayne, IN

This book paves a path back to the roots of The Lutheran Church—Missouri Synod, blocked until now for all those who are not able to read and understand German. But this book is more than just a historical remembrance. It also shows that Lutherans today still sing the old hymns that were sung by the forefathers of the nineteenth century, yes even by the Lutheran Church of the centuries before. *Walther's Hymnal* enables readers to rediscover hymns no longer in use. They are now able to join in words and melodies that make accessible experiences and testimonies of Christian faith that may be underemphasized in our days.

—Prof. Dr. Christoph Barnbrock
Professor of Practical Theology
Lutherische Theologische Hochschule Oberursel, Germany

This resource is a wonderful packet of "Heirloom Seeds" for all who wish to learn more about the spirit and song of the Lutheran confessional revival of the nineteenth century. Those who study and sing the hymns in this collection will be treated to an experience of living theological and liturgical history that gives a glimpse into the faith expressions of those who passed a lively confession to us. This will be a welcome addition to the library of all who appreciate the Lutheran chorale, and for composers who are searching for "new" texts to inspire musical settings for use in the church, school, and home.

—Rev. Prof. Dennis Marzolf, MDiv, MM
Music Department Chair
Bethany Lutheran College, Mankato, MN

Much rings familiar here. But it is fascinating to explore the different accents and emphases of the early Missouri Synod piety that Walther's hymnal embodies. Hymns for warfare, severe drought, dangerous storms. Numerous hymns about sudden death and inescapable woes, from an age that knew these all too well. And throughout, hymns that express a deep confidence in Christ our Savior and the joyous mystery of His presence in worship. Dozens of the more than four hundred hymns, along with the prayers, are Matthew Carver's original translations, most appearing in English for the first time. In this labor of love, Carver has provided a wonderful resource for historians, pastors, and homes—and a wonderful tribute to Walther and our Lutheran hymnody.

—Rev. Thomas Egger
Assistant Professor of Exegetical Theology
Concordia Seminary, St. Louis
Contributing author to *C. F. W. Walther: Churchman and Theologian* (CPH, 2011)

Matthew Carver's masterful translation of C. F. W. Walther's 1847 collection of German-language hymns opens a window on the mid-nineteenth-century revival of confessional Lutheranism in America. This translation enables American Lutherans to read the orthodox hymn texts that were so highly prized by Walther and his fellow German immigrants during the 1830s, '40s, and beyond. In so doing, one gains a new appreciation for the power of hymn texts to proclaim the Gospel in its truth and purity.

—Dr. Daniel Zager
Eastman School of Music

Those who treasure American Lutheran hymnody will be forever grateful to Matthew Carver and the team that helped make this pivotal resource available in English. Without a doubt, the *Kirchengesangbuch* turned the ship of American Lutheran hymnody away from the influence of pietism, rationalism, revivalism, and unionism surrounding C. F. W. Walther, the church, and his time, onto a solid confessional course. And by grace, it is a course that lives on today. Jon Vieker's historical introduction alone is worth the price of this book.

—Rev. Richard C. Resch
Kantor and Associate Professor,
Concordia Theological Seminary
Kantor, St. Paul's Lutheran Church, Fort Wayne, IN

What a wondrous treasure trove Matthew Carver has opened for us English speakers with his translation of *Walther's Hymnal*! I think not merely of the beautiful hymns that had not made it into English until now and that he has translated with care and an ear that is able to retain the ruggedness of the German original in English, but also the robust spiritual resources packed into the appendices: prayers of the great Lutheran divines for numerous occasions and needs and the old Saxon liturgy (morning service) which has all but been forgotten in the history of Lutheran liturgics in America. It is a book that will be a blessing to any lover of Lutheran doctrine, liturgy, and hymnody.

—Rev. William C. Weedon, STM
Director of Worship
The Lutheran Church—Missouri Synod

This English-language edition of Walther's Hymnal demonstrates the enduring quality of the Lutheran chorale, both in its strong catechetical theology, vivid imagery, and captivating poetry.

Matthew Carver has recovered translations long hidden away in forgotten books, and he offers many of his own translations, thus giving us the complete poetic texts in a way that is beneficial and useful for pastors, teachers, musicians, congregation members, theologians, and historians. Carver presents translations that are faithful to the original, and yet understandable today without being either archaic or forcefully modernized.

Like any good Lutheran hymnbook, it is a devotional book for prayer and worship, and a doctrinal compendium to teach the Christian faith to young and old.

—Prof. Mark DeGarmeaux, MDiv, STM
Bethany Lutheran College, Mankato, MN

The German hymnal of C. F. W. Walther formed the spirituality of the early Missouri Synod. Many people marked their copy the way Bibles are often marked today, using the hymnal at home in their private and family devotions. Now it is available to a new generation, with over a hundred hymns appearing in English for the first time.

—Dr. Joseph Herl
Associate Professor of Music
Concordia University, Nebraska

Walther's Hymnal

CHURCH HYMNBOOK
FOR EVANGELICAL LUTHERAN CONGREGATIONS
OF THE UNALTERED AUGSBURG CONFESSION

Walther's Hymnal

CHURCH HYMNBOOK
FOR EVANGELICAL LUTHERAN CONGREGATIONS
OF THE UNALTERED AUGSBURG CONFESSION

Containing The Most Popular Hymns
Of The Blessed Dr. Martin Luther
And Other Spiritual Teachers

Translated and Edited by Matthew Carver
from the *Kirchen-Gesangbuch für Evangelisch-Lutherische Gemeinden ungeänderter Augsburgischer Confession* (1892)

CONCORDIA PUBLISHING HOUSE • SAINT LOUIS

Peer Reviewed

Published by Concordia Publishing House
3558 S. Jefferson Ave., St. Louis, MO 63118-3968
1-800-325-3040 • cph.org

Originally published as *Kirchengesangbvuch für Evangelisch-Lutherische Gemeinden ungeänderter Augsburgischer Confession,* St. Louis, Missouri, 1892.

Manufactured in the United States of America

Library of Congress Cataloging-in-Publication Data

Kirchengesangbuch für Evangelisch-Lutherische Gemeinden. English

Walther's hymnal : church hymnbook for Evangelical Lutheran congregations of the unaltered Augsburg confession : containing the most popular hymns of the blessed Dr. Martin Luther and other spiritual teachers / translated and edited by Matthew Carver.

p. cm.

Includes index.

ISBN 978-0-7586-4117-5

1. Lutheran Church--Hymns. 2. Lutheran Church--Missouri Synod--Hymns. I. Walther, C. F. W. (Carl Ferdinand Wilhelm), 1811-1887. II. Luther, Martin, 1483-1546. III. Carver, Matthew. IV. Title.

BV410.K5713 2012

264'.041023--dc23 2012035020

---

7 8 9 10 11 12 13 28 27 26 25 24 23 22

Contents

APPENDICES & INDICES

Historical Introduction

When C. F. W. Walther and the Saxons arrived in Missouri in 1838–39, they brought with them the German-language hymnal they had used in their homeland. That hymnal was the *Dresdnisches Gesangbuch,* first published in 1796 under the oversight of Church Superintendent Karl Christian Tittmann.[1] Concerning this hymnal, hymnologist Christoph Albrecht notes:

> In Dresden there appeared in 1796 a typical Enlightenment hymnal. In the national newspaper, there was an article that demonstrates the over-confidence typical of this period. It noted: "We should have no need of a new hymnal for centuries because Dr. Tittmann has provided the Dresden Hymnal with the greatest possible perfection, and the proper doctrine, as is here submitted in the selected songs, is exalted above all other improvements." Ironically, the Enlightenment's hymnals were among the shortest-lived in hymn-book history.[2]

Tittmann's hymnal, produced under the influence of German Rationalism, continued to be reprinted as late as 1837, just a year before Walther and the Saxons immigrated to Missouri.[3] This was therefore the hymnal that Walther and his young colleagues knew as children, that they and their compatriots brought with them to America, and which was consequently in use at Trinity Congregation, St. Louis, when Walther began service there as pastor in May 1841.

The minutes of Trinity Congregation indicate that for most of 1842 the congregation's attention was almost completely consumed with the details of constructing a new sanctuary. Shortly after the dedication of the sanctuary, however, the congregation resolved in February 1843 that in the public divine services, only pure Lutheran hymns should be used.[4] Toward that end, the congregation resolved in November 1845, at their pastor's encouragement, to publish a new hymnal. Walther was put in charge of the project, along with a number of laymen from the congregation to handle financial matters and several clergy from nearby congregations to assist in hymn selection.[5] Some eighteen months later, the *Kirchengesangbuch für Evangelisch-Lutherische Gemeinden ungeänderter Augsburgischer Confession* (*KELG* 1847)

---

1 A second edition was printed in 1798. See *Dresdnisches Gesangbuch auf höchesten Befehl herausgegeben,* (Dresden: Churfürstl. Hofbuchdruckerey, 1798). See also Paul Tschackert, "Tittmann, Karl Christian," in *Allgemeine Deutsche Biographie* (1894), 387–88.

2 Christoph Albrecht, *Einführung in die Hymnologie* (Göttingen: Vandenhoeck und Ruprecht, 1973), 95. Author's translation.

3 *Dresdner Gesangbuch auf höchsten Befehl herausgegeben* (Dresden and Leipzig: B. G. Teubner, 1837).

4 "Minutes of Trinity Congregation, St. Louis, Missouri," Concordia Historical Institute, St. Louis, Missouri, February 3, 1843.

5 "Minutes of Trinity Congregation, St. Louis, Missouri," November 17, 1845 (p. 344), and January 26, 1846 (p. 353). See also Jon D. Vieker, "'Who from Our Mothers' Arms': The Story of the Hymnals That Came before Us," *Concordia Historical Institute Quarterly* 79, no. 1 (2006), 4.

was printed in New York City and shipped to St. Louis for distribution.[6]

When one examines the *Dresdnisches Gesangbuch* that Walther and the Saxons brought with them, one finds little correspondence to the outline and organization of the hymns found in *KELG* 1847. However, when one examines the older generation of Dresden hymnals—specifically, those published prior to 1796[7]—the outline and organization of the hymns resemble very much the outline that Walther adopted for the hymnal of 1847. Walther's preference for the confessional Lutheran theology he found in such "old" German hymnals is further evidenced in an 1850 article in *Der Lutheraner,* where the writer notes:

> . . . only the *old* hymn books—which are also now and then in this land found among immigrant German Lutherans, such as the *old* Dresden, the *old* Marburg, the *old* Silesian, the Pomeranian, Prussian, Hamburger, Bavarian, etc.—exhibit a sufficiently large stock of the *old* pure Lord's Supper hymns containing the teachings of the Lutheran Church. And whoever has no such *old* hymnal in his possession, this alone should be enough to convince him to get the "St. Louis Lutheran Hymnal."[8]

For Walther, *KELG* 1847 represented a repudiation of the Rationalist hymnals of his day and a restoration of the "old," pre-1796, Dresden line of hymnals, fine-tuned to engage German Lutherans in America as the first hymnal of the Missouri Synod.

Walther's remarks in *Der Lutheraner* announcing the advent of this seminal hymnal disclose the criteria that were used for hymn selection:

> In the selection of the adopted hymns the chief consideration was that they be *pure in doctrine;* that they have almost universal acceptance *within the orthodox German Lutheran Church* and have thus received the almost unanimous testimony that they had come forth from the true spirit [of Lutheranism] . . .[9]

Walther's emphasis on purity of doctrine was fully in keeping with the rise of the Confessional Lutheran Revival during this period. Indeed, Lutheran, Anglican, and Presbyterian traditions—each in their own way—experienced a renaissance of conservative confessionalism during the mid-nineteenth century, both in America and Europe.[10] Walther and the Missouri Synod would play a critical role on the American side of that equation, and the

6 The first edition of *KELG* 1847, contained the following: title page; table of contents; alphabetical hymn index organized by page number; 437 hymns, text only; melodic index consisting of 167 melodies in 103 different meters; and an appendix containing various prayers with an index to their content, a Formula for Emergency Baptism, the Antiphons, the Proper Prefaces, and finally an *Enchiridion*, consisting of the Small Catechism with Luther's Preface, and the "Christian Questions with Their Answers" (*Christliche Fragestücke*), the Augsburg Confession, and the three Ecumenical Creeds. Josephus' *Destruction of Jerusalem* was added in the 1848 printing. In 1857, six additional hymns were added, and an additional 41 hymns were added in 1917. See Carl F. Schalk, *God's Song in a New Land: Lutheran Hymnals in America* (St. Louis: Concordia, 1995), 129–30; and Jon D. Vieker, "C. F. W. Walther: Editor of Missouri's First and Only German Hymnal," *Concordia Historical Institute Quarterly* 65 (1992): 53–69.

7 For example, *Das Privilegirte Ordentliche und vermehrte Dresdnische Gesang-Buch,* (Dresden and Leipzig: Verlegts D. Carl Christian Richter, 1791).

8 "Die Gesang-Bücher," *Der Lutheraner* 7 (1850): 35. Emphasis not original.

9 C. F. W. Walther, "Lutherisches Kirchen-Gesangbuch," *Der Lutheraner,* June 1, 1847 as translated in Carl S. Meyer, *Moving Frontiers: Readings in the History of The Lutheran Church—Missouri Synod* (St. Louis: Concordia, 1964), 182. Emphasis added.

10 See Walter H. Conser, *Church and Confession: Conservative Theologians in Germany, England, and America, 1815-1866* (Macon, GA: Mercer University Press, 1984), passim.

selection of hymns reflecting this "Old Lutheran" emphasis on purity of doctrine helped to ensure the spread of that commitment among German American Lutherans.

Walther's second consideration—that the hymns be universally accepted by "the orthodox German Lutheran Church"—likewise reflected his commitment to Lutheran orthodoxy, but particularly to Lutheran orthodoxy in its *German* form. As Walther further explained in his *Der Lutheraner* announcement:

> The editors have been fully conscious of the difficulty of their task . . . . They can give the assurance that they approached the task with fear and trembling and from the Christian church's *voluminous treasury of German hymnody,* according to the grace which God had given them, selected only those hymns which they recognized as particularly worthy of transmission from children to children's children and of preservation as a treasure, as an *inalienable possession of the German-speaking church.*[11]

That Walther, on the one hand, would be focusing his efforts on the production of a German-language hymnal for his German-speaking congregation is, in itself, unremarkable. Other German Lutheran immigrants were doing much the same. Yet, Walther was clearly keen that the hymns selected for Trinity's hymnal contain only those that were deemed "particularly worthy" among the tens of thousands available, in order to transmit to and preserve them for future generations as an "inalienable possession of the German-speaking church."

What Walther could not foresee was the way in which this "voluminous treasury" would one day transcend its German-language boundaries and be transmitted to a generation of "children's children" who would sing them not in German, but in English. Walther's *KELG* became the first and only German hymnal the Missouri Synod would ever have, available for purchase from Concordia Publishing House even into the 1960s.[12] Compiled and edited by the synod's founding president and foremost theologian, *KELG* would profoundly shape the piety and hymnological ethos of the Missouri Synod for generations to come.

Matthew Carver has, for the first time, provided for English speakers a complete metrical translation of Walther's "voluminous treasury." For by the time the Missouri Synod had transitioned to an English-language hymnal just a century ago,[13] more than half of the hymns from *KELG* had already been left behind.

May this welcomed volume serve as a gold mine for the discovery and recovery of treasures, "both new and old" (Matthew 13:52).

Jon D. Vieker
Irenaeus of Lyons, Pastor
28 June AD 2012

---

11 Walther, "Lutherisches Kirchen-Gesangbuch," as translated in Meyer, *Moving Frontiers,* 182. Emphasis added.

12 James L. Brauer, "The Hymnals of The Lutheran Church—Missouri Synod" (STM Thesis, Concordia Seminary, 1967), 42.

13 *Evangelical Lutheran Hymn-Book, with Tunes* (St. Louis: Concordia, 1912).

Translator's Note

This book is a translation of a German hymnal, viz., the *Kirchen-Gesangbuch* of the Missouri Synod as it appeared until its second major revision in 1917. This translation is not an official hymnal of the LCMS. The intent is to make intelligible to the average speaker of English a historical artifact which at one time served the church well, and which, it is hoped, may still be found useful today for the private and public devotion and edification of the church.

A few things should be noted. Most importantly, the confessional and lectionary material originally included after the hymns has been omitted. This is not to suggest that those central texts of our liturgy and confession (which are after all readily available in other resources) are of lesser import, but it results from a practical decision to offer a relatively economical resource containing the more original content—the hymns, prayers, and two composite readings—intact and unabridged from the German. Of these, the prayers are largely my own translation, except for those of Luther, many of which have been based on those of C. A. Kistler, Luther's Prayers (Pilger, 1917). Notes describing in greater detail the what has been omitted, as well as what formed the basis for the prose readings, are included in their place.

The text of the hymns has been taken overwhelmingly from CPH publications, with a strong preference for those exhibiting more accurate and more harmonious language, though some exceptions to this rule have been allowed where a particular rendering was deemed to be too much a fixture to change or replace. I am indebted to *The Lutheran Hymnal* (1941) for the bulk of our present text, and it is in continuity with that book that the style of this one has been cultivated. Alterations have been made on occasion for greater fidelity to the original sense, rhyme scheme, or meter (e.g., Miss Winkworth's translation, "Lord, hear the voice of my complaint," altered in #273), or because of centoizing, when multiple stanzas had been combined into fewer (e.g., Praise the Almighty, my soul adore Him," #441). In a very few cases, a less than ideal translation has been retained because of its overwhelming popularity. For many hymns for which no translation was discoverable, and for not a few in which the original sense was so obscured, or the meter and rhyme so altered, as to render them unfit for a book that purports to have translation among its chief aims, it was found necessary to invent a substitute. Thus about 120 hymns, and an uncounted number of additional stanzas, are original to this hymnal.

Before the hymns, sequentially speaking, the antiphons and prefaces, omitted from this translation, originally held their place; these are mentioned together with other omissions after the prayer appendix following the hymns. For the sake of cross-reference, not only the order of the thematic sections of the hymnody, but also the sequence of the hymns within each section, has been maintained from the German, though the English titles now necessarily obscure the fact that, within each section, the hymns were arranged not haphazardly or by order of importance or preference, but alphabetically.

This more or less objective arrangement was facilitated by the fact that there was no musical notation to deal with when laying out the hymns. With notation, often two shorter hymns must go together on a page, or one long hymn may need to occupy two facing pages, and throw everything out of order. Because of the added time and cost of including music, the present translation follows the precedent set by the German hymnbook. Most of the tunes needed to sing the hymns will be found in four-part settings in *The Lutheran Hymnal, The Worship Supplement* (1969), *Lutheran Worship,* and *Lutheran Service Book,* etc. References to these settings are included in brackets before each hymn. Some, marked "mel.," provide the melody only. Settings for tunes that could not be found in current hymnals, have, as far as possible, been included in the musical appendix. One exception is a setting of Luther's Te Deum, which because of length had to be omitted. A setting for that is found in *The Worship Supplement* (1969) in a somewhat abbreviated form. For many hymns, an asterisk has been placed in the tune references to indicate alternate tunes not appointed in the original hymnal but having a (usually greater) history of use with the lyrics in question, or else being an acceptable in tone as a substitute where the singers are too unfamiliar with the proper tune. Many of these alternates are based on suggestions by the commission tasked with revising the old hymnal (see their reports in *Lehre und Wehre,* vol. 55, pp. 198ff.). Alternate tunes can also be found by using the tune reference number (a number between 1 and 103) which follows each hymn tune name. The reader then refers to this number in the hymn tune index, where the other hymn tunes of the same meter are found. Some corrections to authors and dates have been silently introduced in keeping with their recommendations as well as with more recent sources.

Many capable persons contributed meaningfully to the completion and quality of this book. My wife Amanda donated her hours and expertise to design and lay out the book. Revs. Joel Baseley and Richard Stuckwisch spent precious time reviewing its contents and made many helpful suggestions which greatly improved it and clarified its purpose. Rev. Jon D. Vieker generously contributed the fruits of his ongoing research as well as other essential materials and criticism. Everything else right and good in this book is largely owing to the kind contributions and help of many other ministers of the holy office, including Revs. Mark Braden, Mark DeGarmeaux, Dan Harmelink, Ken Howes, Benjamin Mayes, Mark Preus, Jacob Sutton, and Brian Westgate; also to Rev. Sem. Micah Schmidt. Further assistance with and criticism of the musical appendix was provided by Mrs. Carol Butler, Rev. Sean Daenzer, Dr. Joe Herl, and Mr. Kevin J. Hildebrand.

Matthew Carver
Nativity of St. John the Baptist
24 June AD 2012

Abbreviations and Terms

BIBLIOGRAPHICAL ABBREVIATIONS

An	Anding, J.: *Vierstimmiges Choralbuch* . . . (Hildburghausen, 1868)
Br	Brauer, K.: *Mehrstimmiges Choralbuch* (St. Louis, 1906)
ELHB	*Evangelical Lutheran Hymn-Book* (St. Louis, 1912)
HELM	*Hymnal for Evangelical Luth. Missions* (St. Louis, 1905)
HTLH	*The Handbook to the Lutheran Hymnal* (St. Louis, 1942)
Hö	Hölter, H.: *Choralbuch: eine Sammlung* . . . (St. Louis, 1902)
LHy	*Lutheran Hymnary* (Minneapolis, 1913)
LK	Layriz, F.: *Kern des deutschen*. . . (Nördlingen, 1854)
LSB	*Lutheran Service Book* (St. Louis, 2006)
LW	*Lutheran Worship* (St. Louis, 1982)
Mor. H.-B.	*Moravian Hymn-Book* (various eds.)
Ohio	*Evangelical Lutheran Hymnal* (Columbus, 1880)
TLH	*The Lutheran Hymnal* (St. Louis, 1941)
WS69	*Worship Supplement* (St. Louis, 1969)

SPECIAL TERMS

Ab.	Abbreviated or abridged (one stanza omitted).
Ad.	Adapted.
Ca.	Circa.
Cento	Multiple stanzas omitted, parts of original stanzas may be combined into a new stanza.
Composite	Based on the work of multiple authors without clear delineation; often includes editor's work.
Fl.	Flourished (was active in the time period).
Mel.	Melody line only.
Rep.	Repeats.
St(s).	Stanza (stanzas), also known as verse(s), strophe(s).
Tr.	Translated / Translation (by).
Trad.	Traditional.
Alt.	Altered.
Anon.	Anonymous.
†	Year of death.
=	In tune references, indicates that another tune is apparently meant.
*	Different (form of) tune from that appointed in original text.

Sunday

1

Tune: Allein Gott in der Höh sei Ehr. 49. [*TLH* 237; *LW* 215; *LSB* 947]

1. All glory be to God on high,
Who hath our race befriended!
To us no harm shall now come nigh,
The strife at last is ended.
God showeth His good will to men,
And peace shall reign on earth again;
Oh, thank Him for His goodness!

2. We praise, we worship Thee, we trust,
And give Thee thanks forever,
O Father, that Thy rule is just
And wise and changes never.
Thy boundless pow'r o'er all things reigns,
Done is whate'er Thy will ordains:
Well for us that Thou rulest.

3. O Jesus Christ, Thou only Son
Of God, Thy heav'nly Father,
Who didst for all our sins atone
And Thy lost sheep dost gather:
Thou Lamb of God, to Thee on high
From out our depths we sinners cry,
Have mercy on us, Jesus!

4. O Holy Ghost, Thou precious Gift,
Thou Comforter unfailing,
O'er Satan's snares our souls uplift
And let Thy pow'r availing
Avert our woes and calm our dread.
For us the Savior's blood was shed;
We trust in Thee to save us.

—N. Decius, 1522; tr., C. Winkworth, 1863, alt.

2

Tune: Ach, bleib mit deiner Gnade. [p. 395]
Or Christus der ist mein Leben. 2. [*TLH* 53; *LW* 287; *LSB* 919]

1. Abide, O dearest Jesus,
Among us with Thy grace
That Satan may not harm us
Nor we to sin give place.

2. Abide, O dear Redeemer,
Among us with Thy Word
And thus now and hereafter
True peace and joy afford.

3. Abide with heav'nly brightness
Among us, precious Light;
Thy truth direct and keep us
From error's gloomy night.

4. Abide with richest blessings
Among us, bounteous Lord;
Let us in grace and wisdom
Grow daily through Thy Word.

5. Abide with Thy protection
Among us, Lord, our strength,
Lest world and Satan fell us
And overcome at length.

6. Abide, O faithful Savior,
Among us with Thy love;
Grant steadfastness and help us
To reach our home above.

—J. Stegmann, 1627; tr., A. Crull, †1923, alt.

3

Tune: Amen! wir habn gehöret. 4. [p. 396; *or* *TLH* 122*; *LW* 184* (no rep.)]

1. Amen! With truth most precious
Did God again refresh us.
His Spirit, sent / from heaven, (*x3*)
Confirm it in us. Amen. (*x2*)

2. Amen! To God be glory.
Christ Jesus, we adore Thee.
Thy Spirit, Lord, / unite us (*x3*)
In bliss eternal. Amen. (*x2*)

—Anon., Erfurt, 1611; tr., *HELM*, 1905.

4

Tune: Herr Jesu Christ, dich zu uns wend. 11. [*TLH* 3; *LW* 201; *LSB* 902]

1. Lord Jesus, Christ, be present now,
Our hearts in true devotion bow,
Thy Spirit send with grace divine,
And let Thy truth within us shine.

2. Unseal our lips to sing Thy praise,
Our souls to Thee in worship raise,
Make strong our faith, increase our light
That we may know Thy name aright:

3. Until we join the hosts that cry,
"Holy art Thou, O Lord, most high!"
And in the light of that blest place
Fore'er behold Thee face to face.

4. Glory to God the Father, Son,
And Holy Spirit, Three in One!
To Thee, O blessèd Trinity,
Be praise throughout eternity!

—W. A. II von Sachsen-Weimar, 1648; st. 4, Gotha, 1651; tr., C. Winkworth, 1863, alt.

5

Tune: Erhalt uns, Herr, bei deinem Wort. 11. [*TLH* 261; *LW* 334; *LSB* 655]

1. Lord, open Thou my heart to hear
And through Thy Word to me draw near;
Let me Thy Word e'er pure retain;
Let me Thy child and heir remain.

2. Thy Word doth deeply move the heart;
Thy Word doth perfect health impart,
Thy Word my soul with joy doth bless,
Thy Word brings peace and happiness.

3. To God, the Father, God the Son,
And God the Spirit, Three in One,
Shall glory, praise, and honor be
Now and throughout eternity.

—J. Olearius, 1671; tr., M. Loy, 1880.

6

Tune: Erschienen ist der herrlich Tag. 21. [*TLH* 108; *LW* 147]

1. This is the day of holy rest,
This is the day the Lord hath blest!
Away our cares, our griefs away:
Seek we our God upon His day.
Alleluia!

2. On bended knee let all adore;
Let all the Lord most High implore:
This is His holy resting-place—
Here, sinners, see His house of grace!
Alleluia!

3. Though none His anger can endure,
He hears our supplications poor;
So sing we all His praises true:
This is the Christian's labor due.
Alleluia!

4. Praise God for all His creatures great
Which He from nothing did create,
The earth, the heavens wide behold,
And everything which they enfold.
Alleluia!

5. When earth was ready made and fair,
He made mankind and set him there;
Upon him He his image laid:
Wise, good, and holy man was made.
Alleluia!

6. Behold with heart of thankfulness
How God alone, by wondrous grace,
Still daily keeps and feeds us well;
Misfortunes all His arms repel.
Alleluia!

7. Recall how on this day, once slain,
Christ Jesus rose from death again,
True gladness He for us hath won,
Though trials all against us run.
Alleluia!

8. He bore Judea's scorn and hate
And suffered such a shameful fate;
They hoped that all His words would die,
His teachings cease, His foll'wers fly.
Alleluia!

9. Yet, rising, He with glory appeared
And His disciples greatly cheered,
Who loved Him even in their loss,
And grieved when He was on the cross.
Alleluia!

10. To them He came in body fresh;
They saw Him, heard Him, felt His flesh,
Their senses all were reassured,
The pow'rful curse of death was cured.
Alleluia!

11. So let us celebrate with praise
And Christian joy this day of days,
And with our lips our tribute pay,
And from the heart rejoicing say,
Alleluia!

12. O God, who made the heav'ns and earth
For Thine own glory, praise, and worth,
Still be our stay from year to year
In every danger, grief, and fear.
Alleluia!

13. Help us Thy works, God, to confess:
All-wise, all full of righteousness,
Almighty, good and true always,
Alone deserving of all praise.
Alleluia!

14. O Jesus Christ, our Savior dear,
Who didst arise in triumph clear:
Direct our hearts, and work within,
And stir us from the sleep of sin!
Alleluia!

15. Give us Thy resurrection's pow'r,
To comfort us in every hour;
May we alone in this confide,
Though by the circling world denied.
Alleluia!

16. O Holy Ghost, Thy Word outpour
On us this day and evermore,
Thus by Thy teaching to increase
Faith, hope, and love, and never cease.
Alleluia!

17. Enlighten us, O Light of light,
Take not from us Thy favor bright,
So guide our works and all our ways,
That we may ever sing God's praise.
Alleluia!

18. O Father, Son, and Spirit, God,
This day be hallowed with Thy laud:
Grant us as well Thy joys to gain
In Thine eternal Sabbath reign.
Alleluia!

—N. Selnecker, 1676; tr. sts. 1, 2, 11, A. T. Russell, 1851, alt; sts. rest, M. Carver.

7

Tune: Kyrie! Gott Vater. 103. [*TLH* 6; *LW* 209; *LSB* 942]

1. Kyrie, God, Father in heav'n above,
Great art Thou in grace and love,
Of all things the Maker and Preserver.
Eleison, eleison!

2. Kyrie, O Christ, our King,
Salvation for sinners Thou didst bring.
O Lord Jesus, God's own Son,
Our Mediator at the heav'nly throne,
Hear our cry and grant our supplication.
Eleison, eleison!

3. Kyrie, O God the Holy Ghost,
Guard our faith, the gift we need the most;
Do Thou our last hour bless;
Let us leave this sinful world with gladness.
Eleison, eleison! Amen.

—Anon., Naumburg, 1537, after *Kyrie fons bonitatis;* tr., W. G. Polack, 1939.

8

Tune: Liebster Jesu, wir sind hier. 34. [*TLH* 16; *LW* 202; *LSB* 904]

1. Blessed Jesus, at Thy word
We are gathered all to hear Thee;
Let our hearts and souls be stirred
Now to seek and love and fear Thee,
By Thy teachings, sweet and holy,
Drawn from earth to love Thee solely.

2. All our knowledge, sense, and sight
Lie in deepest darkness shrouded,
Till Thy Spirit breaks our night
With the beams of truth unclouded.
Thou alone to God canst win us;
Thou must work all good within us.

3. Glorious Lord, Thyself impart,
Light of light, from God proceeding;
Open Thou our ears and heart,
Help us by Thy Spirit's pleading;
Hear the cry Thy people raises,
Hear and bless our pray'rs and praises.

4. Father, Son, and Holy Ghost,
Praise to Thee and adoration!
Grant that we Thy Word may trust,
And obtain true consolation
While we here below must wander,
Till we sing Thy praises yonder.

—T. Clausnitzer, 1663, sts. 1–3; Berlin, 1707, st. 4;
tr. sts. 1–3, Winkworth, 1863, alt.; st. 4, Anon., alt.

9

Tune: Liebster Jesu, wir sind hier. 34. [*TLH* 16; *LW* 202; *LSB* 904]

1. Now, the hour of worship o'er,
Teaching, hearing, praying, singing,
Let us gladly God adore,
For His Word our praises bringing;
For the rich repast He gave us
Bless the Lord, who deigned to save us.

2. Now the Blessing cheers our heart,
By His grace to us extended.
Let us joyfully depart;
Be our souls to God commended.
May His Spirit ever guide us
And with all good gifts provide us!

3. Bless our going out, we pray,
Bless our entrance in like measure;
Bless our bread, O Lord, each day,
Bless our toil, our rest, our pleasure;
Bless us when we reach death's portal,
Bless us then with life immortal.

—H. Schenck, 1674; tr. sts. 1–2, *TLH,* 1941; st. 3, O. Kaiser, 1938.

10

Tune: Herr Gott, dich loben alle wir. 11. [*TLH* 13; *LW* 216; *LSB* 923]

1. Now shout unto the Lord, O lands!
Yield to His service lips and hands;
Come forth with singing, hasten now,
And in His holy presence bow.

2. Know that our Lord is God, and He
Created us Himself, not we;
And by our Maker's grace alone
Each man has life, God's name to own.

3. He further calls us by His will
To be His sheep, His fold to fill,
And as our Shepherd ready waits
To pasture us in green estates.

4. Come, all who would with Him abide,
Into His gates, now opened wide,
With praise and psalter's sweet report;
Come singing to His glorious court.

5. Give thanks to God and sing His praise,
To spread His name your voices raise;
Give thanks and bless Him, all as one,
For thus our worthy work is done.

6. His goodness and His grace abound
With ceaseless faith and love profound;
His mercy is our heritage,
His truth endures from age to age.

7. To God the Father on His throne,
And Jesus Christ, His only Son,
With God the precious Spirit be
All praise now and eternally.

—D. Denicke, 1646; tr., M. Carver.

CLOSING VERSES

11

Tune: An Wasserflüssen Babylon. 85. [*TLH* 142; *LW* 111; *LSB* 438]

1. To Father, Son, and Spirit be
All thanks and praise forever,
And unto us eternally
Be all His grace and favor,
That we amid this vale of grief
Withstand the world and false belief,
And with true faith supplant it,
That the good warfare may be fought,
For which we here are formed and taught,
Amen. By grace God grant it.

—Anon., Strassburg, 1547; tr., M. Carver.

12

Tune: Es ist das Heil uns kommen her. 49. [*TLH* 377; *LW* 355; *LSB* 555]

1. To Father, Son, and Spirit be
All thanks and praise forever,
And unto us eternally
Be all His grace and favor,
That we may walk upon His way,
And not let sin our souls delay,
Amen. By grace God grant it.

—L. Oeler, 1525; tr., M. Carver.

Advent and Nativity of Christ

13

Aus meines Herzens Grunde. 58. [*TLH* 69; *LW* 25; *LSB* 354]

1. Arise, sons of the Kingdom!
The King is drawing nigh;
Arise and hail with gladness
The Ruler from on high.
Ye Christians, hasten forth!
Your praise and homage bring Him
And glad hosannas sing Him;
Naught else your love is worth.

2. Arise, ye drooping mourners!
The King is very near;
Away with grief and sorrow!
For, lo, your Help is here.
Behold, in many‿a place—
Oh, blessed consolation!—
You find Him, your Salvation,
Within His means of grace.

3. Arise, ye much afflicted!
The King is not afar.
Rejoice, ye long dejected,
Behold the Morning Star!
The Lord will give you joy;
Though troubles now distress you,
With comfort He will bless you,
E'en death will He destroy.

4. Now hear, ye bold transgressors,
The King full well gives heed
To all that ye are doing,
And to the life ye lead,
Enthralled by sin and hell;
There's naught in all creation
Escapes His observation,
He marketh all things well.

5. Be righteous, ye his subjects,
The King is just and true;
Prepare for Him a highway,
Make all things straight and new.
For, lo, He means it well;
Then willing bear the crosses
That He Himself imposes,
Nor let your courage fail.

6. Though war and conflagration
Take all our goods away;
The Lord is our salvation
And heritage for aye.
E'en though our loved ones die,
Yet they are not forsaken,
But from this world are taken
To live with God on high.

7. Arise, ye poor and needy!
The King provides for you;
He comes with succor speedy,
With mercy ever new.
Receive your gracious King,
The Giver of all blessing,
Hail Him, His name confessing,
And glad hosannas sing.

8. He nevermore forsaketh
A child that feels the rod,
Who Him his refuge maketh,
And puts his trust in God,
From whom all bounties flow;
E'en death itself shall never
Those from their Master sever;
His Hand is not too slow.

9. Arise, ye faint and fearful!
The King now comes with might;
His heart hath long since loved us,
He makes our darkness light.
Now are our sorrows o'er;
No wrath shall e'er befall us,
Since God in grace doth call us
His children evermore.

10. Haste then, with eager footsteps,
To see your Savior there!
He rides as King of Zion,
Strong, glorious, meek, and fair.
Draw near the Lord and give
To Him your salutation,
Who bringeth great salvation,
And bids the sinner live.

11. The King in grace remembers
His loved ones here below
With gifts of royal treasures,
Yea, doth Himself bestow
Through His blest Word and grace.
O King, arrayed in splendor,
To Thee all praise we'll render
Here and there face to face.

12. Oh, rich the gifts Thou bringest,
Thyself made poor and weak!
O Love beyond expression,
That thus can sinners seek!
For this, O Lord, will we
Our joyous tribute bring Thee
And glad hosannas sing Thee
And ever grateful be.

—J. Rist, 1651; tr., C. Winkworth, 1858, alt.

14

Tune: Ermuntre dich, mein schwacher Geist. 67. [*LSB* 378]

1. Arise, my soul, and through the air
Thy flight of gladness winging,
Aloft with choirs of angels fair
Be lifted up in singing!
For lo, God's one begotten Son,
Descending from His lofty throne,
Is made a gift so pleasant,
And here with thee is present.

2. O Jesus, Savior, truest Heart,
I stagger now to ponder
That Thou, who small and lowly art,
Hast filled with heav'nly wonder
The humble frame that houses Thee.
Be welcome, Guest of clemency!
Be welcome, Trespass-Sweeper,
O lovely Heaven-Keeper!

3. O Jesus, Prince of Souls, I find
Thou took'st our flesh upon Thee,
Becoming less than angel-kind:
'Twas love to this that won Thee!
Thou wilt beyond in heaven's realm
Our flesh with angel-flesh o'erwhelm;
To earth Thy heart was driven,
That we might be like heaven.

4. Thou art a stranger to our race,
Thy life is scant of solace,
But thus Thou givest us a place
In heaven's richest palace.
And Thou art born in dark of night
That we at last may see Thy light;
By Thee we have been wrested
From tombs by gloom infested.

5. In bitter winter Thou hast brought
Thy heav'nly summer's lightness;
In stable dim Thou mak'st Thy cot,
That we might shine in brightness
And ever share Thy gentle rest.
In cloth Thy mother winds Thy breast
For so Thou wilt unbind us
Where chains of death entwined us.

6. Thou criest, in Thy manger laid,
To give us heav'nly laughter.
Thou, Highest One, art lowest made,
To lift us up hereafter.
Thou, O my Savior, Mercy-Seat,
And Son of God, whom here I greet,
Art born of earthly mother
To be our elder Brother.

7. Thou, Lord of lords, art servant born
To set us free for heaven;
Though owning all, of all art shorn,
That we might all be given.
Thou bear'st with patience every pain;
Oh, evermore my soul sustain
Whenever troubles find me,
To bear the cross behind Thee.

8. O Jesus, kind and merciful,
Grant grace, the poor to favor,
And let me be available
To help the needy ever;
Grant me sincere humility,
And Christian kindness work in me,
To love, despite my weakness,
My neighbors with true meekness.

9. O bounteous Savior, grant to me
The good that will not fail me.
O mighty Lord, I trust in Thee,
Thy refuge will avail me;
When human help is far away,
When comes at last my dying day,
Death's bondage Thou wilt sever;
To Thee I'll sing forever.

—G. W. Sacer, †1699; tr., M. Carver.

15

Tune: Christum wir sollen loben. 11. [*TLH* 104; *LW* 43]

1. Now praise we Christ, the Holy One,
The blessed virgin Mary's Son,
Far as the glorious sun doth shine,
E'en to the world's remote confine.

2. He who Himself all things did make
A servant's form vouchsafed to take
That He as man mankind might win
And save His creatures from their sin.

3. The grace and pow'r of God the Lord
Upon the mother was outpoured;
A virgin pure and undefiled
In wondrous wise conceived a child.

4. The holy maid became th' abode
And temple of the living God;
And she, who knew not man, was blest
With God's own Word made manifest.

5. The noble mother bore a Son,—
For so did Gabriel's promise run,—
Whom John confessed and leaped with joy
Ere yet the mother knew her Boy.

6. Upon a manger filled with hay
In poverty content He lay;
With milk was fed the Lord of all,
Who feeds the ravens when they call.

7. The heav'nly choirs rejoice and raise
Their voice to God in songs of praise.
To humble shepherds is proclaimed
The Shepherd who the world hath framed.

8. All honor unto Christ be paid,
Pure Offspring of the favored maid,
With Father and with Holy Ghost,
Till time in endless time be lost.

—M. Luther, 1524, after Sedulius; tr., R. Massie, 1854, alt.

16

Tune: Der Bräutgam wird bald rufen [p. 398]
Or Ach Gott vom Himmelreiche. 59. [*TLH* 67; *LW* 176; *LSB* 514]

1. The Bridegroom soon will call us:
Come, all ye wedding-guests!
May not His voice appall us
While slumber binds our breasts!
May all our lamps be burning
And oil be found in store
That we, with Him returning,
May open find the door!

2. There shall we see delighted
Our dear Redeemer's face,
Who leads our souls benighted
To glory by His grace.
The patriarchs shall meet us,
The prophets' holy band,
Apostles, martyrs, greet us
In that celestial land.

3. They will not blush to own us
As brothers, sisters dear;
Love ever will be shown us
When we with them appear.
We all shall come before Him
Who for us man became,
As Lord and God adore Him,
And ever bless His name.

4. Our Father, rich in blessing,
Will give us crowns of gold
And, to His bosom pressing,
Impart a bliss untold,
Will welcome with embraces
Of never-ending love,
And deck us with His graces
In blissful realms above.

5. In yonder home shall never
Be silent music's voice;
With hearts and lips forever
We shall in God rejoice.
The angels shall adore Him,
All saints shall sing His praise
And bring with joy before Him
Their sweetest heav'nly lays.

6. In mansions fair and spacious
Will God the feast prepare
And, ever kind and gracious,
Bid us its riches share.
There bliss that knows no measure
From springs of love shall flow,
And never-changing pleasure
His bounty will bestow.

7. Thus God shall from all evil
Forever make us free,
From sin, and from the devil,
From all adversity,
From sickness, pain, and sadness,
From troubles, cares, and fears,
And grant us heav'nly gladness
And wipe away our tears.

—J. Walther, 1552 (trad. cento); tr., M. Loy, 1880.

17

Tune: Der Tag der ist so freudenreich. 81. [p. 400]

1. O hail this brightest day of days,
All ye good Christian people!
For Christ hath come upon our ways,
So ring it from the steeple.
Of maiden pure is He the Son;
Thou, Mary, art the chosen one,
Him in thy womb to carry.
Ever was there news so great?
God's own Son from heav'n's high state
Is born the Son of Mary.

2. This day the wondrous Child is born,
Lent unto us from heaven.
The virgin's womb He doth not scorn,
That we might help be given.
Without this Child and glorious birth
Forsaken were our fallen earth:
He brings for all salvation.
Oh, sweet Jesus Christ, we pray,
All hell's torments turn away
By Thine incarnation!

3. As from above the sun his rays
E'er poureth down upon us,
And with his glow renews our days,
And health and life are shown us;
E'en so the Christ Child was He sent,
A maiden's Babe, for our content,
And for our consolation.
In a manger was He laid,
And for us afflicted made
In this lowly station.

4. The shepherds in amazement stand,
As from the heav'ns come streaming
Bright angels in a flaming band,
Christ's glorious birth proclaiming:
The King above all kings is He!
False Herod, raging mightily,
Everywhere Him seeketh,
And by cunning arts devised
'Gainst the infant Jesus Christ,
Infants' lives he taketh.

—Anon., Wittenberg, 1524; tr., C. S. Terry, 1921, alt.

18

Tune: Freuet euch, ihr Christen alle. 82. [*TLH* 96; *LW* 40; *LSB* 897]

1. Oh, rejoice, ye Christians, loudly,
For our joy hath now begun;
Wondrous things our God hath done.
Tell abroad His goodness proudly,
Who our race hath honored thus
That He deigns to dwell with us.
Joy, O joy, beyond all gladness,
Christ hath done away with sadness!
Hence, all sorrow and repining,
For the Sun of Grace is shining!

2. See, my soul, thy Savior chooses
Weakness here and poverty,
In such love He comes to thee,
Nor the hardest couch refuses;
All He suffers for thy good,
To redeem thee by His blood:
Joy, then, joy, beyond all gladness!
Christ hath done away with sadness!
Hence, all sorrow and repining,
For the Sun of Grace is shining!

3. Lord, how shall I thank Thee rightly?
I acknowledge that by Thee
Every blessing flows to me.
Let me not forget it lightly,
But to Thee through all times cleave;
So my heart and mind receive.
Joy, yea, joy, beyond all gladness!
Christ hath done away with sadness!
Hence, all sorrow and repining,
For the Sun of Grace is shining!

4. Jesus, guard and guide Thy members,
Fill Thy brethren with Thy grace,
Hear their pray'rs in every place,
Quicken now life's faintest embers;
Grant all Christians, far and near,
Holy peace, a glad New Year!
Joy, O joy, beyond all gladness!
Christ hath done away with sadness!
Hence, all sorrow and repining,
For the Sun of Grace is shining!

—C. Keimann, 1645; tr., C. Winkworth, 1863.

19

Tune: Vom Himmel hoch da komm ich her. 11. [*TLH* 85; *LW* 37; *LSB* 358]

1. Rejoice, ye sons of men alway!
God comes to you from heav'n today;
The Lord is born a little child
Of Mary, chosen virgin mild.

2. He is the Branch of Jesse's tree,
The Lion out of Judah He,
The Gentiles' Light, the promised Seed
Who was to bruise the serpent's head.

3. He brings us peace and happiness
And heals all sorrows and distress
Which on account of Adam's fall
Forever weighed upon us all.

4. Through His low birth and holy blood
We all are saved by Christ, true God;
The angels' glory we shall share
And in His kingdom live fore'er.

—C. Freund, †1591; tr., A. Crull, †1923.

20

Tune: Fröhlich soll mein Herze springen. 63. [*TLH* 77; *LW* 39; *LSB* 360]

1. All my heart this night rejoices,
As I hear, / Far and near
Sweetest angel voices.
"Christ is born," their choirs are singing.
Till the air / Everywhere
Now with joy is ringing.

2. Forth today the Conqu'ror goeth,
Who the foe, / Sin and woe,
Death and hell, o'erthroweth.
God is man, man to deliver;
His dear Son / Now is one
With our blood forever.

3. Shall we still dread God's displeasure,
Who, to save, / Freely gave
His most cherished Treasure?
To redeem us, He hath given
His own Son / From the throne
Of His might in heaven.

4. Should He who Himself imparted
Aught withhold / From the fold,
Leave us broken-hearted?
Should the Son of God not love us,
Who, to cheer / Suff'rers here,
Left His throne above us?

5. If our blessèd Lord and Maker
Hated men, / Would He then
Be of flesh partaker?
If He in our woe delighted,
Would He bear / All the care
Of our race benighted?

6. He becomes the Lamb that taketh
Sin away / And for aye
Full atonement maketh.
For our life His own He tenders
And our race, / By His grace,
Meet for glory renders.

7. Hark! a voice from yonder manger,
Soft and sweet, / Doth entreat:
"Flee from woe and danger;
Brethren, come; from all that grieves you
Ye are freed; / All ye need
I will surely give you."

8. Come, then, banish all your sadness,
One and all, / Great and small;
Come with songs of gladness.
Love Him Who with love is glowing;
Hail the Star / Near and far
Light and joy bestowing.

9. Ye whose anguish knew no measure,
Weep no more; / See the door
To celestial pleasure.
Cling to Him, for He will guide you
Where no cross, / Pain, or loss,
Can again betide you.

10. Hither come, ye heavy-hearted,
Who for sin, / Deep within,
Long and sore have smarted;
For the poisoned wounds you're feeling
Help is near, / One is here
Mighty for their healing.

11. Hither come, ye poor and wretched;
Know His will / Is to fill
Every hand outstretchèd;
Here are riches without measure;
Here forget / All regret,
Fill your hearts with treasure.

12. Let me in my arms receive Thee;
On Thy breast / Let me rest,
Savior, ne'er to leave Thee!
Since Thou hast Thyself presented
Now to me, / I shall be,
Evermore contented.

13. Guilt no longer can distress me;
Son of God, / Thou my load
Bearest to release me.
Stain in me Thou findest never;
I am clean, / All my sin
Is removed forever.

14. I am pure, in Thee believing,
From Thy store / Evermore
Righteous robes receiving.
In my heart I will enfold Thee,
Treasure rare, / Let me there,
Loving, ever hold Thee.

15. Dearest Lord, Thee will I cherish;
Though my breath / Fail in death,
Yet I shall not perish;
But with Thee abide forever,
There on high, / In that joy
Which can vanish never.

—P. Gerhardt, 1656; tr., C. Winkworth, 1858, alt., but sts. 13–14, J. Kelly, 1867, alt.

21

Tune: Gelobet seist du, Jesu Christ. 17. [*LW* 35; *LSB* 382]

1. O Jesus Christ, all praise to Thee,
Who art pleased a man to be;
The virgin's womb Thou dost not scorn,
And angels shout to see Thee born.
Kyrieleis!

2. Th' eternal Father's only Son
Takes a manger for His throne;
The everlasting fount of good,
Assumes our mortal flesh and blood.
Kyrieleis!

3. He whom the world cannot enclose
Doth in Mary's lap repose;
To be a little Child He deigns
Who all things by Himself sustains.
Kyrieleis!

4. Th' eternal Light to us descends,
Brightness to the earth it lends,
And purely shines upon our night,
To make us children of the light.
Kyrieleis!

5. The only Son, true God confessed,
To His world now comes a Guest;
And through this vale of tears our guide,
Doth in His heav'n our home provide.
Kyrieleis!

6. In poorest guise to us He came,
Bears Himself our sin and shame,
That, as His heirs in heav'n above,
We may with angels share His love.
Kyrieleis!

7. His love to show, surpassing thought!
God's Son this great work hath wrought;
Then let us all unite to raise
Our song of glad, unceasing praise.
Kyrieleis!

—St. 1, Anon., 15th c.; st. 2–7, Luther, 1524; tr., A. T. Russell, 1851, alt.

22

Tune: Gottes Sohn ist kommen. 28. [*TLH* 74; *LW* 30; *LSB* 333]

1. Once He came in blessing,
All our ills redressing;
Came in likeness lowly,
Son of God most holy;
Bore the cross to save us,
Hope and freedom gave us.

2. Still He comes within us,
Still His voice would win us
From the sins that hurt us;
Would to Truth convert us
From our foolish errors,
Ere He comes in terrors.

3. Thus, if thou hast known Him
Not ashamed to own Him,
But wilt trust Him boldly,
Nor hast spurned Him coldly,
He will then receive thee,
Heal thee, and forgive thee.

4. All these gifts are given
In His pledge from heaven:
Bread and wine deliver
Christ to the receiver;
Here He surely shows us
That He loves and knows us.

5. They who thus unshaking
Cleave without forsaking,
And in every measure
Seek the Master's pleasure,
Shall depart with gladness
From this vale of sadness.

6. Fast the end is nearing,
Judgment day's appearing,
When from cause of grievance
He shall grant deliv'rance,
And shall take us yonder
To celestial wonder.

7. On that day of blessing
And of wrath distressing,
All the dead shall waken
And from earth be taken,
There to stand before Him,
And fear or adore Him.

8. Then the faithful-hearted
Shall to bliss be parted,
But the foul deniers
To hell's bitter fires,-
There to burn in terror
For their sin and error.

9. Come then, O Lord Jesus,
From our sins release us;
Keep our hearts believing,
That, Thy grace receiving,
We may e'er confess Thee,
Till in heav'n we bless Thee.

—J. Horn, 1544; tr. sts. 1–3, 9, Winkworth, 1863, alt.; sts. 4–8, M. Carver.

23

Tune: Nun komm, der Heiden Heiland. 5. [*TLH* 91; *LW* 13; *LSB* 352]

1. Let the earth now praise the Lord,
Who hath truly kept His word
And the sinners' Help and Friend
Now at last to us doth send.

2. What the fathers most desired,
What the prophets' heart inspired,
What they longed for many‿a year,
Stands fulfilled in glory here.

3. Abram's promised great Reward,
Zion's Helper, Jacob's Lord,—
Him of twofold race behold,—
Truly came, as long foretold.

4. Welcome, O my Savior, now!
Hail! My Portion, Lord, art Thou.
Here, too, in my heart, I pray,
Oh, prepare Thyself a way!

5. King of Glory, enter in;
Cleanse it from the filth of sin,
As Thou hast so often done;
It belongs to Thee alone.

6. As Thy coming was in peace,
Quiet, full of gentleness,
Let the same mind dwell in me
That was ever found in Thee.

7. Comfort my desponding heart;
Thou my Strength and Refuge art.
I am weak, and cunningly
Satan lays his snares for me.

8. Bruise for me the Serpent's head,
That, set free from doubt and dread,
I may cleave to Thee in faith,
Safely kept through life and death,

9. And when Thou dost come again
As a glorious King to reign,
I with joy may see Thy face,
Freely ransomed by Thy grace.

—H. Held, 1658; tr., C. Winkworth, 1863, but st. 7, Anon.

24

Tune: Herr Christ, der einig Gotts Sohn. 48. [*LW* 72; *LSB* 402]

1. Lord Christ, the Sole-Begotten
Of God the Father's heart,
Eternal without turning
As Scripture says Thou art;
The Morning Star of heaven,
Of radiance never riven,
The brightest Star of all.

2. For us of flesh partaking,
In time by Spirit sown,
Of virgin born, not breaking
The chasteness of His throne,
Death for our sake He shattered,
The bars of hell He battered,
And life to us restored.

3. Lord, let in us increasing
Thy love and knowledge be,
That we, the faith confessing,
In spirit wait on Thee;
That, tasting of Thy favor,
Our hearts may know its savor,
And always thirst for Thee.

4. Thou Maker of each creature
The Father's Arm and Might,
Who rulest o'er all nature
In Thine own Name and right:
Our hearts to Thee be turning,
Lest by our dull discerning
We ever stray from Thee.

5. Subdue us by Thy kindness,
Sustain us by Thy grace,
Destroy our sin and blindness,
New life within us place
That, while we here are dealing,
Our heart and mind and feeling,
May firmly rest in Thee.

—E. Creuziger, 1524; tr., M. Carver, but sts. 3, 4a, *Mor. H.B.*, 1754, alt.

25

Tune: Nun danket alle Gott. [*TLH* 36; *LW* 174; *LSB* 794]
Or O stilles Gotteslamm. 55. [p. 413]

1. O Lord, I welcome Thee,
My heart for joy is leaping.
Thou, Jesus, dearest Child,
Thy precious promise keeping,
Art come from heav'n to earth
To be my Brother dear;
Thou gracious Son of God,
Wilt banish all my fear.

2. The mighty Son of God,
His majesty concealing,
Dwells with our fallen race
To give us balm and healing.
The everlasting God
Descends from realms above,
Becomes a winsome Child,
Reveals His Father's love.

3. Ah, sweet and gentle Name!
Its echoes far are sounding,
It pierces hearts of stone
And tells of love abounding.
O Jesus, dearest Child,
On Thee will I rely,
And, calling on Thy name,
I die not when I die.

4. To Thee alone I cling,
For Thee all else forsaking;
On Thee alone I build
Though heav'n and earth be quaking.
To Thee alone I live,
In Thee alone I die;
O Jesus, dearest Lord,
With Thee I reign on high.

—C. Ziegler, 1648; tr., *TLH*, 1941, alt.

26

Tune: Meinen Jesum laß ich nicht. 33.
[p. 411; *or TLH* 324; *LW* 269; *LSB* 350]

1. Come, Thou precious Ransom, come,
Only Hope for sinful mortals!
Come, O Savior of the world!
Open are to Thee all portals.
Come, Thy beauty let us see;
Anxiously we wait for Thee,

2. Enter now my waiting heart,
Glorious King and Lord most holy.
Dwell in me and ne'er depart,
Though I am but poor and lowly.
Ah, what riches will be mine
When Thou art my Guest Divine!

3. My hosannas and my palms
Graciously receive, I pray Thee;
Evermore, as best I can,
Savior, I will homage pay Thee,
And in faith I will embrace,
Lord, Thy merit through Thy grace,

4. Hail, hosanna, David's Son!
Help, Lord, hear our supplication!
Let Thy kingdom, scepter, crown,
Bring us blessing and salvation,
That forever we may sing:
Hail, hosanna! to our King,

—J. Olearius, 1664; tr., A. Crull, 1923.

27

Tune: Lobe den Herren, den mächtigen. 24. [*TLH* 39; *LW* 444; *LSB* 790]

1. Comest Thou, Jesus, from heaven to earth now descending?
Can it be heaven and earth are in harmony blending?
O God indeed, / Can my distress and my need
Cause Thee so low to be bending?

2. All that in Adam and Eve by death's power was riven,
Thou by Thy life and Thy torments, O Jesus, hast given!
God of all grace, / By this Thy birth to our race
All grief away hath been driven.

3. Satan and Hell in their rage are conspiring together,
Seeking my fall, that I perish from Thee, Lord, forever.
God of all might, / Stamp out hell's smoldering quite,
Grief and distress from me sever.

4. Jesus, O grant me, alone Thy good mercies to ponder;
Teach my frail flesh in Thy holiness only to wander.
God most divine, / Grant me by faith to assign
Thanks unto Thee here and yonder.

5. Jesus, when finally this life Thou gavest is ending,
Raise up Thy faithful again, Thy true promise defending;
There, God, to see / Grief and distress made to flee,
Gladness forever ascending.

—C. F. Nachtenhöfer, 1667; tr. st. 1a, E. M. Fowler; sts. rest, M. Carver.

28

Tune: Laßt uns alle fröhlich sein. 3. [*TLH* 97; *LW* 42; *LSB* 390]

1. Let us all with gladsome voice
Praise the God of heaven,
Who, to bid our hearts rejoice,
His own Son hath given.

2. To this vale of tears He comes,
Here to serve in sadness,
That with Him in heav'n's fair homes
We may reign in gladness.

3. We are rich, for He was poor;
Is not this a wonder?
Therefore praise God evermore
Here on earth and yonder.

4. O Lord Christ, our Savior dear,
Be Thou ever near us.
Grant us now a glad new year.
Amen, Jesus, hear us!

—Wittenberg, 1611; tr., C. Winkworth, 1863, alt

29

Tune: Lob sei dem allmächtigen Gott. 11. [p. 410; *or LW* 17*; *LSB* 351*]

1. To God we render thanks and praise,
Who pitied mankind's fallen race
And gave His dear and only Son,
That us as children He might own.

2. He came to seek and save the lost;
We sinned, and He would bear the cost,
That we might share eternal bliss;
O what unbounded love was this!

3. What grace, what great benevolence,
What love, surpassing human sense!
For this great work no angel can
Him duly praise, much less a man.

4. God took our nature and our frame,
The Maker to His creature came,
Nor scorned that He should Man become
Within a lowly virgin's womb.

5. The Father's Word Eternal thence
Took flesh in purest innocence;
The Alpha and Omega gave
Himself to mis'ry, us to save.

6. But what is all the human race,
That God should show such matchless grace,
To give His Son, that we might claim
Life everlasting in His name?

7. How wretched they who Thee forsake,
And will not of Thy grace partake!
Those who neglect to hear the Son
The wrath of God from heav'n are shown.

8. Why, sinner, dost thou then delay
To meet Thy king upon His way,
Who unto Thee so humbly comes
And faithfully thy cause assumes?

9. O come, and put away thy care
And in thy heart His way prepare:
"I'll dwell with thee," our Savior saith;
Receive Him and His grace by faith.

10. Thy crimes and self-made holiness,
Thy carnal reason and distress
Give up, and trust to Christ alone,
Who did for all thy sins atone.

11. If this thou do, then thine is He;
Beware of hell's great agony,
For if thou do not, heaven's door
Is barred to thee forevermore.

12. The Lord's first coming to our race
Was in the form of gentleness;
His second shall the heathen see
With terror and anxiety.

13. But those who in Christ Jesus stand
With gladness shall possess the land
And with the choirs of angels rest
Where evil no more can molest.

14. To God the Father on His throne
And Jesus Christ, His only Son,
And Holy Ghost all glory be
With thanks and praise eternally.

—M. Weisse, 1531; tr. sts. 1–3, 6, 9–10, *Mor. H.-Book,* 1789, alt.; sts. rest, M. Carver.

30

Tune: Lobt Gott, ihr Christen allzugleich. 6. [*TLH* 105; *LW* 44; *LSB* 389]

1. Praise God the Lord, ye sons of men,
Before His highest throne;
Today He opens heav'n again
And gives us His own Son,
And gives us His own Son.

2. He leaves His heavenly Father's throne,
Is born an infant small,
And in a manger, poor and lone,
Lies in a humble stall,
Lies in a humble stall.

3. He veils in flesh His pow'r divine
A servant's form to take;
In want and lowliness must pine
Who heav'n and earth did make,
Who heav'n and earth did make.

4. He nestles at His mother's breast,
Receives her tender care,
Whom angels hail with joy most blest,
King David's royal Heir,
King David's royal Heir.

5. 'Tis He who in these latter days
From Judah's tribe should come,
By whom the Father would upraise
The Church, His Christendom,
The Church, His Christendom.

6. A wondrous change which He doth make!
He takes our flesh and blood,
And He conceals for sinners' sake
His majesty of God,
His majesty of God.

7. He serves that I a lord may be;
A great exchange indeed!
Could Jesus' love do more for me
To help me in my need?
To help me in my need?

8. He opens us again the door
Of Paradise today;
The angel guards the gate no more.
To God our thanks we pay,
To God our thanks we pay.

—N. Herman, 1560; tr., A. Crull, 1923, alt

31

Tune: Macht hoch die Tür, die Tor macht weit. 71.
[*TLH* 73, first tune; *or LW* 23*; *LSB* 340*]

1. Lift up your heads, ye mighty gates!
Behold, the King of Glory waits;
The King of kings is drawing near,
The Savior of the world is here.
Life and salvation He doth bring,
Wherefore rejoice and gladly sing:
We praise Thee, Father, now,
Creator, wise art Thou!

2. A Helper just He comes to thee,
His chariot is humility,
His kingly crown is holiness,
His scepter, pity in distress.
The end of all our woe He brings,
Wherefore the earth is glad and sings:
We praise Thee, Savior, now,
Mighty in deed art Thou!

3. O blest the land, the city blest,
Where Christ the Ruler is confessed!
O happy hearts and happy homes
To whom this King in triumph comes!
The cloudless Sun of joy He is,
Who bringeth pure delight and bliss.
We praise Thee, Spirit, now,
Our Comforter art Thou!

4. Fling wide the portals of your heart;
Make it a temple set apart
From earthly use for heav'n's employ,
Adorned with pray'r and love and joy.
So shall your King come in to you
With life and with salvation true.
To Thee, O God, be praise
For word and deed and grace!

5. Redeemer, come! I open wide
My heart to Thee; here, Lord, abide!
Let me Thy inner presence feel,
Thy grace and love in me reveal;
Thy Holy Spirit guide us on
Until our glorious goal is won.
Eternal praise and fame
We offer to Thy name.

—G. Weissel, 1623; tr., C. Winkworth, 1855, alt.

32

Tune: Gottes Sohn ist kommen. 28. [*TLH* 74; *LW* 30; *LSB* 333]

1. Mark, O mortal, duly
What thy life is truly,
And why God hath given
His own Son from heaven,
With our flesh arrayed Him,
Here among us laid Him:

2. He the truth would show thee,
As His convert know thee,
Be from sin thy Savior,
And win thee God's favor,
Pleading with the Father,
E'er to be thy Brother.

3. He would send His Spirit,
Couns'lor of great merit,
Through His proclamation
For thy consolation,
In thee make His dwelling,
All thy grief expelling.

4. Let Him then indwell thee!
Do as God doth tell thee:
Open thy heart's portal,
That, through Word immortal,
Christ therein may enter
And remain its center.

5. Let thy heart be pliant,
On His will reliant;
Lead a pure existence,
Making no resistance,
But all things fulfilling
After His own willing.

6. Prove His love amazing,
With thy works Him praising;
Ever without swerving
Be awake, observing,
That in each endeavor
Thou may'st please Him ever.

7. Then in Him abiding,
Thou shalt have His guiding;
In His peace He'll keep thee
Resting ever deeply,
Witness sure extending
Of the life unending.

8. Much thou now must suffer;
To God's will thine offer,
By His kind assisting
Satan's wiles resisting.
Is thy faith unbending,
Well shall be thine ending.

9. Then the Lord will cheer thee
And in death be near thee,
Bear thy soul from sadness
To eternal gladness,
Till all flesh's springing
At the trumpet's ringing.

10. Then in manner splendid,
He, from heav'n descended,
With all might and glory
Shall conclude the story,
And with joy address them
Who did here confess Him:

11. "Come, ye blest believers,
Of My grace receivers!
Enter, chosen nation,
My new-born creation!
Where My Father waiteth,
And no bliss abateth."

12. Joyful thou wilt waken,
From all sorrow taken,
Living in perfection,
God's by pure election,
Bliss and gladness knowing,
Like the sunlight glowing.

13. Blest, who hear God's preaching
And receive the teaching
Of the Holy Spirit
When by grace they hear it,
Owning Christ their Savior,
Trusting Him forever!

14. But who shun God's calling,
Faith in Christ forestalling,
Shall receive the sentence
For their unrepentance:
Leaving all they cherish,
They in hell must perish.

15. Come, Lord, our Salvation!
Help Thy congregation
To obey Thy teaching,
Till, Thy refuge reaching,
We to Thee shall tender
Endless praise and splendor.

—M. Weisse, 1531; tr., M. Carver.

33

Tune: Von Gott will ich nicht lassen. 58.
[*TLH* 393; *LW* 409; *LSB* 713; *or TLH* 112*]

1. Ye sons of men, oh, hearken:
Your heart and mind prepare;
To hail th' Almighty Savior,
O sinners, be your care.
He who of grace alone
Our Life and Light was given,
The promised Lord from heaven,
Unto our world is shown.

2. Prepare the way before Him;
Prepare for Him the best.
Cast out whate'er offendeth
This great, this heav'nly Guest.
Make straight, make plain, the way:
The lowly valleys raising,
The heights of pride abasing,
His path all even lay.

3. The humble heart and lowly
God lifteth up on high;
Beneath His feet in anguish
The haughty soul shall lie.
The heart, sincere and right,
That heeds God's invitation
And makes true preparation,
It is the Lord's delight.

4. Prepare my heart, Lord Jesus,
Turn not from me aside,
And grant that I receive Thee
This blessèd Advent-tide.
From stall and manger low
Come Thou to dwell within me;
Loud praises will I sing Thee
And forth Thy glory show.

—V. Thilo, 1642, but st. 4, Hannover, 1657; tr. based on A. T. Russell, 1851.

34

Tune: Nun danket alle Gott. [*TLH* 36; *LW* 174; *LSB* 794]
Or Was frag ich nach der Welt. 55. [*TLH* 99; *LW* 187; *LSB* 346]

1. Now are the days fulfilled,
God's Son is manifested,
Now His great majesty
In human flesh is vested.
Behold the mighty God,
By whom all wrath is stilled,
The woman's promised Seed—
Now are the days fulfilled.

2. Now are the days fulfilled,
Lo, Jacob's Star is shining;
The gloomy night has fled
Wherein the world lay pining.
Now, Israel, look on Him
Who long thy heart hath thrilled;
Hear Zion's watchmen cry:
Now are the days fulfilled.

3. Now are the days fulfilled,
Now Aaron's rod has budded,
To which the holy ark
By figure once alluded.
The Counselor of Might
Is born a feeble child
And clothed in humble dust—
Now are the days fulfilled.

4. Now are the days fulfilled,
The child of God rejoices;
No bondage of the Law,
No curses that it voices,
Can fill our hearts with fear;
On Christ our hope we build.
Behold the Prince of Peace—
Now are the days fulfilled.

—Rochlitz, 1746; tr. sts. 1–2, 4, F. W. Herzberger, †1930; st. 3, A. Crull, 1866, alt

35

Tune: Erschienen ist der herrlich Tag. 21. [*TLH* 108; *LW* 147]

1. The new church-year again is come,
This wakes the joy of Christendom;
Thy King, O Zion, comes to thee;
Rejoice, rejoice eternally!
Alleluia!

2. Now in our midst anew are heard
The lessons of God's gracious Word,
That lead the way to life and heav'n;
Lord, praise to Thee for this be giv'n!
Alleluia!

3. What Thy truth teaches o'er and o'er,
By which our faith is strengthened more,
Let it abide in us, that we
May render endless praise to Thee.
Alleluia!

—J. Olearius, 1671; tr., E. Cronenwett, †1931, alt.

36

Tune: Nun komm, der heiden Heiland. 5. [*TLH* 95; *LW* 13; *LSB* 332]

1. Savior of the nations, come,
Virgin's Son, make here Thy home!
Marvel now, O heav'n and earth,
That the Lord chose such a birth.

2. Not by human flesh and blood,
By the Spirit of our God,
Was the Word of God made flesh—
Woman's Offspring, pure and fresh.

3. Wondrous birth! O wondrous Child
Of the Virgin undefiled!
Though by all the world disowned,
Still to be in heav'n enthroned.

4. Lo, He comes, the Lord of all;
Leaves His bright and royal hall;
God and man, with giant force,
Hastèning to run His course.

5. From the Father forth He came,
And returneth to the same,
Captive leading death and hell—
High the song of triumph swell!

6. Thou, the Father's only Son,
Hast o'er sin the vict'ry won.
Boundless shall Thy kingdom be;
When shall we its glories see?

7. Brightly doth Thy manger shine,
Glorious is its light divine.
Let not sin o'ercloud this light;
Ever be our faith thus bright.

8. Praise to God the Father sing,
Praise to God the Son, our King,
Praise to God the Spirit be
Ever and eternally.

—M. Luther, 1524, after Ambrose; tr., W. M. Reynolds, 1860, alt.

37

Tune: In dulci jubilo. 54. [*TLH* 92; *LW* 47; *LSB* 386]

1. Now sing we, now rejoice,
Now raise to heav'n our voice;
He from whom joy streameth
Poor in a manger lies;
Not so brightly beameth
The sun in yonder skies.
Thou my Savior art!
Thou my Savior art!

2. Come from on high to me;
I cannot rise to Thee.
Cheer my wearied spirit,
O pure and holy Child;
Through Thy grace and merit,
Blest Jesus, Lord most mild,
Draw me unto Thee!
Draw me unto Thee!

3. Now through His Son doth shine
The Father's grace divine.
Death o'er us had reignèd
Through sin and vanity;
He for us obtainèd
Eternal joy on high.
May we praise Him there!
May we praise Him there!

4. Oh, where shall joy be found?
Where but on heav'nly ground?
Where the angels singing
With all His saints unite,
Sweetest praises bringing
In heav'nly joy and light.
Oh, that we were there!
Oh, that we were there!

—Anon., 14th c.; tr., A. T. Russell, 1851, alt

38

Tune: Wie schön leuchtet der Morgenstern. 86. [*TLH* 343; *LW* 325; *LSB* 395]

1. O Prince of David's lineage born!
O Bridegroom of my soul forlorn!
My Life and my Salvation:
How can I e'er give thanks to Thee,
Who in my mis'ry soughtest me—
How make due reparation?
Now is / All bliss:
Grief, man seeth, / Wholly fleeth;
Joy is thriving
For the Prince of Peace arriving.

2. Though full of gladness now I sing,
No fitting gift I know to bring
The Child of God's selection!
Receive, dear Son of God's own heart,
My heart, and claim it, every part,
And kindle mine affection!
Let me / Kiss Thee,
Son and Savior! / Hold me ever,
Fill and move me,
That I ever hold and love Thee.

3. Stay, worthiest Treasure, Crown of pride!
O Thou my Bliss, with me abide,
Thou Hope of hearts afflicted!
Thou Dew of heav'n, Thy fruit endow;
O sweetest Manna, visit now
The humble and dejected!
Keep Thy / Light nigh,
Lest earth darken; / Let us hearken,
And forever
See it shine and lose it never.

—P. von Zesen, †1689; tr., M. Carver.

39

Tune: O Jesu Christ, dein Kripplein ist. 26. [*TLH* 81]

1. O Jesus Christ, / Thy manger is
My paradise at which my soul reclineth.
For there, O Lord, / Doth lie the Word
Made flesh for us; herein Thy grace forth shineth.

2. He Whom the sea / And wind obey
Doth come to serve the sinner in great meekness.
Thou, God's own Son, / With us art one,
Dost join us and our children in our weakness.

3. Thou, highest Good, / Dost lift our blood
Up to the throne of God, Thy heav'nly Father.
Thou, Lord, with us / (Who are as grass)
Art both the Pow'r of God and our own Brother.

4. How can it be, / The enemy
Of souls should harm us with his bitter raging?
His only ruse / Is to accuse
And keep us in our inborn sin engaging.

5. Be still, O foe! / Dost thou not know:
My Friend, my flesh and blood, in heav'n is seated?
What thou didst smite / The Prince of might
From Jacob's root to glory elevated!

6. Thy light and grace / Our guilt efface,
Thy heav'nly riches all our loss retrieving.
Immanuel, / Thy birth doth quell
The pow'r of hell and Satan's bold deceiving.

7. Thou Christian heart, / Whoe'er thou art,
Be of good cheer and let no sorrow move thee!
For God's own Child, / In mercy mild,
Joins thee to Him; how greatly God must love thee!

8. Remember thou / What glory now
The Lord prepared thee for all earthly sadness.
The angel host / Can never boast
Of greater glory, greater bliss or gladness.

9. There dost thou see / In front of thee
Thy flesh and blood which steer the clouds of heaven?
What then can rise / To steal this prize,
And leave thy soul by fear and sorrow driven?

10. Thy mind so weak / Will seldom seek
Its comfort in the midst of sin and danger.
So turn thine eyes / Down from the skies
And find thy comfort in a lowly manger.

11. Though plagues thou bear, / Do not despair!
Thy Brother will not spurn thy grief and sighing.
His heart is meek / And loves the weak,
Nor can He see our suff'ring without crying.

12. To Him make haste! / Seek help and rest!
Thou soon wilt thank Him for His peace and patience.
He knows full well / The pangs of hell,
And understands the sick and sinner's conscience.

13. For this indeed / Did He once bleed
And bear the cross's fury in His body,
So that His pain / Might still remain
Of all our misery a constant mem'ry.

14. To say no more, / He is the Door
To all the joys true life could ever offer.
He soon will send / A blessed end
To all that faithful Christians here must suffer.

15. The world may hold / Her wealth and gold;
But thou, my heart, keep Christ as thy true Treasure.
To Him hold fast / Until at last
A crown be thine and honor in full measure.

—P. Gerhardt, 1653; tr. sts. 1–2, 6–8, 15, *TLH,* 1941; sts. 3, 5, 9–14 M. Preus, 2010, alt.; st. 4, M. Carver.

40

Tune: Vom Himmel hoch da komm ich her. 11. [*TLH* 85; *LW* 37; *LSB* 358]

1. Behold, behold, what wonder's here!
The gloomy night turns bright and clear,
A brilliant light dispels the shade,
The stars before it pale and fade.

2. A wondrous light it is, I trow,
And not the ancient sun shines now,
For, contrary to nature, night
Is turned by it to day so bright.

3. What means He to announce to us,
Who nature's course can alter thus?
A mighty work designed must be
When such a mighty sign we see.

4. Oh, can it be that on this e'en
The Sun of Righteousness is seen,
The Star from Jacob's stem so bright,
The woman's Seed, the Gentile's Light?

5. 'Tis even so—for from the sky
Heav'n's hosts with joyful tidings hie,
That He is born in Bethl'hem's stall,
Who Savior is and Lord of All!

6. O blessedness! The goodly throng
Of sainted fathers waited long
To see this day, with hope deferred,
As we may learn from God's own Word.

7. Awake, ye sons of men, awake!
Up, up, and now your journey take
With me! Let us together go
To where the blessèd angels show.

8. Behold, there in yon gloomy stall
He lies who ruleth over all;
Where once their food the cattle sought,
The Virgin's child for rest is brought!

9. O child of Adam, ponder well
And stumble not at what I tell!
He who appears in this low state
For us both is and shall be great.

10. In mortal flesh we Him behold,
Who all things made and doth uphold.
The Word who was with God is He;
Himself is God whom now we see.

11. It is God's sole-begotten Son
Thro' whom we now approach His throne:
The First and Last, Almighty God,
The Conqu'ror, Lord of Sabaoth.

12. The times predicted are fulfilled,
God's fiery wrath must now be stilled;
His Son, made man, doth bear our guilt,
God's favor gains by His blood spilt.

13. It is a time of joy today;
With mourning and with woe away!
Woe, woe to him who us reviled!
God's seen in flesh—we're reconciled.

14. The Canceler of sin is here;
The Serpent-Crusher now is near.
The Death of death—the Woe of hell—
The Lord of Life with us doth dwell.

15. All foes are put our feet beneath,
For sin and Satan, hell and death
Are brought to shame and put to flight
Upon this great, this wondrous night.

16. Oh, happy world, thrice happy they
Who with this lowly Infant stay;
Oh, happy they who by faith's eyes
In Him their Savior recognize!

17. Now praise the Lord, whoe'er can praise,
Who from their low estate to raise
His enemies, from His high throne
Sent down His loved, His only Son.

18. Up, join the angel host and cry,
"Now glory be to God most High;
Let peace prevail the world around,
Good-will to men and joy abound."

—P. Gerhardt, †1676; tr., J. Kelly, 1867, alt.

41

Tune: Vom Himmel hoch da komm ich her. 11. [*TLH* 85; *LW* 37; *LSB* 358]

1. "From heav'n above to earth I come
To bear good news to every home;
Glad tidings of great joy I bring,
Whereof I now will say and sing:

2. "To you this night is born a child
Of Mary, chosen virgin mild;
This little child, of lowly birth,
Shall be the joy of all the earth.

3. "This is the Christ, our God and Lord,
Who in all need shall aid afford;
He will Himself your Savior be
From all your sins to set you free.

4. "He will on you the gifts bestow
Prepared by God for all below,
That in His kingdom, bright and fair,
You may with us His glory share.

5. "These are the tokens ye shall mark:
The swaddling clothes and manger dark;
There ye shall find the Infant laid
By whom the heav'ns and earth were made."

6. Now let us all with gladsome cheer
Go with the shepherds and draw near
To see the precious Gift of God,
Who hath His own dear Son bestowed.

7. Give heed, my heart, lift up thine eyes!
What is it in yon manger lies?
Who is this child, so young and fair?
The blessèd Christ-child lieth there.

8. Welcome to earth, Thou noble Guest,
Through whom the sinful world is blest!
Thou com'st to share my misery;
What thanks shall I return to Thee?

9. Ah, Lord, who hast created all,
How weak art Thou, how poor and small,
That Thou dost choose Thine infant bed
Where humble cattle lately fed!

10. Were earth a thousand times as fair,
Beset with gold and jewels rare,
It yet were far too poor to be
A narrow cradle, Lord, for Thee.

11. For velvets soft and silken stuff
Thou hast but hay and straw so rough,
Whereon Thou, King, so rich and great,
As 'twere Thy heav'n, art throned in state.

12. And thus, dear Lord, it pleaseth Thee
To make this truth quite plain to me,
That all the world's wealth, honor, might,
Are naught and worthless in Thy sight.

13. Ah, dearest Jesus, holy Child,
Make Thee a bed, soft, undefiled,
Within my heart, that it may be
A quiet chamber kept for Thee.

14. My heart for very joy doth leap,
My lips no more can silence keep;
I, too, must sing with joyful tongue
That sweetest ancient cradle-song:

15. Glory to God in highest heav'n,
Who unto us His Son hath giv'n!
While angels sing with pious mirth
A glad new year to all the earth.

—M. Luther, 1535; tr., C. Winkworth, 1855, alt.

42

Tune: Vom Himmel hoch da komm ich her. 11. [=*TLH* 85; *LW* 37; *LSB* 358]

1. To shepherds as they watched by night
Appeared a host of angels bright;
Behold the tender Babe, they said,
In yonder lowly manger laid.

2. At Bethlehem, in David's town,
As Micah did of old make known;
'Tis Jesus Christ, your Lord and King,
Who doth to all salvation bring.

3. Oh, then rejoice that through His Son
God is with sinners now at one;
Made like yourselves of flesh and blood,
Your Brother is th' eternal God.

4. What harm can sin and death then do?
The true God now abides with you.
Let hell and Satan rage and chafe,
Christ is your Brother—ye are safe.

5. Not one He will or can forsake
Who Him his confidence doth make.
Let all his wiles the Tempter try,
You may his utmost powers defy.

6. Ye shall and must at last prevail;
God's own ye are, ye cannot fail.
To God forever sing your praise
With joy and patience all your days.

—M. Luther, 1543; tr., R. Massie, 1854.

43

Tune: Vom Himmel hoch da komm ich her. [*TLH* 85; *LW* 37; *LSB* 358; *or LSB* 655*]
Or Lob sei dem allmächtigen Gott. 11. [p. 410*]

1. Since Adam's age, so long have we
Been cursed in our iniquity,
Corrupt in body, soul, and mind,
With nothing living left to find.

2. By great distress we were hemmed in,
And subjects all of death and sin,
Consigned to hell's abysmal grave,
And there was none to help or save.

3. God searched the cities of mankind
For someone to His will aligned,
A man whose heart reflected God,
Yet nothing found but flesh and blood.

4. For perfect, godly sanctity
And righteousness were thoroughly
Corrupt and lost in Adam's fall,
From whom descend we sinners all.

5. When God beheld our sickness sore
That no physician could restore,
He thought upon His kindness vast,
And kept His Word from first to last.

6. He said, "I will display My grace
And give My Son to save this race,
To heal them as their Doctor true,
To bless them, and to make them new."

7. He swore this great and precious oath
To Abraham and David both,
And promised them His only Son,
By whom redemption would be won.

8. God also sent the prophets word,
And through their lips He made it heard
What godly men, both high and low,
For ages past desired to know.

9. Though well they wished in life to see
The promise kept and come to be,
They yet took comfort in true faith
That God would save them out of death.

10. Then came the time ordained of old,
As Jacob in his day foretold:
God chose a virgin pure and fine,
Betrothed to one of David's line.

11. The Spirit's pow'r on Mary came,
And took her virgin blood to frame
The pure and blessed Crown of youth,
In whom are found all grace and truth.

12. O Christ, Thou Fruit forever blest,
Conceived in manner wholly chaste,
Bestow Thy blessing, set us free,
Our Savior, Salve, and Comfort be.

—M. Weisse, 1533; tr., M. Carver.

44

Tune: Valet will ich dir geben. 59.
[*TLH* 58, first tune; *LW* 79; *LSB* 442; or *TLH* 58, second tune*; *LW* 19*; *LSB* 334*]

1. O Lord, how shall I meet Thee,
How welcome Thee aright?
Thy people long to greet Thee,
My Hope, my heart's Delight!
O kindle, Lord, most holy,
Thy lamp within my breast
To do in spirit lowly
All that may please Thee best.

2. Thy Zion strews before Thee
Green boughs and fairest palms,
And I, too, will adore Thee
With joyous songs and psalms.
My heart shall bloom forever
For Thee with praises new
And from Thy name shall never
Withhold the honor due.

3. What hast Thou e'er neglected
For my good here below?
When heart and soul dejected,
Were sunk in deepest woe,
When lost from that high station
Where peace and pleasure reign,
Thou camest, my Salvation,
And mad'st me glad again.

4. I lay in fetters, groaning,
Thou com'st to set me free;
I stood, my shame bemoaning,
Thou com'st to honor me;
A glory Thou dost give me,
A treasure safe on high,
That will not fail or leave me
As earthly riches fly.

5. Love caused Thy incarnation,
Love brought Thee down to me;
Thy thirst for my salvation
Procured my liberty.
O love beyond all telling,
That led Thee to embrace,
In love all love excelling,
Our lost and fallen race!

6. Rejoice, then, ye sad-hearted,
Who sit in deepest gloom,
Who mourn o'er joys departed
And tremble at your doom.
Despair not, He is near you,
Yea, standing at the door,
Who best can help and cheer you
And bids you weep no more.

7. Ye need not toil nor languish
Nor ponder day and night
How in the midst of anguish
Ye draw Him by your might.
He comes, He comes all willing,
Moved by His love alone,
Your woes and troubles stilling;
For all to Him are known.

8. Sin's debt, that fearful burden,
Let not your souls distress;
Your guilt the Lord will pardon
And cover by His grace.
He comes, for men procuring
The peace of sin forgiv'n,
For all God's sons securing
Their heritage in heav'n.

9. What though the foes be raging,
Heed not their craft and spite;
Your Lord, the battle waging,
Will scatter all their might.
He comes, a King most glorious,
And all His earthly foes
In vain His course victorious
Endeavor to oppose.

10. He comes to judge the nations,
A terror to His foes,
A Light of consolations
And blessed Hope to those
Who love the Lord's appearing.
O glorious Sun, now come,
Send forth Thy beams most cheering,
And guide us safely home.

—P. Gerhardt, 1653; tr., *TLH,* 1941., st. 3, J. Kelly, 1863, alt

45

Tune: Wir Christenleut habn jetzund Freud. 26. [p. 418; *or TLH* 107* (no rep.)]

1. We Christians may (*x2*) / Rejoice today
When Christ was born to comfort and to save us.
Who thus believes / No longer grieves,
For none are lost who grasp the hope He gave us.

2. Oh, wondrous joy (*x2*) / That God most high
Should take our flesh and thus our race should honor!
A virgin mild / Hath borne this Child;
Such grace and glory God hath put upon her.

3. Sin brought us grief, (*x2*) / But Christ relief,
When down to earth He came for our salvation.
Since God with us / Is dwelling thus,
Who dares to speak the Christian's condemnation?

4. Then hither throng (*x2*) / With happy song
To Him whose birth and death are our assurance;
Through whom are we / At last set free
From sins and burdens that surpassed endurance.

5. Yea, let us praise (*x2*) / Our God and raise
Loud alleluias to the skies above us.
The bliss bestowed / Today by God
To ceaseless thankfulness and joy should move us.

—C. Füger, before 1586; tr., C. Winkworth, 1863, alt

46

Tune: Erschienen ist der herrlich Tag. 21. [*TLH* 108; *LW* 147]

1. We sing, Immanuel, Thy praise,
Thou Prince of Life and Fount of grace,
Thou Flow'r of heav'n and Star of morn,
Thou Lord of lords, Thou virgin-born.
Alleluia!

2. With all Thy saints to Thee we sing,
Praise, honor, thanks to Thee we bring,
That Thou, O long-expected Guest,
Hast come at last to make us blest!
Alleluia!

3. For Thee, since first the world was made,
So many hearts have watched and prayed;
The patriarchs' and prophets' throng
For Thee have hoped and waited long.
Alleluia!

4. Above all others longed for Thee
Thy people's king and shepherd, he
With whom Thou, Lord, so well wert pleased,
When with his harp Thy name he praised.
Alleluia!

5. Oh, that the Savior soon would come
To break our bonds and lead us home!
Oh, that He might salvation bring,
Then Jacob would rejoice and sing.
Alleluia!

6. Now art Thou here, Thou ever Blest!
In lowly manger dost Thou rest.
Thou, making all things great, art small;
So poor art Thou, yet clothest all.
Alleluia!

7. All heav'ns are Thine, yet Thou dost come
To sojourn in a stranger's home;
A mother's milk dost not despise,
Who art the Joy of angels' eyes.
Alleluia!

8. Thou hast set bounds to earth and sea,
Yet swaddling-bands encircle Thee;
Thou'rt God—a bed of straw Thou hast;
Thou'rt man—yet art the First and Last.
Alleluia!

9. From Thee above all gladness flows,
Yet Thou must bear such bitter woes;
The Gentiles' Light and Hope Thou art,
Yet findest none to soothe Thine heart.
Alleluia!

10. The sweetest Friend of man Thou art.
Yet many hate Thee in their heart;
By Herod's heart Thou art abhorred,
Yet Thou art our Salvation, Lord.
Alleluia!

11. But I, Thy servant, Lord, today
Confess my love and freely say,
I love Thee truly, but I would
That I might love Thee as I should.
Alleluia!

12. I have the will, the pow'r is weak;
Yet, Lord, my humble off'ring take
And graciously the love receive
Which my poor heart to Thee can give.
Alleluia!

13. Thou to be weak dost not disdain,
Dost choose the things the world deems vain,
Art poor and needy and content
To suffer poverty and want.
Alleluia!

14. Thou sleepest on the lap of earth;
The manger where Thou at Thy birth
Wast laid to rest, the hay, the stall
Were mean and misèrable all.
Alleluia!

15. And therefore doth my courage rise,
Me also wilt Thou not despise;
O dearest Lord, Thy tender grace
Fills me with hope and happiness.
Alleluia!

16. Although I've passed in sin my days,
And wandered far from wisdom's ways,
Yet Thou for this to earth hast come,
To bring the wand'ring sinner home.
Alleluia!

17. Had I no load of sin to bear,
Thy grace, O Lord, I could not share;
In vain hadst Thou been born for me
If from God's wrath I had been free.
Alleluia!

18. Now fearlessly I come to Thee;
From every grief Thou mak'st me free;
Thou bear'st the wrath, dost death destroy,
And turnest sorrow into joy.
Alleluia!

19. Thou art my Head, my Lord divine,
I am Thy member, wholly Thine,
And by Thy Spirit's gracious pow'r
Will seek to serve Thee evermore.
Alleluia!

20. Thus will I sing Thy praises here
With joyful spirit year by year;
And when we reckon time no more,
May I in heav'n Thy name adore.
Alleluia!

—P. Gerhardt, 1653; tr., sts. 1, 3, 6, 9, 12, 17, 20, *TLH*, 1941; sts. rest, C. Winkworth, alt.

Circumcision of Christ and New Year

47

Tune: O Gott, du frommer Gott. 55. [*TLH* 395; *LW* 385; *LSB* 696]

1. O Jesus, for whose truth
And faithfulness undying,
No mouth in heav'n or earth
Meet praise can be supplying:
I thank Thee, that Thou, Lord,
A true Man wast conceived,
Didst hide Thy majesty,
That I might be relieved.

2. The anguish in my heart
Is truly stilled and ended,
When by the gentle balm
Of Thy sweet name attended;
No comfort is as dear
As that Thy name affords,
O Jesus, David's Heir,
Thou Prince and Lord of lords.

3. O Jesus, Treasure true,
Thou bringest joy abounding;
No song more joys the ear
Than Jesus' name there sounding;
No sorrow can I have,
So great is Jesus' name:
Redeemer, Savior, Lord,
Who mighty is to save.

4. When Satan seeks my soul
With tribulation pressing,
Then Jesus' name is peace,
Protection, salve, and blessing,
With counsel wise and cure
For every fear and ill,
That devil, death, and hell
No terror may instill.

5. I am a son of wrath—
For so hath sin repaid me,—
Yet, Jesus, Thy dear name
A child of grace hath made me.
From me it takes away
All guilt and sin's disgrace,
And gives salvation true,
And all Thy Father's grace.

6. Oh, may the sacred name
Of Jesus sanctify me,
For all my stains and shame
A covering supply me!
May this repeal the curse,
The blessing to me send,
And be my strength and pow'r,
All weakness to amend.

7. His name my lantern be,
My path through gloom to lighten;
My heav'nly dew to slake
My thirst when blazes heighten;
My shelter, shade, and shield,
My castle, tow'r, and wall,
My riches, glory,‿and fame,
My highest good of all.

8. His name be still my Life
And Truth and Way to heaven;
And may I this receive
And by His grace be given:
That I in Jesus' name
May have a blessed end,
And in my final hour
My soul to Him commend.

9. Till then this grant me aid,
As long as here I wander,
Of faithfulness and truth
Forever to grow fonder;
This be my help and stay
With God the Spirit's grace,
When I some task must do
Within my given place.

10. O Jesus, in Thy name
I have this day arisen,
And in Thy name complete
Each daily, new commission;
For as in Thy dear name
A task has been begun
So rightly in Thy name
The means and end will run.

11. To Thee, in Thee, I live,
In Thee I yield my spirit;
In Thee, Lord, I will die,
In Thee I will inherit
Eternal life in heav'n,
Which Thou hast won for me,
Where, by Thee glorified,
I'll serve Thee endlessly.

—J. Heermann, 1630, cento; tr., M. Carver.

48

Tune: Das alte Jahr vergangen ist. 11. [p. 397; *or TLH* 125*; *LW* 201*; *LSB* 623*]

1. The old year now hath passed away;
We thank Thee, O our God, today
That Thou hast kept us through the year
When danger and distress were near.

2. We pray Thee, O eternal Son,
Who with the Father reign'st as One,
To guard and rule Thy Christendom
Through all the ages yet to come.

3. Take not Thy saving Word away,
Our souls' true comfort, staff, and stay.
Abide with us and keep us free
From errors, foll'wing only Thee.

4. Oh, help us to forsake all sin,
A new and holier course begin!
Mark not what once was done amiss;
A happier, better year be this,

5. Wherein as Christians we may live
Or die in peace that Thou canst give,
To rise again when Thou shalt come
And enter Thine eternal home.

6. There shall we thank Thee and adore
With all the angels evermore.
Lord Jesus Christ, increase our faith
To praise Thy Name thro' life and death.

—sts. 1–2, Erfurt, 1568; sts. 3–6, J. Steurlein, 1588; tr., C. Winkworth, 1863.

49

Tune: Das neugeborne Kindelein. 11. [p. 398; *or TLH* 85*; *LW* 37*; *LSB* 358*]

1. The new-born Child this early morn,
The dear Christ-Child of Virgin born,
Again brings from His heav'nly home
A New Year to all Christendom.

2. This causes joy to angels fair,
Who love to keep us in their care;
They sing that in this wondrous Child
God now with man is reconciled.

3. Since God is reconciled with men,
What harm can Satan do us then?
O'er Satan and the gates of hell
This Christ-child shall for us prevail.

4. He brings the year of jubilee!
Why doubt we yet despondently?
Rejoice! This is a happy day.
The Christ-child drives all care away.

—C. Schneegaß, 1597; tr., E. Cronenwett, 1880, alt.

50

Tune: Helft mir Gotts Güte preisen. 58. [*TLH* 112]

1. To God the anthem raising,
Sing, Christians, great and small;
Sing out, His goodness praising,
Oh, thank Him one and all!
Behold how God this year,
Which now is safely ended,
Hath in His love befriended
His children far and near.

2. Let us consider rightly
His mercies manifold
And let us not think lightly
Of all His gifts untold.
Let thankfulness recall
How God this year hath led us,
How He hath clothed and fed us,
The great ones and the small.

3. To Church and State He granted
His peace in every place,
His vineyard He hath planted
Among us by His grace.
His ever bounteous hand
Prosperity hath given
And want and famine driven
From this our native land.

4. Our God hath well defended,
Hath kept us through His grace;
But if He had contended
With us our sins to trace
And given us our meed,
We all would then be lying
In sin and sorrow dying,
Each one for his misdeed.

5. His Father heart is yearning
To take us for His own
When, our transgressions mourning,
We trust in Christ alone;
When in His name we pray
And humbly make confession,
He pardons our transgression
And is our faithful Stay.

6. O Father dear in heaven,
For all Thy gifts of love
Which Thou to us hast given
We lift our thanks above.
In Jesus' name we here,
To Thee our pray'rs addressing,
Still ask Thee for Thy blessing:
Grant us a joyful year.

7. God, Father, Son, and Spirit,
Be worshiped and adored,
Whose mighty grace and merit
This passing year outpoured;
Sustained us far and near;
May He yet deign to give us
Life free from things that grieve us
And peace in this New Year.

—P. Eber, 1569, but st. 7, Anon.; tr., C. Døving, 1907, but st. 7, M. Carver.

51

Tune: Nun freut euch, lieben Christen. 49. [*TLH* 124; *LW* 353; *LSB* 556]

1. O Lord, our Father, thanks to Thee
In this new year we render,
For every evil had to flee
Before Thee, our Defender.
Our life was nourished, we were fed
With rich supplies of daily bread,
And peace reigned in our borders.

2. Lord Jesus Christ, our thanks to Thee
In this new year we render;
Thy reign hath kept Thy people free,
Hath shown Thy mercies tender.
Thou hast redeemed us with Thy blood,
Thou art our Joy, our only Good,
In life and death our Savior.

3. Lord Holy Ghost, our thanks to Thee
In this new year we render,
For Thou hast led our eyes to see
Thy truth in all its splendor
And thus enkindled from above
Within our hearts true faith and love
And other Christian virtues.

4. Our faithful God, we cry to Thee:
Still bless us with Thy favor,
Blot out all our iniquity,
And hide our sins forever.
Grant us a happy, good new year
And, when the hour of death draws near,
A peaceful, blest departure.

—C. Schneegaß, 1597; tr., A. Crull, 1880, alt.

52

Tune: Zion klagt mit Angst und Schmerzen. 66.
[*TLH* 268; or *TLH* 207*; *LW* 263*; *LSB* 548*]

1. Help, Lord Jesus, let Thy blessing
Rest upon this op'ning year.
May we now, new strength possessing,
Walk in love and holy fear.
Dearest Savior, speed our way!
Strength bestow from day to day.
With new life and fortune dress us;
Hear us in Thy grace and bless us!

2. Let this be a year of pardon,
Let me all my sins confess;
Grant no sins my heart to harden,
But Thy mercy me to bless;
Also grant Thy grace that I
May repent them heartily;
In Thy grace, O Lord, receive me;
Thou alone canst all forgive me.

3. Grant Thy love and consolation;
God, my urgent pray'r receive
When I suffer tribulation
And in anguish come to grieve.
Sleeping, waking, watch me, Lord;
Help my cause and strength afford,
In my need my welfare cherish,
Lest in sin and death I perish.

4. Let this year to me be holy,
Let Thy grace fill every thought,
Let my life be pure and lowly,
Truthful, as a Christian's ought;
Let me to my neighbor be
Loving in all honesty;
Make me while on earth yet dwelling
Year by year in grace excelling.

5. Jesus, when this year is closing,
Marked by mercies large and free,
May I, in Thy hands reposing,
Gladly leave all things with Thee;
In all need Thy care provide,
Be my stay when ills betide!
Leave me not when life is over,
Let me then Thy life discover.

—J. Rist, 1642, cento, alt.; tr., C. H. Dunn, 1857, alt., but st. 3, M. Carver.

53

Tune: Ich dank dir schon durch deinen Sohn. 7. [*TLH* 431]

1. Rejoice, O Church, I say, rejoice!
Sing out in fitting measure!
This day of grace lift up thy voice,
With praise that gives God pleasure.

2. From east to west the world is filled
With heaven's wealth and gladness:
Sweet show'rs of comfort freely spilled
On spirits weighed by sadness.

3. For God the Father hath His Son
In human vesture given,
And by this Mercy-Seat hath won
For us the joys of heaven.

4. To suffer pain God's righteous Child
Is taken from the manger,
To let us men, by sin defiled,
Escape the curse and danger.

5. Here doth His precious infant blood,
Our heav'nly ransom buying,
Appease the Father for our good,
Our price of guilt supplying.

6. No better name that child could have
Than Jesus, only Jesus,
Whose blood, outpoured, doth sinners save,
Whose perfect ransom frees us.

7. Here for us all salvation blooms,
Here all our blessings flourish,
For Jesus here His work assumes,
Our souls with life to nourish.

8. Whatever good our hearts desire
To us is freely given,
While every weight and burden dire
By Jesus far is driven.

9. So through the year there may no ill
Nor trouble terrify us,
For Jesus has the greatest skill
With shelter to supply us.

10. He watches us by day and night;
When harm and woe are brewing,
He keeps us from their wicked might,
His help to us renewing.

11. Thy name, O Jesus, we adore
For Thy devout affection;
Grant us to know forevermore
Thy comfort and protection.

12. Receive into Thy hand of love
All those Thy name confessing;
Look graciously from heav'n above
And give our land Thy blessing.

—S. Liscow, †1689; tr., M. Carver.

54

Tune: Nun laßt uns Gott, dem Herren. 4. [*TLH* 122; *or LW* 184*]

1. Now let us come before Him,
With song and pray'r adore Him,
Who to our life hath given
All needed strength from heaven.

2. The stream of years is flowing,
And we are onward going,
From old to new surviving
And by His mercy thriving.

3. In woe we often languish
And pass through times of anguish,
Of wars and trepidation
Alarming every nation.

4. As mothers watch are keeping
O'er children who are sleeping,
Their fear and grief assuaging
When angry storms are raging,

5. So God His own is shielding
And help to them is yielding.
When need and woe distress them,
His loving arms caress them.

6. O Thou who dost not slumber,
Remove what would encumber
Our work, which prospers never
Unless Thou bless it ever.

7. We praise Thee for returning
Thy faithfulness each morning,
And for Thy hands' averting
What would our hearts be hurting

8. O God of Mercy, hear us;
Our Father, be Thou near us;
Mid crosses and in sadness
Be Thou our Fount of gladness.

9. To all who bow before Thee
And for Thy grace implore Thee,
Oh, grant Thy benediction
And patience in affliction.

10. O speak Thy richest blessing
Where'er our way is pressing;
And let Thy Sun of favor
Shine on all men whatever.

11. Be Thou a Helper speedy
To all the poor and needy,
To all forlorn a Father;
Thy erring children gather.

12. Be with the sick and ailing,
Their Comforter unfailing;
Dispelling grief and sadness,
Oh, give them joy and gladness!

13. Above all else, Lord, send us
Thy Spirit to attend us,
Within our hearts abiding,
To heav'n our footsteps guiding.

14. All this Thy hand bestoweth,
Thou Life whence our life floweth.
To all Thy name confessing
Grant, Lord, Thy New Year's blessing!

—P. Gerhardt, 1653; tr., J. Kelly, 1867, alt., but sts. 7, 10, M. Carver.

55

Tune: Vater unser im Himmelreich. 44. [*TLH* 458; *LW* 431; *LSB* 766]

1. Now we begin the glad new year,
Lord Jesus, with Thy help be near;
Defend us in this evil age
From war and plague and famine's rage.
We pray Thee, with Thy mighty arm
Keep church and home and state from harm.

2. Thy Word and Sacrament extend
Throughout our land until the end;
This new year with Thy goodness crown,
And pour Thy richest blessing down.
"Amen, dear Lord, hear us this day,"
With fervent hearts Thy Christians pray.

—G. Werner, †1643; tr., *HELM,* 1905, alt.

56

Tune: Freu dich sehr, o meine Seele. 66. [*TLH* 61; *LW* 28; *LSB* 347]

1. Why should they such torment give Thee,
Why so pain Thee, dearest Christ?
Why by such a rite so grieve Thee,
With their hearts uncircumcised?
Jesus, only Thou art free
From the law's severity,
For, although man's nature wearing,
Thou art free from sin and erring.

2. For Thyself Thou dost not bear it,
Of the Cov'nant Thou art Head;
'Tis our debts that make Thee share it,
That like grievous weights of lead
Lie upon us, and Thy heart
Pierce unto the inmost part;
These Thou bearest to deliver
Those who could have paid them never.

3. Let your hearts be glad, ye debtors!
Let the world rejoice today!
For God's Son now breaks your fetters,
Now the price begins to pay.
This day is the Law fulfilled,
This day is God's anger stilled.
Now are we, to death once given,
Made by Christ the heirs of heaven.

4. Who can tell this grace and favor,
Or in measure grateful be?
Heart and mouth, O Savior, ever
Shall exalt and honor Thee!
We shall praise with all our pow'r
All Thy goodness, Thee adore,
While in weakness here we wander,
And Thy praises echo yonder!

—P. Gerhardt, 1653; tr., J. Kelly, 1867, alt.

Epiphany of Christ

57

Tune: O Welt, ich muß dich lassen. 31. [*TLH* 126; *LW* 85; *LSB* 396]

1. Arise and shine in splendor,
Let night to day surrender;
Thy Light is drawing near,
Above thee day is beaming
In matchless beauty gleaming;
The glory of the Lord is here.

2. See earth in darkness lying,
The heathen nations dying
In hopeless gloom and night.
To thee the Lord of heaven —
Thy Life, thy Hope—hath given
Great glory, honor, and delight.

3. The world's remotest races,
Upon whose weary faces
The sun looks from the sky,
Shall run with zeal untiring,
With joy thy Light desiring
That breaks upon them from on high.

4. Lift up thine eyes in wonder;
See, nations gather yonder,
They all come unto thee;
The world has heard thy story,
Thy sons come to thy glory,
And daughters haste thy Light to see.

5. Thy heart will leap for gladness
When, from the realms of sadness,
They come o'er land and sea.
Thine eyes will wake from slumber
When people without number
Come thronging from afar to thee.

6. From Ephah and far nations
Come mounted delegations,
On Midian's camels drawn;
With gold shall Sheba cheer thee,
With incense drawing near thee;
They all shall make thy praises known!

—M. Optiz, 1628; tr. sts. 1–5, G. Gieschen, 1937; st. 6, A. Crull, 1880, alt.

58

Tune: In dich hab ich gehoffet, Herr. 40. [*TLH* 177; *LW* 108; *LSB* 734; *or* p. 406]

1. Now is the time, dear soul, awake!
With joy and bliss thy slumber break:
Behold what God hath given:
His Son most dear, / To mis'ry here,
Sent from His throne in heaven.

2. Not for the Jews alone is meant
This child, their kinsman by descent,
But those in darkness pining
Are giv'n the sight / Of heav'nly Light,
For their elation shining.

3. The firstfruits of the heathen are
Referred to Him by wondrous star,
And so behold their Savior,
And to the Lord / Their gifts afford
And own Him King forever.

4. Now ye who, heathen once, did sleep:
The feast of Gentiles thankful keep,
Let every voice be ringing
To glorify / The Lord most High
With loud and joyful singing.

5. O Jesus, Light and Savior blest!
Thy gracious count'nance on us rest;
With all Thy beams enfold us,
And by Thy grace / Our hearts embrace,
And in Thy light sustain us.

6. All darkness with Thy ray disperse,
The gloomy night to light reverse;
Upon Thy way still guide us,
And let Thy light / And glory bright
Forevermore betide us.

—J. C. Arnschwanger, †1696; tr., M. Carver.

59

Tune: Ich dank dir, lieber Herre. 59. [*TLH* 334; *LSB* 689]

1. O Jesus, King of Glory,
Both David's Lord and Son!
Thy realm endures forever,
In heav'n is fixed Thy throne.
Help that in earth's dominions,
Throughout from pole to pole,
Thy reign may spread salvation
To each benighted soul.

2. The Eastern sages, bringing
Their tribute gifts to Thee,
Bear witness to Thy kingdom
And humbly bow the knee.
To Thee the star is pointing,
And the prophetic Word;
Hence joyously we hail Thee:
Our Savior and our Lord!

3. Thou art a mighty Monarch,
As by Thy Word is told,
Yet carest Thou but little
For earthly goods or gold;
On no proud steed Thou ridest,
Thou wear'st no jewèl'd crown
Nor dwell'st in lordly castle,
But bearest scoff and frown.

4. Yet art Thou decked with beauty,
With rays of glorious light;
Thy works proclaim Thy goodness,
And all Thy ways are right.
Vouchsafe to shield Thy people
With Thine almighty arm
That they may dwell in safety
From those who mean them harm.

5. Ah, look on me with pity
Though I am weak and poor;
Admit me to Thy kingdom
To dwell there, blest and sure.
I pray Thee, guide and keep me
Safe from my bitter foes,
From sin and death and Satan;
Free me from all my woes.

6. And bid Thy Word within me
Shine as the fairest star;
Keep sin and all false doctrine
Forever from me far.
Help me confess Thee truly
And with Thy Christendom
Here own Thee King and Savior
And in the world to come.

—M. Behm, 1606; tr., C. Winkworth, 1863, alt.

60

Tune: Was fürchtst du Feind Herodes sehr. 11.
[p. 415; *or TLH* 63*; *LW* 14*; *LSB* 344*]

1. Why, Herod, unrelenting foe!
Doth Christ the Lord's birth move thee so?
He doth no earthly kingdom crave
Who unto us heav'n's kingdom gave.

2. The star before the wise men goes
This light to them the true Light shows;
They by the three gifts which they bring
Declare this Child: God, Man, and King.

3. He was baptized in Jordan's flood
The holy, heav'nly Lamb of God,
And He who did no sin, thereby
Cleansed us from all iniquity!

4. And now a miracle was done:
Six waterpots stood there of stone;
Christ spake the word with pow'r divine,
The water reddened into wine.

5. All honor, praise to Thee be paid,
O Christ, born of the virgin maid,
With Father and with Holy Ghost,
Till time in endless time be lost.

—M. Luther, 1541, after Sedulius; tr., R. Massie, 1854, alt.

61

Tune: Vom Himmel hoch da komm ich her. [*TLH* 85; *LW* 37; *LSB* 358]
Or Lob sei dem allmächtigen Gott. 11. [p. 410*]

1. We thank Thee, Lord, with one accord
For granting us Thy precious Word
That shines so clearly in our night
And gives our weary heart delight.

2. In death's dark valley bound we lay
And for escape could find no way.
O dearest Jesus, thanks to Thee
Who now hast made us pris'ners free!

3. We pray Thy light may ever shine
Till breaks that glorious day of Thine.
Grant us to wander evermore
The narrow path to heaven's door.

4. Thou very man and God's own Son,
Thou King of kings on glory's throne,
Not one of us, corrupt with sin,
Such love, such bounteous grace could win.

5. Thy goodly Spirit be our guide
That in true service we abide;
For Thou, O Friend of man, dost know
How powèrless we are below.

6. Accept as off'rings of our praise,
O dearest Lord, the pray'rs we raise,
Wherein we Gentiles would adore
Thy wondrous name forevermore.

—P. Hagen, †1620; tr., F. W. Herzberger, †1930, alt.

Purification of Mary

FEBRUARY 2

62

Tune: Herr Jesu Christ, meins Lebens Licht. 11.
[*TLH* 7; *LW* 373; *LSB* 704; or *TLH* 3*; *LW* 201*; *LSB* 902*]

1. O dearest Jesus, Thee I pray:
Within my heart now make Thy stay,
That I, like Simèon of old,
By faith may gladly Thee enfold.

2. Thou art my Life and Happiness,
Whom God hath sent, my soul to bless:
O cleanse and purify my heart,
That from Thy paths I ne'er depart.

3. Lord, with Thy light show me the way,
That never I may go astray;
Ward off all sorrow and despair,
And let me be Thine own fore'er.

4. Lift up Thy face upon me, Lord,
In life and death Thy help afford;
Then I'll depart most cheerfully
This life, whene'er it pleaseth Thee.

—B. Helder, †1635; tr., A. Crull, 1898.

63

Tune: Nun freut euch, lieben Christen. 49. [*TLH* 124; *LW* 353; *LSB* 556]

1. Thank God! My Jesus cleanseth me
From all sins I committed,
He paid my debt and set me free,
I, therefore, am acquitted
Of sin's and Satan's bondage fell;
My faith now laughs at death and hell,
Because my life is Jesus.

2. Why should I grieve? He who fulfilled
The Law, thus to release us,
He who His Father's wrath has stilled
By His own death, this Jesus
Still liveth, and all that He hath
He giveth unto me through faith;
Is there a greater treasure?

3. Because my Jesus cleanseth me
From sin by His own merit,
I am from pain and fear set free,
Death cannot daunt my spirit;
I trust in Jesus' righteousness,
His innocence and blessedness
Are now my life and treasure.

4. Now I, like Simèon, can end
My life in peace and gladness,
And to my God I can commend
My spirit without sadness;
For when my weary eyes I close,
My death becomes a sweet repose,
I see the joys of heaven.

4. How happy, therefore, shall I be,
When life's frail thread is broken;
When holy angels carry me
To joys that ne'er were spoken;
When I behold Him face to face,
When I have gained that blessed place,
Prepared for me by Jesus.

6. Lord, grant that e'er prepared I be,
That naught from Thee me sever.
And when I die, let me with Thee
In glory live forever;
Come quickly to deliver me,
Lord, by Thy death and agony,
Yea, come, Lord Jesus! Amen.

—J. Olearius, 1671; tr., A. Crull, †1923.

64

Tune: Ich dank dir, lieber Herre. 59. [*TLH* 334; *LSB* 689]

1. Thou Light of gentile nations,
Thou Savior from above,
Drawn by Thy Spirit's leading,
We come with joy and love
Into Thy holy temple
And wait with earnest mind
As Simèon once had waited
His God and Lord to find.

2. Yea, Lord, Thy servants meet Thee
In ev'ry holy place
Where Thy true Word has promised
That we should see Thy face.
Today Thou still dost grant us
Who gather round Thee here
In arms of faith to bear Thee
As did that agèd seer.

3. Be Thou our Joy and Brightness,
Our Cheer in pain and loss,
Our Sun in darkest terror,
The Glory round our cross,
A Star for sinking spirits,
A Beacon in distress,
Physician, Friend in sickness,
In death our Happiness.

4. Let us, O Lord, be faithful
Like Simeon to the end,
So that his prayer exultant
May from our hearts ascend:
"O Lord, now let Thy servant
Depart in peace, I pray,
Since I have seen my Savior
And here beheld His day."

5. My Savior, I behold Thee
With faith's enlightened eye;
Of Thee no foe can rob me,
His threats I can defy.
Within Thy heart abiding,
As Thou, O Lord, in me,
Death can no longer frighten
Nor part my soul from Thee.

6. Lord, here on earth Thou seemest
At times to frown on me,
And through my tears I often
Can scarce distinguish Thee;
But in the heav'nly mansions
Shall nothing dim my sight;
There shall I see Thy glory
In never-changing light.

—J. Franck, 1674; tr., C. Winkworth, 1863, alt.

65

Tune: Mit Fried und Freud ich fahr dahin. 35. [*TLH* 137; *LW* 185; *LSB* 938]

1. In peace and joy I now depart
At God's disposing;
For full of comfort is my heart,
Soft reposing.
So the Lord hath promised me,
And death is but a slumber.

2. 'Tis Christ that wrought this work for me,
My faithful Savior,
Whom Thou hast made mine eyes to see
By Thy favor.
Now I know He is my Life,
My Help in need and dying.

3. Him Thou hast unto all set forth
Their great Salvation
And to His kingdom called the earth,
Every nation,
By Thy dear and wholesome Word,
In every place resounding.

4. He is the Hope and saving Light
Of lands benighted;
By Him are they who dwelt in night
Fed and lighted.
He is Israel's Praise and Bliss,
Their Joy, Reward, and Glory.

—M. Luther, 1524; tr., L. Bacon, 1884, alt.

Annunciation of Mary

MARCH 25

66

Tune: Durch Adams Fall ist ganz verderbt. 83. [p. 401]

1. Rejoice this day, dear Christendom!
For Jesus, the Anointed,
Our Lord and Savior, now is come,
The One whom God appointed
By His own grace / And for His praise.
O God, now grant Thy blessing!
And strengthen us / Thine anthem thus
To Thee to be addressing!

2. Our God is just in all He says;
His promises, once spoken,
Endure, though often He delays,
And some may think them broken.
God's Son we greet, / Our Mercy-Seat!
Her Savior earth beholdeth.
O wondrous sign! / A Guest divine
The Virgin's womb enfoldeth.

3. She shall her Lord, Christ Jesus, bear,
She hears the angel telling:
Immanuel her flesh will share,
The Lord, all lords excelling.
The maid demure, / All chaste and pure,
Though wond'ring at the story,
The Word receives / And well believes
In God's great pow'r and glory.

4. How blest, this age of grace to see!
What honor like no other,—
That Thou, God from eternity,
Shouldst thus become our Brother!
Thy Church now prays, / Teach us always
To trust Thy Word as given,
Until we view / With vision new
That wondrous work in heaven.

—P. Hagen, ca. 1600; tr., M. Carver.

67

Tune: Herr Christ, der einig Gotts Sohn. 48. [*LW* 72; *LSB* 402]

1. Now let us gravely ponder
Salvation's blessed Ground,
And pay Him every honor
Who hath our souls unbound
From sin, death, and damnation,
And did not scorn His Passion,
The devil to confound.

2. 'Twas Jesus that God named Him,
Born of the Virgin blest,
And so have we acclaimed Him,
And as the Christ confessed,
Who frees us from transgression
And grants us consolation
Whene'er our soul is pressed.

3. The name of Christ He carried,
For He the world would save,
And suff'ring, dead, and buried,
Crush Satan and the grave;
And thus, hell's gates all riven,
He fills the courts of heaven,
Howe'er the foe may rave.

4. This Jesus, overthrowing
Iniquity and sin,
And righteousness bestowing,
Would be, to death's chagrin,
Of death itself th' Undoing,
All things to right renewing
Which to us lost had been.

5. To Him God gave the scepter
Of all divine command
To rule the Kingdom ever
Enthroned at God's right hand
To govern all our spirits
Which through His bloody merits
He bears to heaven's land.

6. By God was He appointed
High Priest with holy pow'r,
And pledged as the Anointed,
Upon the glorious hour
His people's souls to nourish,
And evermore to flourish
As Sharon's fairest flow'r.

7. As Lord shall men address Him,
All thrones on Him bestow,
And thus shall they confess Him,
That all the earth may know:
He is true God forever,
And still our only Savior
Within this vale of woe.

8. The Holy Scriptures name Him
Jehovah, King divine;
All knees shall bend to claim Him,
All earth in praise combine,
All tongues shall loud adore Him
With songs of thanks before Him
As far as sun doth shine.

9. His throne shall last forever,
His scepter never shake,
The walls of Zion never
Be breached, or crumbling, break;
With oil of gladness, o'er us
He rose on high, victorious,
Nor doth His flock forsake.

10. Since God in flesh drew nigh us,
And keeps us e'er secure,
With blessings doth supply us,
Then let us not demur,
True God and Man to name Him
And Undivided claim Him,
The God-Man's praise assure.

11. To Jesus it was given
The rocky earth to rear
And spread the scroll of heaven
And by His counsel clear
The angel hosts engender,
Which act as our defender
And need not shield nor spear.

12. This Jesus, too, shall wake us
From death with pow'r and might,
From tyranny shall take us,
The wicked put to flight.
He sees our hearts and knows them,
And He His heaven shows them
Who share His heart contrite.

13. Let us in spirit lowly
Adore the Son and Heir
Of God Most High, Most Holy,
Whose is the crown to bear,
To whom all rule is given.
Grant, Lord, Thy grace from heaven,
And bring us to Thee there.

—J. Rist, 1656; tr., M. Carver.

68

Tune: O Herre Gott, dein göttlich Wort. 83. [*TLH* 266; *LW* 341]

1. O wonder high! / This day doth lie
In Mary's womb Salvation!
Almighty God / In flesh and blood,
Man's Life and Consolation!
O wondrous mirth! / This day on earth
God is a Man conceivèd;
The human mind / Must be resigned,
And God's true Word believèd.

2. Now God mine is / And I am His!
Himself as Man He gives me:
My flesh and blood, / My Highest Good
In heaven's ranks receives me.
Praise God above, / Whose tender love
Uplifts me by descending;
His Son I greet, / My Mercy-Seat,
Where I find life unending.

—J. Olearius, 1665; tr., M. Carver.

Passion of Christ

69

Tune: Christe, du Lamm Gottes. 98. [*TLH* 147; *LW* 7; *LSB* 198]

1. O Christ, Thou Lamb of God,
That takest away the sin of the world,
Have mercy upon us!

2. O Christ, Thou Lamb of God,
That takest away the sin of the world,
Have mercy upon us!

3. O Christ, Thou Lamb of God,
That takest away the sin of the world,
Grant us Thy peace! Amen.

—Anon., Braunschweig, 1528, after the Lat. *Agnus Dei;* tr. trad.

70

Tune: Da Jesus an dem Kreuze stund. 19. [*TLH* 177; *LW* 108;]

1. Our blessèd Savior sev'n times spoke
When on the cross our sins He took
And died lest man should perish.
Let us His last and dying words
In our remembrance cherish.

2. "Father, forgive these men; for, lo,
They truly know not what they do."
So far His love extended.
Forgive us, Lord, for we, too, have
Through ignorance offended.

3. Now to the contrite thief He cries:
"Thou, verily, in Paradise
Shalt meet Me ere tomorrow."
Lord, take us to Thy kingdom soon
Who linger here in sorrow.

4. To weeping Mary, standing by,
"Behold thy Son," now hear Him cry;
To John, "Behold thy mother."
Provide, O Lord, for those we leave;
Let each befriend the other.

5. The Savior's fourth word was "I thirst."
O mighty Prince of Life, Thy thirst
For us and our salvation
Is truly great; do help us, then,
That we escape damnation.

6. The fifth, "My God, My God, O why
Forsake Me?" Hark, the awful cry!
Lord, Thou wast here forsaken
That we might be received on high;
Let this hope not be shaken.

7. The sixth, when victory was won,
"'Tis finished!" for Thy work was done.
Grant, Lord, that, onward pressing,
We may the work Thou dost impose
Fulfill with Thine own blessing.

8. The last, as woe and suff'rings end,
"O God, My Father, I commend
Into Thy hands My Spirit."
Be this, dear Lord, my dying wish;
O heav'nly Father, hear it.

9. Whoe'er, by sense of sin oppressed,
Upon these words his thoughts will rest,
He joy and hope obtaineth
And through God's love and boundless grace
A peaceful conscience gaineth.

10. O Jesus Christ, Thou Crucified,
Who hast for our offenses died,
Grant that we e'er may ponder
Thy wounds, Thy cross, Thy bitter death,
Both here below and yonder.

—J. Böschenstain, 1515, alt; tr., F. E. Cox, 1841, alt.

71

Tune: Werde munter mein Gemüte. 66.
[*TLH* 207; *LW* 263; *LSB* 548; *or TLH* 144*; *LW* 95*; *LSB* 421*]

1. Jesus crucified possesses
My love's homage evermore.
Sin and Satan, your caresses,
World, thy pleasures I abhor.
Who your godless way pursue
Will in death their folly rue.
Jesus crucified possesses
My love, as my faith confesses.

2. Jesus crucified possesses
My love—doth it anger thee,
Scoffer, what my heart confesses?
Jesus gave Himself for me!
Thus my saving Shield He proves,
Whose example me behooves.
Jesus crucified possesses
My love, as my faith confesses.

3. Jesus crucified possesses
My love—thou art conquered, Sin.
Woe, if aught His Law transgresses
Whose blood did my pardon win!
Would I not His cross disdain,
His atoning blood profane?
Jesus crucified possesses
My love, as my faith confesses.

4. Jesus crucified possesses
My love—Conscience, cease thy sting!
With His pardon God suppresses
His accusing handwriting.
See how dear my Bondsman pays,
How His blood all fear allays!
Jesus crucified possesses
My love, as my faith confesses.

5. Jesus crucified possesses
My love—tyrant, rack and burn!
Hunger, nakedness, distresses,
Naught my love from Him shall turn;
Neither power, gold, or fame,
Neither angels, death, or shame.
Jesus crucified possesses
My love, as my faith confesses.

6. Jesus crucified possesses
My love—come, Death, dearest friend.
When I turn to dust and ashes,
To those mansions I'll ascend
Where my Bridegroom I behold,
Live with Him in bliss untold.
Jesus crucified possesses
My love, as my faith confesses.

—Anon., *Jesuslieder,* 1668; tr., *HELM,* 1905.

72

Tune: Nun laßt uns den Leib begraben. 11. [*TLH* 596; *LW* 382; *LSB* 759]

1. Thy soul, O Jesus, hallow me,
Thy Spirit steep me all in Thee;
Thy body, pierced by ruthless steel,
My wretched soul and body heal.

2. The water from Thy side that poured
For me a cleansing bath afford,
And all Thy blood, with life divine,
Revive this weakened heart of mine.

3. The sweat of death upon Thy face
Deliver me from death's embrace,
And all Thy Passion, cross, and pain,
With strength my feebleness sustain.

4. O Christ, turn not away from me,
Receive and hide me all in Thee,
Within Thy holy wounds enclose,
And keep me safe from all my foes.

5. In death's dark hour with me abide
And place me, Savior, at Thy side,
Where with Thy saints I shall adore
And praise Thee, Lord, forevermore.

—J. Scheffler, 1657; tr., M. Loy, 1880, alt.

73

Tune: An Wasserflüssen Babylon. 85. [*TLH* 142; *LW* 111; *LSB* 438]

1. A Lamb goes uncomplaining forth,
The guilt of all men bearing;
And, laden with the sins of earth,
None else the burden sharing!
Goes patient on, grows weak and faint,
To slaughter led without complaint,
That spotless life to offer;
Bears shame and stripes and wounds and death,
Anguish and mockery, and saith,
"Willing all this I suffer."

2. This Lamb is Christ, the soul's great Friend,
The Lamb of God, our Savior;
Him God the Father chose to send
To gain for us His favor.
"Go forth, My Son," the Father saith,
"And free men from the fear of death,
From guilt and condemnation.
The wrath and stripes are hard to bear,
But by Thy Passion men shall share
The fruit of Thy salvation."

3. "Yea, Father, yea, most willingly
I'll bear what Thou commandest;
My will conforms to Thy decree,
I do what Thou demandest."
O wondrous Love, what hast Thou done!
The Father offers up His Son!
The Son, content, descendeth!
O Love, how strong Thou art to save!
Thou beddest Him within the grave
Whose word the mountains rendeth.

4. Thou lay'st Him, Love, upon the cross,
With nails and spear Him bruising;
Thou slay'st Him as a lamb, His loss
From soul and body oozing;
From body 'tis the crimson flood
Of precious sacrificial blood,
From soul, the strength of anguish.
My gain it is; sweet Lamb, to Thee
What can I give whose love to me
For me doth make Thee languish?

5. Lord, all my life I'll cleave to Thee,
Thy love fore'er beholding,
Thee ever, as Thou ever me,
With loving arms enfolding.
Yea, Thou shalt be my Beacon-light,
To guide me safe through death's dark night,
And cheer my heart in sorrow;
Henceforth myself and all that's mine
To Thee, my Savior, I consign,
From whom all things I borrow.

6. From morn till eve my theme shall be
Thy mercy's wondrous measure;
To sacrifice myself for Thee
Shall be my aim and pleasure.
My stream of life shall ever be
A current flowing ceaselessly,
Thy constant praise outpouring.
I'll treasure in my memory,
O Lord, all Thou hast done for me,
Thy gracious love adoring.

7. Enlarge, my heart's own shrine, and swell,
To thee shall now be given
A treasure that doth far excel
The worth of earth and heaven.
Away with the Arabian gold,
With treasures of an earthly mold!
I've found a better jewèl.
My priceless treasure, Lord, my God,
Is Thy most holy, precious blood,
Which flowed from wounds so cruèl.

8. This treasure ever I'll employ,
This every aid shall yield me;
In sorrow it shall be my joy,
In conflict it shall shield me;
In joy, the music of my feast,
And when all else has lost its zest,
This manna still shall feed me;
In thirst my drink; in want my food;
My company in solitude,
To comfort and to lead me.

9. Of death I am no more afraid,
New life from Thee is flowing;
Thy cross affords me cooling shade
When noonday's sun is glowing.
When by my grief I am oppressed,
On Thee my weary soul shall rest
Serenely as on pillows.
Thou art my Anchor when by woe
My bark is driven to and fro
On trouble's surging billows.

10. And when Thy glory I shall see
And taste Thy kingdom's pleasure,
Thy blood my royal robe shall be,
My joy beyond all measure.
When I appear before Thy throne,
Thy righteousness shall be my crown—
With these I need not hide me.
And there, in garments richly wrought
As Thine own bride, I shall be brought
To stand in joy beside Thee.

—P. Gerhardt, 1647; tr., *HTLH,* 1942.

74

Tune: Herr Jesu Christ, du höchstes Gut. 49. [p. 404; *or TLH* 406*; *LSB* 625*]

1. Lord Jesus, let Thy grief and pain
And all Thy dreadful Passion
Before mine eyes unmoved remain
To turn me from transgression;
And while I live, upon Thy great
Affliction, death, and bitter fate
Let me devoutly ponder.

2. Grant that the anguish of Thy heart,
Thy sweat as blood distilling,
And every sorrow, sting, and smart
Which Thou to bear wast willing,
Be often burnt within my breast,
A deathless warning there impressed
Against sin's multiplying.

3. Of every rod that broke Thy skin
My hand hath been a holder,
Mine was the pond'rous weight of sin
Laid on Thy tender shoulder.
O dearest Savior, spare my soul,
Cast guilt beyond the farthest pole!
Let judgment yield to mercy!

4. Thou hast from heaven's glorious throne
To agony descended,
To bear our strokes and scorns alone,
Upon the cross suspended;
All this Thou didst, our souls to win
And make atonement for our sin
Before Thy heav'nly Father.

5. Therefore will I in thankfulness
Now lift my heart to praise Thee,
And then, when to Thy blessed place
Thou deign'st some day to raise me,
Much more will I in realms above
With heaven's host for all Thy love
Sing praise to Thee unceasing.

6. Lord Jesus, let Thy grief and pain
And all Thy dreadful Passion
My refuge be, my last refrain,
When closes life's brief session.
Oh, grant me by Thy death to know
A peaceful ending to my woe,
A blessed death receiving!

—T. Clausnitzer, 1662, alt.; tr., M. Carver.

75

Tune: Herzliebster Jesu, was hast du gebrochen. 13. [*TLH* 143; *LW* 119; *LSB* 439]

1. O dearest Jesus, what law hast Thou broken
That such sharp sentence should on Thee be spoken?
Of what great crime hast Thou to make confession—
What dark transgression?

2. They crown Thy head with thorns, they smite, they scourge Thee;
With cruèl mockings to the cross they urge Thee;
They give Thee gall to drink, they still decry Thee;
They crucify Thee.

3. Whence come these sorrows, whence this mortal anguish?
It is my sins for which Thou, Lord, must languish;
Yea, all the wrath, the woe, Thou dost inherit,
This I do merit.

4. What punishment so strange is suffered yonder!
The Shepherd dies for sheep that loved to wander;
The Master pays the debt His servants owe Him,
Who would not know Him.

5. The sinless Son of God must die in sadness;
The sinful child of man may live in gladness;
Man forfeited his life and is acquitted—
God is committed.

6. There was no spot in me by sin untainted;
Sick with sin's poison, all my heart had fainted;
My heavy guilt to hell had well-nigh brought me,
Such woe it wrought me.

7. O wondrous love, whose depth no heart hath sounded,
That brought Thee here, by foes and thieves surrounded!
All worldly pleasures, heedless, I was trying
While Thou wert dying.

8. O mighty King, no time can dim Thy glory!
How shall I spread abroad Thy wondrous story?
How shall I find some worthy gifts to proffer?
What dare I offer?

9. For vainly doth our human wisdom ponder—
Thy woes, Thy mercy, still transcend our wonder.
Oh, how should I do aught that could delight Thee!
Can I requite Thee?

10. Yet unrequited, Lord, I would not leave Thee;
I will renounce whate'er doth vex or grieve Thee
And quench with thoughts of Thee and pray'rs most lowly
All fires unholy.

11. But since my strength will nevermore suffice me
To crucify desires that still entice me,
To all good deeds, oh, let Thy Spirit win me
And reign within me!

12. I'll think upon Thy mercy without ceasing,
That earth's vain joys to me no more be pleasing;
To do Thy will shall be my sole endeavor
Henceforth forever.

13. Whate'er of earthly good this life may grant me,
I'll risk for Thee; no shame, no cross, shall daunt me.
I shall not fear what man can do to harm me
Nor death alarm me.

14. But worthless is my sacrifice, I own it;
Yet, Lord, for love's sake Thou wilt not disown it;
Thou wilt accept my gift in Thy great meekness
Nor shame my weakness.

15. And when, dear Lord, before Thy throne in heaven
To me the crown of joy at last is given,
Where sweetest hymns Thy saints forever raise Thee,
I, too, shall praise Thee.

—J. Heermann, 1630; tr., C. Winkworth, 1863, alt.

76

Tune: Jesu Leiden, Pein und Tod. 60. [*TLH* 140; *LW* 109; *LSB* 440]

1. Jesus, I will ponder now
On Thy holy Passion;
With Thy Spirit me endow
For such meditation.
Grant that I in love and faith
May the image cherish
Of Thy suff'ring, pain, and death,
That I may not perish.

2. Make me see Thy great distress,
Anguish, and affliction,
Bonds and stripes and wretchedness
And Thy crucifixion;
Make me see how scourge and rod,
Spear and nails, did wound Thee,
How for man Thou diedst, O God,
Who with thorns had crowned Thee.

3. Yet, O Lord, not thus alone
Make me see Thy Passion,
But its cause to me make known
And its termination.
Ah! I also and my sin
Wrought Thy deep affliction;
This indeed the cause hath been
Of Thy crucifixion.

4. Grant that I Thy Passion view
With repentant grieving
Nor Thee crucify anew
By unholy living.
How could I refuse to shun
Every sinful pleasure
Since for me God's only Son
Suffered without measure?

5. If my sins give me alarm
And my conscience grieve me,
Let Thy cross my fear disarm,
Peace of conscience give me.
Grant that I may trust in Thee
And Thy holy Passion.
If His Son so loveth me,
God must have compassion.

6. Grant that I may willingly
Bear with Thee my crosses,
Learning humbleness of Thee,
Peace mid pain and losses.
May I give Thee love for love!
Hear me, O my Savior,
That I may in heav'n above
Sing Thy praise forever.

—S. von Birken, 1653; tr., A. Crull, 1889, alt.

77

Tune: Jesu, deine heilgen Wunden. 66. [p. 406; *or TLH* 144*; *LW* 95;* *LSB* 421*]

1. Jesus, grant that balm and healing
In Thy holy wounds I find,
Every hour that I am feeling
Pains of body and of mind.
Should some evil thought within
Tempt my treach'rous heart to sin,
Show the peril, and from sinning
Keep me ere its first beginning

2. Should some lust or sharp temptation
Prove too strong for flesh and blood,
Let me think upon Thy Passion,
And the breach is soon made good.
Or should Satan press me hard,
Let me then be on my guard,
Saying: "Christ for me was wounded,"
That the Tempter flees, confounded.

3. If the world my heart entices
On the broad and easy road
With its mirth and luring vices,
Let me think upon that load
Thou didst carry and endure
That I flee all thoughts impure,
Banishing each wild emotion,
Calm and blest in my devotion.

4. Every wound that pains or grieves me,
By Thy stripes, Lord, is made whole;
When I'm faint, Thy Cross revives me,
Granting new life to my soul.
Yea, Thy comfort renders sweet
Ev'ry bitter cup I meet;
For Thine all-atoning Passion
Has procured my soul's salvation.

5. O my God, my Rock and Tower,
Grant that in Thy death I trust,
Knowing death has lost his power
Since Thou trodd'st him in the dust.
Savior, let Thine agony
Ever help and comfort me;
When I die, be my Protection,
Light and Life and Resurrection.

6. Jesus, grant that balm and healing
In Thy holy wounds I find,
Every hour that I am feeling
Pains of body and of mind;
And when I this world must leave,
Grant that, Lord, to Thee I cleave,
In Thy wounds find consolation,
And obtain my soul's salvation.

—J. Heermann, 1644, alt.; tr., *TLH,* 1941, but st. 6, *ELHB,* 1912.

78

Tune: Jesu, der du meine Seele. 68. [p. 407; *or TLH* 151*; *LW* 94*; *LSB* 420*]

1. Jesus, Thou whose heart was willing
For a world of sin to pay
By Thy precious blood's outspilling,
And, for sinners gone astray,
As a Lamb Thyself didst offer,
Lest the heirs of Adam suffer:
Let Thy Passion's agony
Not have been in vain for me.

2. Save me by Thy sore vexation
When my heart is vexed by sin;
Leave me not in desperation,
Thou whose soul was grieved within!
Let Thy sweat of blood relieve me,
When the cross's fevers grieve me.
Let Thy Passion's agony
Not have been in vain for me.

3. By the bonds that once restrained Thee,
From the devil set me free;
Let the ridicule that pained Thee
Be my crown and majesty.
Balm of souls, and earth's Salvation!
Save me from humiliation.
Let Thy Passion's agony
Not have been in vain for me.

4. Do Thy silence not refuse me:
Jesus, let it plead my cause,
When my sin and guilt accuse me,
Ever pointing to Thy laws—
When my conscience, full of evil,
Cries and threatens hell and devil.
Let Thy Passion's agony
Not have been in vain for me.

5. Gladd'ning roses cause to flourish,
Dearest Jesus, Crown divine,
From the thorns Thy wounds did nourish;
These, O Jesus, deftly twine,
Crowns of love and grace to bring me,
Lest some thorn of sin should sting me.
Let Thy Passion's agony
Not have been in vain for me.

6. Bring my wounded conscience healing,
Take from me my burden sore
By the scourges o'er Thee reeling,
By the stripes Thy shoulders bore,
That, though oft from Thee diverging,
I may flee the devil's scourging.
Let Thy Passion's agony
Not have been in vain for me.

7. Let Thy gaping wounds be flowing
As a fresh and living spring,
When all strength from me is going,
When my soul is languishing;
In Thy love's abysses vanquish
All my guilt and heavy anguish.
Let Thy Passion's agony
Not have been in vain for me.

8. Oh, the rod of judgment shatter!
Let Thy grace and favor show;
With Thy blood expunge and scatter
All my sin that presses so!
Terrors for my crimes enclose me,
Let me at Thy side repose me.
Let Thy Passion's agony
Not have been in vain for me.

9. Let Thy holy thirst avail me,
Which aggrieved Thee on the tree;
When the plagues of drought assail me,
When my sins are haunting me,
Let me profit from Thy thirsting,
Let Thy streams of life be bursting.
Let Thy Passion's agony
Not have been in vain for me.

10. Jesus, free me at my dying
By Thy loud and anguished cry,
When ten thousand sin are crying,
Be with me my Helper nigh;
When my pow'r of speech is failing,
Let me hence be gently sailing—
Let Thy Passion's grievous pain
Life and heaven for me gain.

—Anon., Gotha, 1699; tr., M. Carver.

79

Tune: Jesu, Meines Lebens Leben. 68. [*TLH* 151; *LW* 94; *LSB* 420]

1. Christ, the Life of all the living,
Christ, the Death of death, our foe,
Who Thyself for me once giving
To the darkest depths of woe,—
Through Thy suff'rings, death, and merit
I eternal life inherit:
Thousand, thousand thanks shall be,
Dearest Jesus, unto Thee.

2. Thou, ah! Thou, hast taken on Thee
Bonds and stripes, a cruèl rod;
Pain and scorn were heaped upon Thee,
O Thou sinless Son of God!
Thus didst Thou my soul deliver
From the bonds of sin forever.
Thousand, thousand thanks shall be,
Dearest Jesus, unto Thee.

3. Thou hast borne the smiting only
That my wounds might all be whole;
Thou hast suffered, sad and lonely,
Rest to give my weary soul;
Yea, the curse of God enduring,
Blessing unto me securing.
Thousand, thousand thanks shall be,
Dearest Jesus, unto Thee.

4. Heartless scoffers did surround Thee,
Treating Thee with shameful scorn
And with piercing thorns they crowned Thee.
All disgrace Thou, Lord, hast borne
That as Thine Thou mightest own me
And with heav'nly glory crown me.
Thousand, thousand thanks shall be,
Dearest Jesus, unto Thee.

5. Thou hast suffered men to bruise Thee
That from pain I might be free;
Falsely did Thy foes accuse Thee,—
Thence I gain security;
Comfortless Thy soul did languish
Me to comfort in my anguish.
Thousand, thousand thanks shall be,
Dearest Jesus, unto Thee.

6. Thou hast suffered great affliction
And hast borne it patiently,
Even death by crucifixion,
Fully to atone for me;
Thou didst choose to be tormented
That my doom should be prevented.
Thousand, thousand thanks shall be,
Dearest Jesus, unto Thee.

7. That Thou wast so meek and stainless
Doth atone for my proud mood;
And Thy death makes dying painless,
And Thy ills have wrought our good.
Yea, Thy deep humiliation
Tendeth to my exaltation.
Thousand, thousand thanks shall be,
Dearest Jesus, unto Thee.

8. Then, for all that wrought my pardon,
For Thy sorrows deep and sore,
For Thine anguish in the Garden,
I will thank Thee evermore,
Thank Thee for Thy groaning, sighing,
For Thy bleeding and Thy dying,
For that last triumphant cry
And shall praise Thee, Lord, on high.

—E. C. Homburg, 1659; tr., C. Winkworth, 1863, alt.

80

Tune: Herzliebster Jesu, was hast du gebrochen. 13. [*TLH* 143; *LW* 119; *LSB* 439]

1. Come and behold, come with your hearts attending
Christ's suff'ring, pain, and sorrows without ending.
Surely alone God's winepress He is treading,
His life-blood shedding.

2. See how our sins by such great pains are thwarted:
On Olivet, He, like a worm contorted,
Writhes in such anguish, drops of grief expressing,
Blood's form possessing.

3. God here Himself collapses in the Garden,
Angels must bear Him up who bears our burden,
All creatures see their Maker fall asunder;
Mark well this wonder.

4. All sins by us and Adam e'er committed
The Lord all-blameless will not leave acquitted;
That burning anger which was our unmaking
Here He is taking.

5. Treacherous Judas runs without delaying,
For filthy lucre now His Lord betraying,
Giving the secret sign upon their meeting:
False kiss of greeting.

6. Armed with their sticks and clubs, the foul abettors
To Caiaphas conduct the Lord in fetters;
He holds His peace while they interrogate Him,
And, foiled, berate Him.

7. Though no deceit is in His mouth detected,
By lying witnesses He is rejected.
Spitting with scorn, a crown of thorn they plait Him
To coronate Him.

8. With thickly braided whips the Lord is beaten,
His back with bloody stripes is torn and eaten;
Down from His head, all pierced with spines and slivers,
Blood flows in rivers.

9. Blood-covered thus a spectacle they lead Him,
In robe of royal purple forth they speed Him,
Scornfully hailing Him, upon Him spitting,
To death committing.

10. He is condemned, And so they crucify Him,
With vinegar and bitter gall supply Him,
Thus as His spirit at the last subsided,
Still they derided.

11. We must accuse ourselves, it was our failing;
Him on the tree of wood our hands were nailing,
Since from a tree old Adam by seduction
Wrought our destruction.

12. Oh, see our sin, the cause of His affliction!
We for our crimes required His crucifixion;
Therefore should we, as long we as are living,
Seek His forgiving.

13. Lord Jesus, all man's thanks he then must show Thee!
For Thy redemption ceaseless praise we owe Thee!
And yet too poor is mortal comprehension,
That price to mention.

14. Kindly accept for now the hymn I raise Thee,
Till by the gate of angels we who praise Thee
Are granted praises better that conceive Thee
Ever to give Thee.

15. Grant, Jesus, that, as Thy soul was commended
To God, mine, too, may be when life is ended,
And in Thy blood and name and sainted number
Find blessed slumber.

—M. Bapzien, †1693; tr., M. Carver.

81

Tune: Meine Seel, ermuntre dich. [p. 411]
Or Liebster Jesu, wir sind hier. 34. [*TLH* 16; *LW* 202; *LSB* 904]

1. O my soul, awake thee now,
On the love of Jesus ponder.
Upward to Mount Calv'ry's brow
Let thy meditations wander.
Know how boundless is His favor,
And adore thy faithful Savior.

2. Crowned with thorns, the Son of God
On the cross for thee is dying.
See His body stained with blood,
Hear Him in deep anguish sighing.
Oh, how deep His love's emotion!
Canst thou fathom His devotion?

3. Lost in sin, thy penalty,
O my soul, is death eternal;
Hell's dominion yawns for thee
With its vast abyss infernal.
But thy Lord for thee doth suffer
Grace and life to thee to offer.

4. Now the wrath of God is stilled,
Jesus bore thy condemnation.
He the Law's demands fulfilled,
Cleansed thy sin, and brought salvation.
Death and hell from pow'r are driven,
Thou art now an heir of heaven!

5. What must now be done, my heart,
What should be thy due behavior?
Jesus' suff'ring is no art,
No deception thy dear Savior,
So take thought for what thou owest
To the One whose love thou knowest.

6. Jesus, I can nevermore
Recompense Thy love and kindness.
My transgression grieves me sore;
Oft in loveless carnal blindness
Have I wounded Thee, my Savior.
Pardon Thou my ill behavior!

7. What I did before is past;
Nevermore such things I'll ponder.
Let my mind be settled fast
On a straighter way to wander,
Seeking Christ alone, my Gladness,
Cursing what would cause Him sadness.

8. Sins, begone and hasten hence!
I'll not strive with you forever.
Fain would ye by impudence
Part me from my Lord and Savior,
And so doing, have me driven
From forgiveness, life, and heaven.

9. Jesus, Savior without peer,
Wholly I to Thee commend me,
That from Thee, my Portion dear,
All dissemblers may not bend me;
Unto Thee all things I tender,
Life and death and self surrender.

10. Jesus, Lord, alone for Thee
Will my heart and mind be aching;
Let me Thine forever be,
And Thou mine, with bond unbreaking;
I shall love whate'er Thou lovest,
Hating what Thou disapprovest.

11. Thy blest will my will shall be,
And Thy Word shall ever guide me
When Thy rod reproveth me
In Thy love's pavilion hide me!
Precious truth, sealed by Thy Spirit,—
Heaven's home I shall inherit,

12. Henceforth let me firmly own
Thee my choicest, dearest Treasure;
Jesus, in Thy love alone
Let me find my highest pleasure.
Thou, I know, wilt leave me never;
Let me be Thine own forever!

13. Oh, what joy and peace I find,
When in pray'r's divine communion
I can leave life's cares behind,
Seeking Thee in faith's sweet union!
If on earth such bliss is given,
How can tongue describe Thy heaven?

14. Oh, what happiness and life,
Oh, what joy and jubilation,
Oh, what peace beyond the strife,
Oh, what glorious celebration!
Never shall my song be halted,
When in God I am exalted!

15. Oh, what rapture fills my days,
What delight to be confessing
With my heart and mouth Thy praise,
Jesus, for Thy plenteous blessing!
Keep my faith in Thee unfailing,
And Thy pow'r within me dwelling.

—J. C. Schade, 1675; tr. sts. 1–4, 6, 11–13, A. Hoppe, 1921; sts. rest, M. Carver.

82

Tune: Herzliebster Jesu, was hast du gebrochen. 13. [*TLH* 143; *LW* 119; *LSB* 439]

1. Oh, that I might sufficient tears be shedding!
O ye mine eyes, your bitter floods be spreading,
And thou mine heart, no longer stone resemble;
Oh, weep and tremble!

2. He who to save thee entered His creation,
Chose thee to be His bride and holy nation,
Sinless, for us the sinful and the lesser,
Dies as transgressor.

3. For lawless men the righteous Man hath suffered,
The true Lord's life for servants false is offered,
For the unclean the Spotless takes the scourging,
Our filth expurging.

4. Lo, what a man, O man, is this thy Savior,
Bloody and wracked for thy heart's foul behavior;
See, Jesus wins for thee by crucifixion
True benediction.

5. Thy haughty head in pride is unrestricted,
His head is bowed and painfully afflicted.
Thine eye offendeth, His is swollen thickly,
Bloody and sickly.

6. Thy face fore'er escapes its due disgraces,
His face for thine is bruised in countless places;
Thy count'nance oft is vainly celebrated,
His desecrated.

7. By worldly charms thine ears would be enchanted,
His are by shouts for crucifixion haunted:
All of the curses which thy tongue did merit,
He doth inherit.

8. Oft is thy mouth with wine and water bursting,
Thy Savior lacks a draught to ease His thirsting,
A sponge of bitter gall they offer solely
The Lamb so holy.

9. Velvet and satin are thy sumptuous raiment,
Thy Jesus' nakedness, the poor repayment;
Thy Lord, to robe thee with eternal blessing
In chains is dressing.

10. To loose thee from eternal condemnation,
Thy Ransom bears His cross and takes His station;
Nails deeply pierce His hands and feet so flawless,
So art thou lawless.

11. There by a spear His heart in twain is cloven,
For callous works which thy cold heart hath woven,
His holy flesh, by blisters, scars, and bruises,
Thy health infuses.

12. For all the sins which thou hast perpetrated,
Christ hangs upon the cross, humiliated;
That for thy sake the perfect means be taken,
He is forsaken.

13. He thus to make thee heir of life in heaven,
To death upon the cross is sadly given;
And that thou mightest up to heav'n be carried,
He low is buried.

14. Most precious Jesus, grant Thy love to stir me
And ever onward by Thy Passion spur me
To fight and vanquish every fleshly longing
Within me thronging.

15. Thou who hast once into the grave descended,
When Thy redeeming work for me was ended,
Oh, grant me peace and rest when I am carried
Hence to be buried.

16. Give sweet repose, Lord, through Thy bitter sorrow,
Lift up my soul to that eternal morrow,
Which Thou, O Savior, for my sake suppliedst,
The day Thou diedst.

—G. W. Sacer, 1665; tr. sts. 1–14, M. Carver; sts. 15–16, N. L. Frothingham, †1870, alt.

83

Tune: Du großer Schmerzensmann. 55. [p. 401; *or TLH* 395*; *LW* 385*; *LSB* 731*]

1. Thou Man of Sorrows, hail!
Receive my adoration:
On Thee the Father laid
Grief for my consolation.
Thanks for Thy anguish, Lord,—
Bonds, stripes endured by Thee:
Thanks, Lord for all Thy grief,
Thy last sad agony!

2. Alas, that all these woes
Thou borest in Thy Passion
In place of sinful men
Were due to our transgression.
Naught put Thee on the cross
Except our sin alone.
O spotless Lamb of God,
What else couldst Thou have done?

3. The kindness of Thine heart
Unto our heart revealeth
How dear we were to Thee;
Thy death and suff'ring healeth
The rift that once from man
Thy Father did divide,
Brings us the grace of God,
And makes Him satisfied.

4. Thy conflict is our crown;
Thy death our life in heaven:
Lord, by Thy bonds to us
Is endless freedom given.
Thy cross our solace is;
Thy wounds salvation give:
Thy blood our ransom-price;—
By this we sinners live.

5. Help us like Thee to face
All pain and tribulation,
And as we bear our cross,
Keep us from desperation.
Grant by Thy crown of thorns
That with a patient mood
We may endure the loss
Of honor, name, and blood.

6. Thy sweat, Lord, let avail,
When we to grief are driven;
Grant vict'ry over death,
As Thou with death hast striven;
Lord, let us by Thy bonds
Be bound as pleases Thee;
Thy cross help us both world
And flesh to crucify.

7. Oh, may Thy wounds, we pray,
Be to our sins for healing:
Sustain us at the last,
Hope through Thy death revealing:
O Jesus, grant to us
Through all Thine agony,
Thy suff'rings, cross, and pain,
We ne'er forsaken be.

—A. Thebesius, †1652; tr. sts. 1, 4, 7, A. T. Russell, 1851, alt.; sts. 2–3, 5–6, M. Carver.

84

Tune: Herzlich tut mich verlangen. 59. [*TLH* 172; *LW* 113; *LSB* 450]

1. O sacred Head, now wounded,
With grief and shame weighed down,
Now scornfully surrounded
With thorns, Thine only crown.
O sacred Head, what glory,
What bliss, till now was Thine!
Yet, though despised and gory,
I joy to call Thee mine.

2. Men mock and taunt and jeer Thee,
Thou noble countenance,
Though mighty worlds shall fear Thee
And flee before Thy glance.
How art thou pale with anguish,
With sore abuse and scorn!
How doth Thy visage languish
That once was bright as morn!

3. Now from Thy cheeks has vanished
Their color, once so fair;
From Thy red lips is banished
The splendor that was there.
Grim Death, with cruèl rigor,
Hath robbed Thee of Thy life;
Thus Thou has lost Thy vigor,
Thy strength, in this sad strife.

4. My burden in Thy Passion,
Lord, Thou hast borne for me,
For it was my transgression
Which brought this woe on Thee.
I cast me down before Thee;
Wrath were my rightful lot.
Have mercy, I implore Thee;
Redeemer, spurn me not!

5. My Shepherd, now receive me;
My Guardian, own me Thine.
Great blessings Thou didst give me,
O Source of gifts divine.
Thy lips have often fed me
With words of truth and love;
Thy Spirit oft hath led me
To heavenly joys above.

6. Here I will stand beside Thee,
From Thee I will not part;
O Savior, do not chide me
When breaks Thy loving heart!
When soul and body languish
In death's cold, cruèl grasp,
Then, in Thy deepest anguish,
Thee in mine arms I'll clasp.

7. The joy can ne'er be spoken,
Above all joys beside,
When in Thy body broken
I thus with safety hide.
O Lord of Life, desiring
Thy glory now to see,
Beside Thy cross expiring,
I'd breathe my soul to Thee.

8. What language shall I borrow
To thank Thee, dearest Friend,
For this, Thy dying sorrow,
Thy pity without end?
Oh, make me Thine forever!
And should I fainting be,
Lord, let me never, never,
Outlive my love for Thee.

9. My Savior, be Thou near me
When death is at my door;
Then let Thy presence cheer me,
Forsake me nevermore!
When soul and body languish,
Oh, leave me not alone,
But take away mine anguish
By virtue of Thine own!

10. Be Thou my Consolation,
My Shield, when I must die;
Remind me of Thy Passion
When my last hour draws nigh.
Mine eyes shall then behold Thee,
Upon Thy cross shall dwell,
My heart by faith enfold Thee.
Who dieth thus dies well.

—P. Gerhardt, 1656, after Bernard; tr., *TLH,* 1941.

85

Tune: O Jesu Christ, meins Lebens Licht. 11.
[*TLH* 148; *LW* 314; *LSB* 839; *or LW* 382*; *LSB* 759*]

1. Lord Jesus Christ, my Life, my Light,
My Strength by day, my Trust by night,
On earth I'm but a passing guest
And sorely with my sins oppressed.

2. Far off I see my fatherland,
Where through Thy blood I hope to stand.
But ere I reach that Paradise,
A weary way before me lies.

3. My heart sinks at the journey's length,
My wasted flesh has little strength;
My soul alone still cries in me:
"Lord, take me home, take me to Thee!"

4. Oh, let Thy suff'rings give me pow'r
To meet the last and darkest hour!
Thy blood refresh and comfort me;
Thy bonds and fetters make me free.

5. The blows and stripes that fell on Thee
Heal up the wounds of sin in me;
Thy crown of thorns, Thy foes' mad spite
Let be my glory and delight.

6. That thirst and bitter draught of Thine
Cause me to bear with patience mine;
Thy piercing cry uphold my soul,
When floods of anguish o'er me roll.

7. Oh, let Thy holy wounds for me
Clefts in the rock forever be
Where as a dove my soul can hide
And safe from Satan's rage abide.

8. And when my lips grow white and chill,
Thy Spirit cry within me still,
And help my soul Thy heav'n to find,
When these poor eyes grow dark and blind!

9. And when my spirit flies away,
Thy dying words shall be my stay.
Grant that no evil work be mine
As I in death my head incline.

10. Thy cross shall be my staff in life,
Thy holy grave my rest from strife;
The winding-sheet that covered Thee,
Oh, let it be a shroud for me.

11. Lord, in Thy nail-prints let me read
That Thou to save me hast decreed
And grant that in Thine opened side
My troubled soul may ever hide.

12. Since Thou hast died, the Pure, the Just,
I take my homeward way in trust.
The gates of heav'n, Lord, open wide
When here I may no more abide.

13. And when the last Great Day shall come
And Thou, our Judge, shalt speak the doom,
Let me with joy behold the light
And set me then upon Thy right.

14. Renew this wasted flesh of mine
That like the sun it there may shine
Among the angels pure and bright,
Yea, like Thyself in glorious light.

15. Ah, then I'll have my heart's desire,
When, singing with the angels' choir,
Among the ransomed of Thy grace,
Forever I'll behold Thy face!

—M. Behm, 1608, but st. 7, Anon., 1644; tr., C. Winkworth, 1863, alt., but st. 9b, M. Carver.

86

Tune: O Lamm Gottes unschuldig. 50. [*TLH* 146; *LW* 208; *LSB* 434]

1. Lamb of God, pure and holy,
Who on the cross didst suffer,
Ever patient and lowly,
Thyself to scorn didst offer.
All sins Thou borest for us,
Else had despair reigned o'er us:
Have mercy on us, O Jesus! O Jesus!

2. Lamb of God, pure and holy,
Who on the cross didst suffer,
Ever patient and lowly,
Thyself to scorn didst offer.
All sins Thou borest for us,
Else had despair reigned o'er us:
Have mercy on us, O Jesus! O Jesus!

3. Lamb of God, pure and holy!
Who on the cross didst suffer,
Ever patient and lowly,
Thyself to scorn didst offer.
All sins Thou borest for us,
Else had despair reigned o'er us:
Thy peace be with us, O Jesus! O Jesus!

—N. Decius, 1522, after the Lat. *Agnus Dei;* tr., *TLH,* 1941.

87

Tune: O Lamm Gottes unschuldig. 50. [*TLH* 146; *LW* 208; *LSB* 434]

1. Lamb of God, pure and holy!
Who on the cross didst suffer,
Ever patient and lowly,
Thyself to scorn didst offer.
All sins Thou borest for us,
Else had despair reigned o'er us:
Have mercy on us, O Jesus! O Jesus!

2. Heartfelt thanks, Lord, we give Thee
For all Thy mercy tow'rd us,
When we did but aggrieve Thee!
Oh, sorrow true afford us,
That we may shun transgression
In honor of Thy Passion:
Have mercy on us, O Jesus! O Jesus!

3. In the true faith uphold us,
Lord, by Thy blood and dying;
Firm in Thy wounds enfold us
When death at hand is lying,
O bless us through Thy merit
That we may heav'n inherit!
Thy peace be with us, O Jesus! O Jesus!

—N. Decius, 1541; tr. st. 1, *TLH,* 1941; sts. 2–3, M. Carver.

88

Tune: O Traurigkeit, O Herzeleid! 14. [*TLH* 167; *LW* 122; *LSB* 448]

1. O darkest woe! / Ye tears, forth flow!
Has earth so sad a wonder?
God the Father's only Son
Now is buried yonder.

2. O sorrow dread! / Our God is dead!
But by His expiation
Of our guilt upon the cross
Gained for us salvation.

3. O sinful man! / It was the ban
Of death on thee that brought Him
Down to suffer for thy sins
And such woe hath wrought Him.

4. Lo, stained with blood, / The Lamb of God,
The Bridegroom, lies before thee,
Pouring out His life that He
May to life restore thee.

5. O Ground of faith, / Laid low in death.
Sweet lips, now silent sleeping!
Surely all that live must mourn
Here with bitter weeping.

6. O Virgin-born, / Thy death we mourn,
Thou lovely Star of gladness!
Who could see Thy reeking blood
Without grief and sadness?

7. Oh, blest shall be / Eternally
Who oft in faith will ponder
Why the glorious Prince of Life
Should be buried yonder!

8. O Jesus blest, / My Help and Rest
With tears I now entreat Thee:
Make me love Thee to the last,
Till in heav'n I greet Thee.

—J. Rist, 1641, sts. 2–8; st. 1, Anon.; tr., C. Winkworth, 1863, alt.

89

Tune: O Welt, sieh hier dein Leben. 31.
[*TLH* 171; *LW* 120; *or TLH* 126*; *LW* 85*; *LSB* 396*]

1. Upon the cross extended,
See, world, thy Lord suspended.
Thy Savior yields His breath.
The Prince of Life from heaven
Himself hath freely given
To shame and blows and bitter death.

2. Come hither now and ponder,
'Twill fill thy soul with wonder,
Blood streams from every pore.
Through grief whose depth none knoweth,
From His great heart there floweth
Sigh after sigh of anguish o'er.

3. Who is it that hath bruised Thee?
Who hath so sore abused Thee
And caused Thee all Thy woe?
While we must make confession
Of sin and dire transgression,
Thou deeds of evil dost not know.

4. I caused Thy grief and sighing
By evils multiplying
As countless as the sands.
I caused the woes unnumbered
With which Thy soul is cumbered,
Thy sorrows raised by wicked hands.

5. 'Tis I who should be smitten,
My doom should here be written:
Bound hand and foot in hell.
The fetters and the scourging,
The floods around Thee surging,
'Tis I who have deserved them well.

6. The load Thou takest on Thee,
That pressed so sorely on me,
It crushed me to the ground.
The cross for me enduring,
The crown for me securing,
My healing in Thy wounds is found.

7. A crown of thorns Thou wearest,
My shame and scorn Thou bearest,
That I might ransomed be.
My Bondsman, ever willing,
My place with patience filling,
From sin and guilt hast made me free.

8. Into death's jaws Thou springest,
Deliv'rance to me bringest
From such a monster dire.
My death away Thou takest,
Thy grave its grave Thou makest;
O love, O unexampled fire!

9. Thy cords of love, my Savior,
Bind me to Thee forever,
I am no longer mine.
To Thee I gladly tender
All that my life can render
And all I have to Thee resign.

10. Not much can I be giving
In this poor life I'm living,
But one thing will I do:
Thy death and sorrows ever,
Till soul from body sever,
Keep in my heart's remembrance new.

11. Thy cross I'll place before me,
Its saving power be o'er me,
Wherever I may be;
Thine innocence revealing,
Thy love and mercy sealing,
The pledge of truth and constancy.

12. How God at our transgression
To anger gives expression,
How loud His thunders roll,
How fearfully He smiteth,
How sorely He requiteth,—
All this Thy suff'rings teach my soul.

13. From these I shall be learning,
How I may be adorning,
My heart with quietness,
And how I still should love them
Whose spite and malice move them
My heart by evils to distress.

14. When evil men revile me,
With wicked tongues defile me,
I'll curb my vengeful heart.
The unjust wrong I'll suffer,
Unto my neighbor offer
Forgiveness for each bitter smart.

15. I'll take Thy cross in measure,
Renouncing every pleasure
For which my passions sigh;
Thy cause in me for grieving
I'll flee, forever leaving,
As much as in my strength doth lie.

16. Thy groaning and Thy sighing,
Thy bitter tears and dying,
With which Thou was oppressed,—
They shall, when life is ending,
Be guiding and attending
My way to Thine eternal rest.

—P. Gerhardt, 1647; tr., J. Kelly, 1867, alt.

90

Tune: Freu dich sehr, o meine Seele. 66. [*TLH* 61; *LW* 28; *LSB* 347]

1. Boast, O world, of all thy learning,
Glory in its lofty heights.
All thy carnal knowledge spurning,
My heart still finds pure delights.
In my Savior's cross and pain,
I find wisdom's highest gain.
The blest faith His grace has given
Seals to me the bliss of heaven.

2. Let the worldly-minded treasure
Carnal knowledge here below,
Finding not in Him their pleasure
Who true wisdom can bestow.
He who died on Calv'ry's cross
Grants me gain for earthly loss;
Higher than earth's wisdom reaches
Is the love His Passion preaches.

3. Others shape their comprehension
By the lore of shifty sage,
Seeking glory and attention
From the nobles of our age;
I will only seek the fame
Of my Savior's humble shame.
'Tis for Christian mouths unfitting,
Idols' lore to be repeating.

4. When the world seeks exaltation,
Wealth, esteem, and honors great,
On my Lord's humiliation
I in faith will meditate.
What is earthly gain to me,
When in Christ my All I see?
Carnal vanities shall never
From His fellowship me sever.

5. Come, my Life, my Lord, my Savior,
Come and teach me as Thou wilt.
Take my heart as Thine forever,
Thou for me Thy blood hast spilt.
Boundless wisdom, love divine,
Strength omnipotent is Thine;
Let all earth-born knowledge perish!
Thee alone my soul shall cherish!

6. Earth no lasting comfort knoweth,
When sin-burdened conscience speaks!
Earth no lasting place bestoweth,
When my heart for solace seeks.
What availeth earthly weal,
When the curse of law I feel?
But Thy blood to me has given
Pardon, peace, redemption, heaven!

7. Dearest Jesus, plant, I pray Thee,
Thine own wisdom in my heart!
Dwell in me, let naught delay Thee,
Come, and nevermore depart!
Thou hast suffered death for me
On the cross of Calvary.
Love divine, let Thy salvation
Be my sweetest meditation.

8. At the end, when thoughts of dying
All thoughts else with fear suspend,
Let mine eyes, the cross espying,
There my Comforter attend.
Let thy suff'ring, cross, and pain
In my mind at last remain!
Grant me this, O Jesus, Savior:
Let me worship Thee forever.

—J. Job, 1724; tr. sts. 1–2, 4–7, A. Hoppe, 1922; sts. 3, 8, M. Carver.

91

Tune: Jesu, deine heilgen Wunden. 66. [p. 406; *or TLH* 144*; *LW* 95;* *LSB* 421*]

1. Thousand times by me be greeted,
Jesus, who hast cherished me,
And Thyself to death submitted
For my treason against Thee.
Oh, how happy do I feel,
When before Thee low I kneel,
See Thee on the cross expiring,
My salvation there acquiring!

2. Jesus, Thee I view in spirit,
Covered o'er with blood and wounds:
Now salvation through Thy merit
For my sin-sick soul abounds.
O Thou fairest Prince of Peace,
Who didst thirst for our release,
Who can fathom all that's treasured
In Thy love's design unmeasured?

3. Heal me, O my soul's Physician,
Wheresoe'er I'm sick or sad;
All the woes of my condition
By Thy balm be now allayed.
Heal the hurts which Adam wrought,
Or which on myself I've brought;
If Thy blood but touch me solely,
My distress will vanish wholly.

4. On my heart Thy wounds forever
Be inscribed indelibly,
That I ne'er forget, dear Savior,
What Thou hast endured for me.
Thou'rt indeed my highest Good,
End of all solicitude;
Let me at Thy feet here savor
And enjoy Thy love and favor.

5. With the deepest adoration
Humbly at Thy feet I lie,
And with fervent supplication
Unto Thee for succor cry.
My petition kindly hear,
Say in answer to my pray'r,
"I will change thy grief and sadness
Into comfort, joy, and gladness."

—P. Gerhardt, 1653, after Bernard; tr., J. Gambold, 1754, alt.

92

Tune: So gehst du nun, mein Jesu, hin. 83. [*TLH* 150]

1. (*Soul:*) Lord Jesus, Thou art going forth
For me Thy life to offer;
For me, a sinner from my birth,
Who caused all Thou must suffer.
So be it, then, / Thou Hope of men;
Thee I shall follow weeping,
Tears flowing free / Thy pain to see,
Watch o'er Thy sorrows keeping.

2. (*Jesus:*) O Soul, attend thou and behold
The fruit of thy transgression!
My portion is the curse of old
And for man's sin My Passion.
Now comes the night / Of sin's dread might,
Man's guilt I here am bearing.
Oh, weight it, Soul; / I make thee whole,
No need now of despairing.

3. (*Soul:*) 'Tis I, Lord Jesus, I confess,
Who should have borne sin's wages
And lost the peace of heav'nly bliss
Through everlasting ages.
Instead 'tis Thou / Who goest now
My punishment to carry.
Thy death and blood / Lead me to God;
By grace I there may tarry.

4. (*Jesus:*) O Soul, I take upon Me now
The pain thou shouldst have suffered.
Behold, with grace I thee endow,
Grace freely to thee offered.
The curse I choose / That thou might'st lose
Sin's curse and guilt forever.
My gift of love / From heav'n above
Will give thee blessing ever.

5. (*Soul:*) What can I for such love divine
To Thee, Lord Jesus, render?
No merit has this heart of mine;
Yet while I live, I'll tender
Myself alone, / And all I own,
In love to serve before Thee;
Then when time's past, / Take me at last
To Thy blest home in glory.

—K. F. Nachtenhöfer, 1651, but st. 4, M. Omeis, 1699; tr., W. G. Polack, 1940.

93

Tune: O Traurigkeit, O Herzeleid! 14. [*TLH* 167; *LW* 122; *LSB* 448]

1. So rest, my Rest, / Thou ever Blest!
Thy grave with sinners making;
By Thy precious death from sin
My dead soul awaking.

2. After Thy strife, / Life of my life,
Thou'rt in the tomb reposing,
Round Thee now a rock-hewn grave,
Rock of ages, closing.

3. How cold art Thou, / My Savior, now!
Thy fervent love hath driven
Thee into the cold, dark grave,
That I might gain heaven.

4. Breath of all breath! / I know, from death
Thou wilt my dust awaken;
Wherefore should I dread the grave,
Or my faith be shaken?

5. To me the tomb / Shall be a room,
Where I lie down on roses;
Who by faith hath conquered death,
Sweetly there reposes.

6. The body dies— / Naught else—and lies
In dust, until victorious
From the grave it shall arise
Beautiful and glorious!

7. Meantime I will, / My Jesus, still
Deep in my bosom lay Thee,
Ever musing on Thy death:
Leave me not, I pray Thee!

—S. Franck, 1685; tr., R. Massie, 1857, alt.

94

Tune: Wenn meine Sünd mich kränken. 48. [*TLH* 152; *or LW* 72*; *LSB* 402*]

1. When o'er my sins I sorrow,
Lord, I will look to Thee
And hence my comfort borrow
That Thou wast slain for me;
Yea, Lord, Thy precious blood was spilt
For me, O most unworthy,
To take away my guilt.

2. Oh, what a marv'lous offering!
Behold, the Master spares
His servants, and their suff'ring
And grief for them He bears.
God stoopeth from His throne on high;
For me, His guilty creature,
He deigns as man to die.

3. My manifold transgression
Henceforth can harm me none
Since Jesus' bloody Passion
For me God's grace hath won.
His precious blood my debts hath paid;
Of hell and all its torments
I am no more afraid.

4. Therefore I will forever
Give glory unto Thee,
O Jesus, loving Savior,
For what Thou didst for me.
In songs of thanks I'll spend my breath
For Thy sad cry, Thy suff'rings,
Thy wrongs, Thy guiltless death.

5. Then let Thy woes, Thy patience,
My heart with strength inspire
To vanquish all temptations,
And spurn all low desire;
This thought I fain would cherish most—
What pain my soul's redemption
To Thee, O Savior, cost!

6. Whate'er may be the burden,
The cross here on me laid;
Be shame or want my guerdon,
I'll bear it with Thine aid;
Give patience, give me strength to take
Thee for my bright example,
And all the world forsake.

7. And let me do to others
As Thou hast done to me,
Love all men as my brothers,
And serve them willingly,
With ready heart, nor seek my own,
But as Thou, Lord, hast helped us,
From purest love alone.

8. And let Thy cross upbear me
With strength when I depart;
Tell me that naught can tear me
From my Redeemer's heart,
But since my trust is in Thy grace
Thou wilt accept me yonder,
Where I shall see Thy face.

—J. Gesenius, 1646; tr., st. 1, C. Winkworth, 1855, st. 2–4, *TLH,* 1941.

95

Tune: Nun laßt uns den Leib begraben. 11. [*TLH* 596; *LW* 382; *LSB* 759]

1. Lord Jesus, we give thanks to Thee
That Thou hast died to set us free;
Made righteous thro' Thy precious blood,
We now are reconciled to God.

2. By virtue of Thy wounds we pray,
True God and Man, be Thou our Stay,
Our Comfort when we yield our breath,
Our Rescue from eternal death.

3. Defend us, Lord, from sin and shame;
Help us by Thine almighty name
To bear our crosses patiently,
Consoled by Thy great agony,

4. And thus the full assurance gain
That Thou to us wilt true remain
And not forsake us in our strife
Until we enter into life.

— C. Vischer, 1568; tr., A . Crull, †1923, alt.

Easter, or Resurrection of Christ

96

Tune: Also heilig ist der Tag. 62. [p. 395]

1. This is such a holy day,
That no man can ever its due praise repay,
Since the holy Son of God
On this day conquered hell
And there bound up the wretched devil well.
So hath the Lord delivered Christendom,
This was Christ Himself:
Kyrieleïson!

—Anon., 15th c., after Fortunatus; tr. C. Winkworth, 1869, alt.

97

Tune: Auf, auf, mein Herz, mit Freuden. 57. [*TLH* 192, *LW* 128; *LSB* 467]

1. Awake, my heart, with gladness,
See what today is done;
Now, after gloom and sadness,
Comes forth the glorious Sun.
My Savior there was laid
Where our bed must be made
When to the realms of light
Our spirit wings its flight.

2. The foe, exulting, shouted
When Christ lay in the tomb,
But, lo, he now is routed,
His boast is turned to gloom.
For Christ again is free;
In glorious victory
He who is strong to save
Has triumphed o'er the grave.

3. Upon the tomb is standing
The Hero, looking round;
The foe, his crafts unhanding,
Lies beaten on the ground
And must his hellish pow'r
To Christ deliver o'er,
And to the Victor's bands
Must yield his feet and hands.

4. This is a sight that gladdens;
What peace it doth impart!
Now nothing ever saddens
The joy within my heart.
No gloom shall ever shake,
No foe shall ever take,
The hope which God's own Son
In love for me hath won.

5. Now hell, its prince, the devil,
Of all their pow'rs are shorn;
Now I am safe from evil,
And sin I laugh to scorn.
Grim Death with all his might
Cannot my soul affright;
He is a pow'rless form,
Howe'er he rave and storm.

6. The world against me rageth
Its fury I disdain;
Though bitter war it wageth,
Its work is all in vain.
My heart from care is free,
No trouble troubles me.
Misfortune now is play,
And night is bright as day.

7. Now I will cling forever
To Christ, my Savior true;
My Lord will leave me never,
Whate'er He passeth through.
He rends Death's iron chain,
He breaks through sin and pain,
He shatters hell's dark thrall,—
I follow Him through all.

8. To halls of heav'nly splendor
With Him I penetrate;
And trouble ne'er may hinder
Nor make me hesitate.
Let tempests rage at will,
My Savior shields me still;
He grants abiding peace
And bids all tumult cease.

9. He brings me to the portal
That leads to bliss untold,
Whereon this rhyme immortal
Is found in script of gold:
"Who there My cross hath shared
Finds here a crown prepared;
Who there with Me hath died
Shall here be glorified."

—P. Gerhardt, 1647; tr., J. Kelly, 1867, alt.

98

Tune: Christ ist erstanden von der Marter allen. 99. [*TLH* 187; *LW* 124; *LSB* 459 (mel.)]

1. Christ is arisen
From the grave's dark prison.
We now rejoice with gladness;
Christ will end all sadness.
Kyrieleis!

2. All our hopes were ended
Had Jesus not ascended
From the grave triumphantly.
For this, Lord Christ, we worship Thee.
Kyrieleis!

3. Alleluia, alleluia, alleluia!
We now rejoice with gladness;
Christ will end all sadness.
Kyrieleis!

—Anon., Wittenberg, 1529, after 11th c. orig.; tr., W. G. Polack, 1939.

99

Tune: Christ lag in Todesbanden. 61. [*TLH* 195; *LW* 123; *LSB* 458]

1. Christ Jesus lay in death's strong bands,
For our offenses given;
But now at God's right hand He stands,
And brings us life from heaven;
Therefore let us joyful be
And sing to God right thankfully
Loud songs of alleluia. Alleluia!

2. No son of man could conquer Death,
Such mischief sin had wrought us,
For innocence dwelt not on earth,
And therefore Death had brought us
Into thralldom from of old
And ever grew more strong and bold
And kept us in his bondage. Alleluia!

3. But Jesus Christ, God's only Son,
To our low state descended,
The cause of Death He has undone,
His pow'r forever ended,
Ruined all his right and claim
And left him nothing but the name,—
His sting is lost forever. Alleluia!

4. It was a strange and dreadful strife
When Life and Death contended;
The victory remained with Life;
The reign of Death was ended;
Holy Scripture plainly saith
That Death is swallowed up by Death,
In vain it rages o'er us. Alleluia!

5. Here the true Paschal Lamb we see,
Whom God so freely gave us;
He died on the accursèd tree—
So strong His love!—to save us.
See, His blood doth mark our door;
Faith points to it, Death passes o'er,
And Satan cannot harm us. Alleluia!

6. So let us keep the festival
Whereto the Lord invites us;
Christ is Himself the Joy of all,
The Sun that warms and lights us.
By His grace He doth impart
Eternal sunshine to the heart;
The night of sin is ended. Alleluia!

7. Then let us feast this Easter Day
On Christ the Bread of heaven;
The Word of Grace hath purged away
The old and evil leaven.
Christ alone our souls will feed,
He is our meat and drink indeed;
Faith lives upon no other. Alleluia!

—M. Luther, 1524; tr., R. Massie, 1854, alt.

100

Tune: Christus ist erstanden von des Todes Banden. 15. [*TLH* 190; *LSB* 459]

1. Christ the Lord is ris'n again,
Christ hath broken death's strong chain.
Hark, the angels shout for joy,
Singing evermore on high:
Alleluia!

2. He who gave for us His life,
Who for us endured the strife,
Is our Paschal Lamb today.
We, too, sing for joy, and say:
Alleluia!

3. He who bore all pain and loss
Comfortless upon the cross
Lives in glory now on high,
Pleads for us and hears our cry.
Alleluia!

4. He whose path no records tell,
Hath descended into hell;
He the strong man armed hath bound,
Now in highest heav'n is crowned.
Alleluia!

5. He who slumbered in the grave
Is exalted now to save;
Now through Christendom it rings
That the Lamb is King of kings.
Alleluia!

6. Now He bids us tell abroad
How the lost may be restored,
How the penitent forgiv'n,
How we, too, may enter heav'n.
Alleluia!

7. Thou our Paschal Lamb indeed,
Christ, today Thy people feed;
Take our sins and guilt away
That we all may sing for aye:
Alleluia!

—M. Weisse, 1531; tr., C. Winkworth, 1863.

101

Tune: Helft mir Gotts Güte preisen. 58. [*TLH* 112]

1. Though death indeed had swallowed
The glorious Lord and Son,
What disappointment followed
For death that Easter dawn!
This day hath Christ appeared:
The Sun, bright grace revealing,
Brings gladness, life, and healing;
Who then would not be cheered?

2. An angel came from heaven
And from the tomb's great door
The stone aside was driven,
The seal was there no more.
And they, O Christ our Lord,
Who for Thy death were baited
And by Thy chamber waited—
Where now is fled that horde?

3. In every land is chanted
By hearts with joy made bold,
How Christ has death supplanted,
As He Himself foretold.
His Word's fulfillment see;
Now for this joy most wondrous,
Sing all with voices thund'rous:
Lord Christ, our thanks to Thee!

4. With hope our hearts Thou filledst
Through Thy most precious blood,
To us Thou heaven willedst
And won'st for us great good;
So let us do our best,
And joyfully be keeping
For all Thy pains and weeping
This gladsome Easter feast!

5. Lord, who didst crush the powèr
Of Hell, his host, and death,
Bestow in our last hoùr
A peaceful final breath;
To heaven lead us on,
Where grief away is taken,
On Thy Great Day to waken,
O Jesus, God's true Son!

—G. Werner, †1643; tr., M. Carver.

102

Tune: Herr Gott, dich loben alle wir. 11. [*TLH* 13; *LW* 216; *LSB* 923]

1. Lord Jesus Christ, strong Hero Thou,
Grim death Thou hast o'erpowered now,
Thou dost destroy hell's gate and chain,
Dost on the third day rise again.

2. Thou grantest to Thy friends the grace
To look again upon Thy face,
And showest them the glorious prize,
Won when from death Thou didst arise.

3. Grant that we and all Christians may
Partake of this great joy today,
Which by Thy resurrection Thou
To all men freely givest now.

4. Grant us that we may rise from sin,
A holy life to lead begin,
Till we, from sin and pain set free,
In endless Easter live with Thee.

—J. Mylius, 1596; tr., A. Crull, †1923, alt.

103

Tune: Erschienen ist der herrlich Tag. 21. [*TLH* 108; *LW* 147]

1. The day hath dawned—the day of days,
Transcending all our joy and praise;
This day our Lord triumphant rose,
This day He captive led our foes.
Alleluia!

2. The Serpent's craft, sin, Death, and hell,
This day before the Conqu'ror fell:
All suff'ring, sorrow, ill, the name
Of Jesus ris'n this day o'ercame.
Alleluia!

3. At break of dawn with spice and balm
The Marys Three came to the tomb
To Mary's Son they did suppose,
Who from the dead already rose.
Alleluia!

4. "Whom seek ye here?" the Angel said,
"Christ is arisen from the dead;
Here see His napkin, here His cloth;
To tell His foll'wers, run ye forth!"
Alleluia!

5. Th' Eleven's anguish as they mourned
This day to utter joy was turned;
As soon as they beheld their Lord,
All fear and doubting was ignored.
Alleluia!

6. The Lord spoke tenderly this day
With two disciples on the way.
Their hearts for joy within them burned,
Till in the meal they Him discerned.
Alleluia!

7. Our Samson He, our Hero great,
Christ sealed the mighty Lion's fate,
Laid low the gates of Death and hell,
Broke all the devil's pow'r as well.
Alleluia!

8. Like Jonah under whale and wave,
Three days lay Christ within the grave,
Till Death inside its belly dim
No moment more could hinder Him.
Alleluia!

9. Then Death must render up its prey;
Life held the crown and won the day.
Destroyed is all Death's might and reign;
Christ hath restored our life again.
Alleluia!

10. This day from Egypt forth we go,
And Pharoah's bondage off we throw;
The Paschal Lamb, the Lord Divine
This day we eat in bread and wine.
Alleluia!

11. We also take the manna sweet
Which Moses bade God's people eat,
Nor suffer leaven sour therein,
That we may live all free from sin.
Alleluia!

12. The vengeful Angel passes o'er,
No first-born dies behind our door,
Upon our lintel Jesus' blood
Has been applied, our shield holds good.
Alleluia!

13. The sun, the earth, and all are glad,
Which at His death before were sad:
All own with joy upon this day
The foe's dominion passed away.
Alleluia!

14. Then, as is meet, we now will sing
Glad alleluias to our King:
To Thee, Lord, doth our praise pertain,
Who for our joy art ris'n again.
Alleluia!

—N. Herman, 1560; tr. sts. 1–2, 13–14, A. T. Russell, 1851, alt.; sts. 9–10, G. Walker, 1860, alt; sts. rest, M. Carver.

104

Tune: Freuet euch, ihr Christen alle. 82. [*TLH* 96; *LW* 40; *LSB* 897]

1. Oh, rejoice, ye Christians, loudly,
For our joy is now begun;
Wondrous things our God hath done.
Tell abroad His goodness proudly
Who, to save us from death's sting,
Gave His life an offering:
Joy, O joy, beyond all gladness,
Christ hath done away with sadness!
Hence, all sorrow and repining,
For the Sun of Grace is shining!

2. See, my soul, thy Savior risen,
All-triumphant in the war;
Health and peace He doth restore.
From the chamber of death's prison
Resurrected for thy good,
He has freed thee by His blood:
Joy, O joy, beyond all gladness,
Christ hath done away with sadness!
Hence, all sorrow and repining,
For the Sun of Grace is shining!

3. Lord, how shall I thank Thee rightly?
I acknowledge that from Thee
Every blessing flows to me.
Let me not forget it lightly
But to Thee through all things cleave,
So shall heart and mind receive:
Joy, O joy beyond all gladness,
Christ hath done away with sadness!
Hence, all sorrow and repining,
For the Sun of Grace is shining!

4. Jesus, guard and guide Thy members,
Fill Thy brethren with Thy grace,
Hear their pray'rs in every place,
Quicken now life's faintest embers;
To all Christians, far and near,
Let thy boundless love appear:
Joy, O joy, beyond all gladness,
Christ hath done away with sadness!
Hence, all sorrow and repining,
For the Sun of Grace is shining!

— C. Keimann, 1662; tr., C. Winkworth, 1863, ad. / M. Carver.

105

Tune: Heut triumphieret Gottes Sohn. 44. [*LW* 136]

1. Lo, with this morning's dawning ray,
My Savior rose to endless day!
Alleluia, alleluia!
Past is sin's dark and dreary reign;
Life, light, and peace are ours again!
Alleluia, alleluia!

2. Though oft in night of great dismay
Enclosed as in death's tomb I lay.
Alleluia, alleluia!
Thou mak'st all soon Thy sun of grace
To rise, and joys the sadness chase.
Alleluia, alleluia!

3. 'Twas but three days, the blessed length
My Savior lay in Death's grim strength.
Alleluia, alleluia!
The third day dawned, He cracked the tomb,
His vict'ry banners pierced the gloom.
Alleluia, alleluia!

4. Today I live through days of loss,
Enduring worldly scorn and cross.
Alleluia, alleluia!
Then comes my Sabbath in the grave,
And peace and rest are mine to have.
Alleluia, alleluia!

5. Soon I shall wake to heaven's sun,
Shall view the Easter Day begun.
Alleluia, alleluia!
Arising at my Savior's voice,
Death's name, a long-forgotten noise.
Alleluia, alleluia!

6. Upon the cross Christ freely gave
His life, the lives of all to save.
Alleluia, alleluia!
Since He hath Death's dark prison felled,
No man need more by Death be held.
Alleluia, alleluia!

7. Christ's kingdom is not of this world,
He craves not silk nor flag unfurled.
Alleluia, alleluia!
The humble, poor, and lowly here
Shall be His well-beloved peer.
Alleluia, alleluia!

8. Here cannot fully be explained
What He who conquered Death obtained.
Alleluia, alleluia!
What treasures from His tomb He brought,
What gifts with joy and blessing fraught.
Alleluia, alleluia!

9. The last great day alone will show
What to this wondrous act we owe.
Alleluia, alleluia!
How He hath bruised the serpent's head,
How Death by Him was stricken dead!
Alleluia, alleluia!

10. Then shall I see Christ's glorious state
With joy eternal, full, and great.
Alleluia, alleluia!
I shall behold all wicked foes
Hurled down to Hell's eternal woes.
Alleluia, alleluia!

11. The Lord hath stricken Death's demise,
Because He died and yet did rise.
Alleluia, alleluia!
With pow'r divine He scours the tomb
Death, devil, hell must all succumb.
Alleluia, alleluia!

12. O stronger Thou than Death and hell,
Where is the foe Thou canst not quell?
Alleluia, alleluia!
What heavy stone Thou canst not roll
From off the prisoned, anguished soul?
Alleluia, alleluia!

13. No cross or grief can weigh too sore
To frustrate Christ my Savior's pow'r.
Alleluia, alleluia!
His hand delivers me from all;
Who stands against in shame will fall.
Alleluia, alleluia!

14. The Lord is risen now for you!
Yea, doubt it not, the word is true.
Alleluia, alleluia!
The angel witnesseth to this
The empty tomb, the wondrous bliss.
Alleluia, alleluia!

15. Christ liveth; where is room for fear?
His life, His love my spirit cheer.
Alleluia, alleluia!
What though all worlds should fade and die,
It is enough that He is nigh.
Alleluia, alleluia!

16. He feeds me, comforts, and defends,
And when I die His angel sends.
Alleluia, alleluia!
To bear me whither He is gone,
For of His own He loseth none.
Alleluia, alleluia!

17. He rose again and death withstood,
To grant me angel-brotherhood,
Alleluia, alleluia!
He did the Father's wrath allay,
All enmity is done away.
Alleluia, alleluia!

18. No more to fear or grief I bow,
God and the angels love me now;
Alleluia, alleluia!
The joys prepared for me today
Drive fear and mourning far away;
Alleluia, alleluia!

19. Strong Champion! for this comfort see
The whole world brings her thanks to Thee.
Alleluia, alleluia!
And once we too shall raise above
More sweet and loud the song we love!
Alleluia, alleluia!

—J. Heermann, 1630; tr. sts. 1, 8–9, 15, A. T. Russell, 1851, alt.; sts. 12, 16, 18–19, C. Winkworth, 1863, alt.; sts. rest, M. Carver.

106

Tune: Erschienen ist der herrlich Tag. 21. [*TLH* 108; *LW* 147]

1. All thanks and praise to God this day!
The time of joy has come our way,
When Jesus Christ our Savior hath
Arisen from the realm of death.
Alleluia!

2. Then cease, my soul, to mourn, and leave
Hell, death, and Satan now to grieve;
Thy Lord hath wrought their reckoning.
So worship God, rejoice, and sing:
Alleluia!

3. Not yet in full those spoils we see
That He, by marks of victory,
Hath brought thee for thy utter good,
Won in the battle waged with blood.
Alleluia!

4. I am content, my Lord doth live,
And in His heav'nly joys I thrive!
I know He loves me heartily,
When I am grieved He comforts me.
Alleluia!

5. There is no trial, cross, or need
That can His mighty pow'r exceed,
No heavy stone He cannot roll
To bare the prison of my soul.
Alleluia!

6. Yea, though I die and take my tomb,
'Twill be my restful Sabbath-room.
He shall awake me on that Day
And gather me to heav'n away.
Alleluia!

7. Then shall I see my Easter Day,
Free from all trouble and dismay,
And there behold His glorious state
With joys eternal, full, and great.
Alleluia!

8. This wondrous solace pleases me
As oft, Lord Christ, I think on Thee.
When I must die, this I believe,
Thy hands my spirit shall receive.
Alleluia!

—J. Crüger or J. Niedling, ca. 1658, asc.; tr., M. Carver.

107

Tune: Heut triumphieret Gottes Sohn. 44. [*LW* 136]

1. Today in triumph Christ arose
And conquered all His hellish foes.
Alleluia, alleluia!
Great splendor marks His victory.
Sing praise to God eternally!
Alleluia, alleluia!

2. Now hell has lost its pow'r and might;
Our Lord puts all its hosts to flight.
Alleluia, alleluia!
He brings the end of all our woe;
He routs our foes and lays them low.
Alleluia, alleluia!

3. O Christ, our Savior, Helper, Friend,
Be with us till our journey's end.
Alleluia, alleluia!
In mercy guide us by Thy grace
Till we behold Thy glorious face.
Alleluia, alleluia!

4. Though Satan rage, his pow'r is gone;
His thund'ring roar can harm us none.
Alleluia, alleluia!
Our strong Defender hurls him down
But wins for us a heav'nly crown.
Alleluia, alleluia!

5. Here all is grief and misery.
He who would trust and follow Thee—
Alleluia, alleluia!–
Must bear the world's disdain and scorn,
And often die a death forlorn.
Alleluia, alleluia!

6. Wherefore we all give thanks to Thee,
And long Thy kingdom soon to see.
Alleluia, alleluia!
God save us, for the end draws nigh!
Now let us sing our glad reply.
Alleluia, alleluia!

7. To God the Lord, on highest throne,
To Christ, the Father's own dear Son,
Alleluia, alleluia!
To God the Holy Spirit be
All praise and thanks eternally.
Alleluia, alleluia!

—K. Stolshagen, 1591; tr. sts. 3, 5, M. Carver, sts. rest, O. Rupprecht, 1982, alt.

108

Tune: Es ist genug, so nimm, Herr. 52. [*TLH* 196; *LW* 145; *LSB* 468]

1. I am content! My Jesus liveth still,
In whom my heart is pleased.
He hath fulfilled the Law of God for me,
God's wrath He hath appeased.
Since He in death could perish never,
I also shall not die forever.
I am content! I am content!

2. I am content! My Jesus is my Head;
His member I will be.
He bowed His head when on the cross He died
With cries of agony.
Now death is brought into subjection
For me, too, by His resurrection.
I am content! I am content!

3. I am content! My Jesus is my Lord,
My Prince of Life and Peace;
His heart is yearning for my future bliss
And for my soul's release.
The home where He, my Master, liveth
He also to His servant giveth.
I am content! I am content!

4. I am content! My Jesus is my Light,
My radiant Sun of Grace.
His cheering rays beam blessings forth for all,
Sweet comfort, hope, and peace.
This Easter sun doth bring salvation
And everlasting exultation.
I am content! I am content!

5. I am content! Lord, draw me unto Thee
And wake me from the dead
That I may rise forevermore to be
With Thee, my living Head.
The fetters of my body sever,
Then shall my soul rejoice forever.
I am content! I am content!

—J. Möller, 1704; tr., A. Crull, †1923, alt.

109

Tune: Gott des Himmels und der Erden. 37. [*TLH* 549]

1. Jesus, Thou who open breakest
Hades' gates and bars of steel,
Who, entombed, so lightly takest
Pond'rous stone and Roman seal:
Let my heart be so disposed,
That it ne'er to Thee be closed.

2. Cast aside its stony curtain—
Stone no mortal hand can heave—
Of Thy wonders make me certain,
When the mind would scarce believe;
Yea, Thy teachings right and good
Let me trust as trust I should.

3. Though in doubting Thomas wavered,
Though Cleòpas mourned with pain,
Let Thou all my fears be severed,
Rend all unbelief in twain;
In mine every grief be Thou
Still my Lord and God as now.

4. Lost are death's and devil's scepter,
Now Thy triumph share with me;
E'en as Thou didst foil Thy captor,
Take me from this world to Thee,
That, released from Satan's might,
I may be with God in light.

5. I myself have died within me,
Now, my Savior, waken me,
May the Spirit Thou didst win me
Daily guide my course in Thee,
That on pathways far from sin,
Life anew I may begin.

6. Nearer now the time is growing
When in flesh we shall arise
And, to Thee in bodies going
From our graves, ascend the skies.
Then vouchsafe me, Lord, I pray,
Cause for endless joy that day!

7. Lift Thy poor and lowly members,
Ailing spirits, meek and mild,
From earth's bosom, bright as embers,
And so fashion me, Thy child,
On Thy Father's kingly height
After Thine own body bright.

8. Then to me Thy wounds revealing,
Hands and feet, as Thomas knew,
Let me kiss them, humbly kneeling,
As on earth no man can do;
Sinless then, grant me to sip
Thine immortal fellowship.

—C. Neumann, 1715; tr., M. Carver.

110

Tune: Jesus Christus, unser Heiland, der den Tod. 16. [p. 408]

1. Jesus Christ, our Savior and King,
Conquered death, broke its sting,
Is now arisen
And sin hath bound in prison.
Kyrieleison!

2. He, born free of sin and its stain,
Took God's wrath, bore our pain,
Became our Savior,
And brings to us God's favor.
Kyrieleison!

3. Life and mercy, trespass and death,
All in His hands He hath;
He can deliver
All who trust Him forever.
Kyrieleison!

—M. Luther, 1524; tr., L. W. Bacon, †1881, alt., but sts. 1a, 2a, F. S. Janzow, 1978, alt.

111

Tune: Jesus, meine Zuversicht. 33. [*TLH* 206; *LW* 266; *LSB* 741]

1. Jesus Christ, my sure Defense
And my Savior, ever liveth;
Knowing this, my confidence
Rests upon the hope it giveth
Though the night of death be fraught
Still with many‿an anxious thought.

2. Jesus, my Redeemer, lives;
I, too, unto life shall waken.
Endless joy my Savior gives;
Shall my courage, then, be shaken?
Shall I fear, or could the Head
Rise and leave His members dead?

3. Nay, too closely I am bound
Unto Him by hope forever;
Faith's strong hand the Rock hath found,
Grasped it, and will leave it never;
Even death now cannot part
From its Lord the trusting heart.

4. I am flesh and must return
Unto dust, whence I am taken;
But by faith I now discern
That from death I shall awaken
With my Savior to abide
In His glory, at His side.

5. Glorified, I shall anew
With this flesh then be enshrouded;
In this body I shall view
God, my Lord, with eyes unclouded;
In this flesh I then shall see
Jesus Christ eternally.

6. Then these eyes my Lord shall know,
My Redeemer and my Brother;
In His love my soul shall glow—
I myself, and not another!
Then the weakness I feel here
Shall forever disappear.

7. They who sorrow here and moan
There in gladness shall be reigning;
Earthly here the seed is sown,
There immortal life attaining,
Here our sinful bodies die,
Glorified to dwell on high.

8. Then take comfort and rejoice,
For His members Christ will cherish.
Fear not, they will hear His voice;
Dying, they shall never perish;
For the very grave is stirred
When the trumpet's blast is heard.

9. Laugh to scorn the gloomy grave
And at death no longer tremble;
He, the Lord, who came to save
Will at last His own assemble.
They will go their Lord to meet,
Treading death beneath their feet.

10. Oh, then draw away your hearts
Now from pleasures base and hollow.
There to share what He imparts,
Here His footsteps ye must follow.
Fix your hearts beyond the skies,
Whither ye yourselves would rise.

—Anon, Berlin, 1653; tr., C. Winkworth, 1863.

112

Tune: Es ist das Heil uns kommen her. 49. [*TLH* 377; *LW* 355; *LSB* 555]

1. O Death, where is thy cruèl sting?
O grave, where is thy powèr?
What harm to us can Satan bring
Though threat'ning to devoùr?
Thanks be to God, of glorious might,
Who conquered for us in this fight
Through Jesus Christ our Captain.

2. How fiercely the arch-serpent raged,
When Christ his might contested!
Yet Christ, though all hell's hosts engaged,
Their prowess from them wrested.
And though the serpent pricked His heel,
Yet was he made its weight to feel;
His head is bruised forever.

3. And now Christ comes to life again,
And breaks death's chain asunder;
He binds the foe, takes hell amain,
And wrests from him his plunder.
No pow'r can stay the Victor's march,
He enters the triumphal arch:—
All must succumb before Him.

4. A death to death, to hell a pest,
Christ is become by dying;
Still Satan rages without rest
With murd'rous will and lying.
And since he cannot come with might,
He turns accuser, day and night;
But judged, he stands rejected.

5. The Lord's right hand, His holy arm,
The victory retaineth;
No might of foes can Him disarm,
The glory His remaineth.
Now sin and Satan, death and hell,
Are ousted from their citadel;
Their wrath is fierce, yet pow'rless.

6. The Christ of God, God's Son, was dead;
But lo, He ever liveth!
As He arose, our living Head,
So life to us He giveth.
Now, who believes on Jesus' Word
From death and grave shall be restored,
And live, e'en though he dieth.

7. He who with Christ arises here
By faith and daily sorrow,
The second death need never fear:
Heav'n's his eternal morrow.
Death's swallowed up in victory,
And life and immortality
Are brought to light by Jesus.

8. Forgiveness, peace, joy, righteousness,
On earth and there in heaven—
These are the Easter-spoils that bless
The hearts to Jesus given.
So we, His heirs, wait patiently
Until our bodies fashioned be
Like His own glorious body.

9. The ancient dragon, with his brood,
Is hurled to degradation;
They lay a mock, with scorn subdued,
When Christ rose with salvation.
The gain of our triumphant Head
Is ours, His members; hence we dread
No more the serpent's powèr.

10. O Death, where is thy cruèl sting?
O grave, where is thy powèr?
What harm to us can Satan bring,
Though threat'ning to devoùr?
Thanks be to God, of glorious might,
Who conquered for us in this fight
Through Jesus Christ our Captain.

—G. Weissel, 1644, alt., Hannover, 1657; tr., *Ohio*, 1880.

113

Tune: Nun freut euch, lieben Christen. 49. [*TLH* 387; *LW* 353; *LSB* 556]

1. Be joyful all, both far and near,
Who lost were and dejected:
Today the Lord of glory here,
Whom God Himself elected
As our Redeemer, who His blood
Upon the cross shed for our good,
Hath from the grave arisen.

2. How well succeeded hath thy might,
Thou foe of life unruly,
To kill the Lord of life and light;
Through Him thy arrow truly
Did pass in vain, O worthless foe!
Thou tho't'st when thou hadst laid Him low,
He'd lie in dust forever.

3. No, no! On high His head is borne,
His mighty pow'r asunder
Thy gates hath burst, thy bands hath torn,
Thyself hath trodden under,
That who alone in Him confide,
Thy pow'r and claims may now deride
And say, "Thy sting, where is it?"

4. Thy pow'r is gone, 'tis broken quite,
And now no man offendeth
Who to this Prince with constant sight
His heart and soul commendeth;
Who speaks with joy, "I live, and ye
Shall also live for aye with Me;
For I have won this for you."

5. "The reign and pow'r of death are o'er,
He never need affright you;
I am his Lord and Conqueror,
And this may well delight you;
If ye in Me, your Head, believe,
To you this blessing I will give,
To dwell with Me as members."

6. "Of hell I've wrought the overthrow,
And its destruction speeded.
None need in death fear endless woe,
Who Me and My word heeded;
For now the devil's guile and might
Are crushed, and his head trampled quite,
And he can never harm him."

7. Now praised be God, who vict'ry hath
To us through Jesus given,
Who peace for war and life for death
Hath won for us in heaven,
Who hath o'ercome sin, death, and woe,
The wicked world, and evil foe,
And all our troubles vanquished.

—P. Gerhardt, 1656; tr., J. Kelly, 1867, alt.

114

Tune: O Herre Gott, dein göttlich Wort. 83. [*TLH* 266; *LW* 341]

1. Our voice we raise / With joy and praise
To sing God's vict'ry-story.
This day our own / Good Shepherd won—
'Tis Christ, the King of Glory!
Now every foe / Has been laid low,
And none is left remaining.
Our faithful Lord / Repelled Death's sword,
Our heav'nly triumph gaining.

2. For Christendom / Release has come,
The foe in chains is smitten;
The serpent's crown / Has been cast down,
His head is crushed; he's beaten!
Tho' he did pierce / With fang so fierce
The heel of Christ our Savior,
Yet ris'n is He / With victory;
His Passion wins God's favor.

3. The Law's great might / Bro't us the plight
Of sin and guilt increasing:
Our sin's distress / And death did press
Our souls in bonds unceasing.
There was no mirth / In all the earth,
With wrath our God was rumbling;
The Lord be praised, / Who hath us raised
To glory by His humbling.

4. The pit of hell / And death so fell
Were threat'ning us to swallow,
But in the strife / The pow'r of Life
Left all their boasting hollow:
Despite his rage / The dragon's cage
Was burst—a freedom glorious!
The war is done, / And we have won,
Through Jesus Christ victorious.

5. Good Christian men, / Rejoice again!
The spoils are our possession,
True righteousness / Our treasure is;
We're freed from fear's oppression.
Our prize is hence / True innocence,
God's heirs we are forever.
Therefore we raise / Our voice of praise:
Thanks be to Christ our Savior!

—G. Reimann, †1615; tr., M. Carver.

115

Tune: Herr Jesu Christ, meins Lebens Licht. 11.
[*TLH* 288; *LW* 262; *LSB* 704; *or TLH* 197*; *LW* 344*; *LSB* 585*]

1. Where wilt Thou go since night draws near,
O Jesus Christ, Thou Pilgrim dear?
Lord, make me happy, be my Guest,
And in my heart, oh, deign to rest.

2. Grant my request, O dearest Friend,
For truly I the best intend;
Thou knowest that Thou ever art
A welcome Guest unto my heart.

3. The day is now far spent and gone,
The shades of night come quickly on;
Abide with me, Thou heav'nly Light,
And do not leave me in this night.

4. Enlighten me that from the way
That leads to heav'n I may not stray,
That I may never be misled,
Though night of sin is round me spread.

5. And when I on my death-bed lie,
Help me that I in peace may die.
Abide! I will not let Thee go.
Thou wilt not leave me, Lord, I know.

—Anon., Plön, 1674; tr., A. Crull, †1923, alt.

Ascension of Christ

116

Tune: Wie schön leuchtet der Morgenstern. 86. [*TLH* 343; *LW* 73; *LSB* 395]

1. O wondrous Conqueror and great,
Scorned by the world Thou didst create,
Thy work is all completed!
Thy toilsome course is at an end;
Thou to the Father dost ascend,
In royal glory seated.
Lowly, / Holy,
Now victorious, / High and glorious:
Earth and heaven
To Thy rule, O Christ, are given.

2. To Thee bow down the Cherubim,
And myriad mighty Seraphim
Own Thee the Victor ever;
For Thou the blessing hast restored,
And now in majesty, our Lord,
Art raised to joy and favor.
Sing out, / Ring out,
The ascending / Lord attending
With elation,
Trumpet's sound and adoration.

3. Thou, Lord, art now our Head, and we
Thy members are, and draw from Thee
Our life and full salvation.
For comfort, peace, joy, light, and pow'r,
For balm to heal in sorrow's hour,
We yield Thee adoration.
Kneeling, / Feeling
Thou art nearest, / Lord, and dearest:
So believing
Grace is ours beyond conceiving.

4. Lord Jesus, keep our eyes on Thee;
Help us Thy servants true to be,
Fulfilling Thy good pleasure,
Set Thou our minds on things above,
Let this vain world ne'er win our love,
Be Thou our only treasure.
Wholly, / Lowly,
We would own Thee, / And enthrone Thee:
Wisdom learning,
All Thy perfect ways discerning.

5. Thou, Jesus, art our Shield and Guide,
O let Thy words in us abide,
Directing all our going.
Teach us to love Thy blessed will,
To suffer meekly and be still,
Nor fear grief's tide o'erflowing.
Weeping, / Keeping
Low before Thee, / We adore Thee.
Midst our sorrow,
Lord, we hail the coming morrow.

6. Lord Jesus, hasten Thy return;
Our longing hearts expectant yearn
To prove the joys of heaven.
Thy precious blood has set us free,
We owe our present all to Thee,
For us Thy life was given.
Singing, / Bringing
Praise abounding, / Now we're sounding
Never-ending
Triumph, Lord, in Thy ascending.

—E. C. Homburg, 1658; tr., H. K. Burlingham, 1865, alt., but st. 2, M. Carver.

117

Tune: Nun freut euch, lieben Christen. 49. [*TLH* 124; *LW* 353; *LSB* 556]

1. On Christ's ascension I now build
The hope of mine ascension;
This hope alone has ever stilled
All doubt and apprehension;
For where the Head is, there full well
I know his members are to dwell
When Christ shall come and call them.

2. Since He returned to claim His throne,
Great gifts for men obtaining,
My heart shall rest in Him alone,
No other rest remaining;
For where my Treasure went before,
There all my thoughts shall ever soar
To still their deepest yearning.

3. Oh, grant, dear Lord, this grace to me,
Recalling Thine ascension,
That I may ever walk with Thee,
Adorning Thy redemption;
And then, when all my days shall cease,
Let me depart in joy and peace
In answer to my pleading.

—J. Wegelin, 1636, alt., Hannover, 1660; tr., W. M. Czamanske, 1938.

118

Tune: Auf diesen Tag bedenken wir. 49.
[p. 396; *or TLH* 33;* *LW* 181*; *LSB* 947*]

1. Today our Lord went up on high,
And so our thanks we render:
To Him with strong desire we cry
To be our great defender;
For we poor sinners here beneath
Are dwelling still mid woe and death.
All hope in Him we tender:
Alleluia, alleluia!

2. Praise God that now the way is made!
In that great door to heaven,
Through Him on whom our help was laid,
An opening hath been riven;
Who knoweth this is glad at heart,
And swift prepares Him to depart
Where Christ before hath driven:
Alleluia, alleluia!

3. Who follows not, nor doth His will,
Trusts not the Lord and Savior;
Who doth his flesh's lusts fulfill
From heav'n himself doth sever;
For if our faith is right and true,
Then our life also must congrue
With God the Father's pleasure.
Alleluia, alleluia!

4. Our heav'nward course begins when we,
To God the Father nearing,
Conjoin us to His sons, and flee
From paths of sin and erring;
For He looks down, and they look up:
They feel His love, they live in hope,
Until their Lord's appearing.
Alleluia, alleluia!

5. Then we shall know the joyful day
When we by God are taken,
Made like His Son with bright array
Whom we confess unshaken,
For then shall gladness fill our mood
In glory, with the highest Good:
God grant us there to waken!
Alleluia, alleluia!

—J. Zwick, 1538; tr., C. Winkworth, 1858, alt.; st. 3, A. Crull, 1867, alt.

119

Tune: Christ fuhr gen Himmel. 100. [*TLH* 187; *LW* 124; *LSB* 459 (mel.)]

1. Christ rose to heaven
And unto us hath given
The Comforter, the Holy Ghost,
To comfort His poor Christian host.
Kyrieleis!

2. Alleluia, alleluia, alleluia!
We now rejoice with gladness;
Christ will end all sadness.
Kyrieleis!

—C. Söll / 15th c.; tr. st. 1, M. Carver; st. 2, W. G. Polack, 1939.

120

Tune: Ermuntre dich, mein schwacher. 67. [*LSB* 378]

1. O Prince of life, Christ Jesus, Lord,
Ascended King of heaven:
Thou with the Father art adored
By all Thy flock forgiven.
How best can I the vict'ry sing,
Which to us Thy great might doth bring?
What strains can I be raising,
Thy love and pow'r appraising?

2. Both hell and sin Thou hast o'er-hurled,
With warfare true and fearless,
Besetting Satan, death, and world,
Through sacrifice all-peerless,
Thy vict'ry echoes far and wide.
How can I, as I here abide,
Exalt Thy lordship duly,
O Lord, or praise Thee truly?

3. Thou at the Father's own right hand
Art now in power sitting,
All things are giv'n to Thy command
When Thou, the foe outwitting,
With scarce a wound, didst bring Him down
To take the triumph and the crown,
Which grace Thy march victorious
As treasures bright and glorious.

4. All things are cast beneath Thy feet,
Alone Thou hast no master;
Thy servants are the angels' fleet
In heav'n's immortal pasture:
Thy train of prince and potentate
With willing heart themselves prostrate.
Air, earth and fire and water
In fealty join all matter.

5. Thou, Ruler strong, dost mount the sky
Mid shouts of acclamation,
And thronging chariots round Thee fly
Beyond enumeration;
Thou risest, wrapped in hymnic tone
And trumpets blast from cloud to throne:
Now God, for all Thy graces
I, too, will hymn Thy praises.

6. Thou hast ascended heaven's peak
To lead Thy host from prison;
O'er dire laments that drowned our cheek
And aches we shall have risen,
And so is sung our anthem sweet
O mighty God, from street to street—
By us who here are given
Such plenteous gifts from heaven.

7. Thou art our common Head and Crown,
And we Thy limbs dependent;
Thou art the Shield and shelt'ring Gown
Of those on Thee attendant,
Thy light and comfort give us strength;
Should fear assail our heart at length,
Thou canst in fullest measure
Give life and peace and pleasure.

8. Thou by the Spirit mark'st our head,
And mak'st true shepherds flourish
As teachers who with heav'nly bread
Our souls sustain and nourish.
Thou dost reveal, O great High Priest,
Salvation in Thy mighty fist
From whence hell cannot take us,
Its slaves again to make us.

9. Thou hast by climbing heaven's stair
Our final road made ready,
And to the Father thus laid bare
The path secure and steady,
And therefore, O Lord Christ, since Thou,
In realms of bliss art seated now,
Thy saints who would pursue Thee
Shall also come unto Thee.

10. Since then our Head in heaven stands,
As by th' Apostles written,
Then we, made new like angel bands,
Shall not outside be smitten.
Nor wilt Thou, God, desert at all
Thy children, howsoever small,
Who here in faith adore Thee
And hope to see Thy glory.

11. Lord Jesus, draw us ceaselessly,
That we in mind and spirit
May ever dwell above with Thee
Amid Thy grace and merit.
Our life and conversation ground
Where peace and truth are ever found,
Salvation ever seeing
Within Thy heav'nly being.

12. Help us those treasures not to seek
Which in this life are buried,
But there where all God's children meek
Shall home by Thee be carried
Oh, let us strive with heart and mind
For that which is to come, and find
In Christ our true salvation,
Thy heav'nly habitation.

13. Draw us to Thee, that haste we may,
And ply faith's mighty pinion!
Help us to turn from earth away
To Zion's bright dominion.
My God, when thither may I soar,
Where gladness dwells forevermore?
When may I stand before Thee,
When in the flesh adore Thee?

14. When shall I come to Paradise?
O Jesus, there to hear Thee?
The joy of angels when apprise?
When rise to worship near Thee?
My Savior, come and draw me out,
For gladly would I noise and shout
And cease that worship never:
Alleluia forever.

—J. Rist, 1641; tr. sts. 1, 13, Novello & Co., 1888, alt.; sts. rest, M. Carver.

121

Tune: Zeuch ein zu deinen Toren. 58. [*TLH* 228; *or TLH* 69*; *LW* 25*; *LSB* 354*]

1. Lo, God to heav'n ascendeth!
Throughout its regions vast
With shouts triumphant blendeth
The trumpet's thrilling blast:
Sing praise to Christ the Lord;
Sing praise with exultation,
King of each heathen nation,
The God of hosts adored!

2. With joy is heav'n resounding
Christ's glad return to see;
Behold the saints surrounding
The Lord who set them free.
Bright myriads, thronging, come;
The cherub band rejoices,
And loud seraphic voices
All welcome Jesus home.

3. From cross to throne ascending,
We follow Christ on high
And know the pathway wending
To mansions in the sky.
Our Lord is gone before;
Yet here He will not leave us,
But soon in heav'n receive us
And open wide the door.

4. Our place He is preparing;
To heav'n we, too, shall rise,
With Him His glory sharing,
Be where our Treasure lies.
Bestir thyself, my soul!
Where Jesus Christ has entered,
There let thy hope be centered;
Press onward toward the goal.

5. Let all our thoughts be winging
To where Thou didst ascend,
And let our hearts be singing:
"We seek Thee, Christ, our Friend,
Thee, God's exalted Son,
Our Life, and Way to heaven,
To whom all pow'r is given,
Our Joy and Hope and Crown."

6. Farewell with all thy treasures,
O world, to falsehood giv'n!
Thy dross gives no true pleasures;
We seek the joys of heav'n.
The Savior is our Prize;
He comforts us in sadness
And fills our hearts with gladness;
To Him we lift our eyes.

7. When, on our vision dawning,
Will break the wished-for hour
Of that all-glorious morning
When Christ shall come with pow'r?
Oh, come, thou welcome day,
When we, our Savior meeting,
His second advent greeting,
Shall hail the heav'n-sent ray.

—G. W. Sacer, 1661; tr., F. E. Cox, 1841, alt.

122

Tune: Erschienen ist der herrlich Tag. 21. [*TLH* 108; *LW* 147]

1. O children of your God, rejoice:
In praise lift to the Lord your voice:
With shouts of joy He to the skies
Ascends: to Him our praise shall rise.
Alleluia!

2. Lo, all th' angelic company
Christ with glad anthems glorify!
Their blessèd armies all proclaim,
With shouts of joy, His sacred Name.
Alleluia!

3. Because our Savior, God's true Son,
Christ Jesus, hath become a man,
The angels all are glad and sing
And unto us such honor bring.
Alleluia!

4. The Lord a home prepares on high,—
Our mansion in eternity!
Sing praise to Him, sing praise, rejoice,
Sing praise to Him and raise your voice.
Alleluia!

5. We are His heritage in heav'n:
The angels' joys to us are giv'n.
For this that host, awaiting long,
Gives thanks to God and joins our song.
Alleluia!

6. No more distress our spirit hath:
The devil, sin, and endless death
Are put to shame and overthrown
By God's and Mary's mighty Son.
Alleluia!

7. He sent the Holy Spirit here,
Our hearts to feed and fill with cheer,
Us to console by God's good Word,
Against the devil's wrath secured.
Alleluia!

8. Thus doth He build the Church, His fold,
And to eternal bliss uphold:
God's true confession is alone
To trust in Jesus Christ His Son.
Alleluia!

9. The Holy Spirit strengthens faith,
Builds up our patient hope o'er death,
Enlightens and emboldens hearts,
True consolation He imparts.
Alleluia!

10. All that God's holy majesty
Won for us on the sacred tree
The Holy Spirit doth imbue,
Therefore He is our Teacher true.
Alleluia!

11. The Father sent His Son, the Christ;
The Son cannot else be confessed,
Unless the Holy Spirit first
Doth cleanse our hearts, by sin accursed.
Alleluia!

12. These many godly gifts so fair
Are but the Spirit's own to share,
Who turns the devil's works to naught:
All this the Lord's ascension brought.
Alleluia!

13. So thank we now our precious Lord
With praises from our hearts outpoured;
With angel-choirs then sing ye here,
That those in heaven too may hear.
Alleluia!

14. O God the Father! Praise to Thee
Throughout the world forever be:
With all our pow'rs to Thee we raise
Our song of glory, thanks, and praise.
Alleluia!

15. Lord Jesus Christ! the Son most High!
Full of all might and majesty,
Thy Church o'er all the earth thanks Thee
Now and to all eternity!
Alleluia!

16. O Holy Ghost, true God, be nigh
With heav'nly comfort from on high;
Thee may we praise, and Thee adore,
When earth and time shall be no more.
Alleluia!

—E. Alber, 1549, cento; tr. sts. 1–2, 4a, 5a, 14–16, A. T. Russell, 1851, alt.; sts. rest, M. Carver.

123

Tune: Erschienen ist der herrlich Tag. 21. [*TLH* 108; *LW* 147]

1. We thank Thee, Jesus, dearest Friend,
That Thou didst into heav'n ascend.
O blessed Savior, bid us live
And strength to soul and body give.
Alleluia!

2. Now His disciples all rejoice
And sing His praise with cheerful voice:
Come, let us grateful off'rings bring;
Our Brother is our God and King.
Alleluia!

3. Ascended to His throne on high,
Hid from our sight, yet always nigh;
He rules and reigns at God's right hand
And has all pow'r at His command.
Alleluia!

4. Above the heav'ns in glory raised,
By angel hosts forever praised,
All creatures His dominion own,
He holds an everlasting throne.
Alleluia!

5. He rules and reigns at God's right hand
And has all pow'r at His command;
All things are subject to His rod—
The Son of Man and Son of God.
Alleluia!

6. The world and sin and Satan fell
He overthrew, with death and hell;
Dispute who will His mighty reign,
He still the Victor must remain.
Alleluia!

7. The man who trusts in Him is blest
And finds in Him eternal rest;
This world's allurements we despise
And fix on Christ alone our eyes.
Alleluia!

8. We therefore heartily rejoice
And sing His praise with cheerful voice;
He captive led captivity,
From bitter death He set us free.
Alleluia!

9. With deepest joy our voice we raise
And sing our grateful song of praise;
Our Brother, our own flesh and bone,
Is God and King, our Joy alone.
Alleluia!

10. Through Him we heirs of heav'n are made;
O Brother, Christ, extend Thine aid
That we may firmly trust in Thee
And through Thee live eternally.
Alleluia!

11. Amen, amen, O Lord, we cry;
Do Thou, who art exalted high,
In Thy pure faith preserve our hearts
And shield us from all Satan's darts.
Alleluia!

12. Come, blessed Lord, to Judgment come
And take us to our glorious home
That all our woes on earth may cease
And we may dwell in heav'nly peace.
Alleluia!

13. A glad Amen shall close our song;
Our souls for rest in glory long,
Where we with angel hosts again
Shall sing in nobler strains Amen.
Alleluia!

—N. Selnecker, 1587 / Anon., 1607; tr., M. Loy, 1880, alt.

124

Tune: Ach Gott und Herr (Ion.). 25. [*TLH* 215; *LW* 153; *LSB* 701]

1. Draw us to Thee, / For then shall we
Walk in Thy steps forever
And hasten on / Where Thou art gone
To be with Thee, dear Savior.

2. Draw us to Thee, / Lord, lovingly;
Let us depart with gladness
That we may be / Forever free
From sorrow, grief, and sadness.

3. Draw us to Thee; / Oh, grant that we
May walk the road to heaven!
Direct our way / Lest we should stray
And from Thy paths be driven.

4. Draw us to Thee / That also we
Thy heav'nly bliss inherit
And ever dwell / Where sin and hell
No more can vex our spirit.

5. Draw us to Thee / Unceasingly,
Into Thy kingdom take us;
Let us fore'er / Thy glory share,
Thy saints and joint heirs make us.

—F. Funcke, 1686; tr., A. Crull, †1923, alt.

125

Tune: Nun freut euch, lieben Christen. 49. [*TLH* 124; *LW* 353; *LSB* 556]

1. From everlasting God so loved
The world with deep affection,
That, though, by Satan's guile removed,
It bore His due rejection,
Yet never did His love subside,
But from His heart He hath supplied
The greatest Good of heaven.

2. He gave His sole-begotten Son,
His dearest Heir He offered;
Who, being sent from heaven's throne,
Death for the world hath suffered,
That all mankind both far and wide
Who faithfully in Him confide
Should never have to perish.

3. But when our time on earth is o'er,
We'll live with Him forever,
And Him in heav'nly joy adore
With every true believer.
For God hath sent His Son to men
Not as their Judge, all to condemn,
But to become their Savior.

4. Those who repent and to Him turn,
E'er trusting in His merit,
Shall find a wealth they could not earn,
And heaven's realm inherit.
They shall not know the Father's wrath,
Nor ever taste the second death,
But life eternal enter.

5. Those who in Him do not believe
That day shall go before Him,
Their awful sentence to receive,
And vainly shall implore Him.
But they must pay for all they wrought,
Esteeming God and Scripture not.
To hell this will condemn them.

6. O Jesus Christ, true Son of God,
We praise Thy love sincerely,
For Thou hast suffered pain and rod
And paid for us most dearly,
And by Thy death hast set us free
From death and Satan's tyranny
And sin's oppressive burden.

7. Grant us strong faith to trust in Thee,
In weakness strength conferring;
Let no believer fall away,
Turn all the lost and erring.
Grant us to stand before Thy face
On judgment day, and by Thy grace
Forevermore behold Thee.

—J. Niedling, †1668; tr., M. Carver.

126

Tune: Der Heilge Geist hernieder kam. 21. [p. 399; *or TLH* 108*; *LW* 147*]

1. The Holy Ghost made His descent,
Into th' Apostles hearts He went,
He filled them with His holy grace
And taught them tongues of many‿a race.
Alleluia!

2. He sent them forth with heav'nly flame,
God's mighty wonders to proclaim,
To teach God's love in Christ from heav'n,
That sin and guilt are now forgiv'n.
Alleluia!

3. Praise be to God upon His throne,
And praise to Christ, His only Son,
And to the Spirit whom He gave;
Us may He ever guide and save.
Alleluia!

—Anon., after *Spiritus sancti gratia,* ab.; tr., M. Carver.

127

Tune: Erschienen ist der herrlich Tag. 21. [*TLH* 108; *LW* 147; *or as* #126 *above*]

1. The Holy Ghost's abundant grace
Found in th' Apostles' hearts a place;
The fullest blessing there was shown,
That they might speak in tongues unknown.
Alleluia!

2. Christ sent them once to every land
With wondrous power and command,
For where they went, the people heard
In native tongue God's Holy Word.
Alleluia!

3. To them He said: "This day receive
The Spirit, that men may believe,
For He shall teach you when in need
All things that follow and precede."
Alleluia!

4. "When forth ye go, my Word to bring
And stand before both prince and king,
Fear not, nor strive to comprehend
How ye My honor shall defend."
Alleluia!

5. "The Holy Ghost will guide your speech,
All skill and wisdom He will teach,
That never craft nor might at all
From preaching Me shall make you fall."
Alleluia!

6. To God the Comforter be praise,
Who guides the Church from error's ways
To look in faith to Christ above,
And kindles hearts with flames of love.
Alleluia!

7. Therefore, rejoicing loud, we sing,
To bless the Lord and praise to bring
To God the Holy Trinity,
To whom be thanks eternally.
Alleluia!

—J. Leon, †1597, after *Spiritus sancti gratia;* tr., M. Carver.

128

Tune: Helft mir Gotts Güte preisen. 58. [*TLH* 112]

1. Rejoice, all Christians, proudly!
God gives us His own Son;
Sing praises to Him loudly,
For from His heav'nly throne
He sends His Holy Ghost,
Who through the Word instructs us,
To greater faith conducts us,
To Jesus points His host.

2. The holy Word of heaven
From God, our Refuge high,
Has now to us been given
Who did in folly lie:
Of grace how great a store!
For now our heart can claim Him
And heav'nly Father name Him,
Our Guardian evermore.

3. O God of greatest kindness
Grant us to hold Thee dear,
Nor grieve Thee by our blindness;
Our sinful record clear,
Lead us on pathways true,
Help us to hear Thy preaching
And follow in Thy teaching,
Which is our office due.

4. From heaven hither send us
Thy Spirit, our dear Guest,
To strengthen and attend us,
When by our crosses pressed,
To comfort in death's woe,
Our souls to carry thither
In heaven's gates together,
Thy glorious light to know.

—G. Werner, 1639; tr., M. Carver.

129

Tune: Werde munter, mein Gemüte. 66. [*TLH* 207; *LW* 263; *LSB* 548]

1. Send, O God, a gentle shower,
For my heart is dry as sand;
Father, bathe Thy drooping flower,
Water Thou Thy thirsty land;
Let Thy Holy Spirit's boon
O'er me from Thy heav'nly throne
Like abundant streams be flowing,
Blessings on my heart bestowing.

2. By a human father, even
Though he is by sin defiled,
Only good gifts will be given
Unto a belovèd child;
How much more dost Thou the same,
For "Good Father" is Thy name!
Thou wilt send to me Thy Spirit,
Thy good gifts I shall inherit.

3. Jesus, who for my salvation
To the Father didst ascend,
Hear my earnest supplication,
Unto me Thy Spirit send;
Let the Comforter for aye
Bide with me, my strength and stay,
That in faith I may not waver,
Steadfast in the truth forever.

4. Holy Ghost, strength of the simple,
O make Thine abode with me,
Let me ever be Thy temple;
Cheerfully I welcome Thee.
Do Thou purify my heart,
Cast out all things that might part
Me from those sweet joys of heaven
Which by Thee to faith are given.

5. With Thy gifts my heart endowing,
Make it new and clean and fair;
Let in true love it be glowing.
Living in Thy grace fore'er;
Give me courage bold and good,
Sanctify my flesh and blood,
Let me, trusting in Christ's merit,
Worship God in truth and spirit.

6. Thus myself I will deliver,
Lord, to Thee; my soul shall strive
Only after heav'n forever
Until there I shall arrive
Where the Father and the Son
And Thyself in heav'n's high throne
I shall praise and all Thy treasures
In angelic, heavenly measures.

—M. Kramer, 1683; tr., A. Crull, 1923.

130

Tune: Kommt her zu mir, spricht Gottes Sohn. 41. [*TLH* 263; *LSB* 666 (mel.)]

1. O Father, send Thy Spirit down
From heaven's height, for whom Thy Son
Bade us to pray unfearing;
We ask Thee even as He taught,
Oh, let us from Thy throne go not
Without a gracious hearing!

2. No earthly mortal dwelling here
Is worthy of this gift so dear,
No work of merit owning;
That love and grace alone avail
Which Jesus Christ by His travail
Obtained, our sins atoning.

3. O Father, much it grieves Thy mind,
Us in such woeful plight to find,
As Adam's fall hath wrought us;
The evil one by this same fall
O'erpowered Adam and us all
And into slavery brought us.

4. In our salvation we confide,
Assured, Lord, that we shall abide
Through Christ Thy portion ever;
And thro' His death and precious blood
Our mansions fair and highest good
We look for, doubting never.

5. This is a work of grace indeed,
The Holy Spirit's strength we need,
Our pow'r is unavailing;
Our faith and hope, however high,
Would soon, O Lord, in ashes lie,
Were not Thy help unfailing.

6. Of faith Thy Spirit keeps the light,
Though all the world against us fight,
And storm with every weapon.
Although the prince of this world come
To take the field 'gainst Christendom,
No ill through him can happen.

7. The Spirit's is the winning side,
And where He helps, the battle's tide
Before us soon must founder.
What is the devil's mighty band?
When God's own kingdom lifts its hand,
It all will fall asunder.

8. The chains of hell He rends in twain,
Consoles and frees the heart again
From everything that grieveth;
And when misfortunes o'er us low'r
He shields us better in their hour,
Than ever heart conceiveth.

9. The bitter cross He maketh sweet,
In darkness lights our wand'ring feet,
And like His sheep He leads us,
Holds o'er His flock His shield and might,
And in the dark and gloomy night
To peaceful slumber bids us.

10. The Spirit from God's heav'nly hall
Directs in ways of safety all
Whose love for Him He knoweth;
He guides our goings every day,
Lest from that path we ever stray
That in His blessing goeth.

11. He maketh fit and furnishes
The ministers appointed His,
The Lord's house here sustaining;
Adorns their minds and mouths and hearts,
And light to them for us imparts,
What's dark to us explaining.

12. Our hearts He opens secretly
As they His Word with constancy,
Like precious seed, are sowing;
This Word He with His pow'r supplies
That it take root and spring and rise,
And so He tends its growing.

13. The fear of God He teacheth well,
Loves purity and loves to dwell
In faithful souls and holy;
The contrite, who all good revere,
Repent, and turn to Him in fear
And love, He chooseth solely.

14. He's true, and true doth e'er abide,
In death's dark hour He's at our side,
When all things else forsake us;
He soothes our sorrows when we die,
And to the halls of bliss on high
With peace and joy shall take us.

15. Oh, happy are the souls and blest,
Who while on earth permit this Guest
To make in them His dwelling;
Those who receive Him in this day
To endless bliss He will convey—
God's tabernacle filling.

16. Now Lord and Father of all good,
Hear our request, and like a flood
Pour in our hearts this Blessing;
Thy Spirit give, that here He may
Rule us, and there in endless day
Refresh us without ceasing.

—P. Gerhardt, 1653; tr., J. Kelly, 1867, alt.

131

Tune: Herr, auf dein Wort solls sein gewagt. 75. [=*TLH* 262; *LW* 298; *LSB* 656]

1. Lord, I will venture on Thy Word;
No blame will then offend me,
For there Thy promise is conferred,
The Holy Ghost to send me:
So I come to Thee;
Keep, O Christ, to me
Thy pledge, I request,
Send down Thy precious Guest,
The prize of all who love Thee.

2. Lo, here am I, and seek but this:
Thee and Thy Word immortal,
I know naught else so full of bliss:
So open my heart's portal
And Thy Breath confer,
Mighty Comforter,
Fire and Fountain both,
Dew, Breeze, and Binding Oath,
Anointing, God's own Finger.

3. Come Comforter, my Help and Stay,
Come Fire, ignite compassion,
Come Dew, my thirsty soul allay,
Come Seal, and bind salvation;
Come Breath, be revealed,
Come Fount, waters yield,
Come Oath, ills dispel,
Come, me with gladness fill!
God's Finger, come descending!

4. Come, Holy Ghost and very God!
Come, heav'nly love awaken;
Help me thro' life and death's dark road,
Grant faith in God unshaken,
Renew heart and will,
Penitence instill,
Be my spirit's peace,
From grief my heart release,
Teach me Thy living wisdom.

5. Grant faith, nor let me ridicule
God's favor still by sinning,
Make patience, love, and hope my rule,
My heart to meekness winning.
Let no pray'r be numb
When to God I come;
Oh, grant heart and mind
That Source to seek and find
Whence all my help arises.

6. O gracious Light, now shed Thy rays,
My gloomy heart enlighten.
Scorn not to claim this dwelling-place,
Descend, my soul to heighten.
Lord, let me be sent
Strength and nourishment;
Be my aid and pow'r,
My help, my Counselor
Grant joy and perfect quick'ning.

7. Remove from me blind, godless sense,
Help me my flesh to smother;
Take all my wicked passions hence,
And grant above all other,
That my Jesus' love,
I may daily prove,
Ready morn and eve,
This wilderness to leave,
Thy kingdom then to enter.

—G. W. Sacer, †1699; tr., M. Carver.

132

Tune: Komm, Gott Schöpfer, Heiliger Geist. 10.
[*ELHB* 249; *or LSB* 498 (slur beats 5 and 6 of last line)]

1. Come, God, Creator, Holy Ghost,
Visit the hearts of all Thy men;
Fill them with grace the way Thou know'st:
What was Thine, make so again.

2. Our Comforter Thy name we call,
Sweet Gift of God most high above!
A holy Unction to us all,
Living Fountain, Fire, and Love.

3. Oh, kindle in our minds a light!
Set in our hearts love's glowing gift;
Our weak flesh, known to Thee aright,
With Thy strength and grace uplift.

4. In gifts Thou, Lord, art sevenfold—
The Finger Thou on God's right hand!
His Word by Thee is swiftly told
With bright tongues in every land.

5. Drive far the cunning of the foe;
Thy grace bring peace and make us whole,
That we glad after Thee may go,
And shun that which hurts the soul.

6. Teach us to know the Father well,
And Jesus Christ, his Son, that so
True faith within our hearts may dwell,
Spirit of both, Thee to know!

7. Praise God the Father, and the Son,
Who from the dead arose in pow'r;
Like praise to the Consoling One,
Evermore and every hour!

—Luther, 1524, after *Veni creator Spiritus;* tr., G. Macdonald, 1897, alt.

133

Tune: Komm, Heiliger Geist, erfüll die Herzen. 105. [p. 409]

1. Come, Holy Spirit, fill the hearts of Thy faithful people,
And kindle in them The fire of Thy godly love:
Thou who through the diversity of tongues
Hast gathered together the nations of the world
In the unity of the faith. Alleluia, alleluia!

—Anon., after the antiphon *Veni Sancte Spiritus;* tr., M. Carver.

134

Tune: Komm, heiliger Geist! Herre Gott. 79. [*TLH* 224; *LW* 154; *LSB* 497]

1. Come, Holy Ghost, God and Lord!
Be all Thy graces now outpoured
On each believer's mind and heart;
Thy fervent love to them impart.
Lord, by the brightness of Thy light
Thou in the faith dost men unite
Of every land and every tongue;
This to Thy praise, O Lord, our God, be sung.
Alleluia, alleluia!

2. Thou holy Light, Guide Divine,
Oh, cause the Word of Life to shine!
Teach us to know our God aright
And call Him Father with delight.
From every error keep us free;
Let none but Christ our Master be
That we in living faith abide,
In Him, our Lord, with all our might confide.
Alleluia, alleluia!

3. Thou holy Fire, Comfort true,
Grant us the will Thy work to do
And in Thy service to abide;
Let trials turn us not aside.
Lord, by Thy pow'r prepare each heart
And to our weakness strength impart
That bravely here we may contend,
Through life and death to Thee, our Lord, ascend.
Alleluia, alleluia!

—M. Luther, 1524, after *Veni sancte Spiritus;* tr., *TLH,* 1941.

135

Tune: Jesus, Jesus, nichts als Jesus. 37. [*TLH* 348; *or TLH* 226*]

1. Come, oh, come, Thou quick'ning Spirit,
God from all eternity!
May Thy powèr never fail us;
Dwell within us constantly.
Then shall truth and life and light
Banish all the gloom of night.

2. Grant our hearts in fullest measure
Wisdom, counsel, purity,
That they ever may be seeking
Only that which pleaseth Thee.
Let Thy knowledge spread and grow,
Working error's overthrow.

3. Show us, Lord, the path of blessing;
When we trespass on our way,
Cast, O Lord, our sins behind Thee
And be with us day by day.
Should we stray, O Lord, recall;
Work repentance when we fall.

4. With our spirit bear Thou witness
That we are the sons of God
Who rely upon Him solely
When we pass beneath the rod;
For we know, as children should,
That the cross is for our good.

5. Prompt us, Lord, to come before Him
With a childlike heart to pray;
Sigh in us, O Holy Spirit,
When we know not what to say.
Then our prayer is not in vain,
And our faith new strength shall gain.

6. If our soul can find no comfort
And despondency grows strong
That the heart cries out in anguish:
"O my God, how long, how long?"
Comfort then the aching breast,
Grant us courage, patience, rest.

7. Holy Spirit, strong and mighty,
Thou who makest all things new,
Make Thy work within us perfect
And the evil foe subdue.
Grant us weapons for the strife
And with vict'ry crown our life.

8. Guard, O God, our faith forever;
Let not Satan, death, or shame
Ever part us from our Savior;
Lord our Refuge is Thy name.
Though our flesh cry ever: Nay!
Be Thy Word to us still Yea!

9. And when life's frail thread is breaking,
Then assure us more and more,
As the heirs of life unending,
Of the glory there in store,
Glory never yet expressed,
Glory of the saints at rest.

—H. Held, 1658; tr., C. W. Schaeffer, 1866, alt.

136

Tune: Nun bitten wir den Heiligen Geist. 23. [*TLH* 231]

1. We now implore God the Holy Ghost
For the true faith, which we need the most,
That in our last moments He may befriend us
And, as homeward we journey, attend us.
Kyrieleis!

2. Shine in our hearts, O most precious Light,
That we Jesus Christ may know aright,
Clinging to our Savior, whose blood hath [bought us.
Who again to our homeland hath brought us.
Kyrieleis!

3. Thou sacred Love, grace on us bestow,
Set our hearts with heav'nly fire aglow
That with hearts united we love each other,
Of one mind, in peace with every brother.
Kyrieleis!

4. Thou highest Comfort in every need,
Grant that neither shame nor death we heed,
That e'en then our courage may never fail us
When the foe shall accuse and assail us.
Kyrieleis!

—st. 1, Anon.; st. 2–4, M. Luther, 1524; tr., *TLH,* 1941, alt.

137

Tune: Wer weiß, wie nahe mir mein Ende. 45.
[*TLH* 65; *LSB* 598; or *TLH* 194*; *LW* 429*; *LSB* 750*]

1. O mighty God, Thou purest Essence,
Who didst pure hearts predestinate,
That they should ever house Thy presence:
A clean heart now in me create,
A heart from every worldly stain
Pure and unspotted to remain.

2. First grant me to repent sincerely,
And cleanse my heart so soiled and scathed;
In both Thy favor bought so dearly
And Jesus' blood let it be bathed.
Then for a life of purity
Equipped and ready let me be.

3. Lord, with Thy Spirit rule and guide me,
Assisting, aiding faithfully,
May He my every need provide me;
Reach, God, Thy gracious hand to me,
A certain spirit grant me, too,—
A spirit willing, free, and new.

4. My weakness ever is before me,
Yet, Father, do not turn Thy face;
Do not for all my faults abhor me
Or cast me from Thy throne of grace.
Thy mercy here let be my share,
And then at last Thy heaven there.

5. Take not Thy Spirit of affection,
Nor let Thy Spirit go away,
But guide my way by His direction,
Yea, by His helping every day,
And through this time conduct my tour
Unto the realm of gladness pure.

—J. Olearius, †1684, asc.; tr., M. Carver.

138

Tune: Herr, wie du willst, so schicks mit mir. 49. [*TLH* 406; *LW* 248; *LSB* 625]

1. O Holy Ghost, Thou Gift divine,
And Giver of all blessing,
Thou, with the Father and the Son,
True Godhead art possessing,
And from them both art shed abroad,
Eternal Spirit, Lord and God,
In Thee all Christians glory.

2. O Spirit blest, we Thee entreat;
O grant us that we ever,
With heart and soul, as it is meet,
May serve our Lord and Savior,
And Him confess till our last breath,
As Lord of life and Lord of death,
And give Him praise and honor.

3. Our hearts let new-created be,
Our walk make pure and holy;
Help us offense and sin to flee,
And ever serve God solely,
So that our faith in Christ our Lord
May prove itself in deed and word
Before the world about us.

4. Thy gracious heav'nly dew let fall,
The fainting Church to quicken;
Thy soothing ointment pour on all
Whose souls are sad and stricken;
Sustain us, Lord, in evil days,
And let our lives in all our ways,
Abound in love and mercy.

5. Give strength and courage to contend
Against the hosts of evil,
That we may vanquish, in the end,
The world, the flesh, the devil;
And when death's billow o'er us rolls,
Bear Thou to heav'n our ransomed souls ,
While dust to dust returneth.

—B. Ringwaldt, †1599; tr., O. H. Smeby, †1929.

139

Tune: Herr Gott, dich loben alle wir. 11.
[*TLH* 13; *LW* 216; *LSB* 923; *or TLH* 3*; *LW* 201*; *LSB* 902*]

1. O Holy Ghost, eternal God,
Blest Comfort for life's rugged road,
With all my heart I pray to Thee;
Hear my entreaty graciously.

2. O Lord, be Thou my Comforter,
Lest in my sins I might despair;
Protect me from the snares of hell,
Grant that in Jesus Christ I dwell.

3. That always I may ready be
To serve this Master faithfully,
And own Him in true living faith
My Lord and Savior unto death.

4. O lead me in the narrow way,
And from the fold let me not stray,
That when this mortal frame I leave,
The crown of life I may receive.

—B. Helder, †1635; tr., A. Crull, †1923.

140

Tune: Wie schön leuchtet der Morgenstern. 86. [*TLH* 235; *LW* 325; *LSB* 395]

1. O Holy Spirit, enter in,
Among these hearts Thy work begin,
Thy temple deign to make us;
Sun of the soul, Thou Light divine,
Around and in us brightly shine,
To joy and gladness wake us.
That we, / In Thee
Truly living, / To Thee giving
Pray'r unceasing,
May in love be still increasing.

2. Give to Thy Word impressive pow'r
That in our hearts, from this good hour,
As fire it may be glowing;
That we confess the Father, Son,
And Thee, the Spirit, Three in One,
Thy glory ever showing.
Stay Thou, / Sway now
Our souls ever / That they never
May forsake Thee,
But by faith their Refuge make Thee.

3. Thou Fountain whence all wisdom flows
Which God on pious hearts bestows,
Grant us Thy consolation
That in our pure faith's unity
We faithful witnesses may be
Of grace that bring salvation.
Hear us, / Cheer us
By Thy teaching; / Let our preaching,
And our labor
Praise Thee, Lord, and serve our neighbor.

4. Left to ourselves, we shall but stray;
Oh, lead us on the narrow way,
With wisest counsel guide us
And give us steadfastness, that we
May ever faithful prove to Thee,
Whatever woes betide us.
Come, Friend, / And mend
Hearts now broken, / Give a token
Thou art near us,
Whom we trust to light and cheer us.

5. Thy heav'nly strength sustain our heart
That we may act the valiant part
With Thee as our Reliance,
Be Thou our Refuge and our Shield
That we may never quit the field,
But bid all foes defiance.
Descend, / Defend
From all errors / And earth's terrors;
Thy salvation
Be our constant consolation.

6. O mighty Rock, O Source of life,
Let Thy dear Word, mid doubt and strife,
Be strong within us burning,
That we be faithful unto death,
In Thy pure love and holy faith,
From Thee true wisdom learning.
Thy grace / And peace
On us shower; / By Thy power
Christ confessing,
Let us win our Savior's blessing.

7. O gentle Dew, from heav'n now fall
With pow'r upon the hearts of all,
Thy tender love instilling,
That heart to heart more closely bound,
In kindly deeds be fruitful found,
The law of love fulfilling;
Dwell thus / In us;.
Envy banish; / Strife will vanish
Where Thou livest.
Peace and love and joy Thou givest.

8. Grant that our days, while life shall last,
In purest holiness be passed,
Be Thou our Strength and Tower.
From sinful lust and vanity
And from dead works set Thou us free
In every evil hoùr.
Keep Thou / Pure now
From offenses / Heart and senses;
Blessèd Spirit!
Let us heav'nly life inherit.

—M. Schirmer, 1640, alt; tr., C. Winkworth, 1863, alt.

141

Tune: Zeuch ein zu deinen Toren. 58. [*TLH* 228]

1. Oh, enter, Lord, Thy temple,
Be Thou my spirit's Guest,
Who gavest me, the earth-born,
A second birth more blest.
Thou in the Godhead, Lord,
Though here to dwell Thou deignest,
Forever equal reignest,
Art equally adored.

2. Oh, enter, let me know Thee
And feel Thy pow'r within,
The pow'r that breaks our fetters
And rescues us from sin;
Oh, wash and cleanse Thou me
That I may serve Thee truly
And render honor duly
With perfect heart to Thee.

3. An olive wild by nature,
Thou graftedst me anew;
Death preyed upon my vitals
And claimed me as his due:
But Christ's atoning blood,
In death true comfort granting,
Drowned death with all his vaunting,
In His baptismal flood.

4. Thou art, O Holy Spirit,
The true anointing Oil,
Through which are consecrated
Soul, body, rest, and toil
To Christ, whose guardian wings,
Where'er their lot appointed,
Protect His own anointed,
His prophets, priests, and kings.

5. 'Tis Thou, O Spirit, teachest
The soul to pray aright;
Thy songs have sweetest music,
Thy pray'rs have wondrous might.
Unheard they cannot fall,
They pierce the highest heaven
Till He His help hath given
Who surely helpeth all.

6. Thy gift is joy, O Spirit,
Thou wouldst not have us pine;
In darkest hours Thy comfort
Doth aye most brightly shine.
And, oh, how oft Thy voice
Hath shed its sweetness o'er me
And opened heav'n before me
And bid my heart rejoice!

7. All love is Thine, O Spirit;
Thou hatest enmity;
Thou lovest peace and friendship,
All strife wouldst have us flee;
Where wrath and discord reign,
Thy whisper kindly pleadeth
And to the heart that heedeth
Brings love and light again.

8. The whole wide world, O Spirit,
Upon Thy hands doth rest;
Our wayward hearts Thou turnest
As it may seem Thee best;
Once more Thy pow'r make known,
As Thou hast done so often,
Convert the wicked, soften
Thou all the hearts of stone.

9. O Holy Spirit, hear us
And make our sorrow cease,
Thy scattered flock restoring
To union, joy, and peace;
Let flourish as before
The lands by men forsaken,
The churches spoiled and shaken
By ruthless fire and war.

10. On those that rule our country
Oh, show'r Thy blessings down,
And in Thy loving-kindness
Adorn as with a crown
With piety our youth,
With godliness our nation,
That all, to gain salvation,
May know Thy heav'nly truth.

11. With holy zeal then fill us,
To keep the faith still pure;
And bless our lands and houses
With wealth that may endure;
The evil Foe make flee,
Who e'er against Thee striveth;
From out our heart he driveth
Whate'er delighteth Thee.

12. Grant steadfastness and courage,
That bravely we contend
Against the wiles of Satan;
O Lord, Thy flock defend!
Help us to battle well,
To triumph o'er the Devil,
To overcome the evil
And all the pow'rs of hell.

13. Our path in all things order
According to Thy mind,
And when this life is over
And all must be resigned,
Oh, grant us then to die
With calm and fearless spirit
And after death inherit
Eternal life on high.

—P. Gerhardt, 1653; tr., C. Winkworth, 1863, alt.

Holy Trinity

142

Tune: All Ehr und Lob soll Gottes sein. 44. [*TLH* 236; *LW* 167; *LSB* 948]

1. All glory be to God alone,
For evermore the Highest One,
Who doth our sinful race befriend
And grace and peace to us extend.
Among mankind may His good will
All hearts with deep thanksgiving fill.

2. We praise Thee, God, and Thee we bless;
We worship Thee in humbleness;
From day to day we glorify
Thee, everlasting God on high.
Of Thy great glory do we sing,
And e'er to Thee our thanks we bring.

3. Lord God, our King on heaven's throne,
Our Father, the Almighty One;
O Lord, the Sole-begotten One,
Lord Jesus Christ, the Father's Son,
True God from all eternity,
O Lamb of God, to Thee we flee:

4. Thou dost the world's sin take away;
Have mercy on us, Lord, we pray.
Thou dost the world's sin take away;
Give ear unto the pray'r we say.
Thou sitt'st at God's right hand for aye;
Have mercy on us, Lord, we pray.

5. Thou only art the Holy One,
Thou art o'er all things Lord alone;
O Jesus Christ, we glorify
Thee only as the Lord Most High;
Thou art, the Holy Ghost with Thee,
One in the Father's majesty.

6. Amen, this ever true shall be,
As angels sing adoringly.
By all creation, far and wide,
Thou, Lord, art ever glorified;
And Thee all Christendom doth praise
Now and through everlasting days.

—M. Luther, 1537; tr., W. G. Polack, 1940.

143

Tune: Der du bist drei in Einigkeit. 11. [p. 399]

1. Thou who art Three in unity,
True God from all eternity,
The sun is fading from our sight,
Shine Thou on us with heav'nly light.

2. We praise Thee with the dawning day,
To Thee at even also pray;
With our poor song we worship Thee
Now, ever, and eternally.

3. Let God the Father be adored,
And God the Son, the only Lord,
And God the Holy Spirit be
Adored throughout eternity!

—M. Luther, 1543, after *O lux beata Trinitas;* tr., R. Massie, 1854.

144

Tune: Nun danket alle Gott. 55. [*TLH* 38; *LW* 174; *LSB* 794]

1. The Lord, my God, be praised,
My Light, my Life from heaven;
My Maker, who to me
Hath soul and body given;
My Father, who doth shield
And keep me day by day,
Doth make each moment yield
New blessings on my way.

2. The Lord, my God, be praised,
My Trust, my Life from heaven,
The Father's own dear Son,
Whose life for me was given,
Who for my sin atoned
With His most precious blood,
Who giveth me by faith
The highest heav'nly good.

3. The Lord, my God, be praised,
My Hope, my Life from heaven,
The Spirit, whom the Son
In love to me hath given.
'Tis He revives my heart,
'Tis He that gives me pow'r,
Help, comfort, and support
In sorrow's gloomy hour.

4. The Lord, my God, be praised,
My God, who ever liveth,
To whom the heav'nly host
All praise and honor giveth.
The Lord, my God, be praised,
In whose great name I boast,
God Father, God the Son,
And God the Holy Ghost.

5. To Him with joyful song
Our praises we are bringing
And with the angel throng
Thrice "Holy" we are singing.
With one united voice
The Church doth Him adore,
The Lord, my God, be praised
Now and forevermore.

—J. Olearius, 1665; tr., A. Crull, †1923, alt.

145

Tune: Gott der Vater wohn uns bei. 96. [*TLH* 247; *LW* 170; *LSB* 505]

1. God the Father, be our Stay,
Oh, let us perish never.
Cleanse us from our sins, we pray,
And grant us life forever.
Keep us from the evil one;
Uphold our faith most holy,
Grant us to trust Thee solely
With humble hearts and lowly.
Let us put God's armor on:
With all true Christians running
Our heav'nly race and shunning
The devil's wiles and cunning.
Amen, Amen, this be done,
So sing we, Alleluia!

2. Jesus Christ, be Thou our Stay . . .
3. Holy Ghost, be Thou our Stay . . .

—M. Luther, 1524, after Anon., 15th c.; tr., R. Massie, 1854, alt.

146

Tune: Wie schön leuchtet der Morgenstern. 86. [*TLH* 546; *LW* 325; *LSB* 395]

1. Alleluia! Let praises ring!
To God the Father let us bring
Our songs of adoration.
To Him through everlasting days
Be worship, honor, power, and praise,
Whose hand sustains creation.
Singing, / Ringing:
Holy, holy, / God is holy,—
Spread the story
Of our God, the Lord of Glory.

2. Alleluia! Let praises ring!
Unto the Lamb of God we sing,
In whom we are elected.
He bought His Church with His own blood,
He cleansed her in that blessed flood,
And as His Bride selected.
Holy, / Holy,
Is our union / And communion,
His befriending
Gives us joy and peace unending.

3. Alleluia! Let praises ring!
Unto the Holy Ghost we sing
For our regeneration.
The saving faith in us He wrought
And us unto the Bridegroom brought,
Made us His chosen nation.
Glory! / Glory!
Joy eternal, / Bliss supernal;
There is manna
And an endless, glad hosanna.

4. Alleluia! Let praises ring!
Unto our Triune God we sing;
Blest be His name forever!
With angel hosts let us adore
And sing His praises more and more
For all His grace and favor!
Singing, / Ringing;
Holy, holy, / God is holy,—
Spread the story
Of our God, the Lord of Glory!

—Anon., Darmstadt, 1698; tr., *TLH,* 1941.

147

Tune: Jesaia dem Propheten das geschah. 102. [*TLH* 249; *LW* 214; *LSB* 960]

1. Isaiah, mighty seer, in days of old
The Lord of all in spirit did behold
High on a lofty throne, in splendor bright,
With flowing train that filled the Temple quite.
Above the throne were stately seraphim,
Six wings had they, these messengers of Him.
With twain they veiled their faces, as was meet,
With twain in rev'rent awe they hid their feet,
And with the other twain aloft they soared,
One to the other called and praised the Lord:
"Holy is God, the Lord of Sabaoth!
Holy is God, the Lord of Sabaoth!
Holy is God, the Lord of Sabaoth!
Behold, His glory filleth all the earth!"
The beams and lintels trembled at the cry,
And clouds of smoke enwrapped the throne on high.

—M. Luther, 1526; tr., *TLH,* 1941.

148

Tune: Helft mir Gotts Güte preisen. 58. [*TLH* 112]

1. My mouth will sing, rejoicing,
My heart at every hour
Due praise to God be voicing,
Who made us by His pow'r;
His glorious praises e'er
Be with all force abounding
And wondrously resounding
By Christians everywhere.

2. His name is blest and heightened
Where it in faith is heard,
And all the earth is brightened
By Spirit and the Word;
For thus He doth renew
And cleanse us from transgression,
That heav'n be our possession,
And we, God's children true.

3. No man could gain salvation
Or saving grace have known,
Save by God's operation—
The boast is God's alone;
Those not by His good grace
Reborn unto salvation
Have endless condemnation:
In heav'n they have no place.

4. Lord, keep me e'er believing,
That to Thy flesh divine
I fruitfully be cleaving
As branch unto the vine;
Rule me in mind and heart,
My old man wholly sever,
And guide my tongue forever,
Thine anthems to impart.

5. Praise to the Father render
Upon His highest Throne,
And thanks and praise and splendor
To His beloved Son,
And to the Spirit be
Unending adoration
From every tongue and nation
Now and eternally.

—G. Weissel, †1635; tr., M. Carver.

149

Tune: Nun freut euch, lieben Christen. 49. [*TLH* 124; *LW* 353; *LSB* 556]

1. O Thou, Most Holy Trinity,
Most glorious and omniscient:
How can Thy Christians give to Thee
Due worship and sufficient?
Thou art most high, most full of fame,
Unfathomed is Thy Holy name,
Inscrutable Thine essence.

2. We thank Thee as on earth we dwell
That by Thy mercy purely
Thou in Thy Holy Word dost tell
Abundantly and surely,
That Thou art God, in being One:
And yet the Father and the Son
And Holy Ghost, three Persons.

3. Thee, God, our Father, we revere,
Creation's Source and Fountain,
For all Thy wonders bright and clear
That sound from Zion's mountain:
Thou Father, ere time had begun,
Begottest Christ, Thine only Son
Thy true, eternal image.

4. Thou didst create the realms of earth
According to Thy pleasure,
And there Thou gavest mankind birth
To praise Thee as his Treasure:
And by Thy word is all ordained,
All granted, governed, and sustained:
This word shall stand forever.

5. Abide, O Father, all life long,
Thy children save from worry,
Forgive us all our sins and wrong
For which our hearts are sorry:
From trouble and from Satan's horde
Release us, help us quickly, Lord,
For this is Thy sure promise.

6. O Jesus Christ, ere worlds began
Begotten of the Father,
In heav'n appointed for all man
The Savior, and none other:
By Thee were made all things in sight,
O God of God, O Light of Light,
True God of God eternal.

7. Thou art the Father's Image true,
Who camest down from heaven,
And when the waiting-time was through
In human flesh wast given;
God's grace for man Thou didst obtain,
And pay for all our sin and stain,
When stainless Thou wast smitten.

8. Uplifted high, the Father's right
In heaven is Thy dwelling,
Whence Thou dost rule all lands with might,
The heathen's anger quelling;
True God and Man, Thy help afford!
We thank Thee for Thy death, O Lord,
And for the good Thou givest.

9. O Holy Ghost, Thou priceless Crown,
With light our hearts Thou feedest,
Who from the Father and the Son
Eternally proceedest,
Almighty art and without end,
The Father and the Son Thee send
In faith and truth to lead us.

10. Lord, by Thy baptism Thou dost give
New life to Thy creation
And so Thou leadest us to live
In increase of compassion,
In Thee our hopes shall see their day,
Though all men else should turn away,
Thou in our hearts abidest.

11. With humble hearts we now implore
That all our groans and sighing
May find with Thee an open door,
And help when times are trying:
And when our final hour is nigh,
Grant us in Jesus Christ to die,
In blessing, peace, and comfort.

12. God Father, Son, and Holy Ghost,
For every grace and blessing
Be praised by all, from least to most,
With joy Thy name confessing:
The hosts of heav'n with one accord
Sing "Holy, Holy, Holy Lord!"
And we on earth join with them.

—J. Gesenius, †1671; tr., M. Carver.

150

Tune: Christ unser Herr zum Jordan kam. 77. [*LW* 223; *LSB* 406]

1. The myst'ry hidden from the mind,
And human tongues confounding,
God now reveals to all mankind
From heaven high resounding:
That He alone is King above
All other gods whatever,
Great, mighty, faithful, full of love,
His people's Shield and Savior,
One Essence in three Persons!

2. God, Father, Son, and Holy Ghost:
Thrice holy thus we name Him,
And with this title, praise, and boast
His righteous seed acclaim Him,
Both Abraham's and Isaac's God,
And Jacob's, whom He favors,
The Lord of hosts, who hath bestowed
All gifts on us believers,
And He alone works wonders.

3. The Father had eternally
His Son ere all creation,
The Son then took at God's decree
His earthly incarnation,
The Spirit timelessly goes forth
From Son and Father faring,
With both of equal praise and worth,
Like crown and glory sharing,
With power undivided.

4. See here, my heart, thy precious Good,
Thy rich, unequaled Treasure,
Thy Friend who bought thee with His blood,
To save thee at His pleasure,
Hath made thee in His image fair,
For all thy guilt was smitten,
And gives true faith of fullest share,
Thy sorrows all to sweeten
Through His own words most holy.

5. Rise, then, to Him, the Ever-blest,
And learn to know Him rightly;
Such knowledge can alone bring rest,
And make thy soul burn brightly,
With purest love to nourish thee
For life and joy in heaven;
Things only heard of here, shall be
To open sight there given
By God to His dear children.

6. But woe to the ungodly race,
Which here are blindly living,
Rejecting God, His rightful praise
To His creation giving.
On them, alas! the heav'nly gate
Shall surely close forever;
For them who God reject and hate
Will God reject and sever
From His eternal kingdom.

7. O Prince of Might, Thy mercy show,
O God of earth and heaven!
That every sinner here below
May turn and be forgiven;
Bring back Thy sheep that go astray,
And blinded eyes enlighten,
Remove whatever blocks our way
Or may confuse and frighten
Thine own, whose faith is weaker.

8. Grant that we may in union throng
Through heav'n's eternal portals,
And join Thy kingdom's endless song
With all the blest immortals:
That Thou above art King alone
Above all gods whatever,
The Father, Son, and Spirit, One,
Thy people's Shield and Savior,
One essence but three persons!

—P. Gerhardt, 1653; tr., composite.

St. John the Baptist

JUNE 24

151

Tune: Was frag ich nach der Welt. 55. [*TLH* 99; *LW* 187; *LSB* 346]

1. When all the world was cursed
By Moses' condemnation,
Saint John the Baptist came
With words of consolation.
With true forerunner's zeal
The Greater One he named,
And Him, as yet unknown,
As Savior he proclaimed.

2. Before he yet was born,
He leaped in joyful meeting,
Confessing Him as Lord
Whose mother he was greeting.
By Jordan's rolling stream,
A new Elijah bold,
He testified of Him
Of whom the prophets told.

3. Behold the Lamb of God
That bears the world's transgression,
Whose sacrifice removes
The Enemy's oppression.
Behold the Lamb of God,
Who beareth all our sin,
Who for our peace and joy
Will full atonement win.

4. Thrice blessèd everyone
Who heeds the proclamation
Which John the Baptist brought,
Accepting Christ's salvation.
He who believes this truth
And comes with love unfeigned
Has righteousness and peace
In fullest measure gained.

5. Oh, grant, Thou Lord of Love,
That we receive, rejoicing,
The word proclaimed by John,
Our true repentance voicing;
That gladly we may walk
Upon our Savior's way
Until we live with Him
In His eternal day.

—J. G. Olearius, †1711; tr., P. E. Kretzmann, 1940.

152

Tune: Herr Gott, dich loben alle wir. 11. [*TLH* 13; *LW* 216; *LSB* 923]

1. Blest be the God of Israel
Who hath redeemed our souls from hell,
And with great mercy visited
His people who once lay in dread.

2. His precious Son to us He sent,
That He from anger might relent,
And for His great deliv'rance now
His people glad before Him bow.

3. When every hope was hid from view,
In David's house, His servant true,
He raised salvation's mighty horn
To comfort Christendom forlorn.

4. This on their lips so long ago
The holy prophets made us know,
As God instructed them to cry
How He would bring salvation nigh.

5. From foes' despite and haters' hands,
Tho' they may rage like burning brands,
He who has pow'r o'er Satan, grave,
And sin, and death, our life would save.

6. His heart with mercy's fire was stirred
To speak a good and gracious word:
Upon His covenant He thought
That with our fathers He had wrought:

7. Fresh in His mind His oath He bore,
Which unto Abraham He swore,
To keep unto those hearts that heard
And to their offspring afterward:

8. To us deliv'rance He would grant,
And Satan, death, and hell supplant,
That we might serve Him all our life,
Released from terror, sin, and strife,

9. In righteousness and purity,
As pleases God continually,
Not as by human mind devised,
Which works are vainly realized.

10. This name, O child, shall be thine own:
The Prophet of the Highest One,
The Master's advent to declare,
His way to straighten and prepare,

11. Thro' God's most tender mercy shown
To us poor men, in sin who groan,
For whom the Dayspring from on high,
The Gift and Fruit of love, drew nigh;

12. To lighten all in darkness wrapped
And in death's gloomy shadow trapped,
That they may be the sons of light
By virtue of His radiance bright;

13. Their feet the level ground to show,
And in the way of peace to go,
That all at last may come as one
In bliss before God's golden throne.

—J. Heermann, 1635, cento; tr., M. Carver.

153

Tune: Herr Jesu Christ, meins Lebens Licht. 11. [*TLH* 288; *LW* 262; *LSB* 704]

1. O Jesus, Lamb of God who art
The Life and Comfort of my heart,
I, wretched sinner, come to Thee
And bring so many sins with me.

2. O God, my sinfulness is great,
I groan beneath a dreadful weight;
Yet be Thou merciful, I pray,
Take guilt and punishment away.

3. Saint John the Baptist biddeth me
To cast my burden, Lord, on Thee,
Since Thou hast left Thy heav'nly throne,
That for our sins Thou might'st atone.

4. Help me amend my ways, O Lord,
And willingly obey Thy Word;
Do always, then, abide with me,
And when I die take me to Thee.

—B. Helder, †1635; tr., A. Crull, 1880, alt.

Visitation of Mary

JULY 2

154

Tune: Herr Gott, dich loben alle wir. 11. [*TLH* 13; *LW* 216; *LSB* 923]

1. My soul, O God, gives praise to Thee,
With joy my Savior here I see.
No worldly splendor dost Thou seek,
Regarding me, the poor and weak.

2. Uplifted is my lowly place;
Behold, henceforth shall every race
And every generation sing
Thy grace to me, this blessed thing.

3. Thou mighty art, dear Lord on high,
Thy godly might shall never die,
Thy name is worthy of all praise,
Its anthems all do well to raise.

4. Thy mercy is on every one
Who bows in fear to Thee alone;
Thou helpest all Thy children poor
Whene'er they suffer danger sore.

5. The pride of man must pass away,
Against Thine arm can nothing stay.
Who trusts alone in throne or crown,
The same shalt Thou put quickly down.

6. Thou makest naught of man's desire,
This wonder, Lord, I must admire,
For all their thoughts opposed to Thee
Are cast into obscurity.

7. The humble souls of honor slight
Thou crownest with Thy godly might
Exalting them to royal pitch,
Reversing purse of poor and rich.

8. Lord, this Thou dost in our own day,
Remembering Thy gracious way
To help Thy servant Israel,
And make Thy chosen people well.

9. We have not earned this gift from Thee,
'Tis Thou who dealest graciously,
As to our fathers Thou didst swear,
Esteeming them with promise fair.

10. To Abraham, the man of worth
Thou mad'st an everlasting oath,
Vouchsafing him and all his line
Thy kingdom endless and divine.

11. All glory now and ever be
To God the Holy Trinity:
The Father, Son, and Holy Ghost,
Who daily blesses all His host.

12. May God on us His grace bestow,
Defend us from eternal woe,
And when this fleeting world is o'er,
Grant us salvation evermore.

—H. Bonnus, 1547; tr., M. Carver.

St. Michael

SEPTEMBER 29

155

Tune: Aus Lieb läßt Gott der Christenheit. 49. [p. 396]

1. God shows His love to Christendom
With blessings ever mounting,
Among which He hath made for them
Bright hosts beyond all counting;
So let us all with gladness sing,
This day to God our thanks we bring
For our angelic guardians.

2. They dress for war when dangers near,
And to the battle hasten,
To rescue all who God revere,
And all the foe to chasten;
So let us all with gladness sing,
This day to God our thanks we bring
For our angelic watchmen.

3. They keep the path from peril free,
For all men, great and humble,
Lest any suffer injury,
Or on the pathway stumble;
So let us all with gladness sing,
This day to God our thanks we bring
For our angelic keepers.

—G. Reimann, 1597, ab.; tr., M. Carver.

156

Tune: Herr Gott, dich loben alle wir. 11. [*TLH* 13; *LW* 216; *LSB* 923]

1. Lord God, we all to Thee give praise,
Thanksgivings meet to Thee we raise,
That angel hosts Thou didst create
Around Thy glorious throne to wait.

2. They shine with light and heav'nly grace
And constantly behold Thy face;
They heed Thy voice, they know it well,
In godly wisdom they excel.

3. They never rest nor sleep as we;
Their whole delight is but to be
With Thee, Lord Jesus, and to keep
Thy little flock, Thy lambs and sheep.

4. The ancient Dragon is their foe;
His envy and his wrath they know.
It always is his aim and pride
Thy Christian people to divide.

5. As he of old deceived the world
And into sin and death was hurled,
So now he subtly lies in wait
To ruin school and Church and state.

6. A roaring lion round he goes,
No halt nor rest he ever knows;
He seeks the Christians to devour
And slay them in his dreadful pow'r.

7. But watchful is the angel band
That follows Christ on every hand
To guard His people where they go
And break the counsel of the Foe.

8. From Daniel this may well be seen
When he sat in the lion's den,
And likewise angels rescued Lot,
That the ungodly harmed him not.

9. When, too, those faithful three were cast
Into the fiery furnace blast,
No pow'r had fiercest flames to harm
Against the rescuing angel's arm.

10. And thus our God, still at this day,
From harm and many‿an evil way
Keeps us by His dear angel guard,
Placed over us as watch and ward.

11. For this, now and in days to be,
Our praise shall rise, O Lord, to Thee,
Whom all the angel hosts adore
With grateful songs forevermore.

12. We also pray Thee to defend
By them unto the latter end,
Thy fold, that little flock, O Lord,
That holds in honor Thy blest Word.

—P. Eber, 1561, after Melanchthon, 1539; tr., E. Cronenwett, 1880, alt.

157

Tune: Nun freut euch, lieben Christen. 49.
[*TLH* 124; *LW* 353; *LSB* 556; *or TLH* 377*; *LW* 355*; *LSB* 555*]

1. O God, who dost Thy children love,
Yea, who dost so adore them,
That every moment from above
Thou pour'st Thy graces o'er them:
We thank Thee that Thy faithfulness
Is every morning new to us,
As long as we are living.

2. We praise Thee now especially
For Thine angelic armies
Which Thou hast made to honor Thee
And watch that nothing harm us,
Lest any foot upon a stone
Should come to harm or break a bone,
As on Thy path we travel.

3. What is a man upon the earth?
So greatly dost Thou love him,
To Thee so precious is his worth,
That thou hast set above him
Thy heav'nly spirits in their place
To be for man a wondrous grace,
And serve as his defenders.

4. O Lord, for this unequaled taste
Of charity and blessing,
Thou by all hearts art to be praised
With gratitude unceasing;
Wherefore we sing and shout abroad
Thy wondrous love, with thanks, O God,
For such unfailing goodness.

5. Th' almighty Champion's forces strong
Are stationed fast beside us,
And in these times of grievous wrong
A hard-won rest provide us,
Maintaining church and stately sword
And everyone with one accord
In every proper station.

6. Keep us, O Lord, by Thy good grace
In Thee securely dwelling,
And never by our wickedness
Thine angel bands repelling:
Grant us upright and pure to be,
In humbleness and honesty
Our neighbors gladly serving.

7. Grant us as well to fill Thy praise
As all Thy hosts are bidden,
And with them all as shining rays
Thy wonders spread and widen,
Which unto us and all the earth
Thou in Thy Word hast given forth,
With wisdom, might, and goodness.

8. As out of troubles oft Thou hast
By these Thine angels brought us,
And kept us safe from first to last
Lest plagues and snares had caught us;
So henceforth still our souls upbear,
Command Thine angels everywhere
To keep a hedge about us.

9. Lord, keep Thy Church and this our land
Within Thine angels' shielding,
That round us everywhere may stand
Thy peace and health unyielding!
Empow'r Thine angels to destroy
The devil's every murd'rous ploy,
And crush his crown and legions.

10. Bid them, when, dying, hence we fare,
To banish the deceiver,
Our souls to Abr'hams bosom bear
And to Thy hands deliver,
Where all the hosts Thy praises ring
And "Holy, Holy, Holy" sing
Without a moment's ceasing.

—J. Gesenius, 1648; tr., M. Carver.

Festival of the Reformation

OCTOBER 31

158

Tune: Ein feste Burg ist unser Gott. 75. [*TLH* 262; *LW* 298; *LSB* 656]

1. A mighty Fortress is our God,
A trusty Shield and Weapon;
He helps us free from every need
That hath us now o'ertaken.
The old evil Foe
Now means deadly woe;
Deep guile and great might
Are his dread arms in fight;
On earth is not his equal.

2. With might of ours can naught be done,
Soon were our loss effected;
But for us fights the Valiant One,
Whom God Himself elected.
Ask ye, Who is this?
Jesus Christ it is,
Of Sabaoth Lord,
And there's none other God;
He holds the field forever.

3. Though devils all the world should fill,
All eager to devour us.
We tremble not, we fear no ill,
They shall not overpow'r us.
This world's prince may still
Scowl fierce as he will,
He can harm us none,
He's judged; the deed is done;
One little word can fell him.

4. The Word they still shall let remain
Nor any thanks have for it;
He's by our side upon the plain
With His good gifts and Spirit.
And take they our life,
Goods, fame, child, and wife,
Let these all be gone,
They yet have nothing won;
The Kingdom ours remaineth.

—M. Luther, 1529, after Psalm 46; tr., composite.

159

Tune: Erhalt uns, Herr, bei deinem Wort. 11. [*TLH* 261; *LW* 334; *LSB* 655]

1. Lord, keep us in Thy word and work,
Restrain the murd'rous pope and Turk,
Who fain would tear from off Thy throne
Christ Jesus, Thy beloved Son.

2. Lord Jesus Christ, Thy pow'r make known,
For Thou art Lord of lords alone;
Defend Thy Christendom that we
May evermore sing praise to Thee.

3. O Comforter of priceless worth,
Send peace and unity on earth.
Support us in our final strife
And lead us out of death to life.

4. Destroy their counsels, Lord our God,
And smite them with an iron rod,
And let them fall into the snare
Which for Thy Christians they prepare.

5. So that at last they may perceive
That, Lord our God, Thou still dost live,
And dost deliver mightily
All those who put their trust in Thee.

—M. Luther, 1541; sts. 4–5, J. Jonas, 1544; tr., C. Winkworth, 1863, alt.

160

Tune: Durch Adams Fall ist ganz verderbt. 83.
[p. 401; *or* *TLH* 437*; *LW* 414*; *LSB* 714*]

1. O Lord, Thy blessed, saving Word
In darkness long lay hidden,
And seldom was it seen or heard,
While man-made laws were bidden;
Thus we could not faith's pow'r conceive,
Nor trust Thee, God most holy,
And heeding nothing else, believe
And build on Jesus solely.

2. The saints were long invoked and named
For pray'r and intercession,
And power soon was even claimed
To be in their possession;
Yet, God, Thou art the Mighty One,
Our Helper ever near us,
Who wilt in Jesus' name alone
Be prayed to, and wilt hear us.

3. When Christ ordained His holy meal,
His flesh and blood were given,
With bread and wine, to strengthen, seal,
And give us life and heaven,
A sacrifice they called this food
God's word they contradicted,
As sacramental holy blood
Was from the folk restricted.

4. The works which were required of men
Were by their minds created,
As superstitions seized them, then
False doctrines were instated;
Yet every law of Thine, O God,
Remained in darkness ever,
Men eagerly endured the load,
Of their own vain endeavor.

5. What led us down this dreadful path?
One sin all else exceeding:
They took from men the rule of faith,
Forbidding Scriptures' reading.
Thus many by this one offense
Were tricked with little plying;
And could not tell the difference
Between the truth and lying.

6. Men in their fantasies devised
Abuses to God's service,
And golden lucre was more prized
Than words that could preserve us,
The Holy Scriptures, locked away,
But rarely came to hearing,
While human frills and vain display
Were daily new appearing.

7. For many ages men did grope
Behind a heavy curtain,
Beneath a yoke, bereft of hope
They wondered all uncertain,
If what they did sufficed to find
An entry into heaven,
And, dying, doubted in their mind,
What end they would be given.

8. To Thee, O Lord, be endless praise
For Thou the truth hast brought us,
Thou hast removed our blinding haze,
And purest doctrine taught us:
We know that he who Christ shall trust,
Eternal life inherits;
We look to Him in faith, and just
Are rendered for His merits.

9. And by His grace we do His will,
Within the Spirit's power,
All God's commandments to fulfill,
With good works every hour,
All patience, peacefulness, and joy,
All chasteness, meekness, kindness,
All mildness now we can employ
Without deceit or blindness.

10. All this from God's own mouth we learn,
And nothing hence can shake us,
Yea, from this rock shall nothing turn
Nor even angel take us;
And for this grace more fair than all,
Which God hath demonstrated,
With grateful hearts our voices shall
Sing praises unabated.

11. O Lord, we pray Thee graciously,
Turn those in error pining,
Subdue all those who slander Thee,
Thy grace, O God, maligning;
Let no one hide Thy precious Word
Or stay its promulgation
But keep it plainly seen and heard,
Through every generation.

—J. Gesenius, †1671; tr., M. Carver.

161

Tune: O Herre Gott, dein göttlich Wort. 83. [*TLH* 266; *LW* 341]

1. O God, our Lord, / Thy holy Word
Was long a hidden treasure
Till to its place / It was by grace
Restored in fullest measure.
The words of Paul, / Th' Apostles all,
Which they cannot deny Thee,
We hear today, / And thanks we say
And gladly glorify Thee.

2. For now with might / Thy Word shines bright
And every eye reviews it.
O God my Lord, / Thy grace afford
To those who still refuse it,
Who follow blind / The human mind,
Whereby they would but perish:
Then, lest they die, / Eternally
Teach them Thy Word to cherish.

3. Salvation free / By faith in Thee,
That is Thy Gospel's preaching,
The heart and core / Of Bible-lore
In all its sacred teaching.
In Christ we must / Put all our trust,
Not in our deeds or labor;
With conscience pure / And heart secure
Love Thee, Lord, and our neighbor.

4. Thou, Lord, alone / This work hast done
By Thy free grace and favor.
All who believe / Will grace receive
Through Jesus Christ, our Savior.
And though the Foe / Would overthrow
Thy Word with grim endeavor,
All he hath wro't / Must come to naught,—
Thy Word will stand forever.

5. Thy Spirit send / Those near life's end
That they may soon be turning,
Who, worldly wise, / Thy Word despise,
Nor will its truth be learning,
Which, they object, / Is incorrect,
And yet have not inspected
Or ever heard / the noble Word
Which they like imps rejected.

6. I firmly hold / That truth of gold
Which Paul's dear script maintaineth:
Though night and day should pass away,
Thy holy Word remaineth
Nor e'er shall pass, / Though should, alas!
All stubborn hearts and callous
Refuse to turn, / And thereby earn
Great pains for all their malice.

7. My Lord art Thou, / And for me now
Death holds no dreadful terrors;
Thy precious blood, / My highest good,
Hath blotted out my errors.
My thanks to Thee! / Thou wilt to me
Fulfill Thy promise ever
And mercy give / While here I live
And heav'nly bliss forever.

8. O Lord I pray, / Cast not away
To any dread oppression
Those who believe / Thy Word and cleave
By faith to this confession!
Their hearts caress / With blessedness
And let them know no sadness.
I pray, thro' Thee, / Lord, grant Thou me
To die in joy and gladness.

—Anon., Erfurt, 1527; tr. sts. 1, 3–4, 7, W. G. Polack, 1939, alt.; sts. 2, 5–6, 8, M. Carver.

162

Tune: Wär Gott nicht mit uns diese Zeit. 49. [*TLH* 267]

1. If God had not been on our side
And had not come to aid us,
The foes with all their pow'r and pride
Would surely have dismayed us;
For we, His flock, would have to fear
The threat of men both far and near
Who rise in might against us.

2. Their furious wrath, did God permit,
Would surely have consumed us
And as a deep and yawning pit
With life and limb entombed us.
Like men o'er whom dark waters roll
Their wrath would have engulfed our soul
And, like a flood, o'erwhelmed us.

3. Blest be the Lord, who foiled their threat
That they could not devour us;
Our souls, like birds, escaped their net,
They could not overpow'r us.
The snare is broken—we are free!
Our help is ever, Lord, in Thee,
Who madest earth and heaven.

—M. Luther, 1524, after Ps. 124; tr., *TLH,* 1941.

163

Tune: Wir danken dir, Gott! für und für. 44. [p. 418]

1. We praise Thee, Lord, / For Thy dear Word
Which, by Thy grace, / We at this place
Have with us pure / Unto this hour;
O keep it sound, / And let abound
Forevermore / Thy Gospel pure
Thy name to laud from shore to shore.

2. How great its worth! / Preserve on earth
Its precious light. / Let not the might
Of murd'rous foe / Thy reign o'erthrow!
Let not their arm / Betide us harm;
Restrain their will, / That though they still
Try day and night, they do no ill.

3. With pastors now / Thy church endow,
Who show aright / Thy Word's pure light;
Who faithfully / Would lead to Thee
All who are giv'n / Thy love from heav'n
Lest, great of might, / That dreadful night
Of unbelief return to sight:

4. Which bears forsooth / No gleam of truth,
No joy or gain / In cross or pain;
Thy Word alone / Can cheer Thine own.
Keep its pure gold / For young and old,
Till heav'nward sent! / Those works prevent
Which fight Thy Word and Sacrament.

—J. Heermann, †1647; tr., J. T. Mueller, 1921, alt. / M. Carver.

Commemorations of Holy Apostles

164

Tune: Kommt her zu mir, spricht Gottes Sohn. 41.
[*TLH* 263; *LW* 261; *LSB* 666 (mel.)]

1. Lord Jesus, Refuge of mankind,
Whose Holy Word shows sinners blind
The only way to heaven,
We sing aloud Thy wondrous grace,
Which not to our own day we trace,
But long before was given.

2. In days of yore it was that Thou
Didst in humiliation bow
To bring Thy Word unto us,
That Word that gives our spirits ease
Proclaiming healing homilies
To strengthen and renew us.

3. But when the perfect time had come
To rise to heav'n, Thy royal home,
And pass to men Thy preaching
With wisdom deep Thou didst ordain
A chosen few to keep, sustain,
And speak to us Thy teaching.

4. The office of the ministry
Thou didst ordain initially
In Thine Apostles gathered.
So every seed that Thou hadst sown
By them was tended, fed, and grown
And thus Thy Church was furthered.

5. O faithful God, what faithfulness
At every turn they did possess
And in their service give Thee,
Who, though endangered and in need,
Despised, afflicted, made to bleed,
Yea, dying, would not leave Thee!

6. What agonies by men devised
Fell not upon these saints of Christ
When they proclaimed His blessing?
With rods of iron they were bruised,
With stones and crosses sorely used,
And perished, Him confessing.

7. O fearless heart! O dauntless gaze,
That suffered even fiery blaze
And punishments more fearful!
They fought, Thy glories wide to spread,
And for Thy truth their blood was shed
Till death they greeted cheerful.

8. So too, when, in the course of time,
The devil wove his web of crime
With terrorizing power,
Yet Christian teachers, wise and sage,
And Christendom of every age
He could not bring to cower.

9. Through hill and valley they were sought
In great distress and anguish caught,
In fetters to awaken,
As prey for wolf and lions' jowl,
And so by many means more foul
Their lives from them were taken.

10. And yet, O Lord, Thy precious Word
By no such trials was deterred,
But all the more was nourished,
By martyrdom they did increase
Thy word of healing, life, and peace
And rich its fruits have flourished.

11. Thus all the world has come to know
That in Thy hands the Church shall grow,
And follow Thee, her Master,
Nor can the threat of fire or sword
Chase off the sheep within Thy ward
Or turn them from Thy pasture.

12. Now, Lord, how must Thy heritage
With highest thanks in every age
Exclaim Thy fitting praises!
To see how this Thy Word was sent
To bring us very nourishment
Our humble mind amazes:

13. And so this pray'r we ask of Thee:
That Thou, O Lord, wouldst graciously
Thy Word be still securing
Within Thy shelter, safe from woe
And from the cunning of the foe;
Give us Thy help enduring.

14. Lord, let Thy Gospel, full of cheer,
That Thou hast granted us to hear
In times of peace and quiet
Confirm our faith and trust in Thee,
Instill in us Thy charity,
Nor let us e'er deny it.

15. But if in time there come to be
New persecutions, tyranny,
Oppression, pain, and sadness,
Oh, help us then with willing heart
Like the Apostles at the start,
To bear our cross with gladness.

16. May we with hearts as martyrs bold
Nor flesh nor blood of ours withhold,
Thy doctrine pure defending,
That in the battle's aftermath
And goodly testing of our faith
Thy glory be extended.

17. O Lord, to Thee we now commend
The holy Church from end to end;
Oh, let her perish never,—
In war and peace, in joy and woe,—
Until hereafter we shall know
Thy heav'nly glories ever.

—J. C. Arnschwanger, †1696; tr., M. Carver.

God's Word and the Christian Church

165

Tune: Ach, bleib bei uns, Herr Jesu Christ. 11. [*TLH* 197; *LW* 344; *LSB* 585]

1. Lord Jesus Christ, with us abide,
For round us falls the eventide;
Nor let Thy Word, that heav'nly light,
For us be ever veiled in night.

2. In these last days of sore distress
Grant us, dear Lord, true steadfastness
That pure we keep, till life is spent,
Thy holy Word and Sacrament.

3. Lord Jesus, help, Thy Church uphold,
For we are sluggish, thoughtless, cold.
Oh, prosper well Thy Word of grace
And spread its truth in every place!

4. Oh, keep us in Thy Word, we pray;
The guile and rage of Satan stay!
Oh, may Thy mercy never cease!
Give concord, patience, courage, peace.

5. O God, how sin's dread works abound!
Throughout the earth no rest is found,
And falsehood's spirit wide has spread,
And error boldly rears its head.

6. The haughty spirits, Lord, restrain
Who o'er Thy Church with might would reign
And always set forth something new,
Devised to change Thy doctrine true.

7. And since the cause and glory, Lord,
Are Thine, not ours, to us afford
Thy help and strength and constancy,
With all our heart we trust in Thee.

8. A trusty weapon is Thy Word,
Thy Church's buckler, shield, and sword.
Oh, let us in its power confide
That we may seek no other guide!

9. Oh, grant that in Thy holy Word
We here may live and die, dear Lord;
And when our journey endeth here,
Receive us into glory there.

—Anon., 1579, after the Latin of P. Melanchthon, 1551;
but sts. 2–9, N. Selnecker, 1572; tr., composite.

166

Tune: Ach Gott vom Himmel, sieh darein. 49. [*TLH* 260]

1. O Lord, look down from heav'n, behold
And let Thy pity waken:
How few are we within Thy fold,
Thy saints by men forsaken!
True faith seems quenched on every hand,
Men suffer not Thy Word to stand;
Dark times have us o'ertaken.

2. With fraud which they themselves invent
Thy truth they have confounded;
Their hearts are not with one consent
On Thy pure doctrine grounded.
While they parade with outward show,
They lead the people to and fro,
In error's maze astounded.

3. May God root out all heresy
And of false teachers rid us
Who proudly say: "Now, where is he
That shall our speech forbid us?
By right or might we shall prevail;
What we determine cannot fail;
We own no lord and master."

4. Therefore saith God, "I must arise,
The poor My help are needing;
To Me ascend My people's cries,
And I have heard their pleading.
For them My saving Word shall fight
And fearlessly and sharply smite,
The poor with might defending."

5. As silver tried by fire is pure
From all adulteration,
So through God's Word shall men endure
Each trial and temptation.
Its light beams brighter through the cross,
And, purified from human dross,
It shines through every nation.

6. Thy truth defend, O God, and stay
This evil generation;
And from the error of their way
Keep Thine own congregation.
The wicked everywhere abound
And would Thy little flock confound;
But Thou art our Salvation.

—M. Luther, 1523, after Ps. 12; tr., *TLH,* 1941.

167

Tune: Christe, du Beistand deiner Kreuzgemeine. 13.
[p. 397; *or TLH* 143*; *LW* 119*; *LSB* 439* (no rep.)]

1. O Christ, Thou Champion of Thy congregation,
Haste Thee to save Thy Church in tribulation!
Cast down the mighty foes that e'er alarm us,
And strive to harm us. (*x2*)

2. For Thy poor children do Thou battle ever,
O vanquish Satan! Stem his foul endeavor!
All those who strive to bring Thy Church disaster,
O'erthrow, dear Master! (*x2*)

3. Grant us Thy peace in Church and school, dear Savior,
And with Thy peace do Thou our rulers favor.
May heart and conscience, Thy sweet peace possessing,
Rest in Thy blessing. (*x2*)

4. O let us laud Thy love while here we wander,
And sing Thy praises, faithful Shepherd, yonder!
Heaven and earth shall give Thee endless glory,
And bow before Thee. (*x2*)

—M. A. von Löwenstern, 1644; tr., C. Winkworth, 1855, alt.

CONSECRATION OF A CHURCH

168

Tune: Es ist das Heil uns kommen her. 49. [*TLH* 377; *LW* 355; *LSB* 555]

1. Thrice Holy God, incline Thy sight
From heaven's height; O Father,
See how to Thee, the Lord of might,
Thy little flock doth gather:
Receive the bidding sigh and groan
Which here we offer to Thy throne,
And consecrate Thy dwelling.

2. We build this temple in Thy name;
We are but Thy attendants.
Without Thee, 'tis an empty frame.
Here we and our descendants
In habitations hallowed Thine
Will hear Thy laws and words divine,
Yea, hear Thy saving Gospel.

3. Christ is its Corner-stone and base,
The prophets and apostles
On Him its noble pillars raise,
No storm their teaching jostles,
Though strong and sly the foe may be
God's city standeth happily
Around the font of Zion.

4. Here shall our child be made secure
In Jesus by baptizing,
Their little hearts in kernels pure
Of doctrine catechizing,
As sprouts of heaven them to rear
In Christian love and godly fear,
True faith and its fruition.

5. Here shall we bow in penitence,
Here humbly, too, be kneeling,
Confessing every dark offense,
And to the cross appealing,
In sorrow own our bloody guilt,
And seek forgiveness in what spilt
From Christ's afflicted body.

6. Here at this holy altar shall
Souls famished come to dinner
Where Jesus, Savior of us all,
Will grace each sorry sinner
With His true body and true blood,
To death devoted for our good
And shed for our salvation.

7. Here shall the man and wife be blest,
The sick have supplication,
The beams and gables oft be pressed
With praise and jubilation,
Here shall our leaders in command,
Our church, our home, our school and land
Be aye to Thee commended.

8. Lord, now this house that bears Thy name
We to Thy keeping offer,
From ruthless foe preserve its frame,
Nor let it ruin suffer.
Make all retreat who treat us ill,
Grant us in Zion's calmness still
To sing Thy hymns forever.

9. Thanks, honor, splendor, pow'r, and praise
To Thee, O Lord, be chanted,
That in the toil of many days
A goodly end was granted!
May that on which we now embark
Still prove a good and sturdy ark
Till earth and heaven perish.

—H. von Assig, †1694; tr., M. Carver.

169

Tune: Herzlich tut mich verlangen. 59.
[*TLH* 172; *LW* 113; *LSB* 450; *or TLH* 334*; *LSB* 689*]

1. Preserve Thy Word, O Savior,
To us this latter day
And let Thy kingdom flourish,
Enlarge Thy Church, we pray.
Oh, keep our faith from failing,
Keep hope's bright star aglow.
Let naught from Thy Word turn us
While wand'ring here below.

2. Preserve, O Lord, Thine honor,
The bold blasphemer smite;
Convince, convert, enlighten,
The souls in error's night.
Reveal Thy will, dear Savior,
To all who dwell below—
Thou Light of all the living—
That men Thy name may know.

3. Preserve, O Lord, Thy Zion
Bought dearly with Thy blood;
Protect what Thou hast chosen
Against the foes' dread brood.
Be Thou her great Defender
When dangers gather round;
E'en though the earth be crumbling,
Safe will Thy Church be found.

4. Preserve, O Lord, Thy pastures,
The savage wolf is nigh;
Awake, Lord, when we slumber,
And keep Thy sheep close by,
For Thou alone canst save us,
And to Thy meadows guide,
Feed, freshen, and defend us
Throughout this desert wide.

5. Preserve, O Lord, Thy children,
Thine own blest heritage;
Resist, disperse, and scatter
Those who against Thee rage.
Let Thy commandments guide us,
Grant us Thy heav'nly food;
Clothe us in Thy rich garments
Bought with Thy precious blood.

6. Preserve Thy Word and preaching,
The truth that makes us whole,
The mirror of Thy glory,
The pow'r that saves the soul.
Oh, may this living water,
This dew of heav'nly grace,
Sustain us while here living
Until we see Thy face!

7. Preserve in wave and tempest
Thy storm-tossed little flock;
Assailed by wind and weather,
May it endure each shock.
Take Thou the helm, O Pilot,
And set the course aright;
Thus we shall reach the harbor
In Thine eternal light.

—A. Gryphius, †1664; tr., W. J. Schaefer, 1938, alt., but st. 4, M. Carver.

170

Tune: Es spricht der unweisen Mund wohl. 49. [p. 402]

1. The mouth of fools doth God confess,
But while their lips draw nigh Him
Their heart is full of wickedness,
And all their deeds deny Him.
Corrupt are they, and every one
Abominable deeds hath done;
There is not one well-doer.

2. The Lord looked from His heav'nly throne
On all mankind below Him,
To see if there were any one
Who truly sought to know Him,
And all his understanding bent
To search His holy Word, intent
To do His will in earnest.

3. But none there was who walked with God,
For all aside had slidden,
Delusive paths of folly trod,
And followed lusts forbidden;
Not one there was who practiced good,
Though many deemed, in haughty mood,
Their deeds to God were pleasing.

4. How long, by folly blindly led,
Will they oppress the needy,
And My own flock devour like bread?
So fierce are they and greedy!
In God they put no trust at all,
Nor will on Him in trouble call,
But be their own providers.

5. Therefore their heart is never still,
A constant fear dismays them;
God is with him who doth His will,
Who trusts Him and obeys Him;
Ye shame the counsel of the poor
And mock him when he doth assure
That God is e'er his refuge.

6. Who shall to Israel's outcast race
From Zion bring salvation?
God will Himself at length show grace,
And loose the captive nation;
That will He do by Christ their King;
Let Jacob then be glad and sing,
And Israel be joyful.

—M. Luther, 1524, after Ps. 14; tr., R. Massie, 1854, alt.

171

Tune: Es woll uns Gott genädig sein. 77. [*TLH* 500; *LW* 288; *LSB* 823]

1. May God bestow on us His grace,
With blessings rich provide us,
And may the brightness of His face
To life eternal guide us
That we His saving health may know,
His gracious will and pleasure,
And also to the heathen show
Christ's riches without measure
And unto God convert them.

2. Thine over all shall be the praise
And thanks of every nation,
And all the world with joy shall raise
The voice of exultation;
For Thou shalt judge the earth, O Lord,
Nor suffer sin to flourish;
Thy people's pasture is Thy Word
Their souls to feed and nourish,
In righteous paths to keep them.

3. Oh, let the people praise Thy worth,
In all good works increasing;
The land shall plenteous fruit bring forth,
Thy Word is rich in blessing.
May God the Father, God the Son,
And God the Spirit bless us!
Let all the world praise Him alone,
Let solemn awe possess us,
Now let our hearts say, Amen.

—M. Luther, 1524, after Ps. 67; tr., R. Massie, 1851, alt.

172

Tune: Gott sei uns gnädig und barmherzig. 108. [p. 403]

1. God be merciful unto | us and bless us,
And give us His spir- | itual blessing.

2. God cause His face to | shine upon us,
That His way may be | known upon earth.

3. God, even our | own God, bless us.
God bless us and grant us | His peace. Amen.

—Anon., after Ps. 67:1–2, 6; tr. after KJV.

173

Tune: Durch Adams Fall ist ganz verderbt. 83. [p. 401]

1. O Lord of Hosts, Thy holy Word
Which here Thou hast provided
Lest we should ever be allured
To thought or deed misguided—
Thou didst proclaim, / Thy lips did frame,
And by Thee was it given
Pure, right, and true / Thro' servants who
Were by Thy Spirit driven.

2. This Word, which written leaves display,
Stands fast and changes never.
Though heav'n and earth shall pass away,
God's Word abides forever:
Nor hell nor strife / Nor end of life
Is mighty to destroy it:
All's well therefore / Forevermore
For those who well employ it.

3. How perfectly and brightly glows
This rule of purest teaching:
How openly to us it shows
God's works and praise far-reaching,
And us would tell / How here to dwell,
Faith, hope, and love to practice:
Our hearts are stirred / By this good Word;
Its truth doth e'er attract us.

4. It soothes our wounds and in our grief
Springs up a well of gladness,
It gives the sin-weighed heart relief,
And flight from hell and sadness,
Its comforts stay, / It shows the way
To die with cheerful spirit,
And so be giv'n / The joys of heav'n
Obtained by Christ's own merit.

5. Behold God's Word! beyond account
In potency to bless us
With help and strength of such amount
That loss need not distress us
Of wealth and gold, / Nor need we hold
So dear all worldly pleasures,
But ever go / In weal or woe
To seek this pearl and treasure.

6. Therefore Thy Holy Word sustain,
Lord, let us know its powèr,
In every place its foe restrain,
And freely let it showèr:
And evermore / Our hearts will pour
True thanks upon Thine altar,
Our Rock and Lord! / May we Thy Word
Hold firm, nor from it falter.

—Anon., 1698; tr., M. Carver.

174

Tune: Ich dank dir, lieber Herre. 59. [*TLH* 334; *LW* 257; *LSB* 689]

1. Let me be Thine forever,
Thou faithful God and Lord;
Let me forsake Thee never,
Nor wander from Thy Word.
Lord, do not let me waver,
But give me steadfastness,
And for such grace forever
Thy holy Name I'll bless.

2. Lord Jesus, my Salvation,
My Light, my Life divine,
My only Consolation,
Oh, make me wholly Thine!
For Thou hast dearly bought me
With blood and bitter pain.
Let me, since Thou hast sought me,
Eternal life obtain.

3. And Thou, O Holy Spirit,
My Comforter and Guide,
Grant that in Jesus' merit
I always may confide,
Him to the end confessing
Whom I have known by faith.
Give me Thy constant blessing
And grant a Christian death.

—N. Selnecker, 1572, but sts. 2–3, Anon., 1688; tr., M. Loy, 1880, alt.

175

Tune: Herr Jesu Christ, meins Lebens Licht. 11. [*TLH* 288; *LW* 262; *LSB* 704]

1. O Christ, our true and only Light
Enlighten those who sit in night;
Let those afar now hear Thy voice
And in Thy fold with us rejoice.

2. Fill with the radiance of Thy grace
The souls now lost in error's maze
And all whom in their secret minds
Some dark delusion haunts and blinds.

3. Oh, gently call those gone astray
That they may find the saving way!
Let every conscience sore oppressed
In Thee find peace and heav'nly rest.

4. Oh, make the deaf to hear Thy Word
And teach the dumb to speak, dear Lord,
Who dare not yet the faith avow,
Though secretly they hold it now.

5. Shine on the darkened and the cold,
Recall the wand'rers to Thy fold,
Unite all those who walk apart,
Confirm the weak and doubting heart,

6. So they with us may evermore
Such grace with wond'ring thanks adore
And endless praise to Thee be giv'n
By all Thy Church in earth and heav'n.

—J. Heermann, 1630; tr., C. Winkworth, 1858, alt.

176

Tune: Erhalt uns, Herr, bei deinem Wort. 11. [*TLH* 261; *LW* 334; *LSB* 655]

1. Thine honor save, O Christ, our Lord!
Hear Zion's cries and help afford;
Destroy the wiles of mighty foes
Who now Thy Word and truth oppose.

2. Their craft and pomp indeed are great,
And of their pow'r they boast and prate;
Our hope they scornfully deride
And deem us nothing in their pride.

3. Forgive, O Lord, our sins forgive;
Grant us Thy grace and let us live.
Convince Thy foes throughout the land
That godless counsels shall not stand.

4. That Thou art with us, Lord, proclaim
And put our enemies to shame;
Confound them in their haughtiness
And help Thine own in their distress.

5. Preserve Thy little flock in peace,
Nor let Thy boundless mercy cease;
To all the world let it appear
That Thy true Church indeed is here.

—J. Heermann, 1630; tr., M. Loy, 1880, alt.

177

Tune: Verleih uns Frieden gnädiglich. 107. [p. 416; *or LW* 219*, *LSB* 778* (st. 1 only)]

1. Grant us Thy peace in mercy, Lord;
Peace in our times assure us!
None other could our help afford,
None other could fight for us,
But Thou, O our God, Thou only.

2. Give to our land and all authority
Peace and good government,
That under their guidance we may lead
An honest, peaceful, Christian existence
In all truth and God-pleasing devotion.
Amen.

—Trad., ad. M. Luther, 1529; st. 2, ad. Anon., 1573; tr., M. Carver.

178

Tune: Es ist das Heil uns kommen her. 49. [*TLH* 377; *LW* 355; *LSB* 555]

1. We men, O God, are all unsound,
Thy heav'nly things unheeding;
Thy will and law are too profound,
Our feeble minds exceeding.
Forever lost the world would be,
Hadst Thou not given graciously
Thy Word and Light to guide us.

2. So didst Thou send in days of old
To Israel Thy teachers,
That by their mouth Thy Law be told,
Thy will by holy preachers.
At last Thine own beloved Son
Came down, O God, from heaven's throne,
Thy saving truth to teach us.

3. For such great love we praise Thee, Lord,
And ask Thy Spirit's blessing,
That we may ever trust Thy Word,
And render true confession.
Grant that with meekness, love, and joy,
With honor we Thy Word employ,
Not as ours but Thine only.

4. Assist us lest the scornful flocks
From Holy Scripture turn us,
For such must die and change their mocks
To screams in error's furnace,
Give Thou Thy Word a thunder-blast
To lodge in us Thy doctrines fast
And dwell within us richly.

5. Lord, open Thou our hearts and ears,
That rightly we receive it,
And that in gladness, pains, and fears,
We always may believe it.
Grant that we hear it not alone,
But do it as it should be done,
And bear Thee fruit abundant.

6. The seed that lands upon the way
Is by the devil taken:
In rocky soil the Word scarce may
A goodly root awaken.
The seed that falls amongst the thorn
By worldly cares away is borne,
Amid earth's joys to perish.

7. Oh, help us, Lord, resemble here
That fertile, good foundation,
In virtues rich, with godly fear
Fulfilling our vocation,
With patience, plenteous fruit to bear,
And to preserve in hearts made fair
Thy teachings and Thy favors.

8. As long as here we dwell, may we
Avoid the path of sinning;
Grant us to fasten fast on Thee
Through pain and trial winning:
Eradicate the thorny herb,
Help us all earthly cares to curb,
And quash all wicked pleasures.

9. Thy Word, O Lord, let be always
A lamp to light our going,
Sustain its clear and flawless rays,
That we may thus be knowing
Its wisdom, strength, and help in need,
And neither life nor death may heed,
Unmoved therein confiding.

10. God, Father, to Thy glory spread
Abroad Thy Word and preaching,
O Jesus, make us to be led,
Enlightened by Thy teaching:
O Holy Ghost, in Thine elect
Make this Thy Word divine effect
Faith, hope, love, and forbearance.

—D. Denicke, †1680; tr. sts. 1–3, 5, J. T. Mueller, 1922, alt.; sts. rest, M. Carver.

Catechism

179

Tune: Herr Gott, erhalt uns für und für. 11. [p. 403; *or TLH* 261*; *LW* 334*; *LSB* 655*]

1. Lord, help us ever to retain
The Catechism's doctrine plain
As Luther taught the Word of Truth
In simple style to tender youth.

2. Help us Thy holy Law to learn,
To mourn our sin, and from it turn
In faith to Thee and to Thy Son
And Holy Spirit, Three in One.

3. Hear us, dear Father, when we pray
For needed help from day to day
That as Thy children we may live,
Whom Thou in Baptism didst receive.

4. Lord, when we fall and sin doth stain,
Absolve and lift us up again;
And through the Sacrament increase
Our faith till we depart in peace.

—L. Helmbold, 1594; tr., M. Loy, 1880, alt.

1. GOD'S LAW

180

Tune: Dies sind die heilgen zehn Gebot. 20. [*TLH* 287; *LW* 331; *LSB* 581]

1. That man a godly life might live,
God did these Ten Commandments give
By His true servant Moses, high
Upon the Mount Sinaï.
Kyrieleis!

2. I am thy Lord and God alone,
No other god beside Me own:
Put thy whole confidence in Me
And love Me e'er cordially.
Kyrieleis!

3. By idle word and speech profane
Take not My holy name in vain
And praise but that as good and true
Which I Myself say and do.
Kyrieleis!

4. Hallow the day which God hath blessed
That thou and all thy house may rest;
Keep hand and heart from labor free
That God may so work in thee.
Kyrieleis!

5. Give to thy parents honor due,
Be dutiful and loving, too,
And help them when their strength decays,
So shalt thou have length of days.
Kyrieleis!

6. In sinful wrath thou shalt not kill,
Nor hate nor render ill for ill;
Be patient and of gentle mood,
And to thy foe do thou good.
Kyrieleis!

7. Be faithful to thy marriage vows,
Thy heart give only to thy spouse;
Thy life keep pure and, lest thou sin,
Use temp'rance and discipline.
Kyrieleis!

8. Steal not; all usury abhor,
Nor wring their life-blood from the poor;
But open wide thy loving hand,
To all the poor in the land.
Kyrieleis!

9. Bear not false witness, nor belie
Thy neighbor by foul calumny.
Defend his innocence from blame;
With charity hide his shame.
Kyrieleis!

10. Thy neighbor's house desire thou not,
His wife, nor aught that he hath got,
But wish that his such good may be
As thy heart doth wish for thee.
Kyrieleis!

11. God these commandments gave therein
To show thee, child of man, thy sin
And make thee also well perceive
How man unto God should live.
Kyrieleis!

12. Help us, Lord Jesus Christ, for we
A Mediator have in Thee;
Our works cannot salvation gain;
They merit but endless pain.
Kyrieleis!

—M. Luther, 1524; tr., R. Massie, 1854, alt.

181

Tune: Mensch, willt du leben seliglich. 20. [p. 412; *or as* #180 *above*]

1. Wilt thou, O man, live happily,
And dwell with God eternally?
The Ten Commandments keep, for thus
Our God Himself biddeth us.
Kyrieleis!

2. I am thy Lord and God! take heed
Lest other gods do thee mislead;
Thy heart shall trust alone in Me,
Thou shalt My own kingdom be.
Kyrieleis!

3. Honor My name in word and deed,
And call on Me in time of need;
Hallow the Sabbath, that I may
Work in thy heart on that day.
Kyrieleis!

4. Obedient always, next to Me,
To father and to mother be;
Kill no man, but to wrath be slow;
Be true to thy marriage-vow.
Kyrieleis!

5. Steal not, nor do thy neighbor wrong
By bearing witness with false tongue;
Thy neighbor's wife desire thou not,
Nor grudge him aught he hath got.
Kyrieleis!

—M. Luther, 1525; tr., R. Massie, 1854, alt.

182

Tune: Erschienen ist der herrlich Tag. 21. [*TLH* 108; *LW* 147]

1. Almighty Lord of earth and heav'n,
The Ten Commandments Thou hast giv'n
Reveal how wicked I have been,
And make me dread the curse of sin.
Kyrieleis!

2. I've loved the creature more than Thee,
And sinned against Thy majesty;
My love and trust to Thee denied,
On self and man my soul relied.
Kyrieleis!

3. My lips have oft, from heart profane,
Employed Thy holy name in vain;
Forgetful of Thy cov'nant grace,
How seldom have I sought Thy face!
Kyrieleis!

4. In sinful cares, or work, or play,
I've often spent Thy holy day,
Despised Thy Word, strayed from Thy fold,
And left Thy benefits untold.
Kyrieleis!

5. I have not always sought to please
My parents and authorities;
Their faithful care I have disdained,
Nor served them with a will unfeigned.
Kyrieleis!

6. My neighbor little love I've shown,
But envied him and made him groan;
I've started quarrels, broken faith,
And sinned by vengefulness and wrath.
Kyrieleis!

7. Impurity I have desired,
And not to holiness aspired;
In food and drink I've frequently
Exceeded bounds of gluttony.
Kyrieleis!

8. I have not acted faithfully
As duty would demand of me;
I've gotten things by lawless deed,
And have not helped the poor in need.
Kyrieleis!

9. I've listened to blaspheming men,
And have not set them right again.
I have not always truth pursued,
Or pled the cause of rectitude.
Kyrieleis!

10. I've sought through seemly, false deceit
My neighbor out of wealth to cheat,
And with a smile deprive his hand
Of name, house, servant, beast, and land.
Kyrieleis!

11. Eternal God, Thou well dost see
The man who scorns Thy Law and Thee;
Thy wrath and curse shall be his wage,
Unto the third and fourth man's age.
Kyrieleis!

12. But thousand generations hence
May look for gracious recompense,
For those who love Thee, Lord, and hold
Thy Law above all joy and gold.
Kyrieleis!

13. Alas, no such resolve is here;
Naught good in me there doth appear;
No faith or store have I here set
By this Thy promise and Thy threat.
Kyrieleis!

14. My doings since mine infancy
Have wicked been continually;
Corrupted is my being whole,
From hardened head to straying sole.
Kyrieleis!

15. Who knows how oft he fails the right
Before his conscience pricks him quite?
Should I be brought to testify,
I could not one in thousands spy.
Kyrieleis!

16. Ah, Father, mark my misery;
What I have done, forgive it me!
Let grace to judgment be preferred;
Remove the curse I have incurred.
Kyrieleis!

17. Remember Jesus Christ, Thy Son,
Made on the cross a Cursèd One
For all my foul iniquity,
Which as His own He bore for me.
Kyrieleis!

18. Now as in Christ I am made fit,
Good works to do, I pray, commit
To me Thy Spirit's grace, that I
From every wicked thing may fly.
Kyrieleis!

19. So let me live as Thou dost will,
Resisting sinful passions till
The war be done and life abate;
Then take me through the narrow gate.
Kyrieleis!

—D. Denicke; tr. sts. 1–4, 16b, C. H. L. Schuette, †1926, alt.; sts. rest, M. Carver.

2. THE CHRISTIAN CREED

183

Tune: Wir glauben all an einen Gott, Schöpfer. 87. [*TLH* 251; *LW* 213; *LSB* 954]

1. We all believe in one true God,
Who created earth and heaven,
The Father, who to us in love
Hath the right of children given.
He both soul and body feedeth,
All we need He doth provide us;
He through snares and perils leadeth,
Watching that no harm betide us.
He careth for us day and night,
All things are governed by His might.

2. We all believe in Jesus Christ,
His own Son, our Lord, possessing
An equal Godhead, throne, and might,
Source of every grace and blessing;
Born of Mary, virgin mother,
By the power of the Spirit,
Made true man, our elder Brother,
That the lost might life inherit;
Was crucified for sinful men
And raised by God to life again.

3. We all confess the Holy Ghost,
Who sweet grace and comfort giveth
And with the Father and the Son
In eternal glory liveth;
Who the Church, His own creation,
Keeps in unity of spirit.
Here forgiveness and salvation
Daily come through Jesus' merit.
All flesh shall rise, and we shall be
In bliss with God eternally. Amen.

—Anon., ad. M. Luther, 1524; tr., *TLH,* 1941.

184

Tune: Wir glauben all an einen Gott, Vater. 87. [*TLH* 252; *LW* 212; *LSB* 953]

1. We all believe in one true God,
Father, Son, and Holy Ghost,
Ever-present Help in need,
Praised by all the heav'nly host,
By whose mighty pow'r alone
All is made and wrought and done.

2. We all believe in Jesus Christ,
Son of God and Mary's Son,
Who descended from His throne
And for us salvation won;
By whose cross and death are we
Rescued from all misery.

3. We all confess the Holy Ghost,
Who from both fore'er proceeds;
Who upholds and comforts us
In all trials, fears, and needs.
Blest and holy Trinity,
Praise forever be to Thee!

—T. Clausnitzer, 1668; tr., C. Winkworth, 1863, alt.

3. THE HOLY OUR FATHER

185

Tune: Vater unser im Himmelreich. 44. [*TLH* 458; *LW* 234; *LSB* 766]

1. Our Father, Thou in heav'n above,
Who biddest us to dwell in love,
As brethren of one family,
To cry in every need to Thee,
Teach us no thoughtless words to say,
But from our inmost heart to pray.

2. Thy name be hallowed. Help us, Lord,
In purity to keep Thy Word,
That to the glory of Thy name
We walk before Thee free from blame.
Let no false doctrine us pervert;
All poor, deluded souls convert.

3. Thy kingdom come. Thine let it be
In time and in eternity.
Let Thy good Spirit e'er be nigh
Our hearts with graces to supply.
Break Satan's power, defeat his rage;
Preserve Thy Church from age to age.

4. Thy gracious will on earth be done
As 'tis in heav'n before Thy throne;
Obedience in our weal and woe
And patience in all grief bestow.
Curb flesh and blood and every ill
That sets itself against Thy will.

5. Give us this day our daily bread
And let us all be clothed and fed.
From war and strife be our Defense,
From famine and from pestilence,
That we may live in godly peace,
Free from all care and avarice.

6. Forgive our sins, Lord, we implore,
Remove from us their burden sore,
As we their trespasses forgive
Who by offenses us do grieve.
Thus let us dwell in charity
And serve our brother willingly.

7. Into temptations lead us not.
When evil foes against us plot
And vex our souls on every hand,
Oh, give us strength that we may stand
Firm in the faith, a well-armed host,
Through comfort of the Holy Ghost!

8. From evil, Lord, deliver us;
The times and days are perilous.
Redeem us from eternal death,
And when we yield our dying breath,
Console us, grant us calm release,
And take our souls to Thee in peace.

9. Amen, that is, So shall it be.
Confirm our faith and hope in Thee
That we may doubt not, but believe
What here we ask we shall receive.
Thus in Thy name and at Thy word
We say: Amen. Oh, hear us, Lord!

—M. Luther, 1539; tr., *TLH*, 1941.

4. HOLY BAPTISM

186

Tune: Christ unser Herr zum Jordan kam. 77. [*ELHB* 401; *LW* 223; *LSB* 406]

1. To Jordan came our Lord the Christ,
To do God's pleasure willing,
And there was by Saint John baptized,
All righteousness fulfilling;
There did He consecrate a bath
To wash away transgression,
And quench the bitterness of death
By His own blood and Passion;
He would a new life give us.

2. So hear ye all, and well perceive
What God doth call Baptism,
And what a Christian should believe
Who error shuns and schism:
That we should water use, the Lord
Declareth it His pleasure;
Not simple water, but the Word
And Spirit without measure;—
He is the true Baptizer.

3. To show us this, He hath His word
With signs and symbols given;
On Jordan's banks was plainly heard
The Father's voice from heaven:
"This is My well-beloved Son,
In whom My soul delighteth;
Hear Him." Yea, hear Him every one,
Whom He Himself inviteth,
Hear and obey His teaching.

4. In tender manhood God the Son
In Jordan's water standeth;
The Holy Ghost from heaven's throne
In dovelike form descendeth;
That thus the truth be not denied,
Nor should our faith e'er waver,
That the Three Persons all preside,
At Baptism's holy laver,
And dwell with the believer.

5. Thus Jesus His disciples sent:
Go, teach ye every nation,
That, lost in sin, they must repent,
And flee from condemnation;
He that believes and is baptized,
Shall thereby have salvation;
A new-born man he is in Christ,
Freed from death and damnation,
He shall inherit heaven.

6. Who in this mercy hath not faith
Nor aught therein discerneth,
Is yet in sin, condemned to death
And fire that ever burneth;
His holiness avails him not,
Nor aught which he is doing;
His inborn sin brings all to naught,
And maketh sure his ruin;
Himself he cannot succor.

7. The eye of sense alone is dim,
And nothing sees but water;
Faith sees Christ Jesus, and in Him
The Lamb ordained for slaughter;
It sees the cleansing fountain, red
With the dear blood of Jesus,
Which from the sins, inherited
From fallen Adam, frees us,
And from our own misdoings.

—M. Luther, 1541; tr., R. Massie, 1854, alt.

187

Tune: Es ist das Heil uns kommen her. 49. [*TLH* 377; *LW* 355; *LSB* 555]

1. Ye baptized people, one and all,
 Who know your God in heaven,
 Who have received a holy call,
 To you Christ's name is given.
 Forget ye not, but ponder well
 The precious gifts no tongue can tell,
 The blessing of Baptism.

2. Ye were before your day of birth,
 Indeed, from your conception,
 Condemned and lost with all the earth,
 None good, without exception.
 For like your parents' flesh and blood,
 Turned inward from the highest Good,
 Ye constantly denied Him.

3. Your soul and body were soaked through,
 With pois'nous sin pervaded,
 No more were ye God's children true,
 His image long had faded
 Which our Creator did instill
 When He made Adam, pure of will,
 Full of His light and splendor.

4. The wrath, the curse, and endless hell,
 Misfortune and all anguish
 Upon their heels then quickly fell
 And caused you all to languish;
 Each man was Satan's wretched slave,
 And servant destined for the grave,
 Held in his dungeon captive.

5. But all of that was washed away—
 Immersed and drowned forever.
 The bath of your baptismal day
 Restored again whatever
 Old Adam and his sin destroyed
 And all our wicked selves employed,
 According to our nature.

6. From sin this washing sets us free
 And heavn'ly beauty giveth.
 Those once in Satan's tyranny
 God, loosing thus, receiveth
 As His own sons into His care,
 And that to which His Son is heir
 They too with Him inherit.

7. Our sinful nature is renewed,
 The curse of God is lifted;
 By choicest blessings thus endued,
 And with the Spirit gifted,
 We unto sin are pledged to die
 And by the pow'r of God on high
 The gates of hell can conquer.

8. Here we with Jesus Christ are clad,
 His righteousness receiving,
 Which covers what in us is bad,
 Our innocence achieving;
 His holy blood, for sinners spilt,
 Releases us from sin and guilt,
 And we with God find favor.

9. O wondrous work, O sacred bath,
 O water thou of blessing,
 The world nowhere thy equal hath,
 Such healing grace possessing.
 Thou hast indeed a pow'r divine,
 According to God's own design,
 And with His Word connected.

10. Thou art no water such as we
 Can draw from well or river.
 In thee the life of God we see,
 Who is of grace the Giver.
 His Holy Spirit in thee dwells,
 Who every evil lust dispels
 That in our hearts would linger.

11. O Christians, bear this well in mind,
And thank the Lord sincerely
For all the gifts that here ye find,
And that ye prize so dearly.
When nothing else can soothe the soul,
These gifts lend comfort till the goal
Of life on earth appeareth.

12. So use it well! Ye are made new—
In Christ a new creation!
As faithful Christians, live and do,
In Christ keep your vocation,
Until that day when ye possess
His glorious robe of righteousness
To dress your souls forever!

—P. Gerhardt, 1676; tr. sts. 1, 7–11, H. Brueckner, 1916;
sts. 2, 5, 12, J. Vieker, 2004, alt.; sts. rest, M. Carver.

188

Tune: Nun freut euch, lieben Christen. 49. [*TLH* 124; *LW* 353; *LSB* 556]

1. O Father, Son, and Holy Ghost,
O God of bounteous giving:
To Thee be every glorious boast
And thanks while I am living,
Since Thou by grace and for my cure,
Hast washed me in Thy waters pure,
My sinfulness absolving.

2. Lord, I confess that I was raised
From my conception sinning,
A child of wrath, I never praised
Thy name from the beginning;
I know that I by nature lack
All fear of Thee, and turn my back,
God, on Thy Word and counsel.

3. O Father, when I was forlorn
And lost, devoid of merit,
Yet Thou didst cause me to be born
Anew by Thy good Spirit;
Thy holy washing then did prove
The channel of Thy soothing love
To cleanse my soul's uncleanness.

4. Lord Jesus Christ, Thy precious blood
Has cleansed me from transgression,
And rendered now this gracious flood
The pow'r to grant remission
From curses due my inborn stain—
The Father's favor I regain
Once forfeited by Adam.

5. O Holy Ghost! my thanks to Thee
I give for this dear treasure;
Behold, I now possess in me
Thy witness in rich measure.
And thus my Maker now I may
With confidence address and say
Rejoicing: Abba, Father!

6. Since in this Baptism I have donned
And wear Christ Jesus fully,
Let not the lies, by Satan spawned,
My mind deceive or sully;
For those who are God's temple pure
Shall 'gainst the wicked foe endure
Unharmed within Thy favor.

7. O Lord, this worthy righteousness
Which Thou hast freely given
Let never once in my distress
From memory be driven,
But to my heart new courage lend,
That evermore I may depend
Upon Thy sworn assistance.

8. In Baptism I am also bound
To serve Thee with due action,
So let in me no sin be found
To be the ruling faction;
Grant me obedience ever new
For all Thy blessings good and true,
For I this pledge have taken.

9. May I receive Thy pardon kind
Whene'er I stray in weakness;
Oh, do not store it in Thy mind!
Grant grace, and give me meekness,
Unswervingly with Thee to stay,
Until Thou take this soul away
To live to Thee forever.

—J. Gesenius, 1672; tr., M. Carver.

189

Tune: Was mein Gott will, das gscheh. 83. [*LW* 414; *LSB* 714 (mel.); *or TLH* 437* (iso.)]

1. Lord, make us all as children small,
A clean and new creation,
By Thy baptismal waters call
And build Thy chosen nation—
For they, Lord Christ, / Who are baptized,
From sin to Thee are given,
So when they die, / We need not cry,
For they are Thine in heaven.

—T. Blaurer, 1540; tr., M. Carver.

190

Tune: Liebster Jesu, wir sind hier. 34. [*TLH* 300; *LW* 202; *LSB* 904]

1. Dearest Jesus, we are here,
Gladly Thy command obeying;
With this child we now draw near
In accord with Thine own saying
That to Thee it shall be given,
As a child and heir of heaven.

2. Yea, Thy word is clear and plain,
And we would obey it duly:
"He who is not born again,
Heart and life renewing truly,
Born of water and the Spirit,
Can My kingdom not inherit."

3. Therefore hasten we to Thee,
In our arms this infant bearing;
Let us here Thy glory see,
Let this child, Thy mercy sharing,
In Thine arms be shielded ever,
Thine on earth and Thine forever.

4. Wash it, Jesus, in Thy blood,
From the sin-stain of its nature;
Let it rise from out this flood
Clothed in Thee, a newborn creature;
May it, washed as Thou hast bidden,
In Thine innocence be hidden.

5. Turn its darkness into light,
To Thy grace receive and save it;
Heal the Serpent's venomed bite
In the font where now we lave it;
Here let flow a Jordan river
And from Leprosy deliver.

6. Gracious Head, Thy member own;
Shepherd, take Thy lamb, and feed it;
Prince of Peace, make here Thy throne;
Way of Life, to heaven lead it;
Precious Vine, let nothing sever,
From Thy side this branch forever.

7. Now into Thy heart we pour
Pray'rs that from our hearts proceeded.
Our petitions heav'nward soar;
May our warm desires be heeded!
Write the name we now have given,
Write it in the book of heaven.

—B. Schmolck, 1704; tr., C. Winkworth, 1863, alt.

191

Tune: Christ unser Herr zum Jordan kam. 77. [*LW* 223; *LSB* 406]

1. O God, I had no will or pow'r
To bring myself salvation,
But Thou didst send Thy cleansing show'r
And wash me of transgression;
This to the eye Thou hast disclosed
By plain and tactile token;
O Father, Son, and Holy Ghost,
Thy loving grace here spoken
All other things surpasses!

2. Thou didst mine infant form accept
When I was brought before Thee,
Thy bond of gracious favor wrapped
My soul, which did deplore Thee.
Thou couldst have justly in Thy scorn
Both punished and despised me,
Yet, mighty God! Thou hast forborne,
And lovingly baptized me
Into Thy blest communion.

3. Now by This bath I am Thy child,
An heir of grace securely,
Though sometimes tempted and defiled
Thou wilt defend me surely.
A childlike faith Thou givest me;
I come into Thy temple,
And pour my heart out, God, to Thee,
In pray'r by Thine example,
Assured that Thou wilt hear me.

4. But I am also pledged and bound,
Pure conscience to be keeping,
With faith's assurance as my ground
And diligence unsleeping:
Thee as my God I shall confess
Forever, and none other,
Joined with Thy precious Church I bless
And name Thee Lord and Father,
One God with Son and Spirit.

5. I have renounced the wicked foe
With all his works and cunning;
This bond that chased him doth bestow
That I may him be shunning;
O God, I am Thy temple now,
Reborn and fresh-anointed,
That I may do good works which Thou
For me hast here appointed,
And with Thy lips commanded.

6. The old man now must pass away
The new must now be living,
With wicked lusts of yesterday
Still bitter is my striving.
I cannot help but grow in good,
Thy will shall be my doing,
To ponder it as well I should,
That fruit may be ensuing
Alone by Thine empow'ring.

7. God, Father, Son and Spirit, grant
That I may doubt Thee never;
With peace and joy my spirit plant
Inside this bond forever,
That I the devil's works may hate,
Stamp out each wicked pleasure,
Nor Christ neglect to imitate,
But still defend this treasure,
Till I possess Thy kingdom.

—J. Bornschürer, 1676; tr., M. Carver.

5. HOLY ABSOLUTION

192

Tune: Wenn wir in höchsten Nöten sein. 11. [*TLH* 141; *LW* 363; *LSB* 615]

1. Yea, as I live, Jehovah saith,
I would not have the sinner's death,
But that he turn from error's ways,
Repent, and live through endless days.

2. To us therefore Christ gave command:
"Go forth and preach in every land;
Bestow on all My pard'ning grace
Who will repent and mend their ways.

3. "All those whose sins ye thus remit
I truly pardon and acquit,
And those whose sins ye do retain
Condemned and guilty shall remain.

4. "What ye shall bind, that bound shall be;
What ye shall loose, that shall be free;
Unto My Church the keys are giv'n
To ope and close the gates of heav'n.

5. "They who believe when ye proclaim
The joyful tidings in My name
That I for them My blood have shed,
Are free from guilt and Judgment dread."

6. The words which absolution give
Are His who died that we might live;
The minister whom Christ has sent
Is but His humble instrument.

7. However great our sin may be,
The Absolution sets us free,
Appointed by God's own dear Son
To bring the pardon He has won.

8. When ministers lay on their hands,
Absolved by Christ the sinner stands;
He who by grace the Word believes
The purchase of His blood receives.

9. This is the pow'r of Holy Keys,
It binds and doth again release;
The Church retains them at her side,
Our mother and Christ's holy Bride.

10. Let those who stings of conscience bear,
Whom sin would drive to dark despair,
To Jesus come with trustful mind,
And peace in absolution find.

11. All praise, eternal Son, to Thee
For absolution full and free,
In which Thou showest forth Thy grace;
From false indulgence guard our race.

12. Praise God the Father and the Son
And Holy Spirit, Three in One,
As 'twas, is now, and so shall be
World without end, eternally!

—N. Herman, 1560; tr., M. Loy, 1880, alt.

193

Tune: Erhalt uns, Herr, bei deinem Wort. 11. [*TLH* 261; *LW* 334; *LSB* 655]

1. O faithful God, thanks be to Thee
Who dost forgive iniquity.
Thou grantest help in sin's distress,
And soul and body dost Thou bless.

2. Thy servant now declares to me:
"Thy sins are all forgiven thee.
Depart in peace, but sin no more,
And e'er My pard'ning grace adore."

3. O Lord, we bless Thy gracious heart,
For Thou Thyself dost heal our smart
Through Christ our Savior's precious blood,
Which for the sake of sinners flowed.

4. Give us Thy Spirit, peace afford
Now and forever, gracious Lord.
Preserve to us till life is spent
Thy holy Word and Sacrament.

—N. Selnecker, 1572; tr., *TLH*, 1941.

6. THE HOLY SUPPER

194

Tune: Nun freut euch, lieben Christen. 49.
[*TLH* 124; *LW* 353; *LSB* 556; *or TLH* 406*; *LW* 248*; *LSB* 625*]

1. Lord Jesus Christ, Thou living Bread,
May I for mine possess Thee.
I would with heav'nly food be fed;
Descend, refresh, and bless me.
Now make me meet for Thee, O Lord;
Now, humbly by my heart implored,
Grant me Thy grace and mercy.

2. Thou me to pastures green dost guide,
To quiet waters lead me;
Thy table Thou dost well provide
And from Thy hand dost feed me.
Sin, weakness, and infirmity
Am I; O Savior, give to me
The cup of Thy salvation.

3. O Bread of Heav'n, my soul's Delight,
For full and free remission
With pray'r I come before Thy sight,
In sorrow and contrition.
With faith adorn my soul that I
May to Thy table now draw nigh
With Thine own preparation.

4. O Lord, now tear from out my heart
All hate and bitter feeling,
Let me detest with holy smart
The sins about me reeling;
O paschal Lamb on roasting coal,
O royal Bridegroom of my soul,
Let me enjoy Thee truly!

5. I merit not Thy favor, Lord,
Sin now upon me lieth;
Beneath my burden, self-abhorred,
To Thee my spirit crieth.
In all my grief this comforts me,
That Thou on sinners graciously,
Lord Jesus, hast compassion.

6. I am a soul death-sick in sin;
Impart Thy hand to heal me!
Unscale my heart, all blind within;
Thy favor let avail me.
I am condemned; have mercy, Lord!
Am lost; oh, let me be restored;
By utter grace assist me!

7. Oh, come, Thou Bridegroom, unto me
My soul take for Thy dwelling;
I long to kiss Thee endlessly,
With marriage-joys excelling!
Oh, be Thy sweetest splendor shared,
Which for my soul Thou hast prepared,
And still my spirit's crying!

8. Lord Jesus Christ, Thou living Bread,
Come now, Thyself to give me!
Before me poured, Thou Blood once shed,
Come, hasten and revive me!
Thou art in me, and I in Thee,
And, with Thyself adorning me,
I shall awake in heaven.

—J. Rist, 1654; tr. st. 1–3, 5, A. T. Russell, 1851, alt.; sts. rest, M. Carver.

195

Tune: Gott sei gelobet und gebenedeiet. 90. [*TLH* 313; *LW* 238; *LSB* 617]

1. O Lord, we praise Thee, bless Thee, and adore Thee,
In thanksgiving bow before Thee.
Thou with Thy body and Thy blood didst nourish
Our weak souls that they may flourish:
Kyrieleison!
May Thy body, Lord, born of Mary,
That our sins and sorrow did carry,
And Thy blood for us plead
In all trial, fear, and need:
Kyrieleison!

2. Thy holy body into death was given,
Life to win for us in heaven.
No greater love than this to Thee could bind us;
May this feast thereof remind us!
Kyrieleison!
Lord, Thy kindness did so constrain Thee
That Thy blood should bless and sustain me.
All our debt Thou hast paid;
Peace with God once more is made:
Kyrieleison!

3. May God bestow on us His grace and favor
To please Him with our behavior
And live as brethren here in love and union
Nor repent this blest Communion!
Kyrieleison!
Let not Thy good Spirit forsake us;
Grant that heav'nly-minded He make us;
Give Thy Church, Lord, to see
Days of peace and unity:
Kyrieleison!

—M. Luther, 1524, but st. 1 after Anon., 15th c.; tr., *TLH,* 1941, alt.

196

Morning Hymn Before Communion

Tune: Freu dich sehr, o meine Seele. 66. [*TLH* 61; *LW* 28; *LSB* 347]

1. Praise the Lord, the day is risen
When with Jesus I am bound,
When, set free from debtor's prison,
In God's favor I am found.
Praise the Lord! the day is come
For the wedding of the Lamb,
When God deigns that life in heaven
In His Son entire be given.

2. God, this morn I come before Thee
As Thine own beloved child,
With my flesh and soul adore Thee,
Hast'ning to Thy bosom mild;
Abba, Father! Me endow
Worthily to meet Thee now
As Thy dinner-guest invited,
And with Jesus be united.

3. Christ, Thou Lamb of God, oh, hear me,
Thou who all my sin didst bear:
Bridegroom, with Thy pledge draw near me!
Shepherd, find Thy sheep with care,
In Thy goodness I confide:
To green pastures be my Guide,
Feed me for my good eternal,
With Thy flesh and blood supernal.

4. Holy Ghost, I now embrace Thee;
Now and ever near abide;
Nothing suffer hence to chase Thee,
Grant me, with Thy help allied,
For God's glory and my good,
To partake of heav'nly food,
Christ to heed in my behavior,
And in death to greet my Savior.

5. At Thy feet, O God, I'm lying!
May Thy love adorn my soul;
Jesus' blood to me supplying,
Make me worthy, pure, and whole,
Help me, Father heart, by faith,
Help me, Jesus, by Thy death,
Help me, Spirit, Consolation,
To obtain Thy blest salvation.

—Ä. J. von Schwarzburg-Rudolstadt, †1706; tr., M. Carver.

197

Tune: Herr Jesu Christ, du höchstes Gut. 49.
[p. 404; *or TLH* 306*; *LW* 246*; *LSB* 622*]

1. Lord Jesus Christ, Thou hast prepared
A feast for our salvation,
It is Thy body and Thy blood;
And at Thy invitation
As weary souls, with sin oppressed,
We come to Thee for needed rest,
For comfort and for pardon.

2. Although Thou didst to heav'n ascend,
Where angel hosts are dwelling,
And in Thy presence they behold
Thy glory all excelling,
And though Thy people shall not see
Thy glory and Thy majesty
Till dawns the Judgment morning,

3. Yet, Savior, Thou art not confined
To any habitation,
But Thou art present everywhere
And with Thy congregation.
Firm as a rock this truth shall stand,
Unmoved by any daring hand
Or subtle craft and cunning.

4. We eat this bread and drink this cup,
Thy precious Word believing
That Thy true body and Thy blood
Our lips are here receiving.
This word remains forever true,
And there is naught Thou canst not do;
For Thou, Lord, art almighty.

5. Though reason cannot understand,
Yet faith this truth embraces;
Thy body, Lord, is everywhere
At once in many places.
How this can be I leave to Thee,
Thy Word alone sufficeth me,
I trust its truth unfailing.

6. Lord, I believe what Thou hast said,
Help me when doubts assail me;
Remember that I am but dust
And let my faith not fail me.
Thy Supper in this vale of tears
Refreshes me and stills my fears
And is my priceless treasure.

7. Grant that we worthily receive
Thy Supper, Lord, our Savior,
And, truly grieving o'er our sins,
May prove by our behavior
That we are thankful for Thy grace
And day by day may run our race,
In holiness increasing.

8. For Thy consoling Supper, Lord,
Be praised throughout all ages!
Preserve it, for in every place
The world against it rages.
Grant that this Sacrament may be
A blessèd comfort unto me
When living and when dying.

—S. Kinner, 1638; tr., E. Cronenwett, 1880, alt.

198

Tune: Gott sei gelobet und gebenedeiet. 90. [*TLH* 313; *LW* 238; *LSB* 617]

1. Lord Jesus Christ, my faithful Shepherd, hear me,
Feed me with Thy grace, draw near me!
In Thee alone are healing, life, and heaven:
All I need by Thee is given.
Kyrieleison!
Thy poor sheep, Lord, bring to Thy fountain,
With great joy on Zion's high mountain.
Lead us by waters clear,
Whence our life is flowing e'er.
Kyrieleison!

2. No other food or drink such pow'r containeth,
Christ, the Food of Life, sustaineth.
No one who eats of Thee shall suffer hunger,
Nor such woe remember longer.
Kyrieleison!
Lord Thou art life's Fountain outspringing,
Unto Thee my vessel I'm bringing,
With Thy peace fill it full,
Grant Thy blessing to my soul.
Kyrieleison!

3. All my transgressions let me now be mourning;
Set faith's fire within me burning—
The one, true faith by which, Lord, I receive Thee.
In Thy merits I will leave me.
Kyrieleison!
Give to me a heartfelt repentance,
Hating sin and fearing its sentence,
Keep me meek and contrite,
Let me never from Thy sight.
Kyrieleison!

4. My conscience, Lord, is full of stain and sorrow,
Let me but a droplet borrow
From all the crimson wounds of Thine affliction,
Giv'n Thee at Thy crucifixion,
Kyrieleison!
Set my heart astir now inside me
And with robes of pureness provide me;
Trusting Thee, by Thy blood,
I shall stand before my God!
Kyrieleison!

5. Doctors are needed by the sick and ailing—
Earnestly we long for healing!
Sweet Jesus, see, how I am wounded vastly
With transgression deep and ghastly!
Kyrieleison!
Unto Thee, Physician, I'm turning,
Hope for whom my spirit is yearning!
God-and-Man, lend Thine aid!
Else I shall be truly dead.
Kyrieleison!

6. Now in Thy mercy to Thy rest are bidden
All the weary, heavy-laden,
Here hast Thou granted all their sins true pardon,
And freed them from every burden:
Kyrieleison!
Oh, come with Thy hand now to loose me
From these iron bands that abuse me,
Set me from sorrows free,
Give me strength to follow Thee.
Kyrieleison!

7. Thou fain wouldst have the heart and soul to heed Thee,
Take and make me Thine, I plead Thee!
Thou art the Vine and I the branch. Oh grant me
In Thyself to grow! There plant me!
Kyrieleison!
Mine are only scandal and sickness,
But in Thee they vanish with quickness,
Mine are hell and unrest,
But in Thee, Lord, I am blest.
Kyrieleison!

8. Come, Crown of Beauty, take me for Thy dwelling,
Jesus, come, all sin dispelling!
Friend of my heart, I long to greet and kiss Thee,
Yea, in faith and love embrace Thee.
Kyrieleison!
Come, Thy loving-kindness to give me,
Naught shall have the pow'r to aggrieve me;
Slow of wrath, kind Thou art;
Come, Thy grace and love impart!
Kyrieleison!

9. These are the flow'rets that alone can cure me,
And of needful strength assure me,
That I may cast away all wicked pleasure,
And serve Thee, my dearest Treasure!
Kyrieleison!
What I need in Thee I am given
Through Thy fount of mercy from heaven;
May I e'er dwell in Thee,
And forever Thou in me!
Kyrieleison!

—J. Heermann, 1630; tr. sts. 1, 6, 7, based on C. Winkworth, 1863, alt.; sts. rest, M. Carver.

199

Tune: Wie schön leuchtet der Morgenstern. 86. [*TLH* 546; *LW* 325; *LSB* 395]

1. Lord Jesus, thanks and praise be Thine,
Who givest in this meal divine
What doth the spirit nourish;
With bread and wine Thy flesh and blood
Are given for our certain good,
That, feeding, hearts may flourish;
Then, we / In Thee
May be holy, / Living solely
As Thou willest:
So with good our soul Thou fillest.

2. O Lord, let us not ill conceive
Thy precious Supper but believe
Its mighty consolation:
That we may by this Bread of Life
Still hold, despite all need and strife,
The Rock of our Salvation:
So we / Owe Thee,
Lord ascended, / Praise unended,
Till Thy bidding
Draws us hence to heaven's wedding.

3. Oh, that we may but persevere
In hope and trust, awaiting here
Salvation's blest appearing,
When we shall bid this earth farewell,
And at God's heav'nly table dwell,
And see Him without fearing,
Neatly, / Sweetly
With Him dining / And reclining
At His pleasure,
Satisfied to fullest measure.

—B. Derschau, †1639; tr., M. Carver.

200

Tune: Nun lob, mein Seel, den Herren. 93. [*TLH* 34; *LW* 453; *LSB* 820]

1. Lord Jesus, my heart's Pleasure!
No rest or peace could ever be
Without that holy treasure
Which Thou hast won and given me;
My heart, Thy laws profaning,
And daily proving worse,
In weakness would be waning
And as a mist disperse,
Except faith's hand did hold me
To Thee, Thy cross and death,
And in true tears enfold me
For Thy last painful breath!

2. Thou knowest all my suff'ring
And wicked Satan's craft and art,
Whose jaws are always off'ring
My tender soul to tear apart,
He has a thousand ruses
To lure my soul from Thee:
His lying tongue accuses
And melts my certainty,
He soon makes my affection
And mind from Thee estranged,
And drives me to rejection
Of gifts by Thee arranged.

3. Such misery to banish,
Lord, Thou hast decked Thy table here
Where cares are made to vanish
And hearts are filled with joy sincere.
Thou giv'st for life's restoring
Thy precious flesh and blood,
Into my heart outpouring
Thy Word of truth and good:
"O come," Thou say'st, "draw nigh Me,
Approach Me unafraid,
Receive what I supply Thee,
Thy healing here is spread."

4. "Here with the bread is present
My body which was given up
To cross and pain unpleasant,
For all Thy sins. And in this cup
Is what was shed to save Thee
And flows where flows the wine:
It is My blood I gave Thee
In humbleness divine.
Receive this twofold token,
My merits, too, hereby,
And trust what I have spoken:
'Thy Savior true am I.'"

5. Thy mem'ry, Lord, I'm keeping
As long as I have life and breath
Until the day when, sleeping,
I lie within the grave of death.
O Lord, I see Thy yearning,
To give me endless life:
The gruesome cross not spurning,
Nor prongs of sorrow rife
That tortured, shamed, and pricked Thee
And pierced Thy guiltless heart.
Now death cannot afflict me,
It has no pain and smart.

6. Thou also hast directed
That everything to strengthen faith
Should be from Thee expected,
Nor need we doubt or fear for death:
Thy ransom hath acquitted
All sinners of their crime
In all the world committed
In every place and time;
For erstwhile adversaries,
A sacrifice approved
By God, who all things carries,
And in whom all are moved.

7. O Lord, uphold my thinking,
Which, prone to fraud and falsity,
Would else be quickly sinking
In lies and doubts concerning Thee.
Incline Thy hand to give me,
With brightness from Thy face,
Thy gifts, and so receive me
Into Thy pledge of grace,
By eating and by drinking—
O feast that quells all fear!
For all whose trust is shrinking—
What comfort, Thou art here!

8. O Lord, we hear Thy calling
That summons all from east and west,
From Satan's sieges crawling,
To gather in Thy lap of rest.
Oh, help, Lord, help us quickly
Return to Thee, who art
Disposed to heal the sickly
And aid our throbbing heart!
Give holy thirst and longing
For this Thy Meal of love,
Till we, as princes thronging
Shall fill Thy halls above.

—P. Gerhardt, 1667; tr., M. Carver.

201

Tune: O Welt, ich muß dich lassen. 31. [*TLH* 126; *LW* 85; *LSB* 880]

1. I come, O Christ, invited,
With Thee to be united
Here at Thy feast of grace.
But countless sins that stain me
In fear and awe detain me
In coming, Lord, before Thy face.

2. Though I am sore encumbered
With hosts of sins unnumbered,
Like all the sons of man,
Be Thou my Mediator,
Appease my Lord Creator,
And let Thy grace remove the ban.

3. I will repent contritely;
Lord, deal with me most lightly,
From sin my soul now cure.
Thy deep humiliation
Hath wrought my soul's salvation;
So let Thy mercy e'er endure.

4. In faith and trust abiding,
My sinful soul is hiding
Within Thy wounds in peace.
Help, Christ, Thou valiant Winner!
Say to me, Amen, sinner,
From sin thy soul I will release.

—Anon., Dresden, 1694; tr., F. W. Herzberger, 1915, alt.

202

Tune: Wer weiß, wie nahe mir. 45.
[*TLH* 65; *LSB* 598; *or TLH* 315*; *LW* 242*; *LSB* 618*]

1. I come, O Savior, to Thy table,
For weak and weary is my soul;
Thou, Bread of Life, alone art able
To satisfy and make me whole:
Lord, may Thy body and Thy blood
Be for my soul the highest good!

2. Oh, grant that I in manner worthy
May now approach Thy heav'nly Board
And, as I lowly bow before Thee,
Look only unto Thee, O Lord!
Lord, may Thy body and Thy blood
Be for my soul the highest good!

3. Unworthy though I am, O Savior,
Because I have a sinful heart,
Yet Thou Thy lamb wilt banish never,
For Thou my faithful Shepherd art:
Lord, may Thy body and Thy blood
Be for my soul the highest good!

4. Oh, let me loathe all sin forever
As death and poison to my soul
That I through willful sinning never
May see Thy judgment take its toll!
Lord, may Thy body and Thy blood
Be for my soul the highest good!

5. Thy heart is filled with fervent yearning
That sinners may salvation see
Who, Lord, to Thee in faith are turning;
So I, a sinner, come to Thee.
Lord, may Thy body and Thy blood
Be for my soul the highest good!

6. Weary am I and heavy laden,
With sin my soul is sore oppressed;
Receive me graciously and gladden
My heart, for I am now Thy guest.
Lord, may Thy body and Thy blood
Be for my soul the highest good!

7. Thou here wilt find a heart most lowly
That humbly falls before Thy feet,
That duly weeps o'er sin, yet solely
Thy merit pleads, as it is meet.
Lord, may Thy body and Thy blood
Be for my soul the highest good!

8. By faith I call Thy holy Table
The testament of Thy deep love;
For, lo, thereby I now am able
To see how love Thy heart doth move.
Lord, may Thy body and Thy blood
Be for my soul the highest good!

9. What higher gift can we inherit?
It is faith's bond and solid base;
It is the strength of heart and spirit,
The covenant of hope and grace.
Lord, may Thy body and Thy blood
Be for my soul the highest good!

10. This feast is manna, wealth abounding
Unto the poor, to weak ones pow'r,
To angels joy, to hell confounding,
And life for me in death's dark hour.
Lord, may Thy body and Thy blood
Be for my soul the highest good!

11. The weakened faith thou dost empower,
Thou sweet, celestial feast of love.
Then art Thou truly my strong tower,
When frailty me from Christ would move.
Lord, may Thy body and Thy blood
Be for my soul the highest good!

12. Like as a child cries for its mother
And fain would at her bosom lie
I long for Jesus like no other,
Who lays me here beside Him nigh.
Lord, may Thy body and Thy blood
Be for my soul the highest good!

13. Thou art the Cure and I the canker,
Thou art my Father, I Thy child,
My heart's Thy ship, Thou art my Anchor
My Rudder, Sail, and Zephyr mild.
Lord, may Thy body and Thy blood
Be for my soul the highest good!

14. Thy body, giv'n for me, O Savior,
Thy blood which Thou for me didst shed,
These are my life and strength forever,
By them my hungry soul is fed.
Lord, may Thy body and Thy blood
Be for my soul the highest good!

15. With Thee, Lord, I am now united;
I live in Thee and Thou in me.
No sorrow fills my soul, delighted
It finds its only joy in Thee.
Lord, may Thy body and Thy blood
Be for my soul the highest good!

16. Who can condemn me now? For surely
The Lord is nigh, who justifies.
No hell I fear, and thus securely,
With Jesus I to heaven rise.
Lord, may Thy body and Thy blood
Be for my soul the highest good!

17. Though death may threaten with disaster,
It cannot rob me of my cheer;
For He who is of death the Master
With aid and comfort e'er is near.
Lord, may Thy body and Thy blood
Be for my soul the highest good!

18. Thy holy flesh hath pow'r to wake me
And raise me out of death's abyss,
No darksome grave therefore can shake me,
For Thou shalt change it into bliss.
Lord, may Thy body and Thy blood
Be for my soul the highest good!

19. My flesh, tho' dead, again shall flourish,
Though long consumed, it yet shall live
Thy flesh which here doth feed and nourish,
New life to it again will give.
Lord, may Thy body and Thy blood
Be for my soul the highest good!

20. Thus every ache is vanished fully,
For now my heart the taste doth know
Of Jesus, precious, sweet, and holy,
The taste that sweetens every woe:
Lord, may Thy body and Thy blood
Be for my soul the highest good!

21. My heart has now become Thy dwelling,
O blessèd Holy Trinity.
With angels I, Thy praises telling,
Shall live in joy eternally.
Lord, may Thy body and Thy blood
Be for my soul the highest good!

—F. C. Heyder, †1754; tr., *TLH*, 1941; but sts. 11–13, 18–20, M. Carver.

203

Tune: O Traurigkeit, O Herzeleid! 14. [*TLH* 167; *LW* 122; *LSB* 448]

1. Thy table dear / I dare to near;
Help, Father! Mercy lend me!
Let no unrepented sin
To my hurt attend me.

2. I do not hide / My sin and pride,
My wretched bands bewailing;
Contrite hearts are sure to find,
God, Thy grace unfailing!

3. When time shall come / To pay the sum
Of all the debts I gather,
Yet my glorious Lord shall say,
"I have paid My Father."

4. So Christ, to Thee / I trustingly
And, childlike, all things render:
Jesus, whom the cherubim
Long to see in splendor!

5. Thy flesh and blood, / Which for my good
Were once poured out and riven,
Here—O wondrous mystery!—
At Thy feast are given.

6. With mouth and soul / I take Thee whole,
O Christ, nor can I measure,
As I in Thy flesh and blood
Eat Thy wondrous treasure.

7. Search not to see / How this may be
Nor stumble at this wonder;
God can manage vastly more
Than thy mind can ponder.

8. Thy skeptic sense / May sweep it hence
With fancies doubtful-hearted;
Yet my heart from letters plain
Never shall be parted.

9. God's oath I trust, / His pledges must
Transpire as He hath spoken;
He is not of fallen man,
Nor his promise broken.

10. Vouchsafe, O God, / By Jesus' blood,
That neither world nor devil
Shake me from this point of faith,
In their doubts to revel!

11. May I not fail, / Grow weak, or pale,
From morn to evening giving
Thanks to Thee for Thy shed blood,
Dearly life retrieving.

—G. W. Molanus, 1673; tr., M. Carver, after A. Crull, 1880.

204

Tune: Auf meinen lieben Gott. 29. [*TLH* 526; *LW* 421; *LSB* 745]

1. I long at every hour
With all my heart and pow'r,
O God, to praise Thy favor
Which here I taste and savor;
My every vein is yearning
Thy thanks to be returning!

2. O Christ, my highest Good!
Thy very flesh and blood
Are my heart's source of gladness,
My comfort in all sadness;
These gifts, as here they flourish,
My soul and body nourish.

3. All sense that man holds dear
Must be confounded here.
We trust no innovation,
God's Word is our foundation;
He pow'r and wisdom ground it,
Though worlds collapse around it.

4. Here is the Lamb of God
That to Golgotha trod
To make a rich oblation,
And win for us salvation;
Here boundless grace is given,
Here every sin is shriven.

5. Thy pledge, O God, is true!
Appearing ever new
In blessed cup and platter;
Sin, death, and devil, scatter!
God here my grief is mending,
Here giving life unending!

—J. Olearius, †1684; tr., M. Carver.

205

Tune: Jesus Christus, unser Heiland, der von uns. 9.
[*LW* 237; *or TLH* 311; *LW* 236; *LSB* 627]

1. Jesus Christ, our blessèd Savior,
Turned away God's wrath forever;
By His bitter grief and woe
He saved us from the evil foe.

2. As His pledge of love undying
He, this precious food supplying,
Gives His body with the bread
And with the wine the blood He shed.

3. Whoso to this Board repaireth
May take heed how he prepareth;
For if he does not believe,
Then death for life he shall receive.

4. Praise the Father, who from heaven
Unto us such food hath given
And, to mend what we have done,
Gave into death His only Son.

5. Thou shalt hold with faith unshaken
That this food is to be taken
By the sick who are distressed,
By hearts that long for peace and rest.

6. To such grace and mercy turneth
Every soul that truly mourneth;
Art thou well? avoid this Board,
Else wilt thou reap an ill reward.

7. Christ says: "Come, all ye that labor,
And receive My grace and favor;
They who feel no want nor ill
Need no physician's help nor skill.

8. "Useless were for thee My Passion,
If thy works thy weal could fashion.
This feast is not spread for thee
If thine own savior thou wilt be."

9. If thy heart this truth professes
And thy mouth thy sin confesses,
His dear guest thou here shalt be,
And Christ Himself shall banquet thee.

10. But the fruits must not be missing,
Love thy neighbor without ceasing;
That true love let him receive
Which here to thee thy God doth give.

—M. Luther, 1524, after J. Hus, 1415; tr., Anon., but st. 6, R. Massie, 1854, alt.

206

Tune: Herr Jesu Christ, meins Lebens Licht. 11. [*TLH* 288; *LW* 262; *LSB* 704]

1. O Jesus, Bridegroom of my soul,
Whose love found means to make me whole
By dying on the cursèd tree,
Who left'st Thy blood my legacy:—

2. To Thy blest table I draw near,
Full of unworthiness and fear;
Impure, sick, naked, poor, and blind,—
In mercy cast me not behind.

3. My great Physician and my Light,
All's clear before Thy holy sight:
Thou art the Source of sanctity,
My wedding garment comes from Thee.

4. O blessed Lord, prepare Thou me,
And heal my great infirmity;
Wash all the stains of sin away,
And let me taste Thy grace today.

5. Dispel the darkness from beneath,
Endow me with a living faith,
Thy grace enrich my poverty,
And mortify all self in me.

6. Thus feed me with the living bread
Of Thine own flesh that once was dead;
The wine of Thy most precious blood
Refresh my faith, supremest Good.

7. Root out all tendency to sin;
Implant that heav'nly love within
Which honors God, and makes the peace
With men to flourish and increase.

8. What soul and body want, supply;
What's harmful, check and mortify;
Take up Thy residence in me,
Unite me more and more with Thee.

9. By virtue of this heav'nly meal
The law of sin in me repeal;
All my transgressions far remove,
And let me taste Thy Father's love.

10. Send me relief from all my foes
When earth and hell my hopes oppose.
The present purpose I have made,
O Lord, let never be delayed.

11. My life and conversation, Lord,
Direct according to Thy Word,
That not one moment of my days
Be spent without a sense of grace:—

12. Till Thou art pleased, O Prince of life,
To call me from this world of strife,
To taste with all that love Thy name
The glorious Supper of the Lamb.

—J. Heermann, 1630; tr., J. C. Jacobi, †1750, alt.

207

Tune: Nun laßt uns Gott, dem Herren. 4. [*TLH* 122; *or LW* 184*]

1. O Sun of my salvation,
My joy and consolation,
Friend of my soul, her praises
To Thee my spirit raises.

2. How can full worth be given
To these sweet flow'rs of heaven,
These gifts beyond affording,
New strength to us according?

3. How can I thank Thee rightly,
Who sick am and unsightly,
That Thou to me art given,
Thyself, the Bread of heaven!

4. My heartfelt thanks I offer
For all that Thou didst suffer
For all Thy wounds and bleeding,
For all Thy pain exceeding.

5. The griefs that bowed Thy spirit
My thankful praises merit:
My thanks for all Thy yearning
And tears of fervent burning.

6. Thy wondrous love unshaken
To Thee my heart shall waken;
I for Thy death adore Thee,
It is my hope of glory.

7. My heart enjoys Thy treasure
Of goodness without measure,
This pledge, Thy mercy-bearer,
Blots out all sins and error.

8. Lord, fix my vision ever
On Thee, both Gift and Giver,
This food of heav'n conveys Thee,
For which my heart shall praise Thee.

9. The sins that still attend me
Thou wilt drive out, to mend me,
My flesh wilt cleanse and scour,
And dwell in me with power.

10. Redeemed from judgment dreaded,
To Thee I now am wedded;
O Life beyond assessing!
Where is a better blessing?

11. Permit, O Jesus Fairest,
My soul for which Thou carest
While in its fleshly cover
To hang on Thee, my Lover.

12. Grant pow'r against temptations,
In all affliction, patience,
In prayèr, true devotion,
And peace from world's commotion.

13. In whatso task I find me,
Of this, Lord, still remind me—
What splendid celebration,
Yea, heav'nly restoration!

14. I've joined the blessèd number
And shall not die but slumber,
O Christ, till glad Thou raise me
And by Thy light amaze me.

—J. Rist, 1654; tr. sts. 1, 3b, 5a, 6, A. T. Russell, 1851, alt.; sts. rest, M. Carver.

208

Tune: Nun laßt uns Gott, dem Herren. 4. [*TLH* 122; *or LW* 184*]

1. O Shepherd ever caring!
Thou seekest all the erring,
Thou lovest sinners lowly
As though Thy children holy.

2. O Christ, I strayed in error,
Confused by sin and terror;
Then camest Thou to find me,
To soothe me and unbind me.

3. To wrest me from transgression
Thou mad'st me Thy possession,
With love as of a father
Who doth his children gather.

4. Though grieved I Thee so often,
So oft Thy heart did soften,
My pardon was Thy pleasure,
My bath, Thy comfort's measure.

5. O Jesus, Life that savest!
Thyself to me Thou gavest,
My heart Thy house creating,
My soul and mouth elating.

6. Thy flesh and blood releasing,
Thou givest grace unceasing;
With life I am invested,
My death Thou hast ingested.

7. The devil's armies cower
Before Thy quick'ning power,
And limbs by sin disjointed
By Thee are bound, anointed.

8. Now by regeneration
I slip from condemnation;
Now heaven opens for me,
I know God shall restore me.

9. To Thee, Christ, be all praises,
Who feed'st me with such graces,
That though but death I merit,
I now shall life inherit.

10. I thank Thee, Lord, beseeching
To guide me by Thy teaching,
Lest I from Thee turn errant,
Thy path no more apparent.

11. Thy Spirit send to lead me,
On lighted ways to speed me,
That I, Thy love returning,
May goodly fruit be earning.

12. May by this meal be given
The way to Thee in heaven,
That I may serve Thy pleasure
For ages without measure.

—S. Liscow, †1689; tr., M. Carver,.

209

Tune: Schaffe in mir, Gott. 106. [p. 414]

1. Create in me, Lord, O God, a clean heart,
And renew Thou a right spirit within me.
Reject me not / Reject me not
From Thy holy presence, / From Thy holy presence,
And remove Thy Holy Spirit not from me.

2. Comfort me again with Thy salvation,
And do Thou uphold me with Thy free Spirit.
Wash me, O Lord, / Wash me, O Lord,
From all my transgressions, / From all my transgressions,
And cleanse me from all mine iniquities.

—Ps. 51:11–12, 2; tr. *HELM*, 1905.

210

Tune: Schmücke dich, o liebe Seele. 72. [*TLH* 305; *LW* 239; *LSB* 636]

1. Soul, adorn thyself with gladness,
Leave behind all gloom and sadness;
Come into the daylight's splendor,
There with joy thy praises render
Unto Him whose grace unbounded
Hath this woundrous supper founded.
High o'er all the heav'ns He reigneth,
Yet to dwell with thee He deigneth.

2. Hasten as a bride to meet Him
And with loving rev'rence greet Him;
For with words of life immortal
Now He knocketh at thy portal.
Haste to ope the gates before Him,
Saying, while thou dost adore Him,
Suffer, Lord, that I receive Thee,
And I nevermore will leave Thee.

3. He who craves a precious treasure
Neither cost nor pain will measure;
But the priceless gifts of heaven
God to us hath freely given.
Though the wealth of earth were proffered,
Naught would buy the gifts here offered:
Christ's true body, for thee riven,
And His blood, for thee once given.

4. Ah, how hungers all my spirit
For the love I do not merit!
Oft have I, with sighs fast thronging,
Thought upon this food with longing,
In the battle well-nigh worsted,
For this cup of life have thirsted,
For the Friend who here invites us
And to God Himself unites us.

5. In my heart I find ascending
Holy awe, with rapture blending,
As this mystery I ponder,
Filling all my soul with wonder,
Bearing witness at this hoùr
Of the greatness of Thy powèr;
Far beyond all human telling
Is the pow'r within Him dwelling.

6. Human reason, though it ponder,
Cannot fathom this great wonder
That Christ's body e'er remaineth
Though it countless souls sustaineth,
And that He His blood is giving
With the wine we are receiving.
These great mysteries unsounded
Are by God alone expounded.

7. Jesus, Sun of Life, my Splendor,
Jesus, Thou my Friend most tender,
Jesus, Joy of my desiring,
Fount of life, my soul inspiring,—
At Thy feet I cry, my Maker,
Let me be a fit partaker
Of this blessed food from heaven,
For our good, Thy glory, given.

8. Lord, by love and mercy driven
Thou hast left Thy throne in heaven
On the cross for us to languish
And to die in bitter anguish,
To forgo all joy and gladness
And to shed Thy blood in sadness.
By this blood, redeemed and living,
Lord, I praise Thee with thanksgiving.

9. Jesus, Bread of Life, I pray Thee,
Let me gladly here obey Thee.
By Thy love I am invited,
Be Thy love with love requited;
From this Supper let me measure,
Lord, how vast and deep love's treasure.
Through the gifts Thou here dost give me
As Thy guest in heav'n receive me.

—J. Franck, 1649; tr., composite based on C. Winkworth, 1858.

Repentance and Confession

211

Tune: Kommt her zu mir, spricht Gottes Sohn. 41. [*TLH* 263; *LW* 261; *LSB* 666 (no harm.)]

1. Grant us, O God, Thy grace, that we
May ever own repentantly
Our sin and our transgression,
And faith in Christ unswerving claim,
Who gives Himself the glorious name:
The Master of Salvation.

2. Make us obedient to Thy Word,
In godly living undeterred,
And glorify Thee ever;
Thy gracious Spirit be our stay
To guide us on the heav'nly way,
Through Christ our Lord and Savior.

—S. Zehner, 1633; tr., M. Carver.

212

Tune: Ach Gott und Herr (Ion.). 25. [*TLH* 215; *LW* 153; *LSB* 701]

1. Alas, my God, / How great my load!
My conscience doth upbraid me;
And I have found / Myself so bound,
No man hath pow'r to aid me.

2. Were I to flee / In misery,
In some lone spot to hide me,
Still grief and care / Would haunt me there,
And peace be still denied me.

3. Nay, Thee I seek, / for I am weak,
Yet pity and restore me;
Just God, make not / Thy wrath my lot,
Thy Son hath suffered for me.

4. If sin must owe / The rod of woe,
Then be my path still rougher,
Oh, spare no pain; / If heav'n I gain,
On earth I gladly suffer.

5. Lord, curb my will, / Forgive my ill,
Make Thou my patience firmer,
Let me not groan / As I have done,
Nor at Thy chast'ning murmur.

6. Then deal with me / As pleases Thee,
Thy grace will help me bear it,
If but at last / I see Thy rest,
And with my Savior share it.

7. Christ, where Thou art / All doubts depart,
Thou won'st for me salvation
Upon the cross, / By pain and loss
And by Thy bitter Passion.

(8. To God alone: / The Father, Son
And Holy Ghost be given
All laud and praise / Thro' troublous days
On earth, and e'er in heaven.)

9. And like a bird, / When storm is heard,
Will seek a tree-trunk hollow
And sheltered stay / From all dismay
In which the world must wallow:

10. So, Jesus Christ, / My refuge prized
In Thy dear wounds is hidden:
When sin and hell / Would hope dispel,
There shall my soul be bidden.

11. There I shall bide / Till Thou decide,
And flesh and soul are parted,
Then I with Thee, / My Prize, shall be
Forever, joyful-hearted.

12. Christ Jesus, Lord, / Thy help afford
Until my days are finished,
When I must leave, / My soul receive
To glory undiminished.

13. All praise alone, / God, Father, Son,
And Holy Ghost, we give Thee!
Nor doubt nor dread, / For Thou hast said,
We're saved who here believe Thee!

—sts. 1–6, M. Rutilius, 1604; sts. 9, 11, 13, J. Major, 1613;
tr. sts. 1–6, C. Winkworth, alt.; sts. 7–13, M. Carver.

213

Tune: Allein zu dir, Herr Jesu Christ. 78. [*TLH* 319; *LW* 357; *LSB* 972 (dig.)]

1. In Thee alone, O Christ, my Lord,
My hope on earth remaineth;
I know Thou wilt Thine aid afford,
Naught else my soul sustaineth.
No strength of man, no earthly stay,
Can help me in the evil day;
Thou, only Thou, canst aid supply.
To Thee I cry;
On Thee I bid my heart rely.

2. My sins, O Lord, against me rise,
I mourn them with contrition;
Grant, through Thy death and sacrifice,
To me a full remission.
Lord, show before the Father's throne
That Thou didst for my sins atone;
So shall I from my load be freed.
Thy Word I plead;
Keep me, O Lord, each hour of need.

3. O Lord, in mercy stay my heart
On faith's most sure foundation
And to my inmost soul impart
Thy perfect consolation.
Fill all my life with love to Thee,
Tow'rd all men grant me charity;
And at the last, when comes my end,
Thy succor send.
From Satan's wiles my soul defend.

4. All praise to God in highest heav'n,
The Father ever gracious;
And to the Son, for sinners giv'n,
Who guards His children precious;
And to the Holy Ghost on high;
Oh, may He keep His comfort nigh,
And teach us, free from sin and fear,
To please Him here,
And serve Him in the sinless sphere!

—J. Schneesing, 1542; tr. sts. 1–3, A. T. Russell, 1851, alt.; st. 4, C. Winkworth, 1863, alt.

214

Tune: Aus tiefer Not schrei ich zu dir. 49. [*LW* 230; *TLH* 329; *LSB* 607]

1. From depths of woe I cry to Thee,
Lord, hear me, I implore Thee.
Bend down Thy gracious ear to me,
My pray'r let come before Thee.
If Thou rememb'rest each misdeed,
If each should have its rightful meed,
Who may abide Thy presence?

2. Thy love and grace alone avail
To blot out my transgression;
The best and holiest deeds must fail
To break sin's dread oppression.
Before Thee none can boasting stand,
But all must fear Thy strict demand
And live alone by mercy.

3. Therefore my hope is in the Lord
And not in mine own merit;
It rests upon His faithful Word
To them of contrite spirit
That He is merciful and just;
This is my comfort and my trust.
His help I wait with patience.

4. And though it tarry till the night
And till the morning waken,
My heart shall never doubt His might
Nor count itself forsaken.
Do thus, O ye of Israel's seed,
Ye of the Spirit born indeed;
Wait for your God's appearing.

5. Though great our sins and sore our woes,
His grace much more aboundeth;
His helping love no limit knows,
Our utmost need it soundeth.
Our Shepherd good and true is He,
Who will at last His Israel free
From all their sin and sorrow.

—M. Luther, 1524, after Ps. 130; tr., C. Winkworth, 1863, alt.

215

Tune: Wo Gott der Herr nicht bei uns hält. 49. [p. 418;
or TLH 124*; *LW* 353*; *LSB* 556*]

1. So great, Lord, is Thy faithfulness
That we must be astounded;
We lie before Thy feet of grace,
Though poor, yet not confounded.
While daily evils rise anew,
Yet art Thou still our Shepherd true,
And shalt not let us perish.

2. Sin seems to teem beyond control,
Thou see'st what pain it causes,
Thou know'st the wounds of every soul
Beneath its veiling gauzes;
The load of guilt grows day by day,
And never rest or peace have they
Who turn their back to heaven.

3. Thine eyes are turned against all those
Who, boldly disobeying,
Till death prefer the way that goes
Awry and widely straying,
Who seek amid the haunts of sin
To purge their carnal lust within
Through wills corrupt and godless.

4. Creation sinks in agony
And groans for liberation,
It waits in fear with woeful plea;
God, look on Thy creation,
Thy handiwork, Thy dear domain,
Yea, all that heav'n and earth contain,
Bewail the utter ruin!

5. Our hope is yet unmoved from Thee,
Who hear'st our every sentence;
We beg, Thee, Father, ceaselessly,
To fill with true repentance
The sinners blind from east to west
Who count their cursèd nature blest
As hellwards they are wending.

6. Have mercy, O Thou faithful God,
Who dost the world so cherish—
Upon this world, which earns Thy rod
And, dead in sin, should perish!
Endue Thy precious Word with pow'r
To pierce its heart, so hard and dour,
And break its stony nature.

7. May all who stray in error's smoke
Be blest with vision holy,
To know how mild and light Thy yoke
For sinners poor and lowly
Who feel transgression's weight and shame,
And, in true faith repenting, claim
Christ's Passion and Thy favor.

8. Thy chosen flock preserve intact,
No goodly blessing sparing;
Bestow what things till now it lacked
To tread Thy paths unerring;
Thy faithfulness, Thine eye, Thy hand
Make clear to Thine in every land,
Who trust Thee for Thy goodness.

9. Both kings and fathers have a mind
To govern with compassion,
But God, Thou art than both more kind,
Thy heart no ill can fashion;
So Thee alone we trust and praise;
Oh, lead us, Father, in Thy ways,
Thy perfect will and counsel.

10. As branches here to Thee who cleave,
This joy Thou dost afford us:
That Thou Thy crown of grace wilt give
And in Thy love award us!
We hope all soon to see Thy face
Beyond in ceaseless beams of grace,
Where Thou, our Lamb, shalt feed us.

—J. Weidenheim, before 1698; tr., M. Carver.

216

Tune: Herr Jesu Christ, du höchstes Gut. 49. [p. 404]

1. Lord Jesus Christ, Thou highest Good,
Thou Fount of grace and pardon,
Behold how heavy is my mood,
Of sin how great my burden;
How sore my conscience is beset
With keenest arrows of regret,
That never cease to pierce me.

2. Have mercy, Lord, and hear my plea,
My heart's sore weight relieving,
For Thou hast paid my debt for me
By death, by cross and grieving.
Of Thee alone I crave relief;
Leave me not now in fear and grief
And dark despair to perish.

3. Alas, when I remember all
That I in life committed
A stone upon my heart doth fall,
In robes of terror fitted,
I know not where to take my flight;
Ah Lord! I must despair outright,
But for Thy word of mercy.

4. But when I hear it sweetly sing
Of peace for ever after,
My heart almost begins to spring,
And fills with joyous laughter,
To know how merciful Thou art
To all who, with a contrite heart,
Will come to Thee, O Jesus!

5. And ever when I look within,
As I've lamented ever,
I find a wretched man of sin,
A conscience resting never,
And, earnest for Thy blood, I long
To be absolved of every wrong,
Like David and Manasseh;

6. So I, too, dare to come to Thee,
And at Thy feet I cede Thee
My burden, while with bended knee
And earnest heart I plead Thee,
Forgive me, heal my conscience' strife,
For all the sins of all my life
Forgive, dear Lord, forgive me!

7. Yea, Lord and God, I pray Thee now,
For Thy Name's sake forgive me,
And of this yoke that makes me bow
Do Thou in grace relieve me!
So shall my heart have peace at last,
And to Thy praise my years be passed
In childlike, glad obedience.

8. Thy joyful Spirit give me strength,
And with Thy wounds, oh, mend me,
When my last hour must come at length,
Thy bath of anguish send me,
And take me when it seems Thee best,
In the true faith to heav'nly rest
To Thine elect forever.

—B. Ringwaldt, †1598; tr., C. Winkworth, 1869, alt., but st. 2, F. W. Young, 1877, alt.; st. 5, M. Carver.

217

Tune: Höchster König, Jesu Christ. 32. [p. 405]

1. Jesus Christ, Thou King supreme,
Great and fearsome dost Thou seem,
Yet Thou grantest every Christian
Healing, life, and sin's remission:
Fountain whence all good is giv'n—
Grant me, too, the joys of heav'n!

2. Faithful Lord, receive my plea,
Hold in gracious memory
Thy uniting with creation,
Suff'ring bitter pain and Passion,
That in heav'n on yonder day
We might leave this earth's dismay.

3. Never didst Thou rest or sleep
Till Thou found'st Thy wand'ring sheep,
But Thou bor'st the cross to save me;
Thus Thy death my freedom gave me:
Oh, may all Thine agony
Never prove misspent on me.

4. Just Avenger of all ill,
How I crave Thy kind goodwill!
Grant me in Thy kind compassion
Pardon for my sore transgression,
Ere that dreadful day I face,
Set for judging Adam's race.

5. For my deeds I sigh and mourn;
Rightly have they earned Thy scorn;
All my sins, each bold omission,
Makes me blush with true contrition:
God, I beg Thy clemency;
Spare me in my misery!

6. Mary found Thy grace immense
Through her tearful penitence;
And the thief, contrite in dying,
Mercy found in Thy replying.
May I also, as is just,
Fix on Thee my hope and trust.

7. Such a grace my humble plea
Scarcely hopes to merit me;
Oh, my Crown, of grace unending,
Ever be my soul defending,
That I may not come to dwell
In the endless woes of hell.

8. Grant that I may closely keep
Where Thou wilt dispose Thy sheep;
Save me from the goats in error,
Whom Thy judgments fill with terror;
Bid me enter on the right,
And behold Thy glorious light.

9. When in wrath Thou shalt inflict
By the lips of judgment strict
Fiery flames of condemnation
On the cursèd congregation,
Say to me as to a son,
"Come, oh, come, thou blessèd one!"

10. That in heaven's halls I may
Mid Thy hallowed number stay,
Whom Thy hands have reinstated,
And with pureness coronated,
Full of joy and free of pain,
Thine forever to remain.

—J. Heermann, asc., 1659, cento, after *Dies irae, dies illa;* tr., M. Carver.

218

Tune: Wer nur den lieben Gott läßt walten. 45. [*TLH* 194; *LW* 429; *LSB* 750]

1. A wretched man and wretched debtor
Before Thy face, O God, I stand:
Judge not according to the letter!
Stretch forth to me Thy lenient hand.
Have mercy, God, I cry to Thee:
Have mercy, gracious God, on me!

2. Oh, how my heart with fear is quailing,
As I behold my myriad sin!
Therefore I beg Thy grace availing
Thy poor, lost child to soothe within;
Have mercy, God, I cry to Thee:
Have mercy, gracious God, on me!

3. Receive my cry and loud petition,
O Father, to Thy heart so dear!
Grant for my every sin remission;
What pains my heart, let disappear:
Have mercy, God, I cry to Thee:
Have mercy, gracious God, on me!

4. How long shall I lament unheeded?
How canst Thou not my cries perceive?
How then ignore what I have pleaded?
Oh, hear Thy wretched sinner grieve!
Have mercy, God, I cry to Thee:
Have mercy, gracious God, on me!

5. Indeed, my wounds are deathly serious,
And none can bind them save for Thee:
Oh, grace! Oh, grace! I cry, delirious,
For this alone I make my plea:
Have mercy, God, I cry to Thee:
Have mercy, gracious God, on me!

6. Lord, not as I have earned repay me,
Deal not according to my sin.
O faithful Father, do not slay me!
Receive Thy wicked child again.
Have mercy, God, I cry to Thee:
Have mercy, gracious God, on me!

7. But speak the word, and open heaven,
Speak now to me, a sinner poor,
"Go forth, Thy sins have been forgiven.
Go forth, O man, and sin no more."
Have mercy, God, I cry to Thee:
Have mercy, gracious God, on me!

8. My pray'r hath been accepted surely,
I have been heard, and have no doubt:
My heart is filled with comfort purely,
No more need I to cry and shout:
Have mercy, God, I cry to Thee:
Have mercy, gracious God, on me!

—C. Tietze, ca. 1664; tr., M. Carver.

219

Tune: Durch Adams Fall ist ganz verderbt. 83. [p. 401]

1. A sinner poor, I come to Thee,
My heart is filled with groaning,—
O God of boundless clemency!—
I come in sorrow owning
My misdeeds all / And every fall
Which I have e'er committed,
Since earliest times— / One mass of crimes!—
Like shackles round me fitted.

2. These trespasses that I have wrought
Exceed enumeration,
And yet conceal them I cannot,
So great is their vexation.
Thy dearest Son / My soul hath won
And by His death unbound me,
Alas, but how / I've failed Him now
And let the Foe confound me!

3. So great was my ungratefulness,
Yea, till this moment even,
That at no time did I express
My thanks for graces given:
Thy heart so true / Each morning new,
Thy love I cannot merit,
Yet all in me / I richly see
And carry in my spirit.

4. Above all Thou with patience, Lord,
Hast many ages spared me,
Nor given me my just reward,
Or child of wrath declared me,
But ceaselessly, / O Majesty,
Hast hastened to relieve me,
And all wilt grant, / As is Thy wont,
Till heaven shall receive me.

5. How often Thou hast stirred my heart
With words in Scripture given,
And called me by the Spirit's art
To foretastes of Thy heaven,
And night and day, / In Thy good way,
To true repentance brought me,
And nurtured me / Through agony
And tests till Thou hadst taught me!

6. And yet, Lord, I cannot deny,
I ne'er Thy knocking heeded;
I did not open in reply,
But e'er the voice impeded
With scorn and mock, / Despised Thy knock,
To Thee my back displaying,
While in Thy care / Thou didst forbear
Thy wrath to be conveying.

7. By rights Thou oft, since life began,
My cord of life couldst sever,
And as Thy wicked servant ban
My soul to hell forever,
For without shame / I heaped my blame
Through impudent transgression;
Still dost Thou give / Me space to live,
And peace at Thy discretion.

8. Whene'er my heart considers this,
It's like to burst asunder.
I'm sickened by my pridefulness,
My heart recoils in wonder;
No prong of hell / Could sting so well
That it, too, should not tear me;
I am not worth / That even earth
Should hold me up and bear me.

9. I am not worthy of the name
Of Thy own dear creation;
I should by all that Thou didst frame
Receive my decimation.
So foul hath been / The pow'r of sin
I truly must be shriven;
Didst Thou behold / My errors bold,
What flames I would be given!

10. O Father, merciful, Most High!
I plead and fall before Thee,
Reject not those who to Thee cry;
Repentant, I implore Thee,
With all Thy grace / Incline Thy face,
Let not this sinner languish;
Turn but Thy view / And life imbue
And cast away my anguish.

11. Disclose to me Thy friendly heart,
Love's residence and dwelling.
Forgive my sin, relieve each smart;
Help me to be excelling
In works that please / Thy pure decrees,
And all that's ill to banish,
Until I fly / Where hosts on high
Rejoice, and sorrows vanish.

—J. Heermann, 1630, after J. Tauler; tr., M. Carver.

220

Tune: Es ist gewisslich an der Zeit. 49. [*TLH* 293; *LW* 336; *LSB* 508]

1. I will return unto the Lord
From pathways of transgression.
My God, to me Thy help afford,
Hear Thou my heart's confession.
Thy blessèd Spirit's strength divine
Create anew this heart of mine;
Grant me through grace this blessing!

2. Man fails to see his wretched plight,
So blind is his condition,
Without Thy Holy Spirit's light,
Sin leads him to perdition.
Corrupt in thought and word and deed,
Filled with distress, I come, and plead,
"O Father mine, relieve me!"

3. Knock at my door, and make me feel
My sinfulness and blindness.
The evil I have done reveal,
Win Thou my heart with kindness.
Then, as I comprehend my woe,
Dear Father, let my cheeks o'erflow
With tears of true contrition.

4. For of Thy gifts, ah! what a wealth
Thou hast to me presented!
To Thee I owe my life and health,
For I am well contented
With food and raiment Thou dost grant,
And so much more, that no real want
My pleasure hath prevented.

5. And Thou in Christ hast rescued me
From out hell's flooding surges;
And never am I left by Thee
In destitution's verges
And lest in careless ease I dwell,
Forgetting Him who keeps me well,
Betimes I feel Thy scourges.

6. Who filleth children's hands as Thou?
And yet how have I paid Thee?
Not in obedience, as doth show
My heart, which hath betrayed Thee,
For there a thousand cank'rous sins
Spread rot of death that none can rinse,
By which to death I'm driven.

7. The folly of my younger days,
And all my proud behavior
Indict me with their sneering gaze,
A wretch am I! Oh, Savior!
They call Thy vengeance o'er my head,
The jaws of hell awide to spread
And bring me death forever.

8. Oh, how ashamed I am to own
My horrors, or to frame them;
Of numbering my sins have none,
And scarcely can I name them;
And had I but the smallest tinge
Hell's fires would still have cause to singe,
Nor might I ever tame them.

9. Till now in false security
My conscience said while sleeping:
"There yet is time enough for thee;
God tarries in His reaping,
So strict account He doth not make,
The Shepherd doth forbear to take
His sheep out of safekeeping."

10. But suddenly that sleep was broke,
And now my heart is breaking;
Thy voice in mighty thunders spoke,
Thy lightnings sent me quaking;
I see the realms of death and hell
Advance in pow'r I cannot quell
My soul their captive making.

11. My persecutors chase me on
And madly I am driven;
Where shall I flee? O rising dawn,
Grant me the wings of heaven;
Conceal me, O thou distant sea;
And crumble now and fall on me,
Ye cliffs and hills deep-riven!

12. Oh, futile all! Should I take flight,
Up to the sky ascending,
Or plummet to infernal night,
To creep in shadows blending,
Thine eye would still behold me there,
Exposing in Thy brilliant glare
My sins and shame unending.

13. Lord Jesus, to Thy wounds I flee,
In this blest shelter hide me!
Thy anguish was endured for me,
My guilt has crucified Thee.
On Thee was laid the world's vast load
Of sin, and Thou, blest Lamb of God,
Most willingly didst bear it.

14. Oh, cleanse me by Thy drops of woe,
And scarlet-red affliction,
Thy robes of innocence bestow
White, stainless benediction;
And everything Thou dost destroy
Enliven with Thy comfort's joy,
Lord, by Thy crucifixion.

15. Then with Thy Father intercede,
That He remember never
My every sin and evil deed
That makes me quake and shiver.
Oh, sink the burden of my guilt,
For which such precious blood was spilt,
Beneath the depths forever.

16. And henceforth will I day by day,
Abandon earthly pleasure
By virtue of Thy Spirit's sway,
Thy shared and priceless Treasure,
Whom let assist and rescue me
From sin and all that angers Thee
To live in Christian measure.

—Anon., Berlin, 1653; tr. sts. 4–5, 9–10, 15, C. Winkworth, 1869, alt.;
tr. sts, 1–3, 13, A. Hoppe, 1922; sts. rest, M. Carver.

221

Tune: Jesu, der du meine Seele. 68. [p. 407]

1. Jesus, who in sorrow dying
Didst deliv'rance bring to me,
Whilst my sins for vengeance crying
Nailed Thee to the shameful tree:
Oh, what strength Thou here displayest
And to me what news conveyest
By Thy sweet and soothing word!
Priceless Treasure! God, my Lord!

2. Thou hast found with eyes unfailing
All Thy lost and straying sheep,
As they ran in error flailing
Down to hell's abysses deep.
Thou who Satan's pow'r subduest,
And the sinner's hope renewest,
Biddest me most graciously
To return and come to Thee.

3. Child of sin I am—oh, terror!
Oh, how far astray I've gone;
There is naught in me but error
And unrighteousness, I own;
All my thoughts and observations,
Are to God abominations;
Wicked have my days been here
All devoid of godly fear.

4. Lord, I have to make confession:
There is nothing good in me.
Oft my soul receives suggestion
Of the will that pleases Thee,
Yet the flesh defies submission,
Goodly fruit sees no fruition,
What I would comes not to view;
What I would not, that I do.

5. Yet, O Lord, the lofty number
Of my debts who may obtain?
Countless sins my soul encumber,
Stinging me with grief and pain.
My heart faints beneath its burden,
Oh, my hidden errors pardon!
Reckon not the crimes which have
Wakened, Lord, Thine anger grave.

6. Thou hast canceled my transgression,
Jesus, by Thy precious blood;
May I find therein salvation,
Happiness, and peace with God;
And since Thou, for sinners suff'ring,
On the cross wast made an off'ring,
From all sin deliver me,
That I wholly Thine may be.

7. Often hell's dread apprehension
And the devil's wrathful spite
Rise again with grim intention
To confound me in the fight;
Lying stunned, I scarce can beat them;
Help, Lord Jesus! Come, defeat them!
O my Confidence Thou art,
Let despair not seize my heart.

8. All the pain on Thee inflicted,
All Thy wounds, Thy crown of scorn,
Hands and feet with nails constricted,
The reproach which Thou hast borne;
Thy back, plowed with countless furrows,
Cross and grave and all Thy sorrows,
Thy blood-sweat and agony,
O Lord Jesus, comfort me!

9. When before the court of heaven
I shall come (whence none can flee),
Oh, may there Thy help be given!
May Thou still my Savior be!
Thou alone, Lord, canst defend me
Lest that verdict apprehend me:
"Oh, depart, ye cursèd lot,
Verily, I knew you not."

10. Thou hast fathomed mine affliction,
Thou hast felt my grief and pain,
Thy harsh death and crucifixion
Let my heart alone contain;
Take this heart with suff'ring mingled
In Thy precious blood besprinkled
From Thy cross and wounds outpoured:
It is Thine, O Christ, my Lord.

11. Now I know Thou wilt make quiet
This my conscience that doth mourn;
Faithful art Thou to supply it
With the healing Thou hast sworn,
That in all creation never
Shall a soul be lost forever
But shall live eternally,
If it only trust in Thee.

12. I believe! Lord, help my weakness,
Let me not despairing die;
Strengthen me in faith and meekness,
Sin and death to mortify.
Now I stay me on Thy blessing,
Till, the sight of Thee possessing,
I shall live from conflict free,
Blessed for eternity.

—J. Rist, 1642; tr. sts. 1a, 2b, 12, A. T. Russell, 1851, alt.; sts. 6, 8 *Mor. H.-B.*, 1808, alt; sts. rest, M. Carver.

222

Tune: Meinen Jesum laß ich nicht. 33.
[*TLH* 324; *LW* 269; *LSB* 350; *or* p. 411]

1. Jesus sinners doth receive;
Oh, may all this saying ponder
Who in sin's delusions live
And from God and Heaven wander!
Here is hope for all who grieve—
Jesus sinners doth receive.

2. We deserve but grief and shame,
Yet His words, rich grace revealing,
Pardon, peace, and life proclaim.
Here their ills have perfect healing
Who with humble hearts believe—
Jesus sinners doth receive.

3. Sheep that from the fold did stray
No true shepherd e'er forsaketh;
Weary souls that lost their way
Christ, the Shepherd, gently taketh
In His arms that they may live—
Jesus sinners doth receive.

4. Come, ye sinners, one and all,
Come, accept His invitation;
Come, obey His gracious call,
Come and take His free salvation!
Firmly in these words believe:
Jesus sinners doth receive.

5. I, a sinner, come to Thee
With a penitent confession;
Savior, mercy show to me
Grant for all my sins remission.
Let these words my soul relieve:
Jesus sinners doth receive.

6. Oh, how blest it is to know:
Were as scarlet my transgression,
It shall be as white as snow
By Thy blood and bitter Passion;
For these words I now believe:
Jesus sinners doth receive.

7. Now my conscience is at peace,
From the Law I stand acquitted;
Christ hath purchased my release
And my every sin remitted.
Naught remains my soul to grieve—
Jesus sinners doth receive.

8. Jesus sinners doth receive.
Also I have been forgiven;
And when I this earth must leave,
I shall find an open heaven.
Dying, still to Him I cleave—
Jesus sinners doth receive.

—E. Neumeister, 1718; tr., *TLH*, 1941.

223

Tune: O Gott, du frommer Gott. 55. [*TLH* 395; *LW* 385; *LSB* 696]

1. Now is the time of grace,
Now wide stands heaven's portal,
Now may true blessedness
Be hoped for by each mortal.
He who this day doth waste
Nor will to God repent,
Will mourn himself at last,
When he to hell is sent.

—J. Heermann, 1630; tr., M. Carver.

224

Tune: Kommt her zu mir, spricht Gottes Sohn. 41. [*TLH* 263; *LSB* 666 (mel.)]

1. Oh, come, ye sinners, straying long!
Come hasten, come and join the throng,
Ye weary‿and heavy-laden!
Here Jesus' opened heart receive,
Disclosed for all who weep and grieve
And own their sinful burden.

2. Lo, Jesus sinners doth receive!
So come, He can and will relieve
And fold thee in salvation;
Come weeping, owning thy defeat,
And fall in faith before His feet;
He'll give thee consolation.

3. A shepherd leaves no straying sheep
But ever doth his vigil keep,
And all the field surveyeth;
He leaves the ninety-nine to stand,
And all those in the desert land,
To find the one that strayeth.

4. Our dearest Jesus is the One
Who seeks His sheep in error gone,
And in His fold sustaineth;
Wherefore, dear soul, be found, and flee
To Jesus' wounds that gape for thee
While grace's day remaineth.

5. O Christ, Thy boundless love and care
I seek, though weary, poor, and bare;
Oh, grant me Thy compassion!
I've lost my way; oh, come and aid
A sheep confused, distressed, dismayed,
And caught in its transgression.

6. Oh, woe is me, that I from Thee
Should fall away so speedily!
Lord, let me be returning
To join Thy flock; My bruises nurse,
And free me from the ban and curse—
For this my heart is yearning.

7. May I Thy lamb forever be
And Thou my Shepherd faithfully,—
In life and death my Savior.
Let me forsake the worldly mind
And, as a child of God's own kind,
Adhere to Thee forever.

8. Henceforth the lusts of sin that rave
I will renounce until the grave,
And as a new creation
In holiness and righteousness
Serve Thee this little hour of grace
I'm given for salvation.

9. Take as Thy dove my lowly soul,
And keep it ever safe and whole
Within Thy wounds deep-riven;
Preserve me from the work of sin,
And let Thy Spirit's strength within
My feeble soul be given!

—L. Lorenzen, 1700; tr., M. Carver.

225

Tune: Vater unser im Himmelreich. 44. [*TLH* 318; *LW* 234; *LSB* 766]

1. Remove from us, O faithful God,
Thy dreadful and avenging rod,
The number of our crying crimes
Have well deserved a thousand times.
Sad famine, war, and pestilence
Prevent by Thy good Providence

2. In pity, Lord, look on our race,
We sue for Thine all-saving grace.
For, should Thy judgment, righteous Lord,
Demand for us our just reward,
No man could bear Thy holy sight,
Or plead His guilty cause aright.

3. In Thee we trust, to Thee we sigh,
And lift our heavy souls on high:
Give us an instance of Thy grace
And punish not our evil ways.
By true repentance bring us home,
And save us from the wrath to come.

4. Why wilt Thou raise Thy dreadful storms
Against so vile and feeble worms?
Thou, Author of our being, know'st
That this our frame is filth and dust;
Our best endeavors are but frail:
If Thou dost search, we greatly fail.

5. Sin still besets us everywhere,
Nor Satan fails to lay his snare,
The wicked world, with flesh and blood,
Conspire to rob us of all good.
O Lord, this is not hid from Thee;
Have mercy on our misery!

6. Consider Thy Son's bitter death,
Wounds, agonies, and parting breath.
These dreadful suff'rings of Thy Son
Atoned for sins which we had done.
Oh, for His sake our guilt forgive,
And let the mourning sinners live.

7. O Lord, lead Thou us by Thy hand,
And deign to bless our native land.
Preserve Thy Word amongst us pure,
Keep us from Satan's wiles secure.
Grant us to die in peace and love,
And see Thy glorious face above.

—M. Moller, 1584, after *Aufer immensam;* tr. J. C. Jacobi, †1750, alt.

226

Tune: Wenn wir in höchsten Nöten sein. 11. [*TLH* 141; *LW* 363; *LSB* 615]

1. O God, Thou righteous, faithful Lord,
I have not kept Thy holy Word,
But sinned and oft offended Thee;
Now I repent, it grieveth me.

2. Thou, Father, merciful and kind,
No pleasure in my death dost find,
But strong desire doth in Thee burn,
That I should unto Thee return.

3. Since Thou, dear Father, callest me,
I, poor lost sinner, come to Thee,
Relying on Christ's precious blood
Which from His holy five wounds flowed.

4. I pray through Christ, Thine only Son,
Who for my good our flesh put on;
To me let Thy love never fail;
O'er justice let Thy grace prevail.

5. In mercy, Father, let Thy grace
Through Jesus' blood my sins efface;
Then I, the poor lost child, will be
From all my sins forever free.

6. Grant that, according to Thy Word,
I lead a godly life, O Lord,
And let me, after time is o'er,
Inherit life forevermore.

—Anon., 1643, after J. Leon, 1611; tr., A. Crull, 1866, alt.

227

Tune: Ach Gott und Herr. 25. [*TLH* 215; *LW* 153; *LSB* 701]

1. O God, give heed / In time of need!
Now would I come before Thee;
Do not depart / But hear my heart
And what it doth implore Thee.

2. Withhold Thy wrath, / Give me not death
Because of my transgression,
To Thee I cry / O Lord, supply
Thy grace for my possession.

3. Alas, my heart / Is far apart
From good, and doth revile it;
No hour goes by / But many‿a lie
And wicked deed defile it.

4. This race I've run / From childhood on
Is stained with sin all over;
Yet for my guilt / Christ's blood was spilt,
My guilt with grace to cover.

5. This Christ was He / Who died for me
And carried my transgression,
In which I lay / My price to pay,
And gained for me salvation.

6. Let Him avail / To be my bail,
Let His life be my payment,
His holy blood / My garment good,
My shining crimson raiment.

7. For Thy great love / My guilt remove
Where I Thy laws have broken;
Lo, in Thy Son / Thine oath is done,
Thy grace and balm bespoken.

8. To this I cling / And to Thee bring,
O Lord, my wounds for mending;
Sin heavily / Oppresses me,
Beneath its load I'm bending.

9. Now with Thy hand / Dissolve its band,
Renew my strength and vigor,
Do not o'erthrow / Faith's feeble glow,
Lord, in Thy righteous rigor.

10. For I confess / My wickedness,
The cause of Thy heart's spurning;
Yet as I now / Repentant bow,
I know faith's lamp is burning.

11. So work in me / Continually,
The fire of faith sustaining,
And let this coal / Within my soul
In weakness not be waning.

12. Support me still, / Grant me to will
And do in each endeavor;
My tongue shall then / From deep within
Sing thanks to Thee forever.

—Anon., Chemnitz, before 1727; tr., M. Carver.

228

Tune: Aus tiefer Not schrei ich zu dir. 49. [*LW* 230; *TLH* 329; *LSB* 607]

1. O Lord, my God, by my own pow'r
I only could enrage Thee;
How then shall I at any hour
Be able to assuage Thee?
Yet hope I have: Thy dearest Son
In whom no stain of sin was known,
Became my own Redeemer.

2. With willing heart from heaven's rest
To me He came, descending,
In my own flesh and blood was dressed,
In love my race befriending,
That He might heal and bandage me
And bind my sin-wrought injury
That so provoked Thine anger.

3. One man it was provoked Thy wrath,
One also must appease Thee,
Enduring freely cross and death
To still Thy rage and please Thee.
Upon Thy right His piercings prove
How He hath bound us in His love
And made us Thine forever.

4. This, this my confidence shall be,
My trust and firm reliance.
Art Thou too just to look on me,
My sin, and my defiance,
In grace regard me free of vice;
The merits of Thy Son suffice
To pay for my transgressions.

5. O Father, here Thy Son embrace
And smile on me, Thy servant;
For Him, my Shield, my Throne of Grace,
Withhold Thy rod so fervent.
See Thou His scars of thorn and nail,
For all my sins a glorious veil,
Concealing them forever.

6. His blood so red Thou dost survey
In lavish torrents driven—
Oh, wash my filth of sin away—
For me His blood was given.
As flesh it was that angered Thee,
So let His flesh avail for me
And stir Thy heart to mercy.

7. Great is the debt which oft and deep
I have by sin contracted,
Yet no despair my heart will keep,
Since Christ for me hath acted
And, in obedience suffering,
Endured God's wrath, death's bitter sting,
And won for me salvation.

8. Great, too, is my unrighteousness
Which stirred Thy wrath and steeled it;
His innocence is as the dress
Which amply hath concealed it.
In man is found no sin so ill,
But Jesus' death is greater still,
And blots it out completely.

9. What man in all the world is there
So swollen with pride's leaven,
That, if Christ's humbleness he wear,
He will not be forgiven?
The pow'r of death was not too great
For Christ, God's Son, by bitter fate
Upon the cross to crush it.

10. Let Jesus' grace and love be laid
Against all man's transgression,
And on the balance duly weighed,
And there will be no question—
The first doth so the last outweigh
As far as night is from the day
Or even hell from heaven.

11. Therefore, O God of love replete
And boundless grace, receive me;
Accept Thy Son's blood-off'ring meet
And of my sins forgive me!
His stainlessness for all my stain,
His patience for my proud disdain—
His take to be my merits.

12. Grant me His meekness for my shield
From boasting to defend me;
And help my spiteful heart to yield,
His gentle nature lend me;
Let Him be all that I require,
So shall I not arouse Thine ire,
Nor suffer condemnation.

—J. Heermann, 1630; tr., M. Carver.

229

Tune: Vater unser im Himmelreich. 44. [*TLH* 318; *LW* 234; *LSB* 766]

1. Yea, as I live, thy Maker saith,
I do not wish the sinner's death,
But rather that he turn betimes
From all his evil ways and crimes,
With true repentance come to Me,
And live to all eternity.

2. O man, this word prevail with thee,
Despair not in iniquity,
Lay hold on this free offered grace,
Confirmed by surest promises,
Nay, sealed with God's most solemn oath.
Blest all who their transgressions loathe!

3. Yet, O beware! Think not, secure:
"God's grace I always can procure;
I'll first partake of youthful mirth,
Till I'm convinced how vain this earth,
Then shall my serious thoughts begin
To seek God's pardon for my sin."

4. True, God is ready with His grace
Repenting sinners to embrace,
Yet, who runs up his sinful score
On grace, till he can find no more,
Will learn, to his amazing cost,
Long-suff'ring mercy may be lost.

5. Mercy thy God has promised thee
For Christ, His blood and agony,
Yet in His Word did never say
That thou shouldst live another day.
That thou must die He hath revealed,
But death's dark hour to thee's concealed.

6. Today thou liv'st, today repent,
Lest all thy life should be misspent.
Who laughs today, looks fair and red,
Tomorrow may be sick and dead.
If thou wilt die impenitent,
Then flames will ever thee torment.

7. O blessed Jesus, grant I may
Return to Thee this very day
And live in constant penitence,
Till death appears to call me hence,
That I in every time and place
Be well prepared to end my race.

—J. Heermann, 1630; tr., J. C. Jacobi, 1732, alt.

230

Tune: Auf meinen lieben Gott. 29.
[*TLH* 526; *LW* 421; *LSB* 745; *or TLH* 57; *LW* 20; *LSB* 335]

1. Oh, whither shall I flee,
Depressed with misery?
Who is it that can ease me,
And from my sins release me?
Though all the world should aid me
Of grief they could not rid me.

2. O Jesus, Source of Grace,
I seek Thy loving face,
Upon Thy invitation,
With deep humiliation;
Oh, let Thy blood me cover,
And wash my soul all over.

3. I, Thine unworthy child,
Corrupt throughout and spoiled,
Beseech Thee to relieve me,
And graciously forgive me
My sins, which have abounded,
And my poor soul confounded.

4. Through Thine atoning blood,
That precious healing flood,
Purge off all sin and sadness,
And fill my heart with gladness;
Lord, hear Thou my confession,
And blot out my transgression.

5. Thou shalt my comfort be,
Since Thou hast died for me;
I am by Thee acquitted
Of all I e'er committed,
My sins by Thee were carried,
And in Thy tomb were buried.

6. Though vast my sins may be,
From them I yet am free,
In Thy dear blood confiding
And in true faith abiding.
The soul in Thee located
Finds sorrow soon abated.

7. I know my poverty;
But ne'ertheless, for me
All goodly gifts are offered,
Since Thou Thy death hast suffered;
Thus strengthened, I may banish
All fears; my foes must vanish.

8. Though all the devil's horde
Against me take the sword,
I will not fear to meet them;
With Thee I shall defeat them;
When in Thy blood I hail them,
Their weapons all must fail them.

9. Christ, Thy atoning blood,
The sinner's highest good,
Is mighty to deliver
And free the soul forever
From all claim of the devil,
And cleanse it from all evil.

10. Lord Jesus Christ, in Thee
I trust eternally:
I know I shall not perish,
But in Thy kingdom flourish;
For such Thy merits gave me,
When Thou didst die to save me.

11. Lord, strengthen Thou my heart;
To me such grace impart,
That naught which may await me
From Thee may separate me.
Let me with Thee, my Savior,
United be for ever.

12. Amen! at every hour
I say with all my pow'r.
Oh, ever deign to guide me,
Lord Christ, and stay beside me,
That I may praise forever
Thy name, and finish never.

—J. Heermann, 1630; tr., *Mor. H.-B.*, 1845, alt., but sts. 6, 8, 12, M. Carver.

Faith and Justification

231

Tune: Es ist das Heil uns kommen her. 49. [*TLH* 377; *LW* 355; *LSB* 555]

1. Behold, what right and light I'm taught
By Jesus Christ, my Savior!
My Lord and God forsakes me not,
Nor will be distant ever;
It matters not what ills betide,
With help He hastens to my side,—
My God, my Life, My Jesus.

2. The Father will not me forsake,
Since He doth love me ever;
He will Himself not distant make,
Since He gave me the Savior.
With help He hastens to my side
Because I heartily confide
In Jesus, His beloved.

3. This by His gracious choice I have,
For God so loved creation,
That in His Son to us He gave
His seal of adoration.
The name of every child of God
Is written down in heav'n's abode;
I know He'll not forget me.

4. My faithful Savior paid the cost,
In Him I find completion,
And nothing in Him shall be lost
Except my foul transgression,
For this is sunk beneath the sea,
Beyond the Father's memory,
And I have life eternal.

5. To this poor world our God descends,
Christ's limbs are we, united,
And all those gifts He loves and lends
We offer back, delighted;
He loves us as His heritage,
It is God's praise from age to age,
That He His own defendeth.

6. So when distress or death I know,
I gladly will be singing:
"For God so loved the world," and lo,
The foe will feel its stinging.
Where Christ abides, so, too, shall we;
His life is now our guarantee
That death will not destroy us.

7. God, grant that by Thy Spirit I
May trust in Him sincerely,
And firmly on that hope rely
Within His word set clearly.
For there my certain portion dwells;
There is salvation nowhere else,
No other path to heaven.

8. And so, if I must die today,
No sound my ears will cherish
But what it pleased my God to say:
"Believers shall not perish."
I do believe, Christ doth agree,
Therefore no perishing I'll see,
But life, and life unending!

—C. Weise, 1682; tr., M. Carver.

Tune: Ach, was soll ich Sünder machen. 36. [*TLH* 384; *LW* 364; *LSB* 559]

232

1. Oh, how great is Thy compassion,
Faithful Father, God of grace,
That with all our fallen race
And in our deep degradation
Thou wast merciful that we
Might be saved eternally!

2. Thy great love for this hath striven
That we may from sin be free
And forever live with Thee;
Yea, Thy Son Himself hath given
And extends an earnest call
To His Supper unto all.

3. And for this our soul's salvation
Voucheth Thy good Spirit, Lord,
In Thy Sacraments and Word.
He imparts true consolation,
Granteth us the gift of faith
That we fear nor hell nor death.

4. Lord, Thy mercy will not leave me,—
Truth doth evermore abide,—
Then in Thee I will confide.
Since Thy Word cannot deceive me,
My salvation is to me
Well assured eternally.

5. I will praise Thy great compassion,
Faithful Father, God of grace,
That with all our fallen race
And in our deep degradation
Thou wast merciful that we
Might bring endless praise to Thee.

—J. Olearius, 1671; tr., A. Crull, †1923, alt.

233

Tune: Herr Jesu Christ, meins Lebens Licht. 11. [*TLH* 288; *LW* 262; *LSB* 704]

1. God loved the world so that He gave
His only Son the lost to save
That all who would in Him believe
Should everlasting life receive.

2. Christ Jesus is the Ground of faith,
Who was made flesh and suffered death;
All that confide in Him alone
Are built on this chief Corner-stone.

3. God would not have the sinner die,
His Son with saving grace is nigh,
His Spirit in the Word doth teach
How man the blessèd goal may reach.

4. Be of good cheer, for God's own Son
Forgives all sins which thou hast done;
Thou'rt justified by Jesus' blood,
Thy Baptism grants the highest good.

5. If thou be sick, if death draw near,
This truth thy troubled heart can cheer:
Christ Jesus saves my soul from death,
That is the firmest ground of faith.

6. Glory to God the Father, Son,
And Holy Spirit, Three in One!
To Thee, O blessèd Trinity,
Be praise now and eternally!

—J. Olearius, 1671; tr., A. Crull, 1889, alt.

234

Tune: Wer weiß, wie nahe mir. 45. [*TLH* 65; *LSB* 598; *or TLH* 373*; *LW* 224*; *LSB* 566*]

1. By grace I'm saved, grace free and boundless;
My soul, believe and doubt it not.
Why stagger at this word of promise?
Hath Scripture ever falsehood taught?
Nay; then this word must true remain:
By grace thou, too, shalt heav'n obtain.

2. By grace! None dare lay claim to merit;
Our works and conduct have no worth.
God in His love sent our Redeemer,
Christ Jesus, to this sinful earth;
His death did for our sins atone,
And we are saved by grace alone.

3. By grace! Oh, mark this word of promise
When thou art by thy sins oppressed,
When Satan plagues thy troubled conscience,
And when thy heart is seeking rest.
What reason cannot comprehend
God by His grace to thee doth send.

4. By grace God's Son, our only Savior,
Came down to earth to bear our sin.
Was it because of thine own merit
That Jesus died thy soul to win?
Nay, it was grace, and grace alone,
That brought Him from His heav'nly throne.

5. By grace! This ground of faith is certain;
So long as God is true, it stands.
What saints have penned by inspiration,
What in His Word our God commands,
What our whole faith must rest upon,
Is Grace alone, grace in His Son.

6. By grace! But think not, thou who livest
Securely on in godless ways,
That thou,—though all are called,—receivest
The promised rest that wakes our praise;
By grace none find in heav'n a place
Who live in sin in hope of grace.

7. By grace! They who have heard this sentence
Must all hypocrisy forgo;
For only after deep repentance
Can any soul this treasure know.
To sin free grace a trifle seems,
To faith it bright with glory beams.

8. By grace to timid hearts that tremble,
In tribulation's furnace tried,—
By grace, despite all fear and trouble,
The Father's heart is open wide.
Where could I help and strength secure
If grace were not my anchor sure?

9. By grace! On this I'll rest when dying;
In Jesus' promise I rejoice;
For though I know my heart's condition,
I also know my Savior's voice.
My heart is glad, all grief has flown,
Since I am saved by grace alone.

10. By grace! May sin and Satan hearken!
I bear my flag of faith in hand,
And pass—for doubts my joy can't darken—
The Red Sea to the Promised land.
I cling to what my Savior taught,
And trust it, whether felt or not.

—C. L. Scheidt, 1742; tr., M. Loy, †1915, alt.

235

Tune: Jesus, meine Zuversicht. 33. [*TLH* 206; *LW* 266; *LSB* 741]

1. What a faithful saying this,
Worthy of all acceptation,
Precious promise, full of bliss,
Pledge of all the world's salvation:
That the Father freely gave
Jesus Christ to seek and save.

2. Now we need no longer cry
As the Jews, with grief and sadness:
"Oh, that Christ might soon draw nigh,
Jacob's Star of hope and gladness!"
For Messiah came and drew
Night to all salvation true.

3. Now we see the Prince of peace,
Judah's hero, great and glorious,
Come to gain our full release,
Come to conquer, all victorious.
Now with healing in His hands
To all sinners nigh He stands.

4. Yes, to sinners nigh He stands
With His benefits to bless us,
When the evils of our hands
And our hearts seem to oppress us;
When the conscience, law, and sin
Still accuse us deep within.

5. Hush, O Law, and do not say,
"Sinners, ye are lost forever."
Jesus is our Staff and Stay;
Who can part us, who can sever?
Under law was Jesus born;
What to us thy curse and scorn?

6. Sins and conscience's distress,
Now in peace and quiet leave us!
Why insist that ye possess
Powèr from our God to cleave us?
See how we by His own Son
Now with Him have been made one.

7. Hush, O world, say not that God
Has for man alone displeasure;
Such is foolishness and fraud,
Yea, deceit in fullest measure;
But this word is candid truth:
He is come to save and soothe.

8. Satan, fly and get thee hence!
Christ, the Son of God, hath bound thee.
Death, whose heel knows thine offense?
Jesus' vict'ry did confound thee.
Hell, what use to wage thy war,
Or this triumph to ignore?

9. God, we thank Thee evermore
For Thy blessed gift and favor:
Thy dear Son, whom we adore,
Born to be our Lord and Savior.
What a wonder now unfurled,
To restore a sinful world.

10. Oh, bestow, most precious Son,
That we may in Thee find gladness
And all sinful works may shun
When we meet distress and sadness;
Take us at the proper tide
Into blessing at Thy side.

—J. Möller, 1700; tr. sts. 1–3, 5, 9, W. Czamanske, 1920, alt.; sts. rest, M. Carver.

236

Tune: Durch Adams Fall ist ganz verderbt. 83. [p. 401]

1. By Adam's fall man's frame entire
And nature was infected;
The source, whence came the poison dire,
Was not to be corrected,
The lust accursed, / Indulged at first,
Brought death as its production;
But God's free grace / Hath saved our race
From mis'ry and destruction.

2. Since Eve by Satan was enticed
And, yielding to temptation,
God's Word rejected and despised,
And ruined was creation:
Naught could be done, / But God His Son
Must send in our own nature
That through His death, / We all by faith
Might be a newborn creature!

3. By one man's guilt all men, enslaved,
Were subjects of the devil;
But by another's grace is saved
Mankind from every evil:
And as we all / By Adam's fall
Were sentenced to damnation,
So too hath God / By Christ's own blood
Regained our lost salvation.

4. Since God bestowed His only Son
On His rebellious creatures,
To save our souls, which were undone
And free our sinful natures
From all their guilt / By His blood spilt,
Who rose and high ascended.
Why should we then / Dread any pain,
Or be by death offended?

5. Christ is the Way, the Light, the Door,
The hope and life eternal,
The Father's Word and Counselor,
To conquer pow'rs infernal,
Our strongest Shield / To win the field,
The Helmet of salvation.
What pow'r or might / Then has the right
To cast us to damnation?

6. Man is ungodly and unjust,
And far from his own healing;
Who does in God not put his trust,
But, to mere man appealing,
Would rather frame / Another name
Than Christ's to justify him,
Will banish hence / His confidence,
When Satan comes to try him.

7. But who makes God his hope and trust
Shall never be confounded:
No house built on this Rock is lost,
Though everywhere surrounded
By daring foes / And trying woes;
His faith yet stands unshaken.
Who loves the Lord / Shall by no sword
Nor woe be overtaken.

8. I pray Thee heartily, O Lord,
That of Thy gracious favor,
Thou wouldst not take Thy holy Word
Out of my mouth forever,
That sin and shame / May lose their claim
To hinder my salvation:
Who in Thy grace / His hope will place,
Need fear no condemnation.

9. Thy Word's a lamp unto my feet,
A lantern burning brightly;
My surest guide and path to meet
The way to heaven rightly.
This Star, where'er / It doth appear,
Reveals those heav'nly graces,
Which are laid up / For all that hope
To taste the Lord's embraces.

—L. Spengler, 1524; tr., J. C. Jacobi, 1725, alt.

237

Tune: Es ist das Heil uns kommen her. 49. [*TLH* 377; *LW* 355; *LSB* 555]

1. Salvation unto us has come
By God's free grace and favor;
Good works cannot avert our doom,
They help and save us never.
Faith looks to Jesus Christ alone,
Who did for all the world atone;
He is our one Redeemer.

2. What God did in His law demand
And none to Him could render
Caused wrath and woe on every hand
For man, the vile offender.
Our flesh has not those pure desires
The spirit of the Law requires,
And lost is our condition.

3. It was a false, misleading dream
That God His law had given
That sinners should themselves redeem
And by their works gain heaven.
The Law is but a mirror bright
To bring the inbred sin to light
That lurks within our nature.

4. From sin our flesh could not abstain,
Sin held its sway unceasing;
The task was useless and in vain,
Our guilt was e'er increasing.
None can remove sin's poisoned dart
Or purify our guileful heart,—
So deep is our corruption.

5. Yet as the Law must be fulfilled
Or we must die despairing,
Christ came and hath God's anger stilled,
Our human nature sharing.
He hath for us the Law obeyed
And thus the Father's vengeance stayed
Which over us impended.

6. Since Christ hath full atonement made
And brought to us salvation,
Each Christian therefore may be glad
And build on this foundation.
Thy grace alone, dear Lord, I plead,
Thy death is now my life indeed,
For Thou hast paid my ransom.

7. Let me not doubt, but trust in Thee,
Thy Word cannot be broken;
Thy call rings out, "Come unto Me!"
No falsehood hast Thou spoken.
Baptized into Thy precious name,
My faith cannot be put to shame,
And I shall never perish.

8. The just is he—and he alone—
Who by this faith is living,
The faith that by good works is shown,
To God the glory giving;
Faith gives thee peace with God above,
But thou thy neighbor, too, must love,
If thou art new created.

9. The Law reveals the guilt of sin
And makes men conscience-stricken;
The Gospel then doth enter in
The sinful soul to quicken.
Come to the cross, trust Christ, and live;
The Law no peace can ever give,
No comfort and no blessing.

10. Faith clings to Jesus' cross alone
And rests in Him unceasing;
And by its fruits true faith is known,
With love and hope increasing.
Yet faith alone doth justify,
Works serve thy neighbor and supply
The proof that faith is living.

11. Hope waits for the accepted hour—
Till God give joy for mourning,
When He displays His healing pow'r,
Thy sighs to songs are turning;
Thy needs are known unto thy Lord,
And He is faithful to His word,
This is our hope's foundation.

12. Though it may seem, He hears thee not,
Count not thyself forsaken;
Thy wants are ne'er by Him forgot,
Let this thy hope awaken;
His word is sure, here is thy stay.
And though thy flesh say only nay,
Let not thy faith be shaken.

13. All blessing, honor, thanks, and praise
To Father, Son, and Spirit,
The God that saved us by His grace,—
All glory to His merit!
O Triune God in heav'n above,
Who hast revealed Thy saving love,
Thy blessed name be hallowed.

14. Thy kingdom come, Thy will be done
On earth, as 'tis in heaven:
Keep us in life, by grace led on,
Forgiving and forgiven;
Save Thou us in temptation's hour,
And from all ills; Thine is the pow'r,
And all the glory, Amen!

—P. Speratus, 1523; tr., *TLH*, 1941; but sts. 8, 11–12, 14, Døving, 1904, alt.

238

Tune: Nun freut euch, lieben Christen. 49. [*TLH* 124; *LW* 353; *LSB* 556]

1. Lord Jesus Christ, My Hope and Light,
I give Thee thanks sincerely,
Thou didst not cast me from Thy sight
When my transgressions clearly
Assailed me with relentless woe,
Through Satan's hand, who, as my foe,
Would make me suffer dearly.

2. Thou didst my sighing take to heart,
In grace my sin forgiving,
Though it refuses to depart
Throughout man's earthly living:
Thy servant Thou hast kept in mind,
Who shall Thy heaven come to find,
Thy love on earth receiving.

3. O Lamb of God, Thou Never-stained,
In my own place tormented,
O Bridegroom of my Soul, my Friend,
Now is my death prevented
And life obtained by Thy demise;
I thank Thee that I thus may rise
To live fore'er contented.

4. Lord, give to me Thy Spirit good,
In all Thy truth to guide me,
To beckon me to what He would,
And plant Thy love inside me,
That lips and hands Thy praise impart,
His working in my inmost heart
With songs of joy provide me.

5. Lord, let me henceforth lay aside
All sin and shame completely
And stand against all lust and pride
Which often and discreetly
Seduce me from Thy way to go
To join sin's path, whose steps, I know,
God's blessings lose completely.

6. At last rule Thou my flesh and blood,
Thy will for mine supplying,
For Thou dost work all things for good
To those on Thee relying.
Lord, let my soul to heaven fly,
For there I know for sure that I
Can boldly still my sighing.

7. Lord Jesus, let me seek but Thee,
And ever find Thee even;
From earthly tethers set me free,
And bind my heart to heaven,
And to Thyself, that o'er all woe—
The world, sin, death, hell, and the foe—
I may the crown be given.

—J. Rist, †1667; tr., M. Carver.

239

Tune: Herzlich tut mich verlangen. 59.
[*TLH* 172; *LW* 113; *LSB* 450; *or TLH* 334*; *LW* 257*; *LSB* 689*]

1. Through Jesus' blood and merit
I am at peace with God;
What, then, can daunt my spirit,
However dark my road?
My courage shall not fail me,
For God is on my side;
Though hell itself assail me,
Its rage I may deride.

2. There's naught that me can sever
From the great love of God;
No want, no pain, whatever,
No famine, peril, flood.
Though thousand foes surround me,
For slaughter mark Thy sheep,
They never shall confound me,
The vict'ry I shall reap.

3. Through Jesus, who doth love me,
I now can still my grief,
I now have consolation,
Wise counsel, and relief.
In this sure hope a sharer,
Full is my confidence,
And neither might nor terror
Can ever steal it hence.

4. Yea, neither life's temptation
Nor death's so trying hour,
Nor angels of high station,
Nor any other pow'r,
Nor things that now are present,
Nor things that are to come,
Nor height, however pleasant,
Nor depths of deepest gloom,

5. Nor any creature ever
Shall from the love of God
This wretched sinner sever;
For in my Savior's blood
This love its fountain taketh;
He hears my faithful pray'r
And nevermore forsaketh
His own dear child and heir.

—S. Dach, 1651; tr., A. Crull, †1923, alt., but st. 3, M. Carver.

240

Tune: O daß ich tausend Zungen hätte. 45. [*TLH* 385; *LW* 360; *LSB* 811]

1. Now I have found the firm foundation
Which holds mine anchor ever sure;
'Twas laid before the world's creation
In Christ my Savior's wounds secure;
Foundation which unmoved shall stay
When heav'n and earth will pass away.

2. It is that mercy never ending
Which human wisdom far transcends,
Of Him who, loving arms extending,
To wretched sinners condescends;
Whose heart with pity still doth break
Whether we seek Him or forsake.

3. Our ruin God hath not intended,
For our salvation He hath yearned;
For this His Son to earth descended
And then to heav'n again returned;
For this so patient evermore
He knocketh at our heart's closed door.

4. O depth of love, to me revealing
The sea where my sins disappear!
In Christ my wounds find perfect healing,
There is no condemnation here;
For Jesus' blood through earth and skies
Forever "Mercy! Mercy!" cries.

5. I never will forget this crying;
In faith I'll trust it all my days,
And when o'er all my sins I'm sighing,
Into the Father's heart I'll gaze;
For there is always to be found
Free mercy without end and bound.

6. Though I be robbed of every pleasure
That makes my soul and body glad
And be deprived of earthly treasure
And be forsaken, lone, and sad,
And my desire for help seem vain,
His mercy shall with me remain.

7. Tho' earthly trials should oppress me
And cares from day to day increase;
Tho' earth's vain things should sore distress me
And rob me of my Savior's peace;
Though I be brought down to the dust,
Still in His mercy I will trust.

8. When all my deeds I am reviewing,
The deeds that I admire the most,
I find in all my thought and doing
That there is naught whereof to boast.
Yet this sweet comfort shall abide—
In mercy I can still confide.

9. Let mercy cause me to be willing
To bear my lot and not to fret.
While He my restless heart is stilling,
May I His mercy not forget!
Come weal, come woe, my heart to test,
His mercy is my only rest.

10. I'll stand upon this firm foundation
As long as I on earth remain;
This shall engage my meditation
While I the breath of life retain;
And then, when face to face with Thee,
I'll sing of mercy, great and free.

—J. A. Rothe, 1722; tr., *TLH,* 1941.

241

Tune: Nun lob, mein Seel, den Herren. 93. [*TLH* 381; *LW* 453; *LSB* 820]

1. I know my faith is founded
On Jesus Christ, my God and Lord;
And this my faith confessing,
Unmoved I stand upon His Word.
Man's reason cannot fathom
The truth of God profound;
Who trusts her subtle wisdom
Relies on shifting ground.
God's Word is all sufficient,
It makes divinely sure,
And trusting in its wisdom,
My faith shall rest secure.

2. Increase my faith, dear Savior,
For Satan seeks by night and day
To rob me of this treasure
And take my hope of bliss away.
But, Lord, with Thee beside me,
I shall be undismayed;
And led by Thy good Spirit,
I shall be unafraid.
Abide with me, O Savior,
A firmer faith bestow;
Then I shall bid defiance
To every evil foe.

3. In faith, Lord, let me serve Thee;
Though persecution, grief, and pain
Should seek to overwhelm me,
Let me a steadfast trust retain;
And then at my departure
Take Thou me home to Thee
And let me there inherit
All Thou hast promised me.
In life and death, Lord, keep me
Until Thy heav'n I gain,
Where I by Thy great mercy
The end of faith attain.

—E. Neumeister, 1718; tr., *TLH,* 1941.

242

Tune: Mein Heiland nimmt die Sünder an. 88. [*TLH* 386]

1. My Savior sinners doth receive,
Who find no rest and no salvation,
To whom no man can comfort give,
So great their guilt and condemnation;
For whom the world is all too small,
Their sins themselves and God appall;
With whom the Law itself hath broken,
On whom its judgment hath been spoken,—
To them the Gospel hope doth give:
My Savior sinners doth receive.
My Savior sinners doth receive.

2. A love more deep than mother-love,
With which His heart was overflowing,
Drew Him to earth from heav'n above,
On sinners boundless grace bestowing,
He in their stead a curse became,
He bore the cross with all its shame;
Brought full atonement by His suff'ring,
Gave up His life for them an off'ring.
This comfort doth the Gospel give:
My Savior sinners doth receive.
My Savior sinners doth receive.

3. His loving bosom still remains
A haven for the heavy-laden;
Christ frees them from their guilty stains,
Their burdened hearts doth ease and gladden.
He casts into th' unfathomed sea
The load of their iniquity;
He gives assurance by His Spirit
That they are saved through His own merit.
Yea, they shall live who this believe:
My Savior sinners doth receive.
My Savior sinners doth receive.

4. In arms that flow with blood divine
He bears them to His Father holy
And makes the Father's mind incline
With everlasting mercy solely;
As children doth He make them His,
Yea, everything He hath and is
Into their hands He doth deliver;
The door that leads to life forever
Swings wide to gladden all who grieve:
My Savior sinners doth receive.
My Savior sinners doth receive.

5. Oh, couldst thou but His heart have seen,
And how to lost ones e'er it bore Him,
For those who long in sin had been,
Whose eyes poured out their tears before Him!
He cleansed the publican of blame,
And to Zaccheus' quickly came;
When Magdalene mourned her transgression,
He dried her tears with sweet compassion;
Despite their sins, He would not leave.
My Savior sinners doth receive.
My Savior sinners doth receive.

6. How love-filled was His tender look
When Peter's deep-dyed sin He pondered!
Ah, not alone this course He took
When in this vale of tears He wandered.
Eternal love is still the same,
The Friend of sinners is His name.
As on the cross His love was given,
Thus from His glorious throne in heaven
He gives to sinners kind reprieve:
My Savior sinners doth receive.
My Savior sinners doth receive.

7. O come, then, child of sinful men,
Come well thy griefs and sorrows knowing,
Approach the One who knew no sin
And stoops to sinners, lowly bowing.
What, wilt thou stand in judgment's light
And perish without heart contrite?
Wilt thou let sin and hell enslave thee
When Christ is manifest to save thee?
Oh nay, but from sin's byways leave!—
My Savior sinners doth receive.
My Savior sinners doth receive.

8. Come, all that heavy-laden are;
Come, weary, void of self-assistance;
Though doubting, ready to despair,
To Jesus come without resistance.
Behold His heart with love replete,
Full of desire the worst to meet;
Long hath He sought for thee, tho' wretchèd,
Thee to embrace with arms outstretchèd.
So come, poor soul, thy way here weave;
My Savior sinners doth receive.
My Savior sinners doth receive.

9. Say not: "My sins are far too great,
His mercy I have scorned and slighted,
Now my repentance is too late;
I came not when His love invited."
O trembling sinner, have no fear;
In penitence to Christ draw near.
Come now, tho' conscience still is chiding;
Accept His mercy, e'er abiding.
Come; blest are they who this believe:
My Savior sinners doth receive.
My Savior sinners doth receive.

10. Think not, "'Tis time enough;" nor say,
"God, who is gracious beyond measure,
Shuts not the door of grace today;
I'll first enjoy some carnal pleasure."
No, God forbid! If trouble wise,
Grace offered now do not despise.
Who slights today the invitation
May ever lose his soul's salvation:
Come now to Jesus, come and live;
My Savior sinners doth receive.
My Savior sinners doth receive.

11. Oh, draw us ever unto Thee,
Thou Friend of sinners, gracious Savior;
Help us that we may fervently
Desire Thy pardon, peace and favor.
When guilty conscience doth reprove,
Reveal to us Thy heart of love.
May we, our wretchedness beholding,
See then Thy pard'ning grace unfolding
And say: "To God all glory be:
My Savior, Christ, receiveth me.
My Savior, Christ, receiveth me."

—L. F. Lehr, 1731; tr. sts. 1–3, 9, 11, *TLH*, 1941; sts. 8, 10, *Mor. H.B.*, 1799, alt.;
tr. st. 6, A. Hoppe, 1922, alt.; sts. rest, M. Carver.

243

Tune: Nun freut euch, lieben Christen. 49. [*TLH* 387; *LW* 353; *LSB* 556]

1. Dear Christians, one and all, rejoice,
With exultation springing,
And, with united heart and voice
And holy rapture singing,
Proclaim the wonders God hath done,
How His right arm the vict'ry won;
Right dearly it hath cost Him.

2. Fast bound in Satan's chains I lay,
Death brooded darkly o'er me,
Sin was my torment night and day,
In sin my mother bore me;
Yea, deep and deeper still I fell,
Life had become a living hell,
So firmly sin possessed me.

3. My own good works availed me naught,
No merit they attaining;
Free will against God's judgment fought,
Dead to all good remaining.
My fears increased till sheer despair
Left naught but death to be my share;
The pangs of hell I suffered.

4. But God beheld my wretched state
Before the world's foundation,
And, mindful of His mercies great,
He planned my soul's salvation.
A father's heart He turned to me,
Sought my redemption fervently:
He gave His dearest Treasure.

5. He spoke to His beloved Son:
'Tis time to have compassion.
Then go, bright Jewel of My crown,
And bring to man salvation;
From sin and sorrow set him free,
Slay bitter death for him that he
May live with Thee forever.

6. This Son obeyed His Father's will,
Was born of virgin mother,
And God's good pleasure to fulfill,
He came to be my Brother.
No garb of pomp or pow'r He wore,
A servant's form, like mine, He bore,
To lead the devil captive.

7. To me He spake: Hold fast to Me,
I am thy Rock and Castle;
Thy Ransom I Myself will be,
For thee I strive and wrestle;
For I am with thee, I am thine,
And evermore thou shalt be Mine;
The Foe shall not divide us.

8. The Foe shall shed My precious blood,
Me of My life bereaving.
All this I suffer for thy good;
Be steadfast and believing.
Life shall from death the vict'ry win,
My innocence shall bear thy sin;
So art thou blest forever.

9. Now to My Father I depart,
The Holy Spirit sending
And, heav'nly wisdom to impart,
My help to thee extending.
He shall in trouble comfort thee,
Teach thee to know and follow Me,
And in all truth shall guide thee.

10. What I have done and taught, teach thou,
My ways forsake thou never;
So shall My kingdom flourish now
And God be praised forever.
Take heed lest men with base alloy
The heav'nly treasure should destroy;
This counsel I bequeath thee.

—M. Luther, 1523; tr., R. Massie, 1854, alt.

244

Tune: Ach Gott vom Himmel, sieh darein. 49. [*TLH* 260]

1. Lord Jesus Christ, God's only Son,
In Thee is my salvation;
To Thee I owe my faith alone,
To Thee, my preservation;
Oh, help Thou me from heav'n above,
Keep me in steadfast faith and love,
That ever I may serve Thee.

2. Instruct me, make Thy teachings known,
That I may know the Father,
And Thee confess as God's true Son,
Thee only and none other,
And praise the Holy Spirit's name,
Of equal glory, praise, and fame,
The triune God forever.

3. Of Thy salvation great and free
Afford me true cognition,
That those who but partake of Thee
Of sin have full remission.
Help me to seek it as I should;
Thou art the Way, the level Road,
The Truth, the Life, my Savior.

4. Grant me to trust Thy precious Word,
Its blessings to inherit;
Upon it build my faith, O Lord,
And on Thy holy merit,
That in my sin and sore distress
Thy perfect work and righteousness
May be my consolation.

5. Teach me to view Thy holy blood,
Shed for each vile transgression,
My ever ready, healing flood,
My fount of sure salvation.
So precious let it be to me,
That earth's most valued gifts I flee,
To win and keep it only.

6. Though faith as small as mustard be,
And scarce an eye may view it,
Yet be Thou mighty, Lord, in me,
Through grace with strength imbue it;
The bruisèd reed, oh, do not break;
The smold'ring wick do not forsake,
But show Thy strength in weakness.

7. Help me that I may constant be,
The faith securely keeping,
And hold a conscience good in me
That, though awake or sleeping,
I may be filled in all I do
With righteousness, and ever show
The fruits that issue from it.

8. Lord, by this faith reside in me
And make it strong and healthy,
That it may ever fruitful be,
In good works rich and wealthy,
And that it may abound in love,
All joy and patience know and prove
In service to my neighbor.

9. Above all else, sustain my pow'r
To wage, till life is ended,
The warfare good from hour to hour,
And be to Thee commended
When comes my final dying breath,
And have at last, Lord, by Thy death
The end of faith: Salvation.

10. Lord Jesus, let me trust always
In Thee for my salvation;
Increase my faith through all my days,
Inflame my love to passion;
Thy blessed work begun in me,
Perfect until in heav'n I'll see
And praise Thee there forever.

—D. Denicke, 1657; tr. sts. 1, 4–6, 10, J. T. Mueller, 1920, alt.; sts. rest, M. Carver.

245

Tune: Nun freut euch, lieben Christen. 49.
[*TLH* 124; *LW* 353; *LSB* 556; *or TLH* 383*; *LW* 358*; *LSB* 557*]

1. Seek where ye may / To find a way
That leads to your salvation;
My heart is stilled, / On Christ I build,
He is the one Foundation.
His Word is sure, / His works endure;
He doth o'erthrow / My every foe;
Through Him I more than conquer.

2. Seek whom ye may / To be your stay;
None can redeem his brother.
All helpers failed, / This Man prevailed,
The God-man, and none other.
Our Servant-Lord / Did help afford;
We're justified, / For He hath died,
The Guiltless for the guilty.

3. Seek Him alone, / Who did atone,
Who did your souls deliver;
Yea, seek Him first, / All ye who thirst
For grace that faileth never.
In every need / Seek Him indeed;
To every heart / He will impart
His blessings without measure.

4. My heart's Delight, / My Crown most bright,
Thou, Jesus, art forever.
Nor wealth nor pride / Nor aught beside
Our bond of love shall sever.
Thou art my Lord; / Thy precious Word
Shall be my guide, / Whate'er betide.
Oh, teach me, Lord, to trust Thee!

5. Hide not from me, / I ask of Thee,
Thy gracious face and favor.
Though floods of woe / Should o'er me flow,
My faith shall never waver.
From pain and grief / Grant sweet relief;
For tears I weep, / Lord, let me reap
Thy heav'nly joy and glory.

—G. Weissel, 1623; tr., A. Voss, 1938.

246

Tune: Nun freut euch, lieben Christen. 49. [*TLH* 124; *LW* 353; *LSB* 556]

1. If Thy beloved Son, O God,
Had not to earth descended
And in our mortal flesh and blood
Had not sin's power ended,
Then this poor, wretched soul of mine
In hell eternally would pine
Because of its transgression.

2. But now I find sweet peace and rest,
Despair no more reigns o'er me;
No more am I by sin oppressed,
For Christ has borne sin for me.
Upon the cross for me He died
That, reconciled, I might abide
With Thee, my God, forever.

3. I trust in Him with all my heart;
Now all my sorrow ceases;
His words abiding peace impart,
His blood from guilt releases.
Free grace through Him I now obtain;
He washes me from every stain,
And pure I stand before Him.

4. Saved through my Savior's precious blood,
I am rejoicing ever.
I humbly seek Thy grace, O God;
Now nothing shall us sever.
All that my blest Redeemer's death
Hath won for me is mine through faith;
Of this no foe shall rob me.

5. All righteousness by works is vain,
The Law brings condemnation;
True righteousness by faith I gain,
Christ's work is my salvation.
His death, that perfect sacrifice,
Has paid the all-sufficient price;
In Him my hope is anchored.

6. My guilt, O Father, Thou hast laid
On Christ, Thy Son, my Savior.
Lord Jesus, Thou my debt hast paid
And gained for me God's favor.
O Holy Ghost, Thou Fount of grace,
The good in me to Thee I trace;
In faith do Thou preserve me.

—J. Heermann, 1630, but st. 6, Anon., 1661; tr. sts. 1–3, 5–6, *TLH,* 1941; st. 4, A. Hoppe, 1919, alt.

Jesus

247

Tune: O daß ich tausend Zungen hätte. 45. [*TLH* 30; *LW* 360; *LSB* 811]

1. The truest Friend abides in heaven;
On earth our friends are rare and few;
The world to faithlessness is given;
Her children often prove untrue:
And therefore I must here contend
That Jesus is my truest Friend.

2. Men like a cradle sway and falter,
But Jesus like a rock doth stand;
Though storms of woe my fortune alter,
He holds me firmly by the hand:
Yea, He stands by me to the end,
So Jesus is my truest Friend.

3. The world will sell her love whenever
Fair fortune bribes her selfish heart,
But soon the dearest ties will sever
When fortune's smiling charms depart.
No selfish gains His love suspend,
For Jesus is my truest Friend.

4. For me He suffers crucifixion,
For me He sheds His precious blood,
He lends me help in my affliction,
His counsels all are wise and good:
Upon His word I may depend,
And thus He is my truest Friend.

5. My Friend, such faithfulness possessing;
My Friend, whose own I am for aye;
My Friend, so tender and caressing;
My Friend e'en unto death will stay.
Then let me evermore contend
That Jesus is my truest Friend.

—B. Schmolck, 1704; tr., H. Brueckner, 1918, but st. 3, F. W. Herzberger, 1917, alt.

248

Tune: Nun laßt uns Gott, dem Herren. 4. [*TLH* 122; *or LW* 184*]

1. The Lord who rules creation,
Whose hand holds every nation,
The Fount of grace, defends me
And as my shepherd tends me.

2. As long as He is near me
With every gift He'll cheer me,
Of fullness overflowing,
Abundant wealth bestowing.

3. By pastures green He leads me,
With gladness there He feeds me,
To purest waters guides me,
In need His help provides me.

4. And when my soul is fearful
Through grievous thoughts and careful,
He knows how to restore it
And clear all ills before it.

5. He teaches my behavior,
Leads me the right way ever,
And for His name's sake glorious
Makes me o'er fear victorious.

6. Though left by men to ponder
While in dark vales I wander,
Yet will I fear no evil,
Adversity, nor devil.

7. Thou standest still beside me,
From wicked men dost hide me,
Thy rod and staff protect me,
And no fear can deject me.

8. My table Thou preparest,
For my refreshment carest,
When foes are plotting round me,
And seek to pain and wound me.

9. Thou, Lord, my head anointest,
My empty soul appointest
Of every good and pleasure
A full, o'erflowing measure.

10. The goodness Thou bestowest,
The mercy that Thou showest,
Till life itself forsake me,
Shall glad and joyful make me.

11. Thy service will I never
Forsake, but praise Thee ever
Where Thou dost live in heaven
Where faith's reward is given.

12. I'll praise Thee while I'm granted
Life here, and, when transplanted
To stand in heav'n before Thee,
I'll evermore adore Thee!

—P. Gerhardt, 1657, after Ps. 23; tr., J. Kelly, 1867, alt.

249

Tune: Eins ist not, ach, Herr, dies Eine. 69. [*TLH* 366; *or LW* 277; *LSB* 536]

1. One thing's needful; Lord, this treasure
Teach me highly to regard;
All else, though it first give pleasure,
Is a yoke that presses hard.
Beneath it the heart is still fretting and striving,
No true, lasting happiness ever deriving.
The gain of this one thing all loss can requite
And teach me in all things to find true delight.

2. Wilt thou find this one thing needful,
Turn from all created things
Unto Jesus and be heedful
Of the blessed joy He brings.
For where God and Man both in one are united,
With God's perfect fullness the heart is delighted;
There, there is the worthiest lot and the best,
My One and my All, and my Joy and my Rest.

3. How were Mary's thoughts devoted
Her eternal joy to find
As intent each word she noted,
At her Savior's feet reclined!
How kindled her heart, how devout was its feeling,
While hearing the lessons that Christ was revealing!
For Jesus all earthly concerns she forgot,
And all was repaid in that one happy lot.

4. Thus my longings, heav'nward tending,
Jesus, rest alone on Thee.
Help me, thus on Thee depending;
Savior, come and dwell in me.
Although all the world should forsake and forget Thee,
In love I will follow Thee, ne'er will I quit Thee.
Lord Jesus, both spirit and life is Thy Word;
And is there a joy which Thou dost not afford?

5. Wisdom's highest, noblest treasure,
Jesus, lies concealed in Thee;
Grant that this may still the measure
Of my will and actions be,
Humility there and simplicity reigning,
In paths of true wisdom my steps ever training.
Oh, if I of Christ have this knowledge divine,
The fullness of heavenly wisdom is mine.

6. Naught have I, O Christ, to offer,
Naught but Thee, my highest Good.
Naught have I, O Lord, to proffer
But Thy crimson-colored blood.
Thy death on the cross hath Death wholly defeated
And thereby my righteousness fully completed;
Salvation's white raiments I there did obtain,
And in them in glory with Thee I shall reign.

7. Let my soul, in full exemption,
Wake up in Thy likeness now:
Thou art made to me Redemption,
My Sanctification Thou.
Whatever I need for my journey to heaven,
In Thee, O my Savior, is unto me given;
Oh, let me all perishing pleasures forgo,
And Thy life, O Jesus! alone let me know.

8. Where should else my hopes be centered?
Grace o'erwhelms me with its flood;
Thou, my Savior, once hast entered
Holiest heaven through Thy blood.
Eternal redemption for sinners there finding,
From hell's dark dominion my spirit unbinding,
To me perfect freedom Thy entrance has brought,
And childlike to cry, "Abba, Father," I'm taught.

9. Christ Himself, my Shepherd, feeds me,
Peace and joy my spirit fill;
In a pasture green, He leads me
Forth beside the waters still.
Oh, naught to my soul is so sweet and reviving
As thus unto Jesus alone to be living;
True happiness this, and this only, supplies,
Through faith on my Savior to fasten mine eyes.

10. Therefore Thou alone, my Savior,
Shalt be All in all to me;
Search my heart and my behavior,
Root out all hypocrisy.
Restrain me from wand'ring on pathways unholy
And through all life's pilgrimage keep my heart lowly.
This one thing is needful, all others are vain;
I count all but loss that I Christ may obtain.

—J. H. Schröder, 1695; tr., F. E. Cox, 1841, alt.

250

Tune: Jesu, komm doch selbst zu mir. 5. [p. 407; *or TLH* 95*; *LW* 13*; *LSB* 332*]

1. Jesus, Savior, come to me;
Let me ever be with Thee.
Come and nevermore depart,
Thou who reignest in my heart.

2. Lord, for Thee I ever sigh,
Nothing else can satisfy.
Ever do I cry to Thee:
Jesus, Jesus, come to me!

3. Earthly joys can give no peace,
Cannot bid my longing cease;
Still to have my Jesus near,
This is all my pleasure here.

4. All that makes the angels glad,
In their garb of glory clad,
Only fills me with distress
If Thy presence does not bless.

5. Take Thou all away from me,
I shall still thus minded be,
Thou who madest me Thine own
Shalt be all my Joy alone.

6. None shall claim my heart beside,
None but Jesus crucified;
Savior, I am only Thine,
Other love shall ne'er be mine.

7. Thou alone, my God and Lord,
Art my Glory and Reward.
Thou hast bled for me and died;
In Thy wounds I safely hide.

8. Come, then, Lamb for sinners slain,
Come and ease me of my pain.
Evermore I cry to Thee:
Jesus, Jesus, come to me!

9. Patiently I wait Thy day;
For this gift, O Lord, I pray,
That, when death shall come to me,
My dear Jesus Thou wilt be.

—J. Scheffler, 1657; tr., M. Loy, 1861, alt.

251

Tune: Jesu, meine Freude. 74. [*TLH* 347; *LW* 270; *LSB* 743]

1. Jesus, priceless Treasure,
Source of purest pleasure,
Truest Friend to me;
Ah, how long in anguish
Shall my spirit languish,
Yearning, Lord, for Thee?
Thou art mine, / O Lamb divine!
I will suffer naught to hide Thee,
Naught I ask beside Thee.

2. In Thine arms I rest me;
Foes who would molest me
Cannot reach me here.
Though the earth be shaking,
Every heart be quaking,
Jesus calms my fear.
Lightnings flash / And thunders crash;
Yet, though sin and hell assail me,
Jesus will not fail me.

3. Satan, I defy thee;
Death, I now decry thee;
Fear, I bid thee cease.
World, thou shalt not harm me
Nor thy threats alarm me
While I sing of peace.
God's great pow'r / Guards every hour;
Earth and all its depths adore Him,
Silent bow before Him.

4. Hence all earthly treasure!
Jesus is my Pleasure,
Jesus, is my Choice.
Hence all empty glory!
Naught to me thy story
Told with tempting voice.
Pain or loss, / Or shame or cross,
Shall not from my Savior move me,
Since He deigns to love me.

5. Evil world, I leave thee;
Thou canst not deceive me,
Thine appeal is vain.
Sin that once did blind me,
Get thee far behind me,
Come not forth again.
Past thy hour, / O pride and pow'r;
Sinful life, thy bonds I sever,
Leave thee now forever.

6. Hence, all fear and sadness!
For the Lord of gladness,
Jesus, enters in.
Those who love the Father,
Though the storms may gather,
Still have peace within.
Yea, whate'er / I here must bear,
Thou art still my purest Pleasure,
Jesus, priceless Treasure!

—J. Franck, 1653; tr., *TLH*, 1941, based on C. Winkworth, 1863.

252

Tune: Jesu, meines Herzens Freud. 51. [p. 407]

1. Jesus, Thou my heart's delight,
Sweetest Jesus!
Thrill'st my soul with rapture quite,
Sweetest Jesus!
All cares vanish at Thy sight,
Sweetest Jesus, / Jesus, Sweetest Jesus!

2. Evermore I think of Thee,
My Redeemer!
And I long for none but Thee,
My Redeemer!
Yearns my soul with Thee to be,
My Redeemer, / Jesus, my Redeemer!

3. Feed Thou me and fill my soul,
Heav'nly Manna!
Quench my thirst, my heart make whole,
Help, Hosanna!
Be the rest unto my soul,
Rest of weary, / Jesus, Rest of weary!

4. Naught is lovelier than Thou,
Fairest Lover!
Naught is friendlier than Thou,
Gentle Lover!
And naught sweeter is than Thou,
Sweetest Lover, / Jesus, sweetest Lover!

5. I am weak, come, strengthen me,
Strength in weakness!
Faint am I, refresh Thou me,
Sweetest Jesus!
When I die, console Thou me,
Thou Consoler, / Jesus, my Consoler.

—J. Flittner, 1661; tr., J. A. Rimbach, 1903, alt.

253

Tune: Jesus, Jesus, nichts als Jesus. 37. [*TLH* 348]

1. Jesus, Jesus, only Jesus,
Can my heartfelt longing still.
Lo, I pledge myself to Jesus
What He wills alone to will.
For my heart, which He hath filled,
Ever cries, Lord, as Thou wilt.

2. One there is for whom I'm living,
Whom I love most tenderly;
Unto Jesus I am giving
What in love He gave to me.
Jesus' blood hides all my guilt;
Lord, oh, lead me as Thou wilt.

3. What to me may seem a treasure
But displeasing is to Thee,
Oh, remove such harmful pleasure;
Give instead what profits me.
Let my heart by Thee be stilled;
Make me Thine, Lord, as Thou wilt.

4. Let me earnestly endeavor
Thy good pleasure to fulfill;
In me, through me, with me ever,
Lord, accomplish Thou Thy will.
In Thy holy image built,
Let me die, Lord, as Thou wilt.

5. Jesus, constant be my praises,
For Thou unto me didst bring
Thine own self and all Thy graces
That I joyfully may sing:
Be it unto me, my Shield,
As Thou wilt, Lord, as Thou wilt.

—L. E. von Schwarzburg, 1668; tr., A. Crull, 1880, alt.

254

Tune: Meinen Jesum laß ich nicht. 33. [*TLH* 324; *LW* 269; *LSB* 350; *or* p. 411]

1. Jesus mine I will not leave,
He alone my life remaineth;
They lack naught who to Him cleave,
He their every need sustaineth;
From all trouble He will save,—
E'en from Satan, sin, and grave.

2. Jesus mine I will not leave,
For no earthly friend is greater;
Jesus eases those who grieve,
Making all their troubles better,
Hastens with His remedy,
Loves me for eternity.

3. Jesus mine I will not leave;
Though all men on earth forsake me,
Though my rivals I perceive,
Coming with their hordes to take me
And to crush me 'neath their tides,
Jesus' help for me abides.

4. Jesus mine I will not leave
When sin fills my heart with terrors,
And the Foe his web doth weave:
"Great and countless are thy errors"
Jesus says: "Fear not, my son!
I for all thy sins atone."

5. Jesus mine I will not leave;
When the throes of death attend me
Calmly I'll await reprieve,
Victory He then shall send me.
This world's final judgment He
Will not suffer me to see.

6. Jesus mine I will not leave,
Neither shall He leave me ever;
This I'll trust, to this I'll cleave,
And He will despise me never.
He, my Light, the way will give:
Jesus mine I will not leave!"

—G. Linzner, 1680; tr., M. Carver.

255

Tune: Meinen Jesum laß ich nicht. 33.
[*TLH* 324; *LW* 269; *LSB* 350; *or* p. 411]

1. Jesus I will never leave,
Who for me Himself hath given;
Firmly unto Him I'll cleave
Nor from Him be ever driven.
Life from Him doth light receive,—
Jesus I will never leave.

2. Jesus I will never leave
While on earth I am abiding;
What I have to Him I give,
In all cares in Him confiding.
Naught shall me of Him bereave,—
Jesus I will never leave.

3. Though my sight shall pass away,
Hearing, taste, and feeling fail me;
Though my life's last light of day
Shall o'ertake and sore assail me;
When His summons I receive,
Jesus I will never leave.

4. Nor will I my Jesus leave
When at last I shall come thither
Where His saints He will receive,
Where in bliss they live together.
Endless joy to me He'll give,—
Jesus I will never leave.

5. Not for earth's vain joys I crave
Nor, without him, heaven's pleasure;
Jesus, who my soul did save,
Evermore shall be my Treasure.
He redemption did achieve,—
Jesus I will never leave.

6. Jesus I will not let go,
Gladly by His side I'm staying:
Ever Christ will lead me so,
On to streams of life conveying.
Say, who blessing would receive:
"Jesus I will never leave."**

—C. Keimann, 1658; tr., *TLH,* 1941, but st. 6, M. Carver.

256

Tune: Ich ruf zu dir, Herr Jesu Christ. 76. [p. 405]

1. O Jesus Christ, my fairest Light,
Who in Thy soul dost love me,
With love so measureless of height,
No end I see above me!
Grant that my heart may warm to Thee
With love of ardent burning,
For Thee yearning,
And as Thy property,
To Thee, Lord, only turning.

2. Let nothing dwell within my heart
But Thy sweet love and favor:
Let me account Thy loving art
My crown and prize forever!
Cast all things out, take all away,
That Thee and me would sever,
So that ever
My pow'rs by Thy love may
Be kindled, and cool never!

3. How friendly, blessèd, fair, and kind
Is Thy great love, O Jesus!
Where this is fixed within our mind
What sorrow then can seize us?
So let no thought arise in me,
Nor let me see or hear it
Or revere it,
Except the love from Thee,—
Enlarge it in my spirit!

4. O that this great and highest good
Were ever my possession!
O that it would inflame my blood
To glow with holy passion!
Help me to watch, Lord, day and night,
To keep this heav'nly Treasure
From the seizure
Of Satan's wiles and might,
Who seeks our woe with pleasure.

5. My Savior, Thou in love to me
Hast down to death descended,
And like a murd'rer on the tree
And thief hast been suspended,
Spit on, despised, and wounded sore;
The wounds which Thee have riven,
May I even
Within my very core
With love to feel be given.

6. The blood that hath been shed by Thee
Is ever good and precious.
My heart is wicked desp'rately,
A millstone hard and vicious.
Lord, let the virtue of Thy blood
Subdue the stubborn nature
Of Thy creature,
And spread this living flood
Through every vein and feature.

** J.G.E.O.S.: i.e., "Johann Georg, Elector of Saxony" says: "Jesus I will never leave."

7. O that my heart might open be
To catch the blood then falling,
Pressed out in dark Gethsemane
By all my sins appalling!
O that the fountains of mine eyes
Were oped, and with much sighing,
And sore crying,
Gushed forth, like he who cries
While in love's passion lying.

8. O that I as a child might yearn
And weeping, run and chase Thee,
Until Thy heart with love should burn
And so Thine arms embrace me,
And in my heart Thy soul I see
With sweet love overflowing,
Grace bestowing,
That unity with Thee
I ever may be knowing.

9. Ah, draw me, Dearest, after Thee,
And so shall I be hasting;
I'll run, and in my heart will be
Thy love with rapture tasting;
The gracious words from Thee I'll hear
Whose blessed consolation
Brings salvation,
O'ercoming sin and fear
With ease on each occasion.

10. My Comfort, Treasure, Health, and Light,
My Life and Savior tender!
Ah, take me for Thy portion quite
As I to Thee surrender!
There's naught but pain apart from Thee,
Though all the world may glitter,
All is bitter,
Naught ever comforts me,
Naught than Thyself is sweeter.

11. But Thou the Rest most blessèd art,
In Thee is peace eternal.
O Jesus, ever let my heart
Feed in Thy pastures vernal!
Be Thou My flame and burn in me,
My Balsam, comfort dealing,
Quickly healing
All earthly misery
That causes sighs and wailing.

12. Ah, Fairest One, in Thy great love
What faileth me of blessing?
It is my star and sun above,
My fount, my soul refreshing!
My sweetest wine, my heav'nly bread,
My cov'ring in God's glory,
My crown o'er me,
My shield in every need,
My house and shelter for me!

13. Ah, dearest Love, if Thou remove,
What is my birth and being?
Shouldst Thou withdraw Thy precious love,
Then all my good were fleeing.
So help me, Guest, seek after Thee
With all my best endeavor,
Hold Thee ever;
And holding steadily,
Let Thee go from me never.

14. Thou ever hast had love for me
And to Thyself didst move me;
When still I did no good for Thee,
E'en then did Thy heart love me:
O let Thy love, Almighty Lord!
Continue here to guide me,
Close beside me
Aid ever to afford,
Whatever may betide me.

15. Lord, let Thy love adorn my place,
Whatever be my station,
And, if I wander from Thy ways,
Lead me back to salvation.
From it let me Thy prudence learn,
And wise works to be doing,
Sin eschewing,
And, should I fall, to turn,
For Thy forgiveness suing!

16. Thy love let be my joy in woe,
In frailty, strength to stay me;
And when my course is run below,
And down to rest I lay me,
Then let Thy loving faithfulness
Lord Jesus, stay beside me,
Strength provide me,
Until all joy and bliss
In heaven be supplied me.

—P. Gerhardt, 1653; tr., composite.

257

Tune: Wie schön leuchtet der Morgenstern. 86. [*TLH* 546; *LW* 325; *LSB* 395]

1. O Jesus, Jesus, God's own Son,
My Brother and My Mercy-Throne,
My Joy and sweetest Pleasure;
Thou know'st the truth that I aver,
For in Thy sight no secrets are,
Thou seest me, dearest Treasure.
Alway, / Each day,
Shall I love Thee / That above Thee,
Naught I cherish,
Though all else should fail and perish.

2. This is of all my deepest pain,
That I no greater love can gain,
To love, past love exceeding.
The more I strive, the more I find
How far each hour I fall behind,
How poor is my succeeding.
Let me / From Thee
Gain each hour / Greater powèr
By Thy Spirit,
That Thy love I may inherit.

3. For by Thy strength I shall endure,
And love Thee ever more and more,
Each day in love increasing.
Nor can the world's most garished pride,
Or transient gifts my need provide;
Alone Thy love unceasing—
That will / Fulfill
Wants that grieve me: / Savior, give me
Love untainted,
For my cure, ere I have fainted.

4. For who will love Thee, Thou shalt love,
And shed Thy blessings from above,
Joy, rest, and peace bestowing.
And though life's road be hard and long,
With arduous steeps its way along,
It ends in bliss o'erflowing.
Laughter / After
Earth's brief trials / And denials
There is given,
And an end of grief in heaven.

5. No ear hath ever heard the sound,
No man hath seen or knowledge found,
No tongue may be explaining
What glory yonder them awaits,
Prepared by Thee in heaven's gates,
For those in love remaining.
All this / World's bliss
Is unstable / And unable
E'er to equal
What in heav'n shall be its sequel.

6. This only, Lord, will I allow
To be my heart's obsession now:
That I may love Thee dearly,
And that I may by charity
Abound in all that pleases Thee,
As Scripture tells me clearly,
Until / We will
Hence be parted, / Joyful-hearted,
From all sorrow,
To awake that blissful morrow.

7. Then shall I of Thy sweetness dear,—
Which passes telling in this sphere,—
In flawless love be tasting,
And then Thy lovely presence see,
Where vision cannot faded be
Nor heart in anguish wasting.
Richly / Shall we
Be awarded / And accorded
Life and pleasure:
At Thy throne in endless measure.

—J. Heermann, 1630; tr. sts. 1–4, J. T. Mueller, 1920, alt.; sts. 5–7, M. Carver.

258

Tune: Herr Jesu Christ, meins Lebens Licht. 11. [*TLH* 288; *LW* 262; *LSB* 704]

1. O Jesus sweet, to think on Thee
Fills hearts with sweet felicity,
Yet sweeter still is to the heart
Where Thou Thyself, O Jesus, art.

2. O Jesus, Joy and Bliss in one,
Thou Fount of life, Thou very Sun,
Thou hast no equal on this earth,
In Thee is man's desire and mirth.

3. O Jesus, Love than all more sweet,
No weariness in Thee we meet;
Far nobler is Thy love, I say,
Than man can utter or convey.

4. O Jesus, Fount of graciousness,
Our Hope Thou art of heav'nly bliss,
A River sweet, a Spring of grace,
The heart's true Joy, all grief to chase.

5. O Jesus Christ, sweet Lord, Thy love
The heart's best nourishment doth prove,
It satisfies, yet makes not ill,
And whets the heart with hunger still.

6. O Jesus, crown of angels dear,
How sweet Thy name is to mine ear;
O Honey wondrous to the lips,
This drink all others doth eclipse.

7. O Jesus, gracious Love most high,
My heart's desire and greatest joy;
Unfathomable Grace Thou art,
Thy love enfolds my mind and heart.

8. O Jesus, Thee to love is best,
The one who seeks naught else is blest;
I fain unto myself would die,
Within Thy life alone to lie.

9. O Jesus, sweetest Remedy,
Thou Balm to souls that call on Thee,
For Thee is spilled each fervent tear,
For Thee doth cry the heart sincere.

10. O Jesus, wheresoe'er I be,
I fain would have Thee near to me;
'Tis joy of joys where Thou dost dwell;
If I may have Thee, all is well.

11. O Jesus, what I sought I see,
My longing now fulfilled must be;
For but Thy love I faint and sigh,
For Thee my heart doth burn and cry.

12. O Jesus, he who loves Thee so
Shall surely not abide in woe;
This love no thing can e'er devour;
It grows and burns with deathless pow'r.

13. O Jesus, Flow'r and Virgin's Son,
O heav'nly Love, O Mercy-Throne,
To Thee meet praise and laud ascend,
Thy kingdom nevermore shall end.

14. O Jesus, Lord, in Thee disclosed
My pleasure is, and mine Thou know'st;
In Thee mine every boast is laid,
Man's only Savior, Help, and Aid.

15. O Jesus, Source of clemency,
Thy brightness spreads unceasingly;
Put every gloomy cloud to flight,
Sustain for us Thy glorious light.

16. O Jesus, high in heav'n resounds
Thy praise which every choir propounds;
Thou makest glad the world abroad
Which Thou hast reconciled to God.

17. O Jesus, peaceful is Thy reign,
Exceeding every worldly gain;
Let peace preserve my heart and mind
As long as here my home I find.

18. O Jesus, when my time is come,
Receive me to Thy heav'nly home,
That there in peace and joy I may
Enjoy Thee in eternal day.

19. O Jesus, take my pray'r on high,
O Jesus, hear me as I sigh!
O Jesus, Thou my hope shalt be;
O Jesus, Jesus, rescue me!

—M. Moller, 1584, after Bernard; tr., M. Carver.

259

Tune: Valet will ich dir geben. 59. [*TLH* 58; *LW* 79; *LSB* 442]

1. O Treasure o'er all treasure,
O Jesus, Prize divine;
I love Thee without measure,
For Thee alone I pine.
My heart shall be Thy dwelling,
Sweet Lover of my soul;
My lips be ever telling
That Thou hast made me whole.

2. O Joy, all joys exceeding,
Thou very Bread of heav'n,
My pasture, whereon feeding,
My soul relief is giv'n
My weary life to strengthen,
My fainting heart to stay,
My weak'ning hope to lengthen
With comfort on my way.

3. O Dearest One, afford me
Thy kindly face to see;
A living heart accord me!
Come, gladsome Light, to me;
For to abide without Thee
Would fill my heart with pain;
To live with Thee, nor doubt Thee,
All blessing were to gain.

4. O rich, life-giving Fountain,
O Jesus, sweetest Rest,
Thou faithful Cross-Companion,
Let all Thy rods be pressed;
With patience I will ever
Endure each bitter sting,
I know they shall not sever
Or keep me from my King.

5. My heart in Thee delighted
In life and death shall be
One evermore, united;
For rather be with Thee
In deepest flames perspiring,
Than, lacking Thee, to go
To Paradise untiring,
Despised and full of woe.

6. O worldly pride and leaven,
What good in you is found?
My spirit would to heaven,
And thither shall be bound,
To Jesus' light unfailing;
I long that place to see,
Where He hath built my dwelling;
There it is good to be!

7. O Jesus, sweetest Pleasure,
Come, bring me to the goal,
To rest in Thee, my Treasure,
With Thee to crown my soul;
Come, in Thy grace convey me,
To Zion to reside,
Where nothing shall dismay me,
And I am satisfied.

—S. Liscow, 1672; tr. sts. 1, 2b, 5a, J. T. Mueller, 1918, alt; sts. rest, M. Carver.

260

Tune: Seelenbräutigam. 27. [*TLH* 410; *LW* 386; *LSB* 718]

1. Bridegroom, Thou art mine,
Jesus, Lamb divine;
Saved from sin, to Thee I render
Thanks for love so pure and tender,
That has made me Thine,
Jesus, Lamb divine.

2. Thy love's ardent flame
Heals my mortal frame;
As Thy kindly eye beholds me,
As Thy gentle hand enfolds me;
I with joy proclaim
Thy love's ardent flame.

3. Very man and God,
Comfort 'neath the rod:
Thou wast born in woe to languish,
Saving souls from endless anguish
By Thy crimson blood
Very man and God.

4. Let my faith's pure light
Evermore be bright;
Strengthen me each day and hour,
By Thy Spirit's quick'ning power;
Keep my soul aright
In faith's holy light.

5. So shall I in Thee
Bide eternally,
For Thy love with praise supply Thee,
And within Thee, magnify Thee,
As eternally
I shall bide in Thee.

6. David's Son and Heir,
Let Thy love so fair
Ever nourish and defend me,
For the world doth harm intend me,
From their anger spare,
David's Son and Heir.

7. Prince of Peace once curst,
Heavy was Thy thirst
To save man from his affliction,
When amidst Thy crucifixion,
Thou didst cry: "I thirst!"
Prince of Peace once curst.

8. Grant Thy peace, O Lord,
Of Thy love outpoured
Unto us of Thy confession,
Who by name are Thy possession;
To Thine own adored,
Grant Thy peace, O Lord.

9. They who bear their cross,
Fighting for the cause
Of the faith that's true and living,
Shall not perish in their striving,
Counting all as loss,
As we bear our cross.

10. I will cling to Thee
Who fulfillest me;
Grant me nevermore to leave Thee,
As in faith I did receive Thee;
And thus trustingly
I will cling to Thee.

11. When my tears must flow,
Give me Thine to know,
That with balm they may provide me
And unto Thy wounds may guide me,
That my tears must go
And forbear to flow.

12. When I shall again
Times of joy obtain,
Thou wilt share my jubilation,
Till I join Thy heav'nly nation
And in Thy sweet reign
Endless joy obtain.

13. Here through scorn and frown,
There the glorious crown;
Here in hoping and believing,
There in having and perceiving;
For the glorious crown
Follows scorn and frown.

14. Jesus, dearest Friend,
Help me to contend
Make me o'er all foes victorious;
Through Thy victory so glorious
May I comprehend
How Thou dost contend.

15. Thou my Joy replete,
Sharon's Rose so sweet;
My desire and praise and Treasure,
Naught shall move me but Thy pleasure;
Sharon's Rose so sweet,
Thou my Joy replete!

—A. Drese, 1697; tr. st. 1, 3, 14, M. Loy, 1880, alt.; sts. 2, 4, J. T. Mueller, 1919;
sts. 5–12, M. Carver; sts. 13, 15, E. Cronenwett, 1880.

261

Tune: Wie schön leuchtet der Morgenstern. 86. [*TLH* 343; *LW* 325; *LSB* 395]

1. How lovely shines the Morning Star!
The nations see and hail afar
The light in Judah shining.
Thou David's Son of Jacob's race,
My Bridegroom and my King of Grace,
For Thee my heart is pining.
Lowly, / Holy,
Great and glorious, / Thou victorious
Prince of graces,
Filling all the heav'nly places.

2. O highest joy by mortals won,
True Son of God and Mary's Son,
Thou highborn King of ages!
Thou art my heart's most beauteous Flower,
And Thy blest Gospel's saving power
My raptured soul engages.
Thou mine, / I Thine;
Sing hosanna! / Heav'nly manna
Tasting, eating,
Whilst Thy love in songs repeating.

3. Now richly to my waiting heart,
O Thou, my God, deign to impart
The grace of love undying.
In Thy blest body let me be,
E'en as the branch is in the tree,
Thy life my life supplying.
Sighing, / Crying,
For the savor / Of Thy favor;
Resting never,
Till I rest in Thee forever.

4. A pledge of peace from God I see
When Thy pure eyes are turned to me
To show me Thy good pleasure.
Jesus, Thy Spirit and Thy Word,
Thy body and Thy blood afford
My soul its dearest treasure.
Keep me / Kindly
In Thy favor, / O my Savior!
Thou wilt cheer me;
Thy Word calls me to draw near Thee.

5. Thou, mighty Father, in Thy Son
Didst love me ere Thou hadst begun
This ancient world's foundation.
Thy Son hath made a friend of me,
And when in spirit Him I see,
I joy in tribulation!
What bliss / Is this!
He that liveth / To me giveth
Life forever;
Nothing me from Him can sever.

6. Lift up the voice and strike the string,
Let all glad sounds of music ring
In God's high praises blended.
Christ will be with me all the way,
Today, tomorrow, every day,
Till trav'ling days be ended.
Sing out, / Ring out
Triumph glorious, / O victorious,
Chosen nation;
Praise the God of your salvation.

7. Oh, joy to know that Thou, my Friend,
Art Lord, Beginning without end,
The First and Last, Eternal!
And Thou at length—O glorious grace!—
Wilt take me to that holy place,
The home of joys supernal.
Amen, / Amen!
Come and meet me! / Quickly greet me!
With deep yearning,
Lord, I look for Thy returning.

—P. Nicolai, 1599; tr., *TLH*, 1941.

262

Tune: Wie wohl ist mir. 89. [*TLH* 362]

1. My soul's best Friend, what joy and blessing
My spirit ever finds in Thee!
From gloomy depths of doubt distressing
Into Thine arms for rest I flee.
Then will the night of sorrow vanish
When from my heart Thy love doth banish
All anguish and all pain and fear.
Yea, here on earth begins my heaven;
Who would not joyful be when given
A loving Savior always near!

2. For though the evil world revile me
And prove herself my bitter foe
Or by her smile seek to beguile me,
I trust her not; her wiles I know.
In Thee alone my soul rejoices,
Thy praise alone it gladly voices,
For Thou art true when friendships flee.
The world may hate but cannot fell me;
Would mighty waves of trial quell me,
I anchor in Thy loyalty.

3. Tho' Moses' law with threats be fright'ning,
From awful Sinai's burning hill,
Straightway from its fierce wrath and lightning
My soul through faith mounts higher still;
It throws itself before Thee sighing,
A safe retreat in Thee enjoying,
Where curse and death can never come.
Though all things threaten condemnation,
Yet Jesus, Thou art my Salvation,
For in Thy love I find my home.

4. Through deserts of the cross Thou leadest;
I follow, leaning on Thy hand.
From out the cloud Thy child Thou feedest
And givest water from the sand.
I trust Thy ways, howe'er distressing;
I know my path will end in blessing;
Enough that Thou wilt be my Stay.
For whom to honor Thou intendest
Oft into sorrow's vale Thou sendest;
The night must e'er precede the day.

5. To some, death seems a dark endeavor,
But not, Thou Life of life, to me.
I know Thou wilt forsake him never
Whose heart and spirit rest in Thee.
Oh! who would fear his journey's ending,
If from dark woods and foes offending,
He then find safety and release?
Nay, O my Light, with joyful vision
I would depart this gloomy region
To Thy eternal home of peace.

6. My soul's best Friend, how well contented
Am I, reposing on Thy breast;
By sin no more am I tormented
Since Thou dost grant me peace and rest.
Oh, may the grace that Thou hast given
For me a foretaste be of heaven,
Where I shall bask in joys divine!
Away, vain world, with fleeting pleasures;
In Christ I have abiding treasures.
Oh, comfort sweet, my Friend is mine!

—W. C. Dessler, 1692; tr., *TLH,* 1941; but sts. 3, 5, C. Winkworth, 1855, alt.

The Christian Life

263

Tune: O Gott, du frommer Gott. 55. [*TLH* 395; *LW* 385; *LSB* 696]

1. O God, forsake me not!
Thy gracious presence lend me;
Lead Thou Thy helpless child;
Thy Holy Spirit send me
That I my course may run.
Be Thou my Light, my Lot,
My Staff, my Rock, my Shield—
O God, forsake me not!

2. O God, forsake me not!
Take not Thy Spirit from me
And suffer not the might
Of sin to overcome me.
Increase my feeble faith,
Which Thou Thyself hast wrought.
Be Thou my Strength and Pow'r,—
O God, forsake me not!

3. O God, forsake me not!
Lord, hear my supplication!
In every evil hour
Help me o'ercome temptation;
And when the prince of hell
My conscience seeks to blot,
Be Thou not far from me,—
O God, forsake me not!

4. O God, forsake me not!
Thy mercy I'm addressing;
O Father, God of Love,
Grant me Thy heav'nly blessing
To do when duty calls
Whate'er Thou didst allot,
To do what pleaseth Thee,—
O God, forsake me not!

5. O God, forsake me not!
Lord, I am Thine forever.
Grant me true faith in Thee;
Grant that I leave Thee never.
Grant me a blessèd end
When my good fight is fought;
Help me in life and death,—
O God, forsake me not!

—S. Franck, 1714; tr., A. Crull, †1923.

264

Tune: Herr, ich habe mißgehandelt. 39. [*TLH* 326; *LW* 233; *LSB* 608]

1. Oh, what are we without Jesus?
Needy, mis'rable, and poor!
What are we, but wholly wretched?
Lord, have mercy, we implore!
As in trouble we are lying,
Kindly hear our pray'r and sighing.

2. We are naught without Thee, Jesus,
Here all seems as dark as night,
Here we stand in vicious torment
From the serpent's deadly bite.
To the heart his venom stingeth,
Constant pain and sorrow bringeth!

3. Without Thee, O faithful Jesus,
Hell and Satan work their fear;
Condemnation makes me tremble,
As I stand in terror here;
Lord, my conscience is awoken;
Sharply the abyss hath spoken.

4. Without Thee, most precious Jesus,
From this world none may escape.
Every path is pure temptation,
Every step, a tangling trap;
How it boasts of all its treasures
And ensnares us in its pleasures!

5. Vainly, O life-giving Jesus,
Lifeless souls attempt to rise!
All our strength is but a swooning,
All our might a slow demise:
Who sees not, the more our hurry,
So much more our fault and worry?

6. Therefore help us, dearest Jesus,
In our darkness be our light,
Make our spirit's eyes unblinded,
Bring Thy kindly face to sight;
Glimmer, Sun, where sin hath stricken,
Send Thy beams, our hearts to quicken.

7. Trample Satan, mighty Jesus,
Underneath our feeble feet,
Come to join Thy bride and hail her
With Thy salutation sweet,
That she may know heaven's gladness
Marred no more by grief and sadness.

8. Take our hand, O sweetest Jesus,
Lead us in the pilgrim's way,
That on paths both straight and narrow
We may go and not delay;
Keep us every snare eschewing,
Past ways ne'er with lust reviewing.

9. Let Thy mighty Spirit, Jesus,
Fill our spirits with His strength,
That we fervently may follow
In Thy love, whate'er the length.
Oh, Lord, deign to sanctify us,
With a righteous life supply us.

10. Then our inmost hearts, Lord Jesus,
Shall Thy thanks and praises bring,
Then shall all creation revel,
Heart and mouth rejoice to sing;
Praise excelling earth's in heaven,
Jesus, then Thou shalt be given.

—P. Lackmann, 1704; tr., M. Carver.

265

Tune: Dir, dir, Jehova, will ich singen. 46. [*TLH* 21; *LW* 446]

1. Jehovah, let me now adore Thee,
For where is there a God such, Lord, as Thou?
With songs I fain would come before Thee;
Oh, let Thy Holy Spirit teach me now
To praise Thee in His name through whom alone
Our songs can please Thee, through Thy blessed Son!

2. O Father, draw me to my Savior
That Thy dear Son may draw me unto Thee;
Thy Spirit guide my whole behavior
And rule both sense and reason thus in me
That, Lord, Thy peace from me may ne'er depart,
But wake sweet melodies within my heart.

3. Grant that Thy Spirit prompt my praises,
Then shall my singing surely please Thine ear;
Sweet are the sounds my heart then raises,
My pray'r in truth and spirit Thou wilt hear.
Then shall Thy Spirit raise my heart to Thee
To sing Thee psalms of praise in high degree.

4. For He can plead for me with sighings
That are unspeakable to lips like mine;
He bids me pray with earnest cryings,
Bears witness with my soul that I am Thine,
Joint heir with Christ, and thus may dare to say:
O heav'nly Father, hear me when I pray!

5. When thus my heart in pray'r ascendeth,
Through Thine own Holy Spirit, unto Thee,
Thy heart, O Father, kindly bendeth
Its fervent love and favor unto me,
Rejoicing my petition to fulfill
Which I have made according to Thy will.

6. And what Thy Spirit thus hath taught me
To seek from Thee must needs be such a pray'r
As Thou wilt grant through Him who bought me
And raised me up to be Thy child and heir.
In Jesus' name I boldly seek Thy face
And take from Thee, my Father, grace for grace.

7. O joy! my hope and trust are founded
On His sure Word, and witness in the heart;
I know Thy mercies are unbounded,
And all good gifts Thou freely wilt impart,
Nay, more is lavished by Thy bounteous hand,
Than we can ask or seek or understand.

8. O bliss! In Jesus' name I've tendered
My pray'r; He pleads at Thy right hand for me.
Yea and Amen in Him is rendered
What I in faith and spirit ask of Thee.
O joy for me! and praise be ever Thine,
Whose wondrous love has made such blessings mine!

—B. Crasselius, 1697; tr., C. Winkworth, 1863, alt.

266

Tune: Herr Jesu Christ, meins Lebens Licht. 11. [*TLH* 288; *LW* 262; *LSB* 704]

1. Renew me, O eternal Light,
And let my heart and soul be bright,
Illumined with the light of grace
That issues from Thy holy face.

2. Destroy in me the lust of sin,
From all impureness make me clean.
Oh, grant me pow'r and strength, my God,
To strive against my flesh and blood!

3. Create in me a new heart, Lord,
That gladly I obey Thy Word
And naught but what Thou wilt, desire;
With such new life my soul inspire.

4. Grant that I only Thee may love
And seek those things which are above
Till I behold Thee face to face,
O Light eternal, through Thy grace.

—J. F. Ruopp, 1714; tr., A. Crull, †1923.

267

Tune: Meinen Jesum laß ich nicht. 33.
[*TLH* 324; *LW* 269; *LSB* 350; *or* p. 411]

1. O Thou true and faithful Lord,
From whose heart and mouth proceedeth
Heavn'ly truth and gracious Word,
Which into all wisdom leadeth:
On this true and steady ground
Let my trust and hope be found.

2. Thus declared Thy holy Son,
"Whoso shall on earth deny Me,
At the Father's judgment throne,
Even so I will deny thee,
Nor will I confess thy name,
Nor thee as My child proclaim."

3. 'Neath the banner of His cross
I have vowed to follow ever;
Failing faith shall be my loss,
And the crown I'll lose forever;
Therefore Jesus' name alone
May my mouth forever own.

4. When my flesh and blood despair,
When the world my speech would hinder,
When they drive me here and there
As the tempest blows the cinder,
When they treat me savagely,
Oh, my God, then comfort me!

5. When they ask me, when they seek
Where my hope and faith is founded,
Open Thou my mouth to speak,
Let it in Thy truth be grounded,
Good confession then to make;
Let me of Thy courage take.

6. David's faith and speech were one,
One the twain must be forever.
Thus true Christians e'er have done,
Playing not the false believer.
From such sin deliver me!
Falsity draws wrath from Thee.

7. Lord, uphold me with Thy pow'r,
Faith and walk as one sustaining,
Let these witness every hour
That in Christ I am remaining;—
He's my Shepherd, well He knows
Every sheep that with Him goes.

8. Let me ever till I die
Jesus rightly be confessing,
And as in death's grip I lie,
Count each of His wounds a blessing.
Living, dying in my Lord,
I shall be to bliss restored.

—B. Schmolck, †1737; tr. sts. 1–3, J. T. Mueller, 1921, alt; sts. 4–8, M. Carver.

268

Tune: Liebster Jesu, wir sind hier. 34. [*TLH* 16; *LW* 202; *LSB* 904]

1. From eternity, O God,
In Thy Son Thou didst elect me;
Therefore, Father, on life's road
Graciously to heav'n direct me;
Send to me Thy Holy Spirit
That His gifts I may inherit.

2. Though alive, I'm dead in sin,
Lost to all good things by nature.
Holy Ghost, change me within,
Make of me a new-born creature;
For the flesh works ruination
And can never gain salvation.

3. Drive away the gloomy night
Of my heart's perverse reflection;
Quench all thoughts that are not right,
Hold my reason in subjection;
Grant that I from Thee, with yearning,
Wisdom always may be learning.

4. All desire and thoughts of mine
From my youth are only evil;
Save me by Thy pow'r divine
From myself and from the devil;
Give me strength in ample measure
Both to will and do Thy pleasure.

5. Oh, create a heart in me
That in Thee, my God, believeth
And o'er the iniquity
Of my sins most truly grieveth.
When dark hours of woe betide me,
In the wounds of Jesus hide me.

6. As a branch upon a vine
In my blessed Lord implant me;
Ever of my Head divine
To remain a member grant me.
Oh, let Him, my Lord and Savior,
Be my Life and Love forever!

7. Faith and hope and charity
Graciously, O Father, give me;
Be my Guardian constantly
That the devil may not grieve me;
Grant me humbleness and gladness,
Peace and patience in my sadness.

8. Help me speak what's right and good
And keep silence on occasion;
Help me pray, Lord, as I should,
Help me bear my tribulation;
Help me die and let my spirit
Everlasting life inherit.

—C. Neumann, 1711; tr., A. Crull, †1923.

269

Tune: Herr Christ, der einig Gotts Sohn. 48. [*LW* 72; *LSB* 402]

1. Thou Sun of grace, Lord Jesus,
Thou true and living Light,
Let life and light and gladness
Restore my feeble sight,
Through all Thy grace unfailing,
Renew my spirit ailing,
My God, reveal Thy might.

2. Forgive all my transgression
And cast it far away;
Let wrath yield to compassion,
In grace Thy help display;
Thy gifts of peace let flourish,
My weary heart to nourish.
Lord, hear me as I pray!

3. Dispel my spirit's sorrow—
Old Adam's fallen mind—
And Thy mind let me borrow,
That I may be resigned
To serve and live before Thee
And with my life adore Thee,
Who didst my soul unbind.

4. My soul, O faithful Savior,
With knowledge of Thee fill,
True understanding ever
Through Thy pure Word instill,
In Thee my faith sustaining,
That, in the truth remaining,
I scorn the gates of hell.

5. Of Thee let me be drinking,
My passions crucify
With all unholy thinking,
That I may ceaselessly
This evil world be flying,
And to the flesh be dying,
And live instead in Thee.

6. Oh, kindle Thy love's burning
Within my lowly breast,
That, with an inward yearning,
Its love for Thee not rest,
And I, To Thy pure pleasure,
With steps of constant measure
May walk the pathway blest.

7. O Lord, make me tenacious,
Resilient, strong, and bold,
Which is the office gracious
Thy Holy Ghost doth hold;
My reason and my senses
And all my hand commences,
Were else but dead and cold.

8. Wherefore, O God of goodness,
O Father ever true,
Dispel my spirit's sadness
And daily make me new;
Grant on Thy will I ever
May train my each endeavor;
Grant pow'r to see it through!

—L. A. Gotter, 1695; tr., M. Carver.

270

Tune: Herr, wie du willst, so schicks mit mir. 49. [*TLH* 406; *LW* 248; *LSB* 625]

1. Lord, as Thou wilt, deal Thou with me;
No other wish I cherish.
In life and death I cling to Thee;
Oh, do not let me perish!
Let not Thy grace from me depart
And grant an ever patient heart
To bear what Thou dost send me.

2. Grant honor, truth, and purity,
And love Thy Word to ponder;
From all false doctrine keep me free.
Bestow, both here and yonder,
What serves my everlasting bliss;
Preserve me from unrighteousness
Throughout my earthly journey.

3. When, at Thy summons, I must leave
This vale of sin and sadness,
Give me Thy grace, Lord, not to grieve,
But to depart with gladness.
To Thee my spirit I commend;
O Lord, grant me a blessèd end
Through Jesus Christ, my Savior.

—K. Bienemann, 1574; tr., E. Cronenwett, 1880, alt.

271

Tune: Herzlich lieb hab ich dich, O Herr. 94. [*TLH* 429; *LW* 413; *LSB* 708*]

1. Lord, Thee I love with all my heart;
I pray Thee, ne'er from me depart,
With tender mercy cheer me.
Earth has no pleasure I would share,
Yea, heav'n itself were void and bare
If Thou, Lord, wert not near me.
And should my heart for sorrow break,
My trust in Thee can nothing shake.
Thou art the Portion I have sought;
Thy precious blood my soul has bought.
Lord Jesus Christ,
My God and Lord, My God and Lord,
Forsake me not! I trust Thy Word.

2. Yea, Lord, 'twas Thy rich bounty gave
My body, soul, and all I have
In this poor life of labor.
Lord, grant that I in every place
May glorify Thy lavish grace
And serve and help my neighbor.
Let no false doctrine me beguile
And Satan not my soul defile.
Give strength and patience unto me
To bear my cross and follow Thee.
Lord Jesus Christ,
My God and Lord, My God and Lord,
In death Thy comfort still afford.

3. Lord, let at last Thine angels come,
To Abr'am's bosom bear me home,
That I may die unfearing;
And in its narrow chamber keep
My body safe in peaceful sleep
Until Thy reappearing.
And then from death awaken me
That these mine eyes with joy may see,
O Son of God, Thy glorious face,
My Savior and my Fount of grace.
Lord Jesus Christ,
My pray'r attend, My pray'r attend,
And I will praise Thee without end!

—M. Schalling, 1569; tr., C. Winkworth, 1863, alt.

272

Tune: Das Jesulein soll doch mein. 83. [p. 398]

1. Oh, help me, God, that e'er for Thee
My heart be filled with yearning,
That I may seek Thee fervently,
To Thee, when fearful, turning;
Bestow on me / A glimpse of Thee,
And joy, all fears to banish,
Grant will and sense / To drive from hence
All sins, and make them vanish.

2. Upon Thy grace, by pain and smart,
Affix my whole ambition
To cultivate a lowly heart,
To live in true contrition;
To Thee I flee, / A piteous plea
For all my sins to offer:
Each hour prepare / My heart to bear
The weights of those who suffer.

3. Suppress the fleshly lust in me,
Defeat it with Thy merit,
Let true delight and love for Thee
Be kindled by Thy Spirit;
In all distress / Let me confess
Thy Word till death should take me;
Grant not that ill / Or selfish will
From all Thy truth may break me.

4. Restrain me from all wrath and ire,
Let kindness gleam inside me,
Remove from me all proud desire,
To humbler temper guide me.
Whatever sin / Still lurks within
Let me henceforth be shunning.
Let comfort, peace, / And joy not cease,
But keep me in them running.

5. Confirm my faith, sustain in me
All love, with strength preserving
My hope and trust, for unto Thee
The best is faith unswerving;
Hold back my breath / Lest ever death
Or danger be awoken;
My flesh constrain, / Lest by some stain
Its sober walk be broken.

6. Give faithfulness and zeal, I pray,
To do what works are fitting,
And never to be led astray
Through pride or lust unwitting;
Of envy, strife, / And hatred rife
Leave not a drop within me,
My stubborn sense / Expel from hence,
To honest dealing win me.

7. Oh, grant that I Thy counsel heed,
All wayward thoughts betraying,
Assist my arms in every deed,
For friend and foe e'er praying.
To serve each man / As best I can,
Upright and sober-hearted,
According to / Thy precepts true,
Till from this world I've parted.

—J. Heermann, 1630; tr., M. Carver.

273

Tune: Ich ruf zu dir, Herr Jesu Christ. 76. [p. 405]

1. Lord Jesus Christ, I call to Thee,
I pray Thee, hear my crying.
Drive all despair away from me,
This hour Thy grace supplying.
True faith, O Lord, of Thee I pray;
Oh, let me each day newly
Live life truly
To Thee, Thy Word obey,
And serve my neighbor duly.

2. Yet more from Thee, Lord God, I pray,
Whose goodness is unbounded:
Oh, let me never meet dismay,
My hope be ne'er confounded,
But e'en in death still find Thee true,
And in that hour trust wholly
In Thee solely,
And not in what I do,
For I'd regret that fully.

3. Oh, grant that from my inmost heart
My foes be all forgiven,
And pardon, Lord, to me impart,
And grant new life from heaven;
Thy Word, that blessed food, bestow
As nourishment to mend me
And defend me
Through days of bitter woe,
Which else astray would send me.

4. Let neither worldly lust offend
Nor apprehension sway me,
But make me steadfast to the end,
For in Thy hands I lay me:
And free is all that Thou hast giv'n;
No works of ours can merit
Or inherit
Thy pledge of life in heav'n—
It comes but by Thy Spirit.

5. Help, Lord, for I am weak; I fight,
Yet scarce can battle longer;
I cling but to Thy grace and might;
'Tis Thou must make me stronger.
When tribulations are my lot,
Permit them not to grieve me.
Shelter give me!
With Thee they'll harm me not—
I know Thou wilt not leave me.

—J. Agricola, before 1580; tr., C. Winkworth, 1863, alt.

274

Tune: Ich weiß, mein Gott, daß all mein Tun. 19. [p. 405]

1. My God, my works and all I do
Rest only on Thy will, I know,
Thy blessing prospers ever;
When Thou dost guide, we persevere
In right ways, erring never.

2. It stands not in the pow'r of man
To bring success to any plan,
Or gladness when it endeth:
God's counsel only prospers sure,
'Tis He who blessing sendeth.

3. Man often thinks in haughty mood
That this or that is for his good,
The truth yet far forsaking;
And hurtful oft he thinks the way
Which God Himself is taking.

4. But even wise men frequently
A good work may begin with glee
Yet reach no termination;
They build a castle firm and strong,
But sand is the foundation.

5. How many in their fancy stray
High over mountain peaks away,
And ere they know it ever
Down to the ground they fall, and vain
Has been their great endeavor.

6. Then, O my Father, who the crown
And scepter bear'st on heaven's throne,
Whence lightnings flash before Thee:
Regard my words, and hear my cry,
Upon Thy seat of glory!

7. Vouchsafe to me the noble light
That from Thy countenance so bright
On all Thy suppliants breaketh,
And where the pow'r of wisdom true
Through Thine own pow'r awaketh.

8. Give understanding from on high,
That I may henceforth not rely
And build upon my willing.
Be Thou my Friend and Counselor,
The good to be fulfilling.

9. Prove all things well, give me the good,
But that preferred by flesh and blood,
O Lord, I pray, deny me!
Thy love and glory, my first aim
And fairest part, supply me!

10. Sun of my soul, my chief delight,
Whate'er is pleasing in Thy sight,
Oh, may I choose and do it;
And what's displeasing unto Thee,
May I, O Lord, eschew it!

11. If so a work be Thine, then bless
My poor weak efforts with success;
But if of man, destroy it
And change my mind. What Thou dost not
Will fail ere man enjoy it.

12. But if our common enemy
Begin to rage revengefully
Against what Thou intendest,
My comfort is, Thou from his wrath
My soul with ease defendest

13. Draw near, and let that easy be
Which seems impossible to me,
A happy issue giving
To what Thou didst Thyself begin
All through Thine own conceiving.

14. Though hard at first the work may be,
And I must tread the deepest sea
Of bitter grief and sorrow,
Oh, may I only driven be
To sighs and pray'rs each morrow.

15. Whoever prays and trusts in Thee,
With valiant heart shall victor be
O'er all that else dismayed him;
In thousand pieces soon shall break
The stone of grief that weighed him.

16. The way to good is almost wild,
And high with thorns and hedges piled;
And he who bears the sadness
Lord, by Thy Spirit, comes at last
To realms of bliss and gladness.

17. I am Thy child, my Father Thou.
Thou of Thy fullness canst endow
Whatever I am needing;
So help me well my task to fill,
To glorious vict'ry speeding.

18. Thine be the glory and the praise!
With raptured soul for all my days
I'll tell Thy deeds of wonder
Before Thy people and the world
Until I join Thee yonder.

—P. Gerhardt, 1653; tr., J. Kelly, 1867, alt.

275

Tune: Ach, was soll ich Sünder machen. 36. [*TLH* 384; *LW* 364; *LSB* 559]

1. Jesus Christ, my Pride and Glory,
He, the true and living Light,
Strengthens me with glorious might.
Christ, revealed in sacred story,
Whom I now as Lord confess,
Teaches me true holiness.

2. How in ruins lies my spirit,
Firmly held by bonds of sin
Body, mind and sense within!
What from Adam I inherit,
Sinful being, flesh, and blood,
Still remains, nor worketh good.

3. O my God, I pray Thee, strip me
Of the weeds of envy, hate,
Pride, and wickedness innate;
Let not Satan taunt and trip me.
Make my heart like new each day,
Make me walk the righteous way.

4. Plant my heart and spirit solely
With Thy noble, gentle peace,
Patience, kindness, godliness,
And Thy love and graces holy;
Let me piety possess,
Truth, and faithful holiness.

5. Let me live to praise Thee ever,
Jesus, Thou my heart's Delight,
Thou who leadest me aright.
Let me cling to Thee forever,
All the fleshly lusts deny,
And the devil's host defy.

6. Grant me, Lord, Thy Holy Spirit
That in all I follow Him
Lest the light of faith grow dim.
Let me ever trust Thy merit,
Let Thy blessing me attend,
From all evil me defend.

7. From all pain and imperfection,
Gracious Lord, deliver me,
Heaven's glory let me see.
Keep me under Thy direction
That the grace Thou gavest me
I may praise eternally.

—J. Olearius, 1671; tr. sts. 1, 5–7, P. E. Kretzmann, 1939; sts. 2–4, M. Carver.

276

Tune: Kommt her zu mir, spricht Gottes Sohn. 41.
[*TLH* 263; *LW* 300; *LSB* 666 (mel.)]

1. "Come hither," saith the Son of God,
"All ye who loathe sin's heavy load
And would no longer bear it;
Come hither, young and old, to Me,
For well I know your injury
And gladly would repair it."

2. "My yoke is mild, My burden light,
And all who bear its easy weight,
Release from hell are given.
I'll give them strength when theirs would fail,
And by My strength they shall prevail
And so inherit heaven.

3. "All I have done and suffered here
From womb to cross, do ye revere,
And emulate in measure.
What you may think or say or do
Is neither safe nor good nor true,
But as it seeks My pleasure."

4. The world may wish the bliss to gain
Without the cross, reproach, and pain,
Of which they hear the warning:
It cannot be! The cross is there,
And they must choose its shame to bear,
Or endless shame and mourning.

5. Lo, all creation testifies
That all that is decays and dies—
Earth, sky, and waters languish.
Who then despises God's high name
Shall be the devil's own to claim,
And death shall be his anguish.

6. Man flaunts today the pomps that please,
Tomorrow sickens with disease,
And next, behold, he's dying!
Then, like the blossom's fading bloom,
To him earth's glory sinks in gloom,
Its hopes in ruin lying.

7. No wealth can buy an hour's delay,
Youth pleads in vain for longer stay,
His joys and he must sever.
Though eyes around with pity flow,
Death has no pity to bestow—
Farewell to earth forever!

8. The wise their wondrous skill disdain,
For worldly splendor is but vain
And e'er to dust is tending.
Alas for them who have not found
While there is time, in Christ their ground:
Their death is woe unending.

9. The worldly are afraid of death,
And only when they gasp for breath
Are mindful of devotion.
One toiled for this and one for that,
But each his own poor soul forgot,
In all of earth's commotion.

10. At last, when he must surely die,
He lifts to God an anxious cry,
And makes a forced surrender:—
I sadly fear, God's slighted grace,
Which long with scorn he did efface,
Will scarce a pardon tender.

11. Dear children, ye your God who own
And piety in heart have shown,
Let not your souls be troubled!
Confide in Jesus' holy Word,
The greatest Refuge ever heard,
So shall your joys be doubled.

12. Requite not evil deeds in wrath,
Pursue in love the narrow path,
Heed not the world's seduction;
Revenge and glory yield to God,
Stray not to byways lush and broad—
For there is all destruction.

13. Could but the flesh indulge its mood
In pleasure, pomp, and worldly good,
Your trust full soon would waver:
In mercy sending earthly cares,
By chast'ning God the soul prepares
To greet His endless favor.

14. But seems your cross too much to bear?
Then think of hell—its dark despair—
To which the world is hasting:
Its flame eternally supplies
Each man with torment, groans, and sighs—
Its fuèl never wasting.

15. But ye, beyond this world's annoy,
In Christ shall find your endless joy—
Which ye do well to ponder;
No mortal tongue can realize
What pleasures and eternal prize
Shall swell you with their wonder.

16. For, what the God of changeless truth
Confirms by Spirit and by oath,
Must come, and ye shall see it.
Whoso will trust His proffered grace
Shall in His kingdom find a place
Through Jesus Christ. So be it!

—G. Grünwald, 1530; tr., composite.

277

Tune: Freu dich sehr, o meine Seele. 66. [*TLH* 61; *LW* 28; *LSB* 347]

1. Come and hear our blessed Savior,
All who want instruction, come;
Learn the right and true behavior
For the heirs of Christendom;
Who believe and so confess,
And with hearts and hands express,
That their whole delight and labor
Is to serve both God and neighbor.

2. Blessed are the poor in spirit,
Who all humbleness possess,
Never claiming any merit,
Praising only God's good grace,
And depend in everything
On the Lord, their God and King;
He will there exalt to greatness
Those who here are full of meekness.

3. Blessed are the secret mourners
Who are filled with godly grief,
And like merciful sojourners
Pray for all mankind's relief;
God, who counts their bitter tears,
And their inward groaning hears,
Will not without comfort leave them
But all blessings ever give them.

4. Blessed are the meek and holy,
Filled with godly gentleness,
Bearing with a spirit lowly
All the scorn their foes express,
Leaving vengeance up to God,
Still submitting to His rod—
They shall gain the Lord's protection,
And the land to their subjection.

5. Blest are they who thirst and hunger
After truth and righteousness,
Where oppression is no longer,
And all evil turns to peace.
Such whose words and life agree,
Love in pure simplicity,
Hate self-int'rest and extortion—
Plenteousness shall be their portion.

6. Blest are they who with compassion
Look upon their neighbor's grief,
Help the poor in their oppression,
Pray to God for their relief;
Who assist the suff'rer's need,
Not with word alone, but deed—
They shall never be discarded
But with mercy be rewarded.

7. Blest are they whose heart and center
Always proveth clean and pure,
In whose breast no ill may enter,
In all holiness secure.
Those who scorn the tainted joys
Of the world and all its ploys,
Nor impurities do treasure,
Shall see God, their truest pleasure.

8. Blessed are the true supporters
Of sweet harmony and peace,
In each conflict gentle courters,
Making strife and malice cease;
Who goodwill and concord frame,
Helping others in the same—
They God's children shall be rendered
And that blessed title tendered.

9. Blest are they who bear affliction,
Persecution, and distress,
Without selfish contradiction,
For the sake of righteousness;
Though their cross be full of grief,
They shall find in God relief,
And beyond this passing story
Shall receive the crown of glory.

10. Lord, bestow these heav'nly graces
On this broken heart of mine,
That in their divine embraces
I remain forever Thine:
Grant me true humility,
Let me bring Thee every plea,
And to friend and foe be gracious,
Holding justice dear and precious.

11. Still to serve my needy neighbor,
Cleanness of my heart preserve,
For the restless let me labor,
In affliction never swerve;
Father, from Thy holy throne,
Grant me grace to love Thy Son,
And assist me with Thy Spirit,
Fruits of goodness to inherit.

—J. Heermann, 1630, alt. D. Denicke, †1680; tr., J. C. Jacobi, 1722, alt.

278

Tune: Lasset uns mit Jesu ziehen. 84. [*TLH* 409; *LW* 381; *LSB* 685]

1. Let us ever walk with Jesus,
Follow His example pure,
Flee the world, which would deceive us
And to sin our souls allure.
Ever in His footsteps treading,
Body here, yet soul above,
Full of faith and hope and love,
Let us do the Father's bidding.
Faithful Lord, abide with me;
Savior, lead, I follow Thee.

2. Let us suffer here with Jesus,
To His image, e'er conform;
Heaven's glory soon will please us,
Sunshine follow on the storm.
Though we sow in tears of sorrow,
We shall reap with heav'nly joy;
And the fears that now annoy
Shall be laughter on the morrow.
Christ, I suffer here with Thee;
There, oh, share Thy joy with me!

3. Let us also die with Jesus.
His death from the second death,
From our soul's destruction, frees us,
Quickens us with life's glad breath.
Let us mortify, while living,
Flesh and blood and die to sin;
And the grave that shuts us in
Shall but prove the gate to heaven.
Jesus, here I die to Thee
There to live eternally.

4. Let us gladly live with Jesus;
Since He's risen from the dead,
Death and grave must soon release us.
Jesus, Thou art now our Head,
We are truly Thine own members;
Where Thou livest, there live we.
Take and own us constantly,
Faithful Friend, as Thy dear brethren.
Jesus, here I live to Thee,
Also there eternally.

—S. von Birken, 1653; tr., J. A. Rimbach, 1910.

279

Tune: Straf mich nicht in deinem Zorn. 56. [*TLH* 446; *LW* 302; *LSB* 663]

1. Rise, my soul, to watch and pray,
From thy sleep awaken;
Be not by the evil day
Unawares o'ertaken.
For the Foe, / Well we know,
Oft his harvest reapeth
While the Christian sleepeth.

2. But first rouse thee and awake
From secure indiff'rence;
Else will follow in its wake
Woe without deliv'rance.
O beware! / Soul, take care!
Death in sins might find thee
Ere thou look behind thee.

3. Wake and watch, or else thy night
Christ can ne'er enlighten;
Far off still will seem the light
That thy path should brighten;
God demands / Willing hands,
Hearts His love confessing,—
Such He fills with blessing.

4. Watch against the devil's snares
Lest asleep he find thee;
For indeed no pains he spares
To deceive and blind thee.
Satan's prey / Oft are they
Who secure are sleeping
And no watch are keeping.

5. Watch! Let not the wicked world
With its pow'r defeat thee.
Watch lest with her pomp unfurled
She betray and cheat thee.
Watch and see / Lest there be
Faithless friends to charm thee,
Who but seek to harm thee.

6. Watch against thyself, my soul,
Lest with grace thou trifle;
Let not self thy thoughts control
Nor God's mercy stifle.
Pride and sin / Lurk within
All thy hopes to scatter;
Heed not when they flatter.

7. But while watching, also pray
To the Lord unceasing.
He will free thee, be thy Stay,
Strength and faith increasing.
O Lord, bless / In distress
And let nothing swerve me
From the will to serve Thee.

8. Yea, indeed, He bids us pray,
Promising to hear us,
E'er to be our Staff and Stay,
Ever to be near us.
Ere we plead, / Will He heed,
Strengthen, keep, defend us,
And deliv'rance send us.

9. Courage, then, for all things must
Work for good and bless us
If we but in pray'rful trust
To His Son address us;
For He will / Richly fill
And His spirit send us,
Who to Him commend us.

10. Therefore let us watch and pray,
Knowing He will hear us
As we see from day to day
Dangers ever near us,
And the end / Doth impend,—
Our redemption neareth
When the Lord appeareth.

—J. B. Freystein, 1695; tr., C. Winkworth, 1863, alt.

280

Tune: Mir nach! spricht Christus, unser Held. 38. [*TLH* 421; *LW* 379; *LSB* 688]

1. Come, follow Me, the Savior spake,
All in My way abiding;
Deny yourselves, the world forsake,
Obey My call and guiding.
Oh, bear the cross, whate'er betide,
Take My example for your guide.

2. I am the Light, I light the way,
A godly life displaying;
I bid you walk as in the day,
I keep your feet from straying.
I am the Way, and well I show
How you must sojourn here below.

3. My heart abounds in lowliness,
My soul with love is glowing,
And gracious words My lips express,
With meekness overflowing.
My heart, My mind, My strength, My all,
To God I yield, on Him I call.

4. I teach you how to shun and flee
What harms your soul's salvation,
Your heart from ev'ry guile to free,
From sin and its temptation.
I am the Refuge of the soul
And lead you to your heav'nly goal.

5. But if too hot you find the fray,
I at your side stand ready;
I fight Myself, I lead the way,
At all times firm and steady.
A coward he who will not heed
When the chief Captain takes the lead.

6. Who seeks to find his soul's welfare
Without Me, he shall lose it;
But who to lose it may appear,
In God shall introduce it.
Who bears no cross nor follows hard
Deserves not Me nor My reward.

7. Then let us follow Christ, our Lord,
And take the cross appointed
And, firmly clinging to His word,
In suff'ring be undaunted.
For who bears not the battle's strain
The crown of life shall not obtain.

—J. Scheffler, 1668, but st. 4, Anon., 1695; tr., C. W. Schaeffer, 1896, alt.

281

Tune: O Gott, du frommer Gott. 55. [*TLH* 395; *LW* 385; *LSB* 696]

1. O God, Thou faithful God,
Thou Fountain ever flowing,
Who good and perfect gifts,
In mercy art bestowing,
Give me a healthy frame,
And may I have within
A conscience free from blame,
A soul unhurt by sin!

2. Grant Thou me strength to do
With ready heart and willing
Whate'er Thou shalt command,
My calling here fulfilling;
To do it when I ought,
With all my might, and bless
The work I thus have wrought,
For Thou must give success.

3. Oh, let me never speak
What bounds of truth exceedeth;
Grant that no idle word
From out my mouth proceedeth;
And then, when in my place
I must and ought to speak,
My words grant pow'r and grace
Lest I offend the weak.

4. If dangers gather round,
Still keep me calm and fearless;
Help me to bear the cross
When life is dark and cheerless;
And let me win my foe
With words and actions kind.
When counsel I would know,
Good counsel let me find.

5. And let me with all men,
As far as in me lieth,
In peace and friendship live.
And if Thy gift supplieth
Great wealth and honor fair,
Then this refuse me not,
That naught be mingled there
Of goods unjustly got.

6. If Thou a longer life
Hast here on earth decreed me;
If Thou through many ills
To age at length wilt lead me,
Thy patience on me shed.
Avert all sin and shame
And crown my hoary head
With honor free from blame.

7. Let me depart this life
Confiding in my Savior;
Do Thou my soul receive
That it may live forever;
And let my body have
A quiet resting-place
Within a Christian grave;
And let it sleep in peace.

8. And on that solemn Day
When all the dead are waking,
Stretch o'er my grave Thy hand,
Thyself my slumbers breaking.
Then let me hear Thy voice,
Change Thou this earthly frame,
And bid me aye rejoice
With those who love Thy name.

—J. Heermann, 1630; tr., C. Winkworth, 1858, alt.

282

Tune: Wachet auf, ruft uns die Stimme. 95. [*TLH* 444; *LW* 303; *LSB* 516]

1. Rise! To arms! With pray'r employ you,
O Christians, lest the foe destroy you,
For Satan has designed your fall.
Wield God's Word, a weapon glorious!
Against each foe you'll be victorious;
Our God will set you o'er them all.
Is Satan strong and fell?
Here is Immanuel.
Sing hosanna! / The strong ones yield
To Christ our Shield,
And we as conqu'rors hold the field.

2. Cast afar this world's vain pleasures,
Aye, boldly fight for heav'nly treasures,
And steadfast be in Jesus' might.
He will help, whate'er betide you,
And naught will harm with Christ beside you.
By faith you'll conquer in the fight.
Then shame, thou weary soul!
Look forward to the goal!
Joy awaits you. / The race, then, run,
The combat done,
The crown of glory will be won.

3. Wisely fight, for time is fleeting,
The hours of grace are fast retreating;
Short, short is this our earthly way.
When the trump the dead is waking
And sinners all with fear are quaking,
With joy the saints will greet that Day.
Bless God, our triumph's sure,
Though long we did endure
Scorn and trial. / Thou, Son of God,
To Thine abode
Wilt lead the way Thyself hast trod.

4. Jesus, all Thy children cherish
And keep them that they never perish
Whom Thou hast purchased with Thy blood.
Let new life to us be given
That we may look to Thee in heaven
Whenever fearful is our mood.
Thy spirit on us pour
That we may love Thee more—
Hearts o'erflowing; / And then will we
Be true to Thee
In death and life eternally.

—W. E. Arends, 1714; tr., J. M. Sloan, 1865, alt.

283

Tune: Freu dich sehr, o meine Seele. 66. [*TLH* 61; *LW* 28; *LSB* 347]

1. Be thou faithful to the ending,
Let not danger nor distress
Be thy love for God offending;
Until death His faith confess.
Ah! the suff'ring of this earth
All the glory is not worth,
Which thy Jesus then will give thee
When in joy He shall receive thee.

2. Be thou faithful in believing,
Build thy house on solid ground;
Let no doubts or thoughts deceiving
This baptismal gift confound.
Then, in the o'erflowing wave,
God is with thee, strong to save.
Lost art thou, by God deserted,
If thou falsely hast converted.

3. Be thou faithful in thy loving
Tow'rd thy God who loveth thee,
E'en to them thy love be proving
Who but work thy misery,
Think how Jesus prayed for those
By whose hands His cross arose!
To the height of God's forgiving
Mercy let in thee be living.

4. Be thou faithful in affliction,
Let no sorrow, pain, or loss
Hide thy Savior's benediction,
Murmur not beneath the cross!
Can impatience balm obtain?
Doth it profit to complain?
He who patiently endureth
Comfort from on high secureth.

5. Be thou faithful in thy hoping!
Trust thou firmly in God's Word!
Comes He not when thou art groping?
Seems thy grievous cry unheard?
Hope thou in Him firmly yet!
For the Lord doth not forget,
Yea, to help He oft is minded,
While thine eyes with sin are blinded.

6. Forward then! in God confiding,
Faithful evermore remain,
Keep thee to His faithful guiding,
There is then no shame to gain.
Only call, and God is there,
So is full His heart with care,
Only call, God help will send thee;
Hope shall not with shame offend thee.

7. Be thou faithful, that within thee
E'er thy heart to truth incline;
To a truthful heart let win thee
Joab's kiss and Judas' sign.
Falsehood be thy baneful foe;
Let thy heart thy mouth o'erflow.
In thy faith be wise and clever,
Nor yet false or lying ever.

8. Be thou faithful in each matter,
From the start until the end;
Suffer God all storms to scatter
And all to His purpose bend,
That His glory may increase;
Yea, and thou be filled with peace,
Heaven's goodly path pursuing,
And all sinful ways eschewing.

9. Be thou faithful e'en in dying,
Fighting till the fight is won,
Every devil's trick defying;
Thus the hardest part is done.
Who with Jesus' help will fight,
Putting flesh and sin to flight,
With God as His true defender,
Shall obtain the crown of splendor.

—B. Prätorius, 1659; tr. sts. 1–3, 5–6, A. B. Warner, 1858, alt;
st. 4, A. Hoppe, 1921, alt.; sts. 7–9, M. Carver.

284

Tune: Was mein Gott will, das gscheh allzeit. 83. [*LW* 414; *LSB* 714 (mel.);
or (iso.) *TLH* 437; *LW* 425; *LSB* 758; *or TLH* 266*; *LW* 341*]

1. Be true to God, O man, and keep
Within His cov'nant rooted;
Rely on this foundation deep,
To Him alone devoted.
Recall how He / Laid claim to thee,
His Word with water blending,
A binding oath, / Conferring both
His love and grace unending.

2. Be true to God, let trouble not
Nor cross thee from Him sever;
If He's thy Father and thy God,
What more couldst thou wish ever?
The highest Good / Doth cheer the mood.
Hast thou His grace and pleasure,
Dear Christian mine, / Then more is thine
Than heav'n and earth can measure.

3. Be true to God throughout thy life,
Let of His love bereave thee
No worldly bliss nor sorrow rife,
As long as life He give thee.
His pledge of old / Will daily hold,
His faithfulness fail never.
The words He spake / He shall not break—
This boldly trust forever.

4. Be true to God whatever be
Thy calling, rank, or station.
What harm can come if only He
Gives thee His preservation?
Man's breastplate His / Good favor is;
No devil then can harm him.
That man can boast / God's circling host,
And nothing shall alarm him.

5. Be true to God, His precious Word
With steadfast faith confessing.
Where'er thou be, hold undeterred
By faith that gracious blessing;
The world will have / Its dust and chaff;
They shall together perish;
God's Word o'er earth / Shall still go forth,
And without failure flourish.

6. Be true to God, who evermore
Is faithful, kind, and gracious,
And as His vassal wage the war,
Nor suffer sin rapacious
To steal the rein / Of thy campaign;
Yet, if thy heart be riven,
Do not forestall, / Confess thy fall,
And fight as one forgiven.

7. Be true to God e'en unto death
And suffer naught to turn thee;
He can and shall His help bequeath
When fire and foe would burn thee,
Yea, tho' the realm / Of hell should whelm,
And all its might be meted
Thy soul to grieve, / Yet firm believe,
Thou shalt not be defeated.

8. So if to God thou true adhere,
This proof He too shall render,
That He's thy Father, ever dear,
And His own oath's Defender.
A crown of grace / In yonder place
Shall to thy brow be given,
And evermore / Shalt thou adore
His faithfulness in heaven.

—M. Franck, 1657; tr. sts. 2, 3a, 5b, D. G. Ristad, 1897, alt.; sts. rest, M. Carver.

285

Tune: Was frag ich nach der Welt. 55. [*TLH* 430; *LW* 187; *LSB* 346]

1. What is the world to me
With all its vaunted pleasure
When Thou, and Thou alone,
Lord Jesus, art my Treasure!
Thou only, dearest Lord,
My soul's Delight shalt be;
Thou art my Peace, my Rest,—
What is the world to me!

2. The world is like a cloud
And like a vapor fleeting,
A shadow that declines,
Swift to its end retreating.
My Jesus doth abide,
Though all things fade and flee;
My everlasting Rock,—
What is the world to me!

3. The world seeks to be praised
And honored by the mighty,
Yet never once reflects
That they are frail and flighty.
But what I truly prize
Above all things is He,
My Jesus, He alone,—
What is the world to me!

4. The world seeks after wealth
And all that Mammon offers,
Yet never is content
Though gold should fill it coffers.
I have a higher good,
Content with it I'll be:
My Jesus is my Wealth,—
What is the world to me!

5. The world is sorely grieved
Whenever it is slighted
Or when its hollow fame
And honor have been blighted.
Christ, Thy reproach I bear
Long as it pleaseth Thee;
I'm honored by my Lord,—
What is the world to me!

6. The world with wanton pride
Exalts its sinful pleasures
And for them foolishly
Gives up the heav'nly treasures.
Let others love the world
With all its vanity;
I love the Lord, my God,—
What is the world to me!

7. The world abideth not;
Lo, like a flash 'twill vanish;
With all its gorgeous pomp
Pale death it cannot banish;
Its riches pass away,
And all its joys must flee;
But Jesus doth abide,—
What is the world to me!

8. What is the world to me!
My Jesus is my Treasure,
My Life, my Health, my Wealth,
My Friend, my Love, my Pleasure,
My Joy, my Crown, my All,
My Bliss eternally.
Once more, then, I declare:
What is the world to me!

—G. M. Pfefferkorn, 1667; tr., A. Crull, †1923.

286

Tune: O daß ich tausend Zungen hätte. 45. [*TLH* 373; *LW* 224; *LSB* 566]

1. Soul, what return has God, thy Savior,
For all He gives thee day by day?
Oh, hast thou in thy gift a favor
That can delight and please Him?—Say!
The best of off'rings He requires:
Thy heart it is that He desires.

2. Give unto God thy heart's affection,
Who else can claim thee as His own?
Should Satan hold thee in subjection?
With him but pangs of hell are known.
To Thee alone, O Lord divine,
My heart and all I now resign.

3. Accept the gift which Thou requirest,
My heart and soul, O gracious God,
The first-fruits Thou so much desirest,
For which Thy Son paid with His blood.
To Thee I willingly assign
My heart, dear Lord, for it is Thine.

4. Whom should I give my heart's affection
But Thee, who gavest Thine to faith?
Thy fervent love is my protection;
Lord, Thou hast loved me unto death.
My heart with Thine shall ever be
One heart throughout eternity.

—K. F. Lochner, 1673, ab.; tr., *TLH,* 1941.

287

Tune: O Gott, du frommer Gott. 55. [*TLH* 395; *LW* 385; *LSB* 696]

1. How can I thank Thee, Lord,
For all Thy loving-kindness,
That Thou hast patiently
Borne with me in my blindness?
When dead in many sins
And trespasses I lay,
I kindled, holy God,
Thine anger every day.

2. Lord, Thou hast shown to me
Divine commiseration:
I persevered in sin,
But Thou in great compassion;
I did resist Thee, Lord,
Deferring to repent;
Thou didst defer Thy wrath
And instant punishment.

3. It is Thy work alone
That I am now converted;
O'er Satan's work in me
Thou hast Thy power asserted.
Thy mercy and Thy grace
That rise afresh each morn
Have turned my stony heart
Into a heart new-born.

4. I could but grieve Thee, Lord,
And with my sins displease Thee;
Yet to atone for sin
My works could not appease Thee.
Though I could fall from grace
And choose the way of sin,
I had no strength to rise,
A new life to begin.

5. But Thou hast raised me up
To joy and exultation
And clearly shown the way
That leads me to salvation.
My sins are washed away,
For this I thank Thee, Lord;
And with my heart and soul
All dead works are abhorred.

6. Grant that Thy Spirit's help
To me be always given
Lest I should fall again
And lose the way to heaven;
That He may give me strength
In mine infirmity
And e'er renew my heart
To serve Thee willingly.

7. Oh, guide and lead me, Lord,
While here below I wander
That I may follow Thee
Till I shall see Thee yonder.
For if I led myself,
I soon would go astray;
But if Thou leadest me,
I keep the narrow way.

8. O Father, God of Love,
Hear Thou my supplication;
O Savior, Son of God,
Grant me Thy full salvation;
And Thou, O Holy Ghost,
Be Thou my faithful Guide
That I may serve Thee here
And there with Thee abide.

—D. Denicke, 1648, but st. 6, J. Heermann, 1630, alt.; tr., A. Crull, †1923.

288

Tune: Ach Gott vom Himmel, sieh darein. 49. [*TLH* 260]

1. Thou dust and clay of earthly mold,
Boast not of carnal glory!
Thy misery is manifold,
Conceived in sin, before thee
A way of pain and woe extends,
Until in pain life's journey ends,
Affliction is thy portion.

2. Thy body frail thou dost adorn
Wherein corruption dwelleth,
Thy mind, of true discernment shorn,
In self-indulgence swelleth.
Dost thou not know the day is near,
When death shall end thy brief career,
And worms destroy thy body?

3. Oh, rather beautify thy soul,
True penitence confessing!
The Living Bread of heav'n extol,
The food so rich in blessing.
Redeemed, thy deathless soul shall soar
To dwell with God forevermore,
And all the holy angels.

4. Why give such service to the flesh
And leave the soul to languish?
Doth man heed more the servant's wish
Than all his lady's anguish?
The spirit must be leading first,
Alas, for thee, 'tis all reversed—
Thy flesh rules o'er thy spirit.

5. Such value God the mighty Lord
To all men's souls hath given,
And over all things else adored,
Yea, set them over heaven.
For whose sake else sent He His Son—
His greatest Joy, the blessed One—
Upon the cross to suffer?

6. He did this not for earth and heav'n,
But men, His dear creation.
To them His boundless grace was giv'n,
He yearned for their salvation!
In love He gave the ransom-price,
His only Son, whose sacrifice
Secured complete redemption.

7. O mortal man, since thy great God
Doth deem thy soul so precious,
Canst thou ignore it as the sod,
In base neglect,—ungracious?
Remember that His only Son
Descended from His heav'nly throne,
From death and hell to save it.

8. For when He found them fast in chains
Of guilt, wrought by the devil,
And doomed to suffer endless pains
In hell for all their evil,
His heart within Him, grieving, broke,
He mourned the pain and dev'lish yoke
To which they had been blinded.

9. Yea, more than this, He did not scorn
Death for their sake to suffer,
But pierced Himself with every thorn
Their sinful hand could offer.
His sweat like blood the ransom paid
In coin by coin of crimson shade,
And thus became our Savior.

10. Oh, ponder on His sacrifice
In fervent meditation.
Thy precious soul no more despise,
Resist not God's salvation!
The balm of earth could nevermore
Relieve thy soul's deep wounds so sore,
But Jesus' blood hath healed them.

11. If Satan, worker of all woe,
Had not by lies and cunning
With fatal poison laid them low
In sin and sorrow drowning,
Then 'twere for God's Son wholly loss
To meet His death upon the cross
Through mockery and torture.

12. Wherefore do not despise, O man,
That sore and heavy suff'ring
Which for thy sake o'er Jesus ran,
But thanks to Him be off'ring,
And shun all ill; see how thy Lord
Thy periled soul hath so adored,
Came to thy aid, and saved thee!

13. Oh, help me, God, for all my days
These weighty things to ponder,
And humbly give Thee thanks and praise
For this Thy gift of wonder;
And let me leave the path of sin,
And lift my heart to Thee in heav'n,
My Savior ever seeking.

—J. Heermann, 1630, after Bernard; tr. sts. 1–3, 6–7, 10, A. Hoppe, 1921, alt.; sts. rest, M. Carver.

289

Tune: Was frag ich nach der Welt. 55. [*TLH* 99; *LW* 187; *LSB* 346]

1. Though one possess all skill
And knowledge in creation,
And speak with tongues of men
And angels high in station,
Yet if beside these things
His charity should fail,
In God almighty's eyes
It nothing would avail.

2. He would resemble naught
But brass so clearly sounding,
Yet never in good fruit
Or any use abounding;
Yea rather, such a man,
Though Christian be his name,
Is like an empty shell,
No life or aught to claim.

3. Though one may prophesy,
With faith remove a mountain,
And on the blind and deaf
Pour out life's healing fountain,
Yet if, beside these things,
His charity should fail,
Again I will declare,
This all would naught avail.

4. Though one may feed the poor
And give them every treasure,
Yet if his deed come not
From mercy without measure—
Yea, though his body burn—
If yet his love should fail,
Once more I must declare
This all would naught avail.

5. Love suffers long, is kind
And gentle-hearted ever,
A friend to every man,
And hesitating never
To help in time of need;
No envy doth it know,
But seeks its neighbor's good
And helps him in all woe.

6. Love is not proud or vain,
For no man hatred bearing,
Seeks not its selfish gain,
With all its counsel sharing;
Love is not soon provoked
But helps its fellow man,
It drives all harm away
In every way it can.

7. Love mourns and is aggrieved
When wickedness is courted,
But gladly doth rejoice
When truth is well supported;
Love also covers o'er
Its neighbors flaws and faults,
All things it gladly bears,
True peace and rest exalts.

8. Love faithfully believes,
All matters well construing,
For restoration hopes
When one in evildoing
And sin should hap to fall;
Though love may faultless be,
Yet still it doth endure
Its suff'rings patiently.

9. When earthly lore shall be
In heaven's splendor ceasing,
Yet love will still abide
And ever be increasing;
When faith and hope as well
In time shall pass away,
Yet love abideth still,
Beyond in endless day.

10. O Jesus, Lord, who art
True Love, the Pattern proving:
Grant that I, too, may be
To every neighbor loving;
And make me evermore
Prepared to serve each man
With all my heart and pow'r
As I both ought and can.

— L. Backmeister, asc., Lüneburg, 1661; tr., M. Carver.

290

Tune: Kommt her zu mir, spricht Gottes Sohn. 41. [*TLH* 263; *LW* 261; *LSB* 666 (mel.)]

1. How can I seek, O highest Light,
To enter in Thy presence bright
With flesh and blood so lowly?
How shall my heart be bolder made
To go where all must pale and fade
Before Thy face so holy?

2. What is my flesh but stubble dry?
What is my life? And what am I
But dust and ashes wholly?
What is my pow'r when all is done?
What is my wealth and all I own,
But what Thou givest solely?

3. I am a wretched worm and snail,
A piece of chaff that by a gale
Is quickly tossed and driven,
And if Thy hand that carries all
Should barely touch me, I would fall,
And all my pow'rs be riven.

4. Lord, I am naught; Thou art the Man
Who holdest all things in Thy span;
In Thee I have my being.
If Thou some shock of terror prove,
Nor shield me with Thy grace and love,
My life would soon be fleeing.

5. Thou, Father, faithful art and just,
But I, a wicked fiend, who must
With utter shame be blushing,
In such a state of misery
To take the littlest good from Thee
Whose purse is ever gushing.

6. Since youth I've done naught else to Thee
But roused Thine anger constantly;
In sin my mother bore me,
And hadst Thou not in faithfulness
Redeemed and freed me from distress,
No hope would lie before me.

7. Far be it then that I should boast;
I'll give Thee Thine, the fitting cost,
For all should solely praise Thee;
Lord Jesus, let my spirit here
And all that from it doth appear
Be ever turned to face Thee.

8. And even if some good I do,
I could not start and see it through:
The pow'r by Thee is given;
For which all praise and glory be,
O Savior, evermore to Thee
On earth as 'tis in heaven.

—P. Gerhardt, 1667; tr., M. Carver.

291

Tune: Werde munter, mein Gemüte. 66. [*TLH* 207; *LW* 263; *LSB* 548]

1. Blessèd is the man that never
Doth in godless counsel meet;
Nor in sinners' way stands ever,
Nor sits in the scorner's seat,
But on God's all perfect law
Meditates with holy awe;
Day and night he delves for treasure
In the Word—'tis all his pleasure.

2. As a tree that has been planted
By the flowing waters fair,
In its season e'er is granted
Fruits and foliàge to bear;
So is he, the righteous, seen
Ever fruitful, ever green,
And his leaf shall wither never,
All he does shall prosper ever.

3. To the wicked 'tis not given
Such a happy lot to share;
As the chaff by wind is driven,
So shall the ungodly fare;
They in judgment shall not stand,
Nor be in the righteous band:
These the Lord forsaketh never,
Those shall be cast off forever.

4. For the Lord His people knoweth,
His pure eyes behold their way,
And the blessing He bestoweth
Is their heritage for aye:
But the wicked ever tend
To their doom and to their end:
God will all the righteous cherish,
But the wicked ones shall perish.

—P. Gerhardt, 1653; / M. B. Landstad, †1880, after Psalm 1; tr., C. Døving, 1906.

Morning

292

Tune: Aus meines Herzens Grunde. 58. [*TLH* 548; *LW* 25; *LSB* 354]

1. My inmost heart now raises
In this fair morning hour
A song of thankful praises
To Thine almighty pow'r,
O God, upon Thy throne.
To honor and adore Thee,
I bring my praise before Thee
Through Christ, Thine only Son.

2. For Thou from me hast warded
All perils of the night;
From ev'ry harm hast guarded
My soul till morning light.
To Thee I humbly cry,
O Savior, have compassion
And pardon my transgression;
Have mercy, Lord most high!

3. And shield me from all evil,
O gracious God, this day,
From sin, and from the devil,
From shame and from dismay,
From fire's consuming breath,
From water's devastation,
From need and consternation,
From evil sudden death.

4. My life, my soul—defend them!
My wife, child, goods, and home,—
To Thy hand I commend them,
From Thee my blessings come;
Thy bounteous hand bestows
My household and my treasures,
My parents, friends, and pleasures;
My cup with good o'erflows.

5. Let not Thine angel leave me
While here on earth I stay
Lest Satan's arts deceive me
And lead my soul astray.
Then keep Thine angel near
At night and each new morrow
Lest soul and body sorrow
And falt'ring cost me dear.

6. God shall do my advising,
Whose might with wisdom blends;
May He bless rest and rising,
My efforts, means, and ends!
To God, forever blest,
Will I with mine confide me,
And willing let Him guide me
As seemeth to Him best.

7. Amen I say, not fearing
That God rejects my prayer;
I doubt not He is hearing
And granting me His care.
Thus I go on my way
And do not look behind me,
But ply the task assigned me;
God's help shall be my stay.

—G. Nigidius, before 1585, alt.; tr., C. Winkworth, 1863, alt., but st. 4, E. Cronenwett, 1880, alt.

293

Tune: Geduld, die solln wir haben. 59. [*TLH* 544; *or TLH* 334*; *LW* 257*; *LSB* 689*]

1. While yet the morn is breaking,
I thank my God once more,
Beneath whose care awaking,
I find the night is o'er.
I thank Him that He calls me
To life and health anew;
I know, whate'er befalls me,
His care will still be true.

2. O Israel's Guardian, hear me,
Watch over me this day;
In all I do be near me.
For others, too, I pray;
To Thee I would commend them,
Our Church, our youth, our land,
Direct them and defend them
When dangers are at hand.

3. O gracious Lord, direct us,
Thy doctrine pure defend,
From heresies protect us,
And for Thy Word contend
That we may praise Thee ever,
O God, with one accord
And say: The Lord, our Savior,
Be evermore adored.

4. Oh, grant us peace and gladness,
Give us our daily bread,
Shield us from grief and sadness,
On us Thy blessings shed.
Grant that our whole behavior,
In truth and righteousness,
May praise Thee, Lord, our Savior,
Whose holy name we bless.

5. And gently grant Thy blessing
That we may do Thy will,
No more Thy ways transgressing,
Our proper task fulfill,
With Peter's full assurance
Let down our nets again.
Success will crown endurance
If faithful we remain.

6. With craftiness unceasing
Strives Satan to restrain
What in Thy sight is pleasing
And for Thy Church is gain;
Yet vain is his endeavor,
For Thou, O Christ, our Lord,
Dost rule all things forever
By Thine almighty Word.

7. Thou art the Vine,—oh, nourish
The branches graft in Thee
And let them grow and flourish,
A fair and fruitful tree.
Thy Spirit pour within us
And let His gifts of grace
To such good actions win us
As best may show Thy praise.

—J. Mühlmann, †1613; sts. 1–2, 5–6, tr., C. Winkworth, 1863, alt.; sts. 3–4, *TLH*, 1941.

294

Tune: Die helle Sonn leucht jetzt herfür. 11. [*TLH* 547; *LW* 352]

1. The radiant sun shines in the skies,
With joy from sleep we now arise.
All praise to God, who through this night
Hath kept us from the devil's might.

2. Lord Jesus Christ, guide us this day;
Keep sin and shame far from our way.
Thy guardian angels to us send
And let them to our wants attend.

3. Direct our hearts to do Thy will
And for Thy Word true love instill
That we may do whate'er is right
And ever pleasing in Thy sight.

4. Crown all our labors with success,
Each one in his own calling bless.
May all we do or think or say
Exalt and praise Thee, Lord, this day!

—N. Herman, 1560; tr., *TLH,* 1941.

295

Tune: Herr Jesu Christ, meins Lebens Licht. 11. [*TLH* 288; *LW* 262; *LSB* 704]

1. Since now the night, dear Lord, is o'er,
We thank Thee in this morning hour
For our refreshing sleep, and pray,
That Thou wouldst keep us safe this day.

2. O Thou illuming Light of grace,
Lift Thou on us Thy beaming Face:
In this dark vale be Thou our Stay,
And keep us in Thy paths alway.

3. Grant us Thy peace, and civil rest,
Likewise what Thou deem'st for us best,
And by Thy gracious, mighty hand
Protect us and our native land.

4. Our sins and frailties, Lord, forgive,
And a good conscience ever give;
Help us that we Thy name defend,
And more and more its fame extend.

5. And when at last it shall Thee please
Us from life's burdens here to ease,
Then grant us each a blessed end,—
That we to Thee in heav'n ascend.

6. Dear Savior, Lord, our pray'r hear Thou!
Be merciful and save us now
Thro' Thine own merits and Thy death!—
Be this our pray'r till life's last breath.

—Anon., Frankfurt, 1662; tr., E. Cronenwett, 1925, alt.

296

Tune: Warum betrübst du dich, mein Herz. 18. [p. 415]

1. Arise, heart, mind, and sense, arise!
The silent night before thee flies,
The day is broken now;
Wherefore, my soul, this hour impart
Thy thanks to God with mouth and heart!

2. Oh, what a countless host of ill
The Lord hath routed by His will,
Which Satan set for thee,
But God hath kept them all at bay:
That man is blest who owns it aye.

3. Oh, Lord, I must unworthy be,
For all the things Thou showest me,—
Such things I've never earned;
Yet had I not Thy bounties great,
How piteous then would be my state!

4. Now, Lord, I see, 'tis utter grace
Which in Thine every work I trace,
And which I have enjoyed;
Oh, grant me to return Thy praise
And give Thee thanks for all my days.

5. Grant me each hour of day to fill
According to Thy holy will;
Preserve me safe from harm;
Unfailing hold before mine eye
That mortal day, when I must die.

6. Lest ever I by careless thought
In some ungodly sin be caught,
Let me be warned of death.
My body, soul, and senses be
Commended, O my Lord, to Thee.

7. Now forward to my task I go,
Nor will another helper know
Than my beloved God,
Who hedges me about, that I
The devil boldly may defy.

—J. M. Dilherr, †1669; tr., M. Carver.

297

Tune: Gott des Himmels und der Erden. 37. [*TLH* 549]

1. God who madest earth and heaven,
Father, Son, and Holy Ghost;
Who the day and night has given,
Sun and moon and starry host;
Whose almighty hand sustains
Earth and all that it contains.

2. God, I thank Thee, in Thy keeping
Safely have I slumbered here;
Thou hast guarded me while sleeping
From all danger, pain, and fear;
And the cunning evil foe
Hath not wrought my overthrow.

3. Let the night of my transgression
With night's darkness pass away.
Jesus, into Thy possession
I resign myself today;
In Thy wounds I find relief
From all sorrow, sin, and grief.

4. Help me as the morn is breaking,
In the spirit to arise,
So from careless sloth awaking,
That, when o'er the agèd skies
Shall the Judgment Day appear,
I may see it without fear.

5. Lead me and forsake me never,
Guide my wand'rings by Thy Word;
As Thou hast been, be Thou ever
My Defense, my Refuge, Lord.
Never safe except with Thee,
Thou my faithful Guardian be.

6. O my God, I now commend me
Wholly to Thy mighty hand,
All the pow'rs that Thou dost lend me,
By Thy hand directed be;
Thou my boast, my strength divine,
Keep me with Thee, I am Thine.

7. Send Thine angel for my guarding
From the evil one's dark pow'r,
From his crafts and sieges warding,
Keeping watch o'er me each hour,
Till my final rest be come,
And Thine angel bear me home.

—H. Albert, 1642; tr., C. Winkworth, 1855, alt.

298

Tune: Herr Gott, dich loben alle wir. 11. [*TLH* 13; *LW* 216; *LSB* 923]

1. Praise God, the day is here at last!
We now awake from slumber fast.
God kept us from the devil's might
By angels watching through the night.

2. O God, forgive us, heart and mind,
Be gracious, merciful, and kind;
Thy host about us keep arrayed,
Against the devil lend Thine aid.

3. Bless all the work that we must do
And give us strength to see it through,
Increase our pow'r to understand,
And govern us by Thine own hand.

4. Make us to walk in Thy true way
And ever in it surely stay,
Thy Spirit as our Guide bestow
To keep us from all fear and woe.

5. Protect us from the erring path
When Satan strikes us in his wrath,
Guard us from sin and shameful deed,
And help us out of every need!

6. Amen! to work our way we tread
With God upon our heart and head;
May these our labors all our days
Bring God the glory and the praise.

—N. Selnecker, 1587, alt.; tr., M. Carver.

299

Beginning of the Week

Tune: Herr Jesu Christ, meins Lebens Licht. 11. [*TLH* 7; *LW* 262; *LSB* 704]

1. As we begin another week,
In Jesus' name this boon we seek:
God, grant that through these seven days
No evil may befall our ways.

2. Thy gentle blessings, Lord, outpour
On all our labor evermore;
Our hearts with Thy good Spirit fill
That we may gladly do Thy will.

3. In every season, every place,
May we regard Thy Word of grace
Until, when life's brief day is past,
We reach eternal joy at last

4. And keep with angels in Thy rest
The endless Sabbaths of the blest.
This grant to us through Christ, Thy Son,
Who reigns with Thee upon Thy throne.

—M. Wandersleben, 1668; tr., W. G. Polack, 1940.

300

Tune: Ich dank dir, lieber Herre. 59. [*TLH* 334; *LW* 257; *LSB* 689]

1. I thank Thee, Lord, for keeping
Thy watch throughout the night
And guarding me while sleeping
And putting foes to flight;
When shades on me descended,
And I in danger lay,
Thy hand my life defended
Until I saw the day!

2. With thanks I bow before Thee,
My heav'nly God and Lord,
And urgently implore Thee,
This day Thy help afford;
O Father, hear my pleading,
Yet let Thy will be done,
In Thy good way be leading,
My will with Thine be one!

3. From wand'ring, Lord, prevent me,
That I not slip or stray,
Grant not the Foe to tempt me
To take the erring way.
I pray Thee, help in shunning,
O Lord, by all Thy grace,
The devil's snares and cunning
Which wait in every place.

4. With solid faith endue me,
In Jesus Christ to trust;
Forgive my sins, renew me,
For Him declare me just;
Nor wilt Thou this forbid me,
E'en as Thy lips did swear
That Christ of sin would rid me
And all its burden bear.

5. And with that hope provide me
Which no corruption sees,
Put Christlike love inside me
For all mine enemies,
That I may show compassion,
Nor seek or serve mine own,
But love them in the fashion
That Thou to me hast shown.

6. Thy Word be my confession
Before the world profane,
Nor let me make concession
To fear, might, wealth, or gain,
But make me serve Thee ever
In Thy clear truth, my rock,
Nor my connection sever
With Thy true Christian flock.

7. The day grant me to finish
In glory to Thy name,
Nor let my faith diminish,
But Thee till death acclaim;
Sustain my life to heaven,
Support the fruiting land
What Thou to me hast given
Is all within Thy hand.

8. Lord Christ, I give Thee praises
For all Thy goodness fair,
Which Thou as each day passes
Revealest everywhere;
Thy name, all names exceeding
I'll praise, for Thou art good,
Thou giv'st Thy flesh for feeding,
Thou bidd'st me drink Thy blood.

9. We worship and we bless Thee
We praise Thee, God, alone;
Grant that, as we confess Thee,
Thy blessings may be known;
That we in peace may slumber,
Thy grace upon us pour;
For Satan's darts in number
Grant faith, Thy weapon sure.

—J. Kolross, 1535; tr., M. Carver.

301

Tune: Ich dank dir schon durch deinen Sohn. 7. [*TLH* 431]

1. I thank Thee, Father, through Thy Son,
That Thou didst kindly watch me
And keep me safe till night was done,
Nor suffer harm to touch me.

2. At night I lay in chains of gloom
With darkness all around me,
Afflicted by the sense of doom
In which my sins had bound me.

3. So from my heart to Thee I pray
That Thou wouldst now forgive me
Of all my sins which till this day
I've done, nor let them grieve me.

4. I also pray Thee, Lord, avert
All woe by Thy protection,
Lest Satan cause me any hurt
With all his sly deception.

5. Direct me, God, to do Thy will,
And let me not be falling,
That I Thy pleasure may fulfill
In life and in my calling.

6. My soul and body I commend,
With all things, to Thy keeping;
O Lord, to me Thine angel send
In my distress and weeping.

7. Forbid the devil thus to gain
O'er me the slightest powèr;
For didst Thou not Thy grace sustain,
I'd soon before him cowèr.

8. Have I not always heard men say,
Men's help availeth never?
O faithful God, be Thou my Stay;
Thy help availeth ever.

9. To God the Father, God the Son
Upon the throne of heaven,
With God the Spirit, Three in One,
All praise be ever given.

10. He governs all with mighty pow'r
From starting until ending;
May He upon my final hour
A blessèd death be sending.

—Anon., Leipzig, 1586, but sts. 8, 10 later; tr., M. Carver.

302

Tune: Nun danket all und bringet Ehr. 6. [*TLH* 248; *LW* 200; *LSB* 903]

1. Now that the night hath reached its close
And darkness is no more,
All waken from their sweet repose
Who rushed to sleep before.

2. So wake ye, too, my senses all,
Put off your slumber dour,
Be minded now, on God to call
In this the fitting hour.

3. And thou, dear soul within my breast,
Dear spirit, humbly bow,
To give for all thy gentle rest
Thanks to thy Maker now.

4. How shall I pay, O Light divine,
Thy fitting meed of praise?
My soul and body I resign;
Let them be Thine always.

5. To Thee, O Jesus, I will give
This gift, my pledge to prove,
Since all I have I do receive
From Thy free hand of love.

6. And this Thy hand of love hath e'er
Defended me from fright
And made all dangers disappear
Throughout the gloomy night.

7. When in Thine arms I fell asleep,
The devil, with his art,
Could not succeed to make me weep
Or any wound impart.

8. From harm by fire and flood, O Lord,
Thy grace preserved me hath
And thro' the night hath been my ward
From evil, sudden death.

9. I thank Thee, Jesus, for Thy love
And for Thy faithfulness;
Assist me e'er my thanks to prove
And from the heart confess.

10. O Lord, remember me, I pray,
As through this day I go,
In grace turn every harm away
And banish every woe.

11. O gracious Jesus, hear my pray'r,
Receive my groan and cry,
Direct my step that I may fare
Thy righteous pathways by.

12. Oh, Jesus, keep my courses clear
From all iniquity,
Else, as sin's wretched child, I fear,
I could not stay with Thee.

13. Turn all my glances in Thy grace
From what this world doth crave;
That I may shun all wickedness
Until I reach the grave.

14. On all that I must do this day,
Lord, let Thy blessing rest,
That with rejoicing I may say,
"Who Jesus hath is blest!"

15. Yea, blest is he when Jesus' name
Is on his heart engraved,
His deeds have then a pleasing frame
And he is blest and saved.

16. Thus in God's name I gladly go
My labors to begin.
That I may end them, God bestow
The Spirit's strength within.

—J. F. Möckel, 1691; tr., M. Carver.

303

Tune: Herr Gott, dich loben alle wir. 11. [*TLH* 13; *LW* 216; *LSB* 923]

1. O blessed Holy Trinity,
Divine, eternal Unity,
God Father, Son, and Holy Ghost,
Be Thou this day my Guide and Host.

2. My soul and body keep from harm,
O'er all I have extend Thine arm,
That Satan may not cause distress
Nor bring me shame and wretchedness.

3. The Father's love shield me this day,
The Son's pure wisdom cheer my way,
The Holy Spirit's light divine
Illume my heart's benighted shrine.

4. My Maker, strengthen Thou my heart,
O my Redeemer, help impart,
Blest Comforter, keep at my side,
That faith and love in me abide.

5. Lord, bless and keep Thou me as Thine;
Lord, make Thy face upon me shine;
Lord, lift Thy countenance on me
And give me peace, sweet peace, from Thee.

—M. Behm, 1598, alt. / Wittenberg, 1608, ab.; tr., C. H. L. Schuette, 1880, alt.

304

Tune: Nun laßt uns Gott dem Herren. 4. [*LW* 184; *or TLH* 122*]

1. Awake my heart, be singing,
Praise to thy Maker bringing,
Of all good gifts the Sender,
Of all men the Defender.

2. As shades of night spread over
Myself its darkling cover,
Then Satan sought to have me,
But God was near to save me.

3. Yea, when he would o'erpow'r me,
O Father, to devour me,
I in Thy bosom found me,
Thy shelt'ring wing around me

4. Thou saidst, "I will, relieve thee,
Though much the foe deceive thee,
Sleep well, let naught affright thee,
The sunlight shall delight thee."

5. Thy pledge was made sincerely,
The light I can see clearly,
I'm free from mine affliction,
Renewed by Thy protection.

6. Thou dost desire an off'ring,
My gifts I will be proff'ring:
My pray'rs and hymns as spices
And fitting sacrifices.

7. Such Thou disdainest never,
The heart Thou canst search ever,
Thou know'st none can deceive Thee,
No better can I give Thee.

8. Thy work, Lord, to the ending
Perfect in me, and, sending
The Spirit to uphold me,
Let Him this day enfold me.

9. Say Yes to each endeavor,
All to my good work ever,
Beginning, middle, ending,
Lord, to the good be bending.

10. Thy blessings pour Thou in me,
Thy lodging make within me,
Thy Word as food bestowing,
Till I to heav'n am going.

—P. Gerhardt, 1649; tr. sts. 3, 5–6, 8, 10, M. Carver; sts. rest, J. Kelly, 1867, alt.

305

Tune: Wie schön leuchtet der Morgenstern. 86. [*TLH* 546; *LW* 325; *LSB* 395]

1. How lovely shines the morning star!
In twilight sky it gleams afar;
The reign of night is ended.
Creation stirs to hail the light
Whose glories now with radiance bright
Stream forth in beauty splendid.
Both far / And near
All things living / Thanks are giving,
Praise outpouring,
Earth and sky the Lord adoring.

2. Then haste, my soul, thy song to raise,
Delay thou not thy Lord to praise,
Bow down in adoration.
For glory, Lord, to Thee belongs,
Thy praise resounds in grateful songs,
Thou Lord of all creation.
Let all / Recall
Hymns of gladness / Without sadness,
For Thy favor
And Thy mercy never waver.

3. Unconscious, I securely slept,
Nor saw the cruèl foes which kept
Close watch about my slumber;
Though evil spirits through the night
With hellish craft and watchful spite
Came round me without number;
Whose hands / In bands,
Mischief brewing / For my ruin,
Had enslaved me,
Hadst not Thou stood by and saved me.

4. For, Jesus, Thou with saving pow'r,
Wast near me in that threat'ning hour,
And warded off their fury;
And I reposed in quiet sleep,
Whilst Thou unwearied watch didst keep;
To Thee all praise and glory!
Lord, all / My soul,
Upward springing, / Loudly singing,
Shall adore Thee,
While on earth I walk before Thee.

5. This day my Fortress, Lord, abide,
Now ope Thy gates of mercy wide,
Within their shelter place me;
My Castle and my Rock Thou art,
O let no foeman's treach'rous dart
From Thee, my Stronghold, chase me.
Help, Lord, / Afford!
Near me tarry, / Blows to parry,
While around me
Sword and arrow sore confound me.

6. Pour down Thy grace in cheering streams
And warm my heart with mercy's beams
From heav'n, Thy throne of beauty;
Thy Spirit ever lead and guide
That in my calling I abide
And find my joy in duty.
Send light / And might
That each measure, / Plan, and pleasure,
Heav'nward tending,
E'er in Thee may find its ending.

7. Keep grief, if this may be, away;
If not, Thy will be done, I pray,
My choice to Thine resigning.
O come, and like the morning dew,
Refresh my heart and make it new,
That I may unrepining
Bear cross / And loss,
Till that morrow / Chase all sorrow,
When upraisèd
Where Thy name is ever praisèd.

8. Meanwhile, my heart, both sing and leap,
Mid cross and loss good courage keep,
To heav'n's bright gate you hasten;
Then lay desponding care aside,
God ever thus His own hath tried,
And those He loves doth chasten.
Hope still / Midst ill,
Calm, though grieving / Firm believing
Tribulation
Is the road to sure salvation.

—B. Wiesenmayer, 1640, ad.; tr., F.E. Cox, 1864, alt.

At Table

1. BEFORE THE MEAL

306

Tune: Herr Jesu Christ, meins Lebens Licht. 11. [*TLH* 288; *LW* 262; *LSB* 704]

1. Lord, bless to us these gifts of Thine
That they may nourish those who dine,
And thereby strengthen and refresh
Upon this earth our feeble flesh.

2. For not by bread alone have we
Our sust'nance in eternity;
Thy Holy Word alone can feed
Our soul and give us life indeed.

—Anon., Frankfurt a. O., 1561; tr., M. Carver.

307

Tune: Freu dich sehr, o meine Seele. 66. [*TLH* 61; *LW* 28; *LSB* 347]

1. Mighty God, we sinners lowly
Pray Thee with a heart sincere,
Feed us as our Father holy,
And regard Thy children dear;
Let us no starvation know,
But our daily bread bestow,
Grant to us Thy gracious blessing
For prosperity unceasing.

2. Let us never take for granted
What Thou, dearest Father, hast
Spoken, written, and commanded,
When the hour of need is past;
Grant that we Thy gifts may use
As Thou wouldest have us choose,
That we lift our hearts to heaven,
And so eat what Thou hast given.

3. Let us make a clear confession
And accord Thee endless praise,
Giving Thee all acclamation
For Thy caring father-ways;
Thou wilt never turn Thy back,
And where we may something lack
In this lowly, poor existence,
Thou wilt give us Thine assistance.

4. In Thy name and grace we gather
Round the table, each in place;
Grant us nourishment, O Father,
Keep our bodies in Thy grace;
So refresh us that we may
Gladly do our work today.
Guide our meal in every measure
After Thy most gracious pleasure.

—Anon., Plön, 1672; tr., M. Carver.

308

Tune: Schmücke dich, o liebe Seele. 72. [*TLH* 659; *LW* 468; *LSB* 636]

1. Feed Thy children, God most holy,
Comfort sinners poor and lowly;
O Thou Bread of Life from heaven,
Bless the food Thou here hast given!
As these gifts the body nourish,
May our souls in graces flourish
Till with saints in heav'nly splendor
At Thy feast due thanks we render.

—J. Heermann. 1656, alt.; tr., *TLH,* 1941.

2. AFTER THE MEAL

309

Tune: Nun laßt uns Gott, dem Herren. 4. [*TLH* 122; *or LW* 184*]

1. To God the Lord be praises
For all His wondrous graces,
And thousand countless favors,
Of which we are receivers.

2. Of body, soul, and powèr,
He is alone Endower:
And nothing does He spare them,
That naught may hurt or snare them.

3. Food for our flesh He giveth;
The soul awhile yet liveth,
Though still the fall diffuses
To us such mortal bruises.

4. We have a great Physician,
Life's gift is His true mission:
Christ, who was murdered for us,
Renews our health more glorious.

5. His Word, His Font, His Supper,
From every harm give cover,
So doth in faith the Spirit
Teach us to trust their merit.

6. Through Him is sin forgiven,
And life begun: in Heaven
What gifts we shall inherit!
No tongue can now declare it.

7. Thy mercies, which ne'er alter,
Let henceforth be our shelter—
Both great and small, defend us;
Thou canst not ill intend us.

8. Firm in Thy truth retain us,
In liberty sustain us,
To praise Thy name forever
Through Jesus Christ, our Savior.

—L. Helmbold, 1575; tr., *Mor. H.-B.,* 1789, alt.

310

Tune: Herr Jesu Christ, meins Lebens Licht. 11. [*TLH* 288; *LW* 262; *LSB* 704]

1. We thank and praise our Lord in heav'n
For all the gifts which He has giv'n,
And ask Him also evermore
To feed us all as heretofore.

2. Thy Word our nourishment let be
Now and in all eternity
And let at length us occupy
Our heav'nly mansions when we die.

—E. Alber, 1537; tr., *HELM,* 1905, alt.

Evening

311

Tune: Ach, was soll ich Sünder machen. 36. [*TLH* 384; *LW* 364; *LSB* 559]

1. Oh, my Lord, behold, I greet Thee
As the day to night inclines,
And as shade with shade combines;
Now as at Thy throne I meet Thee,
Let my praying heart and mind
To Thine own be so inclined.

2. Quickly are my moments rushing
Like a shaft tow'rd endless day;
Time and season will not stay;
Past my life their floods are gushing,
Flowing as a ceaseless stream,
Whistling as the wind and steam.

3. Oh, my Lord, behold, how heedless
Of my wretched self I've been,
Of Thy mercy longed to glean!
Day and night, all else is needless;
Thee I've sought so many‿a day,
Wake or sleep, I cannot say.

4. Oh, how shamefully I've acted,
While Thy hand so graciously
Day and night hath guarded me,
Yet my thoughts were too distracted
To pay Thee the thanks I owe
Without vanity or show!

5. Now I come to Thee with yearning,
O Thou kind and gracious Friend:
Let to me Thy light descend.
Since the sun hath hid its burning,
Give Thyself to be my light,
Pierce the deepest shade of night.

6. Teach me now my days to number,
Which to grant me Thou hast willed;
Let my heart by Thee be filled;
Naught may then disturb my slumber,
For where Thou art light and day,
Nights can cause us no dismay.

7. Faithful Savior, be my guardian,
Keep me through the coming night,
Guard my body with Thy might,
Lift me with Thy love and pardon,
Let me, too, my vigil keep,
Even as I go to sleep.

—L. J. Schlicht, 1705; tr., M. Carver.

312

Tune: Christ, der du bist der helle Tag. 11. [p. 397]

1. Lord Christ, Thou art the heav'nly Light
Who dost disperse the shades of night.
All radiant, Thou, the Father's Son,
Dost spread the brightness of His throne.

2. O dearest Lord, e'er guard our sleep,
From foes' assault our slumbers keep,
And let us find in Thee our rest,
Nor be by Satan's wiles oppressed.

3. E'en though our weary eye-lids fall,
O keep our hearts true to Thy call.
Above us stretch Thy shelt'ring hand,
Lest sin or shame our dreams should brand.

4. We pray Thee, Jesus, Christ and Lord,
'Gainst Satan's cunning help afford;
May he who ever seeks our soul
Ne'er bring us under his control.

5. Sure, 'tis Thy heart's most precious Blood
Has won our souls Thy brotherhood;
And so indeed the Father meant
Ere to our world Thyself He sent.

6. Deploy Thine angels round our bed,
And may our thoughts to Thee be led;
That guarded safe, north, south, east, west,
From Satan's lures we find sure rest.

7. Safe in Thy care so shall we sleep,
While wakeful angels vigil keep.
O God Eternal, Three in One,
Forever may Thy praises run.

—E. Alber, 1556; tr., C. S. Terry, 1921, alt.

313

Tune: Christe, der du bist Tag und Licht. 11. [*TLH* 559]

1. Christ, everlasting Source of light,
All things are open to Thy sight;
Thou Splendor of Thy Father's face,
Show us the path of truth and grace.

2. We now implore Thy peerless might
To keep us, Lord, the coming night;
Preserve us, Lord, from all distress;
O God, Thy mercy we address.

3. Remove our sinful drowsiness;
Let Satan not our soul oppress;
Our feeble flesh keep chaste and pure,
And let us rest in Thee secure.

4. And when our eyes are bound in sleep,
The lamp of faith still burning keep;
Thy hand sustain us while we rest;
Remove our sin, and we are blest.

5. Great Guardian of Thy Christian flock,
Thy presence be our saving rock;
Thine agony and holy blood
Be always our support, O God!

6. Remember, Lord, the woes and pains
Which here our body hold in chains;
Our soul, which Thou hast ransomed, Lord,
Oh, comfort with Thy holy Word.

7. To God the Father and the Son
And Holy Spirit, Three in One,
Be glory, praise, and majesty
Now, ever, and eternally.

—W. Meusel, 1526, after *Christe, qui lux es et dies;* tr., J. C. Jacobi, †1850, alt.

314

Tune: Die Nacht ist kommen, drin wir ruhen sollen. 47. [*TLH* 556]

1. O God, be with us, for the night is falling;
For Thy protection we to Thee are calling;
Beneath Thy shadow to our rest we yield us;
Thou, Lord, wilt shield us.

2. May evil fancies flee away before us;
Till morning cometh, watch, O Father, o'er us;
In soul and body Thou from harm defend us,
Thine angel send us.

3. While we are sleeping, keep us in Thy favor;
When we awaken, let us never waver
All day to serve Thee, Thy due praise pursuing
In all our doing.

4. Through Thy Beloved soothe the sick and weeping
And bid the captive lose his grief in sleeping;
Widows and orphans, we to Thee commend them,
Do Thou befriend them.

5. We have no refuge, none on earth to aid us,
Save Thee, O Father, who Thine own hast made us.
But Thy dear presence will not leave them lonely
Who seek Thee only.

6. Thy name be hallowed and Thy kingdom given,
Thy will among us done as 'tis in heaven,
Feed us, forgive us, from all ill deliver
Now and forever.

—P. Herbert, 1566, but. st. 5, Anon. 1627; tr., C. Winkworth, 1863, alt.

315

Tune: Herr Gott, dich loben alle wir. 11. [*TLH* 13; *LW* 216; *LSB* 923]

1. Before Thy throne I now appear,
O Lord, bow down Thy gracious ear
To me, and cast not from Thy face
Thy sinful child that sues for grace.

2. Thou, Father of eternity,
Thine image hast impressed on me;
In Thee I am and live and move,
Nor can exist without Thy love.

3. Oft hast Thou snatched me from distress,
And raised me oft when comfortless,
When but a step, nay, one hair's breadth,
Was 'twixt my tott'ring life and death.

4. My sense and reason come from Thee,
And sustenance Thou givest me;
A faithful friend Thou dost bestow,
To prove his love in weal and woe.

5. Thou hast redeemed me, Son of God,
Hast shed for me Thy precious blood,
The Law for my sake hast fulfilled,
And thus Thy Father's wrath hast stilled.

6. When sin and Satan witness bear
Against me that I must despair,
As Mediator step Thou in
And save me from the curse of sin.

7. Thou art my Advocate for aye,
My Savior, Comfort, and my Stay.
Thine all-sufficient merit is
On earth my peace, in heav'n my bliss.

8. God, Holy Spirit, Pow'r Divine,
Thou workest in this heart of mine;
Naught can be counted good in me
But what proceeds alone from Thee.

9. Through Thee I now my God adore
And call Him Father evermore;
Through Thee His Word and Sacrament
I love and hold till life is spent.

10. Through Thee in trials I am free
From fear and sad despondency;
Through Thee I'm quickened oft to taste
The sweets of Thine eternal rest.

11. And so I now give thanks to Thee
With heart and tongue most joyfully
For all Thy mercies, Lord my God,
Which on my soul Thou hast bestowed.

12. Beseeching Thine almighty grace
To aid me, till I've run my race;
Soul, body, honor, house, and friend
To Thy protection I commend.

13. Give me a heart that is sincere
To love Thy truth and persevere
In faith and Christian piety
And shun all base hypocrisy.

14. My sins and trespasses forgive;
Have patience with me while I live;
O give me faith and charity,
And let my hope rest but in Thee.

15. Grant that in peace I close mine eyes,
But on the Last Day bid me rise
And let me see Thy face fore'er—
Amen, Amen, Lord, hear my pray'r!

—B. von Hodenburg, 1640, alt. by J. Gesenius, 1650; tr., J. C. Jacobi, †1750, alt.

316

Tune: Werde munter, mein Gemüte. 66. [*TLH* 560; *LW* 263; *LSB* 548]

1. Once again, O Lord, is ended
Of my life another day.
Show me where I have offended,
Where I faltered on the way;
Let me by Thy grace divine
Own this sinful life of mine.
Calmly, as the day now closes,
In Thy love my soul reposes.

2. Well I grant that Thou wilt find me
Full of what delights Thee not;
Thoughts and words and deeds remind me,
Sin is still my earthly lot,
And from morning till I sleep
Heart and hand and mouth so keep
In their error ever mounting,
That its sum exceeds my counting.

3. Yet, O gracious God, before Thee
I would bring another plea;
Though unworthy, I implore Thee,
Be Thou merciful to me;
Let Thy face upon me shine
As the fleeting hours decline.
Help me do Thy will and pleasure
Day by day in fuller measure.

4. Sanctify my spirit wholly,
Keep me sinless as I sleep;
Wrap me in Thy goodness fully,
Angels send their watch to keep.
Bid all threat'ning foes begone,
Guard my home and all mine own;
Drive away all gloom and sorrow,
Bless me with a glad tomorrow.

5. All ungodly people bridle,
Who the dark with crime infest!
Should some soul by labors idle
Seek to hurt us as we rest,
Turn to naught his wicked plan,
Hinder all the crimes of man;
From all terrors else defend us
Which the devil dares to send us!

6. Lord, Thy tireless eyes forever
Watch, though darkness hide the view;
Waking always, failing never,
They their loving task pursue.
Gentle Shepherd, as Thy sheep
Now repose in trustful sleep,
So within Thine arms enfold us,
In Thy care securely hold us.

7. Hale and healthy let me waken
To another blessed day
That I may, with faith unshaken,
Serve Thee as my Strength and Stay.
Should instead death's summons come,
Take me to Thy heav'nly home.
To Thy care I thus commend me;
Lord, in life and death attend me.

—C. Neumann, 1711; tr. sts. 1, 3–4, 6–7, J. T. Mueller, 1938, alt.; sts. 2, 5, M. Carver.

317

Tune: Hinunter ist der Sonnenschein. 11. [p. 404; *or TLH* 563*; *LW* 467*; *LSB* 862*]

1. The sun's last beam of light is gone,
The shades of night come swiftly on;
O Christ, our Light, upon us shine
Lest we to sin's dark ways incline.

2. We thank Thee that throughout the day
Thine angels kept all harm away.
Thy grace from care and vexing fear
Hath led us on in safety here.

3. Lord, if we angered Thee today,
Remember not our sins, we pray,
But let Thy mercy o'er them sweep,
And give us calm and restful sleep.

4. Let angels guard our sleeping hours
And drive away all evil pow'rs;
Our soul and body, while we sleep,
In safety, gracious Father, keep.

—N. Herman, 1560; tr., *TLH,* 1941.

318

Tune: Vater unser im Himmelreich. 44. [*TLH* 318; *LW* 234; *LSB* 766]

1. I thank Thee, God, whose loving way
Hath guarded me throughout this day
From scandal, shame, and mockery;
Such is Thy gift of grace to me.
All wretchedness is mine, I own,
Salvation Thine and Thine alone.

2. Didst Thou, O Lord not reach to me
Thy hand, I soon and easily
Would fall into sin's deep abyss,
Like worldly men who do amiss;
Unaided by Thy gracious hand,
The pious, too, in sin would stand.

3. As pure as angels I am not;
Lord Christ, I ever see my blot
And feel old Adam's work in me,
Who goads me unrelentingly
To bend my heart and turn my sight
To wanton sin and vain delight.

4. My negligence I now lament
To Thee, O God, and I repent,
For Thou Thyself dost often see
The shame of my infirmity.
The inner man I've guarded not
As diligently as I ought.

5. I have not kept my senses reined
Or from foul vanity restrained;
I frequently have seen and said
And heard and done and filled my head
With things that merit only blame;
Their sum I cannot know or name.

6. Forgive me by Thy grace, I pray,
Let Thy love's fire purge all away.
Of grace and pureness full Thou art;
Where these I lack, the rest impart,
Pour out Thy blood to make me pure,
Of Thy heart's pleasure me assure.

7. I also thank Thee, dearest Lord,
For every grace that Thou hast poured
Upon my life from infancy,
And pourest yet till heav'n I see;
So richly all Thou hast bestowed,
I cannot count what Thou art owed.

8. I pray Thee, graciously to keep
Thine eyes upon me while I sleep,
That Satan with his craft and might
May not o'erpow'r me in the night.
Guard soul and body from dismay,
Drive woe and danger far away.

9. Grant me, when wonted rest is through,
To wake and rise and gladly do
Whatever Thou hast given me,
And deal with all men honestly;
Assist me by Thy Holy Ghost
That naught in me of sin may boast.

10. From any sudden, evil end,
Good, loving Lord, my life defend!
Preserve me now and constantly;
Let angel hosts watch over me,
That Satan and his wicked kind
No powèr over me may find.

—J. Heermann, 1630; tr., M. Carver.

319

Tune: O Welt, ich muß dich lassen. 31. [*TLH* 554; *LW* 85; *LSB* 880]

1. Now rest beneath night's shadow,
The woodland, field, and meadow,
The world in slumber lies;
But Thou, my heart, awake thee,
To pray'r and song betake thee;
Let praise to thy Creator rise.

2. The radiant sun hath vanished,
His golden rays are banished
By night, the foe of day;
But Christ, the Sun of gladness,
Dispelling all my sadness,
Within my heart holds constant sway.

3. The rule of day is over
And shining jewèls cover
The heaven's boundless blue.
Thus I shall shine in heaven,
Where crowns of gold are given
To all who faithful prove and true.

4. To rest my body hasteth,
Aside its garments casteth,
Types of mortality;
These I put off and ponder
How Christ will give me yonder
A robe of glorious majesty.

5. Head, hands, and feet reposing
Are glad the day is closing,
That work came to an end;
Cheer up my heart, with gladness!
For God from all earth's sadness
And from sin's toil relief will send.

6. Ye weary limbs, now rest you,
For toil hath sore oppressed you,
And quiet sleep ye crave;
A sleep shall once o'ertake you
From which no man can wake you,
In your last narrow bed—the grave.

7. My heavy eyes are closing:
When I lie deep reposing,
Soul, body, where are ye?
To helpless sleep I yield them,
Oh, let Thy mercy shield them,
Thou sleepless Eye, their Guardian be!

8. Lord Jesus, who dost love me,
Oh, spread Thy wings above me
And shield me from alarm!
Though evil would assail me,
Thy mercy will not fail me:
I rest in Thy protecting arm.

9. My loved ones, rest securely,
For God this night will surely
From peril guard your heads.
Sweet slumbers may He send you
And bid His hosts attend you
And through the night watch o'er your beds.

—P. Gerhardt, 1647; tr., *HTLH,* 1942.

320

Tune: Nun sich der Tag geendet hat. 6. [*TLH* 561]

1. Now that the day hath reached its close,
The sun doth shine no more,
In sleep the toil-worn find repose
And all who wept before.

2. But Thou, my God, dost never sleep,
For Thou Thyself art Light;
No darkness, howsoever deep,
Can dim Thy perfect sight.

3. Therefore, O Lord, remember me
Throughout the gloom of night,
Protect Thou me most graciously
And shield me with Thy might.

4. Keep Satan's fury far from me
By many‿an angel arm;
Then shall I be from worry free
And safe from every harm.

5. I know the evil I have done
Doth cry aloud to Thee;
But yet in mercy Thy dear Son
Hath full atoned for me.

6. In Him accepted I shall be
When suppliant at Thy feet.
He is my Surety and my Plea
Before Thy judgment-seat.

7. And so I close my weary eyes,
Sweet peace within my breast.
Why toss about in fears or sighs?
God watches while I rest.

8. Away, vain, idle thoughts, depart!
Roam not, my soul, abroad!
For now I build within my heart
A temple to my God.

9. Should this night prove the last for me
In this sad vale of cares,
Then lead me, Lord, to dwell with Thee
And all Thy chosen heirs.

10. And thus I live and die to Thee,
Strong Lord of hosts indeed.
In life, in death deliver me
From every fear and need.

—J. F. Hertzog, 1670, but st. 1, A. Krieger, 1665; st. 9, Anon., Leipzig, 1693; tr., *HTLH,* 1942.

321

Tune: Werde munter, mein Gemüte. 66. [*TLH* 207; *LW* 263; *LSB* 548]

1. Sink not yet, my soul, to slumber,
Wake, my heart, go forth and tell,
All the mercies without number
That this bygone day befell:
Tell how God hath kept afar
All things that against me war,
Hath upheld me and defended,
And His grace my soul befriended.

2. Father, merciful and holy,
Thee tonight I praise and bless,
Who to labor true and lowly,
Grantest ever meet success;
Many‿a sin and many‿a woe,
Many‿a fierce and subtle foe
Hast Thou checked that once alarmed me,
So that naught today has harmed me.

3. Yes, our wisdom vainly ponders,
Fathoms not Thy loving thought.
Never tongue can tell the wonders
That Thy hand for me hath wrought;
Thou hast guided me today,
That no ill hath crossed my way;
There is neither bound nor measure
In Thy love's o'erflowing treasure.

4. Now the light that nature gladdens,
And the pomp of day is gone,
And my heart is tired and saddens,
As the gloomy night comes on;
Ah, then with Thy changeless light
Warm and cheer my heart tonight;
As the shadows round me gather,
Keep me close to Thee, my Father.

5. Of Thy grace, I pray Thee, pardon
All my sins, and heal their smart;
Sore and heavy is their burden,
Sharp their sting within my heart;
And my foe lays many‿a snare
But to tempt me to despair;
Thou alone canst help me, Savior,
Punish not my ill behavior.

6. Though I have from Thee departed,
Now I seek Thy face again,
For Thy Son, the loving-hearted,
Made our peace through bitter pain.
Yes, far greater than our sin,
Though it still be strong within,
Is Thy love that fails us never,
Mercy that endures forever.

7. Brightness of th' eternal city!
Light of every faithful soul!
Safe beneath Thy shelt'ring pity
Let the tempests past me roll;
Now it darkens far and near,
Still, my God, still be Thou here;
Thou canst comfort, and Thou only,
When the night is long and lonely.

8. From the pow'r of darkness save me,
And from Satan's hellish snares,
Who endeavors to enslave me,
And assails me unawares;
Let me never lose the sight
Of Thy good and gracious light;
Thou canst fill my heart with gladness,
That it feel no pain in sadness.

9. Though my weary eyes are closing
And my senses fall asleep,
Still my soul, on Thee reposing,
Ever might its vigils keep.
Let my spirit longingly
Always dream, my God, of Thee.
Firmly unto Thee e'er cleaving,
Sleeping, yet Thy grace receiving.

10. Lord, the twilight now hath vanished,
Send Thy blessing on my sleep;
Every sin and terror banished,
Let my rest be calm and deep.
Soul and body, mind and health,
Wife and children, house and wealth,
Friend and foe, the sick, the stranger,
Keep Thou safe from harm and danger.

11. O Thou mighty God, now hearken
To the pray'r Thy child hath made;
Jesus, while the night-hours darken,
Be Thou still my hope, my aid;
Holy Ghost, on Thee I call,
Friend and Comforter of all,
Hear my earnest pray'r, oh, hear me!
Lord, Thou hearest, Thou art near me.

—J. Rist, 1642; tr., C. Winkworth, 1863, alt .

End of the Week

322

Tune: Werde munter, mein Gemüte. 66. [*TLH* 207; *LW* 263; *LSB* 548]

1. God, my heart to Thee is sending
Words of honor, thanks, and praise,
For the week hath reached its ending,
Done are all its troublous days:
Past their labor, toil, and care,—
All that I was made to bear;
So to Thee I now would render
Praises for Thy love so tender.

2. 'Twas Thy hand of love sustained me,
Dressed me, fed me, sparing naught;
Sent Thine angels to defend me,
Constant help and safety brought,
Every harm from me deterred,
Soul's and body's good secured.
Let me these enjoy completely,
End this week in blessing sweetly!

3. All my pow'r is insufficient
Meetly to extol and spread
These the gifts of Thine omniscient
Grace in granting daily bread;
Love, protection, care, and food,—
All I have Thou hast bestowed.
Praise forever, God, I'll sing Thee;
All I am as Thine will bring Thee.

4. Oh, grant pardon; Purge and cleanse me
From the daily, ceaseless flood
Of my wanton sin that stains me;
Hallow me in Jesus' blood!
Count to me what Christ hath done
For an everlasting boon.
Every blemish thereby sever;
Grant me blessedness forever.

5. Lord, I am a sinful being,
Trav'ling far the wicked path,
And my mind, with men's agreeing,
Merits not Thy grace but wrath.
Yet Thy father-heart so prized
And the wounds and death of Christ—
These true life and blessing send me.
So to them I now commend me.

6. Joyful now I go to slumber,
May Thy love and Jesus' blood
Never vanish from my chamber,
Keep me by Thy Spirit good.
In the morning bring me there
Where Thy Holy Word I hear;
Feed me with Thyself, uphold me,
Till Thy heav'nly courts enfold me.

—Ä. J. von Schwarzburg-Rudolstadt, 1684; tr., M. Carver.

Estate and Vocation

323

Tune: Alles ist an Gottes Segen. 43. [*TLH* 425; *LW* 415; *LSB* 732]

1. All depends on our possessing
God's abundant grace and blessing,
Though all earthly wealth depart.
He who trusts with faith unshaken
In His God is not forsaken
And e'er keeps a dauntless heart.

2. He who hitherto hath fed me
And to many joys hath led me,
Is and ever shall be mine.
He who did so gently school me,
He who still doth guide and rule me,
Will remain my Help divine.

3. Many spend their lives in fretting
Over trifles and in getting
Things that have no solid ground.
I shall strive to win a treasure
That will bring me lasting pleasure
And that now is seldom found.

4. When with sorrow I am stricken,
Hope my heart anew will quicken,
All my longing shall be stilled.
To His loving-kindness tender
Soul and body I surrender;
For in Him alone I build.

5. Well He knows what best to grant me;
All the longing hopes that haunt me,
Joy and sorrow, have their day.
I shall doubt His wisdom never,—
As God wills, so be it ever,—
I to Him commit my way.

6. If on earth my days He lengthen,
He my weary soul will stengthen;
All my trust in Him I place.
Earthly wealth is not abiding,
Like a stream away is gliding;
Safe I anchor in His grace.

—Anon., Nürnberg, 1676; tr., C. Winkworth, 1858, alt.

324

Tune: Schwing dich auf zu deinem Gott. 60.
[p. 414; *or TLH* 204; or *TLH* 540*; *LW* 483*; *LSB* 869*]

1. With the Lord begin thy task,
Jesus will direct it;
For His aid and counsel ask,
Jesus will perfect it.
Ev'ry morn with Jesus rise,
And when day is ended,
In His name then close thine eyes;
Be to Him commended.

2. Let each day begin with pray'r,
Praise, and adoration;
On the Lord cast ev'ry care,
He is thy Salvation.
Morning, evening, and at night
Jesus will be near thee,
Save thee from the Tempter's might,
With His presence cheer thee.

3. With thy Savior at thy side,
Foes need not alarm thee;
In His promises confide,
And no ill can harm thee.
All thy trust do thou repose
In the mighty Master,
Who in wisdom truly knows
How to stem disaster.

4. If thy task be thus begun
With the Savior's blessing,
Safely then thy course will run,
Naught thy soul distressing.
Good will follow everywhere
While thou here must wander;
Thou at last the joy wilt share
In the mansions yonder.

5. Thus, Lord Jesus, every task
Be to Thee commended;
May Thy will be done, I ask,
Until life is ended.
Jesus, in Thy name begun
Be the day's endeavor;
Grant that it may well be done
To Thy praise forever.

—Anon., Waldenburg, 1734; tr., W. G. Polack, 1937.

325

Tune: Wer nur den lieben Gott läßt walten. 45. [*TLH* 194; *LW* 429; *LSB* 750]

1. Now let my task be undertaken
In Jesus Christ, my God and Lord,
In whom no suppliant is forsaken,
Whose hands our very help afford;
This all will Jesus do, I say,
So I part not from Jesus' way.

2. From Jesus I shall never wander,
He loveth me forevermore;
To Him my heart its thanks will render,
Since He His grace on me doth pour,
On Him my heart is set for aye;
I shall not part from Jesus' way.

3. My Jesus will be ever guiding,
Because in grace with Him I stand.
I will not leave Him, but, confiding,
Cling in all troubles to His hand.
For He remains my Strength and Stay;
I shall not part from Jesus' way.

4. I'll stay with Him who solace gives me;
In Him I dwell, so He is mine;
I leave Him all who never leaves me,
He in my heart shall e'er recline.
By faith it must these words display:
I shall not part from Jesus' way.

5. Though I may oft be weak and falling,
Christ bears me up lest I despair;
He comes to help without my calling,
All things with Him I thus may dare;
Though countless dangers, come they may,
Yet I part not from Jesus' way.

6. The devil cannot terrify me,
Though fiercely he my soul engage;
My Lord shall with His shield supply me
To keep me safe from Satan's rage,
Therefore my heart with joy shall say,
I shall not part from Jesus' way.

7. Creation tow'rd its end is hasting,
Its pride and splendors all must fade;
Naught in this world is everlasting,
But that which Jesus hath re-made;
When heav'n and earth have had their day,
Yet I'll part not from Jesus' way.

8. Though die I must, e'en death shall never
Gain over me the upper hand;
In Christ I will not perish ever,
His pledge eternally shall stand.
Sworn in His Word, so shall it stay;
I shall not part from Jesus' way.

9. In earthly life I'll not be leaving,
In heav'n fore'er with Him I'll be,
And like a burr to Jesus cleaving,
My mouth shall sing His majesty
As I His glorious face survey
With joy more brilliant than the day.

10. My thanks and praise I'll give Him solely,
And at the Most High's lofty throne,
I will sing Holy, Holy, Holy,
Unto the mighty Prince, The Son,
Within His calm and joyful ray,
Nor shall I part from Jesus' way.

—M. Walther, asc., 1662; tr., M. Carver.

326

Tune: Auf meinen lieben Gott. 29. [*TLH* 526; *LW* 421; *LSB* 745]

1. I venture forward now
As well as I know how,
To do the work I'm given
By God Himself in heaven,
Who keeps His blessings falling
Upon me in my calling.

2. O Father, have my praise
For blessing all my days!
So richly hast Thou fed me,
Through gracious pathways led me;
Still cause Thy gifts to flourish,
To strengthen me and nourish.

3. O Jesus Christ my Lord,
All help Thou dost afford!
Now bless my day of labor
With strength to serve my neighbor,
To do Thy will and pleasure
In full and perfect measure.

4. Guard body, soul, and mind,
All evils chase and bind
That else would be distressing
My labor and Thy blessing;
Grant me in peace and gladness
Some day to part from sadness.

—J. H. von Hippen, 1676; tr., M. Carver.

1. MARRIAGE

327

Tune: Werde munter, mein Gemüte. 66. [*TLH* 207; *LW* 263; *LSB* 548]

1. Every soul that seeks to marry
Should begin with earnest pray'r,
And to God the matter carry,
So that, free from grief and care,
It may prosp'rously be done,
And the two in peace made one;
God Himself will unify them
And with every joy supply them.

2. All is rightly undertaken
When both pray'r and counsel wise
By the two are not forsaken:
They will see with their own eyes,
God hath wrought their wedding-band
And preserves it by His hand,
Blessing both and freely giving
Man and wife a peaceful living.

3. With God's grace and peace sustaining,
Honor, joy, and good ensue;
And upon His path remaining,
They will find salvation true.
Happily they shall proceed
When they say, "It is God's deed."
Yea, 'twas God who unified them
And with every joy supplied them.

—J. Olearius, †1684, asc.; tr., M. Carver.

328

Tune: Wo Gott zum Haus nicht gibt sein Gunst. 11. [*TLH* 131; *LW* 467; *LSB* 862]

1. Happy the man who feareth God,
Whose feet His holy ways have trod;
Thine own good hand shall nourish thee,
And well and happy shalt thou be.

2. Thy wife shall like a fruitful vine
Fill all thy house with clusters fine;
Thy children all be fresh and sound,
Like olive plants thy table round.

3. Lo, to that man these blessings cleave
Who in God's holy fear doth live;
From him the ancient curse hath fled
By Adam's race inherited.

4. Out of Mount Zion God shall send
And crown with joy thy latter end,
That thou Jerusalem may'st see
In favor and prosperity.

5. He shall be with thee in thy ways
And give thee health and strength of days:
Yea, thou shalt children's children see,
And peace on Israel shall be.

6. Praise God the Father, God the Son,
And God the Spirit, Three in One;
As 'twas through ages heretofore,
Is now, and shall be evermore.

—Luther, 1524; tr., R. Massie, 1854.

2. TRAVEL

329

Tune: In allen meinen Taten. [p. 406 (omit words in brackets)]
Or O Welt, ich muß dich lassen. 30. [*TLH* 126; *LW* 85; *LSB* 880*]

1. In all my plans, Thou Highest,
If counsel Thou suppliest,
My efforts may succeed:
But ev'ry best endeavor,
Without Thy smile of favor,
Can but to [*surest*] failure lead.

2. No toil by day, nor sorrow
From evening till the morrow,
Nor murm'ring aught avails:
My goings,—I confide them
To Thee, my God, to guide them;
[*Tow'rd faith*] Thy mercy never fails.

3. The path—would I oppose it?
My heav'nly Father chose it
And He shall work my good;
If Thou dost give, I'll take it,
If Thou dost choose, I'll make it
My choice [*as well*] with thankful mood.

4. Pursuing Thy direction,
I'll trust in Thy protection,
Amid surrounding foes;
Thy promise, always near me,
With constant hope will cheer me,
Till Thou the [*promised*] good disclose.

5. From sin's oppressive burden
Relieving me, Thy pardon
From wrath has set me free:
Leave not my soul forsaken,
If now by sin o'ertaken;
In patience [*only*] chasten me!

6. I travel to my station,
My faraway vocation,
Which He hath bid me fill;
His blessing He shall send me,
In His direction tend me,
To serve [*His world*] as is His will.

7. Though deserts wild enwreath me,
Yet Christians friends are with me,
And Christ Himself is near;
He who hath safely kept me,
And from all dangers swept me
Can [*also*] keep me safely here.

8. He on our way will speed us,
And on our journey lead us,
And help us as we live,
Body and health sustaining,
Time, wind, and rain ordaining,—
All things [*we need*] our God shall give.

9. His angel, my protector,
Drives off each foe and specter,
And keeps them far from me.
As we by faith pursue Him,
We make our progress through Him,
Yet how, we scarcely [*know or*] see.

10. When night repose is lending,
Or sun, the skies ascending,
Brings back the toils of day:
When ways of peril offer,
Or I the cross must suffer,
Thy Word abides my [*strength and*] stay.

11. Go with me! and wherever
It be, I'll nothing waver,
Content I'll forward go.
No threatened ill alarms me,
With strength Thy presence arms me,
And will conduct me [*safely*] through.

12. With all Thy will complying,
For living or for dying,
The whole to Thee I leave:
If Thou today should call me
To die, 'twill not appall me,
I'll undismayed [*the call]* receive.

13. But if it please Him mainly,
And if my mind not vainly
Its whisperings express,
God I shall praise in duty
With many strains of beauty
When peace [*at home*] I do possess.

14. Loved ones He will be keeping
Blest while awake and sleeping,
Who is my shield and theirs;
And He will be conceding
Our common wishes, heeding
Our many [*common*] tearful pray'rs.

15. Be His, my spirit, wholly,
And trust His wisdom solely,
Who has Thy being blest:
Whate'er on earth be given,
Thy Father rules in heaven,
Appointing what [*for thee*] is best.

—P. Fleming, 1633; tr., composite.

330

Tune: Dies sind die heilgen. 20. [*TLH* 287; *LW* 331; *LSB* 581]

1. In God's name let us on our way,
His holy angel lead, we pray,
Like Israèl in Egypt-land,
When they fled from Pharaoh's hand.
Kyrieleis!

2. O Lord, be Thou our goodly Guide,
Through all our wand'rings at our side,
Our journey step by step to show
And then dispel ev'ry woe.
Kyrieleis!

3. No hill so high nor dale so deep
Nor water can our errand keep;
With gladness we our goal shall see,
If Thou wilt help graciously.
Kyrieleis!

4. Lord Christ, Thou art the Way alone
And the true Path to heaven's throne;
Bring home Thy pilgrim brotherhood;
Therefore Thou didst shed Thy blood.
Kyrieleis!

—N. Herman, 1562; tr., M. Carver.

331

Tune: Wer nur den lieben Gott läßt walten. 45. [*TLH* 194; *LW* 429; *LSB* 750]

1. With God be thou thy voyage making,
And He all hindrance shall remove;
On paths He will thy soul be taking,
Watched by His eyes of grace and love;
This truth abides in toil and rest:
"Who follows God is ever blest!"

2. God lifted wand'ring Jacob's burden,
When unto Bethel he was led;
And Israèl beside the Jordan
Saw Canaan's land before him spread;
When David through the valley trod,
He leaned upon the staff of God.

3. How dear the pledges God hath given,
That He will never leave His own!
There is no place in earth or heaven
To His omniscient mind unknown.
In fire and flood He will be nigh,
Yea, even when His pilgrims die.

4. He draws me on with caring gesture,
He leads me in His gracious sight,
Good wind He gives and goodly pasture,
And speeds my journey by His might.
His love alone shall shelter me
No matter what the storm may be.

5. My Pillar, He leads at His pleasure,
In fire and cloud, by night and day;
He makes one step of feeblest measure
Traverse the longest, weariest way.
All stones that would my progress cease
He rolls away with gentle ease.

6. The Truth, the Life, the Way to heaven,—
Who follows Him will not be lost.
For He Himself His word hath given:
In Him no harm can us accost;
And though the way with thorns be filled,
Before us ever goes His shield.

7. His circling chariots shall defend us,
Round Dothan's mountain thick-arrayed;
He'll bid His host in arm to tend us,
That never foot may be mislaid;
His angels at our left and right
Shall keep us free from harm and fright.

8. Thus here in earth's sad vale we wander
And only pilgrims poor are we
Till we be heaven's subjects yonder
And enter in, our Lord to see.
A gentle death,—therein doth lie
The pathway to our home on high.

9. Meanwhile we leave to His selection
The way to fare, His will be blest,
For so we've learnt by His direction
That He intends for us the best.
Though strange His way must often seem,
It holds a blessing none can dream.

10. Lord, in Thy name I will be going,
Be Thou my Way, my Staff, my Friend,
And, to mine aid Thy host bestowing,
Let Jacob's helpers now descend;
Mine entrance and mine exit bless,
That I may reach Thy blessedness.

11. Abide with us when night is falling,
And by Thy presence be our light;
If cross be heavy and appalling,
Yet, Thou, my Star, wilt guide aright
And soothe us in that land of rest
When we recline at Jesus' breast.

12. Art Thou mine Escort and Defender
As on this journey forth I go,
And yet to all mine own wilt render
Thy care, that they Thy grace may know—
This off'ring then we shall intone:
Praise be to Thee, the Lord alone!

13. Come, let us raise and build an altar,
Our Ebenezer let it be:
Inscribed with words that ne'er shall falter:
"God leads His children wondrously";
And let therein these words be pressed:
"Who follows God is ever blest."

—B. Schmolck, 1704; tr., M. Carver.

3. HARVEST

332

Tune: Nun danket alle Gott. 55. [*TLH* 36; *LW* 174; *LSB* 794]

1. Sing gladly, one and all,
Both great and small together,
On whom God caused to fall
His mercy and good weather
Throughout this passing year,
With blessings rich and fair;
Your Father's kindly ear
Hath heard your earnest pray'r.

2. To God be thanks and praise,
For peace and preservation;
The Lord hath spared our days
All war and ruination;
No wild and burning fire,
No heavy hailing storm,
No flood, no famine dire,
Nor plague to us hath come.

3. The Lord watched o'er the land,
Its fruit with favor tending;
Who would have food at hand,
Were not His shield defending?
Who sent the dew and rain?
Who made the sun to shine?
What would our labor gain
Without His grace divine?

4. Our work would be in vain,
In vain each kernel planted,
Yea, e'en the smallest grain
We never would be granted;
Though early we may rise
And labor wearily
And seldom shut our eyes,—
In vain it all would be.

5. Yet hath our Lord on high
Been watching and defending,
His blessing keeping nigh,
And all our labors tending;
Earth now at His command
Fulfills the sower's pray'r,
And weighs the reaper's hand
With bounties everywhere.

6. Now that God's gifts of grace
Are (all / soon) in safety sitting,
Ye know and must confess,
God's is the glory fitting,
Whose hand hath richly lent
Our souls both life and cheer,
And to our homeland sent
A goodly harvest-year.

7. The sheaves are gathered in,
Now grain of every measure
In every barn and bin
Incites us, to God's pleasure,
To give Him worship sweet,
Who loves His children true,
And doth their joy complete
With meat in season due.

8. Good is, O Lord, this land
In which Thy love hath placed us,
Great is Thy mighty hand
Which hath so often blessed us,
Unending is Thy pow'r,
Thy glory without bound;
Therefore do we this hour
Thy praise devoutly sound.

9. O faithful God, grant still
Thy grace to rest upon us,
That never fire nor ill
May take our dwellings from us;
Nor let us ever know
Of theft or sorrow's sting,
Flood, famine, plague, or woe,
Or any evil thing.

10. Thy blessing freely give,
Our daily bread affording,
And let us mindful live,
All needy souls supporting;
To all men good impart,
Yet not excessively,
Let them be glad at heart
As Christians out to be.

11. Thy blessing on the seed
And harvest both be given,
Supply Thy plan and deed,
Work in us signs from heaven,
That all may know at heart,
Thou, Lord of Sabaoth,
Our Wonder-worker art,
The true and faithful God.

12. Laud, praise, and glory be
From age to age ascending,
To Thee, the One in Three,
One God, world without ending,
Thee, God the Father, Son,
And Holy Ghost, One Lord,
Both at Thy heav'nly throne
And here on earth adored.

—C. Schmidt, 1737; tr., M. Carver.

4. FOR CHILDREN

333

Tune: Mein lieber Gott, ich bitte dich. 44. [p. 411*]

1. Dear God, I pray Thee, graciously
To make a faithful child of me,
But if this thing cannot be given,
Then lift me up from earth to heaven;
Take me to Thy glorious light,
Make me like Thine angels bright. Amen.

—Anon., *Fibel* (German primer); tr., M. Carver.

334

Tune: Mir ist ein geistlich Kirchelein. 11. [p. 412]

1. There is within this heart of mine
A chapel built with sacred shrine,
And sprinkled ever with the blood
Of Jesus Christ, the Lamb of God.

2. Here dwelleth God the Father, Son,
And Holy Spirit, Three in One;
He is my soul's beloved Guest,
And grants my heart true peace and rest.

3. This little church looks poor and odd;
But, being the abode of God,
It has a glorious, peerless grace:
It is God's royal dwelling-place.

4. This house and chapel I commend,
God, to Thy care and pray defend
And shield it from calamity;
Dwell there now and eternally.

—B. Derschau, †1639, after the Latin of B. Walther; tr., A. Crull, 1890, alt.

335

Tune: In dich hab ich gehoffet, Herr. 40.
[*TLH* 524; *LW* 406; *LSB* 734; *or* p. 406]

1. O faithful God, my thanks to Thee
That Thou hast kindly given me
Such parents dear to raise me,
And, by Thy pow'r / Until this hour,
Hast kept them both to bless me.

2. Forgive me my iniquity
By which I've hurt both them and Thee;
Let me not be rewarded
As I should be! / For frequently
Thy law I've disregarded.

3. Give me a heart of thanks sincere,
My parents' righteous wrath to fear
And nothing do to earn it;
Let me hate not / What I am taught,
Nor out of mischief spurn it.

4. Bring often to my memory
What toil my mother's borne for me
Since on the day she bore me,
What sweat and blood / My father good,
Has spent in labor for me.

5. Give both my parents peace and rest,
Grant grace to be their cov'ring blest,
And in their cross support them,
Defend their days / From grief always
And from whate'er may hurt them.

6. And when the perfect time has come,
Then lead them from this mortal home
Up to Thy realm of glory;
Oh, hear my plea, / And let it be;
For that I will adore Thee!

—Anon., Frankfurt, 1693; tr., M. Carver.

Praise and Thanksgiving

336

Tune: Allein Gott in der Höh sei Ehr. 49. [*TLH* 33; *LW* 215; *LSB* 947]

1. The Lord hath helped me hitherto
By His surpassing favor;
His mercies every morn were new,
His kindness did not waver.
God hitherto hath been my Guide,
Hath pleasures hitherto supplied,
And hitherto hath helped me.

2. I praise and thank Thee, Lord, my God,
For Thine abundant blessing
Which heretofore Thou hast bestowed
And I am still possessing.
Inscribe this on my memory:
The Lord hath done great things for me
And graciously hath helped me.

3. Help me henceforth, O God of grace,
Help me on each occasion,
Help me in each and every place,
Help me through Jesus' Passion;
Help me in life and death, O God,
Help me through Jesus' dying blood;
Help me as Thou hast helped me!

—Ä. J. von Schwarzburg-Rudolstadt, 1699; tr., A. Crull, 1882.

THE TE DEUM

*Note: The first choir sings the non-indented lines,
the second choir sings the indented lines.
On lines marked "Both," the first and second choirs sing together.*

337

Tune: Herr Gott, dich loben wir. 101. [*WS69* 745 (mel., ab.)]

I. Lord God, Thy praise we sing;
    II. Lord God, our thanks we bring;
I. Father in eternity,
    II. All the world worships Thee.
I. Angels all and heav'nly host
    II. Of Thy glory loudly boast;
I. Both Cherubim and Seraphim
    II. Sing ever with loud voice this hymn:
I. Holy art Thou, our God!
    II. Holy art Thou, our God!
(Both:) Holy art Thou, our God, the Lord of Sabaoth!

I. Thy majesty and godly might
II. Fill earth and all the realms of light.
I. The twelve apostles join in song
II. With the dear prophets' goodly throng.
I. The martyrs' noble army raise
II. Their voice to Thee in hymns of praise.
I. The universal church doth Thee
II. Throughout the world confess to be
I. The Father, on Thy highest throne,
II. Thy worthy, true, and only Son.
I. Also of Thee she makes her boast,
II. The Comforter the Holy Ghost.

I. To Thee, O Christ, all creatures, bow,
II. The everlasting Son art Thou.
I. To save mankind Thou hast not, Lord,
II. The Virgin Mary's womb abhorred;
I. Thou overcamest death's sharp sting,
II. Believers unto heav'n to bring;
I. At God's right hand Thou sittest, clad
II. In th' glory which the Father had;
I. Thou shalt in glory come again,
II. To judge both dead and living men.
I. Thy servants help whom Thou, O God,
II. Hast ransomed with Thy most precious blood;
I. Grant that we share the heav'nly rest
II. With the all the saints etern'lly blest.

I. Help us, O Lord, from age to age,
II. And bless Thy chosen heritage.
I. Nourish and keep them by Thy pow'r,
II. And lift them up forevermore.
I. Lord God, we praise Thee day by day
II. And sanctify Thy name alway.
I. Keep us this day, and at all times,
II. From secret sins and open crimes;
I. Be gracious to us, Lord, we plead,
II. Be gracious in our ev'ry need.
I. Thy loving mercy let us see,
II. As our trust is fixed on Thee.
I. In Thee, Lord, have we put our trust;
II. O never let our hope be lost!
(Both:) Amen.

—M. Luther, 1529, after *Te Deum laudamus;* tr., R. Massie, 1854, alt.

338

Tune: In dich hab ich gehoffet, Herr. 40. [*TLH* 524; *LW* 406; *LSB* 734; *or* p. 406]

1. O God, my Father, thanks to Thee
I bring with deep humility,
That Thou Thy wrath hast ended,
And sent Thy Son, / Our Joy and Crown,
Who unto us descended.

2. He hath appeared, His precious blood
He hath poured forth in such a flood,
That all our sins it washes.
Who to Him cleaves, / He soon relieves
Of burdens, and refreshes.

3. I come, O Lord, as best I may;
Receive me in the band, I pray,
Of those who are forgiven,
Who thro' this blood / Are just and good,
And shall be blest in heaven.

4. Oh, let mine eye and hand of faith
This noble pledge retain till death
And let it leave me never
And let this light / Lead me aright
To light that lasts forever.

5. The mansion of my soul prepare,
Cast out whate'er is evil there,
And build in me Thy dwelling:
Thy grace so free / Reveal to me,
My soul with Thy love filling.

6. All things are mine when I have Thee,
Thou void of gifts canst never be;
Thy ways and methods flourish
On earth to keep / Thy feeble sheep,
And them to feed and nourish.

7. Grant me, that in my calling here
Thee in Thy Word I ever fear,
And so fulfill my station
That constancy / And truth may be
My lifelong decoration.

8. Give me contented heart and sense,
For that indeed is gain immense,
To lie in fast devotion,
At peace to live / As God will give
According to His notion.

9. The little that by God's great grace
The righteous as his portion has,
Possesses far more honors
Than all the gold / The world doth hold,
And with proud spirit squanders.

10. The faithful, Lord, to Thee are known,
Thou art their Joy, and they Thine own,
To shame Thou putt'st them never;
Comes scarcity, / Their bread from Thee
They find in all lands ever.

11. God loves the man who Him doth fear,
He wipes away his mournful tear,
Joy in his ways possessing;
And if he slide, / God doth abide,
And keeps him in His blessing.

12. God's eye is on all those who wait
And hope in Him both soon and late,
In all need to deliver,
Yea, even when / Death threatens men
And would devour them ever.

13. Lord, Thou canst only gracious be,
Thou givest them to know and see
Thy goodness and Thy favor,
Who with their mouth / And heart in truth
Own Thee their only Savior.

14. Preserve our dear and native land
In Thine embrace and mighty hand;
Protect us altogether
From heresies / And enemies,
Fire, plague, and evil weather.

15. All whom I love, keep every day,
Let all the hosts of hell away
From young and old be driven!
Thy faithful sheep / Defend and keep
Here now, and there in heaven!

—P. Gerhardt, 1686, ab.; tr., J. Kelly, 1867, alt.

339

Tune: Lobt Gott, ihr Christen allzugleich. 6.
[*TLH* 105; *LW* 44; *LSB* 389; or *TLH* 569*; *LW* 424*; *LSB* 737*]

1. O Lord, I sing with lips and heart,
Joy of my soul, to Thee;
To earth Thy knowledge I impart,
As it is known to me. (*x2*)

2. Thou art the Fount of grace, I know,
And Spring so full and free
Whence saving health and goodness flow
Each day so bounteously. (*x2*)

3. For what have all that live and move
Through this wide world below
That does not from Thy bounteous love,
O heav'nly Father, flow? (*x2*)

4. Who built the lofty firmament?
Who spread th' expanse of blue?
By whom are to our pastures sent
Refreshing rain and dew? (*x2*)

5. Who warmeth us in frost and cold,
Who shields us from the wind,
Who doth the wine and grain uphold
Which we in season find? (*x2*)

6. Who is it life and health bestows,
Who keeps us with His hand
In golden peace, wards off war's woes
From our dear native land? (*x2*)

7. O Lord, of this and all our store
Thou art the Author blest;
Thou keepest watch before our door
While we securely rest. (*x2*)

8. Thou feedest us from year to year
And constant dost abide;
With ready help in time of fear
Thou standest at our side. (*x2*)

9. Thou ever wilt with patience chide,
Nor long Thine anger keep,
But castest all our sins aside
Into the ocean deep. (*x2*)

10. When silent woe our bosom rends,
Thy pity sees our grief,
Supplies what to Thy glory tends
And to our own relief. (*x2*)

11. Thou know'st how oft a Christian weeps
And why his tears now fall;
And in the book Thy mercy keeps
These things are noted all. (*x2*)

12. Our deepest need dost Thou supply,
And all that lasts for aye;
Thou leadest to our home on high,
When hence we pass away. (*x2*)

13. Rejoice, my heart, be glad and sing,
A cheerful trust maintain;
For God, the Source of everything,
Thy Portion shall remain. (*x2*)

14. He is thy Treasure, He thy Joy,
Thy Life and Light and Lord,
Thy Counselor when doubts annoy,
Thy Shield and great Reward. (*x2*)

15. Why spend the day in blank despair,
In restless thought the night?
On thy Creator cast thy care;
He makes thy burdens light. (*x2*)

16. Did not His love and truth and pow'r
Watch o'er thy childhood day?
Has He not oft in threat'ning hour
Turned dreaded ills away? (*x2*)

17. His wisdom never plans in vain,
Ne'er falters or mistakes;
All that His counsels did ordain
A happy ending makes. (*x2*)

18. Upon thy lips, then, lay thy hand
And trust His guiding love;
Then like a rock thy peace shall stand
Here and in heav'n above. (*x2*)

—P. Gerhardt, 1653; tr., J. Kelly, 1867, alt.

340

Aus meines Herzens Grunde. 58. [*TLH* 69; *LW* 25; *LSB* 354]

1. With thanks I fain would enter
The faithful company
That holds God's Word its center
And worships fervently
His wisdom and His ways,
And in that blest communion
Would pray in perfect union
And offer heartfelt praise.

2. Great is the Lord and mighty,
And great His every deed.
Whoever ponders rightly
His works, and pays good heed,
Therein will take delight.
All that God's mind ordaineth
With grace His church sustaineth
And all is done aright!

3. His grace and His salvation
Stand fast and undisturbed,
And He gives confirmation,
Lest, by our doubts perturbed,
We be to error swayed,—
A sure memorial token
That gives what He hath spoken
He in His realm hath made.

4. With gifts beyond all measure
God's hand doth freely feed,
Conferring life and pleasure
On all His heirs indeed;
His cov'nant He doth keep,
And from the heathen nations
He gathers rich possessions
To pasture all His sheep.

5. All that the Lord commands us
And that His hands create
To every good advance us,
And comfort and elate
In truth without deceit.
His servants, all upbearing,
He leads the way unerring,
That life above shall meet.

6. His heart He changes never
When once His mouth has sworn;
He will restore forever
All that from us was torn;
Intrepid, without fear,
He works our great deliv'rance
From cross and every grievance
Which vex His children here.

7. His Word is surely grounded,
His lips are clean and pure,
All oaths by Him propounded
He seals and keeps secure.
Naught shall His pow'r confound.
The name which He bears solely
Is beautiful and holy,
With praise and honor crowned.

8. The first and best foundation
Of wisdom He holds dear
And brings Him jubilation
Is holy, godly fear.
That soul, oh, how 'tis wise
Which this good truth possesses,
And in it e'er progresses!
Its glory never dies.

—P. Gerhardt, 1653, after Ps. 111; tr., M. Carver.

341

Tune: Lobe den Herren, den mächtigen. 24.
[*TLH* 39; *LW* 444; *LSB* 790]

1. Praise to the Lord, the Almighty, the King of creation!
O my soul, praise Him, for He is thy Health and Salvation!
Join the full throng, / Wake, harp and psalter and song;
Sound forth in glad adoration!

2. Praise to the Lord, who o'er all things so wondrously reigneth,
Who, as on wings of an eagle, uplifteth, sustaineth.
Hast thou not seen / How thy desires e'er have been
Granted in what He ordaineth?

3. Praise to the Lord, who hath fearfully, wondrously, made thee;
Health hath vouchsafed and, when heedlessly falling, hath stayed thee.
What need or grief / Ever hath failed of relief?—
Wings of His mercy did shade thee.

4. Praise to the Lord, who doth prosper thy work and defend thee,
Who from the heavens the streams of His mercy doth send thee.
Ponder anew / What the Almighty can do,
Who with His love doth befriend thee.

5. Praise to the Lord! Oh, let all that is in me adore Him!
All that hath life and breath, come now with praises before Him!
Let the Amen / Sound from His people again;
Gladly for aye we adore Him.

—J. Neander, 1679; tr., C. Winkworth, 1863, alt.

342

Tune: Herr Jesu Christ, meins Lebens Licht. 11.
[*TLH* 288; *LW* 262; *LSB* 704; *or TLH* 13*; *LW* 216*; *LSB* 923*]

1. Praise, laud, and honor be to God
Who such great love on us bestowed,
His only Son He sent our race,
To be our saving Throne of grace.

2. Praise be to Thee, Lord Jesus Christ,
Our Brother born, whose blood sufficed
To save us from the fires of hell
And Satan's pow'r o'er us to quell.

3. Praise be to Thee, O Holy Ghost,
Who comfortest Thy Christian host,
And crownest them with perfect faith
That pleases God and quells His wrath.

4. No tongue of man can e'er express
What we in Thee, our God, possess.
Therefore to Thee, our Rock, we sigh:
Still grant us that for which we cry!

5. Be mindful, Father, of Thine own;
We put our trust in Thee alone;
Give us good health and government;
All famine, war, and plague prevent.

6. Lord Jesus Christ, Thou Champion bold,
Restrain the prince who rules this world,
Destroy his kingdom, send us peace,
And make Thy holy Church increase.

7. O priceless Comfort, Holy Ghost,
Our every weakness well Thou know'st,
Stay nigh to help us all, that we
May serve our God unceasingly.

8. O everlasting Trinity,
One God and Lord eternally,
Illuminate us by Thy face,
And keep us steadfast in Thy grace.

—M. Moller, 1591; tr., M. Carver.

343

Tune: Lobet den Herren, denn er ist sehr freundlich. 13. [p. 410]

1. Praise ye Jehovah *(x2)*
For He is all-gracious;
And it is pleasant
To give God our praises. (*x*2)
His praise is comely, sweet the sound it raises.
Praise ye Jehovah. (*x*2)

2. Sing, voice and chorus, *(x2)*
Sing with glad thanksgiving,
With harp resounding
Sing to God our Father, (*x*2)
Great is our Lord, and great is He of powèr.
Praise ye Jehovah. (*x*2)

3. He decks the heavens, *(x2)*
Cloud on cloud outspreading;
Rain He prepareth
All the earth to water, (x2)
He makes the grasses grow upon the mountains.
Praise ye Jehovah. (*x*2)

4. To all creation *(x2)*
Nourishment He giveth,
To all the cattle,
With a father's kindness, (*x*2)
To the young ravens which to Him are crying.
Praise ye Jehovah. (*x*2)

5. The Lord delighteth *(x2)*
Not in strength of horses,
He takes not pleasure
In the legs of humans; (*x*2)
But He takes pleasure in all those who trust Him.
Praise ye Jehovah. *(x2)*

6. Thank ye Jehovah *(x2)*
Who all things created.
Life's rushing Fountain
From our God forth springeth, (*x*2)
High in the heavens, from His heart begotten:
Praise ye Jehovah. (*x*2)

7. O Christ, our Savior, *(x2)*
Son of God the Highest,
Grace give Thou ever
To Thy faithful Christians, (*x*2)
That we with common voice may praise Thee! Amen.
Praise ye Jehovah. (*x*2)

—Leipzig, 1565, after Ps. 147; tr., M. Carver.

344

Tune: Nun freut euch, lieben Christen. 49. [*TLH* 124; *LW* 353; *LSB* 556]

1. Now praise the Lord, ye Gentiles all,
In fervent adoration;
Praise Him, ye nations great and small,
Extol His rich salvation
For making you His chosen race
And sending on you His dear grace
In Christ, His Son incarnate.

2. His tender mercy day by day
O'er us, His children, reigneth.
His love and truth and grace alway
Both young and old sustaineth,
And through the ages doth endure,
Our bliss and glory to assure.
Then sing ye: Alleluia!

—Anon., *Praxis Pietatis Melica,* 1664; tr., *HELM,* 1906.

345

Tune: Herr Gott, dich loben alle wir. [*TLH* 13; *LW* 216; *LSB* 923]
Or Lob sei dem allmächtigen Gott. 11. [p. 410*]

1. My God, I thank Thee heartily
For all Thy benefits to me
Which Thou hast rained in ample show'r
From earliest youth until this hour.

2. Thou hast by means of wondrous might
Brought me into Thy heav'nly light,
Adorned my spirit, soul, and heart,
And made me of Thy Church a part.

3. The sin which I inherited
Hath lost o'er me its pow'r and dread,
For in Thy waters I was born
Thine own dear child, no more Thy scorn.

4. And though, alas, iniquity
Still often shows its stain in me,
Yet for Thy Son I long have been
Forgiven of my every sin.

5. So many thousand graces Thou
Hast ever shown me, e'en till now,
In every way, as e'er before,
That I must now declare once more:

6. My God, I thank Thee heartily
For all Thy benefits to me
Which Thou hast rained in ample show'r
From earliest youth until this hour.

7. To God the Father, God the Son,
And God the Spirit, Three in One,
Be glory as it was before,
Is now, and shall be evermore.

—J. H. Keulisch, 1676; tr., M. Carver.

346

Tune: Nun danket alle Gott. 55. [*TLH* 36; *LW* 174; *LSB* 794]

1. Now thank we all our God
With heart and hands and voices,
Who wondrous things hath done,
In whom His world rejoices;
Who from our mothers' arms
Hath blessed us on our way
With countless gifts of love,
And still is ours today.

2. Oh, may this bounteous God
Through all our life be near us,
With ever joyful hearts
And blessèd peace to cheer us;
And keep us in His grace
And guide us when perplexed
And free us from all ills
In this world and the next.

3. All praise and thanks to God
The Father now be given,
The Son, and Him who reigns
With them in highest heaven:
The one eternal God,
Whom earth and heav'n adore!
For thus it was, is now,
And shall be evermore.

—M. Rinckart, 1636; tr., C. Winkworth, 1858.

347

Tune: Nun danket all und bringet Ehr. 6. [*TLH* 581; *LW* 200; *LSB* 903]

1. All ye who on this earth do dwell,
Give thanks and glorify
The Lord whose praises ever swell
In seraph songs on high.

2. Lift up your hearts in praise to God,
Himself best Gift of all,
Who works His wonders all abroad,
Upholding great and small.

3. Since first our life began to be,
He has preserved our frame;
And when man's strength was vanity,
He as our Helper came.

4. Though often we His patience try
And well deserve His frown,
In grace He lays His anger by
And pours new blessings down.

5. 'Tis He revives our fainting soul,
Gives joyful hearts to men;
And when great waves of trouble roll,
He drives them back again.

6. May He adorn with precious peace
Our own, our native, land
And crown with joys that never cease
The labors of our hand.

7. His love and goodness may He let
In and around us be,
All that may frighten us and fret
Cast far into the sea.

8. Long as we tarry here below
Our saving Health is He;
And when from earth to heav'n we go,
May He our portion be!

9. He giveth His belovèd sleep
When these frail heart-beats cease;
And in His presence then will keep
Our souls His endless peace.

—P. Gerhardt, 1647; tr., A. Ramsey, †1926, alt.

348

Tune: Nun lob, mein Seel, den Herren. 93. [*TLH* 34; *LW* 453; *LSB* 820]

1. My soul, now bless thy Maker!
Let all within me bless His name
Who maketh thee partaker
Of mercies more than thou dar'st claim.
Forget Him not whose meekness
Still bears with all thy sin,
Who healeth all thy weakness,
Renews thy life within;
Whose grace and care are endless
And saved thee through the past;
Who leaves no suff'rer friendless,
But rights the wronged at last.

2. He shows to man His treasure
Of judgment, truth, and righteousness,
His love beyond all measure,
His yearning pity o'er distress,
Nor treats us as we merit,
But lays His anger by,
The humble, contrite spirit
Finds His compassion nigh;
And high as heav'n above us,
As break from close of day,
So far, since He doth love us,
He puts our sins away.

3. For as a tender father
Hath pity on his children here,
He in His arms will gather
All who are His in childlike fear.
He knows how frail our powers
Who but from dust are made;
We flourish like the flowers,
And even so we fade;
The wind but o'er them passes,
And all their bloom is o'er,—
We wither like the grasses,
Our place knows us no more.

4. God's grace alone endureth,
And children's children yet shall prove
How He with strength assureth
The hearts of all that seek His love.
In heav'n is fixed His dwelling,
His rule is over all;
Angels, in might excelling,
Bright hosts, before Him fall.
Praise Him, who ever reigneth,
All ye who hear His Word,
Nor our poor hymns disdaineth—
My soul, oh, bless the Lord!

5. To Father, Son, and Spirit
Be glory, honor, laud, and praise!
May we the fruit inherit
Of all He promised us by grace:
That we may trust Him wholly,
With will to His resigned,
Relying on Him solely;
With heart and soul and mind
To Him forever cleaving.
Now let us gladly sing,
Amen! With hearts believing,
Let God fulfillment bring!

—J. Gramann, 1525; st. 5, Anon., 1555; tr., C. Winkworth, 1863, alt.; st. 5, M.Carver.

349

Tune: O daß ich tausend Zungen hätte. 45. [*TLH* 88; *LW* 224; *LSB* 811; or *LW* 448*]

1. Oh, that I had a thousand voices
To praise my God with thousand tongues!
My heart, which in the Lord rejoices,
Would then proclaim in grateful songs
To all, wherever I might be,
What great things God hath done for me.

2. Oh, that my voice might high be sounding,
Far as the widely distant poles;
My blood run quick with rapture bounding,
Long as its vital current rolls,
And every pulse thanksgiving raise,
And every breath, a hymn of praise!

3. O all ye pow'rs that God implanted,
Arise, and silence keep no more;
Put forth the strength that He hath granted,
Your noblest work is to adore.
O soul and body, be ye meet
With heartfelt praise your Lord to greet!

4. Ye forest leaves so green and tender,
That dance for joy in summer air;
Ye meadow grasses, bright and slender;
Ye flow'rs so wondrous sweet and fair;
Ye live to show His praise alone,
With me now make His glory known.

5. All creatures that have breath and motion,
That throng with life earth, the sea, and sky,
Now join me in my heart's devotion,
Help me to raise His praises high.
My utmost pow'rs can ne'er aright
Declare the wonders of His might.

6. Dear Father, endless praise I render
For soul and body, strangely joined;
I praise Thee, Guardian kind and tender,
For all the noble joys I find
So richly spread on every side,
And freely for my use supplied.

7. What equal praises can I offer,
Dear Jesus, for Thy mercy shown?
What pangs, my Savior, didst Thou suffer,
And thus for all my sins atone!
Thy death alone my soul could free
From Satan, to be blest with Thee.

8. Glory and praise, still onward reaching,
Thine be it, Spirit of all grace,
Whose holy pow'r and faithful teaching
Give me among Thy saints a place!
Whate'er of good in me may shine
Comes only from Thy light divine.

9. Who grants abundant gifts to bless me?
Who, but Thyself, O God of love?
Who guards my ways lest fears oppress me?
'Tis Thou, Lord God of hosts above!
And when my sins Thy wrath provoke,
Thy patience, Lord, forbears the stroke.

10. I kiss the rod too, unrepining,
When God His chast'ning makes me feel,
My graces call for His refining,
The trial works no lasting ill:
It purifies and makes it known
That He regards me as a son.

11. In life I often have discovered,
With gratitude and glad surprise,
When clouds of sorrow o'er me hovered,
God from them sent my best supplies:
In troubles He is ever near,
And shows me all a father's care.

12. Why not, then, with a faith unbounded,
Forever in His love confide?
Why not, with earthly grief surrounded,
Rejoicing still in hope abide?
Until I reach that blissful home
Where doubt and sorrow never come?

13. No more low vanities regarding,
To Thee, in whom I find my rest,
I cry—my inmost soul according,—
"My God, Thou art the highest, best;
Strength, honor, praise, and thanks, and pow'r
Be Thine, both now and evermore!"

14. Lord, I will tell while I am living,
Thy goodness forth with every breath
And greet each morning with thanksgiving
Until my heart is still in death;
Yea, when at last my lips grow cold,
Thy praise shall in my sighs be told.

15. O Father, deign Thou, I beseech Thee,
To listen to my earthly lays;
A nobler strain in heav'n shall reach Thee,
When I with angels hymn Thy praise
And learn amid their choirs to sing
Loud alleluias to my King.

—J. Mentzer, 1704; tr. sts. 1, 3–5, 14–15, *TLH,* 1941; sts. rest, *ELHB,* 1912.

350

Tune: Es ist das Heil uns kommen her. 49. [*TLH* 377; *LW* 355; *LSB* 555]

1. All praise to God, who reigns above,
The God of all creation,
The God of wonders, power, and love,
The God of our salvation!
With healing balm my soul He fills,
The God who every sorrow stills,—
To God all praise and glory!

2. The angel host, O King of kings,
Thy praise forever telling,
In earth and sky all living things
Beneath Thy shadow dwelling,
Adore and praise their Maker's might,
Whose wisdom orders all things right;
To God all praise and glory!

3. What God's almighty pow'r hath made
His gracious mercy keepeth;
By morning dawn or evening shade
His watchful eye ne'er sleepeth;
Within the kingdom of His might
Lo, all is just and all is right,—
To God all praise and glory!

4. I cried to Him in time of need:
Lord God, oh, hear my calling!
For death He gave me life indeed
And kept my feet from falling.
For this my thanks shall endless be;
Oh, thank Him, thank our God, with me,—
To God all praise and glory!

5. The Lord forsaketh not His flock,
His chosen generation;
He is their Refuge and their Rock,
Their Peace and their Salvation.
As with a mother's tender hand
He leads His own, His chosen band,—
To God all praise and glory!

6. When earth can comfort us no more
Nor human help availeth,
The Maker comes Himself, whose store
Of blessing never faileth,
And bends on them a Father's eyes
Whom earth all rest and hope denies;
To God all praise and glory!

7. Thus all my pilgrim way along
I'll sing aloud Thy praises
That men may hear the grateful song
My voice unwearied raises:
Be joyful in the Lord, my heart!
Both soul and body, bear your part!
To God all praise and glory!

8. Ye who confess Christ's holy name,
To God give praise and glory!
Ye who the Father's pow'r proclaim,
To God give praise and glory!
All idols under foot be trod,
The Lord is God! The Lord is God!
To God all praise and glory!

9. Then come before His presence now
And banish fear and sadness;
To your Redeemer pay your vow
And sing with joy and gladness:
Though great distress my soul befell,
The Lord, my God, did all things well,—
To God all praise and glory!

—J. J. Schütz, 1673; tr., C. Winkworth, 1858, 1863, alt.

351

Tune: Sollt ich meinem Gott nicht singen. 84. [*TLH* 25; *LW* 439; *LSB* 977 (digital)]

1. I will sing my Maker's praises
And in Him most joyful be,
For in all things I see traces
Of His tender love to me.
Nothing else than love could move Him
With such sweet and tender care
Evermore to raise and bear
All who try to serve and love Him.
All things else have but their day,
God's great love abides for aye.

2. As an eagle spreadeth over
Her young brood her shelt'ring wings,
So the arm of God did cover
Me against affliction's stings.
He who life and being gave me,
Even in my mother's womb,
From the cradle to the tomb
He shall ever guard and save me.
All things else have but their day,
God's great love abides for aye.

3. Yea, so dear did He esteem me
That His Son he loved so well
He hath given to redeem me
From the quenchless flames of hell.
O Thou Spring of boundless blessing,
How could e'er my feeble mind
Of Thy depth the bottom find
Though my efforts were unceasing?
All things else have but their day,
God's great love abides for aye.

4. God His Spirit to instruct me
In His holy Word hath giv'n,
That He safely may conduct me
Through this weary world to heav'n.
He my heart's dark chamber filleth
With the clear pure light of faith,
Which destroys the pow'r of death,
Yea, e'en hell itself it stilleth.
All things else have but their day,
God's great love abides for aye.

5. All that for my soul is needful
He with loving care provides,
Nor of that is He unheedful
Which my body needs besides.
When my strength cannot avail me,
When my pow'rs can do no more,
Doth my God His strength outpour;
In my need He doth not fail me.
All things else have but their day,
God's great love abides for aye.

6. All the hosts of earth and heaven
Wheresoe'er I turn mine eye,
For my benefit are given,
That they may my need supply.
All that's living, all that's growing,
On the heights or in the woods,
In the vales or in the floods,
God is for my good bestowing,
All things else have but their day,
God's great love abides for aye.

7. When I sleep, He still is near me,
O'er me rests His guardian eye;
And new gifts and blessings cheer me
When the morning streaks the sky.
Were it not for God's protection,
Had His countenance not been
Here my guide, I had not seen
E'er the end of my affliction.
All things else have but their day,
God's great love abides for aye.

8. Ah! how often doth the devil
Cause some great calamity!
But my life from all such evil
Till this moment has been free.
For the angel whom God sendeth,
Wardeth off each threat'ning hurt,
Every evil doth avert
That mine enemy intendeth.
All things else have but their day,
God's great love abides for aye.

9. As a father never turneth
Wholly from a wayward child,
For the prodigal still yearneth,
Longing to be reconciled,
So my many sins and errors
Find a tender, pard'ning God,
Chast'ning frailty with His rod,
Not in vengeance, with His terrors.
All things else have but their day,
God's great love abides for aye.

10. All His strokes and scourges truly
For the moment grievous prove,
And yet, when I weigh them duly,
Are but tokens of His love:
Proofs that He is watching o'er me,
And by crosses to His fold,
From the world that fain would hold
Soul and body, would restore me.
All things else have but their day,
God's great love abides for aye.

11. On this thought I dwell with pleasure;
For it granteth joy and peace.
Christ's cross hath its time and measure,
And at last will wholly cease.
When the winter disappeareth,
Lovely summer comes again;
Joy is giv'n for woe and pain
Who His cross in patience beareth.
All things else have but their day,
God's great love abides for aye.

12. Since, then, neither change nor coldness,
In my Father's love can be,
Lo! I lift my hands with boldness,
As Thy child I come to Thee.
Grant me grace, O God, I pray Thee,
That I may with all my might,
All my lifetime, day and night,
Love and trust Thee and obey Thee
And, when this brief life is o'er,
Praise and love Thee evermore.

—P. Gerhardt, 1653; tr. sts. 1, 3, 5, 7, 9, 12, *TLH,* 1941; sts. rest, *ELHB,* 1912.

Cross and Comfort

352

Tune: Herr Jesu Christ, meins Lebens Licht. 11. [*TLH* 288; *LW* 262; *LSB* 704]

1. O God, my days are dark indeed,
How oft this aching heart must bleed;
The narrow way,—how filled with pain,
That I must pass ere heav'n I gain!

2. How hard to teach this flesh and blood
To seek alone th' eternal Good!
Ah! whither now for comfort turn?
For Thee, my Jesus, do I yearn.

3. In Thee have I, howe'er distressed,
Found ever counsel, aid, and rest!
I cannot all forsaken be
While still my heart can trust in Thee.

4. Thine office and Thy person show
That Thou great miracles canst do;
Miraculous was, Lord, Thy birth
When Thou wert born a child on earth.

5. And by Thy death Thou mak'st me free
So strangely from all misery.
Jesus, my only God and Lord,
What sweetness in Thy name is stored!

6. No grief can ever be so sore
But Thy sweet name can cheer me more;
So keen no sorrows' rankling dart
But Thy sweet name can heal my heart.

7. Although my flesh and heart may fail,
I'll heed it not, I shall not quail;
My Savior, if I have but Thee,
I shall be blest eternally.

8. In Thee my soul and body dwell;
What harm can sin and death and hell?
Earth holds no truth more to be prized
Than that in Thee, Lord Jesus Christ.

9. I know Thou wilt forsake me not,
Thy truth is fixed, though dark my lot;
Thou art my Shepherd, and Thy sheep
From harm forever Thou wilt keep.

10. Jesus, my Boast, my Light, my Joy,
The Treasure naught can e'er destroy,
No words, no song that I can frame
Speak half the sweetness of Thy name.

11. They only all its pow'r shall prove
Whose hearts have learnt Thy faith and love.
How many‿a time I've sadly said,
Far better were it I were dead;

12. Far better ne'er the light to see
If I had not this joy in Thee;
For he who hath not Thee in faith,
His very life is merely death.

13. Jesus, my Bridegroom and my Crown,
If Thou but smile, the world may frown,
In Thee lie depths of joy untold,
Far richer than the richest gold.

14. Whene'er I do but think of Thee,
Thy dews drop down and solace me;
Whene'er I hope in Thee, my Friend,
Thy comfort and Thy peace descend.

15. Whene'er in grief I pray and sing,
I feel new courage in me spring;
Thy Spirit witnesses that this
Is foretaste of eternal bliss.

16. Therefore, while life remains in me,
I'll bear Thy cross and follow Thee.
Grant me a patient, willing mood;
I know that it shall work my good.

17. Help me to do my task aright,
That it may stand before Thy sight;
Let me this flesh and blood control,
From sin and shame preserve my soul.

18. Oh, keep me steadfast in the faith,
Then I am Thine in life and death;
Jesus, my Comfort, bend to me,
Ah, would I were e'en now with Thee!

—M. Moller, 1587 / K. Hojer, 1597; tr., C. Winkworth, 1863, alt.; st. 8, M. Carver.

During an Epidemic

353

Tune: Wo Gott der Herr nicht bei uns hält. 49. [p. 418]

1. Dear Christians, put away your fears!
What cause for such despairing?
Now as God's hand so harsh appears,
Our hearts should be declaring
That we these scourges merited,
The guilt hangs over every head,
And none may claim exception.

2. Into Thy hands ourselves we give,
O God, beloved Father,
For 'tis in Thee we move and live;
Earth is vain altogether;
While in this dwelling we remain,
All is affliction, grief, and pain,
And we await Thy gladness.

3. Except to earth a grain should fall
No fruit shall it be earning:
So must our earthly bodies all
To dust and ash be turning
Ere in that glory they may share
Which Thou, Lord, didst for us prepare,
Up to Thy throne ascending.

4. How should we then know such dismay
Or dread the death assigned us?
For everyone must die some day—
What blessing then shall find us!—
Like Simèon, our sin confessed,
Our hand on Christ, our dying blest,
Our death, a gentle slumber!

5. Look to thy body and thy soul,
Let God the Father watch thee;
His angels shall preserve thee whole,
Lest any evil touch thee.
Yea, as the hen her chicks doth bring
And shelter underneath her wing,
Such is our Lord's compassion.

6. So, if we wake or fall asleep,
We are the Lord's possession.
Baptized in Christ, He doth us keep
And foil the Foe's aggression.
Through Adam death came to us all,
But Christ hath saved us from its thrall,
And so we glorify Him.

—D. Spaiser, 1521, but sts. 2–6, J. Heune, 1561; tr., M. Carver.

354

Tune: Auf meinen lieben Gott. 29. [*TLH* 526; *LW* 421; *LSB* 745]

1. In God, my faithful God,
I trust when dark my road;
Though many woes o'ertake me,
Yet He will not forsake me.
His love it is doth send them
And, when 'tis best, will end them.

2. My sins assail me sore,
But I despair no more.
I build on Christ, who loves me;
From this Rock nothing moves me.
To Him I all surrender,
To Him, my soul's Defender.

3. If death my portion be,
Then death is gain to me
And Christ my Life forever,
From whom death cannot sever.
Come when it may, He'll shield me,
To Him I wholly yield me.

4. O Jesus Christ, my Lord,
So meek in deed and word,
Thou once didst die to save us
Because Thy love would have us
Be heirs of heav'nly gladness
When ends this life of sadness.

5. "So be it," then, I say
With all my heart each day.
We, too, dear Lord, adore Thee.
We sing for joy before Thee.
Guide us while here we wander
Until we praise Thee yonder.

—Anon., Lübeck, before 1603; tr., C. Winkworth, 1863, alt.

355

Tune: Herzlich tut mich verlangen. 59. [*TLH* 520; *LW* 113; *LSB* 450]

1. Commit whatever grieves thee
Into the gracious hands
Of Him who never leaves thee,
Who heav'n and earth commands.
Who points the clouds their courses,
Whom winds and waves obey,
He will direct thy footsteps
And find for thee a way.

2. On Him place Thy reliance
If thou wouldst be secure;
His work thou must consider
If thine is to endure.
By anxious sighs and grieving
And self-tormenting care
God is not moved to giving;
All must be gained by prayer.

3. Thy truth and grace, O Father,
Most surely see and know
Both what is good and evil
For mortal man below.
According to Thy counsel
Thou wilt Thy work pursue;
And what Thy wisdom chooseth
Thy might will always do.

4. Thy hand is never shortened,
All things must serve Thy might;
Thine every act is blessing,
Thy path is purest light.
Thy work no man can hinder,
Thy purpose none can stay,
Since Thou to bless Thy children
Wilt always find a way.

5. Though all the pow'rs of evil
The will of God oppose,
His purpose will not falter,
His pleasure onward goes.
Whate'er God's will resolveth,
Whatever He intends,
Will always be accomplished
True to His aims and ends.

6. Then hope, my feeble spirit,
And be thou undismayed;
God helps in every trial
And makes thee unafraid.
Await His time with patience,
Then shall thine eyes behold
The sun of joy and gladness
His brightest beams unfold.

7. Arise, my soul, and banish
Thy anguish and thy care.
Away with thoughts that sadden
And heart and mind ensnare!
Thou art not lord and master
Of thine own destiny;
Enthroned in highest heaven,
God rules in equity.

8. Leave all to His direction;
In wisdom He doth reign,
And in a way most wondrous
His course He will maintain.
Soon He, His promise keeping,
With wonder-working skill,
Shall put away the sorrows
That now thy spirit fill.

9. A while His consolation
He may to thee deny,
And seem as though in trial
He far from thee would fly;
A while distress and anguish
May compass thee around,
Nor to thy supplication
An answ'ring voice be found.

10. But if thou perseverest,
Thou shalt deliv'rance find.
Behold, all unexpected
He will thy soul unbind
And from the heavy burden
Thy heart will soon set free;
And thou wilt see the blessing
He had in mind for thee.

11. O faithful child of heaven,
How blessèd shalt thou be!
With songs of glad thanksgiving
A crown awaiteth thee.
Into thy hand thy Maker
Will give the victor's palm,
And thou to thy Deliv'rer
Shalt sing a joyous psalm

12. Give, Lord, this consummation
To all our heart's distress;
Our hands, our feet, e'er strengthen,
In death our spirits bless.
Thy truth and Thy protection
Grant evermore, we pray,
And in celestial glory
Shall end our destined way.

—P. Gerhardt, 1653; tr., *TLH*, 1941.

356

Tune: Jesu, meine Freude. 74. [*TLH* 347; *LW* 270; *LSB* 743]

1. God brings restoration
From all tribulation;
All to Him I'll leave.
I was His elected
Ere in womb detected,
Ere my heart did grieve.
Likewise He / Will come to me
And my soul from woe deliver;—
'Tis His manner ever.

2. God brings restoration,
Laughter, jubilation,
Joy, and happiness.
E'er His thoughts attend me,
Daily He doth send me
Needful food and dress.
E'en when great / The cross's weight
Hid from sight His favor dully,
He restored me fully.

3. God brings restoration;
Storm and fulmination
Well may have their way.
Mid the noise and quaking
Of the billows breaking,
He will by my stay.
Jonah, tombed, / Was yet exhumed;
Though adversity dismays thee,
God again will raise thee.

4. God brings restoration,
Keeping observation
Over thy distress.
Is thy hope near failing
For thy plagues assailing?
Faithful is His grace.
He is there / With timely care;
Soon thy worries once that mattered
Like a mist are scattered.

5. God brings restoration;
In His weak creation
He is ever strong.
What was left unheeded
That His children needed
When they suffered wrong?
So, my heart, / Forget Thy smart.
All is God's, let Him arrange it;
He has pow'r to change it.

6. God brings restoration,
Though with dread sensation
Jaws of death swing wide;
Though life's years, expended,
Lie on bier extended,
Heav'nward He will guide.
'Tis the way, / All has its day:
Saints must first in death be buried
Ere to heaven carried.

7. God brings restoration,
Who brought devastation
To that dragon old.
Lonely ways He leads us,
Often thorn impedes us,
Ere we reach the fold;
Yet fear not, / Whate'er thy lot,
Leave to God thy tribulation,
He'll bring restoration.

—E. Stockmann, 1701; tr., M. Carver.

357

Tune: In dich hab ich gehoffet, Herr. 40. [*TLH* 524; *LW* 406; *LSB* 734; *or* p. 406]

1. God leads His saints by wondrous ways,
And yet the courses which He lays
Are paved with hidden graces;
By day and night / He keeps in sight
Their wand'ring steps and paces.

2. From time to time He harsh appears,
And hides His presence at their tears,
And leave His own in sadness;
Alone their pain / Shall brief remain;
God means it for their gladness.

3. Regard what ways with God we fare!
His dearest child must often bear
The hardest, heaviest crosses;
Our earthly lot / In life is but
A storm of plagues and losses.

4. Our mighty God delivers those
Who own Him, by such grievous woes,
From out of sin and blindness,
And thus our God / Turns cross and load
To cords of loving-kindness.

5. So let us evermore be glad,
And should some evil hour be had,
We need not weep with terror.
God's little one / Can swiftly run
To God, his burden-bearer.

6. And when draws nigh our dying breath
We know how we should look at death,
If Jesus we have carried:
Our home is His; / Our healing, bliss,
And life in Him are buried.

7. And so, dear God, I look to Thee;
By wondrous ways Thou hast led me,
Through joy and sorrow driven.
Ah, help me now / To do all Thou
Unto Thy saints hast given!

8. God, I commend into Thy hand
My family and native land:
Thou wilt be their Defender.
Thou, Lord, art my / Great Help on high,
To Thee all things I render.

—Anon., Chemnitz, 1759; tr., M. Carver.

358

Tune: O Gott, du frommer Gott. 55.
[*TLH* 395; *LW* 385; *LSB* 696; *or TLH* 38*; *LW* 174*; *LSB* 794*]

1. God ever true remains;
His heart with love is breaking.
Though oft He tests His own,
He'll never be forsaking;
He burdens with the cross
To purge our faith of stains
And prove our patience firm;
God ever true remains.

2. God ever true remains,
Whatever grief attends us;
He helps us all to bear
The burdens that He sends us;
He often wields the rod,
Yet all the while retains
A father's love for us:
God ever true remains.

3. God ever true remains,
He knows what we can handle,
His load is light to bear,
He snuffs no smold'ring candle;
He sets His people free
From all their weights and chains;
When great distress appears,
God ever true remains.

4. God ever true remains
And comforts after sadness,
He fills the sunless night
At last with stars of gladness;
The cross's raging storm
Will pass like summer rains;
O soul, be of good cheer:
God ever true remains.

5. God ever true remains
And stills thy deepest yearning;
He tries thy faith as gold
In sorrow's furnace burning;
So from God's hand accept
The cup of cross and pains,
The cup of life will come.
God ever true remains.

6. God ever true remains,
Though storms the sky be rending,
God yet shall cause thy grief
To have a measured ending;
And cross, distress, and need
Shall yield eternal gains.
The Most High loves thee so
And ever true remains.

—Anon., *Kirchen-Echo,* 1695; tr., M. Carver.

359

Tune: Gott lebet noch! Seele. 80. [p. 402]

1. God liveth still!
Soul, despair not, fear no ill!
God is good; from His compassion
Earthly help and comfort flow;
Strong is His right hand to fashion
All things well for men below:
Trial, oft the most distressing,
In the end have proved a blessing,
Wherefore, then, my soul, despair?
God still lives, who heareth pray'r.

2. God liveth still!
Soul, despair not, fear no ill!
He who gave the eye its vision,
Shall He slumber once or sleep?
He who gave the ear its mission,
Hears He not His children weep?
God is God; His ear attendeth,
When the sigh or bosom rendeth.
Wherefore then, my soul, despair?
God still lives, who heareth pray'r.

3. God liveth still!
Soul, despair not, fear no ill!
He who gives the cloud their measure,
Stretching out the heav'ns alone;
He who stores the earth with treasure,
Is not far from every one.
God in hour of need defendeth
Him whose heart in love ascendeth.
Wherefore then, my soul, despair?
God still lives, who heareth pray'r.

4. God liveth still!
Soul, despair not, fear no ill!
Is thy cross too great and pond'rous,
Cast on Him thy grievous load;
God is great, His love is wondrous,
He will speed thee on thy road.
For His truth endureth ever,
And His mercy ceaseth never:
Wherefore then, my soul, despair?
God still lives, who heareth pray'r.

5. God liveth still!
Soul, despair not, fear no ill!
Is thy yoke of sin too galling?
Christ Himself has set you free,
Borne for thee their weight appalling,
Cast them in oblivion's sea!
In thy deepest grief and sadness
He can grant thee joy and gladness:
Wherefore then, my soul, despair?
God still lives, who heareth pray'r.

6. God liveth still!
Soul, despair not, fear no ill!
When the world would let thee perish,
Pathless all thy tangled way,
God the nearer draws, to cherish
Him who makes the Lord his stay.
Children oft that most He loveth
Thus with strictest rod He proveth.
Wherefore then, my soul, despair?
God still lives, who heareth pray'r.

7. God liveth still!
Soul, despair not, fear no ill!
Be thy life, until its ending,
Full of thorns, of grief or need,
God, in love the trial sending,
Thus His child would heav'nwards lead:
For this life's long night of sadness
He will give thee peace and gladness.
Wherefore then, my soul, despair?
God still lives, Who heareth pray'r.

—J. F. Zihn, 1682, ab.; tr., F. E. Cox, 1864, alt.

360

Tune: Vater unser im Himmelreich. 44. [*TLH* 318; *LW* 234; *LSB* 766]

1. O Lord, Redeemer of Thy host,
God, Father, Son, and Holy Ghost,
Most Holy Trinity, most Blest,
On Christendom Thy mercy rest!
Good Lord, our faithful God, we plead,
Have mercy in our every need.

2. Oh, spare us, God, Thy wrath forgo,
Do not reward us as we owe.
Do not Thy mercy's depths forget,
Our errors and our sins remit;
Help soul and body, goods and name,
To be preserved from hurt and shame.

3. O Father, earnestly we pray
Through Jesus Christ, Thy help convey,
By His birth, blood, sweat, failing breath,
Five wounds and Passion, cross and death,
His resurrection and ascent,
Deliver us who here repent.

4. By teaching pure on us bestow
That godly fear may sprout and grow,
That youth be raised in decency
And from all sin and evil flee;
Make all who would Thy Word efface
To meet with failure and disgrace.

5. Let all who have authority
Fulfill their office carefully;
Our magistrates protect and guide,
Their work with blessings all provide;
Grant wholesome, peaceful government,
All famine, plague, and strife prevent.

6. Deliver all the suffering,
To them Thy help and comfort bring;
Destroy their yoke, their weight remove
By which Thou dost their mettle prove;
So prove Thy grace and constancy,
From plague and bondage set them free.

7. O Jesus Christ, God's very Son,
O Jesus Christ, Thou Mercy-Throne,
O Jesus Christ, Thou Lamb of God,
That borest the world's sinful load,
Have mercy on us, hear our pleas,
Have mercy, Lord, and grant us peace.

8. O Lord, Redeemer of Thy host,
God, Father, Son, and Holy Ghost,
Most Holy Trinity, most Blest,
On Christendom Thy mercy rest!
Good Lord, our faithful God, we plead,
Have mercy in our every need.

—J. Freder, †1562, ab. Hannover, 1657; tr., M. Carver.

361

Tune: Herr Gott, der du mein Vater bist. 11. [p. 403]

1. Lord God, who art my Father dear,
I pray in Jesus' name: O hear
What, trusting in His promised word,
I humbly ask of Thee, good Lord.

2. Grant us Thy Word, Thy Spirit give,
That by His grace we godly live,
Give shelter, peace, good friends, and food,
Protect our native land, O God!

3. Save us from sin and Satan's fraud,
Deliver us from evil, God!
Be with us in our dying hour;
Thine is the kingdom, glory, pow'r.

4. Lord, at Thy word, Amen, I say;
Increase my feeble faith, I pray.
Thou lead'st me with a father's care,
Oh, let me be Thy child and heir!

—J. Mathesius, 1564; tr., A. Crull, †1923.

362

Tune: Herr Jesu Christ, wahr Mensch und Gott. 11.
[p. 404; *or TLH* 141*; *LW* 363*; *LSB* 615*]

1. Help, Helper, help, in fear and need;
Have mercy, to my pray'r give heed!
I know Thou lov'st me still as Thine,
Though 'gainst me world and hell combine.

2. My God and Lord, I trust in Thee;
What need I, if Thou art with me?
And Thou, Lord Jesus Christ, art mine;
My God and Savior, I am Thine.

3. Therefore my happiness is great,
I am content, for Thee I wait,
Trust wholly in Thy name, and then
I pray: Help, Helper, help! Amen.

—M. Moller, 1596, after N. Selnecker, 1565; tr., E. Cronenwett, †1923, alt.

363

Tune: Es ist genug, so nimm, Herr. 52. [*TLH* 196; *LW* 145; *LSB* 468]

1. I am content! Christ Jesus is my Lord;
No better lord I know.
Who will be His, and service true afford,
Need never worry so.
So I to God will cleave completely;
This world can never please as sweetly.
I am content. I am content.

2. I am content! From care and sorrow free,
My heart no longer strains.
I'm satisfied in God, who shelters me
And soothes all earthly pains.
I worry not, whate'er betide me;
All things the Most High can provide me.
I am content. I am content.

3. I am content! God, who the sparrows feeds,
And all the world upholds;
Who still the grass and flowèrs grows and heeds,
And with sweet charm enfolds,—
The Same my body, too, sustaineth,
My food and clothing still ordaineth.
I am content. I am content.

4. I am content! And though my purse be light,
To me 'tis all the same.
I have my God;—to what more fortune bright
Can all the world lay claim?
For Jesus is my Crown and Coffer,
And doth the wealth of heaven offer.
I am content. I am content.

5. I am content! If God my body dress,
And make all well to fare,
It is enough. Though days may come apace
When closets all lie bare,
And though the clouds of want may hover,
My soul and body God shall cover!
I am content. I am content.

6. I am content! My faithful Father sees,
Where other men are blind:
He guards His child, ensuring me of peace,
In body, soul, and mind;
So I will let my Father tend me;
Tomorrow's cares cannot offend me.
I am content. I am content.

7. I am content! God grant a spirit meek,
All else shall added be;
His heav'n alone, which Jesus bids me seek,
Can truly comfort me.
I'm seeking only by the Spirit
To do the Father's will and fear it.
I am content. I am content.

8. I am content, on Jesus' breast I lie
In God the Father's heart;
What need I more? This gives me utter joy,
This sweetens every smart.
If but a foretaste here is given,
What greater things await in heaven?
I am content. I am content.

—Anon., Halle, 1714; tr., M. Carver.

364

Tune: Wer nur den lieben Gott läßt walten. 45. [*TLH* 194; *LW* 429; *LSB* 750]

1. I leave all things to God's direction,
He loveth me in weal and woe;
His will is good, true His affection.
With tender love His heart doth glow.
My Fortress and my Rock is He:
What pleaseth God, that pleaseth me.

2. My God hath all things in His keeping,
He is the ever faithful Friend;
He grants me laughter after weeping,
And all His ways in blessings end.
His love endures eternally:
What pleaseth God, that pleaseth me.

3. The will of God shall be my pleasure
While here on earth is mine abode;
My will is wrong beyond all measure,
It doth not will what pleaseth God.
The Christian's motto e'er must be:
What pleaseth God, that pleaseth me.

4. God knows what must be done to save me,
His love for me will never cease;
Upon His hands He did engrave me
With purest gold of loving grace.
His will supreme must ever be!
What pleaseth God, that pleaseth me.

5. My God desires the soul's salvation,
Me also He desires to save;
Therefore with Christian resignation
All earthly troubles I will brave.
His will be done eternally:
What pleaseth God, that pleaseth me.

—S. Franck, 1685; tr., A. Crull, †1923, alt.

365

Tune: In dich hab ich gehoffet, Herr. 40. [*TLH* 524; *LW* 406; *LSB* 734; *or* p. 406]

1. In Thee, Lord, have I put my trust;
Leave me not helpless in the dust,
Let me not be confounded.
Let in Thy Word / My faith, O Lord,
Be always firmly grounded.

2. Bow down Thy gracious ear to me
And hear my cries and pray'rs to Thee,
Haste Thee for my protection;
For woes and fear / Surround me here.
Help me in mine affliction.

3. My God and Shield, now let Thy pow'r
Be unto me a mighty tow'r
Whence bravely I defend me
Against the foes / That round me close.
O Lord, assistance lend me.

4. Thou art my Strength, my Shield, my Rock,
My Fortress that withstands each shock,
My Help, my Life, my Treasure.
Whate'er the rod, / Thou art my God;
Naught can resist Thy pleasure.

5. The world for me has falsely set
Full many‿a secret snare and net
To tempt me and to harm me.
Lord, make them fail, / Do Thou prevail,
Let their disguise not charm me.

6. With Thee, Lord, have I cast my lot;
O faithful God, forsake me not,
To Thee my soul commending.
Lord, be my Stay, / Lead Thou the way
Now and when life is ending.

7. All honor, praise, and majesty
To Father, Son, and Spirit be,
Our God forever glorious,
In whose rich grace / We'll run our race
Till we depart victorious.

—A. Reusner, 1533, after Ps. 31; tr., C. Winkworth, 1863, alt.

366

Tune: Valet will ich dir geben. 59.
[*TLH* 58; *LW* 79; *LSB* 442; *or LW* 407*; *LSB* 724* (mel.)]

1. If God Himself be for me,
I may a host defy;
For when I pray, before me
My foes, confounded, fly.
If Christ, my Head and Master,
Befriend me from above,
What foe or what disaster
Can drive me from His love?

2. This I believe, yea, rather,
Of this I make my boast,
That God is my dear Father,
The Friend who loves me most,
And that, whate'er betide me,
My Savior is at hand
Through stormy seas to guide me
And bring me safe to land.

3. I build on this foundation,
That Jesus and His blood
Alone are my salvation,
The true, eternal good.
Without Him all that pleases
Is valueless on earth;
The gifts I owe to Jesus
Alone my love are worth.

4. My Jesus is my Splendor,
My Sun, my Light, alone;
Were He not my Defender
Before God's lofty throne,
I never should find favor
And mercy in His sight,
But be destroyed forever
As darkness by the light.

5. He canceled my offenses,
Delivered me from death;
He is the Lord who cleanses
My soul from sin through faith.
In Him I can be cheerful,
Bold, and undaunted aye;
In Him I am not fearful
Of God's great Judgment Day.

6. Naught, naught, can now condemn me
Nor set my hope aside;
Now hell no more can claim me,
Its fury I deride.
No sentence e'er reproves me,
No ill destroys my peace;
For Christ, my Savior, loves me
And shields me with His grace.

7. His Spirit in me dwelleth,
And o'er my mind He reigns.
All sorrow He dispelleth
And soothes away all pains.
He crowns His work with blessing
And helpeth me to cry,
"My Father!" without ceasing,
To Him who dwells on high.

8. And when my soul is lying
Weak, trembling, and oppressed,
He pleads with groans and sighing
That cannot be expressed;
But God's quick eye discerns them,
Although they give no sound,
And into language turns them
E'en in the heart's deep ground.

9. To mine His Spirit speaketh
Sweet word of holy cheer,
How God to him that seeketh
For rest is always near
And how He hath erected
A city fair and new,
Where what our faith expected
We evermore shall view.

10. In yonder home doth flourish
My heritage, my lot;
Though here I die and perish,
My heav'n shall fail me not.
Though care my life oft saddens
And causeth tears to flow,
The light of Jesus gladdens
And sweetens every woe.

11. Who clings with resolution
To Him whom Satan hates
Must look for persecution;
For him the burden waits
Of mockery, shame, and losses,
Heaped on his blameless head;
A thousand plagues and crosses
Will be his daily bread.

12. From me this is not hidden,
Yet I am not afraid;
I leave my cares, as bidden,
To whom my vows were paid.
Though life and limb it cost me
And everything I won,
Unshaken shall I trust Thee
And cleave to Thee alone.

13. Though earth be rent asunder,
Thou'rt mine eternally;
Not fire nor sword nor thunder
Shall sever me from Thee;
Not hunger, thirst, nor danger,
Not pain nor poverty
Nor mighty princes' anger
Shall ever hinder me.

14. No angel and no gladness,
No throne, no pomp, no show,
No love, no hate, no sadness,
No pain, no depth of woe,
No scheme of man's contrivance,
However small or great,
Shall draw me from Thy guidance
Nor from Thee separate.

15. My heart for joy is springing
And can no more be sad,
'Tis full of mirth and singing,
Sees naught but sunshine glad.
The Sun that cheers my spirit
Is Jesus Christ, my King;
That which I shall inherit
Makes me rejoice and sing.

—P. Gerhardt, 1653; tr., R. Massie, 1857, alt.; but sts. 4–6, 10 based on J. Kelly, 1867.

367

Tune: Keinen hat Gott verlassen. 59. [p. 408; *or TLH* 172*; *LW* 113*; *LSB* 450*]

1. Know well that none's forsaken
Whose trust in God is set;
Though he by foes be shaken,
He shall not have regret,
For God His own sustaineth,
To raise them at the last,
And all their need ordaineth
Beyond, as here and past.

2. Alone to God I'll leave it
To govern as He will,
My poor soul will receive it
For good;—though cross and ill
In this sad land we suffer,
Yet so it must remain:
Those joys which earth can offer
Will end in endless pain.

3. To God, my great Advisor
Continually I'll cry;
In every need He's wiser
And knows far more than I.
I'll cleave with resignation,
No matter what may be;
He'll rule me with compassion,
And help me faithfully.

4. Adversity and favor
Come from my God most dear;
I'll pray, and will not waver
When darker roads appear.
How will He not relieve me—
My Father ever true?
When greatest troubles grieve me,
He'll surely guide me through.

5. Resplendence, wealth, and treasure,
And all the world esteems—
In them I find no pleasure,
Death mocks their fading gleams;
My Treasure reigns in heaven—
My Joy, my richest Crown
Is Christ, who all hath given,
And pours His Spirit down.

6. Inside my heart is seated
As in a paltry shrine,
My Lord who, sorely treated,
Once shed His blood divine—
For me, a worm but worthless,
That, by His death and pain,
I might from torments deathless
Release and heaven gain.

7. Now then my life I'm spending
In thanks and praise to Him,
All to His hands commending—
All that I have and am.
What want this life may give me
I leave to Him to fill,
Of worries to relieve me,
And answer as He will.

8. Amen, this the conclusion
Of my poor anthem be;
Lord, by Thy blood's effusion,
Let me belong to Thee:
Thus I'll await, possessing
True bliss while I am here,—
The time, when the unceasing
Bright crown of grace I'll wear.**

–Anon., ca. 1590; tr. M. Carver, but st. 8, *Mor. H.-B.*, 1859, alt.

THE LITANY, OR COMMON PRAYER OF THE CHURCH

Note: Lines marked (I.) are sung by the first choir,
those marked (II.) by the second.

368

Tune: [*TLH* 661]

I. Kyrie — *II.* Eleison.
Christe — Eleison.
Kyrie — Eleison.
O Christ, — Hear Thou us.
Lord God, the Father in heaven; — Have mercy upon us.
Lord God, the Son, Redeemer of the world; — Have mercy upon us.
Lord God, the Holy Ghost: — Have mercy upon us.

I. Be gracious unto us, — *II.* Spare us, good Lord.
Be gracious unto us, — Help us, good Lord.

** Note: The stanzas form the acrostic *KATARINA* in honor of Lady Katharina of Brandenburg.

I. From all sin;	*II.* Good Lord, deliver us.
From all error;	Good Lord, deliver us.
From all evil;	Good Lord, deliver us.
From the crafts and assaults of the devil;	Good Lord, deliver us.
From sudden and evil death;	Good Lord, deliver us.
From pestilence and famine;	Good Lord, deliver us.
From war and bloodshed;	Good Lord, deliver us.
From sedition and rebellion;	Good Lord, deliver us.
From hail and tempest;	Good Lord, deliver us.
From all calamity by fire and water;	Good Lord, deliver us.
From everlasting death:	Good Lord, deliver us.
I. By Thy holy nativity;	*II.* Help us, good Lord.
By Thine agony and bloody sweat;	Help us, good Lord.
By Thy cross and death;	Help us, good Lord.
By Thy holy resurrection and ascension;	Help us, good Lord.
In our last distress;	Help us, good Lord.
And at the Last Judgment:	Help us, good Lord.
I. We poor sinners do beseech Thee	*II.* To hear us, O Lord God,
And to rule and govern Thy holy [Christian Church;	We beseech Thee to hear us, good Lord.
To preserve all bishops, pastors, and [ministers of Thy Church in the [wholesome Word and holiness of life;	We beseech Thee to hear us, good Lord.
To end to all schisms and causes of offence;	We beseech Thee to hear us, good Lord.
To bring back all the erring and deceived;	We beseech Thee to hear us, good Lord.
To beat down Satan under our feet;	We beseech Thee to hear us, good Lord.
To send faithful laborers into Thy harvest;	We beseech Thee to hear us, good Lord.
To give to Thy Word Thy Spirit and power;	We beseech Thee to hear us, good Lord.
[And to comfort and help the weak- [hearted and the distressed:	We beseech Thee to hear us, good Lord.
I. To give to all kings and rulers peace and [concord;	*II.* We beseech Thee to hear us, good Lord.
To restrain our foes and all tyrants;	We beseech Thee to hear us, good Lord.
To direct and defend our land and all [authorities;	We beseech Thee to hear us, good Lord.
To bless and keep our council and [congregation;	We beseech Thee to hear us, good Lord.
To behold and be of help to all who are in [danger and all who travel:	We beseech Thee to hear us, good Lord.

I. To grant all those with child and all that nurse [infants a happy result and good success; *II.* We beseech Thee to hear us, good Lord.
To treat and attend to all children and the sick; We beseech Thee to hear us, good Lord.
To loose and release all innocent prisoners; We beseech Thee to hear us, good Lord.
To protect and provide for all widows [and orphans; We beseech Thee to hear us, good Lord.
To have mercy upon all men: We beseech Thee to hear us, good Lord.
To forgive our enemies, persecutors, and [slanderers, and to convert them; We beseech Thee to hear us, good Lord.
To grant and preserve the fruits of the field; We beseech Thee to hear us, good Lord.
And graciously to hear our prayers: We beseech Thee to hear us, good Lord.

I. O Lord Jesus Christ, Son of God, *II.* We beseech Thee to hear us.
O Lamb of God, that takest away the sin [of the world, Have mercy upon us.
O Lamb of God, that takest away the sin [of the world, Have mercy upon us.
O Lamb of God, that takest away the sin [of the world, Grant us Thy peace.
O Christ, Hear us.
Kyrie Eleison.
Christe Eleison.

(*Both:*) Kyrie Eleison. Amen.

—M. Luther, 1529; tr., composite.

369

Tune: Jesu, meine Freude. 74. [*TLH* 347; *LW* 270; *LSB* 743]

1. Still my soul abideth,
In God's will confideth,—
In His mighty hand;
I have satisfaction
In His course of action,
All my heart will stand;
If but heav'n / I may be giv'n,
And from Jesus never parted,
Then I am glad-hearted.

2. Thee my soul desireth,
And but this requireth:
God, to be with Thee,—
Thee on each occasion,—
Nor will heed persuasion
From this loyalty;
Worldly main / And wealth and gain—
Though the many hunger for them,
My soul doth deplore them.

3. Nay, oh, nay! One solely
Doth my soul love wholly,
There's none else but He:
Christ, my faithful Savior,
Source of joy forever,
Gives Himself to me.
He alone / My soul shall own,
My life is His gift requited,
With His life united.

4. On God's goodness ponder,
And in faith and wonder
Lay thee at His breast.
There, reliance learning,
Thou wilt be discerning
With what healing rest
And repose / His Spirit flows;
Souls to Him for slumber crying
Shall have rest undying.

5. Still my soul abideth,
Deep itself it hideth
In Christ's bosom true;
Strong in hope's conviction,
It will face affliction
And pass joyful through.
To the last / It holds Him fast,
Patiently by faith adhering
Till His glad appearing.

6. Yea, amen, and surely,
Those who trust Christ purely,
Verily shall find
Crosses' weight diminished,
And, when life is finished,
Greater bliss consigned;
God shall mend / Them in the end,
Making of their former sorrow
Joy upon the morrow.

—J. C. Schade, 1690; tr., M. Carver.

370

Tune: Schwing dich auf zu deinem Gott. 60.
[*TLH* 204; or *TLH* 540*; *LW* 483*; *LSB* 869*]

1. Look up to thy God again,
Soul, sunk in affliction!
Shall He be reproached by men
Through thy sore dejection?
Satan's wiles dost thou not see,
Who by sore temptation
Gladly would keep far from thee
Jesus' consolation?

2. Shake thy head, bid Satan, "Flee!
Wouldst thou, O deceiver,
With thy thrusts renewed at me
Make me fear and shiver?
Serpent! Bruised thy head I see;
Christ my Savior freed me
From thee by His agony,
And to joy will lead me.

3. "Dost thou charge my sin to me?
When hath God in heaven
Ordered that my judgment be
From thee sought and given?
Who did pow'r on thee bestow,
Sentence to deliver,
Who thyself art sunk so low
In hell's flames forever?"

4. Though I've not done as I should,
And it grieves me truly,
I lay claim to Jesus' blood,
Death, and Passion fully.
These the ransom price repay
Set for my transgression,
These before God's throne I lay,—
Choicest intercession!

5. Rage then, devil, and thou, death!
How can ye afflict me?
In the trials of my path
God's hand shall protect me.
He hath giv'n His Son to me
Moved by love and favor,
That to endless misery
Naught may drive me ever.

6. Cry then, foolish world, and say
That God nothing gives me,
But delusion, false display,—
Yea, with lies deceives me.
Had God been averse to me,
Would He then provide me
With the gifts so rich and free
Which He hath supplied me?

7. What is good in sky or sea,
What the wide earth over,
Which is yet not good for me?
Canst thou then discover?
For whose sake do stars supply
Beauteous light from heaven?
Why but for my good am I
Air and water given?

8. I am God's, and God is mine,
Who can us then sunder?
Though beneath the cross I pine,
And it press me under,
Let it press! The hand of love
Hath the cross laid on me,
He the burden will remove
When the good is done me.

9. Children whom a father would
To all good be guiding,
Seldom grow in manner good
Without rod and chiding.
If then I'm a child of God,
Why should I be fleeing
When on sin He wields the rod
For my own well-being?

10. Gracious are God's heart and mind
In the pain He's sending,
Who through present days hath pined
Reaps not woe unending,
But eternal joy shall taste
In Christ's garden dwelling,
Joy he shall know there at last,—
Now assurance feeling.

11. Often God's own children here
Sow in tears and sadness,
But at length the longed-for year
Comes to joy and gladness;
For the reaping time appears,
All their labors after,
When are turned their grief and tears
Into joy and laughter.

12. Come then, Christian heart, today,
Take thy desperation,
Cast it joyfully away;
Let God's consolation
Burn within thee more and more,
Praise and honor giving
To thy God's great name and pow'r,
Source of thy relieving.

—P. Gerhardt, 1653, cento; tr., J. Kelly, 1867, alt., but st. 4, M. Carver.

371

Tune: Sollt es gleich bisweilen scheinen. 8. [p. 415]

1. Seems it only in my anguish
As though God would let us languish,
Yet I hold this knowledge fast:
God will surely help at last.

2. Though by some delay He try us,
He will not His aid deny us,
Though it come not oft with speed,
It will surely come at need.

3. As no father giveth surely
Gifts to children prematurely,
So our God gives when He will;
Wait His leisure and be still.

4. Rest I find, upon Him thinking,
When all courage else is sinking,
For I know my soul shall prove
His is more than father's love.

5. What if Satan chase me after?
All his might I scorn with laughter.
What if cross be pressing sore,
God, my God, lives evermore!

6. What of death, whose fangs await me?
What of all the men who hate me?
Foes my heart may pierce and rend;
God in heav'n is still my Friend.

7. All the world may be denied me,
Men may never long abide me,
Yet I will not ask for more;
God my Judge shall all restore.

8. Earth may grudge me all her pleasures,
Safe on high still wait my treasures,
And if heav'n at last be mine,
All things else I can resign.

9. World, I willingly would cease thee,
How I hate the things that please thee!
Baneful every gift of thine,
Only be my God still mine.

10. Ah, Lord, if I have Thee solely,
I crave not creation wholly;
Bright is even death's dark road,
If but Thou art there, my God.

—C. Tietze, 1663; tr., C. Winkworth, 1863, alt., but st. 7, M. Carver.

372

Tune: Jesu Leiden, Pein und Tod. 60. [*TLH* 140; *LW* 109; *LSB* 440]

1. Father God, provide for me,
For my needs and sorrow,
For my true tranquility
Now and on the morrow.
God, provide for all my own,
Keep them in Thy favor;
Tender God, be Thou alone
My Provider ever.

2. God, provide at break of day,
Soul and body tending,
That to Thee alone I may
E'er be these commending;
O Most High, provide for aye
For my mind and senses,
That they may not Thee betray
By undue offenses.

3. God, provide Thy Holy Word
To be with us ever
With Thy Sacraments, O Lord,
And deny us never.
Lord, provide for those who preach
Those who rule the nation;
In Thy grace provide for each
In his place and station.

4. Friend of man, provide for us,
Called Thy children holy;
Lord, provide for friends and foes,
And us sinners lowly.
God, provide our daily bread,
Help the poor and sickly,—
Those like me by grief dismayed;
When I fall, come quickly!

5. God, provide when eyelids close
And my rest I'm taking,
When to bed my body goes
And again is waking.
God, provide for word and thought,
Duty, work, and reason,—
All that I must do or not
In its time and season

6. God, provide for all I own,
Name, and reputation;
For my heart, when made to groan
By man's foul transgression.
God, provide when to disgrace
Flesh would fain allure me.
God, provide when death I face—
Of the crown assure me.

7. Lord, provide when Satan seeks
Viciously to break me;
When Thy final judgment speaks,
Lest perdition take me;
Lord, provide Thou for my dust
And my life here given,
For my spirit when it must
Go to Thee in heaven.

—L. E. von Schwarzburg-Rudolstadt, 1687; tr., M. Carver.

373

Tune: Freu dich sehr, o meine Seele. 66. [*TLH* 61; *LW* 28; *LSB* 347]

1. Faithful God, my heart's affliction
Now I must relate to Thee,
Though Thou knowest my condition
More than I myself can see:
Utter weakness oft I sense
In temptations and offense,
When the devil would bereave me
Of all faith, and hopeless leave me.

2. Thou, my God, who art omniscient,
Know'st that nothing good is mine;
All my labors are deficient,
Every gift, O Lord, is Thine;
Every good I find in me
I've received alone from Thee;—
Thine my faith and Thine each treasure,
Giv'n according to Thy pleasure.

3. O my God, I come before Thee
In my grave necessity;
Hear how strongly I implore Thee,
Leave me not to mockery;
Gird my faith so weak and frail,
Make the foe's devices fail,
That despair may take me never,
But that Christ be mine forever.

4. Jesus, Fount of grace and pardon,
Thou hast never cast away
Those who cannot bear their burden,
But Thy foll'wers dost allay,
Saying, though their faith exceed
Not the lowly mustard-seed,
Yet so worthy wilt Thou count them,
That they may remove a mountain.

5. Let me find Thy grace, O Savior,
In my depth of grief and woe;
Come Thyself, my soul deliver,
Help me overcome the foe.
Daily multiply my faith
And the Spirit's sword bequeath,
That I Satan may be quelling
And his arrows all repelling.

6. Holy Ghost, enthroned in heaven,
Very God eternally,
From the Son and Father given,
One with them in Majesty;
Thou art Balm to all who grieve,
Fire by which I now believe;
With Thy grace on me remaining,
Ever be my faith sustaining!

7. Help confer in Thy descending,
Noble Guest, upon my heart,
Grant Thy work a perfect ending,
Which by faith Thou gav'st a start;
Blow and stoke the spark with force,
That I may complete the course,
And with all the saints in heaven
Faith's awaited end be given.

8. God of gods, Most High forever,
Holy, blessed Trinity!
Save for Thee there is no Savior,
Therefore save me speedily
When the devil's arrows come
And my flesh feels weak and numb,
When he seeks my consolation,
Casting me in desperation.

9. Guard me lest his traps ensnare me,
Where he strews them in my way;
Bring to naught his plots and spare me
From his dealings night and day.
In the battle brace my hand,
That I valiantly may stand,
And whenever I must face him,
Send Thy help to curb and chase him.

10. Swiftly to Thy child so fragile,
Sinking wearily and fast,
Reach Thy hand of graces agile
Till the fearful storm be past.
Guide Thy child that needs Thee most
Lest the foe should wildly boast
That he hath a heart confounded
Which its hope in Thee had grounded.

11. Thou my Life and my Defender,
Thou my Rock, my Confidence,
Life and limb to Thee I tender;
God, my God, oh, go not hence!
Hasten to my side, remain,
Dash the devil's darts in twain,
Break him, send him devastated
Back to hell, humiliated.

12. Till my days on earth shall languish,
I will praise Thy hand of might,
Which hath put all need and anguish,
By Thy grace, to shame and flight.
Yet not only ere I die
Shall Thy glories multiply,
But hereafter for Thy favor
I will sing Thy praise forever!

—J. Heermann, 1630; tr., M. Carver.

374

Tune: Von Gott will ich nicht lassen. 58. [*TLH* 393; *LW* 409; *LSB* 713]

1. From God shall naught divide me,
For He is true for aye,
And on my path will guide me,
Who else should often stray.
His right hand holdeth me;
For me He truly careth,
My burdens ever beareth
Wherever I may be.

2. When man's help and affection
Shall unavailing prove,
God grants me His protection
And shows His pow'r and love.
He helps in ev'ry need,
From sin and shame redeems me,
From chains and bonds reclaims me,
Yea, e'en from death I'm freed.

3. God shall be my Reliance
In sorrow's darkest night;
Its dread I bid defiance
When He is at my right.
I unto Him commend
My body, soul, and spirit,—
They are His own by merit,—
All's well then at the end.

4. Whate'er shall be His pleasure
Is surely best for me;
He gave His dearest treasure
That our weak hearts might see
His good and gracious will;
In His own Son He gave us
Whate'er could bless and save us.
Praise Him who loves us still!

5. Oh, praise Him, for He never
Forgets our daily need;
Oh, blest the hour whenever
To Him our thoughts can speed;
Yea, all the time we spend
Without Him is but wasted,
Till we His joy have tasted,
The joy that hath no end.

6. Yea, when the world shall perish
With all its pride and pow'r,
Whatever worldlings cherish
Shall vanish in that hour.
But though in death they make
The deepest grave our cover,
When there our sleep is over,
Our God will us awake.

7. Our soul shall never perish,
But in yon paradise
The joys of heav'n shall cherish;
Our body shall arise
Pure, holy, new-born, free
From every sin and evil;
The tempting of the devil
We then no more shall see.

8. What though I here must suffer
Distress and trials sore,
I merit ways still rougher;
And yet there is in store
For me eternal bliss,
Yea, pleasures without measure,
Since Christ is now my Treasure
And shall be evermore.

9. Such is His will that made us,
The Father seeks our good;
The Son of sin doth rid us,
And saves us by His blood;
The Spirit rules our ways,
Through faith in us abiding,
To heav'n our footsteps guiding;
To Him be thanks and praise!

—L. Helmbold, 1563; tr., C. Winkworth, 1863, alt.

375

Tune: Warum sollt ich denn grämen. 63. [*TLH* 523; *LW* 423; *LSB* 756]

1. Why should cross and trial grieve me?
Christ is near / With His cheer;
Never will He leave me.
Who can rob me of the heaven
That God's Son / For my own
To my faith hath given?

2. Naked was I, nothing owning,
When on earth / At my birth
My breath came with groaning,
Naked hence shall I betake me,
When I go / From earth's woe
And my breath forsake me.

3. Naught—not e'en the life I'm living,
Is mine own, / God alone
All to me is giving.
Must I then His own restore Him?
Though bereft / Of each gift
Still shall I adore Him.

4. Though a heavy cross I'm bearing
And my heart / Feels the smart,
Shall I be despairing?
God, my Helper, who doth send it,
Well doth know / All my woe
And how best to end it.

5. God oft gives me days of gladness;
Shall I grieve / If He give
Seasons, too, of sadness?
God is good, and tempers ever
All my ill; / And He will
Wholly leave me never.

6. Though united world and devil,
All their pow'r / Can no more
Do than mock and cavil.
Let derision now employ them,
Christ e'en here / Will appear
And in full destroy them.

7. Hopeful, cheerful, and undaunted
Everywhere / They appear
Who in Christ are planted.
Death itself cannot appall them,
They rejoice / When the voice
Of their Lord doth call them.

8. Death cannot destroy forever;
From our fears, / Cares, and tears
It will us deliver.
It will close life's mournful story,
Make a way / That we may
Enter heav'nly glory.

9. There I'll reap enduring pleasure,
After woe / Here below
Suffered in large measure.
Lasting good we find here never,
All the earth / Deemeth worth
Vanisheth forever.

10. What is all this life possesses?
But a hand / Full of sand
That the heart distresses.
Noble gifts that pall me never
Christ, our Lord, / Will accord
To His saints forever.

11. Lord, my Shepherd, take me to Thee.
Thou art mine; / I was Thine
Even ere I knew Thee.
I am Thine, for Thou hast bought me;
Lost I stood, / But Thy blood
Free salvation bought me.

12. Thou art mine; I love and own Thee.
Light of Joy, / Ne'er shall I
From my heart dethrone Thee.
Savior, let me soon behold Thee
Face to face,— / May Thy grace
Evermore enfold me!

—P. Gerhardt, 1653; tr. *TLH,* 1941, based on J. Kelly, 1867.

376

Tune: Was Gott tut, das ist wohlgetan. 64. [*TLH* 521; *LW* 422; *LSB* 760]

1. What God ordains is always good;
His will abideth holy.
As He directs my life for me,
I follow meek and lowly.
My God indeed / In every need
Doth well know how to shield me;
To Him, then, I will yield me.

2. What God ordains is always good.
He never will deceive me;
He leads me in His own right way,
And never will He leave me.
I take content / What He hath sent;
His hand that sends me sadness
Will turn my tears to gladness.

3. What God ordains is always good.
His loving thought attends me;
No poison can be in the cup
That my Physician sends me.
My God is true; / Each morn anew
I'll trust His grace unending,
My life to Him commending.

4. What God ordains is always good.
He is my Friend and Father;
He suffers naught to do me harm,
Though many storms may gather.
Now I may know / Both joy and woe,
Some day I shall see clearly
That He hath loved me dearly.

5. What God ordains is always good.
Though I the cup am drinking
Which savors now of bitterness,
I take it without shrinking.
For after grief / God grants relief,
My heart with comfort filling
And all my sorrow stilling.

6. What God ordains is always good.
This truth remains unshaken.
Though sorrow, need, or death be mine,
I shall not be forsaken.
I fear no harm, / For with His arm
He shall embrace and shield me;
So to my God I yield me.

—S. Rodigast, 1675; tr., *TLH*, 1941.

377

Tune: Was mein Gott will, das gscheh allzeit. 83. [*TLH* 517 (iso.); *LW* 414; *LSB* 714 (mel.)]

1. The will of God is always best
And shall be done forever;
And they who trust in Him are blest,
He will forsake them never.
He helps indeed / In time of need,
He chastens with forbearing;
They who depend / On God, their Friend,
Shall not be left despairing.

2. God is my Comfort and my Trust,
My Hope and Life abiding;
And to His counsel, wise and just,
I yield, in Him confiding.
The very hairs, / His Word declares,
Upon my head He numbers.
By night and day / God is my Stay,
He never sleeps nor slumbers.

3. Lord Jesus, this I ask of Thee,
Deny me not this favor:
When Satan sorely troubles me,
Then do not let me waver.
Keep watch and ward, / O gracious Lord,
Fulfill Thy faithful saying:
Who doth believe / He shall receive
An answer to His praying.

4. When life's brief course on earth is run
And I this world am leaving,
Grant me to say: "Thy will be done,"
By faith to Thee still cleaving.
My heav'nly Friend, / I now commend
My soul into Thy keeping,
O'er sin and hell, / And death as well,
Through Thee the vict'ry reaping.

—Anon., Nürnberg, ca. 1554, asc.; tr., *TLH*, 1941.

378

Tune: Von Gott will ich nicht lassen. 58. [*TLH* 393; *LW* 409; *LSB* 713]

1. My soul, why such affliction?
What can thy grief compel?
On Him set thine affection
Who's called Immanuel;
Confide in Him alone.
All wrongs to thee redressing,
He'll work thy greater blessing
From all that makes thee groan.

2. God leaves not His elected,
Nor is He left by them;
His own are not neglected,
Who firmly trust in Him;
Though strange His way appears,
Let not thyself be saddened,
Thy spirit shall be gladdened
When thy deliv'rance nears.

3. On Him thou mayest wager,
Courageous in thy mood;
He'll balance out thy ledger
With what for thee is good.
For when God wills to move,
No men or armies ever
Can hinder the endeavor,
However vast they prove.

4. Yea, though the devil bellow
And rush defiantly
With every hellish fellow
To wage his war on thee,
He soon shall be destroyed,
For 'gainst him God shall arm thee;
His scheming cannot harm thee
Since God is on thy side.

5. He does this for His glory
And also thee to save;
'Tis God's to write the story,
No matter how men rave.
But where God hath not willed,
The cause must be forsaken,
God's nay cannot be shaken.
His yea must be fulfilled.

6. To God, then, I commend me,
I trust His expertise;
All purposes offend me
But those which Him may please.
His will is ever best,
And is my purpose purely,
This I believe most surely.
Who doeth so is blest.

—J. Heermann, 1630; tr., M. Carver.

379

Tune: Zion klagt mit Angst und Schmerzen. 66. [*TLH* 268]

1. Hence, my heart, with such a notion,
As that thou art cast away!
Rein with Scripture thy devotion,
That far otherwise doth say.
Even though thou wicked art,
True and faithful is God's heart.
Though thy due is death forever,
Faint not! Christ hath gained His favor.

2. Thou art, as is every other,
Tainted by the poison, sin,
That the serpent, and our father,
Adam, by the fall brought in.
But if thou wilt turn to God
And forsake the erring road,
Fear thou not, this comfort owning:
He will not despise thy groaning.

3. He is not a bear nor lion
Only thirsting after blood,
Faithful is thy God in Zion,
Gentle ever is His mood.
Father's love His being fills,
He's afflicted by our ills,
Our misfortune sorrow gives Him,
And our dying ever grieves Him.

4. "Yea, as surely as I'm living,
No man's death do I desire,
But that he, himself up-giving,
May be rescued from sin's mire."
God's heart then with rapture burns,
When a wanderer returns,
Wills that not the least one even
Ever from His flock be driven.

5. Shepherd was so faithful never,
Seeking every sheep that strays;
Couldest thou God's heart see ever,
How for them it cares always,
How it thirsts and sighs and burns
After him who from Him turns,
From His people's midst doth wander,—
Love would make thee weep and ponder.

6. God not only loves the pious
Who within His temple dwell,
But those, too, without all bias,
Who have been made slaves to hell,
By its prince, the soul's arch-foe,
Who makes hearts with hatred glow
'Gainst the One whose step so humble
Makes the world to shake and rumble.

7. Deep His love is and enduring,
His desire is ever great;
He is calling and alluring
Us to enter heaven's gate.
When they come, whoe'er they be,
Seeking after liberty,
And the devil's yoke is riven,
God and angels joy in heaven.

8. God and all the host there dwelling,
In whose sight fails heaven's voice,
Praises to the Maker swelling,
O'er our penitence rejoice,
And God's pardon covers o'er
All the evil done before,
All by which we have offended,—
All is buried, all is mended.

9. Never ocean was so gushing,
Never depth so deep did fall,
Never flood so strong was rushing;
Next to God all things are small—
Next to God and all His love,
Which He poureth from above
Daily on our debts, assuaging
Those who still life's war are waging.

10. Why, then, art thou sad and dreary?
Rest, my soul, and be content!
Why wilt thou thyself so weary?
There's no need for such lament.
Though thy sins appear to thee
Like a vast and shoreless sea,
If thou with God's heart compare them,
'Twill a trifle seem to bear them.

11. Had a thousand worlds been fashioned
By the Most High's majesty,
And of all their sins impassioned,
Every one been done by thee,
Still they would by far be less
Than what His full light of grace
Could on earth extinguish ever!
God from greater could deliver.

12. Open, God, thy gates of favor,
Whence such tender mercies flow;
Everywhere and aye, my Savior,
Let me all Thy sweetness know.
Love me, Lord, and let me be
Nearer ever drawn to Thee,
That I may embrace and love Thee,
Nor again to anger move Thee!

—P. Gerhardt, 1653; tr., composite, but st. 9, M. Carver.

380

Tune: Freu dich sehr, o meine Seele. 66. [*TLH* 61; *LW* 28; *LSB* 347]

1. When afflictions sore oppress you,
Low with grief and anguish bowed,
Then to earnest pray'r address you;
Pray'r will help you, through the cloud
Still to see your Savior near,
Under every cross you bear;
By the light His Word doth lend you,
Pray'r will joy and comfort send you.

2. None shall ever be confounded,
Who in God will freely trust;
Though they be by woes surrounded,
God's a rock to all the just:
Though you deem He hears you not,
Still your wants are ne'er forgot:
Cry to Him when storms assail you,
Let your courage never fail you.

3. Call on God, knock, seek, implore Him,
'Tis the Christian's noblest skill;
He who comes with faith before Him,
Meets with help and favor still:
Who on God most firmly rest,
Are the wisest and the best;
God will with such strength imbue them,
Ne'er shall any foe subdue them.

4. Learn to mark God's wondrous dealing
With the people that He loves;
When His chast'ning hand they're feeling,
Then their faith the strongest proves:
God is nigh, and notes their tears,
Though He answers not, He hears;
Pray with faith, for though He try you,
No good thing can God deny you.

5. Ponder all God's truth can teach you,
Let His Word your footsteps guide;
Satan's wiles shall never reach you,
Though he draw the world aside:
Lo! God's truth is thy defense,
Light, and hope, and confidence:
Trust in God, He'll not deceive you,
Pray, and all your foes will leave you.

6. For His grace give God your praises;
His great goodness, ever true,
Stays the hand each rival raises,
Every morning it is new;
Therefore all my thanks and laud
I shall render to my God
Every moment I am living,
Joyous alleluias giving.

—J. Olearius, 1671; tr., F. E. Cox, 1841, but st. 6, M. Carver.

381

Tune: Wer Gott vertraut hat wohl gebaut. 92. [p. 417]

1. Who trusts in God / A strong abode
In heav'n and earth possesses; (*x2*)
Who looks in love / To Christ above,
No fear his heart oppresses. (*x2*)
In Thee alone, / Dear Lord, we own
Sweet hope and consolation,
Our Shield from foes, / Our Balm for woes,
Our great and sure Salvation. (*x2*)

2. Though Satan's wrath / Beset our path
And worldly scorn assail us, (*x2*)
While Thou art near, / We will not fear;
Thy strength shall never fail us. (*x2*)
Thy rod and staff / Shall keep us safe
And guide our steps forever;
Nor shades of death / Nor hell beneath
Our souls from Thee shall sever. (*x2*)

3. In all the strife / Of mortal life
Our feet shall stand securely; (*x2*)
Temptation's hour / Shall lose its pow'r,
For Thou shalt guard us surely. (*x2*)
O God, renew / With heav'nly dew
Our body, soul, and spirit
Until we stand / At Thy right hand
Through Jesus' saving merit. (*x2*)

—st. 1, J. Magdeburg, 1572; sts. 2–3, Anon., Leipzig, 1597; tr., B. H. Kennedy, 1863.

382

Tune: Wer nur den lieben Gott läßt walten. 45. [*TLH* 194; *LW* 429; *LSB* 750]

1. If thou but suffer God to guide thee
And hope in Him through all thy ways,
He'll give thee strength, whate'er betide thee,
And bear thee through the evil days.
Who trusts in God's unchanging love
Builds on the Rock that naught can move.

2. What can these anxious cares avail thee,
These never-ceasing moans and sighs?
What can it help if thou bewail thee
O'er each dark moment as it flies?
Our cross and trials do but press
The heavier for our bitterness.

3. Be patient and await His leisure
In cheerful hope, with heart content
To take whate'er thy Father's pleasure
And His discerning love hath sent,
Nor doubt our inmost wants are known
To Him who chose us for His own.

4. God knows full well when times of gladness
Shall be the needful thing for thee.
When He has tried thy soul with sadness
And from all guile has found thee free,
He comes to thee all unaware
And makes thee own His loving care.

5. Nor think amid the fiery trial
That God hath cast thee off unheard,
That he whose hopes meet no denial
Must surely be of God preferred.
Time passes and much change doth bring
And sets a bound to everything.

6. All are alike before the Highest;
'Tis easy to our God, we know,
To raise thee up, though low thou liest,
To make the rich man poor and low.
True wonders still by Him are wrought
Who setteth up and brings to naught.

7. Sing, pray, and keep His ways unswerving,
Perform thy duties faithfully,
And trust His Word, though undeserving,
Thou yet shalt find it true for thee.
God never yet forsook in need
The soul that trusted Him indeed.

—G. Neumark, 1640; tr.,C. Winkworth, 1863, alt.

383

Tune: Herr, wie du willst, so schicks mit mir. 49. [*TLH* 406; *LW* 248; *LSB* 625]

1. As God shall lead I'll take my way,
And trust His wise direction.
The path He chooses cannot stray,
Nor needs it my correction.
His guidance I will ever keep,
And cheerful follow step by step,—
As child would trust a father.

2. As God shall lead I'll follow still,
Imploring His assistance,
Though far too often my self-will
Might wish to make resistance.
Let God the way for me explore,
And I will now, and evermore,
His counsel seek to honor.

3. If God will lead me, 'tis enough,—
On Him is my reliance;
And let the road be smooth or rough,
I yield a glad compliance.
Into His hands I all commit,
That He should guide as He sees fit,
While living or while dying.

4. God leads me,—and my every change
I leave to His good pleasure:
Though Reason may pronounce it strange,
His course reveals the measure
Of good He had decreed for me
Ere ever I this world did see.
Can I refuse his guidance?

5. God leads me,—I will true remain,
Nor faith nor hope shall waver:
My spirit, if His strength sustain,
Who from His love can sever?
With confidence I'll hold it fast,
And ills, endured from first to last,
Shall work my greater blessing.

6. As God shall lead I'll onward go,
E'en where death's shadows lower.
But death shall prove a conquered foe,
His terrors lose their power;
For He, my Savior, will be there,
Who died that faith might nothing fear;—
This is my soul's firm-anchor.

—L. Gedicke, 1711; tr., H. Mills, 1856, alt.

384

Tune: Wenn wir in höchsten Nöten sein. 11. [*TLH* 141; *LW* 363; *LSB* 615]

1. How long already, highest God,
Been made to bear my heavy load!
How long my soul in misery
Has cried its ceaseless cry to Thee!

2. And yet Thou gavest no relief,
But greater only grows my grief;
With every hour it doth increase,
Nor day nor night will give me peace.

3. I've often pondered in my soul
How trickling rain can bore a hole
E'en through the hardest porphyry;
Thy heart seems harder yet to me.

4. My tears of grief like rain distill,
And o'er my cheeks in rivers spill;
Upon Thy heart they freely fall,
But cannot soften it at all.

5. O God, Thou Fountain full of grace,
Whose faithful love doth never cease,
Drop down the goodness of Thy heart,
Thy mercy to my pain impart.

6. If Thou refuse to set me free
From all my cross and misery,
Then, Lord, do Thou but mitigate
My pain, that I may bear its weight.

7. So shalt Thou do some blessed day;
Give me but patience that I may
Endure my woe, as it should be,
Nor be by sorrow turned from Thee.

8. I know that merciful Thou art,
That full of pity is Thy heart;
Therefore, O God, no longer prove
More callous than a stone to love..

9. If not to Thee my mis'ry grieve,
Who else could swear such balm to give?
And should some even deign to swear,
Who hath the pow'r my soul to spare?

10. But Thou, O God, canst mightily
From all distress deliver me;
There's no adversity too great
For Thy least word to dissipate.

11. I have sinned oft and grievously;
What man may plead His case with Thee?
Yet since Thou, Lord, hast promised grace,
Upon Thy Word I'll rest my case.

12. I'll call and cry, I'll trust in Thee,
Till from my pain I shall be free;
Though these so roughly now aggrieve,
Thy Word can never once deceive.

13. Although the world shall pass away,
Immovable and firm shall stay
What Thou hast promised in Thy Word;
Thou wilt not fail to help, O Lord!

14. And when my grief shall ended be,
I will forever joyfully
Thy helping grace and mercy praise,
Which never left me in distress.

—J. Heermann, 1630; tr., A. Crull, 1866 / M. Carver.

385

Tune: Zion klagt mit Angst und Schmerzen. 66. [*TLH* 268]

1. Zion mourns in fear and anguish,
Zion, city of our God.
"Ah," she says, "how sore I languish,
Bowed beneath the chast'ning rod!
For my God forsook me quite
And forgot my sorry plight
Mid these troubles now distressing,
Countless woes my soul oppressing."

2. "Once," she mourns, "He promised plainly
That His help should e'er be near;
Yet I now must seek Him vainly
In my days of woe and fear.
Will His anger never cease?
Will He not renew His peace?
Will He not show forth compassion
And again forgive transgression?"

3. "Zion, surely I do love thee,"
Thus to her the Savior saith,
"Though with many woes I prove thee
And thy soul is sad to death,
Yet now cast thy griefs behind;
Where wilt thou a mother find
For her own child not providing,
Or in hatred with it chiding?"

4. "And if thou couldst find a mother
Who forgot her infant's claim,
Or whose wrath her love could smother,
Yet would I be still the same;
For my truth is pledged to thee,
Zion, thou art dear to Me,
I within My heart have set Thee,
And I never can forget thee."

5. "Let not Satan make thee craven;
He can threaten, but not harm.
On My hands thy name is graven,
And thy shield is My strong arm.
How, then, could it ever be
I should not remember thee,
Fail to build thy walls, My city,
And look down on thee with pity?"

6. "Ever shall Mine eyes behold thee;
On My bosom thou art laid.
Ever shall My love enfold thee;
Never shalt thou lack Mine aid.
Neither Satan, war, nor stress
Then shall mar thy happiness:
With this blessèd consolation
Be thou firm in tribulation."

—J. Heermann, 1636; tr.,C. Winkworth, 1869, alt.

Particular Times of Need

1. GENERAL NATIONAL CALAMITY

386

Tune: Wend ab deinen Zorn. 13. [p. 417]

1. Turn back Thy wrath, dear God, and have compassion!
   Bid not Thy bloody rod to rage forever;
   Judge us not strictly after our transgression
   But Thy good favor.

2. For, didst Thou judge us after our own merit,
   What man could bear Thy fury, wrath, and lightning?
   All that Thou madest would but death inherit
   With torments fright'ning.

3. Graciously, Lord, our mortal debts forgive us,
   Let justice to Thy mercy's rule surrender;
   For as Thou lov'st us, so wilt Thou reprieve us,
   Thine be the splendor.

4. Are we but worms, yea, only dust and ashes,
   Burdened from birth by sin, by sorrows battered,
   Mortal and frail? Why, then, in wrath ungracious
   Should we be shattered?

5. Look on Thy Son, His cross, His bitter Passion,
   Who by His holy blood hath us delivered,
   Whose heart and side, for all the world's salvation,
   Freely were severed.

6. Therefore, O Father, leave us not confounded,
   Through Christ bestow Thy grace and Holy Spirit;
   Let us with Him all heav'nly joys unbounded
   Come to inherit.

—B. Gesius, asc., 1583, after *Aufer immensam*; tr., M. Carver.

387

Tune: Wenn wir in höchsten Nöten sein. 11. [*TLH* 522; *LW* 363; *LSB* 615]

1. When in the hour of utmost need
   We know not where to look for aid;
   When days and nights of anxious thought
   Nor help nor counsel yet have brought,

2. Then this our comfort is alone,
   That we may meet before Thy throne
   And cry, O faithful God, to Thee
   For rescue from our misery;

3. To Thee may raise our hearts and eyes,
Repenting sore with bitter sighs,
And seek Thy pardon for our sin
And respite from our griefs within.

4. For Thou hast promised graciously
To hear all those who cry to Thee
Through Him whose name alone is great,
Our Savior and our Advocate.

5. And thus we come, O God, today
And all our woes before Thee lay;
For sorely tried, cast down, we stand,
Perplexed by fears on every hand.

6. Ah! hide not for our sins Thy face,
Absolve us through Thy boundless grace,
Be with us in our anguish still,
Free us at last from every ill.

7. That so with all our hearts we may
To Thee our glad thanksgiving pay,
Then walk obedient to Thy Word
And now and ever praise Thee, Lord.

—P. Eber, before 1560, after J. Camerarius; tr., C. Winkworth, 1858, alt.

2. WARTIME

388

Tune: Das Jesulein soll doch mein. 83.
[p. 398; *or TLH* 437* (iso.); *LW* 414; *LSB* 714 (mel.)]

1. Grant peace, O God of faithfulness,
O Father of salvation!
Avert our great and clear distress,
Prevent all devastation.
The foe with might / Has set his sight
To battle Thy believer,
Who lauds Thy Son, / The Blessed One,
And owns Him Lord and Savior.

2. Grant peace, O Jesus, Savior dear,
Of all Thy flock Defender;
Preserve Thy pleasing worship here,
Thy work, Thy name, Thy splendor!
All this the foe / Would fain o'erthrow
And utterly abolish;
So be our Stay, / Lord Christ, this day;
In shame their works demolish.

3. Grant peace, O Holy Ghost divine,
Of all who faint Reliever,
Both now and e'er Thy help consign,
Thy Church from death deliver.
Our pray'r incite, / Our faith ignite,
To true repentance lead us;
Defeat The foe, / Thine aid bestow,
In endless joy to speed us.

—C. Schneegaß, 1595; tr., M. Carver.

389

Tune: Freu dich sehr, o meine Seele. 66. [*TLH* 61; *LW* 28; *LSB* 347]

1. God, grant peace to this Thy nation,
Where Thou dwellest with Thy Word;
Grace and health in every station,
In all places, be conferred.
Haste the war to timely end
And to us Thy concord send;
Be our Keeper and Defender,
Nothing let Thy Gospel hinder.

2. God, grant peace in Thy communion
Which extols Thy pow'r and fame,
Owning Christ in blessed union
As the only-saving Name.
Let her be at peace and safe,
Never of those blows to chafe
Which her ruthless foes endeavor;
On all sides support her ever.

3. God, grant peace in every quarter,
Where Thy Gospel is proclaimed,
Take Thy Word not from our border,
For Thy glory there is framed;
Scatter doctrines false and proud
Which Thy Word pervert and cloud;
Never let its light forsake us,
But Thy blessed children make us.

4. God, grant peace! Each moment send us
Peace while yet our life we own;
For none other can defend us,
By man's might can naught be done.
Rise, then, Christ our Lord, and come,
Captain of Thy Christendom!
Fight for us, Thy children lowly,
And defeat the foe unholy.

5. God, grant peace, and break asunder
All our foes who, fierce and wild,
Will not spare from death and plunder
E'en the young, defenseless child.
Those avenge who wrongly die,
Hear their blood for vengeance cry!
Give the foe the judgment fitted
For each sin and shame committed.

6. God, grant peace, all else surpassing,
As the godless world cannot,
Waging wars and wealth amassing,—
Thrones that fade, and robes that rot.
Prince of Peace, O Christ our Lord,
If Thou but Thy peace afford,
So shall we give Thee the glory,
Gladly praise and tell Thy story.

—Anon., Altenburg, 1655; tr., M. Carver.

3. PERSECUTION

390

Tune: Herzliebster Jesu, was hast du gebrochen. 13. [*TLH* 143; *LW* 119; *LSB* 439]

1. O Lord, our Father, shall we be confounded
Who, though by trials and by woes surrounded,
On Thee alone for help are still relying,
To Thee are crying?

2. Lord, put to shame Thy foes who breathe defiance
And vainly make their might their sole reliance;
In mercy turn to us, the poor and stricken,
Our hope to quicken.

3. Be Thou our Helper and our strong Defender;
Speak to our foes and cause them to surrender.
Yea, long before their plans have been completed,
They are defeated.

4. 'Tis vain to trust in man; for Thou, Lord, only
Art the Defense and Comfort of the lonely.
With Thee to lead, the battle shall be glorious
And we victorious.

5. Thou art our Hero, all our foes subduing;
Save Thou Thy little flock they are pursuing.
We seek Thy help; for Jesus' sake be near us.
Great Helper, hear us!

—J. Heermann, 1630; tr.,C. Winkworth, 1869, alt.

391

Tune: Ach, was soll ich Sünder machen. 36. [*TLH* 384; *LW* 364; *LSB* 559]

1. All my trust in God is grounded,
Who loves me so tenderly,
As a Father cares for me.
All my faith on Him is founded,
On my Rock that never shakes,
Nor His children e'er forsakes!

2. He knows all things that oppress me,
All my worries and dismay,
Till I die He is my Stay.
He with comforts doth caress me,
His dear love and loyalty
Ever new remain to me.

3. He who all the birds doth nourish,
Clothes the grass and tree and flow'r
Splendidly at every hour,
Grants us goods and makes us flourish,—
Shall He e'er my need forget?
Nay, I'll trust Him surely yet,

4. Seeking first His heav'nly pleasure,
By His righteousness alone
Trusting to behold His throne,
Heeding not all earthly treasure,—
Thus I find from morn to eve
Grace to prosper and believe.

5. Let each morrow bring its bother!
Ills that come can shake me not:
Christian is my happy lot!
I leave all to God my Father,
To provide whate'er I need,
For His comforts all exceed.

6. God be praised for strength and patience
In this knowledge to abide,
That my God will still provide!
God be praised for consolations
Ever new, to know that He
Loves me for eternity!

—J. Olearius, 1671; tr., M. Carver.

4. SEVERE STORM

392

Tune: Auf meinen lieben Gott. 29. [*TLH* 526; *LW* 421; *LSB* 745]

1. A tempest fills the skies!
My heart, to God arise!
Fall swiftly down before Him,
Repentant now implore Him
To cleanse thee of transgression
Through Jesus' death and Passion.

2. O Lord of clemency,
I come in faith to Thee,
With Christ in arm, to pray Thee
To let Thy mercy sway Thee;
For Him Thy grace afford me,
Nor for my sins reward me.

3. Through Jesus' precious blood,
Give me a heart, O God,
That will not doubt or waver,
But trust Thy pledge forever
With innocent persuasion,
And hope in Thy salvation.

4. Myself, my family,
I now commend to Thee;
Thy wing shall safe enfold us,
From fright and fear withhold us,
And in Thy graces arm us
Lest any storm should harm us.

5. Do not forsake us now!
Our confidence be Thou;
Give us Thy love so tender
And be our great Defender;
To Thee we'll then be giving
All praise while we are living.

—Ä. J. von Schwarzburg-Rudolstadt, 1699; tr., M. Carver.

393

Tune: Wenn wir in höchsten Nöten sein. 11. [*TLH* 141; *LW* 363; *LSB* 615]

1. The thunder peals! dear God, we plead,
Be with us in this hour of need!
Let not the tempest long abide,
For we are sorely terrified.

2. Alas, our sins, which we deplore,
Have earned this wrath and yet far more;
They add new terror day by day,
And at our conscience gnaw away.

3. O faithful God, strike not so hard;
The death of Christ our Lord regard;
The lightning bid no grievous woe
To work upon us here below.

4. O Jesus, Lord, our words convey;
So speak, that what we humbly pray
May move Thy Father; let Him see
That Thou hast done sufficiently.

5. Most Holy Trinity and blest,
Within Thy mercies let us rest,
Ensure the safety of our soul
And keep our life and being whole.

6. Oh, turn Thy wrath from us away,
And keep from ruin and decay
Our precious produce where it grows,
As roughly now this tempest blows.

7. From sea to sea our nation bless
With fortune, health, and happiness;
Let all that serves our good and gain
From heav'n in drops of mercy rain.

8. This year with goodness crown from hence,
And stir in us true confidence
With childlike faith Thy flash to see
And know that there Thy work must be.

9. Remove from us unfounded fear
Thy thunder's crashing peal to hear,
And suffer us again to view
The placid sunlight's golden hue.

10. So praying, firmly we believe
That Thou art pleased and wilt receive
Our supplication to Thy heart,
Which humbly we by hymn impart.

11. To Thee, O God the Father, Son,
And Holy Spirit, Three in One,
Divine and Holy Trinity
Be laud and praise eternally.

—J. Säubert, 1676; tr., M. Carver.

394

After the Storm

Tune: Wer nur den lieben Gott läßt walten. 45. [*TLH* 194; *LW* 429; *LSB* 750]

1. Who is a God like Thee, Jehovah?
O Lord of hosts, what God indeed
So pardons sin, forgives transgression,
And stays beside us in all need,
And even makes the dead to be?
O God, there is none else like Thee.

2. Thou hast unleashed Thy blasts of thunder,
Thy bolts of lightning called to strike,
As if to rend us all asunder.
Our sins are great and without like,
Too vast for us to understand,
More num'rous than the grains of sand.

3. We feared for lack of consolation,
Thy countenance we could not see,
We thought Thee hid from all creation,
We feared Thy wrath might boundless be.
Yet soon from sin Thou gav'st relief;
Thine anger lasts a moment brief.

4. Dear God, according to Thy pleasure,
We live, we were not left for dead;
We still enjoy Thy gracious treasure,
Thy gift to us of daily bread,
Of house and home, of beast and grain,
And all things else that life sustain.

5. For in the storm we would have perished,
Hadst Thou not held us close to Thee,
And harbored us like children cherished,
With father-hearted charity;
Thy loving nature moved Thee so:
Oh, how Thou dost Thy kindness show!

6. And now, my soul, let adoration
O'erspill thy heart to God in heav'n,
Be mindful here amid thy station
Of all the blessings He hath giv'n;
God by His hand omnipotent
Hath stilled the storm, the fury rent.

7. All that is in us swells to give Thee
Sincerest thanks, O Father true,
For though we frequently aggrieve Thee
And earn Thy rage, yet ever new
Thy tender mercies daily prove,
The hourly comforts of Thy love.

8. Oh, might we only heed Thy warning
And by our actions and our speech
Thy name with praises be adorning,
And live as Thy commandments teach;
If only we might have the pow'r
To pay our vows to Thee this hour!

9. Alas, we sinners, poor and lowly,
Though now perhaps in heightened state,
Are only men, and fragile wholly,
Too soon our pious thoughts abate,
And, heedless, we again will fall
When we had scarcely stood at all.

10. Therefore, when our life's conversation
Is not as it should rightly be,
Enclose our every bare transgression
Within Thy robes of purity;
Oh, deal with us in gracious care
And patiently our faults forbear!

11. When heaven's trumps, their duty keeping,
To men shall sound the final eve,
Let us on earth, or in it sleeping,
Thine echoing cry of grace perceive:
"Come, O ye blest in Jesus' name,
Your readied kingdom now to claim!"

12. Oh, might we only now behold Thee
Within Thy presence, face to face,
And join Thy flocks that round enfold Thee
Where Thou shalt keep them in Thy grace!
Yet in this time our hearts prepare
And bring us to salvation there.

—L. E. von Schwarzburg-Rudolstadt, †1672; tr., M. Carver.

5. SEVERE DROUGHT

395

Tune: Wo Gott der Herr nicht bei uns hält. 49. [p. 418]

1. Alas, O Lord, Thou righteous God,
'Tis just that for our sinning
The heavens should withhold their flood,
Nor field its fruit be winning,
And sorrow fill both man and beast;
When at Thy will the rains are ceased
We quickly must be fainting.

2. Our sins, O Lord, to Thee we own,
And pray Thee to forgive us;
Our hope we find in Thee alone,
So comfort and relieve us.
Our thirsty land with showers slake
And bless us for Thy good name's sake
O Lord, our God and Comfort.

3. Recall, O Lord, Thy covenant,
For Thy name's sake we're crying;
Receive our deepest heart's lament
And still our cause for sighing
By sending rain from heaven down,
For heav'n is subject to Thy crown,
And cannot rain without Thee.

4. There is no other God but Thou,
Who hast the pow'r to will it,
Who heaven dost with rain endow,
And with Thy presence fill it.
Almighty is Thy name on high,
All this alone Thou canst supply,
O Lord, our God and Comfort.

5. May we henceforth devoted be
O God, to Thee forever!
Equip us by Thy Spirit free
Thy will to trespass never,
Peace-offerings to lift on high,
Thy name to laud and glorify,
Through Christ our Savior. Amen.

—Anon., Greifswald, 1592; tr., M. Carver.

Death and Burial

396

Prayer for a Peaceful and Blessed Death

Tune: Herr Jesu Christ, du höchstes Gut. 49. [p. 404]

1. Oh, God! as now I contemplate
How all that's flesh must wither,
And mark how piteous is the fate
Of many‿a soul gone thither,—
O Father, now on Thee I call,
Whose grace and pow'r are best of all
And who alone canst help me.

2. That I must die, this well I know,
Though yet the hour be hidden;
So grant me faith, and let me show
Repentance, as I'm bidden;
Both now and ever let me be
Prepared to journey home to Thee,
Whenever Thou wilt call me.

3. Lay not presumption to my charge
If I would fain endeavor
To ask of Thee what is too large
For man to grant me ever.
Oh, keep, I pray, by grace alone
My body free from ache and groan,
And let me not grow weary.

4. O God, whatever happens hence,
From sudden death defend me;
Let not impatience, loss of sense,
Or dark despair attend me.
Grant me a space sufficient long
That over all my sin and wrong
I may in faith have sorrow.

5. Thy precious Holy Spirit send
To govern and to guide me,
To comfort me until my end,
And with true faith provide me,
That but the blood of Christ my Lord,
Which for my sake was freely poured,
May for my good avail me.

6. Help, Savior, help in death's distress,
Nor grant me long to suffer;
May Thou in faithful grace possess
My soul, which here I offer.
Make brief my woe, my pain allay,
That when I see my end, I may
Depart in peace and gladness.

—Anon., Hannover, 1646; tr., M. Carver.

397

Tune: Alle Menschen müssen sterben. 68. [*TLH* 601]

1. All men living are but mortal,
Yea, all flesh must fade as grass;
Only through death's gloomy portal
To eternal life we pass.
This frail body here must perish
Ere the heav'nly joys it cherish,
Ere it gain the free reward
For the ransomed of the Lord.

2. Therefore, when my God doth choose it,
Willingly I'll yield my life
Nor will grieve that I should lose it,
For with sorrows it was rife.
In my dear Redeemer's merit
Peace hath found my troubled spirit,
And in death my comfort this:
Jesus' death my source of bliss.

3. Jesus for my sake descended
My salvation to obtain;
Death and hell for me are ended,
Peace and hope are now my gain;
Yea, with joy I leave earth's sadness
For the home of heav'nly gladness,
Where I shall forever see
God, the Holy Trinity.

4. There is joy beyond our telling,
Where so many saints have gone;
Thousands, thousands, there are dwelling,
Worshiping before the throne,
There the Seraphim are shining,
Evermore in chorus joining:
"Holy, holy, holy, Lord!
Triune God, for aye adored!"

5. Patriarchs of sacred story
And the prophets there are found;
The apostles, too, in glory
On twelve seats are there enthroned.
All the saints that have ascended
Age on age, through time extended,
There in blissful concert sing
Alleluias to their King.

6. O Jerusalem, how glorious
Dost thou shine, thou city fair!
Lo, I hear the tones victorious
Ever sweetly sounding there.
Oh, the bliss that there surprises!
Lo, the sun of morn now rises,
And the breaking day I see
That shall never end for me.

7. Yea, I see what here was told me,
See that wondrous glory shine,
Feel the spotless robes enfold me,
Know a golden crown is mine.
Thus before the throne so glorious
Now I stand a soul victorious,
Gazing on that joy for aye
That shall never pass away.

—J. G. Albinus, 1652; tr., C. Winkworth, 1863, alt., but st. 5, *Ohio,* 1880, alt.

398

Tune: Valet will ich dir geben. 59. [*TLH* 58; *LW* 79; *LSB* 442]

1. The end, O mortal, ponder,
Yea, ponder now thy death;
Death soon may draw thee under
And steal away thy breath;
Today thy lip is ruddy,
Tomorrow it may sigh;
So, sinner, make thy study
Each day, how thou shalt die.

2. The end, O mortal, ponder,
Oh, ponder judgment day!
When great and small shall yonder
Their judge in Christ survey;
Excuse will not be given,
Each man must thither go
To be repaid in heaven
As he hath done below.

3. The end, O mortal, ponder,
Hell's anguish and distress,
Lest thou thy vision squander
With Satan's pridefulness.
Here brief is every gladness,
But ever echoes there
The howls of pain and sadness;
Oh, sinner, then beware.

4. The end, O mortal, ponder,
Oh, ponder e'er the days
Lest Thou of aught be fonder
Than that most glorious grace
Which to the soul is given,
To stand before God's throne,
Where faithful souls in heaven
Receive the victor's crown.

5. O Lord, teach me to ponder
All that the End shall bring,
That naught my heart may sunder
From following my King;
Instruct me to think rightly
Of death and Judgment Day,
Nor let me reckon lightly
Hell's flame without decay.

6. O Christ, with sorrow steady
Supply me that I may
For death stand ever ready,
To meet it any day!
In death be my Defender,
In judgment be my Stay,
That I in heaven's splendor
May dwell with Thee for aye.

—S. Liscow, asc., Braunschweig, 1686; tr., M. Carver.

399

Tune: Vater unser im Himmelreich. 44. [*TLH* 318; *LW* 234; *LSB* 766]

1. Christ is the Truth and Life, and He
The resurrection brings to be.
He that believes in Him shall live,
Though here his flesh must death receive;
Who lives, believes, and gives Him praise
Shall never die for endless days.

—M. Luther, 1542, after John 11:25; tr., M. Carver.

400

Tune: Christus, der ist mein Leben. 2. [*TLH* 597; *LW* 267; *LSB* 742]

1. For me to live is Jesus,
To die is gain for me;
Then, whensoe'er He pleases,
I meet death willingly.

2. For Christ, my Lord and Brother,
I leave this world so dim
And gladly seek that other,
Where I shall be with Him.

3. My woes are nearly over,
Though long and dark the road;
My sin His merits cover,
And I have peace with God.

4. Lord, when my pow'rs are failing,
My breath comes heavily,
And words are unavailing,
Oh, hear my sighs to Thee!

5. When mind and thought, O Savior,
Are flick'ring like a light
That to and fro doth waver
Ere 'tis extinguished quite,

6. In that last hour, oh, grant me
To slumber soft and still,
No doubts to vex or haunt me,
Safe anchored on Thy will;

7. And so to Thee still cleaving
Through all death's agony,
To fall asleep believing
And wake in heav'n with Thee.

8. Amen! Thou, Christ, my Savior,
Wilt grant this unto me.
Thy Spirit lead me ever
That I fare happily.

—Anon., 1609, 1612; tr. sts. 1–7, C. Winkworth, 1863, alt.; st. 8, Anon.

401

At the Burial of Children and Infants
(For a Son)

Tune: Ermuntre dich, mein schwacher Geist. 67. [*LSB* 378]

1. Mine art thou still, and mine shalt be,
Who will this be denying?
Yet I lay not sole claim to thee;
The Lord of Life undying,
Who hath a stronger right than mine,
Hath called thee hence, and I resign
Thee, O my son, my treasure,
My heart's delight and pleasure!

2. If wish availed, my soul's sweet star!
Thee would I rather cherish,
And lose what riches else there are,
And let earth's pleasures perish;
Oh, fain I'd say: Abide with me,
The glory of my house to be,
I shall love thee forever,
Till death itself us sever.

3. So speaks my heart, and means it well,
But God doth mean still better;
And though in me great love may dwell,
In God there dwells still greater.
I am a father, nothing more,
Of fathers He the crown and pow'r,
The fount and loving tether
Of young and old together.

4. I long full sorely for my child,
But He who once hath given,
Wills that, no more by sin defiled,
He live with Him in heaven.
I say, "Alas! my light is gone!"
God says, "I bid thee welcome, son!
Here I'll be ever near thee
And ever richly cheer thee!"

5. O kind decree, O word of grace,
More holy than conceiving;
With God no evil has a place,
No sorrow, no bereaving.
There come no sickness, want, or care,
No hurt can ever reach him there;
Those in God's love and caring
Will never be despairing.

6. We men much thought and time expend
On our dear ones' adorning;
And all our anxious efforts bend
By evening, noon, and morning,
To gain for them a happy place;
And yet how seldom 'tis the case
They reach the destination
We had in contemplation.

7. How many‿a young and noble heart,
By bad example straying,
Has come to choose the baser part,
The Christian way betraying;
Oh, fearful are his wages then,
The wrath of God, the scorn of men!
The father must with grieving
Regret his child thus leaving.

8. Now such can never be my case,
My son is safely yonder,
Where he may stand before God's face,
And in Christ's garden wander,
There his is pleasure unexpressed,
From every heartache he hath rest;
He sees and hears so glorious
The hosts who here watch o'er us.

9. He sees and hears the angels sing,
With them his voice is blending;
He drinks of wisdom from the Spring;
He speaks of things transcending
What we can ever learn or know
With all our searching here below;
To none on earth 'tis given,
Reserved it is for heaven.

10. Ah! if afar I could but stand,
And hear a moment faintly
Thy voice upraised amid the band
That sings the praises saintly
To th' holy, holy, holy God
Who hallows thee, His name to laud,
So glad, I know, 'twould make me,
That tears would overtake me.

11. Then would I say, "There blest abide,
And I will cease repining."
Alas, wert thou but by my side!
Nay, rather, come thou shining
Swift chariot of Elijah on,
And bear me thither where my son,
With all the blest surrounding,
Doth speak of things astounding.

12. So let it be, and so remain!
No more these tears I'll pour thee;
Thou liv'st in bliss that will not wane,
Pure sunlight shines before thee;—
The sun of endless joy and rest,
Abide thou, then, where thou art blest;
God willing, I will wander
Ere long to find thee yonder.

—P. Gerhardt, 1650; tr., composite.

402

Tune: Wenn mein Stündlein vorhanden ist. 49.
[*TLH* 594; *or LW* 230*; *TLH* 329*; *LSB* 607*]

1. A wretched thing, and full of woe,
Here I in death must languish;
In life and death no balm I know
To rid me of this anguish,
Save this alone, Lord Jesus Christ:
Thou, too, wast wretched and despised!
O God, receive my crying!

2. O Christ my Lord, let me abide
A branch in Thee, and flourish;
When soul and body must divide,
Thy Spirit send to nourish
My soul, and let Him be my stay,
When life departs and limbs decay
And naught on earth remaineth.

3. Then let me not in this distress
Despair and sadly languish;
But come, O God of faithfulness,
And help me bear my anguish;
Rememb'ring me, Thy member own,
A sprig upon Thy body grown,
And in Thy peace receive me.

4. Thine oath, O Lord, do not forget,
Thy promise keep and cherish:
As surely as Thou livest yet,
I surely shall not perish,
Nor e'er to condemnation fall,
Nor taste eternal death at all;
Salvation Thou wilt show me.

5. O God, Thy Word let be my light,
To life eternal guiding;
Bestow a blessed end and bright.
In Thee I'll be confiding;
Lord, Thee alone I'll trust and heed,
For Thou forsakest none in need
Who hope in Thee to help them.

6. Now I commend into Thy hand
My soul through Jesus' merit;
O faithful God, beside me stand,
Take not away Thy Spirit;
And when I may no longer speak,
Accept my final sigh, though weak,
Through Jesus Christ, my Savior.

—B. Frölich, 1587; tr., M. Carver.

403

Tune: Es ist genug, so nimm, Herr. 52. [*TLH* 196; *LW* 145; *LSB* 468]

1. It is enough! O Lord, my soul now take
To Zion's home on high;
Dissolve the bonds that slowly, slowly break,
And let my spirit fly,
Which for its God is sorely sighing,
With nightly tears and daily crying,
It is enough! It is enough!

2. It is enough of this my wretchedness!
Old Adam's gluttony,
That bane of sin, doth all my life oppress.
No good thing dwells in me.
Of that which me from God doth sever,
Of that which me defileth ever,
It is enough. It is enough.

3. It is enough of cross, and its disgrace,
And back bent lowly down;
O God, how harsh, how heavily it weighs!
How many‿a night I drown
My couch with bitter tears and weeping.
When shall I cease this vigil keeping?
When is enough? When is enough?

4. It is enough when Jesus so decides;
My heart He knoweth well.
I cling to Him, my soul in peace abides
Until He shall dispel
From out my breast this gnawing sorrow
And say to me some joyous morrow:
"It is enough! It is enough!"

5. It is enough! Lord, when Thou thinkest right,
Take me from worldly woe!
My Jesus comes! I bid thee, world, good night!
To heaven I will go!
I will depart in peace and gladness,
And leave on earth my tears of sadness.
It is enough! It is enough!

—F. J. Burmeister, 1662; tr., M. Carver, but st. 2, A. Crull, 1866, alt.

404

Tune: Freu dich sehr, o meine Seele. 66. [*TLH* 61; *LW* 28; *LSB* 347]

1. O rejoice, my soul, and rid thee
Of all ling'ring pain and woe,
Christ thy Lord doth call, and bid thee
From this vale of mis'ry go—
Go from sorrow and distress,
Into joy and happiness,
Such as ear hath heard of never,
And that will endure forever.

2. Day and night I have been crying
To my dearest Lord and God,
That He might be help supplying
In my heavy cross and load.
As a pilgrim long who wends
Yearns for when his journey ends,
Even so is my desiring
Now from earth to be retiring.

3. Like as mingled are the roses
In among the prickly thorn,
So the Christian's way imposes
Through the thick of fear and scorn;
Like as waves of water roll
And the restless breezes howl,
So on earth our conversation
Overflows with aggravation.

4. World and sin, hell, death, and devil,
Flesh and blood that in us dwell,
Never cease to work their evil,
Grant our souls no quiet spell;
Ours is anguish and dismay,
Naught but cross from day to day;
Earth is full of pain and aching,
Even at our first awaking.

5. When the morning dawn hath broken,
Driving slumber from our eyes,
Cares and sorrows, too, are woken,
From each shadow worries rise.
Here our weeping is the bread
On which we are ever fed;
When the sun withdraws its shining,
All is but lament and pining.

6. Christ, Thou Morning Star, I pray Thee,
Dayspring of eternity,
Close beside me now convey me,
For Thy blood hath ransomed me.
Help me now in peace and joy
To depart from earth's annoy;
Be my Light and Path to take me,
Be my Escort, ne'er forsake me.

7. In Thy side my refuge taking,
I will walk death's bitter path,
Through Thy wounds I will be waking
Home in heaven after death;
And fair Paradise I'll see,
Where the robber came to be;
Thou, Lord Jesus, wilt receive me
And eternal glory give me.

8. Though mine eyes grow dim and darken,
Though my tongue lose pow'r to speak,
Though mine ears no longer hearken,
Though my mind and sense grow weak,
Thou shalt be my Light and Stay,
Gate of heav'n, and living Way,
Graciously Thou wilt direct me
To my home, and well protect me.

9. Let Thine angels close attend me
On Elias' chariot red,
Refuge for my soul then send me,
As Thou didst for Laz'rus dead;
Let it in Thy bosom rest,
Give it joys and comforts best,
Till with flesh, from dust returning,
It is joined and ceases yearning.

10. O rejoice, my soul, and rid thee
Of all ling'ring pain and woe;
Christ thy Lord doth call, and bid thee
From this vale of mis'ry go;
Thou shalt see His joy and pow'r
And His glory evermore,
With the choirs of angels blending
Songs of triumph never-ending.

—Freiberg (Sax.), before 1620; tr., M. Carver, but st. 9, C. S. Terry, 1917, alt.; st. 10b, Anon., alt.

405

At the Burial of Young Infants

Tune: O Welt, ich muß dich lassen. 31. [*TLH* 126; *LW* 85; *LSB* 880]

1. Praise God, this hour of sorrow
Shall bring a brighter morrow:
I go to Paradise.
My mother dear and father,
When round my grave you gather,
Lay me to rest with songs of praise.

2. What better can befall me
Than that the Lord doth call me
From hence, where sin holds sway?
Who is on earth a stranger
Must ever be in danger,
Till God hath closed life's fleeting day.

3. My days of grief are ended,
The aches and pains amended
Which weighed so heavily;
God from the world withdrew me
Before they could subdue me
With ever-mounting agony.

4. Brief though my earthly dwelling,
God gives me life excelling
In His eternity;
There I will know no dying,
Nor in distress be lying:
My life will utter gladness be.

5. God takes His own from anguish
And pain, in which they languish
Within this vale of tears,
And gives them to inherit
The crown that Christ did merit:
The joy of heav'n's eternal years.

6. Often temptation taketh
A child, and he forsaketh
All piety and right;
The world, with craft abetting,
Its hidden snares is setting
At every hour, by day and night.

7. Now what of their devices?
I have escaped their guises,
My soul they cannot lure;
Now who can harm or fret me,
Since Christ hath safely set me
Within His castle strong and sure?

8. I was on earth your treasure;
When now I know but pleasure
Ye weep in bitter woe;
Believe, whate'er betideth,
God's love in all abideth,
And soon your tears shall cease flow.

9. Our days the Lord appointeth,
He woundeth and anointeth,
He knoweth all things well.
No evil He effected,
No good He e'er neglected,
And all His works His glory tell.

10. When ye shall see me nearing
The throne of God, appearing
Adorned and crowned a bride,
My palms of vict'ry swinging,
Midst alleluias ringing,
In beauteous grace the Lamb beside:

11. Ye both shall rue the sadness
That made you weep, and gladness
E'er in your hearts shall reign.
Who follows where God guideth,
And takes what He provideth,
Shall know surcease from all his pain.

12. Farewell, I now must leave you;
The grief this day doth give you
Soon others, too, shall bear.
Be ye to God commended;
In heav'n all woe is ended,
And we shall meet in glory there.

—J. Heermann, 1634. / H. A. Brorson, 1714; tr. sts. 1–2, 5, 8–12, O. H. Smeby, 1904; sts. rest, M. Carver.

406

(See # 85.)

407

Tune: Herr Jesu Christ, wahr Mensch und Gott. 11.
[p. 404; *or TLH* 141*; *LW* 363*; *LSB* 615*]

1. Lord Jesus Christ, true Man and God,
Who borest anguish, scorn, the rod,
And diedst at last upon the tree,
To bring Thy Father's grace to me:

2. I pray Thee, through that bitter woe,
Let me, a sinner, mercy know,
When comes the hour of failing breath,
And I must wrestle, Lord, with death,

3. When from my sight all fades away,
And when my tongue no more can say,
And when mine ears no more can hear,
And when my heart is racked with fear,

4. When all my mind is darkened o'er,
And human help can do no more;
Then come, Lord Jesus, come with speed,
And help me in the hour of need.

5. Lead me from this dark vale beneath,
And shorten then the pangs of death;
All evil spirits drive away,
But let Thy Spirit with me stay,

6. Until my soul the body leave;
Then in Thy hands my soul receive,
And let the earth the body keep,
Till the Last Day shall break its sleep.

7. Joyful my resurrection be,
Thou in the Judgment plead for me,
And hide my sins, Lord, from Thy face,
And give me Life, of Thy dear grace!

8. Implicitly I trust Thee, Lord,
For Thou hast promised in Thy Word:
"In truth I tell you, who receives
My Word, and keeps it, and believes,

9. Shall never fall God's wrath beneath,
Shall never taste eternal death;
Though here he must return to dust,
He still is noways therefore lost;

10. For I will with a mighty hand
Deliver him from death's strong band,
And lift him hence that he shall be
Forever in My realm with Me,

11. Forever living there in bliss."
O let us not that glory miss!
Dear Lord, forgive us all our guilt,
Help us to wait until Thou wilt

12. That we depart; and let our faith
Be brave and conquer e'en in death,
Firm resting on Thy sacred Word,
Until we sleep in Thee, our Lord.

—P. Eber, 1557; tr., C. Winkworth, 1861, alt.

408

Tune: Nun laßt uns den Leib begraben. 11. [*TLH* 596; *LW* 382; *LSB* 759]

1. Now hush your cries and shed no tear,
On such death none should look with fear;
He died a faithful Christian man,
And with his death true life began.

2. The grave and coffin decked with care,
His body rev'rently we bear;
It is not dead, but rests in God,
And softly sleeps beneath the sod.

3. It seems as all were over now,—
The heavy limbs, the soulless brow,—
Yet through these rigid limbs once more
A noble life, ere long, shall pour.

4. These bones, now dead, again shall feel
New warmth and vigor thro' them steal;
And reunited they shall soar
On high to live forevermore.

5. This body, lying stiff and stark,
Shall soon rise upward from the dark,
And swiftly mount up to the skies,
E'en as the spirit heav'nward flies.

6. The buried grain of wheat must die,
Withered and worthless long must lie,
Yet springs to light all sweet and fair,
And proper fruits shall richly bear:

7. E'en so this body, made of dust,
To earth we once again entrust,
Where it shall slumber free from pain,
Till from the dead it rise again.

8. God breathed into this house of clay
The spirit that hath passed away;
The righteous mind, the noble heart,
The living faith did Christ impart.

9. Now earth has hid it from our eyes,
Till God shall bid it wake and rise,
Who ne'er the creature will forget,
On whom His image He hath set.

10. Ah! would that promised Day were here
When Christ will once again appear
And bring them to their heav'nly home
Who have been buried in the tomb!

—Anon., Frankfurt a. O., 1561, after Prudentius; tr., C. Winkworth, 1861, alt.

409

Tune: Herzlich tut mich verlangen. 59. [*TLH* 172; *LW* 113; *LSB* 450]

1. A Pilgrim and a stranger
On earth I journey here;
Through many‿a mile and danger
My fatherland I near.
On ranging paths I wander
Oft weary and oppressed,
But God shall lead me yonder
To everlasting rest.

2. What hath my whole existence
From youth been to this day,
But toiling with persistence
And trouble all the way?
How many‿a morn of anguish,
How many‿a weary night
In sorrow did I languish,
My heart by care squeezed tight!

3. I've met with storms and danger,
With thunder, wind, and rain,
With foe and hostile stranger,
With fightings, fears, and pain.
No comfort was I offered
But spite and enmity,
Which wrongly I have suffered,
And yet borne patiently

4. So lived the honored fathers
In whose footsteps we tread,
From whom the saint oft gathers
The wisdom he may need.
Of trial what full measure
Had father Abraham,
Ere he attained his pleasure,
To his right dwelling came!

5. How rough, too, and uneven
The way that Isaac trod!
And Jacob, who had striven
And had prevailed with God,—
What bitter grief and wearing
Felt he, what woe and smart!
In fear and in despairing
Oft sank his fainting heart.

6. The saints were ever driven,
And onward made to roam;
With agony, for heaven
To leave their wonted home,
They went by roads asunder,
Great crosses bore each day,
Till death had put them under
And in the grave they lay.

7. To e'en such joy and sadness
My days devoted are;
Or should I know more gladness
Than men more famed by far?
Here must we suffer ever,
Here must we onward press;
Who strives not here shall never
Find rest in blessedness.

8. My life, tow'rd heav'n excelling,
Shall thus on earth be plied;
Within this foreign dwelling
I would not long abide.
Along the paths I wander
That lead me to my home,
God boundless comfort yonder
Will give me when I come.

9. My home is high above me,
Where all the angel bands
Praise Him who deigns to love me,—
The Ruler, in whose hands
All things in all creation
Are held and harbored still,
In every generation
According to His will.

10. For home my heart has fainted,
'Tis there I long to be,
The world by time so tainted
Now almost wearies me.
The longer I remain here
The less delight I taste,
My spirit to allay here;—
Nigh all is arid waste.

11. Too faulty is the dwelling,
Too many the laments,
Come, God, when Thou art willing,
And free my heart from hence!
Come, make a blessed ending
Of this my pilgrim hour,
My every ill amending,
Lord, by Thine arm and pow'r.

12. This present habitation
Is not my proper home;
When I have filled my station,
Then forth from it I'll come.
What here I've needed ever
I'll then put all away;
When soul and body sever,
Me in the grave they'll lay.

13. Thou, O my Joy and Glory,
Thou of my life the Light,
Wilt usher me before Thee
To mansions glad and bright,
Where in joy everlasting
E'en as the sun I'll shine,
With all my brethren tasting
Of pleasures all divine.

14. There I shall dwell forever,
No more a parting guest,
With all whom Thou, our Savior,
Wilt crown and cause to rest.
I'll sing with voice exalted
Thine every mighty deed,
Enjoying peace unhalted,
From earthly sorrows freed.

—P. Gerhardt, 1666; tr., composite.

410

Tune: O Ewigkeit, du Donnerwort. 70. [p. 412]

1. O Lord I lie within Thy might;
Thou broughtest me to see Thy light,
My life not once forsaking.
Thou know'st the number of my years,
Know'st, too, when from this vale of tears
I must my leave be taking;
Where, how, and when I am to die—
These all within Thy knowledge lie.

2. Whom have I now but Thee alone,
Who knowest how to soothe the groan
Of death with comforts living?
Who else could my weak soul defend
As soon with death I must contend
In battle unforgiving,
As all my powèrs dwindle now?
O God, my Savior, who but Thou?

3. It seems I see me, lying still,
In fever dire, so faint and ill,
With anguish sorely stricken;
My voice, my senses all grow numb,
My eyes to gravish dark succumb,
Sin's plagues around me thicken;
The foe's accusings never end,
Temptations sore my soul offend.

4. I hear the trumpet's blast and see
God's Judgment closing speedily,
With peals of condemnation;
My conscience cries its ghastly verse,
In chorus with the Law's dread curse:
"O child of sore transgression!
To hell with thee, where evermore
The sinner doth his pain deplore."

5. No wealth or wares our freedom gain,
A brother's offer stands in vain;
His death cannot reprieve us.
And so it is eternally:
We nevermore shall wander free,
Once Hades' jaws receive us.
Who'll save me from their venomed breath,
If not Thou, God, O Death of death?

6. The devil hath no right to me;
'Gainst Thee I've sinned, yea, only Thee,
And Thou my sin remittest.
What cause hath Satan then to rage?
He cannot sue, nor sin allege;
Thou, Judge, in my stead sittest.
So let him take what's his alone;
I know that Christ my soul doth own.

7. Lord Jesus, as Thy treasure good
I testify this with Thy blood:
Sin hath no powèr o'er me;
Yet Satan grants me no relief
From Sinaï and all its grief!
Oh, save Thy Passion's glory!
Thou canst surrender me to none,
For all Thy death hath cost and won.

8. Nay, nay, my Savior, well I know,
That I, Thine heir, can safely go
Where Thou wast cut asunder,
And safely in Thy hollows hide,
All worldly terrors to deride,
Though hell and death may thunder.
While yet I lived I e'er was Thine;
To no Lord else can I resign.

—S. Dach, 1648; tr., M. Carver.

411

Tune: Herzlich tut mich verlangen. 59. [*TLH* 172; *LW* 113; *LSB* 450]

1. A little child born lately
Upon this earth was I,
Yet God had long appointed
That I so soon should die.
I have no worldly knowledge,
Know not its thoughts and ways,
Learned not of good and evil,
Of curses and of praise.

2. My father, dearest father,
'Twas thou begottest me,
And oh, my tend'rest mother,
I nurtured was by thee!
Farewell ye both now bid me
With bitter, heavy sighs,
Yet Jesus Christ, my Savior,
Has claimed me as His prize.

3. He brings me to His kingdom
An heir in grace arrayed;
Death has no pow'r to hurt me,
Like angels I am made;
My flesh again shall quicken
In peace and endless joy,
And, with my soul united,
Know bliss without alloy.

4. God bless you, O my parents!
Of troubles I know naught,
A tender shoot transplanted
To Paradise's plot.
There we shall see each other,
Our joy shall not be small,
When God His own shall gather,
And be our All in all.

—Anon., Freiberg (Sax.), 1620; tr., M. Carver.

412

Tune: Vater unser im Himmelreich. 44. [*TLH* 318; *LW* 234; *LSB* 766]

1. I fall asleep in Jesus' wounds,
There pardon for my sins abounds;
Yea, Jesus' blood and righteousness
My jewèls are, my glorious dress.
In these before my God I'll stand
When I shall reach the heav'nly land.

2. With peace and joy I now depart;
God's child I am with all my heart.
I thank thee, death, thou leadest me
To that true life where I would be.
So cleansed by Christ, I fear not death.
Lord Jesus, strengthen Thou my faith.

—Anon., Leipzig, 1638; tr., C. Winkworth, 1869, alt.

413

Tune: Zion klagt mit Angst und Schmerzen. 66. [*TLH* 268]

1. Cease, oh, cease, my friends, your weeping,
Let your grief no more endure.
Why your sorrow thus be keeping,
Since for me this thing is sure?
All my pain and trouble past,
I am home with God at last,
Where, in joy that ceases never,
With the blest I live forever.

2. Save your sorrow and lamenting
For the dead in hell aggrieved,
In such tortures unrelenting
As can scarcely be conceived;
For those souls whom God doth call
To Himself in heaven's hall,
All their thirsts with joy relieving—
Who for them could e'er be grieving?

3. In the wounds of Christ my Savior
Safely closed, I take my rest;
Here my soul possesses ever
That which makes it saved and blessed.
Christ, my Righteousness, avails
In God's sight and never fails;
Naught from heaven may be bringing
Those in faith to Jesus clinging.

4. Let none call me thus forsaken,
Though by death I have been slain;
'Tis but God my soul hath taken
And made death my utter gain.
From distress and tragedy
God my Father rescued me;
Nevermore in grief to languish,
I've forgotten all my anguish.

5. On its bed my body slumbers,
Free from sorrow, soft and still,
Deaf to what the ear encumbers,—
Earthly noises, empty thrill,—
While my soul that face beholds,
Who His own in love enfolds,
Who into His bosom draws me,
And with highest bliss endows me.

6. All the world is full of horrors:
Famine, pestilence, and strife,
And all manner else of sorrows
With which sinful man is rife.
Without warning flies a dart
And impales a Christian's heart.—
Oh, but thus to die in blessing
Far excels that life distressing.

7. Rescue from all woe hath found me,
Here is nothing more to fear;
Peace and gladness now surround me,
There's no foe can hurt me here.
Now forevermore I stand
Safe within My Savior's hand,
Who made me His own possession
By His bitter crucifixion.

8. Now to Him I here commend you,
Called your Father God above,
Who counts all the tears that stained you,
And whose heart burns hot with love.
Comforts He shall send sublime
In your woes, and, in His time,
He to where I am shall take you
And with highest glory deck you.

9. O my dearest friends, still weeping
In the world, your Champion see!
Safe your souls the Son is keeping
From your every enemy.
Only to your Lord be true,
Daily are His mercies new.
They that harm the grieved and shattered
Like the stubble shall be scattered.

10. Then not even death shall sever
Or divide us, like as now.
God Himself will feed us ever
With delight on Zion's brow:
Here we shall in paradise
Join as one our joyous cries
To our God with glad thanksgiving,
Like the angels, ever-living.

—J. Heermann, 1636; tr., M. Carver.

414

Tune: Lasset die Kindlein kommen. 58. [p. 409]

1. "Suffer the children tender
To come to Me," Christ says;
"They are My joy and splendor,
I am their Shield and Praise;
Yea, I who love them well
Was born a child and given
To make them Mine in heaven,
And rescue them from hell."

2. The Lord His children loveth,
And greets them tenderly,
And with sweet pledges proveth
That heaven theirs shall be,
For His most precious blood,
Which from His wounds so holy
Flowed for all sinners lowly,
Is also for their good.

3. So as our Lord desireth,
Let them to Him be brought,
Where each His grace acquireth:
Forbid the children not!
Let Christ their keeper be;
He will His mercy show them,
And in His arms endow them
With peace eternally.

4. Though here in time they perish,
God doth their souls receive
And high in heaven cherish,
As worldly woes they leave,
To be His very own:
No longer here they suffer,
But praises gladly offer
With angels round God's throne.

—C. Becker, 1611; tr., M. Carver.

415

To Be Sung by a Young Child Near Death

Tune: Herr Jesu Christ, meins Lebens Licht. 11. [*TLH* 288; *LW* 262; *LSB* 704]

1. With joy my journey now I take,
Death is my gain for Jesus' sake,
My goal, praise God! that place I make
Where I in utter bliss shall wake—

2. To my dear Father, God alone,
To Christ, true Man and God in one,
To angels bright around the throne,
With whom eternal joy is known.

3. Though sep'rate ways we here must go,
Above shall meet who part below;
Amen, Amen, God make it so,
And save us all from every woe!

—Anon., Gotha, 1648; tr., M. Carver.

416

Tune: Mitten wir im Leben sind. 27. [*TLH* 590; *LW* 265; *LSB* 755 (mel.)]

1. In the midst of earthly life
Snares of death surround us;
Who shall help us in the strife
Lest the foe confound us?
Thou only, Lord, Thou only!
We mourn that we have greatly erred,
That our sins Thy wrath have stirred.
Holy and righteous God!
Holy and mighty God!
Holy and all-merciful Savior!
Eternal Lord God!
Save us lest we perish
In the bitter pangs of death.
Kyrieleison!

2. In the midst of death's dark vale
Pow'rs of hell o'ertake us.
Who will help when they assail,
Who secure will make us?
Thou only, Lord, Thou only!
Thy heart is moved with tenderness,
Pities us in our distress.
Holy and righteous God!
Holy and mighty God!
Holy and all-merciful Savior!
Eternal Lord God!
Save us from the terror
Of the fiery pit of hell.
Kyrieleison!

3. In the midst of utter woe
When our sins oppress us,
Where shall we for refuge go,
Where for grace to bless us?
To Thee, Lord Jesus, only!
Thy precious blood was shed to win
Full atonement for our sin.
Holy and righteous God!
Holy and mighty God!
Holy and all-merciful Savior!
Eternal Lord God!
Lord, preserve and keep us
In the peace that faith can give.
Kyrieleison!

—M. Luther, 1524; st. 1 after *Media vita in morte*; tr., *TLH*, 1941.

417

To Be Sung at the Grave

Tune: Nun laßt uns den Leib begraben. 11. [*TLH* 596; *LW* 382; *LSB* 759]

CHOIR

1. This body in the grave we lay,
There to await that solemn Day
When God Himself shall bid it rise
To mount triumphant to the skies.

2. And so to earth we now entrust
What came from dust and turns to dust
And from the dust shall rise that Day
In glorious triumph o'er decay.

3. The soul forever lives with God,
Who freely hath His grace bestowed
And through His Son redeemed it here
From every sin, from every fear.

4. All trials and all griefs are past,
A blessed end has come at last.
Christ's yoke was borne with ready will;
Who dieth thus is living still.

5. We have no cause to mourn or weep;
Securely shall this body sleep
Till Christ Himself shall death destroy
And raise the blessed dead to joy.

6. For they who with Him suffered here
Shall there be healed from woe and fear;
And when eternal bliss is won,
They'll shine in glory like the sun.

7. Then let us leave this place of rest,
And homeward turn, for they are blest
Who heed God's warning and prepare
Lest death should find them unaware.

RESPONSE

1. Ye bear me to my earthly grave,
My body for an age to save,
Till God, who doth my spirit keep,
Shall come and rouse me from my sleep.

2. Yea, having died, indeed I must
Return to ashes and to dust,
Yet God shall take this bone and flesh
So frail, and make it new and fresh.

3. My body is by worms despised,
My soul in heav'n by Jesus prized,
Who did by bitter suffering
My soul redeem and thither bring.

4. The griefs that caused me great annoy
Give way to heaven's highest joy;
The world was but a vale of tears;
Beyond it, true delight appears.

5. When all the world must pass away
And God proclaims His Judgment Day,
My body glorified shall rise
To meet my soul beyond the skies.

6. How many‿a vile and dread offense
I suffered ere I journeyed hence!
But there no other thing is known
By God's elect but bliss alone.

7. So leave me now in peace to rest
And seek again your dwellings blest;
Let each man daily keep in mind
How he such blessed death may find.

8. So help us Christ, our only Good,
Who hath redeemed us by His blood
From endless death and misery;
To Him alone all glory be.

—sts. 1–7 "Choir," M. Weisse, 1531; tr., C. Winkworth, 1858, alt.
—st. 8, Anon., Magdeburg, 1540; tr., W. M. Czamanske, 1938.
—sts. 1–7 "Response," G. Neumark, 1657; tr., M. Carver.

418

Tune: Herr Jesu Christ, wahr Mensch und Gott. 11. [p. 404; *or as* #417]

1. A lowly thing, I lie at rest
Within my little chamber blest;
I have escaped by death serene
Your griefs, but briefly known and seen.

2. What harm if this my flesh and bone
Lie buried in this grave of stone?
My spirit dwells bereft of woe
In glory high, in heaven's glow.

3. Adorned in righteousness and love,
I shine before God's throne above.
My Jesus is my greatest Good,
My Joy, my Life, my heav'nly Food.

4. What is the wretched world to me?
My Jesus holds me tenderly;
In Him alone my soul I bless,
Without Him have no happiness.

5. With tears I came into the earth
But into heav'n with shouts of mirth;
The angels ever sing with me
The endless year of jubilee.

6. No sweeter song my tongue can sing,
My ears can hear no purer ring,
There is no name all grief to mend,
But Jesus Christ, my dearest friend.

7. Dear father, mother, therefore cease
To mourn my life cut short in peace;
For thus soon was I glorified:
He's old enough who blest hath died.

8. Compare my present gladness won
With how the world is wont to run:
There rumors spread of war and strife,
Here concord reigns and endless life.

9. As long as man on earth doth dwell,
Sin cleaves and vexes him as well;
With flesh and blood he oft must war,
And suffer many‿a fearful sore.

10. Yea, his are trial, cross, and care,
And long and weary death to bear;
For struggle brief was I ordained,
And then the crown of glory gained.

11. How many die by recklessness,
How many drown in great distress,
How many suffer years and years,
Before they leave this vale of tears!

12. So should it not your comfort be
That I should sleep so tranquilly,
That my beloved Jesus hath
Cut short my pains by blessed death?

13. So hush your cries beneath your hands
And look to God, who ready stands
That, having hurt you, He may heal
And work this for your commonweal.

14. That final day we'll take the road
(When great and small shall know their God)
To heav'nly bliss, where joys abound,
With honor and great glory crowned.

—M. Schirmer, 1648; tr., M. Carver.

419

Tune: Wenn mein Stündlein vorhanden ist. 49. [*TLH* 594]

1. Be glad, my heart! now fear no more,
Let nothing ever grieve thee;
Christ lives, who loved thee long before
Thy being He did give thee,
And ere He made thy wondrous frame;
E'en now, as death thy life would claim,
He surely cannot hate thee.

2. Fear not, my heart, thy nearing end,
There's nothing to appall thee.
Thy dear Lord's hands to thee extend
And from this world would call thee,—
From all the thousand forms of woe
That in this vale of tears below
Thou hadst to suffer ever.

3. Men call this death and agony,
But yet it is no dying;
The death of death is Christ, for He
Prevents it from destroying,
That though it puts forth all its pow'r,
It will not hurt one hair the hour
When I from hence am taken.

4. The pow'r of death in sin doth lie,
And in our evil doing,
Which, as a child of Adam, I
Have ever been pursuing.
In Jesus' blood now sin is drowned,
Choked, blotted out, no more is found,
No more brings condemnation.

5. My sin is gone and I am clean,
Despite who would deprive me!
Henceforth is life eternal mine;
The thought no more may grieve me
That sin's dread wages stain my hands:
Who's reconciled in favor stands,
And nothing has against him.

6. Now God's free grace with me I take
And all His joy and gladness
On this last journey that I make,
And know no grief or sadness.
The raging foe is but a sheep,
His wrath and ire a blessèd sleep,
Yea, but a gentle slumber.

7. Thou, Jesus, dearest Friend to me,
My Light and Life art ever!
Thou keep'st me safe; no enemy
From me Thy hold can sever.
In Thee I am, and Thou in me,
As we are here, we'll ever be,
Naught here or there can part us.

8. My body down to rest doth lie,
Fatigued with life's sad story;
The soul ascends to heaven high;
With chosen ones in glory
It mingles, and keeps joyfully,
The endless year of Jubilee
With all the holy angels.

9. Oh, Highest Prince of great and small,
May that blest day be nearing
When at the last Thy trump shall call,
And all the dead be hearing.
Then soul and body shall as one
Go forth with Thee, the joying Son,
Into Thy Father's kingdom.

10. If 'tis Thy will, O Lord, appear,
To endless bliss to take me,
Forever Thee may I be near,—
How joyful would it make me!
Be opened wide, O gate of death,
That I may pass through thee by faith
To yonder bliss and glory.

—P. Gerhardt, 1664; tr., J. Kelly, 1867, alt.

420

Prayer to the Holy Trinity at Death

Tune: O Herre Gott, in meiner Not. [p. 413]
Or Vater unser im Himmelreich. 44. [*TLH* 600; *LW* 234; *LSB* 766]

1. O God and Lord, / Thy help afford!
I cry to Thee; / Thou helpest me.
As hence I fare, / All to Thy care
I do commend. / Thine angel send,
Me safe to keep / When to my sleep
Thou bidd'st me go / From earthly woe.

2. O Jesus Christ, / Whose life unpriced
To death was giv'n, / God's Lamb from heav'n.
Thy wounds so red, / The blood they shed,
In every need / For me succeed;
Thy cross and death / Make me by faith
Thy heav'nly heir, / Like angels there.

3. O Spirit pure, / My Comforter,
Thy solace send / When life must end;
Forsake me not / When I am sought
By Satan's might, / Hell's endless fright;
My Rock, my Lord, / Fulfill Thy Word,
Thy blessing give, / Fore'er to live.

—N. Selnecker, 1572; tr., M. Carver.

421

Tune: Vater unser im Himmelreich. 44. [*TLH* 318; *LW* 234; *LSB* 766]

1. Thy days, O mortal, number well
Prepare for death and flee from hell;
Give ear to God and turn to Him,
Let not thy heart be weighed with sin.
Here none can stay; thou too must hence
To take thy fitting recompense.

2. Where are the children of the dust
With all their riches, pride, and lust?
Where now are they who moments past
We saw to vaunt in pleasure vast?
Oh, they are dead, and theirs is naught
Except a grave in which they rot.

3. O child of man, this contemplate,
And ponder what hath been their fate:
For they were mortals, as thou art,
And spent of life the greater part
Pursuing pleasures, yet at last
How suddenly to hell they passed!

4. While vermin here the flesh accost,
There pines the soul in fire and frost,
Till God the twain shall reunite
On Judgment Day, and with affright
Cast both into eternal flame,
To fearsome devils, grief, and shame.

5. For if in rankest riches they
Were Satan's servants in their day,
And heeded not repentance, faith,
Or e'en the gloomy night of death,
How justly then shall they as one
In Satan's realm travail and groan!

6. What now avail their goods and fame?
Their pleasures, pow'r, and lofty name?
Where is their leisure, laugh, and jest?
Their proud conceit and puffed-up breast?
All these have turned to utter pain
That never shall be turned again.

7. In this God's work of judgment see
That He can do the same to thee;
For earth thou art, on earth dost tread,
From earth dost bring thy daily bread;
So back to earth thou shalt decay
In death, like so much dust and clay.

8. Mark well this warning, nor forget
Thy day of death approaches yet,
And suddenly may come to sight,
Yea, even on this very night.
Death will no bargain make with thee.
So what if it come presently?

9. This much is certain: come it will,
Though time and place be hidden still.
Yet every moment, everywhere,
Death casts about its net and snare;
Wouldst thou be wise, then ready stand
To meet it when thy time's at hand.

10. Put not thy trust in prideful flesh,
Nor spin the wheel of sin afresh.
If on thy wicked path thou stay,
The gates of hell will come thy way;
God's just, and justly punisheth
The sinful man with endless death.

11. He who this world to God prefers,
Esteeming godliness a curse,
And, as the rich man, slaves each hour
In gluttony with all his pow'r;
As Satan's servant, he will share
His master's fate in judgment there.

12. Lord Jesus Christ, who graciously
Hast from deep darkness summoned me
Into Thy light; Oh, kindly send
Thy help, that I may not befriend
The wicked world, nor imitate
Its ways perverse, and share its fate.

13. Grant me to scorn all human might,
And count as naught its vain delight,
But seek Thy kingdom constantly,
Where like Thine angels I shall be,
Yea, where Thy chosen heirs are found,
In highest gladness gathered round.

—J. Heermann, 1630; tr., M. Carver.

422

Tune: O Welt, ich muß dich lassen. 31.
[*TLH* 126; *LW* 85; *LSB* 880; *or TLH* 171*; *LW* 120*]

1. O Death, thou dost not frighten!
The Lord, my Sun, will brighten,
And bid my body rise
From earth's deep bosom sleeping;
Alive I shall be leaping
By His good Spirit through the skies.

2. Oh, friends, refrain from crying!
What woe betides my dying?
I only go before;
And where I go, ye thither
Must follow altogether
Through death and its beshadowed door.

3. Earth for my bed I borrow,
To slumber through all sorrow
And without all dismay,
And weary heart, and illness
To rest in peace and stillness,
Until the Lord's awaited Day.

4. Though I be ashes wholly,
God shall restore me fully
When Christ, my Shepherd true,
My dust and bones shall gather
And bring me to His Father,
Enrobed in glory, bright and new.

5. Though made of clay so tender
My flesh will share the splendor
Of Christ, who also died;
No longer will I sorrow,
For on that joyful morrow
I'll shine like angels, glorified.

6. Come, then, sweet hour of gladness,
When I shall fly from sadness,
And breathe my final breath,
My body cold be carried
And by my loved ones buried
In its appointed bed of death.

7. There will I safely slumber
With Jesus' chosen number,
And none disturb my rest,
For round mine ashes lowly
The angels high and holy
Shall stand the watch at God's behest.

8. When I have used completely
My tomb of rest, then sweetly
My Lord will waken me;
And as He from the prison
Of death again is risen,
I, too, shall fly from misery.

9. O Lord, when life must fail me,
Then let Thy cross avail me
And be my monument,
Whereunder I will lay me
Until Thou wilt convey me
To heaven through a blest ascent.

10. Good night, my friends, I bid you;
Of bitter weeping rid you,
For quiet rest I pine;
In days but few of number
Ye'll bear me to my slumber,
And on my couch my form recline.

11. Soon dirges soft and gentle
In chorus reverential
Will lull to sleep my heart;
The earth so cool and somber
Will be my resting-chamber.
Farewell, for soon our path must part.

—J. Quirsfeld, †1686; tr., M. Carver.

423

Tune: O Welt, ich muß dich lassen. 31. [*TLH* 126; *LW* 85; *LSB* 880]

1. O world, I now must leave thee,
But little doth it grieve me,
I seek my native land;
True life I there inherit,
And here I yield my spirit
With joy to God's all-gracious hand.

2. My time on earth is finished,
My faculties diminished
Death's gain awaits my heart;
The things of earth are failing,
Eternal things unveiling,
With peace and joy I now depart.

3. This godless world has grieved me
And often times deceived me
With shame and trickery.
Yet will I never waver
In faith, but answer ever:
My sins have been forgiven me.

4. So on His Word relying,
I know while I am dying
I soon shall see His face
Thro' Christ whose death hath bought me,
The Father's love He brought me,
And now prepares for me a place.

5. The grave hath lost its terrors
Since for my sins and errors
My Savior doth atone:
My works can naught avail me,
But His work cannot fail me,
I rest in faith on Him alone.

6. My service cannot merit
That I should e'er inherit
Eternal life with Christ:
But He hath freely given
A share with Him in heaven
Of that fair heritage unpriced.

7. And so I hence am going
In peace, full surely knowing
With Him is perfect rest;
I feel Death's icy finger,
My soul here cannot linger,
Now would I stay—to go is best.

8. O world, I yet would teach thee
That Death will surely reach thee,
That thou must follow me;
Then while thy days are lengthened
Pray that thy faith be strengthened
That God have mercy too on thee!

9. Now is my end beginning,
Leave off thy shame and sinning,
And hold the narrow way,
With watch and supplication,
Let go of earth's temptation,
With joy await the final day.

10. This I say at my ending.
Farewell! I'll soon be wending
To God, my sole desire!
Beware eternal suff'ring
And ponder this last off'ring;
My stay on earth must now expire.

—Anon., Nürnberg, 1555; tr. sts. 1, 4–8, C. Winkworth, 1863; sts. 2–3, 9–10, M. Carver.

424

Dialog between the Living and the Dead

Tune: O wie selig seid ihr doch, ihr Frommen. 12. [*TLH* 589; *LW* 268; *LSB* 679]

1. Oh, how blest are ye whose toils are ended,
Who thro' death have unto God ascended!
Ye have arisen
From the cares which keep us still in prison.

1. Truly, I to glory have arisen,
From all cares that held me in a prison,
Earthly toil ended,
I unto my God am now ascended.

2. We are still as in a dungeon living,
Still oppressed with sorrow and misgiving;
Our undertakings
Are but toils and troubles and heart-
[breakings.

2. I no more as in a dungeon wander;
God has taken me to heaven yonder.
Tears and frustrations
Are the sum of earthly expectations.

3. Ye meanwhile are in your chambers
[sleeping,
Quiet, and set free from all our weeping;
No cross or sadness
There can hinder your untroubled gladness.

3. Oh, my destiny, how blest, how wondrous,
To be free from earthly pain so pond'rous!
Naught but rejoicing
Fills me now, my thanks and praises voicing.

4. Christ has wiped away your tears forever;
Ye have that for which we still endeavor;
To you are chanted
Songs that ne'er to mortal ears were granted.

4. Ah, what words, what language might I
[borrow
To describe my freedom from all sorrow?
Naught else but singing
Of the angels in my ears is ringing!

5. Ah, who would, then, not depart with
[gladness
To inherit heav'n for earthly sadness?
Who here would languish
Longer in bewailing and in anguish?

5. In the world man's heart is torn with anguish,
Constantly his soul in pain must languish;
But Jesus' merit,
Death a door has made, life to inherit.

6. Come, O Christ, and loose the chains that [bind us:
Lead us forth and cast this world behind us.
With Thee, th' Anointed,
Finds the soul its joy and rest appointed.

—S. Dach, 1635; tr., H. Longfellow, 1845, alt.

6. Dearest friends, I say farewell with [gladness;
May my death not cause you grief or sadness.
By Christ invited,
Someday we again shall be united!

—P. Pfeffer, 1737; tr., K. Runge, 1945, alt.

425

At the Burial of Children and Infants

Tune: Herzlich tut mich verlangen. 59. [*TLH* 172; *LW* 113; *LSB* 450]

1. My course is run; in glory
A victor now I dwell.
Farewell life's fleeting story,
A thousand times farewell!
Loved ones, who pine and languish,
Oh, bid your sorrows flee!
What good your bitter anguish
When all is well with me?

2. Think, father, of the sorrows,
Of all the nights awake,
Of all the gloomy morrows
Which oft a child can make!
Who loves him well may worry
What woes it may receive;
Let not your heart be sorry,
For neither do I grieve!

3. O mother, cease your weeping
And let your tears be stilled;
The Lord His plan is keeping,
And it must be fulfilled.
That ye in grief are leaning,
And now lament so sore,
Is surely all well-meaning.
God will all things restore.

4. That joy, all joys transcending,
That fills a pilgrim's soul
When he, his journey ending,
Has fin'lly reached his goal;
The joy that fills the sailor
Who quickly hath discerned
A harbor free from danger—
Of this I now have learned.

5. Away, all pain and weeping,
Begone forevermore!
For joy my heart is leaping,
To think your rule is o'er.
Now thousand joys I borrow
From my Creator's hand,
And earthly pain and sorrow
Come not in this fair land.

6. 'Tis but in lisping measure
That they on earth who roam
Can tell what tides of pleasure
Fill heav'n's eternal home.
I'd rather be with Jesus
Than live on earth below,
For death forever frees us
From all our earthly woe.

7. Then strew my bier with flowers,
As 'twere a conqu'ror's car;
I gain from vernal bowers,
That bloom in heav'n afar,
A crown that ne'er shall wither;
And He who ever lives,—
God's Son, who bears me thither,—
The victor's chaplet gives.

8. And still the tears are springing,
And flowing down amain;
With grief your hearts are wringing,
And like to burst in twain.
My father's looks still languish
Where sleeps the silent clay.
My mother stands in anguish,
And turns her eyes away.

9. I was but briefly lent you,
And then by God called home;
So now, no more lament you
Because my hour is come;
God gave of His good pleasure,
And now God takes away;
He fixes our life's measure,
We must His will obey.

10. My years let not confound you,
But keep before your eye
How once I lived around you,
A mortal bound to die,
And then was called to leave you,
In greener bud of youth;
How then should that aggrieve you
Which God your Master doth?

11. My grave but shows too clearly
We are a pilgrim band,
And that it comes so early,
Is by a Father's hand.
Say not that prematurely
My soul has passed on high.
Who dies in God is surely
Mature enough to die.

12. Seems death too quickly given?
Let men reply and say,
"What hour's too soon for heaven?"
It is God's wonted way:
He doth His children hurry
To heaven's glories bright;
So who for him should worry
Who shares in heav'n's delight?

13. Farewell, then, dearest spirit,
To brighter mansions go,
And there a bliss inherit
Which mortals cannot know.
When dawns that day of splendor,
When death resigns his prey,
We'll mix embraces tender—
Oh, would it were today!

—G. W. Sacer, 1665; tr. sts. 1, 5–9, 11, 13, composite; sts. 2–4, 10, 12, M. Carver.

426

Tune: Valet will ich dir geben. 59. [*TLH* 407; *LW* 79; *LSB* 442]

1. Farewell I gladly bid Thee,
False, evil world, farewell.
Thy life is vain and sinful,
With thee I would not dwell.
I long to be in heaven,
In that untroubled sphere
Where they will be rewarded,
Who served their God while here.

2. By Thy good counsel lead me,
O Son of God, my Stay;
In each perplexing trial
Help me, O Lord, I pray.
Mine hour of sorrow shorten,
Support my fainting heart,
From every cross deliver,
The crown of life impart.

3. When darkness round me gathers,
Thy name and cross, still bright,
Deep in my heart are sparkling
Like stars in blackest night.
O heart, this image cherish:
The Christ on Calvary,
How gen'rously in suff'ring
He shed His blood for me!

4. Lord, hide my soul securely
Deep in Thy wounded side;
From every danger shield me
And to Thy glory guide.
He has been truly blessèd
Who reaches heav'n above;
He has found perfect healing
Who rests upon Thy love.

5. Lord, write my name, I pray Thee,
Now in the Book of Life
And with all true believers
Take me where joys are rife.
There let me bloom and flourish,
Thy perfect freedom prove,
And tell, as I adore Thee,
How faithful was Thy love.

—V. Herberger, 1613; tr., C. Winkworth, 1863, alt.

427

Tune: Jesu, meine Freude. 74. [*TLH* 347; *LW* 270; *LSB* 743]

1. What is our existence,
What our heart's persistence,
Seeking futile gain;
What is all our doing,
Planning, and pursuing?
Toil and effort vain!
Vain the strife / Of earthly life,
Vain the dreams for which we languish,
Vain our pain and anguish.

2. Ah! how void and cheating,
Ah! how quickly fleeting
Is our course on earth!
Scarcely do we quicken
And by griefs are stricken
From our very birth!
Life but stings / And sadness brings,
Wickedness of men increasing,
Conflict never ceasing.

3. This our life commences
Ever with offenses,
With great cross and woe;
Vain its paltry off'ring:
Anguish, sorrow, suff'ring,
And death's final blow.
This life's lot / Delights me not;
Of that life my heart is fonder
Which awaits me yonder.

4. World, I would not know thee!
Fain would I forgo thee,
And thy vain annoy!
These have I rejected,
And instead selected
Heaven's fadeless joy,
Thereon yet / My heart is set,
Constantly my thoughts are driven
To the bounds of heaven.

5. May I have Thee only,
Lord, I am not lonely;
For naught else I pine.
Though my soul be ailing
And my body failing,
Thou, O Christ, art mine.
To my heart / All Joy Thou art,
Thou my Life and Portion ever,
Thou, my precious Savior.

—C. Tietze, 1664; tr., M. Carver.

428

Tune: Wenn mein Stündlein vorhanden ist. 49. [*TLH* 594]

1. When my last hour is close at hand,
Lord Jesus Christ, attend me;
Beside me then, O Savior, stand
To comfort and defend me.
Into Thy hands I will commend
My soul at this my earthly end,
And Thou wilt keep it safely.

2. My sins, dear Lord, disturb me sore,
My conscience cannot slumber;
But though as sands upon the shore
My sins may be in number,
I will not quail, but think of Thee;
Thy death, Thy sorrow, borne for me,
Thy suff'rings, shall uphold me.

3. I am a branch in Thee, the Vine,
And hence the comfort borrow
That Thou wilt surely keep me Thine
Through fear and pain and sorrow;
And when I die, I die to Thee,
Thy precious death hath won for me
The life that never endeth.

4. Since Thou the pow'r of death didst rend,
In death Thou wilt not leave me;
Since Thou didst into heav'n ascend,
No fear of death shall grieve me.
For where Thou art, there shall I be
That I may ever live with Thee;
That is my hope when dying.

5. My spirit I commend to Thee
And gladly hence betake me;
Peaceful and calm my sleep shall be,
No human voice can wake me.
But Christ is with me through the strife,
And He will bear me into life
And open heav'n before me.

—N. Herman, 1560, but st. 5, Anon., Bonn, 1575; tr., C. Winkworth, 1869, alt.

429

Tune: Wer weiß, wie nahe mir. 45. [*TLH* 598; *LSB* 598]

1. Who knows when death may overtake me!
Time passes on, my end draws near.
How swiftly can my breath forsake me!
How soon can life's last hour appear!
My God, for Jesus' sake I pray
Thy peace may bless my dying day.

2. The world that smiled when morn was [breaking
May change for me ere close of day;
For while on earth my home I'm making,
Death's threat is never far away.
My God, for Jesus' sake I pray
Thy peace may bless my dying day.

3. My end to ponder teach me ever
And, ere the hour of death appears,
To cast my soul on Christ, my Savior,
Nor spare repentant sighs and tears.
My God, for Jesus' sake I pray
Thy peace may bless my dying day.

4. Help me now set my house in order
That always ready I may be
To say in meekness on death's border:
Lord, as Thou wilt, deal Thou with me.
My God, for Jesus' sake I pray
Thy peace may bless my dying day.

5. Reveal the sweetness of Thy heaven,
Earth's galling bitterness unfold;
May I, amid this turmoil riven,
Thy blest eternity behold.
My God, for Jesus' sake I pray
Thy peace may bless my dying day.

6. My many sins blot out forever
Since Jesus has my pardon won;
In mercy robed, I then shall never
Fear death, but trust in Thee alone.
My God, for Jesus' sake I pray
Thy peace may bless my dying day.

7. His blood and wounds are my salvation,
My blessed bed within the grave
There I find light and consolation,
And everything I fain would have.
My God, for Jesus' sake I pray
Thy peace may bless my dying day.

8. Naught shall my soul from Jesus sever;
In faith I touch His wounded side
And hail Him as my Lord forever.
Nor life nor death shall us divide.
My God, for Jesus' sake I pray
Thy peace may bless my dying day.

9. Once in the blest baptismal waters
I put on Christ and made Him mine;
Now numbered with God's sons and daughters,
I share His peace and love divine.
My God, for Jesus' sake I pray
Thy peace may bless my dying day.

10. His body and His blood I've taken
In His blest Supper, feast divine;
Now I shall never be forsaken,
For I am His, and He is mine.
My God, for Jesus' sake I pray
Thy peace may bless my dying day.

11. Then may death come today, tomorrow,
I know in Christ I perish not;
He grants the peace that stills all sorrow,
Gives me a robe without a spot.
My God, for Jesus' sake I pray
Thy peace may bless my dying day.

12. And thus I live in God contented
And die without a thought of fear;
My soul has to God's plans consented,
For through His Son my faith is clear.
My God, for Jesus' sake I pray
Thy peace may bless my dying day.

—Ä. J. von Schwarzburg-Rudolstadt, 1686; tr., *TLH,* 1941, but st. 7, C. Winkworth, 1869, alt.

430

Tune: Wer nur den lieben Gott läßt walten. 45. [*TLH* 194; *LW* 429; *LSB* 750]

1. How short man's life, how brief the measure,
How wretched till his dying day!
On every side death has his pleasure,
Life's essence ever seeps away;
We fade as quickly as we bloom,
We leave the crib to greet the tomb.

2. But blest is he who finds an ending
That causes neither fear nor fret,
Whose spirit, saved from death impending,
God in a better life doth set,—
In paradise beside His throne,
Where sorrow nevermore is known.

3. Drown not my death with lamentation,
My health is now in whole regained;
What Jesus won for my salvation,
I have at last in death obtained;
I have been merely brought release
To where the soul delights in peace.

4. 'Tis sweet in heaven to be sharer,
'Tis sweet to lie at Jesus' breast.
The fray of anguish holds no terror
Where now I dwell in holy rest.
Through suff'rings brief I've come to see
The treasures of eternity.

5. The quicker death my vision shaded,
The sooner God my soul could keep,
My body, though grown cold and faded,
Lies not in death, but gentle sleep.
God set me safe behind His wall
And pulled me out of troubles all.

6. How highly have I been exalted,
What providence my God hath shown!
For this I sing His praise unhalted.
Oh, life with you was but a loan;
Now God from earth hath bid me rise,
And granted me the heav'nly prize.

7. Begrudge me not this blessed fortune,
Which greater is than ye conceive;
Your tearful gazes curb and shorten,
I lie in comforts none should grieve.
So stem affliction's bitter tide:
In wondrous glory I reside.

8. Though in the earth the body wither,
Its bloom will come another day,
When Jesus shall these ashes gather
And robe them in His bright array;
Then like an angel I shall be—
Oh, let this please you heartily!

9. The wicked world I have departed,
In which ye stand afflicted still;
My Jesus holds me, tender-hearted,
With greater love than ye could will;
My Savior's face I now adore,
So think on this and weep no more.

—Z. Herrmann, 1697; tr., M. Carver.

Eternity, Resurrection, and Judgment

431

Tune: Es ist gewisslich an der Zeit. 49. [*TLH* 293; *LW* 336; *LSB* 508]

1. For Thy return, O Christ our Lord,
We wait with expectation;
The day when all shall be restored
Draws near with our salvation.
Oh, help us but to wake aright,
When Thou with all Thine angels bright
Shalt come to render judgment!

—N. Herman, 1560, cento; tr., M. Carver.

432

Tune: Auf meinen lieben Gott. 29. [*TLH* 526; *LW* 421; *LSB* 745]

1. The time is very near
When, Lord, Thou wilt be here;
The signs by which, discerning,
We'd know of Thy returning—
Have been so oft appearing,
Thine advent must be nearing.

2. What shall I do then, Lord,
But rest upon Thy Word,—
The promise Thou hast given
That Thou wilt come from heaven,
Me from the grave deliver
And from all woe forever!

3. O Jesus Christ, how fair
Will be my welcome there!
Thy glances will address me
With quick'ning pow'r to bless me,
When I the earth forsaking,
My flight to Thee am taking.

4. Oh, what will be the word
I'll hear from Thee, my Lord!
What then will be Thy greeting,
Me and my brethren meeting,
When, Thy heart being shown us,
Thy members Thou wilt own us!

5. How shall I have the pow'r
In such a gracious hour,
To keep my eyelids tearless,
My heart and senses cheerless?
My joy from flowing over,
My cheeks with floods to cover?

6. With what a beauteous light
Thy face, so fair and bright,
Will light me then in heaven,
When sight of Thee is given!
What joy Thy grace and merit
Will give my heart and spirit!

7. Thine eyes, Thy mouth, Thy lips,
Thy body bruised with whips,
On which our faith is founded,—
I'll then behold, astounded;
With gaze devout will follow
In hands and feet each hollow.

8. Thou only know'st the joy,
The bliss without alloy,
The food of souls forgiven
Within Thy realm of heaven;
Though well before Thou show them,
By faith alone I know them.

9. What I've believed stands sure,
My portion is secure,
Surpassing every treasure
In which the rich take pleasure.
By wealth they'll be forsaken,
My portion stands unshaken.

10. O Lord, my fairest Part!
How will my bounding heart
With joy be overflowing,
That newness to be knowing,
When Thou wilt open for me
Thy door to heaven's glory!

11. "Come, come, My child elect,
And taste without defect
Free graces like no other
From Me and from My Father;
Come," Thou wilt say, "And nourish
Thy heart where joys e'er flourish."

12. Alas, poor passing earth!
What are thy treasures worth
Beside these crowns before us
And thrones than gold more glorious
Which Jesus is reserving
For those who are unswerving?

13. Here is the angel's rest,
The station of the blest.
Here I hear naught but singing,
See all with gladness springing;
Here is no cross, no sorrow,
No parting on the morrow.

14. Refrain, my feeble sense!
Why leap thy pond'rings hence,
As if to span the groundless,
As if to bound the boundless?
Here mind must be submitting,
Here mouth its speech be quitting.

15. But Thou, my Glory, know,
I will not let Thee go!
On Thee I'll ever ponder,
O Lord, whose gifts of wonder
To me, forever mounting,
Surpass my pow'r of counting.

16. How sad, O Lord, am I
Till Thee I see on high,
Descending to Thy nation!
Oh, that Thy great salvation
Might e'en this day be granted!
For this my heart hath panted.

17. The time is in Thy hand;
My task is but to stand
Prepared and joyful ever,
To go to Thee, my Savior,—
My heart no moment ceasing
In Thee to be increasing.

18. This grant, Lord, and bestow
Thy truth and grace that so
My heart may ever waken
Lest I by fear be shaken
That Day, when fear and sadness
Shall turn to peace and gladness.

—P. Gerhardt, 1653; tr., J. Kelly, 1867 / M. Carver.

433

Tune: Es ist gewisslich an der Zeit. 49. [*TLH* 293; *LW* 336; *LSB* 508]

1. The day is surely drawing near
When God's Son, the Anointed,
Shall with great majesty appear
As Judge of all appointed.
All mirth and laughter then shall cease
When flames on flames will still increase,
As Scripture truly teacheth.

2. A trumpet loud shall then resound
And all the earth be shaken.
Then all who in their graves are found
Shall from their sleep awaken;
But all that live shall in that hour
By the Almighty's boundless power
Be changed at His commanding.

3. A book is opened then to all,
A record truly telling
What each hath done, both great and small,
When he on earth was dwelling;
And every heart be clearly seen,
And all be known as they have been
In thought and words and actions.

4. Then woe to those who scorned the Lord
And sought but carnal pleasures,
Who here despised His precious Word
And loved their earthly treasures!
With shame and trembling they will stand
And at the Judge's stern command
To Satan be delivered.

5. O Jesus, who my debt didst pay
And for my sin wast smitten,
Within the Book of Life, oh, may
My name be also written!
I will not doubt; I trust in Thee,
From Satan Thou hast made me free
And from all condemnation.

6. Therefore, my Intercessor be
And for Thy blood and merit
Declare my name from judgment free
With all who life inherit,
That I may see Thee face to face
With all Thy saints in that blest place
Which Thou for us hast purchased.

7. O Jesus Christ, do not delay,
But hasten our salvation;
We often tremble on our way
In fear and tribulation.
Then hear us when we cry to Thee;
Come, mighty Judge, and make us free
From every evil! Amen.

—Anon., ca. 1565, after *Dies irae* / B. Ringwaldt, 1586; tr., P. Peter, 1880, alt.

434

The Dread of Eternity

Tune: O Ewigkeit, du Donnerwort. 70. [p. 412]

1. Eternity, thou thund'rous word,
Within the heart a piercing sword,
Beginning without ending!
Eternity, unmeasured time!
I sink beneath the thought sublime
That I to thee am tending:
Deep horror fills my quaking heart,
My lips in speech refuse to part.

2. Here sorrow hath its bound and stay;
Still after night returns the day;
Still hope its solace lendeth:
But everlasting is the grief;—
Nor mercy there, nor sweet relief
From heav'n to man descendeth.
Eternity forevermore
Doth on the soul its terrors pour.

3. Eternity! Oh, what a pang!
Eternity! No serpent's fang
Could send that thrill of terror.
When I revolve thy clanking chains,
Thy dark abyss of deathless pains,
My soul is filled with horror.
Oh, search the universe around,
No equal terror can be found!

4. And what of water, fire, and sword!
No cause for trembling they afford,
They have no lasting power.
What if some tyrant prince appear
(Who scarce will see his fiftieth year),
And trap me in his tower!
No prison, pain, or agony
On earth can last eternally.

5. Could all the torments felt in hell
In years that number not excel
Of human population,
Or of the stars in heaven spread,
Or leaves of foliage overhead—
Yea, all that fills creation—
Those torments still would have an end
And fill the measure so ordained.

6. But there, when thou hast suffered thro'
A countless thousand years anew,
And by the demons, jeering,
Been tortured for so many days,
In many grim and gruesome ways,
No end will yet be nearing.
The time, which never thought can span,
Repeats from whence it once began.

7. Should he who ails recline to rest
Upon a couch for princes dressed
And wrought with many‿a jewel,
He holds its splendor in such spite
That he must suffer all the night
In misery so cruel;
He counts the bells till night is past,
And sighs for day to come at last.

8. But what is that? The pains of hell
Will make all worldly ills seem well,
For there no hour will end them;
The whole assembly of the curst
In boundless flames will be immersed,
And God's great wrath attend them;
And this unfathomed agony
Shall last for all eternity.

9. O God, Thou righteous Judge, how strait
Upon the wicked sinner wait
Thy judgments unrelenting!
Alas! must man sin's little day
Through all eternity repay?
Bethink Thee, Lord, repenting.
Look to it, man, draw in thy breath,
How short is time, how quick is death!

10. Oh, flee the devil's bondage sore!
All earthly lusts can bring no more
Than but a moment's pleasure.
Wouldst thou consign thy sorry soul
To hell to pay the devil's toll
For such a fleeting treasure?
O handsome trade! O dear the debt,
With devils ever to regret!

11. As long as God on high resides
Far over all the cloudy tides,
So will these torments fright'ning
Still send their plagues of frost and fire,
Of anguish, fright, and hunger dire,
Of thunder and of lightning;
Yet ne'er consumed to naught, their sting,
Like God, shall have no lessening.

12. These torments evermore endure
As at the first they fashioned were,—
Their work is never finished;
They labor on and take no rest
O'er souls by Satan's chains oppressed,
Whose groans are not diminished.
O sinner, thine iniquity
No help or comfort e'er shall see.

13. Awake, O man, from sinful sleep;
Arise, thou idle, wand'ring sheep,
Amend, and live more truly.
Wake up, the time is almost o'er,
Eternity is at the door
To pay thy wages duly.
This is perchance thy final day,
For who can tell, when die he may?

14. Not to these worldly hungers hold:
Resplendence, praises, pride, and gold—
Life not for these be waging.
See how secure in lies and crimes
This world remains, how ill the times,
And all the devil's raging.
Above all, keep in constant sight
The long foretold and final night.

15. O mortal and accursèd child,
In spirit blind, in sense defiled,
Thy worldly passion sever!
Alas, must all the pains of hell,
A thousand hangmen which excel,
Aggrieve thy soul forever?
Where is the man of language fair
That can these matters more declare?

16. Eternity, thou thund'rous word,
Within the heart a piercing sword,
Beginning without ending!
Eternity, unmeasured time!
I sink beneath the thought sublime
That I to thee am tending:
Lord Jesus, when it pleaseth Thee,
Grant me Thy blest eternity!

17. O hellish pain no tongue can teach,
O agony transcending speech,
O griefs, the mind defying!
My Jesus, oh, my heart defend
From searing pains that never end;
The joys of heav'n supplying!
Since for my sake Thy blood was poured,
Forsake me not at last, O Lord.

—J. Rist, 1642, but st. 17, V. E. Löscher, 1702; tr. sts. 1–3, 9, 13, 16, composite; sts. rest, M. Carver.

435

Tune: O wie selig seid ihr doch, ihr Frommen. 12. [*TLH* 589; *LW* 268; *LSB* 679]

1. How shall we for earthly joys be sighing,
Evermore ourselves thereby denying
The rest of heaven
And the thousand joys the blest are given?

2. Must we not, like them, be trav'ling yonder,
To the vale of death from hence to wander,
And each be viewing
His reward for all his earthly doing?

3. When the world on Judgment Day has ended
And the righteous Judge from heav'n descended,
He shall uncover
All that we had tried to cover over.

4. Oh, what bitter sentence He shall render
When our deeds appear before His splendor
In solemn session,
Showing how our lives were sheer transgression!

5. O Lord Christ, I pray Thee, grace afford me!
Not as I, a sinner, owe, reward me;
Then every hunger
Of the wicked world I'll heed no longer.

6. Let me live henceforward to Thy glory,
Heedful of Thy Word in sacred story!
I'm Thine forever;
From Thyself no world my soul can sever.

7. Unto none Thy gate of mercy closes,
If in Thee his earthly hope reposes,
But Thy denier,
When he dies, must perish in hell-fire-.

8. Therefore in Thy wounds I will conceal me,
Where is found the balm, of sin to heal me;
Thy body riven
And Thy blood sustain me unto heaven.

—H. Albert, 1640; tr., M. Carver.

436

Tune: Wachet auf, ruft uns die Stimme. 95. [*TLH* 444; *LW* 303; *LSB* 516]

1. "Wake, awake, for night is flying,"
The watchmen on the heights are crying;
"Awake, Jerusalem, arise!"
Midnight hears the welcome voices
And at the thrilling cry rejoices:
"Oh, where are ye, ye virgins wise?
The Bridegroom comes, awake!
Your lamps with gladness take!
Alleluia!
With bridal care / Yourselves prepare
To meet the Bridegroom, who is near."

2. Zion hears the watchmen singing,
And all her heart with joy is springing,
She wakes, she rises from her gloom;
For her Lord comes down all-glorious,
The strong in grace, in truth victorious,
Her Star is ris'n, her Light is come.
"Now come, Thou Blessed One,
Lord Jesus, God's own Son,
Hail! Hosanna!
The joyful call / We answer all
And follow to the nuptial hall."

3. Now let all the heav'ns adore Thee,
Let men and angels sing before Thee,
With harp and cymbal's clearest tone.
Of one pearl each shining portal,
Where, dwelling with the choir immortal,
We gather round Thy radiant throne.
No vision ever brought,
No ear hath ever caught,
Such great glory;
Therefore will we / Eternally
Sing hymns of praise and joy to Thee.

—P. Nicolai, 1599; tr., C. Winkworth, 1863, alt.

437

Tune: Valet will ich dir geben. 59.
[*TLH* 58; *LW* 79; *LSB* 442; *or TLH* 67*; *LW* 176*; *LSB* 514*]

1. When God my soul delivers
From present woes and past,
And from all evil severs
With blessed death at last,
And I, to glory rising,
In heaven's height shall see
The faithful hosts rejoicing,—
How blest I then shall be!

2. My lips will know but laughter,
My tongue the sound intone
Of sweetest hymns hereafter,
Our Savior's praise to own.
To God the honor always
For all His works I'll sing
And all of heaven's hallways
Shall echo with their ring.

3. O Lord, fulfill my yearning,
And set me free, that I
May be these bonds adjourning,
And to Thy freedom fly!
While in this world impounded,
My worries never cease,
I go by sin surrounded,
And find no rest or peace.

4. All that Thy Law commands me,
My spirit longs to do,
And yet my flesh withstands me
And still would ill pursue;
From wishes, dreams, and sighing
I find no liberty;
I cry, these chains defying,
"God, who will rescue me?"

5. Who shall my soul deliver,
From all this grief within,
This body‿of death and fever,
This war with flesh and sin?
Yet all I'll gladly suffer,
O God, if Thou by grace
Thy constant help wilt offer,
And never turn Thy face.

6. Uphold me by Thy Spirit,
Bestow His constant aid
That, being ever near it,
I may no falling dread.
And though I long must sorrow,
The sun I shall behold
More brightly on the morrow
In cloudless rays of gold.

7. Though now on earth I scatter
The seed of pain, and weep,
These tears will little matter
When harvest's bliss I reap.
Now grief must dull my singing,
Now time be my lament;—
Then sheaves I shall be bringing,
In glories never spent.

—S. Dach, †1659; tr., M. Carver.

Addendum

1. FESTIVAL OF THE REFORMATION

Tune: Wo Gott der Herr nicht bei uns hält. 49. [p. 418]

438

1. If God were not upon our side
When round us foes are raging,
Were not Himself our help and guide
When bitter war they're waging,
Were He not Israel's mighty shield,
To whom their utmost craft must yield,
We surely must have perished.

2. But now no human wit or might
His chosen people frighteth,
God sitteth in the highest height,
And He their counsels blighteth;
When craftiest snares and nets they lay,
God doth His work another way,
And makes a path before us.

3. Against our souls they rage and mock,
Exciting great commotion:
As billows meet with angry shock
Out on the stormy ocean,
So they our lives with fury seek;
But God hath pity on the weak,
And Him they have forgotten.

4. They call us heretics, and aye
Their Christian name are flaunting;
They seek to spill our blood, while they
Their fear of God are vaunting.
Ah, God! that precious name of Thine
O'er many a wicked deed must shine,
But Thou wilt once avenge it.

5. They open wide their rav'nous jaws,
And threaten to devour us,
But thanks to God, who rules our cause,
They shall not overpow'r us;
Their snares He yet will bring to naught,
And overthrow what they have taught;
God is too mighty for them.

6. How richly He consoleth those
Whom no one else befriendeth!
The door of grace doth never close;
Sense never comprehendeth
How this may be, and deems all lost,
When through this very cross a host
Of champions God is raising.

7. Our foes, O God, are in Thy hand,
Thou knowest their endeavor;
But only give us strength to stand,
And let us waver never,
Though reason strives with faith, and still
It fears to wholly trust Thy will,
And sees not Thy salvation.

8. But heav'n and earth, O Lord, are Thine,
For Thou alone hast made them;
Thy light let on Thy people shine,
And in their sorrows aid them;
Ignite our hearts to love and faith
That shall be steadfast e'en to death,
Howe'er the world may murmur!

—J. Jonas, 1524; tr., C. Winkworth, 1869, alt.

2. ESTATE AND VOCATION

439

Christian Courage

Tune: Löwen, laßt euch wieder finden. 65. [*TLH* 470]

1. Rise again, ye lion-hearted
Saints of early Christendom.
Whither is your strength departed,
Whither gone your martyrdom?
Lo, love's light is on them,
Glory's flame upon them,
And their will to die doth quell
E'en the lord and prince of hell.

2. These the men by fear unshaken,
Facing danger dauntlessly;
These no witching lust hath taken,
Lust that lures to vanity.
Mid the roar and rattle
Of tumultuous battle
In desire they soar above
All that earth would have them love.

3. To the truth they own adherence,
On the substance train their sight,
Never trusting in appearance,
Judging all by heav'nly light;
Blest in their conviction,
Even in affliction,
Far from human slavery
And its shackles they are free.

4. Great of heart, they know no turning,
Honor, gold, they laugh to scorn,
Quench desires within them burning,
By no earthly passion torn.
Mid the lions' roaring
Songs of praise outpouring,
Joyously they take their stand
On th' arena's bloody sand.

5. Would to God that I might even
As the martyred saints of old,
With the helping hand of heaven,
Steadfast stand in battle bold!
O my God, I pray Thee,
In the combat stay me.
Grant that I may ever be
Loyal, staunch, and true to Thee.

6. But for Thee I weakly cower,
Void of any asset small,
Let alone great feats of power;
On Thee only hangeth all.
Lord, my hope's assurance,
Pledge of my endurance,
Grant me as a champion now
Not to break my knightly vow!

7. Grant me, armored by the Spirit,
In Thy name, O Christ, to fight
With a lions' strength and merit,
Slumb'ring not, but by Thy might
Bravely battle waging,
'Gainst the devil's raging.
Let no rout o'ertake my soul,
But support me till the goal.

8. Time will come when foes, arising,
Rage again to take the field,
Christian souls in war surprising,
Spilling blood on sword and shield;
Ponder well this warning:
Days of shrouds and mourning
Here our homes again shall know—
Yea, and many a martyr's blow.

9. Now at last must come the leaven,
For the measure must be filled,—
Martyrs more be crowned in heaven,
On the cross of glory killed;—
Eve than morn be ruddier,
Church's dusk be bloodier,
As the Lamb at even died
Which at morn was crucified!

10. Courage, brethren! firm and fearless,
Steady in your calling stand:
Follow we that cloud of peerless
Witnesses in warlike band,
Who, the flesh subduing,
Know no cause for ruing;
Flesh must suffer as it will,
And the soul will flourish still.

11. Count we not the Cross, bespattered,
Like the wise, a foolish thing!
Let us not from thence be scattered
When we should proclaim our King;
Let it be our station
When the generation
Of the Foe attacks the faith,
Threat'ning us with swords of death.

12. Slacken not, though thou be slaughtered:
Is it not with martyrs' blood
That the Church's beds are watered,
And bedewed her fertile mud?
From these crimson showers
Spring her countless flowers;
Oh, what bounties here she yields
In her fruitful battlefields!

13. Spirit, as a rain descending!
On our drying hearts be poured,
That for Thee we may unbending
Wilt at neither fire nor sword;
In Thy love surrounded,
Firmly in Thee grounded,
Make Thy Church in faith to be
Rich as in her infancy.

—G. Arnold, asc., 1712; sts. 1–2, 4–5, tr., M. Franzmann, 1940; sts. 3, 6–13, M. Carver.

3. MORNING

440

Tune: Der Tag vertreibt die finstre Nacht. 1. [p. 400]

1. Now day drives off the gloomy night:
O brethren, rise and greet the light,
Serving God, your Master.

2. The angels ever sing and laud
And in their orders worship God,
Who o'er all things reigneth.

3. All flying birds that fill the sky
Sing praise to God with joyful cry,
For He feeds and clothes them.

4. The earth, the sea, the heavens raise
Unto the Lord their laud and praise,
Doing as He bids them.

5. All things that ever have been made,
In all their myriad kinds arrayed,
Worship their Creator.

6. O man, thou soul of noble kind,
O creature crowned with reas'ning mind,
Do not then be idle.

7. Remember that thy God and Lord
His image did to thee accord,
That thou mayest know Him,

8. And that thou mayest love the Same,
And with thy mouth confess His name,
And thereby enjoy Him.

9. Since of His Spirit thou hast known,
And been His wondrous graces shown,
Give Him thanks sincerely.

10. Watch ye and pray with diligence,
And keep the way with permanence
Till the Lord returneth.

11. Thou knowest not the hour or day,
For that Christ willed not to display,
But bade thee be watching.

12. So to His covenant take heed,
Praise Him with heart and mind and deed,
Thank Him for His goodness.

13. Pray: Father in eternity,
I thank Thee that Thou graciously
Keepest me each moment,

14. Through Jesus Christ, Thine only Son,
To whom, with Thee upon Thy throne,
Angels sing their praises.

15. Assist me, Lord, that all my days
I, too, may give Thee laud and praise
Evermore. So be it.

—M. Weisse, 1531; tr., M. Carver.

4. PRAISE AND THANKSGIVING

441 Tune: Lobe den Herren, O meine Seele. 53. [*TLH* 26; *LW* 445; *LSB* 797]

1. Praise the Almighty; my soul, adore Him!
Yea, I will laud Him until death.
With songs and anthems I'll come before Him
As long as He doth give me breath.
From Him my life and all things came;
Bless, O my soul, His holy name.
Alleluia, alleluia!

2. Trust not in princes, they are but mortal;
Earth-born they are and soon decay.
Naught are their counsels at life's last portal,
When the dark grave doth claim its prey.
Since, then, no man can help afford,
Trust ye in Christ, our God and Lord.
Alleluia, alleluia!

3. Blessèd, yea, blessèd is he forever
Whose help is in the Lord most high,
Whom from the saving faith naught can sever,
And who in hope to Christ draws nigh.
To all who trust in Him, our Lord,
Counsel and aid He doth afford.
Alleluia, alleluia!

4. God the Almighty, the great Creator,
Ruler of sky and land and sea,
All things ordainèd, and sooner or later
They come to pass unfailingly.
His rule is over rich and poor,
His promise ever standeth sure.
Alleluia, alleluia!

5. He pleads the cause of the poor forsaken;
Righteous and just are all His ways.
Feeding the hungry, their faith unshaken,
Mercy unfolds its beaming rays.
His grace, as boundless as the sea,
Opens the way to liberty.
Alleluia, alleluia!

6. Unto the blind man new sight supplying,
The lame He makes to walk again;
Penitent sinners, for mercy crying,
Pardon and peace from Him obtain;
He helps His children in distress,
The widows and the fatherless.
Alleluia, alleluia!

7. But when His rivals their steps are taking—
He with His hand confounds them all,
So that, unwilling, their plans forsaking,
They to their own devices fall.
The Lord is King eternally:
Zion, thy God e'er cares for thee.
Alleluia, alleluia!

8. Praise, all ye nations, the name so holy
Of Him who doth such wondrous things!
All that hath being, to praise Him solely,
With happy heart its Amen sings!
Children of God, with angel host
Praise Father, Son, and Holy Ghost!
Alleluia, alleluia!

—J. D. Herrnschmidt, 1714; tr. sts. 1–4, 6b, 8, A. E. R. Brauer, 1925, alt.; st. 5, W. M. Czamanske, 1919, alt.; sts. 6a, 7, M. Carver.

5. ETERNITY, RESURRECTION, AND JUDGMENT

442

Tune: Gott hat das Evangelium. 22. [p. 402]

1. God gave the Gospel that we may
Return to Him in faith today;
The world holds not this treasure fair,
For it the many do not care;
This is a token of the latter day!

2. Its precious doctrine they disdain;
Far rather, greed and sinful gain
In every station rampant run,
While they declare, "No harm is done!"
This is a token of the latter day!

3. Such vice incites the worldly wise
New ruses daily to devise,
For all things that their hearts desire,
To steal or falsely to acquire.
This is a token of the latter day!

4. Men give the Gospel words of laud
And yet refuse to turn to God.
Indeed, He is with mock'ry met
While they declare, "There is no threat!"
This is a token of the latter day!

5. Corruption thrives on every hand;
Men wreak injustice o'er the land
As if there were no God at all.
The poor to their affliction fall.
This is a token of the latter day!

6. The Church's treasures they receive,
But little profit will these give;
They let the needy starve unfed,
And rob their mouths of daily bread.
This is a token of the latter day!

7. The Church's gifts are God-endowed,
Not instituted by their crowd,
Yet they would take the Church's share;
Behold, what will their greed not dare?
This is a token of the latter day!

8. Men care no longer for the Lord,
The world seeks but to be adored,
A haughty spirit wins the prize,
Nor will they blush at tricks and lies.
This is a token of the latter day!

9. Where is the love of fellow men?
The world is but a robber's den.
All faith and hope are gone indeed,
While they declare, "'Tis gold I need!"
This is a token of the latter day!

10. The world will not soon be deterred;
No man will turn to hear God's Word!
Of nothing else they learn or think
But gluttony of food and drink.
This is a token of the latter day!

11. Their greatest knowledge is in feasts
And imitating shameless beasts—
These things they know to high degree;
The world is full of villainy.
This is a token of the latter day!

12. The lovely sun no longer can
Endure this awful sight to scan:
And so it takes away its glow.
Oh, what a dreadful, sorry show!
This is a token of the latter day!

13. The moon and stars are filled with pain,
Their faces in great sorrow strain.
How ardently they long to be
From all this wicked vision free!
This is a token of the latter day!

14. O Jesus Christ, dear Lord, then come!
The earth is weary, sick, and numb
From bearing Satan's kindling dry!
So come and bring their ending nigh,
And grant us all to see the latter day!

—E. Alber, 1548; tr., M. Carver.

443

Joyous Welcome to the Heavenly Jerusalem

Tune: Jerusalem, du hochgebaute Stadt. 73. [*TLH* 619; *LW* 306; *LSB* 674]

1. Jerusalem, thou city fair and high,
Would God I were in thee!
My longing heart fain, fain, to thee would fly,
It will not stay with me.
Far over vale and mountain,
Far over field and plain,
It hastes to seek its Fountain
And leave this world of pain.

2. O happy day and yet far happier hour,
When wilt thou come at last,
When fearless to my Father's love and pow'r,
Whose promise standeth fast,
My soul I gladly render?
For surely will His hand
Lead her with guidance tender
To heav'n, her fatherland.

3. A moment's space, and gently, wondrously,
Released from earthly ties,
Elijah's chariot bears her up to thee,
Through all these lower skies
To yonder shining regions,
While down to meet her come
The blessed angel legions
And bid her welcome home.

4. O Zion, hail! Bright city, now unfold
The gates of grace to me.
How many‿a time I longed for thee of old
Ere yet I was set free
From yon dark life of sadness,
Yon world of shad'wy naught,
And God had giv'n the gladness,
The heritage, I sought.

5. What glorious throng and what resplendent host
Comes sweeping swiftly down?
The chosen ones on earth who wrought the most,
The Church's brightest crown,
Our Lord hath set to meet me,
As in the far-off years
Their words oft came to greet me
In yonder land of tears.

6. The patriarchs' and prophets' noble train,
With all Christ's foll'wers true,
Who bore the cross and could the worst disdain
That tyrants dared to do,
I see them shine forever,
All-glorious as the sun,
Mid light that fadeth never,
Their perfect freedom won.

7. And when within that lovely Paradise
At last I safely dwell,
What songs of bliss shall from my lips arise,
What joy my tongue shall tell,
While all the saints are singing
Hosannas o'er and o'er,
Pure alleluias ringing
Around me evermore!

8. Unnumbered choirs before the shining throne
Their joyful anthems raise
Till heav'n's glad halls are echoing with the tone
Of that great hymn of praise
And all its host rejoices,
And all its blessed throng
Unite their myriad voices
In one eternal song.

—J. M. Meyfart, 1626; tr., C. Winkworth, 1858, alt.

Collects and Prayers

1.
A Christian Preparation for Prayer

O heavenly, faithful God, dear Father, I, a poor, miserable sinner, conceived and born in sin, am not worthy to lift mine eyes and hands up to Thee, or to open my heart and mouth to Thee, or even to be called Thy child. But since Thou hast not only bidden us, Thy poor creatures, to pray earnestly to Thee in all our cares, but also bountifully pledged and promised that Thou wouldst graciously hear us, and furthermore shown and taught us through Thine elect in the Old and New Testament, yet chiefly through Thine only and most beloved Son, our Lord Jesus Christ, both the words and the means whereby to obey Thee in what Thou biddest us, therefore, O God and Father, I come now, relying on Thy gracious pledge and promise, to call on Thee in my cares, and pray Thee in the name and merits of Thy beloved and only-begotten Son graciously and tenderly to hear me. Amen.

2.
Morning Prayer

Merciful, gracious God, Father of eternal light and consolation, whose goodness and faithfulness are new every morning, praise, honor, and thanks be to Thee for the blessed light of day, and for so graciously preserving me through the darkness of night and granting me a peaceful slumber and time of rest. Now let me rise joyfully again in Thy grace and love, protection and keeping, and make profitable and happy use of the blessed light of day. But above all, shine on me with the eternal Light, which is my Lord Jesus Christ, that I may be enlightened with His grace and the knowledge of Him. Guard within my breast the lamp of faith, stoke and strengthen it, stir up Thy love within me, confirm my hope, grant me true humility and gentleness that I may walk in the footsteps of my Lord Jesus Christ, and let Thy godly fear be always before mine eyes in all that I do. Drive out of my heart all spiritual darkness and blindness. Keep me this day and every day from superstition and idolatry, from pride, from blasphemy of Thy name, from contempt of Thy Word, from disobedience, and from violent wrath, that this day the sun may not go down in mine anger. Keep me from hostility, from hatred and envy, from immorality, from unrighteousness, from falsehood and lying, from shameful greed, and from the willing and doing of all that is wicked. Stir up within me a hunger and thirst for Thyself and Thy righteousness. Teach me to do the thing that pleases Thee; let Thy good Spirit lead me upon level ground. Let me behold the host of Thine holy angels, even as Jacob; give them charge over me, to keep me in all my ways, to bear me up in their hands, lest I dash my foot against a stone; that I may be strong to tread upon the lion and adder, and to trample under feet the young lion and the dragon. This day I commend unto Thee my thoughts, heart, mind, senses, and all mine endeavors; I commend unto Thee my lips and all my words; I commend unto Thee all my works: let them redound to the glory of Thy name and to the service of my neighbor. Make me a vessel of Thy mercy and an instrument of Thy grace. Bless all my every deed, give me success in my calling, and curb all who would hinder it. Defend me from the slander and poisonous darts of the deceiver. Unto Thee I commend my body and soul, my honor and property; let Thy grace and goodness be my constant companion. Keep Thine hand upon me when I sit or stand, when I stay or go, when I rise up or lie down. Keep me from the arrow that flieth by day, from the pestilence that walketh in darkness, and from the destruction that wasteth at noonday. Bless the source of my livelihood; give to me in my need whatever is Thy will, nor suffer me to abuse Thy gifts. Preserve us all from war, famine, and pestilence, and from a sudden and evil death. Defend my soul, my going out and my coming in, from this time forth and even forevermore. Bestow on me a blessed end, and let me await the blessed Last Day with longing and joy. God the Father bless me and keep me, God the Son make His face to shine upon me and be gracious unto me, and God the Holy Ghost lift up His countenance upon me and give me peace. Amen.

3.

Brief Morning Prayers

In the name of my Lord Jesus Christ the Crucified, who redeemed me with His precious blood, I now arise. May He defend and preserve me from all evil, and grant me every good in body and soul. O gracious Lord, my only Consolation, Hope, and Life, to Thine eternal majesty and grace I offer and devote myself wholly, humbly beseeching Thee that I and all whom Thou hast committed to my care, together with all the faithful who glorify and confess Thy name, may by Thy help and grace live and walk according to Thy divine will and pleasure all this day and all the days of our life; and that Thou wouldst this day also govern, bless, preserve, and defend me and all my thoughts, words, and works in all good things unto life everlasting. O Lord, I beseech Thee, remove from me whatever is displeasing to Thee, and grant me to do what pleases Thee well; for Thou livest and reignest with the Father and the Holy Spirit, one God, now and forever. Amen.

4.

O Lord God, heavenly Father, I praise and thank Thee for keeping me in Thy watch throughout this night and all time hitherto, and for allowing me in Thy grace to see this present hour. And I pray Thee from my heart graciously to keep me now, this day, and all my life, and to direct me by Thy Holy Spirit, that all the darkness of disbelief and carnal desires may be driven from my heart, and that, justified by perfect faith, I may walk body and soul in the light of Thy divine truth, to the praise of Thee and to the benefit and aid of my neighbor; through Jesus Christ, our Lord. Amen.

5.

Lord Jesus Christ, who alone art the true Sun of the world, ever rising and never setting, who by Thy gracious sight dost bring forth, sustain, nourish, and gladden all that is in heaven and on earth: Shine also upon my heart, I beseech Thee, and drive away the night of sin and the darkness of all error, that, freed from all the works of darkness, I may by Thine inward and gracious enlightening walk in a Christlike manner without any stumbling all the days of my life on this earth; for Thou livest and reignest with the Father and the Holy Ghost, one God, now and forever. Amen.

6.
Evening Prayer

Merciful, gracious God and Father, I give Thee thanks and praise that Thou hast created day and night, dividing the light from the darkness and giving the day for toil and the night for rest, that man and beast may be refreshed. I praise and thank Thee in all Thy benefits and works that, through Thy divine grace and protection, Thou hast allowed me to see the ending of this day and to overcome and leave behind its burdens and travails. Sufficient unto the day, dear Father, is the travail thereof; for Thou wilt ever help us to lay aside one burden after another until at last we come to rest in the eternal day when all travail and heaviness shall cease. I thank Thee from my heart for all the good that I have received from Thy hand this day. O Lord, I am not worthy of the least of all the mercies which Thou hast showed unto me each day. I thank Thee also for averting whatever evil might have met me this day, and for covering and keeping me in the secret place of the Most High and under the shadow of the Almighty, from all misfortune and grievous sin. I, Thy child, also heartily beseech Thee to forgive me all my sins which I have committed this day in thought, word, and deed. Much evil have I done, and much good have I neglected. Be merciful unto me, O God, be merciful unto me! Let all my sins, together with myself, die this day, and grant me to rise again with ever greater fear of God, holiness, godliness, and righteousness, that my sleep not be the sleep of sin, but a holy slumber, that my soul and my spirit within me may wake with Thee, speak with Thee, and be concerned with Thee. Bless my sleep like that of the patriarch Jacob, when in a dream he saw the heavenly ladder and received the blessing and beheld the holy angels; that I may talk of Thee upon my bed, and remember Thee when I wake; so that, whether I sleep or whether I wake, Thy name and remembrance may abide in my heart continually. Grant me not to be afraid for the terror by night, nor for sudden fear, nor for the troubling winds of the ungodly, but that I may sleep in peace. Defend me from frightening dreams, from phantoms and spirits of the night, from the assaults of the enemy, and from calamity by fire and water. Behold, He that keepeth us will not slumber; behold, He that keepeth Israel shall neither slumber nor sleep. Be Thou, O God, my shade upon my right hand, that the sun may not smite me by day, nor the moon by night. Let Thy holy watchers defend me, and Thine angels encamp round about me, and deliver me. Let Thy holy angels rouse me in due season, as they did the prophet Elijah when he slept under the juniper tree, and Peter when he slept in prison between two soldiers. Let the holy angels appear to me in my sleep, as they did to Joseph and to the wise men from the east, that I may know that I, too, have the fellowship of the holy angels. And when my last hour is close at hand, grant me a peaceful sleep and blessed rest in Jesus Christ my Lord. Amen.

7.
Evening Prayer

Lord God, heavenly Father, I give Thee praise and thanks that Thou hast defended, instructed, and sustained me this day in so fatherly a manner, and I beseech Thee to forgive me whatever I have thought, spoken, and done against Thee this day, and to preserve me this night also, that I may rest in Thy name, and in the morning joyfully rise again to Thy praise. Defend also our leaders, teachers, and every man; through Jesus Christ, our Lord. Amen.

8.

Daily Confession before Going to Sleep

My dear Father, I always confess, and Thou seest, that for my own part, in all my comings and goings, inside and out, hide and hair, body and soul, I deserve nothing but the everlasting fire of hell. Taking it all in all, Thou, my Father, indeed knowest that there is nothing good in me, not even a hair on my head. It all deserves nothing but to go to the wretched devil in the pit of hell. Why should I use many words? Nevertheless, O my dear Father, I beseech Thee, in spite of all that I am, do not fix Thine eyes upon me to search me, or I must perish and be destroyed, even if there were a hundred thousand worlds between us. Rather, I pray Thee, fix Thine eyes upon and search the face of Thy dear Son Jesus Christ, Thine Anointed, my Mediator, High Priest, and Advocate, my Savior and Redeemer. For His sake, and not for mine own, I pray Thee, O my Father, be gracious and merciful to me; and grant me a blessed end and a joyful resurrection for the sake of Thy dear Son Jesus Christ, and preserve my body here and my poor soul in the world to come. For the sake of the crimson blood which He, Thy Son Jesus Christ, so generously shed on the gallows of the cross for the forgiveness and remission of my sins, I pray Thee now, O my Father, that Thou wouldst not, according to Thy righteousness, change and alter the blood of the same Jesus Christ, Thy dear Son, and withhold it from me, a poor creature, because of my manifold sins which cannot be named, but according to Thy boundless mercy allow this benefit and fruit to avail for me, for which purpose it was ordained from eternity by Thee and shed by Thy dear Son Jesus Christ on the gallows of the cross; namely, that Thou wouldst let it suffice for me and let it avail for the remission and forgiveness of my sins, so that, at whatever hour or moment, by day or night, Thou wilt come and knock, and wilt require my spirit which Thou first didst breathe into me, so I pray Thee continually, O my Father, to permit this my spirit, that is, my soul, to be commended into Thy hands, for the sake of the blood, Passion, and death of Thy dear Son Jesus Christ. Amen.

9.

On the Seven Petitions of the Holy Our Father

Thou art Our Father, and desirest honor from us, wherefore grant that Thy name may be esteemed as excellent and exalted in all the world; restrain all manner of false faith and worship, the whole of hell, the blasphemous beliefs of the pope, and the factious spirits and heretics who all profane and disgrace Thy name, and in Thy name seek only their own honor.

2. *Thy kingdom come.* Since we have Thy Word and true doctrine and worship, grant also that Thy kingdom may be and abide among us; govern us in this doctrine and life, supporting and sustaining us therein against all the power of the devil and his kingdom, and grant that every kingdom that rages against it may be brought to ruin.

3. *Thy will be done.* Suffer not the will of man, but of Thee alone, to be done, and make Thine own thought and counsel to prosper against all the plans and endeavors of the world, and against whatsoever resists Thy will and counsel, though all the world assemble and strengthen themselves in one body to affirm their cause against it.

4. *Give us this day our daily bread.* Give us all that we need to sustain this life: nourishment, good health, good weather, house, home, wife, child, good government, and peace, and defend us from all manner of plague, sickness, pestilence, famine, war, rebellion, and the like.

5. *Forgive us our trespasses.* Look not on the world's disgraceful abuse and ingratitude

for the blessings which Thou daily and richly givest us, nor deny and remove them from us because of this, nor punish us by the withholding of Thy grace as we deserve, but graciously pardon us, even though we who are called Christians and Thy children do not lead sinless lives as we ought.

6. *Lead us not into temptation.* Because we live on this earth in the midst of all manner of tribulation and offense, where we are beset on all sides by hindrances and under attack not only outwardly by the world and the devil but also inwardly by our own flesh, and cannot live as we ought, nor stand one day in the face of so much peril and tribulation; we therefore pray Thee, sustain us in this danger and distress lest we be overcome by them and perish.

7. *Deliver us from evil.* Bring us at last out of all adversity, and when the time comes for us to depart this life, bestow on us a gracious and blessed death. Amen.

10.
Brief Prayer for Faith

I thank Thee, my dear God, that I have learned that I am not to confront my sins with my own repentance, nor seize faith by my own efforts, nor blot out my own sins. Before men I might well do so; in the eyes of the world and of magistrates such things may avail. But with Thee, O God, there is an everlasting wrath which I cannot appease and before which I would have to despair. Therefore I thank Thee that Another has confronted, borne, atoned for, and blotted out my sins in my stead. All this I would gladly believe, since it seems right and admirable to me, yet I cannot persuade myself to believe it, for I find nothing in mine own powers wherewith to do so, nor can I comprehend it as I ought. Lord, lead Thou me, help me, and give me the power and grace to believe. I plead as David did: "Create in me a clean heart, O God, and renew a right spirit within me." I am unable to create a new and clean heart, for that is Thy work and creation. As little as I am able to make the sun or moon to rise and shine brightly in the heavens, so little can I make my heart clean, and endue myself with a right spirit, and give myself a strong and steadfast heart that is unbending and will not waver, neither doubt nor mistrust Thy Word. Amen.

11.
In Tribulation of Temporal Cares

Almighty God, heavenly Lord, and merciful Father, I come again to Thee as to mine own faithful, beloved Lord and Father, and from my heart lay before Thee my present troubles which urge me to come to Thee, for I am again beset by scandalous unbelief, so that I cannot confide in Thee, nor abandon myself wholly to Thy Word and pledge that Thou wilt provide for me in every trouble. Wherefore, O my God and Lord, I beseech Thee, help Thou my unbelief and increase faith in me, that I may rely on Thy Word and not depart therefrom; and forasmuch as Thou hast bidden me to pray for daily bread, I therefore beseech Thee through Christ, through whom Thou badest us pray in this manner, that Thou wouldst provide me with all that I need in body and soul; and, O my dear Father, forasmuch as my temporal livelihood is each day in great peril, and I cannot confide or take comfort in it, but only in Thee, for Thou alone canst help me, and Thou Thyself dost offer Thy help to me, saying, "Call upon Me in the day of trouble; I will help thee,"— therefore I come to Thee, trusting in Thy comforting pledge which Thou didst swear to me by the mouth of the holy prophet David, saying, "The Lord knoweth the days of them that believe; they shall not be ashamed in the evil time, and in the days of famine they shall be satisfied." Therefore I cast my cares, O Lord, on Thee. Thou wilt provide for me and satisfy the desires of my heart, for Thou, my Lord, hast promised that, if I seek first the kingdom of God and His righteousness, all these things will naturally be added and given unto me. Therefore I will concern myself above all with Thy Word, and leave Thee to worry how Thou wilt support me. Unto Thee do I commend myself, body and soul, house and livelihood; sustain Thou me by Thy grace, here in time and hereafter in eternity; in Jesus Christ, Thy Son, our Redeemer and Savior. Amen.

12.

Against the Persecutors and Enemies of the Church

O heavenly Father, though we have most justly deserved Thy punishment, yet correct us in Thy mercy and not in Thy wrath. Better it is for us, as David pled, that we should fall into the rod of Thy hands than into the hand of man or of our enemy, for Thy mercies are great. We have sinned against Thee, and have not kept Thy commandments. But Thou knowest, O Almighty God our Father, that we have not sinned against the devil or the foes and persecutors of Thy Word, nor have they any right or power to punish us. Howbeit Thou canst and mayest use them against us as Thy stinging rod, for we have sinned against Thee and deserve every misfortune. Yea, O God our heavenly Father, we have committed no sins against them for which cause they might be right to punish us, but much rather do they desire that we should join them in the most execrable sins against Thee, for they care not if we disobey Thee, slander Thee, and commit all kinds of idolatry (as they do), deal in false teaching, disbelief, and lying, adultery, immorality, murder, theft, robbery, sorcery, and do every manner of evil against Thee—for such they have no concern, but rather this is our sin against them, that we proclaim, believe in, and confess Thee, God our Father, the only true God with Thy dear Son, our Lord Jesus Christ, and the Holy Ghost, one everlasting God. Indeed, this is the sin which we commit against them. Yet were we to deny Thee, the devil and the accuser would surely leave Thy church in peace, as Thy dear Son says: "If ye were of the world, the world would love you." Therefore be a merciful Father unto us, and a stern Judge unto our enemies, for they are rather Thine enemies than our own, and when they persecute and afflict us, they persecute and afflict Thee Thyself, for the Word which we proclaim, believe in, and confess is not our own but Thine, and all a working of Thy Holy Spirit in us. The devil cannot endure this, but he would be our god instead of Thee and implant in us falsehood instead of Thy Word. If it so be that it is sin that we hold, confess, and extol Thee, the Father, and Thy Son, and the Holy Ghost as the one true God, then Thou Thyself art the Sinner which workest in us, callest us, and desirest us. Thus when they hate, strike, and punish us for such doctrines, they hate, strike, and punish Thee Thyself. Arise, therefore, dear Lord God, and hallow Thy Name which they profane, strengthen Thy kingdom which they assail, and exert Thy will which they would extinguish in us; nor because of sin do Thou remove Thy feet from those who do not punish our sins in us, but would stamp out Thy holy Word, name, and work in us, that Thou shouldst be no God, nor have any people that proclaims, believes in, and confesses Thee, who art our only Hope, with Thy Son and the Holy Ghost, ever one God, world without end. Amen.

13.

For Ministers

Almighty and gracious God, the Father of our Lord Jesus Christ, who hast earnestly commanded us to pray that Thou wouldst send forth laborers into Thy harvest: we beseech Thee of Thine infinite mercy, give us true teachers and ministers of Thy divine Word, and put Thy saving Word in their hearts and in their minds and on their lips, that they may truly fulfill Thy command, and preach nothing contrary to Thy holy Word; that we, being warned, instructed, nurtured, comforted, and strengthened by that everlasting and heavenly Word, may do those things which are well-pleasing to Thee, and profitable to us. Grant, O Lord, unto Thy Church Thy Holy Spirit, and the wisdom which cometh down from above, that Thy Word, as becometh it, may have free course and be glorified among us, being preached to the joy and edifying of Thy holy Christian Church, that in steadfast faith we may serve Thee, and in the confession of Thy name abide unto the end; through Jesus Christ our Lord. Amen.

14.

For One's Minister at the Beginning of the Service

Almighty, everlasting God, who by Thy dear Son, our Lord and Savior Jesus Christ, didst command us to pray that Thou wouldst send forth faithful laborers into Thy harvest: grant, I heartily beseech Thee, unto my minister so to handle Thy holy Word that, as becometh it, he would fearlessly open his mouth to oppose every false doctrine and abuse, proclaim the mystery of Thy holy Gospel, and instruct and edify Thy Church, that I and all my brothers and sisters assembled with me in the Church, being strengthened by Thy Holy Spirit, may live in Thine obedience here in time, and be saved hereafter in eternity; through the same Thy Son Jesus Christ our Lord. Amen.

15.

Confession to God after the Holy Ten Commandments

Righteous God, merciful Father: I, a poor, miserable sinner, confess not only that I was conceived and born in sin, but also, alas, that I have passed all the days of my life from childhood to this very hour in many grievous sins, during which time I have not feared and loved Thee, my God and Lord, with all my heart, with all my soul, with all my strength, and with all my mind, nor trusted in Thee above all things, nor called upon and worshiped Thy holy name with all my heart, but have frequently taken Thy name in vain. I have often neglected, despised, and refused to be edified by the preaching of Thy holy Word. I have been disobedient to my parents and those in authority over me. I have not occupied my estate and vocation as faithfully and diligently as Thou requirest of me. Neither have I loved my neighbor as myself, but I have hated, despised, offended, and injured him, and allowed him to be injured. I have also acted shamefully and immorally in word and deed. In all my doings I have not been as zealous for righteousness and as eager for speaking the truth as I ought. I have delighted in wickedness; I have been proud, greedy, lustful, wrathful, intemperate, envious, and slothful. Thus I have transgressed the covenant of my holy Baptism. I have sinned against Thee in deed, word, and thought, private and public, and by all my hidden errors which Thou, unto whom all hearts lie bare, dost know better than I myself, who now confess them all with sincere remorse and sorrow. I am an unprofitable servant (maidservant), and have sinned against heaven and before Thee, and am not worthy to be called Thy child or to lift up mine eyes unto Thee. For I have grievously angered Thee with many foul sins, and sorely burdened my poor soul and conscience, which as a great weight heavily oppresses me. I come therefore in the day of grace, appealing Thy strict judgment to Thine infinite mercy. Forgive me of my sins; receive as payment the innocent death of Jesus Christ, Thy dear Son, and grant Thine Holy Spirit for the correction of my sinful life. Amen.

16.
Another Confession

I, a poor sinner, confess unto God, my heavenly Father, that I have sinned grievously and in various ways, not only by outward sins, but also by inward, innate blindness, disbelief, doubt, despondency, impatience, disobedience, pride, evil lusts, avarice, secret envy, hatred, malice and other sins; that in many ways I have transgressed the most holy commandments of God, as my dear Lord and God perceives, and I, alas! cannot as fully discern. But I repent of these sins, and am sorry for them, and from my heart desire grace of God through His beloved Son Jesus Christ, and I pray that He will send me His Holy Spirit for the reformation of my life. Amen.

17.
For a Longing for the Holy Supper

Oh, most beloved Lord Jesus Christ, look upon my sorrow, for I am poor and miserable. I am so slothful and idle toward Thy medicine, for I have no longing to run to the riches of Thy grace. Wherefore I beseech Thee, O Lord, to kindle in me a true desire and longing for Thy grace, and to give me a firm belief in Thy promise, lest I offend Thee with my unholy disbelief and aversion. Amen.

My Lord Jesus Christ, behold my corrupt nature, for I, a needy and miserable man, have no appetite for the medicine that Thou hast ordained for the forgiveness of sins and for salvation. I find in myself no genuine longing for the riches of Thy grace. Kindle in my heart, dear Lord, a longing for Thy mercy and faith in Thy promise, that I might not anger Thee, my most faithful Shepherd, with my shameful disbelief and offensive aversion, but eat and drink worthily of the bread and wine of Thy Body and Blood, and by this saving food be strengthened and sustained unto life everlasting. Amen.

18.
For Steadfast Faith in One's Absolution

Dear God, who in Thy Holy Word hast furnished me with certain proofs assuring me that my Lord Christ's life, grace, and heaven, where He is, have completely removed sin, death, and hell from me: Thou wilt assuredly keep this promise to me, that the words wherewith the minister of Thy Church has absolved me of my sins are as firm and efficacious as if they had been spoken by Thee, O God. If therefore it is God's Word, as indeed it is, then it must and shall certainly happen and be done as the words on which I rely declare; and in this hope and confidence I will gladly die. Amen.

19.
Before Partaking of the Holy Supper

My Lord Jesus Christ, I come once again, a poor sinner indebted to Thee in manifold ways, and meriting nothing but eternal wrath and the punishment of hell. Yet inasmuch as Thou art abundant in mercy, Thou hast no pleasure in the death of the wicked, but that he should turn and live, for which cause Thou didst institute for us a New Testament, promised long ago through Thy prophets, wherein Thou wouldst through Thine own death remove from us our iniquities and remember them no more. Thus before Thy death Thou didst ordain for us Thy last will and testament, promising verily to deliver Thy body up to contemptible death, and to pour out Thy blood for the forgiveness of our sins. For such is Thy gracious promise: "Take, eat, this is My body, given for you; this is the cup of the New Testament in My blood, poured out for the forgiveness of your sins." This Thy pledge I firmly believe, confiding therein as in the true Word of God. Let it be unto me according to Thy words. Therefore, for the greater assurance and strengthening of my faith, I will approach and receive Thy true Body and drink Thy true Blood as Thou hast bidden, and in this way help to show, praise, laud, and honor Thy death, giving thanks for the unspeakable benefit which Thou hast shown and granted me therein. For here, as a generous Treasurer, Thou dost open Thy treasure-store unto me, apportioning Thy blessings, the forgiveness of sins, righteousness, and eternal life. Unto Thee, O Lord, with God Thy heavenly Father and the Holy Ghost, be worship, glory, and honor from everlasting to everlasting. Amen.

20.
Sighs Before Receiving the Holy Supper

My Lord Christ, I have fallen, and would fain be strong; for which purpose Thou hast instituted this Sacrament for us, that with it we may rekindle and strengthen our faith, and thus be helped. Therefore I am here to receive it. — Behold, Lord, here is Thy Word, and here are my failures and infirmities. Thou Thyself hast said, "Come unto Me, all that labor and are heavy laden, and I will give thee rest." Wherefore I now come to be helped.

Lord, it is true that I am not worthy that Thou shouldst come under my roof. Yet I am in need and desirous of Thy help and grace, that I may be healed. Thus I come with no other plea than that I have heard the gracious words of invitation to approach Thy table, assuring me who am unworthy that I shall have forgiveness of all my sins through Thy Body and Blood which I eat and drink in this Sacrament. Amen, dear Lord, Thy Word is true. I do no doubt it, and hereupon I will eat and drink with Thee. Be it unto me according to Thy Word. Amen.

Dear Lord, I feel so weak, sick, and powerless, yet I will not let this cause me to go astray. I will come to Thee, that Thou mayest help me, for Thou art the Shepherd. So accounting Thee, I therefore despair of my own works.

21.
After Partaking of the Holy Supper

Almighty, everlasting God, I praise and thank Thee that of Thy divine generosity Thou hast again fed me with the saving Body and given me to drink of the saving Blood of Thine only Son Jesus Christ, my Lord; and I humbly pray Thee to work in me by Thy Holy Spirit, that, having now by mouth received this Holy Sacrament, I may by firm faith receive and ever hold fast Thy divine grace, forgiveness of sins, unity with Christ, and life everlasting, all of which Thou hast so graciously offered and delivered to me in this Thy Holy Sacrament; through Jesus Christ, Thy dear Son, our Lord. Amen.

22.
To Be Said by the Dying, after Receiving the Holy Supper

Almighty, merciful, everlasting Lord God and Father of our dear Lord Jesus Christ, I am certain that everything that Thou hast said Thou art willing and able also to keep, for Thou canst not lie. Thy Word is true, and from the beginning Thou hast pledged to give me Thy dear and only Son, Jesus Christ, who came and redeemed me from the devil, death, hell, and sin, and thereafter, for my greater assurance, graciously bestowed on me the Sacrament of Baptism and of the Altar, wherein, being proffered the forgiveness of sins, eternal life, and every heavenly good, I have partaken of them, and in faith firmly relied on and received them, for which cause I have no doubt that I am safe and secure from the devil, death, hell, and sin. If this prove to be my hour and Thy divine will, then at Thy word I will gladly depart in peace.

23.
At the Point of Death

I am a poor sinner, as Thou knowest, my dear Lord, yet Thou hast shown me through Thy dear Son Jesus Christ that Thou wilt be gracious to me, forgive my sins, and put away all wrath and condemnation, and biddest me to believe this and not doubt. In this I trust, and will depart from hence in joy. Amen.

Lord, I know no man either in heaven or on earth in whom I could ever have a consoling refuge except in Thee through Christ. I have no choice but to strip myself naked of all other works and merits. Lord, I have no refuge save in Thy divine bosom where Thy Son is seated. Had I not this hope, all would be in vain. Amen.

24.
To Be Said by Those Attending to a Dying Person

Almighty, everlasting God, dear, heavenly, faithful Father, inasmuch as Thou hast pledged and promised us in Thy trustworthy Word mercifully to receive the prayers of them that call upon Thee in the day of trouble: now therefore do we cry to Thee also in this our hour of distress, beseeching Thee through Thy dear Son Jesus Christ, our Lord, not to abandon this Thy poor creature here at his (her) final end. Defend him (her), O Lord and God, from the power of the evil foe; lead him (her) not into temptation; reckon not his (her) frailty against him (her), but pardon and be gracious unto him (her). Leave him (her) not during this great distress, but have mercy on him (her), and grant him (her) the power and strength boldly to resist his (her) enemies, sin, death, the devil, and hell, and to abide steadfast in his (her) Redeemer, and through the Same at last to be saved; for the sake of the Thy dear Son, our Lord Jesus Christ. Amen.

25.

Brief Litany and Prayers for the Dying

O Lord,	Have mercy.
O Christ,	Have mercy.
O Lord,	Have mercy on this sick person.
God, the Father in heaven;	Have mercy upon him (her).
God, the Son, Redeemer of the world;	Have mercy upon him (her).
God, the Holy Ghost;	Have mercy upon him (her).
Holy Trinity, Everlasting God:	Have mercy upon him (her).
O Lord,	Be merciful and spare this dying person.
From the evil one;	Good Lord, deliver him (her).
From the crafts and assaults of the devil;	Good Lord, deliver him (her).
From all evil;	Good Lord, deliver him (her).
From the torment of hell:	Good Lord, deliver him (her).
By Thy holy incarnation and nativity;	Help him (her), good Lord.
By Thine agony and bloody sweat;	Help him (her), good Lord.
By Thy cross and bitter death;	Help him (her), good Lord.
By Thy holy resurrection and ascension;	Help him (her), good Lord.
By the grace of the Holy Ghost;	Help him (her), good Lord.
In the hour of his (her) death;	Help him (her), good Lord.
On the Last Day;	Help him (her), good Lord.
At the Last Judgment:	Help him (her), good Lord.
We poor sinners do beseech Thee	To hear us, O Lord God.
That this sick person may have consolation;	Hear us, O Lord God.
That all his (her) sins may be pardoned;	Hear us, O Lord God.
And that after this misery he (she) may be [granted everlasting life:	Hear us, O Lord God.
O Christ,	Hear us.
O Lamb of God, that takest away the sin [of the world,	Have mercy upon this sick person and grant [him (her) everlasting peace.
O Lord,	Have mercy.
O Christ,	Have mercy.
O Lord,	Have mercy upon him (her).

Our Father, who art in heaven, etc.

Prayer

Almighty, everlasting God, dear, faithful, heavenly Father: comfort and strengthen this Thy poor creature, and in Thy lovingkindness spare him (her); deliver him (her) from all anguish and distress, release him (her) in Thy grace, and receive him (her) to Thyself in Thy kingdom; through Jesus Christ, Thy dear Son, our only Lord, Redeemer, and Savior. Amen.

Another

Almighty, everlasting God: let the anxious sighings and lamentations of this dying person find mercy with Thee. Receive him (her) into the heavenly kingdom which by grace Thou hast prepared for him (her) and for all believers from the foundation of the world. Graciously release him (her), O Lord, and after paying the mortal debt, comfort him (her) forever with Thine elect; through Thy dear Son, our Lord Jesus Christ. Amen.

26. Forms for Baptism in Cases of Necessity

All say: Our Father, who art in heaven, etc.
Hereupon the baptizer says:

O dear Lord Christ, at Thy bidding we offer to Thee this child. Receive it and let it be an heir of Thy kingdom, even as Thou hast said, "Suffer the children to come unto Me, and forbid them not, for of such is the kingdom of heaven."

Those present say:

Amen.

Hereupon the water is administered with the words:

I baptize thee in the name of the Father, and of the Son, and of the Holy Ghost.

Those present say:

Amen.

If there is concern that the preceding form is too long for the fleeting life of the child, the baptizer may say:

O Lord Jesus Christ, mercifully receive this child.

Those present say:

Amen.

The baptizer says:

I baptize thee in the name of the Father, and of the Son, and of the Holy Ghost. Amen.

Those present say:

Amen.

History of the Passion

AND DEATH OF OUR LORD AND SAVIOR JESUS CHRIST

ARRANGED IN FIVE PARTS[14]

First Reading

When they had sung a hymn, Jesus went out with His disciples across the Kidron valley, as was His custom, to the Mount of Olives; and the disciples followed Him. And Jesus said to them, "You will all fall away because of Me this night. For it is written, 'I will strike the shepherd, and the sheep of the flock will be scattered.' But after I am raised up, I will go before you into Galilee." But Peter answered Him, "Though they all fall away because of You, I will never fall away." And Jesus said to him, "Truly, I tell you, this very night, before the rooster crows twice, you will deny Me three times." But He said emphatically, "If I must die with you, I will not deny you." And all the discipl es said the same.

Then Jesus went with them to a place called Gethsemane, where there was a garden which He and His disciples entered. Now Judas, who betrayed Him, also knew the place, for Jesus often met there with His disciples. And Jesus said to them, "Sit here while I go over there and pray."

And He took with Him Peter, and James and John, the two sons of Zebedee, and began to be greatly distressed and troubled, and said to them, "My soul is very sorrowful, even to death; remain here, and watch with Me, that you may not fall into temptation." And He withdrew from them about a stone's throw and knelt down and fell on His face and prayed that, if it were possible, the hour might pass from Him, and said, "Abba, Father, all things are possible for You. Remove this cup from Me. Yet not what I will, but what You will." And He came to His disciples and found them sleeping, and He said to Peter, "Simon, are you asleep? Could you not watch with Me one hour? Watch and pray, that you may not fall into temptation. The spirit indeed is willing, but the flesh is weak." Again, for the second time, He went away and prayed, "My Father, if this cannot pass unless I drink it, Your will be done." And again He came and found them sleeping, for their eyes were heavy, and they did not know what to answer Him. So, leaving them again, He went away and prayed the third time, saying the same words again: "Father, if You are willing, remove this cup from Me. Nevertheless, not My will, but Yours, be done."

And there appeared to Him an angel from heaven, strengthening Him. And being in an agony He prayed more earnestly; and His sweat became like great drops of blood falling down to the ground.

And when He rose from prayer, He came to the disciples and found them sleeping for sorrow and said to them, "Are you still sleeping and taking your rest? Why are you sleeping? It is enough. The hour has come, and the Son of Man is betrayed into the hands of

14 I have tried to follow the ESV as closely as possible in translating the original German text, which is based on Luther's translation of the Bible. Changes and omissions are noted.

sinners. Rise and let us be going; see, My betrayer is at hand. But pray that you may not fall into temptation."

While He was still speaking, Judas, one of the twelve, having procured a band of soldiers and some officers from the chief priests and the Pharisees, came there with lanterns and torches and weapons, going before a great crowd with swords and clubs, from the chief priests and the elders of the people. Now the betrayer had given them a sign, saying, "The one I will kiss is the man; seize Him and lead Him away under guard." Then Jesus, knowing all that would happen to Him, came forward and said to them, "Whom do you seek?" They answered him, "Jesus of Nazareth." Jesus said to them, "I am He." Judas, who betrayed Him, was standing with them. When Jesus said to them, "I am He," they drew back and fell to the ground. So He asked them again, "Whom do you seek?" And they said, "Jesus of Nazareth." Jesus answered, "I told you that I am He. So, if you seek Me, let these men go." (This was to fulfill the word that He had spoken: "Of those whom You gave Me I have lost not one.")

Now Judas drew near to Jesus to kiss Him; and he came up to Him at once and said, "Greetings, Rabbi!" And he kissed Him. And Jesus said to him, "Friend, do what you came to do.[15] Judas, would you betray the Son of Man with a kiss?" And they came up and laid hands on Jesus and seized Him. And when those who were around Him saw what would follow, they said, "Lord, shall we strike with the sword?" Then Simon Peter, having a sword, drew it and struck the high priest's servant and cut off his right ear. (The servant's name was Malchus.)

But Jesus said, "No more of this!" And He said to Peter, "Put your sword into its sheath. For all who take the sword will perish by the sword. Do you think that I cannot appeal to My Father, and He will at once send me more than twelve legions of angels? Shall I not drink the cup that My Father has given Me? But how then should the Scriptures be fulfilled, that it must be so?" And He touched his ear and healed him.

At that hour Jesus said to the chief priests and the rulers of the temple and the elders, "Have you come out as against a robber, with swords and clubs to capture Me? Day after day I sat in the temple teaching, and you did not lay hands on Me. But this is your hour, and the power of darkness, that the Scriptures might be fulfilled. And this has all taken place that the Scriptures of the prophets might be fulfilled."

Then all the disciples left Him and fled. And a young man followed Him, with nothing but a linen cloth about his body. And they[16] seized him, but he left the linen cloth and ran away naked.

Second Reading

So the band of soldiers and their captain and the officers of the Jews arrested Jesus and bound Him. First they led Him to Annas, for he was the father-in-law of Caiaphas, who was high priest that year. It was Caiaphas who had advised the Jews that it would be expedient that one man should die for the people. They led Him to Caiaphas the high priest, where all the chief priests and the elders and the scribes had gathered.

Simon Peter followed Jesus at a distance, right into the courtyard of the high priest, and so did another disciple. Since that disciple was known to the high priest, he entered

15 In the German: "My friend, why have you come?"

16 In the German: "And the young men . . . "

with Jesus into the court of the high priest. But Peter stood outside at the door. So the other disciple, who was known to the high priest, went out and spoke to the servant girl who kept watch at the door, and brought Peter in. Now the servants and officers had made a charcoal fire in the middle of the courtyard, and they were standing and warming themselves. Peter also was with them, standing and warming himself at the fire to see the end. Then the high priest's servant girl who kept watch at the door, seeing Peter as he sat in the light, warming himself, and looking closely at him, said, "You also were with Jesus the Galilean. You also are not one of this man's disciples, are you?" But he denied it before them all, saying, "Woman, I am not; I do not know Him, nor do I understand what you mean."

The high priest then questioned Jesus about His disciples and His doctrine. Jesus answered him, "I have spoken openly to the world; I have always taught in synagogues and in the temple, where all Jews come together. I have said nothing in secret. Why do you ask Me? Ask those who have heard Me what I said to them; they know what I said." When He had said these things, one of the officers standing by struck Jesus with his hand, saying, "Is that how you answer the high priest?" Jesus answered him, "If what I said is wrong, bear witness about the wrong; but if what I said is right, why do you strike me?" Annas then sent Him bound to Caiaphas the high priest.

Now Simon Peter was standing, warming himself. And a while after the first denial, as he went out into the gateway, the rooster crowed. And another servant girl saw him, and began again to say to the bystanders, "This man was with Jesus of Nazareth." Then they said to him, "You are not one of His disciples, are you?" And another said, "You also are one of them." But he again denied it with an oath: "Man, I am not, nor do I know the man." And after an interval of about an hour, still another insisted with the bystanders, saying, "Certainly you also are one of them, for you are a Galilean, and your accent betrays you." One of the servants of the high priest, a relative of the man whose ear Peter had cut off, asked, "Did I not see you in the garden with Him?" But he began to invoke a curse on himself and to swear, "I do not know this man of whom you speak." And immediately, while he was still speaking, the rooster crowed again. And the Lord turned, and looked at Peter. And Peter remembered the saying of the Lord, how He had said to him, "Before the rooster crows twice, you will deny Me three times." And he went out and wept bitterly.

And the chief priests and the elders and the whole Council were seeking testimony against Jesus to put Him to death, but they found none. For many bore false witness against Him, but their testimony did not agree. At last two came forward, saying, "We heard Him say, 'I am able to and will destroy the temple of God, which is made with hands, and in three days build another not made with hands.'" Yet even about this their testimony did not agree.

And the high priest stood up in the midst and asked Jesus, "Have You no answer to make? What is it that these men testify against You?" But He remained silent and made no answer. Again the high priest asked Him, "Are You the Christ, the Son of the Blessed? I adjure You by the living God, tell us if You are the Christ, the Son of God." Jesus said to him, "You say that I am. But I tell you, from now on you will see the Son of Man seated at the right hand of Power and coming on the clouds of heaven." Then the high priest tore his robes and said, "He has uttered blasphemy. What further witnesses do we need? You have now heard His blasphemy. What is your judgment?" They answered, "He deserves death."

Now the men who were holding Jesus in custody were mocking Him, and they spit in His face and struck Him. And some slapped Him, in particular the guards, saying, "Prophesy to us, you Christ! Who is it that struck you?" And they spoke many other blasphemies against Him.

When morning came, all the chief priests and scribes and the elders of the people, with the whole assembly, gathered together and took counsel against Jesus to put Him to death. And they led Him away to their council, and they said, "If You are the Christ, tell us." But He said to them, "If I tell you, you will not believe, and if I ask you, you will not answer Me, nor let Me go.[17] But from now on the Son of Man shall be seated at the right hand of the Power of God." So they all said, "Are You the Son of God, then?" And He said to them, "You say that I am." Then they said, "What further testimony do we need? We have heard it ourselves from His own lips."

Third Reading

And the whole company of them arose and bound Jesus and led Him away from the house of Caiaphas to the governor's headquarters, and delivered Him over to Pontius Pilate the governor.

Then when Judas, His betrayer, saw that Jesus was condemned, he changed his mind and brought back the thirty pieces of silver to the chief priests and elders, saying, "I have sinned by betraying innocent blood." They said, "What is that to us? See to it yourself." And throwing down the pieces of silver into the temple, he departed, and he went and hanged himself, and burst open in the middle, and all his bowels gushed out.

But the chief priests, taking the pieces of silver, said, "It is not lawful to put them into the treasury, since it is blood money." So they took counsel and bought with the silver, the reward of his wickedness, the potter's field as a burial place for strangers. And it became known to all the inhabitants of Jerusalem, so that the field has been called in their own language Akeldama, that is, Field of Blood, to this day. Then was fulfilled what had been spoken by the prophet Jeremiah, saying, "And they took the thirty pieces of silver, the price of him on whom a price had been set by some of the sons of Israel, and they gave them for the potter's field, as the Lord directed me."

Now the Jews themselves did not enter the governor's headquarters, so that they would not be defiled, but could eat the Passover. So Pilate went outside to them and said, "What accusation do you bring against this man?" They answered him, "If this man were not doing evil, we would not have delivered Him over to you." Then Pilate said to them, "Take Him yourselves and judge Him by your own law." The Jews said to him, "It is not lawful for us to put anyone to death." This was to fulfill the word that Jesus had spoken to show by what kind of death He was going to die.

Then the high priest and the elders began to accuse Him with many things, saying, "We found this man misleading our nation and forbidding us to give tribute to Caesar, and saying that He Himself is Christ, a king." So Pilate entered his headquarters again and called Jesus and said to Him, "Are You the King of the Jews?" Jesus answered, "Do you say this of your own accord, or did others say it to you about Me?" Pilate answered, "Am I a Jew? Your own nation and the chief priests have delivered You over to me. What have You

17 The phrase " . . . Me, nor let Me go" is omitted in ESV.

done?" Jesus answered, "My kingdom is not of this world. If My kingdom were of this world, My servants would have been fighting, that I might not be delivered over to the Jews. But My kingdom is not from the world." Then Pilate said to Him, "So You are a king?" Jesus answered, "You say that I am a king. For this purpose I was born and for this purpose I have come into the world—to bear witness to the truth. Everyone who is of the truth listens to My voice." Pilate said to Him, "What is truth?" After he had said this, he went back outside to the Jews and told them, "I find no guilt in Him." And when He was accused by the chief priests and elders, He gave no answer. Then Pilate spoke to Him again, saying, "Do You not hear how many things they testify against You?" And He gave him no answer, not even to a single charge, so that the governor was greatly amazed. But they were urgent, saying, "He stirs up the people, teaching throughout all Judea, from Galilee even to this place."

When Pilate heard this, he asked whether the man was a Galilean. And when he learned that he belonged to Herod's jurisdiction, he sent him over to Herod, who was himself in Jerusalem at that time. And when Herod saw Jesus, he was very glad, for he had long desired to see Him, because he had heard about Him, and he was hoping to see some sign done by Him. So he questioned Him at some length, but He made no answer. The chief priests and the scribes stood by, vehemently accusing Him. And Herod with his soldiers treated Him with contempt and mocked Him. Then, arraying Him in splendid clothing, he sent Him back to Pilate. And Herod and Pilate became friends with each other that very day, for before this they had been at enmity with each other.

Pilate then called together the chief priests and the rulers and the people and said to them, "You brought me this man, as one who was misleading the people. And after examining Him before you, behold, I did not find this man guilty of any of your charges against Him. Neither did Herod, for he sent Him back to us. Look, nothing deserving death has been done by Him. I will therefore punish and release Him. Now at that feast the governor was accustomed to release for the crowd any one prisoner whom they wanted. And they had then a notorious prisoner called Barabbas, who was a robber and a murderer, and had been thrown into prison with the rebels, and had committed murder in the insurrection started in the city. And the crowd came up and began to ask Pilate to do as he usually did for them. So when they were gathered together, Pilate said to them, "You have a custom that I should release one man for you at the Passover. So do you want me to release to you Barabbas, or Jesus, the King of the Jews, who is called Christ?" For he knew that it was out of envy that they had delivered Him up.

Besides, while he was sitting on the judgment seat, his wife sent word to him, saying, "Have nothing to do with that righteous man, for I have suffered much because of Him today in a dream."

Now the chief priests and the elders persuaded the crowd to ask for Barabbas and destroy Jesus. The governor again said to them, "Which of the two do you want me to release for you?" And they all cried out together, "Away with this man, and release to us Barabbas." Pilate addressed them once more, desiring to release Jesus. But they cried out, "Crucify Him, crucify Him!" And he said to them a third time, "Why, what evil has He done? I have found in Him no guilt deserving death. I will therefore punish and release Him." But they cried out all the more, Crucify Him!" And they were urgent, demanding with loud cries that He should be crucified: and their voices[18] prevailed.

18 In the German: ". . . the voices of them and of the chief priests . . ."

Then Pilate took Jesus and flogged Him. And the governor's soldiers led Him away inside the palace, and they called together the whole battalion. And they stripped Him and put a purple robe on Him, and twisting together a crown of thorns, they put it on His head and put a reed in His right hand. And kneeling before Him, they mocked Him and began to salute Him, saying, "Hail, King of the Jews!" And they slapped Him and spit on Him, and took the reed and struck Him on the head with it, and kneeled down in homage to Him.

Pilate went out again and said to them, "See, I am bringing Him out to you that you may know that I find no guilt in Him. So Jesus came out, wearing the crown of thorns and the purple robe. Pilate said to them, "Behold the man!" When the chief priests and the officers saw Him, they cried out, "Crucify Him, crucify Him!" Pilate said to them, "Take Him yourselves and crucify Him, for I find no guilt in Him." The Jews answered him, "We have a law, and according to that law He ought to die because He made Himself the Son of God."

When Pilate heard this statement, he was even more afraid, and entered his headquarters again and said to Jesus, "Where are You from?" But Jesus gave him no answer. So Pilate said to Him, "You will not speak to me? Do You not know that I have authority to release You and authority to crucify You?" Jesus answered, "You would have no authority over Me at all unless it had been given you from above. Therefore he who delivered Me over to you has the greater sin." From then on Pilate sought to release Him, but the Jews cried out, "If you release this man, you are not Caesar's friend. Everyone who makes himself a king opposes Caesar."

So when Pilate heard these words, he brought Jesus out and sat down on the judgment seat at a place called the Stone Pavement, and in the Aramaic, Gabbatha. Now it was the day of Preparation of the Passover, about the sixth hour. He said to the Jews, "Behold your King!" They cried out, "Away with Him, away with Him, crucify Him!" Pilate said to them, "Shall I crucify your King?" The chief priests answered, "We have no king but Caesar."

So when Pilate saw that he was gaining nothing, but rather that a riot was beginning, he, wishing to satisfy the crowd, decided that their demand should be granted, and took water and washed his hands before the crowd, saying, "I am innocent of this man's[19] blood; see to it yourselves." And all the people answered, "His blood be on us and on our children!"

So Pilate released for them Barabbas, who had been thrown into prison for insurrection and murder, for whom they asked. But having scourged and mocked Jesus, he delivered Him over to their will to be crucified.

Fourth Reading

Then the soldiers took Jesus, stripped Him of the cloak and put His own clothes on Him. And they led Him out to crucify Him; and He went out, bearing His own cross. As they went out, they found a passerby of Cyrene, Simon by name, who was coming in from the country, the father of Alexander and Rufus, and laid on him the cross, to carry it behind Jesus.

And there followed Him a great multitude of the people and of women, who were mourning and lamenting for Him. But Jesus turning to them said, "Daughters of Jerusalem, do not weep not for Me, but weep for yourselves, and for your children. For behold, the days are coming when they will say, 'Blessed are the barren and the wombs that never bore and the breasts which never nursed.' Then they will begin to say to the mountains, 'Fall on

19 KJV: " . . . of this just person . . . "

us,' and to the hills, 'Cover us.' For if they do these things when the wood is green, what will happen when it is dry?"

Two others, who were criminals, were led away to be put to death with Him. And they brought Him to the place, which in Aramaic is called Golgotha (which means Place of a Skull). And they offered Him sour wine, or wine mixed with gall, to drink, but when He tasted it, He would not drink it.

And they crucified him on Golgotha, and with Him the two criminals, one on His right and the other on His left, and Jesus between them. And the Scripture was fulfilled that says, "He was numbered with the transgressors."[20] And it was the third hour when they crucified Him.

And Jesus said, "Father, forgive them; for they know not what they do."

Pilate also wrote an inscription of the charge against Him and put it on the cross over His head. It read, "Jesus of Nazareth, the King of the Jews." Many of the Jews read this inscription, for the place where Jesus was crucified was near the city, and it was written in Aramaic, in Latin, and in Greek. So the chief priests of the Jews said to Pilate, "Do not write, 'The King of the Jews,' but rather, 'This man said, I am King of the Jews.'" Pilate answered, "What I have written I have written."

When the soldiers had crucified Jesus, they took His garments and divided them into four parts, one part for each soldier; also His tunic. But the tunic was seamless, woven in one piece from top to bottom. So they said to one another, "Let us not tear it, but cast lots for it to see whose it shall be." This was to fulfill the Scripture which says, "They divided My garments among them, and for My clothing they cast lots." And they sat down and kept watch over Him there. Therefore the soldiers did these things,[21] and the people stood by, watching.

But standing by the cross of Jesus were His mother and His mother's sister, Mary the wife of Clopas, and Mary Magdalene. When Jesus saw His mother and the disciple whom He loved standing nearby, He said to his mother, "Woman, behold, your son!" Then he said to the disciple, "Behold, your mother!" And from that hour the disciple took her to his own home.

And those who passed by derided Him, wagging their heads, and saying, "Aha! You who would destroy the temple and rebuild it in three days, save Yourself. If You are the Son of God, come down from the cross." So also the chief priests, with the scribes and elders, mocked Him to one another with the people, saying, "He saved others; He cannot save Himself. If He is the Christ of God, His Chosen One, the King of Israel, let Him save Himself and come down now from the cross, that we may see and believe in Him. He trusts in God; let God deliver Him now, if He desires Him. For He said, 'I am the Son of God.'" And the robbers who were crucified with Him also reviled Him in the same way. And the soldiers also mocked Him, coming up and offering Him sour wine and saying, "If You are the King of the Jews, save Yourself!"

One of the criminals who were hanged railed at Him, saying, "Are You not the Christ? Save Yourself and us!" But the other rebuked him, saying, "Do you not fear God, since you are under the same sentence of condemnation? And we indeed justly, for we are receiving the due reward of our deeds; but this man has done nothing wrong." And he said to Jesus,

20 This phrase from Mark 15:28, omitted from the ESV, has a parallel in Luke 22:37.

21 This phrase is omitted from the ESV.

"Lord, remember me when You come into Your kingdom." And Jesus said to him, "Truly, I say to you, today you will be with Me in paradise."

It was now about the sixth hour, and there was a darkness over the whole land until the ninth hour, while the sun's light failed. And at the ninth hour Jesus cried out with a loud voice, saying, "Eloi, Eloi, lema sabachthani?" which means, "My God, my God, why have You forsaken Me?" And some of the bystanders hearing it said, "Behold, He is calling Elijah." After this, Jesus knowing that all was now finished, said (to fulfill the Scripture), "I thirst." A jar full of sour wine stood there, and one of them at once ran and took a sponge, filled it with sour wine and hyssop,[22] and put it on a reed, and held it to His mouth and gave it to Him to drink. But the others said, "Wait, let us see whether Elijah will come to take Him down."

When Jesus had received the sour wine, He said, "It is finished." Then Jesus, again calling out with a loud voice, said, "Father, into Your hands I commit My spirit!" And having said this, He bowed his head and gave up His spirit.

And behold, the curtain of the temple was torn in two, from top to bottom. And the earth shook, and the rocks were split. The tombs also were opened. And many bodies of the saints who had fallen asleep were raised, and coming out of the graves after His resurrection, they went into the holy city and appeared to many.

When the centurion and those who were with Him, keeping watch over Jesus, saw the earthquake and what took place, they were filled with awe and praised God and said, "Truly this man was innocent, and the Son of God!" And all the crowds that had assembled for this spectacle, when they saw what had taken place, returned home beating their breasts.

There were also women looking on from a distance, among whom were Mary Magdalene, and Mary the mother of James the younger and of Joses, and Salome, the mother of the sons of Zebedee. When He was in Galilee, they followed Him and ministered to Him, and there were also many other women who came up with Him to Jerusalem.

Since it was the day of Preparation, and so that the bodies would not remain on the cross on the Sabbath (for that Sabbath was a high day), the Jews asked Pilate that their legs might be broken and that they might be taken away. So the soldiers came and broke the legs of the first, and of the other who had been crucified with him. But when they came to Jesus and saw that He was already dead, they did not break His legs. But one of the soldiers pierced His side with a spear, and at once there came out blood and water.

He who saw it has borne witness—his testimony is true, and he knows that he is telling the truth—that you also may believe. For these things took place that the Scripture might be fulfilled: "Not one of His bones will be broken." And again another Scripture says, "They will look on Him whom they have pierced."

Fifth Reading

And when evening had come, since it was the day of Preparation, that is, the day before the Sabbath, Joseph of Arimathea, a respected member of the Council, a good and righteous man (who had not consented to their decision and action), who was looking for the kingdom of God, for he was a disciple of Jesus, but secretly for fear of the Jews, took courage and went to Pilate, and asked that he might take away the body of Jesus.

22 ESV has only "sour wine."

Pilate was surprised to hear that He should have already died. And summoning the centurion, he asked him whether He was already dead. And when he learned from the centurion that He was dead, he granted the corpse to Joseph, and ordered it to be given to him. Nicodemus also, who earlier had come to Jesus by night, came bringing a mixture of myrrh and aloes, about seventy-five pounds in weight. So they took the body of Jesus and wound it in linen cloths with the spices, as is the burial custom of the Jews.

Now in the place where He was crucified there was a garden, and in the garden a new tomb, belonging to Joseph, which he had cut in the rock, and in which no one had yet been laid. So because of the Jewish day of Preparation, when the Sabbath was near, since the tomb was close at hand, they laid Jesus there and rolled a great stone to the entrance of the tomb and went away. Mary Magdalene and Mary the mother of Joses were there, sitting opposite the tomb, and other women also who had come with Him from Galilee followed, and they saw where and how His body was laid. Then they returned and prepared spices and ointments. On the Sabbath they rested according to the commandment.

Next day, that is, after the day of the Preparation, the chief priests and Pharisees gathered before Pilate and said, "Sir, we remember how that impostor said, while He was still alive, "After three days I will rise. Therefore order the tomb to be made secure until the third day, lest His disciples go by night and steal Him away, and tell the people, 'He has risen from the dead,' and the last fraud will be worse than the first. Pilate said to them, "You have a guard of soldiers. Go, make it as secure as you can. So they went and made the tomb secure by sealing the stone and setting a guard.

The Destruction of Jerusalem

DRAWN FROM THE ACCOUNT OF JOSEPHUS[23]

As the time drew near when God wished to release the final wrath upon Jerusalem and the Jewish people, as the prophets and the Lord Christ Himself had threatened and foretold them, the following signs occurred:

A comet was seen in the heavens resembling a sword, which stood over the city for a whole year, and it was seen by every man.

Thus also, in the days of Unleavened Bread, on the eighth day of the month of April,[24] at the ninth hour of night, so great a light shone round the altar of the temple that it appeared to all to be day-time.

Moreover, a heavy and strong bronze gate of the inner temple, which took twenty men to lift whenever one wished to open it, and which was secured with strong bands and bolts of iron, appeared to open of its own accord about the sixth hour of night.

Besides these, on the twenty-first day of June,[25] chariots and troops of soldiers in their armor were seen running about the heavens among the clouds in many places, smiting each other by night with great noise.

Moreover, at the feast of Pentecost, when the priests were going into the temple to ready the things pertaining to the feast, they felt a quaking, and heard a great noise, and after that they heard a voice, calling: "Let us come away from here!" Although some say that it happened during Christ's suffering, at the time when the curtain of the temple was torn.

Likewise, there was one named Jesus, the son of Ananus, a commoner, who, as he went up to Jerusalem on the feast of Tabernacles, began to cry aloud by a particular spirit, "A cry from the east! A cry from the west! A cry from the four winds! A cry against Jerusalem and the temple! A cry of lament against bride and groom! A cry against this whole people!" And this was his mournful cry as he went about, day and night, in all the lanes of the city in a sort of fury. And certain men, indignant at his dire cry against the city, chastised him with whips and rods, but still he went on with the same words which he cried before.

Hereupon this man was brought to the Roman procurator, where he was whipped till his bones were laid bare; yet he did not make any supplication for himself, nor shed any tear, but continually cried aloud, "Woe, woe to Jerusalem!" Albinus the procurator took him to be a madman. He did not go near any of the citizens, nor was seen by them while he spoke thus; but he every day uttered these words: "Woe, woe to Jerusalem." And he continued this call without growing hoarse or tiring of it.

But when the city was under siege by the Romans, as he was going around upon the wall, he kept crying out, "Woe, to the people and to the temple!" and at last he added the unexpected words, "Woe to myself also!" And just as he spoke these words, a stone came out of one of

23 Certain parts have been corrected and improved from their classical source using the translation of William Whiston; this has chiefly affected quantities and a few personal names. I have noted the source of the text, when discoverable.

24 I.e., Nisan, in the Jewish calendar.

25 I.e., Iyar, in the Jewish calendar.

the enemy's engines and struck him and killed him. These and other great signs occurred before the destruction of Jerusalem.

Now let us also briefly describe the city's destruction itself. When, according to Stephanus, the Jews had consigned the righteous and innocent Christ to death as a murderer and traitor, matters grew steadily worse throughout the kingdom of Judea in every quarter. The high priests rebelled and perpetrated tyranny over the other priests. Among those who ruled, all manner of hatred and envy was present, and all rule of law gave way to discord, and it was evident that a great change and dissolution of the kingdom was at hand. As this discord and the hatred of those in power grew, factions and all manner of partisan divisions arose, and from this all sorts of trouble and much plunder and murder in the city and outside Jerusalem, and all affairs were such that the rule of the people both spiritual and secular was about to fall to ruin.

For this reason it came to pass also that Caesar Nero sent Gessius Florus to the Jewish land. And when the Jews saw that he was very harsh with them, exercising greed, arrogance, and selfishness in many affairs, they revolted against him, and meeting him in battle, slew 5,000 of his own men. Such was the raving of the Jews by God's arrangement, that even against the Romans they betrayed themselves and defected. However, when Caesar Nero learned of this, he sent Flavius Vespasian into Syria with his son Titus.

And at this time, as Trinquillus also writes, an old and established belief had spread over all the Orient that it was fated at that time for men coming from Judea to be greatly magnified and to rule over all the world.[26] And although this was fulfilled in Christ's spiritual kingdom, when the name of Christ (who was born of the tribe of Judah) was greatly magnified in all the world through the preaching of the Gospel, nevertheless certain men understood this in regard to the two Vespasians. But the people of Judea took this prediction as concerning themselves. So, after several battles against their enemies had fallen to them, they became proud, chose three captains, and violently attacked the city of Ascalon, where they were defeated in two battles (without the loss of their captains) and some 20,000 of their men perished.

After this, Vespasian, at Caesar's command, entered Galilee, which was a densely populated land, and laid waste and devastated every part of it, and there was no end of murder, rapine, and fire. In that time many thousands of Jews were slain, on one occasion as many as 50,000 armed men, not counting women, children, commoners, and peasants. The soldiers spared neither old nor young, nor those with child, nor infants in the cradle. On one occasion Vespasian sent 6,000 young men, as his own, to Achaia in order to dig through the isthmus. On another occasion, 30,000 Jewish soldiers were sold into slavery. Five thousand cast themselves from high cliffs in despair.

At this time there was among the Jews an excellent and learned man, wise and judicious, of the priestly office, and one of their leaders in the war, by the name of Josephus. And he, having fled with certain few during the earliest terrors into a cave near the city of Galilee which is named Jotapata, was seized and brought before Vespasian. When he prophesied that Vespasian would be Caesar, he was graciously kept in his charge. And this same Joseph wrote what we know of these events.

As these things took place in Galilee, there came up to Jerusalem a motley gang of brazen thieves, which John, a member of the nobility, had assembled, so that through this horde

26 Suetonius *Vespasian* 4.5.

he might secure all rule for himself. Then many cases of concealed murder, robbery, and plunder were again perpetrated in Jerusalem, bringing great misfortune to every quarter, and every part of the miserable city was greatly afflicted. During this time certain high priests were cut down, and blood was frequently shed even in the temple. Josephus writes that 12,000 of the best and eldest of the Jews lost their lives in this chaos, their possessions and houses being given over to plunder by commoners and footmen. Some believe that the Romans contrived these things by secret artifice.

Thus before the true storm had fallen upon Jerusalem, it was already plagued by three separate calamities: the war against Rome, sedition and various mutinies within the city, and the tyrants who through partisan plots overthrew each other, one by one, shedding a great deal of blood in pursuit of supremacy.

At that time the men of Gadara rose up against the Romans, and Vespasian was forced to break his winter camp in haste and take control of the city of Gadara, sending his captain Placidus, who slew all whom he overtook as far as the Jordan. Hand to hand, 15,000[27] of them were slain in the rout, while the number of those peasants and fugitives that were unwillingly forced to leap into the Jordan was prodigious,[28] and Jordan could not be passed over by reason of the dead bodies that were in it. And the lake Asphaltiris, which is called the Dead Sea, also was full of dead bodies that had been carried down into it by the river Jordan.[29] The Jews across the Jordan were all waylaid and overcome with great terror, and [all the men of Perea either surrendered themselves, or were][30] taken by the Romans, as far as Macherus.

Now as winter was ending and spring about to begin, Vespasian was encamped at Caesarea. When he heard that Nero was dead,[31] he quickly broke camp and took all the cities of the Jews[32] and Idumeans, except for a few strongholds that contained a number of a foreign warriors. In every place he set garrisons in the cities so that he might the more easily invade and capture Jerusalem (which was the only one remaining). So after the soldiers, having taken counsel together, declared Vespasian emperor,[33] he went to Egypt, intending to enter Italy from there, for the meantime committing the conduct of the war against the Jews to Titus.

Now as Titus rode toward the city with the purpose of viewing it, he was intercepted and narrowly escaped capture by the Jews.[34] After this Titus removed to a place called Scopus,[35] no more than seven furlongs from the city, and parted his army in order to set about the works for besieging the city from three camps. In the meantime, a very great multitude from all the cities from every region gathered at Jerusalem for the Passover to worship God.[36] There were also, as indicated above, many throngs of various nations there already, as well as bold and worthless folk who had been driven out of Galilee, and there were three factions in the city,[37] which were gradually undoing the concord and rule of law (as is the

27 After Whiston; in the German: "30,000."
28 Josephus *The Jewish War* (JW) 4.7.5.
29 Ibid., 4.7.6.
30 Omitted in the German.
31 JW 4.9.1.
32 Ibid., 4.10.2.
33 Ibid., 4.10.4.
34 Ibid., 5.2.2.
35 Ibid., 5.2.3.
36 Ibid., 5.3.1.
37 Ibid., 5.1.1, 4.

natural result of such things). One faction had control of the temple, and their chief was Eleazar, the son of Simon, who was joined by the Zealots, a wicked, hypocritical faction very hostile to the citizenry. John, who was the cause of all calamity, as discussed above, held the lower city. Simon held the upper city[38] with 5,000[39] Idumeans who had been called to defend the city from the intentions and violent plans of the Zealots. When there was a desire to be rid of all these visitors, it was impossible to do so.

So Titus, perceiving that the city had been overrun by such a countless host of people, gathered equipment and forces in great haste in order to lay siege to the city and to make a blockade around it, as Christ had told them, while the people were together, that hunger might oppress and afflict them the more severely. When the Jews saw this, they tried with all their might to hinder, curb, and prevent it, but it was no use. Fortune was gone. Our Lord God intended to finish them completely, wherefore they were unable to gain ground with any plan or action. Then there was utter disunity, and at this time a mutiny arose in the city, so that a great host of people was slain before the temple.

The city of Jerusalem was well fortified in the parts where it was possible to approach the city.[40] It had three walls around which the Roman forces endeavored with all their might to storm it, and after great toil two walls were conquered and taken.[41] At the same time a countless number of people were dying of famine, as Josephus writes: "the dearest friends fell to fighting and stabbing one with another over food, snatching from each other the most miserable crumb of bread."[42] Children snatched the food from the mouth of their parents, their father and mother. Then neither brother nor sister had mercy on the other. A measure of grain was bought for many pieces of gold. Some persons were driven to such hunger that they ate the dung of cattle. Others did not abstain from belts and shoes; and the very leather which belonged to their shields they pulled off and gnawed. Others had straw in their mouth when they were later found dead. Some persons searched the common sewers to deliver themselves from famine by means of filth and dung. And so great a multitude died of starvation that Manneus, the son of Lazarus,[43] came running to Titus at the time of the siege, and told him that no fewer than 115,880[44] dead bodies had been carried out through the one gate that was entrusted to his care. Egesippus writes that at one gate alone so many thousands of corpses had been carried out, and that about 600,000 men were left dead at this time of the siege.

The Jews still possessed the fortress Antonia, which was a strong fortification, and they possessed the temple as well, from which one bridge went into the city. To conquer this fortification took far more labor than any other part.

But Titus, though certain that the famine would eventually subdue and divide the Jews within the city, grew impatient with waiting, and exhorted the troops to storm the fortification with force. Although there was great danger in this, everything fell to the Romans, and there was neither victory nor fortune for the Jews any longer.

38 Ibid., 5.6.1.
39 The German has "20,000."
40 JW 5.4.1.
41 Ibid., 5.7–5.8.
42 Ibid., 6.3.3.
43 The German reads: "Ananias, the son of Eleazar."
44 The German has "150,000."

Now when the Romans gained entry to the castle, the trumpeter sounded a signal with his trumpet, and the Jews who were inside the castle were all beaten back,[45] some being thrown from the walls, others falling to death of their own accord, and still others escaping quickly from the city by night. Next the soldiers turned in earnest toward those who had possession of the temple.

It is said that Titus was willing to spare the temple,[46] but it was no use. God arranged it so that nothing was spared; for when the fighting and laboring was long and the Jews could not be moved either with threats or exhortations to give up their fortified position,[47] the soldiers perceived that they would not be able to take that quarter except by famine (which would take time) or fire.

And so it happened that some of the infantry threw fire into the temple so that it was kindled, and in this way the most admirable of all the works of which we have seen or heard, both for its marvelous construction and its size, and also for the vast wealth bestowed upon it, as well as for the glorious reputation that it had for its holiness, was burned to ashes that hour.[48]

Of the Jews who held the upper city, one part had retreated into the city, but many more died by fire and sword.

The priests begged and pleaded piteously to save their lives, but there was no grace with either God or the people. Titus, as Egesippus writes, answered that the time of pardon was over for them, and that this very holy house, for which alone they could justly hope to be preserved, was destroyed; and that it was agreeable to their office that priests should perish with the house itself to which they belonged.[49]

The desolation of the temple occurred on the tenth day of the month of August—the date when it was formerly burnt by the king of Babylon. And that day had been an especially fatal day for the temple. The time that passed from when it was first founded by king Solomon until it was destroyed in the second year of the reign of Vespasian is reckoned at 1,130 years, and seven months and fifteen days.[50] But from the time when it was rebuilt by Haggai, in the second year of Cyrus the king, until its destruction under Vespasian, there were 639 years and forty-five days.[51]

Now when the Jews were sorely distressed and there was no hope of deliverance, many thousands died of starvation, yet the rest persisted in their plans. Josephus writes that, on the day when the temple was burned and devastated, a horrid and miserable case occurred which will scarcely be believed among generations to come.[52] There was a certain woman who had dwelt beyond Jordan, who was eminent because of her family and her wealth, and had fled to Jerusalem out of fear. Now when the city was severely oppressed and in anguish with famine, she slew her son, and then roasted him and ate half of him, and kept the other half hidden by her. When the rebels came in, seeking food, she presented it to them. But they were seized with horror and amazement, and stood astonished at the sight, and left

45 JW 6.1.7.

46 Ibid., 6.2.1; 6.4.7.

47 Ibid., 6.2.5.

48 Ibid., 6.4.8.

49 Ibid., 6.6.1.

50 After Whiston: German has "1,101 years."

51 After Whiston: German has "569 years."

52 JW 6.3.4.

the mother. And this tragic story was quickly told to the great rulers of Jerusalem. This miserable event moved them from that day on to consider surrendering and to parley and deal with Titus. But now it was too late to make peace. Though they begged for peace and liberty while they were already starving and in utter anguish, nothing came of it, and for a few days the city was piteously detained. In the meantime, countless persons, out of great anguish and extreme necessity of unbearable hunger, deserted the city for the camps, running into the hands of the enemy, where they were sold cheaply. Meanwhile, the soldiers found among the Syrian deserters a certain person who was caught gathering pieces of gold out of the excrements of the Jews' bellies; for the deserters used to swallow such pieces of gold. But when this ploy was discovered in one instance, the rumor filled the various camps that the deserters came to them full of gold. So the multitude of the Arabians, with the Syrians, cut up those that came as supplicants and searched their bellies. Thus in one night's time about 2,000 of these deserters were dissected.[53] And more would have died also, had not Titus then threatened that he would put to death any such men as were found to be so insolent as to repeat this.[54]

At last the city of Jerusalem was conquered, neither young nor old being spared; but Caesar ordered his soldiers to kill none but those who were armed and resisted them, but to take the rest alive. Nevertheless, along with those whom they had orders to slay, they also slew the aged and the infirm.[55] In this way all Jerusalem was horribly plundered, set afire, and burnt by the enemy, the greater part of it being destroyed and laid waste. But part of the wall was spared, in order to afford a camp for the garrison; as were the towers also spared, in order to demonstrate to posterity what kind of city the valor of the Romans had subdued, and how well fortified it had been.[56]

And thus Jerusalem was destroyed and leveled to its foundations on the eighth day of September,[57] in the fifth month after the siege was begun.

As for the great multitude of captives, Titus put those who were above seventeen years old into bonds, and sent them to the Egyptian mines[58] to carry stones and toil as bondservants in Alexandria.

Titus also sent a great number of Jews into the provinces, as a present to them, that they might be destroyed upon their theaters, by the sword and by the wild beasts; but those that were under seventeen were sold for slaves cheaply like cattle.

Now the number of those that were taken captive during this whole war was collected to be 97,000; as was the number of those that perished during the whole siege 1,100,000, the greater part of whom were indeed of the same nation with the citizens of Jerusalem, but not belonging to the city itself.[59]

So after Titus had taken Jerusalem by force, shattered it, and occupied it, he sent away the rest of his army to the several places where they would be every one best situated; but permitted the tenth legion to stay, as a guard at Jerusalem, and did not send them away beyond Euphrates, where they had been before. And as he remembered that the twelfth

53 Ibid., 5.13.4.
54 Ibid., 5.13.5.
55 Ibid., 6.9.2.
56 Ibid., 7.1.1.
57 I.e., Elul in the Jewish calendar, Gorpiaius in the Macedonian.
58 JW 6.9.2.
59 Ibid., 6.9.3.

legion had given way to the Jews, under Cestius their general, he expelled them out of all Syria, and sent them away to the River Euphrates, which is in the limits of Armenia and Cappadocia,[60] for so far did the Roman Empire extend in those days.

Now at the time that the mighty, renowned, and holy city of Jerusalem was destroyed, 4,034 years had been numbered from the beginning of the world, and 823 years from the founding of the city of Rome, and forty since Christ's suffering. And thus Jerusalem, the most renowned city in all the east, was brought to a miserable and piteous end.

60 JW 7.1.3.

Summary of Omitted Portions

To conserve space and to constrain the scope of this book, some liturgical and confessional materials, which, in view of their importance are readily available elsewhere, have been omitted. These include:

1. Antiphons: a list of responsive versicles used in the divine service, including a few extra-biblical sources as well as a few poetic couplets. Practically identical sets of versicles are found in *HELM* and *ELHB.*
2. Liturgical Prefaces: preceded by the words of preparation, these include the Common Preface (which is also found in Appendix II) and the Prefaces for Christmas; Epiphany; Passion; Easter; Ascension; Pentecost; Holy Trinity.
3. The full text of Luther's Small Catechism, including the Preface.
4. The Augsburg Confession with the three Ecumenical Creeds or symbols.
5. The Epistles and Gospels for all Sundays and chief festivals throughout the year, with the text in full, viz.: Advent I: Rom. 13:11–14, Matt. 21:1–9. Advent II: Rom. 15:4–13, Luke 21:25–36. Advent III: 1 Cor. 4:1–5, Matt. 11:2–10. Advent IV: Phil. 4:4–7; John 1:19–28. Christmas: Titus 2:11–14; Is. 9:2–7; Luke 2:1–14. Second Day of Christmas: Titus 3:4–7, 2:15–20. St. Stephen, Martyr: Acts 6:8–15; 7:54–59; Matt. 23:34–39. Third Day of Christmas: Heb. 1:1–12; John 1:1–14. St. John the Apostle: 1 John 1; John 21:20–24. Sunday after Christmas: Gal. 4:1–7; Luke 2:33–40. New Year's Day: Gal. 3:23–29; Luke 2:21. Sunday after New Year: 1 Peter 4:12–19; Matt. 2:13–23. Baptism of Christ: Matt. 3:13–17. Epiphany: Is. 60:1–6; Matt. 2:1–12. Epiphany I: Rom. 12:1–5;[61] Luke 2:41–52. Epiphany II: Rom. 12:5–16;[62] John 2:1–11; Epiphany III: Rom. 12:17–21; Matt. 8:1–13. Epiphany IV: Rom. 13:8–10; Matt. 8:23–27. Epiphany V: Col. 3:12–17; Matt. 13:24–30. Purification: Mal. 3:1–4; Luke 2:22–32; Epiphany VI: 2 Peter 1:16–21; Matt. 17:1–9. Septuagesimae Sunday: 1 Cor. 9:24–27; 10:1–5; Matt. 20:1–16. Sexagesimae Sunday: 2 Cor. 11:19–33; 12:1–9; Luke 8:4–15. Quinquagesimae / Esto mihi: 1 Cor. 13:1–13; Luke 18:31–43. Lent I / Invocavit: 2 Cor. 6:1–10; Matt. 4:1–11. Lent II / Reminiscere: 1 Thess. 4:1–7; Matt. 15:21–28. Lent III / Oculi: Eph. 5:1–9; Luke 11:14–28. Lent IV / Laetare: Gal. 4:21–31; John 6:1–15. Lent V / Judica: Heb. 9:11–15; John 8:46–59. Annunciation of Mary: Is. 7:10–16; Luke 1:26–38. Lent VI / Palmarum: Phil. 2:5–11; Matt. 21:1–9. Maundy[63] Thursday: 1 Cor. 11:23–32; John 13:1–15. Good Friday: Is. 53; Easter: 1 Cor. 5:6–8; Mark 16:1–8. Easter Monday: Acts 10:34–41; Luke 24:13–35. Easter I / Quasimodogeniti: 1 John 5:4–10; John 20:19–31. Easter II / Misericordias:

61 Originally, "Rom. 12:1–6[a]", with the second half appearing in the next Sunday's Epistle; but in English, the grammar does not allow for a division there without much alteration; the Epistle of the next Sunday therefore begins with verse 6, according to common usage.

62 See n. 61 above.

63 In German, lit., "Green," or "Groaning."

1 Peter 2:21–25; John 10:12–16. Easter III / Jubilate: 1 Peter 2:11–20; John 16:16–23. Easter IV / Cantate: James 1:16–21; John 16:5–15. Easter V / Rogate / Vocem Jucunditatis: James 1:22–27; John 16:23–30. Ascension: Acts 1:1–11; Mark 16:14–20. Sunday after Ascension / Exaudi: 1 Peter 4:8–11; John 15:26–16:4. Pentecost: Acts 2:1–13; John 14:23–31. Pentecost Monday: Acts 10:42–48; John 3:16–21. Pentecost Tuesday: Acts 8:14–17; John 10:1–11. Trinity: Rom. 11:33–36; John 3:1–15. Trinity I: 1 John 4:16–21; Luke 16:19–31. Trinity II: 1 John 3:13–18; Luke 14:16–24. Trinity III: 1 Peter 5:6–11; Luke 15:1–10. St. John the Baptist: Is. 40:1–5; Luke 1:57–80. Trinity IV: Rom. 8:18–23; Luke 6:36–42. Visitation: Is. 11:1–5; Luke 1:39–56. Trinity V: 1 Peter 3:8–15; Luke 5:1–11. Trinity VI: Rom. 6:3–11. Matt. 5:20–26. Trinity VII: Rom. 6:19–23; Mark 8:1–9. Trinity VIII: Rom. 8:12–17; Matt. 7:15–23. Trinity IX: 1 Cor. 10:6–13; Luke 16:1–9. Trinity X: 1 Cor. 12:1–11; Luke 19:41–48. Trinity XI: 1 Cor. 15:1–10; Luke 18:9–14. Trinity XII: 2 Cor. 3:4–11; Mark 7:31–37. Trinity XIII: Gal. 3:15–22; Luke 10:23–37. Trinity XIV: Gal. 5:16–24; Luke 17:11–19. Trinity XV: Gal. 5:25–6:10; Matt. 6:24–34. Trinity XVI: Eph. 3:13–21; Luke 7:11–17. St. Michael: Rev. 12:7–12; Matt. 18:1–11. Trinity XVII: Eph. 4:1–6; Luke 14:1–11. Trinity XVIII: 1 Cor. 1:4–9; Matt. 22:34–46. Trinity XIX: Eph. 4:22–28; Matt. 9:1–8. Trinity XX: Eph. 5:15–21; Matt. 22:1–14. Trinity XXI: Eph. 6:10–17; John 4:47–54. Trinity XXII: Phil. 1:3–11; Matt. 18:23–35. Trinity XXIII: Phil. 3:17–21; Matt. 22:15–22. Trinity XXIV: Col. 1:9–14; Matt. 9:18–26. Trinity XXV: 1 Thess. 4:13–18; Matt. 24:15–28. Trinity XXVI: 2 Peter 3:3–14; Matt. 25:31–46. Trinity XXVII: 1 Thess. 5:1–11; Matt. 25:1–13. St. Andrew: Rom. 10:8–18; Matt. 4:18–22. St. Nicholas: 2 Cor. 1:3–7; Luke 12:35–40. St. Thomas: Eph. 1:3–6; John 20:24–31. Conversion of St. Paul: Acts 9:1–22; Matt. 19:27–30. St. Matthias: Acts 1:15–26; Matt. 11:25–30. Ss. Philip and James: Eph. 2:19–22; John 14:1–14. Ss. Peter and Paul: Acts 12:1–11; Matt. 16:13–20; St. Mary Magdalene: Prov. 31:10–31; Luke 7:36–50. St. James: Rom. 8:28–39; Matt. 20:20–23. St. Lawrence: 2 Cor. 9:6–10; John 12:24–26. St. Bartholomew: 2 Cor. 4:7–10. Exaltation of the Cross: Phil. 2:5–11; John 12:31–36. St. Matthew: Eph. 4:7–14; Matt. 9:9–13. Ss. Simon and Jude: 1 Peter 1:3–9; John 15:17–21. All Saints: Rev. 7:2–3; Matt. 5:1–12. Festival of the Reformation: John 14:6–7; Matt. 11:12–15. Church-Consecration Day: Rev. 21:1–5; Luke 19:1–10.

Appendix I

THE MORNING SERVICE ON SUNDAYS AND FESTIVALS WITH COMMUNION[64]

First, the hymn, "Kyrie, God Father in Heav'n Above" [#7] *is sung. At the close of the singing of this hymn, the minister steps forward to the altar and, facing it, intones:*

Glory to God in the Highest!

Whereupon the congregation begins singing "All Glory be to God Alone" [#1] *and so through to the end. During the last stanza, the preacher again steps forward to the altar and, facing the congregation, sings:*

The Lord be with you!

The congregation responds:

And with thy spirit!

Then the minister intones one suitable Antiphon, on festival days two, e.g., on Advent:

Minister: Prepare the way for the Lord. Allelluia.
Congreg.: Make His paths straight. Alleluia.
Minister: Hosanna to the Son of David. Alleluia.
Congreg.: Hosanna in the highest. Alleluia.

After this, the minister, still facing the altar, sings a suitable Collect, and first, as with all Collects, the invitation to prayer.

Let us pray.

Collect for Advent

Stir us up, Lord God, that we may be ready, when Thy Son cometh, to receive Him with joy and to serve Thee with a pure heart; through the Same Thy Son Jesus Christ our Lord.

Congreg.: Amen.

A Collect for Sundays

Let us pray. Almighty, everlasting God, who through Thy Holy Spirit dost sanctify and govern the whole Christian Church: hear our prayer, and graciously grant that it with all its members may through Thy grace serve Thee in true faith; for the sake of Jesus Christ, Thy beloved Son, our Lord.

---

64 Before its adoption in 1914 of the Common Service of 1888, the Lutheran Church—Missouri Synod used an agenda and order of service derived from those of Saxony. While the service below bears many similarities to the Common Service, of which the heir today is found in *Lutheran Service Book's* Divine Service, setting III (q.v.), there are also important differences. It is hoped that its inclusion will help to shed light on our hymnal by illustrating one part of the context in which it was used. The German is found in the *Kirchen-Agende* (St. Louis, 1856). The translation is that of the *Church Liturgy for Evangelical Lutheran Congregations of the Unaltered Augsburg Confession* (St. Louis, 1881), slightly updated and revised after the German.

The minister then, turning to the congregation, says (e.g., on the first Sunday in Advent):

Let the Christian congregation (*or* Let the Beloved in Christ) hear now with due devout attention the Epistle for the day, the first Sunday of Advent, which is written in St. Paul's Letter to the Romans, in the 13th chapter, from the 11th to the 14th verse, and reads as follows:

The congregation stands.

Beloved brethren, knowing the time, that now it is high time to awake out of sleep . . . , etc.

The Epistle being read, the minister withdraws, and the congregation sings the Chief Hymn, during the last stanza of which the minister appears again at the altar and, turning to the congregation, says:

Let the Christian congregation hear also with due devout attention the Gospel for the day, the first Sunday in Advent, which is written in the Gospel according to St. Matthew, in the 21st chapter, from the 1st to the 9th verse, and reads as follows:

The congregation stands.

Minister: When they drew nigh unto Jerusalem, by Bethphage, etc.

After the reading of the Gospel, the minister withdraws, and the congregation sings "We All Believe in One True God" [#183], *at the close of which, the minister, having entered the pulpit at the words* " . . . the Church, His own Creation . . . ," *commencement is made on festival days with a prayer, on common Sundays with one of the apostolic greeting. Having then ended the commencement by introducing his subject, he invites the congregation to pray the Our Father silently, which is nevertheless preceded by the Pulpit Verse, which he also specifies. After the Pulpit Verse has been sung, the preacher kneels and prays with the whole congregation a silent Our Father, and then stands and says:*

Let the Beloved in Christ hear again the Gospel for the day, which is written in the Gospel according to St. Matthew in the 21st chapter, from the 1st to the 9th verse, and reads as follows:

The congregation stands.

When they drew nigh unto Jerusalem, by Bethphage, etc.

Hereupon follows an overview of the thesis, and, when this and the chief points have been relayed, the sermon is begun on festival days with a prayer ex corde, or else on festivals where a prayer has already been spoken after entering the pulpit, it is begun immediately. After having delivered his sermon, the minister reads the common confession and speaks the Absolution.

Confession

Having heard the Word of God, let us now humble ourselves before the supreme Majesty of God, and make a confession of our sins, saying:

All: O Almighty God, merciful Father, I a poor, miserable, sinner, confess unto Thee all my sins and iniquities with which I have ever offended Thee and justly deserved Thy temporal and eternal punishment; but I am heartily sorry for them, and I pray Thee of Thy boundless mercy, and for the sake of the holy, innocent, bitter sufferings and death of Thy beloved Son, Jesus Christ, to be gracious and merciful to me, a poor, sinful being. Amen.

Absolution

Minister: Upon this your confession, I, by virtue of my office, as a called and ordained servant of the Word, announce the grace of God unto all of you who heartily repent of your sins, believe on Jesus Christ, and earnestly purpose by the assistance of the Holy Ghost henceforth to amend your sinful lives, and in the stead and by the command of my Lord Jesus Christ, I forgive you all your sins in the name of God ☩ the Father, God ☩ the Son, and God ☩ the Holy Ghost. Amen.

Prayer

Let us pray: Almighty, everlasting God and Father of our Lord Jesus Christ, Lord of heaven and earth: we heartily beseech Thee, that Thou by Thy good Spirit wouldst govern Thy Christian Church, with all her teachers and servants, so that it be preserved in the true, unadulterated doctrine of Thy pure Word, here and everywhere, in order that by it Thy kingdom may be spread among us, true faith awakened and strengthened, and love to all men increased in us.

We also pray Thee, Lord of lords, that Thou wouldst graciously look upon this our (new) country, preserve it unimpaired in its liberty, and constantly advance its temporal and spiritual welfare. Take, we pray Thee, all the officers of this country into Thy divine protection and keeping. Make them all a blessing of Thine, and crown them at all times with Thy favor and goodness, so that under their government we may lead a quiet and peaceable life, in all godliness and honesty.

Especially do we beseech Thee, let Thine eyes be open upon this city (region) and all its inhabitants day and night, and graciously also remember our congregation. Almighty Protector of Thy Church, continue to be among us with Thy grace and help, remove not Thine hand away from us, but give Thy divine increase to all that is done for our temporal and eternal welfare. Grant us holy courage, good counsels, and just works.

Into Thy gracious protection and care do we also commend the brethren of our faith abroad. Be gracious unto them, Lord our God, and prosper the work of their hands. Defend them mightily from all dangers which may threaten them, and preserve them in the one thing, to fear Thy name.

Graciously bless the education and instruction of our youth, that they may grow up in Thy fear, to the praise of Thy name. Especially bless in our country also the institutions of the true faith, in preparing faithful laborers in Thy vineyard.

Advance every Christian trade, business, and occupation, and let every one walk in them before Thee in all good conscience, and support himself honestly.

Graciously provide for all sick, poor, widows, and orphans; keep all who are with child, all children, and nursing mothers; be the guide of all who travel by land or by water in the way of their calling; have mercy upon all who are in temptations, and on those who suffer persecution for Thy name's sake. Comfort them, O God, with Thy favor, and finally deliver them according to Thy fatherly pleasure.

Give Thy divine increase to the growth of the fruits of the land; avert all hurtful tempests, scarcity, famine, war, conflagration, inundation, and other calamities. Do thus, O faithful Father, remain with us until our end, and let Thy Spirit never depart from us, that we may live in Thy fear, die in Thy grace, and at last receive the end of our faith, even the salvation of our souls.

All this grant for the sake of Thy beloved Son, Jesus Christ, and His precious blood; who with Thee and the Holy Ghost liveth and reigneth in equal majesty and glory, true God and man, most blessed forever. Amen.

Intercessions and Thanksgivings

[Omitted.]

After the necessary intercessions and thanksgivings, etc., are offered, the announcements are made, whereupon the minister closes with the Lord's Prayer (aloud) and, after a short, suitable scriptural Benediction, leaves the pulpit.

Should there be no Communion, the congregation now sings a short hymn, after which the minister at first, as usual at the close, facing the altar, sings a suitable Antiphon and Collect, then, facing the congregation, the Benediction; after which the congregation closes the whole service by the singing of a closing verse and the Lord's Prayer (silently).

On Communion days, however, the congregation begins to sing: "Create in me, Lord, O God, a clean heart," etc. [#209]

During the singing of this hymn the minister steps forward to the altar, properly arranging all things (the bread on the left hand side of the altar, the wine on the right hand side) for the Consecration and, after the singing of the hymn, facing the congregation, intones:

The Lord be with you.
Congreg.: And with thy spirit.
Minister (facing the altar): Lift up your hearts.
Congreg.: We lift them up unto the Lord.
Minister: Let us give thanks unto the Lord our God!
Congreg.: It is meet and right [so to do].

Then the minister sings either the general preface, or another having reference to the particular time.

The General Preface

It is very meet and right, becoming and salutary, that we should at all times and in all places give thanks unto Thee, O Lord, holy Father, Almighty, everlasting God, through Jesus Christ, our Lord, through whom Thy majesty is praised by the angels, worshiped by the dominions, feared by the powers, celebrated with unanimous rejoicings by the heavens, the powers of all heavens, and the blessed Seraphim; with whom we also join our voices, worshiping Thee and saying:

[Proper prefaces omitted.]

Congreg. Holy, holy, holy is God, the Lord of Sabaoth.
Heaven and earth are full of Thy glory.
Hosanna in the highest!
Blessed is { Mary's Son, *or* the Paschal Lamb } that cometh in the name of the Lord.
Hosanna in the highest!

The minister having sung the Preface and the congregation the Sanctus, the former continues singing:

Minister: Our Father, who art in heaven, hallowed be Thy name; Thy kingdom come; Thy will be done on earth as it is in heaven. Give us this day our daily bread, and forgive us our trespasses as we forgive them that trespass against us; and lead us not into temptation, but deliver us from evil.

Congreg.: For Thine is the kingdom, and the power, and the glory, for ever and ever. Amen.

Minister: Our Lord Jesus Christ, the same night in which He was betrayed, took bread;[65] and when He had given thanks, He brake it, and gave it to His disciples, and said, "Take, eat; this is My ☩ Body,[66] which is given for you. This do in remembrance of Me.

After the same manner also took He the cup, when He had supped, gave thanks, and gave it to them, saying, "Take, drink all ye of it; this cup[67] is the New Testament in My ☩ Blood,[68] which is shed for you for the forgiveness of sins: this do ye, as oft as ye drink of it, in remembrance of Me.

Hereupon the congregation sings "O Christ, Thou Lamb of God" (#69). *Then a Communion hymn is sung while the communicants approach the altar. The minister gives them at first the Bread, three at a time, and says:*

Take and eat; this is the true Body of your Lord and Savior, Jesus Christ, given into death for your sins; this strengthen and preserve you in the true faith unto life everlasting. ☩ Amen.

Having thus given the Bread to a number of communicants, who either kneel around the altar or pass around from the left to the right behind around the Altar, he now gives them the Cup also in the same manner, and says:

Take and drink; this is the true Blood of your Lord and Savior Jesus Christ, shed for the remission of your sins; this strengthen and preserve you in the true faith unto life everlasting. ☩ Amen.

---

65 Here he touches the paten with his hand.

66 At ☩ he makes the sign of the cross over the bread.

67 Here he touches the cup with his hand.

68 At ☩ he makes the sign of the cross over the wine.

When the distribution is finished, the minister, facing the altar, intones a suitable Antiphon and Collect, e.g.:

Minister: As often as ye eat this bread and drink this cup.
Congreg.: Ye do show the Lord's death till He come.
Minister: Let us give thanks unto the Lord and pray:

We thank Thee, O Lord, Almighty God, that Thou hast refreshed us by this wholesome gift, and we beseech Thy mercy, that Thou wouldst cause it to redound in strong faith toward Thee and in fervent love among us all; through Jesus Christ, Thy Son, our Lord.

Congreg.: Amen.
Minister (facing the congregation): The Lord bless thee and keep thee.
The Lord make His face to shine upon thee, and be gracious unto thee.
The Lord lift up His countenance upon thee, and give thee ✠ peace.
Congreg.: Amen.

Then is sung "O Lord, We Praise Thee . . . " [#195] *or some other suitable closing verse* [e.g., #11–12], *and the congregation, after praying the Lord's Prayer silently, leaves the place of worship.*

Appendix II

SUPPLEMENTARY TUNES

Br 13. Amen! wir habn gehöret.
J. von Burgk, 1575.
Br 20. Auf diesen Tag bedenken wir.
Strassburg, 1537.
Br 18. Aus Lieb läßt Gott der Christenheit.
J. Eccard, 1597.

Br 22. Christ, der du bist der helle Tag. Anon., 15th c. / C. Spangenberg, 1568.

Br 27. Christe, du Beistand deiner Kreuzgemeine. M.A. v. Löwenstern, 1644.

Br 35. Das alte Jahr vergangen ist. J. Crüger, 1649.

Br 38, ad. Das Jesulein soll doch mein Trost. B. Helder, 1614.

Br 37. Das neugeborne Kindelein. M. Vulpius, 1609.

Hö 130. Der Bräutgam wird bald rufen. (Herzlich tut mich erfreuen.) Anon., 1542.

Br 40. Der du bist drei in Enigkeit. Anon., 7th c. / Wittenberg, 1543.

Hö 61. Der Heilge Geist hernieder kam. (Des Heilgen Geistes reiche Gnad.) H. Schein, 1627.

Br 36. Der Tag der ist so freudenreich. (orig. meter) — Anon., 14th c. / Wittenberg, 1529.

LK 162. Der Tag vertreibt die finstre Nacht. — Bohemian Brethren, 1531.

LK 416. Du großer Schmerzensmann. M. Janus, 1663.

Br 46. Durch Adams Fall ist ganz verderbt. Wittenberg, 1529.

Br 55, ad. Es spricht der Unweisen Mund wohl.
Wittenberg, 1524.
Br 65. Gott hat das Evangelium.
E. Alber, 1548.
Br 66. Gott lebet noch, Seele, was verzagst du doch. (Alle Menschen müssen sterben, ad.)
J. Crüger, 1678 / F. Layriz, 1844.

Br 68. Gott sei uns gnädig und barmherzig. Traditional / Klug, 1529.

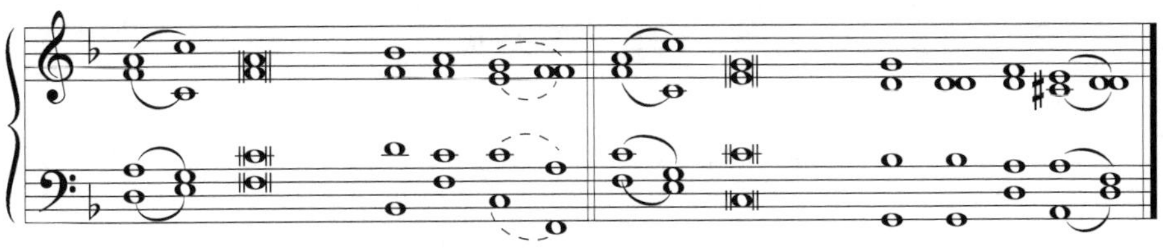

Br 73. Herr Gott, der du mein Vater bist. Anon., 16th c.

Br 75. Herr Gott, erhalt uns für und für. J. von Burgk, 1575.

LK 210. Herr Jesu Christ, du höchstes Gut. J.G. Rhonius, 1587.

Br 80. Herr Jesu Christ, wahr Mensch und Gott. (Nu loben wir mit Innigkeit.) Bohemian Brethren, 1531.

Br 86. Hinunter ist der Sonnenschein. M. Vulpius, 1609.

Br 87. Höchster König, Jesu Christ.
F.E. Hommel, 1844.
ELHB365. Ich ruf zu dir, Herr Jesu Christ.
Wittenberg, 1533.
Br 166. Ich weiß, mein Gott, daß all mein Tun. (Verzage nicht, o frommer Christ.)
C. Buchwälder, 1611 / Dresden, 1625.

Br 219, ad. In allen meinen Taten.
J. Quirsfeld, 1679.
LK 480, ad. In dich hab ich gehoffet, Herr. (Jesus ist ein süßer Nam.)
Anon., 15th c. / H. Fink, 1536.
Hö 160. Jesu, deine heilgen Wunden.
Dresden, 1694.

Br 93. Jesu, der du meine Seele. J. Rist, 1641.

Br 95. Jesu, komm doch selbst zu mir. Unknown.

ELHB 89. Jesu, meines Herzens Freud. Lüneburg, 1686.

Br 100. Jesus Christus, unser Heiland, der den Tod. Wittenberg, 1529.

Hö 172. Keinen hat Gott verlassen. (Lobet Gott, unsern Herren. – Befiehl du deine Wege.) B. Gesius, 1605.

Hö 174, ad. Komm, Heiliger Geist, erfüll die Herzen. Traditional / Erfurt, 1527.

Br 113. Lasset die Kindlein kommen. J.H. Schein, 1627.

Br 117. Lobet den Herren, denn er ist sehr freundlich.
A. Scandelli, 1568.
Br 221. Lob sei dem allmächtigen Gott.
J. Crüger, 1640.

ELHB 88. Meinen Jesum laß ich nicht. (No rep.)
A. Hammerschmidt, 1658 / Nürnberg, 1677.
Hö 197. Meine Seel, ermuntre dich. (Herr, wie lange willt du doch.)
J. Crüger, 1653.
Hö 199. Mein Lieber Gott, ich bitte dich.
J. G. Kunz, 1885.

ELHB 392, ad. Mensch, willt du leben seliglich.
J. Walther, 1524.
Br 128. Mir ist ein geistlich Kirchelein.
C. Fabricius, 1651.
Br 143. O Ewigkeit, du Donnerwort!
J. Schop, 1642 / J. Crüger, 1653.

Br 146. O Herre Gott, in meiner Not. (with rep.)
M. Franck, 1631.
*Repeat last line of text.
*Repeat last four syllables.
Hö 240. O stilles Gotteslamm. (Ich freue mich in dir.)
(1714.) B. König, 1738.

Br 156. Schaffe in mir, Gott, ein reines Herze. G. Wiener, 1648.

Br 155. Schwing dich auf zu deinem Gott. J. Crüger, 1653.

Hö 250. Sollt es gleich bisweilen scheinen. (Allenthalben, wo ich gehe.)
A. Fritsch, 1675.
Br 171, ad. Warum betrübst du dich, mein Herz.
Anon., 1565.
LK 205. Was fürchtst du, Feind Herodes, sehr?
Medieval / F. Layriz, 1854.

Br 167. Verleih uns Frieden gnädiglich.

Medieval / J. Klug, 1529; J. Walther, 1566.

Br 179. Wend ab deinen Zorn, lieber Gott, mit Gnaden.
Anon., 16th c.
LK 124, ad. Wer Gott vertraut hat wohl gebaut.
J. Magdeburg, 1571.
* Repeat last line of text.

LK 345. Wir Christenleut habn jetzund Freud.
Dresden, 1589.
Br 188. Wir danken dir, Gott, für und für. (Von edler Art ein Jungfrau zart.)
Anon., 15th c.
ELHB 284. Wo Gott der Herr nicht bei uns hält.
J. Kluge, 1535.

Index of Tunes

ARRANGED BY REFERENCE NUMBER

99.
Christ ist erstanden von der Marter allen.

100.
Christ fuhr gen Himmel.

101.
Herr Gott, dich loben wir.

102.
Jesaia, dem Propheten, das geschah.

103.
Kyrie, Gott Vater in Ewigkeit.

104.
Kyrie Eleison.

105.
Komm, Heiliger Geist, erfüll die Herzen.

106.
Schaffe in mir, Gott, ein reines Herze.

107.
Verleih uns Frieden gnädiglich.

108.
Gott sei uns gnädig und barmherzig.

Alphabetical Index of First Lines

Alphabetical Index of First Lines (German)

Alphabetical Index of Authors

Alphabetical Index of Translators

Translator — Hymn (Italics indicate partial translation)

Copyrights and Acknowledgments

The following copyrights are acknowledged:
All those hymns, stanzas, and partial stanzas specified above as translated by Matthew Carver. Text: © 2012 Matthew Carver.

Other hymns and stanzas:
#
7. Text: © 1939 Concordia Publishing House.
9. (st. 3). Text: © 1938 Concordia Publishing House.
39. (sts. 3, 5, 9, 10–14). Text: © 2011 Mark A. Preus. Used by permission.
84. Text: © 1941 Concordia Publishing House.
92. Text: © 1927, 1941, Concordia Publishing House.
98. Text: © 1939, Concordia Publishing House.
107. (sts. 1–2, 4, 6–7). Text © 1982 Concordia Publishing House.
110. (sts. 1a, 2a). Text: © 1978 Concordia Publishing House.
117. Text: © 1938 Concordia Publishing House.
119. (st. 2). Text: © 1939, Concordia Publishing House.
134. Text: © 1941 Concordia Publishing House.
142. Text: © 1940, Concordia Publishing House.
147. Text: © 1941 Concordia Publishing House.
161. (sts. 1, 3–4, 7). Text: © 1938 Concordia Publishing House.
162. Text: © 1941 Concordia Publishing House.
187. (sts. 2, 5, 12). Text: © 2004 Jon D. Vieker. Used by permission.
202. (sts. 1–11, 14–17). Text: © 1941 Concordia Publishing House.
237. (sts. 1–7, 9–10, 13). Text: © 1941 Concordia Publishing House.
308. Text: © 1941 Concordia Publishing House.
324. Text: © 1937, Concordia Publishing House.
349. (sts. 1, 3–8, 12, 14–15). Text: © 1941 Concordia Publishing House.
416. Text: © 1941 Concordia Publishing House.
417. (st. 8). Text: © 1938 Concordia Publishing House.
424b. ("Response"). Text: © 2010 Zion Evangelical Lutheran Church, Detroit, Michigan. Used by permission.
429. (sts. 1–5, 7–12). Text: © 1941 Concordia Publishing House.

Concordia Publishing House

Similar to the peer review or "refereed" process used to publish professional and academic journals, the Peer Review process is designed to enable authors to publish book manuscripts through Concordia Publishing House. The Peer Review process is well-suited for smaller projects and textbook publication.

We aim to provide quality resources for congregations, church workers, seminaries, universities, and colleges. Our books are faithful to the Holy Scriptures and the Lutheran Confessions, promoting the rich theological heritage of the historic, creedal Church. Concordia Publishing House (CPH) is the publishing arm of The Lutheran Church—Missouri Synod. We develop, produce, and distribute (1) resources that support pastoral and congregational ministry, and (2) scholarly and professional books in exegetical, historical, dogmatic, and practical theology.

For more information, visit:
www.cph.org/PeerReview.